OFFICIAL 2002

NCAA®
FINAL FOUR TOURNAMENT RECORDS

INDIVIDUAL AND TEAM RECORDS

RECORDS FOR ALL ROUNDS OF THE TOURNMENT

COACHING RECORDS

INCLUDES RECORDS OF EVERY HEAD COACH IN THE TOURNAMENT

COMPLETE TOURNAMENT BRACKETS

SITES, DATES, SEEDS AND SCORES SINCE 1939

THE NATIONAL COLLEGIATE ATHLETIC ASSOCIATION
P.O. Box 6222, Indianapolis, Indiana 46206-6222
317/917-6222
http://www.ncaa.org

December 2001

Researched and Compiled By:
Gary K. Johnson, *Senior Statistics Coordinator.*

Edited By:
Marty Benson, *Communications Coordinator.*

Typesetting/Design By:
Toi Davis, *Production Designer II.*

Cover Design By:
Wayne Davis, *Graphics Manager.*

Cover Photography By:
Rich Clarkson and Associates.

Distributed to Division I men's basketball sports information directors and conference publicity directors.

NCAA, NCAA logo and National Collegiate Athletic Association are registered marks of the Association and use in any manner is prohibited unless prior approval is obtained from the Association.

Copyright, 2001, by the National Collegiate Athletic Association.
Printed in the United States of America.
ISSN 0267-1017
NCAA 16142-12/01

Contents

The Final Four	5
The Early Rounds	29
The Tournament	47
The Coaches	85
Attendance and Sites	103
The Tournament Field	117

NAME CHANGE KEY
(Listed throughout the book by the name on the left)

PLAYER name changes
College name was:	Changed to:
Lew Alcindor	Kareem Abdul-Jabbar
Walt Hazzard	Mahdi Abdul-Rahmad
Chris Jackson	Mahmoud Abdul-Rauf
Akeem Olajuwon	Hakeem Olajuwon
Keith Wilkes	Jamaal Wilkes

SCHOOL name changes
Current name is:	Changed from:
Charlotte	UNC Charlotte
Chattanooga	Tennessee-Chattanooga
Colorado St.	Colorado A&M
Detroit	Detroit Mercy; Detroit Tech
La.-Lafayette	Southwestern La.
La.-Monroe	Northeast La.
Loyola (La.)	Loyola-New Orleans
Memphis	Memphis St.
Oklahoma St.	Oklahoma A&M
UTEP	Texas Western
Towson	Towson St.

ARENA name changes
Current name is:	Changed from:
The Arena	Checkerdome
Coleman Coliseum	Memorial Coliseum
Continental Airlines Arena	Meadowlands Arena
Fogelman Arena	Tulane Gym
Hinkle Field House	Butler Field House
Holt Arena	ISU Minidome
Jon M. Huntsman Center	Special Events Center
The Joyce Center	Athletic & Convocation Center
Pacific Exposition Center	Pacific International Livestock Pavilion
RCA Dome	Hoosier Dome; Indiana Hoosier Dome
Reed Gym	ISU Gymnasium
Tropicana Field	Thunder Dome; Florida Suncoast Dome
Welsh-Ryan Arena/McGaw Hall	McGaw Hall

TOURNAMENT REGION name changes
Current name is:	Changed from:
East	Eastern (1939-50)
South	Midwest (1956), Mideast (1957-84), Southeast (1985-97)
Midwest	West (1956)
West	Western (1939-50), Far West (1956)

The Final Four

Championship Results	6
Final Four Game Records	7
Championship Game Records	9
Semifinals Game Records	11
Final Four Two-Game Records	13
Final Four Cumulative Records	15

Championship Results

Year	Champion	Score	Runner-Up	Third Place	Fourth Place
1939	Oregon	46-33	Ohio St.	† Oklahoma	† Villanova
1940	Indiana	60-42	Kansas	† Duquesne	† Southern California
1941	Wisconsin	39-34	Washington St.	†Pittsburgh	† Arkansas
1942	Stanford	53-38	Dartmouth	† Colorado	† Kentucky
1943	Wyoming	46-34	Georgetown	† Texas	† DePaul
1944	Utah	42-40 +	Dartmouth	† Iowa St.	† Ohio St.
1945	Oklahoma St.	49-45	New York U.	† Arkansas	† Ohio St.
1946	Oklahoma St.	43-40	North Carolina	Ohio St.	California
1947	Holy Cross	58-47	Oklahoma	Texas	CCNY
1948	Kentucky	58-42	Baylor	Holy Cross	Kansas St.
1949	Kentucky	46-36	Oklahoma St.	Illinois	Oregon St.
1950	CCNY	71-68	Bradley	North Carolina St.	Baylor
1951	Kentucky	68-58	Kansas St.	Illinois	Oklahoma St.
1952	Kansas	80-63	St. John's (N.Y.)	Illinois	Santa Clara
1953	Indiana	69-68	Kansas	Washington	LSU
1954	La Salle	92-76	Bradley	Penn St.	Southern California
1955	San Francisco	77-63	La Salle	Colorado	Iowa
1956	San Francisco	83-71	Iowa	Temple	Southern Methodist
1957	North Carolina	54-53 ‡	Kansas	San Francisco	Michigan St.
1958	Kentucky	84-72	Seattle	Temple	Kansas St.
1959	California	71-70	West Virginia	Cincinnati	Louisville
1960	Ohio St.	75-55	California	Cincinnati	New York U.
1961	Cincinnati	70-65 +	Ohio St.	* St. Joseph's	Utah
1962	Cincinnati	71-59	Ohio St.	Wake Forest	UCLA
1963	Loyola (Ill.)	60-58 +	Cincinnati	Duke	Oregon St.
1964	UCLA	98-83	Duke	Michigan	Kansas St.
1965	UCLA	91-80	Michigan	Princeton	Wichita St.
1966	UTEP	72-65	Kentucky	Duke	Utah
1967	UCLA	79-64	Dayton	Houston	North Carolina
1968	UCLA	78-55	North Carolina	Ohio St.	Houston
1969	UCLA	92-72	Purdue	Drake	North Carolina
1970	UCLA	80-69	Jacksonville	New Mexico St.	St. Bonaventure
1971	UCLA	68-62	*Villanova	*Western Ky.	Kansas
1972	UCLA	81-76	Florida St.	North Carolina	Louisville
1973	UCLA	87-66	Memphis	Indiana	Providence
1974	North Carolina St.	76-64	Marquette	UCLA	Kansas
1975	UCLA	92-85	Kentucky	Louisville	Syracuse
1976	Indiana	86-68	Michigan	UCLA	Rutgers
1977	Marquette	67-59	North Carolina	UNLV	Charlotte
1978	Kentucky	94-88	Duke	Arkansas	Notre Dame
1979	Michigan St.	75-64	Indiana St.	DePaul	Pennsylvania
1980	Louisville	59-54	*UCLA	Purdue	Iowa
1981	Indiana	63-50	North Carolina	Virginia	LSU
1982	North Carolina	63-62	Georgetown	† Houston	† Louisville
1983	North Carolina St.	54-52	Houston	† Georgia	† Louisville
1984	Georgetown	84-75	Houston	† Kentucky	† Virginia
1985	Villanova	66-64	Georgetown	† St. John's (N.Y.)	*† Memphis
1986	Louisville	72-69	Duke	† Kansas	† LSU
1987	Indiana	74-73	Syracuse	† UNLV	† Providence
1988	Kansas	83-79	Oklahoma	† Arizona	† Duke
1989	Michigan	80-79 +	Seton Hall	† Duke	† Illinois
1990	UNLV	103-73	Duke	† Arkansas	† Georgia Tech
1991	Duke	72-65	Kansas	† UNLV	† North Carolina
1992	Duke	71-51	Michigan	† Cincinnati	† Indiana
1993	North Carolina	77-71	Michigan	† Kansas	† Kentucky
1994	Arkansas	76-72	Duke	† Arizona	† Florida
1995	UCLA	89-78	Arkansas	† North Carolina	† Oklahoma St.
1996	Kentucky	76-67	Syracuse	*†Massachusetts	† Mississippi St.
1997	Arizona	84-79 +	Kentucky	*†Minnesota	† North Carolina
1998	Kentucky	78-69	Utah	† North Carolina	† Stanford
1999	Connecticut	77-74	Duke	†Michigan St.	†Ohio St.
2000	Michigan St.	89-76	Florida	†North Carolina	†Wisconsin
2001	Duke	82-72	Arizona	†Maryland	†Michigan St.

†tied for third place; +overtime; ‡three overtimes; *later vacated

The year 2001 was a good one for Duke and especially coach Mike Krzyzewski, who captured his third NCAA championship and was inducted into the Naismith Memorial Basketball Hall of Fame.

Photo by Rich Clarkson

Tournament trivia

Question...
How many schools from the state of Georgia have played in the Final Four?

Answer...
Two (Georgia in 1983 and Georgia Tech in 1990)

Final Four Game Records

Statistics for the Division I Men's Basketball tournament have been collected since 1939, the first year of the tournament. Individual rebounds were added in 1951, although team rebounds were not added until 1955. Assists were added in 1984 and blocked shots and steals were added in 1986. Scoring, rebounding, assists, blocked shots and steals are ranked on total number and per-game average; shooting, on percentage. In statistical rankings, the rounding of percentages and/or averages may indicate ties where none exist. In these cases, the numerical order of the rankings is accurate. In 1973, freshmen became eligible to compete on the varsity level.

A national championship game is indicated by (CH), a national semifinal game by (NSF), a national third-place game by (N3d) and record later vacated by (*).

Individual Records

POINTS
58, Bill Bradley, Princeton vs. Wichita St., N3d, 1965
48, Hal Lear, Temple vs. Southern Methodist, N3d, 1956
44, Bill Walton, UCLA vs. Memphis, CH, 1973
42, Bob Houbregs, Washington vs. LSU, N3d, 1953
42, *Jack Egan, St. Joseph's vs. Utah, N3d, 1961 (4 ot)
42, Gail Goodrich, UCLA vs. Michigan, CH, 1965
41, Jack Givens, Kentucky vs. Duke, CH, 1978
39, Oscar Robertson, Cincinnati vs. Louisville, N3d, 1959
39, Al Wood, North Carolina vs. Virginia, NSF, 1981
38, Jerry West, West Virginia vs. Louisville, NSF, 1959
38, Jerry Chambers, Utah vs. UTEP, NSF, 1966
38, Freddie Banks, UNLV vs. Indiana, NSF, 1987

FIELD GOALS
22, Bill Bradley, Princeton vs. Wichita St., N3d, 1965
21, Bill Walton, UCLA vs. Memphis, CH, 1973
18, Jack Givens, Kentucky vs. Duke, CH, 1978
17, Bob Houbregs, Washington vs. LSU, N3d, 1953
17, Hal Lear, Temple vs. Southern Methodist, N3d, 1956
17, *Jack Egan, St. Joseph's vs. Utah, N3d, 1961 (4 ot)
16, Don May, Dayton vs. North Carolina, NSF, 1967
16, Charlie Scott, North Carolina vs. Drake, N3d, 1969
16, Larry Bird, Indiana St. vs. DePaul, NSF, 1979
15, Lew Alcindor, UCLA vs. North Carolina, CH, 1968
15, Lew Alcindor, UCLA vs. Purdue, CH, 1969
15, Ernie DiGregorio, Providence vs. Memphis, NSF, 1973

FIELD-GOALS ATTEMPTED
42, Lennie Rosenbluth, North Carolina vs. Michigan St., NSF, 1957 (3 ot)
36, Rick Mount, Purdue vs. UCLA, CH, 1969
36, Ernie DiGregorio, Providence vs. Memphis, NSF, 1973
34, Elvin Hayes, Houston vs. Ohio St., N3d, 1968
33, *Jack Egan, St. Joseph's vs. Utah, N3d, 1961 (4 ot)
33, *Jerry Dunn, Western Ky. vs. Villanova, NSF, 1971 (2 ot)
32, Elgin Baylor, Seattle vs. Kentucky, CH, 1958
31, Billy McGill, Utah vs. Cincinnati, NSF, 1961
31, Jerry Chambers, Utah vs. UTEP, NSF, 1966
31, Elvin Hayes, Houston vs. UCLA, NSF, 1967

FIELD-GOAL PERCENTAGE
(Minimum 10 FGM)
95.5% (21-22), Bill Walton, UCLA vs. Memphis, CH, 1973
91.7% (11-12), Bill Walton, UCLA vs. Louisville, NSF, 1972
90.9% (10-11), Jerry Lucas, Ohio St. vs. St. Joseph's, NSF, 1961
90.9% (10-11), Billy Thompson, Louisville vs. LSU, NSF, 1986
84.2% (16-19), Larry Bird, Indiana St. vs. DePaul, NSF, 1979
83.3% (10-12), Sidney Wicks, UCLA vs. New Mexico St., NSF, 1970
83.3% (10-12), Udonis Haslam, Florida vs. Michigan St., CH, 2000
82.4% (14-17), Joe Barry Carroll, Purdue vs. Iowa, N3d, 1980
76.5% (13-17), Mike Gminski, Duke vs. Notre Dame, NSF, 1978
76.5% (13-17), James Worthy, North Carolina vs. Georgetown, CH, 1982

THREE-POINT FIELD GOALS
10, Freddie Banks, UNLV vs. Indiana, NSF, 1987
7, Steve Alford, Indiana vs. Syracuse, CH, 1987
7, Dave Sieger, Oklahoma vs. Kansas, CH, 1988
7, Dennis Scott, Georgia Tech vs. UNLV, NSF, 1990
7, Tony Delk, Kentucky vs. Syracuse, CH, 1996
6, Bobby Hurley, Duke vs. Indiana, NSF, 1992
6, Darryl Wilson, Mississippi St. vs. Syracuse, NSF, 1996
6, Mike Bibby, Arizona vs. North Carolina, NSF, 1997
5, 10 tied (most recent: Mike Dunleavy, Duke vs. Arizona, CH, 2001)

THREE-POINT FIELD GOALS ATTEMPTED
19, Freddie Banks, UNLV vs. Indiana, NSF, 1987
14, Dennis Scott, Georgia Tech vs. UNLV, NSF, 1990
13, Dave Sieger, Oklahoma vs. Kansas, CH, 1988
13, Damon Stoudamire, Arizona vs. Arkansas, NSF, 1994
13, Darryl Wilson, Mississippi St. vs. Syracuse, NSF, 1996
12, Steve Kerr, Arizona vs. Oklahoma, NSF, 1988
12, Glen Rice, Michigan vs. Seton Hall, CH, 1989 (ot)
12, John Morton, Seton Hall vs. Michigan, CH, 1989 (ot)
12, Donald Williams, North Carolina vs. Arkansas, NSF, 1995
12, Tony Delk, Kentucky vs. Syracuse, CH, 1996
12, Scott Padgett, Kentucky vs. Arizona, CH, 1997 (ot)

THREE-POINT FIELD-GOAL PERCENTAGE
(Minimum 5 3FGM)
71.4% (5-7), Adonis Jordan, Kansas vs. North Carolina, NSF, 1993
71.4% (5-7), Donald Williams, North Carolina vs. Kansas, NSF, 1993
71.4% (5-7), Donald Williams, North Carolina vs. Michigan, CH, 1993
70.0% (7-10), Steve Alford, Indiana vs. Syracuse, CH, 1987
66.7% (6-9), Bobby Hurley, Duke vs. Indiana, NSF, 1992
62.5% (5-8), Arthur Lee, Stanford vs. Kentucky, NSF, 1998 (ot)
58.3% (7-12), Tony Delk, Kentucky vs. Syracuse, CH, 1996
55.6% (5-9), Anderson Hunt, UNLV vs. Georgia Tech, NSF, 1990
55.6% (5-9), Rex Walters, Kansas vs. North Carolina, NSF, 1993
55.6% (5-9), Mike Dunleavy, Duke vs. Arizona, CH, 2001

FREE THROWS MADE
18, Gail Goodrich, UCLA vs. Michigan, CH, 1965
15, Oscar Robertson, Cincinnati vs. Louisville, N3d, 1959
15, Bill Buntin, Michigan vs. Kansas St., N3d, 1964
14, Hal Lear, Temple vs. Southern Methodist, N3d, 1956
14, Jerry West, West Virginia vs. Louisville, NSF, 1959
14, Bill Bradley, Princeton vs. Wichita St., N3d, 1965
14, Mark Aguirre, DePaul vs. Pennsylvania, N3d, 1979
14, Miles Simon, Arizona vs. Kentucky, CH, 1997 (ot)
13, Don Schlundt, Indiana vs. LSU, 1953
12, Four tied (most recent: Christian Laettner, Duke vs. Kansas, CH, 1991)

FREE-THROWS ATTEMPTED
20, Jerry West, West Virginia vs. Louisville, NSF, 1959
20, Gail Goodrich, UCLA vs. Michigan, CH, 1965
19, Oscar Robertson, Cincinnati vs. Louisville, N3d, 1959
18, Bob Pettit, LSU vs. Indiana, NSF, 1953
17, Don Schlundt, Indiana vs. LSU, NSF, 1953
17, Bob Carney, Bradley vs. La Salle, CH, 1954
17, Paul Hogue, Cincinnati vs. UCLA, NSF, 1962
17, Bill Buntin, Michigan vs. Kansas St., N3d, 1964
17, Miles Simon, Arizona vs. Kentucky, CH, 1997 (ot)
16, Wilt Chamberlain, Kansas vs. North Carolina, CH, 1957 (3 ot)
16, Lew Alcindor, UCLA vs. Drake, NSF, 1969
16, Dennis Wuycik, North Carolina vs. Louisville, N3d, 1972

FREE-THROW PERCENTAGE
(Minimum 10 FTM)
100.0% (12-12), Jim Spanarkel, Duke vs. Notre Dame, NSF, 1978
100.0% (12-12), Christian Laettner, Duke vs. Kansas, CH, 1991
100.0% (11-11), Jeff Lamp, Virginia vs. LSU, N3d, 1981
100.0% (10-10), Ron King, Florida St. vs. North Carolina, NSF, 1972
93.3% (14-15), Bill Bradley, Princeton vs. Wichita St., N3d, 1965
93.3% (14-15), Mark Aguirre, DePaul vs. Pennsylvania, N3d, 1979
92.9% (13-14), *Jim Lynam, St. Joseph's vs. Utah, N3d, 1961 (4 ot)
91.7% (11-12), Dick Estergard, Bradley vs. La Salle, CH, 1954
91.7% (11-12), Bill Walton, UCLA vs. Louisville, NSF, 1972
91.7% (11-12), Earvin "Magic" Johnson, Michigan St. vs. Pennsylvania, NSF, 1979

REBOUNDS
27, Bill Russell, San Francisco vs. Iowa, CH, 1956
24, Elvin Hayes, Houston vs. UCLA, NSF, 1967
23, Bill Russell, San Francisco vs. Southern Methodist, NSF, 1956
22, Elgin Baylor, Seattle vs. Kansas St., NSF, 1958
22, Tom Sanders, New York U. vs. Ohio St., NSF, 1960
22, Larry Kenon, Memphis vs. Providence, NSF, 1973
22, Akeem Olajuwon, Houston vs. Louisville, NSF, 1983
21, Bill Spivey, Kentucky vs. Kansas St., CH, 1951
21, Lew Alcindor, UCLA vs. Drake, NSF, 1969
21, Artis Gilmore, Jacksonville vs. St. Bonaventure, NSF, 1970
21, Bill Walton, UCLA vs. Louisville, NSF, 1972

ASSISTS
18, Mark Wade, UNLV vs. Indiana, NSF, 1987
12, Rumeal Robinson, Michigan vs. Illinois, NSF, 1989
12, Edgar Padilla, Massachusetts vs. Kentucky, NSF, 1996
11, Michael Jackson, Georgetown vs. St. John's (N.Y.), NSF, 1985
11, Milt Wagner, Louisville vs. LSU, NSF, 1986
11, Rumeal Robinson, Michigan vs. Seton Hall, CH, 1989 (ot)
10, Corey Beck, Arkansas vs. North Carolina, NSF, 1995
9, Six tied (most recent: Lazarus Sims, Syracuse vs. Mississippi St., NSF, 1996)

BLOCKED SHOTS
6, Danny Manning, Kansas vs. Duke, NSF, 1988
6, Marcus Camby, Massachusetts vs. Kentucky, NSF, 1996
4, A.J. Bramlett, Arizona vs. Kentucky, CH, 1997 (ot)
4, Andy Kowske, Wisconsin vs. Michigan St., NSF, 2000
4, Shane Battier, Duke vs. Maryland, NSF, 2001
4, Loren Woods, Arizona vs. Duke, CH, 2001
3, 22 tied (most recent: Loren Woods, Arizona vs. Michigan St., NSF, 2001)

STEALS
7, Tommy Amaker, Duke vs. Louisville, CH, 1986
7, Mookie Blaylock, Oklahoma vs. Kansas, CH, 1988
6, Gilbert Arenas, Arizona vs. Michigan St., NSF, 2001
5, Danny Manning, Kansas vs. Oklahoma, CH, 1988
5, Greg Anthony, UNLV vs. Duke, CH, 1990
5, Anthony Epps, Kentucky vs. Minnesota, NSF, 1997
5, Wayne Turner, Kentucky vs. Minnesota, NSF, 1997
4, 15 tied (most recent: Vince Carter, North Carolina vs. Arizona, NSF, 1997)

Team Records

POINTS
127, *St. Joseph's vs. Utah (120), N3d, 1961 (4 ot)
120, Utah vs. St. Joseph's (127), N3d, 1961 (4 ot)
118, Princeton vs. Wichita St. (82), N3d, 1965
108, UCLA vs. Wichita St. (89), NSF, 1965
106, UCLA vs. Rutgers (92), N3d, 1976
106, UNLV vs. Charlotte (94), N3d, 1977
105, North Carolina vs. Louisville (91), N3d, 1972
103, UNLV vs. Duke (73), CH, 1990
101, UCLA vs. Houston (69), NSF, 1968
101, Michigan St. vs. Pennsylvania (67), NSF, 1979

FEWEST POINTS
28, Kentucky vs. Dartmouth (47), NSF, 1942
30, Duquesne vs. Indiana (39), NSF, 1940
30, Pittsburgh vs. Wisconsin (36), NSF, 1941
30, Oregon St. vs. Oklahoma St. (55), NSF, 1949
31, Iowa St. vs. Utah (40), NSF, 1944

WINNING MARGIN
36, Princeton (118) vs. Wichita St. (82), N3d, 1965
34, Cincinnati (80) vs. Oregon St. (46), NSF, 1963
34, Michigan St. (101) vs. Pennsylvania (67), NSF, 1979
32, UCLA (101) vs. Houston (69), NSF, 1968
30, UNLV (103) vs. Duke (73), CH, 1990

SMALLEST WINNING MARGIN
1, 12 tied (most recent: Kentucky [86] vs. Stanford [85], NSF, 1998 [ot])

POINTS BY LOSING TEAM
120, Utah vs. St. Joseph's (127), N3d, 1961 (4 ot)
94, Charlotte vs. UNLV (106), N3d, 1977
93, Pennsylvania vs. DePaul (96), N3d, 1979
93, UNLV vs. Indiana (97), NSF, 1987
92, Rutgers vs. UCLA (106), N3d, 1976

DEFICIT OVERCOME TO WIN
22, Duke vs. Maryland, 17-39 with 6:55 left in 1st half, F: 94-84, NSF, 2001

FIELD GOALS
50, Utah vs. St. Joseph's, N3d, 1961 (4 ot)
48, Princeton vs. Wichita St., N3d, 1965
47, UNLV vs. Charlotte, N3d, 1977
45, *St. Joseph's vs. Utah, N3d, 1961 (4 ot)
45, Drake vs. North Carolina, N3d, 1969

FEWEST FIELD GOALS
9, Oklahoma St. vs. Kentucky, CH, 1949
10, Wisconsin vs. Pittsburgh, NSF, 1941
10, Kentucky vs. Dartmouth, NSF, 1942
11, Duquesne vs. Indiana, NSF, 1940
11, Oregon St. vs. Oklahoma St., NSF, 1949

FIELD GOALS ATTEMPTED
105, *Western Ky. vs. Villanova, NSF, 1971 (2 ot)
103, Utah vs. St. Joseph's, N3d, 1961 (4 ot)
101, *St. Joseph's vs. Utah, N3d, 1961 (4 ot)
100, Rutgers vs. UCLA, N3d, 1976
95, Houston vs. Ohio St., N3d, 1968
95, UNLV vs. Charlotte, N3d, 1977

FEWEST FIELD GOALS ATTEMPTED
28, Villanova vs. Georgetown, CH, 1985
38, Villanova vs. Memphis, NSF, 1985
41, Georgetown vs. Louisville, NSF, 1982
41, Duke vs. Kansas, CH, 1991
42, Houston vs. Virginia, NSF, 1984 (ot)
42, St. John's (N.Y.) vs. Georgetown, NSF, 1985

FIELD-GOAL PERCENTAGE
78.6% (22-28), Villanova vs. Georgetown, CH, 1985
67.4% (31-46), Ohio St. vs. California, CH, 1960
64.5% (40-62), UCLA vs. Memphis, CH, 1973
63.6% (35-55), Kansas vs. Oklahoma, CH, 1988
63.3% (38-60), Ohio St. vs. St. Joseph's, CH, 1961
63.3% (38-60), Michigan St. vs. Pennsylvania, NSF, 1979

LOWEST FIELD-GOAL PERCENTAGE
19.5% (15-77), North Carolina St. vs. Baylor, N3d, 1950
21.5% (14-65), Washington St. vs. Wisconsin, CH, 1941
23.4% (15-64), Baylor vs. Kentucky, CH, 1948
24.5% (13-53), Kentucky vs. Georgetown, NSF, 1984
25.4% (18-71), Oklahoma St. vs. Illinois, N3d, 1951

THREE-POINT FIELD GOALS
13, UNLV vs. Indiana, NSF, 1987
12, Arkansas vs. North Carolina, NSF, 1995
12, Kentucky vs. Syracuse, CH, 1996
11, Kansas vs. North Carolina, NSF, 1993
11, Mississippi St. vs. Syracuse, NSF, 1996
11, Arizona vs. North Carolina, NSF, 1997
11, Stanford vs. Kentucky, NSF, 1998 (ot)
11, Michigan vs. Florida, CH, 2000

FEWEST THREE-POINT FIELD GOALS
0, Michigan vs. Kentucky, NSF, 1993 (ot)
1, Duke vs. UNLV, CH, 1990
1, Michigan vs. Duke, CH, 1992
1, Connecticut, vs. Ohio St., NSF, 1999
2, Seven tied (most recent: Michigan St. vs. Arizona, NSF, 2001)

THREE-POINT FIELD GOALS ATTEMPTED
35, UNLV vs. Indiana, NSF, 1987
34, Arkansas vs. North Carolina, NSF, 1995
32, Arizona vs. Arkansas, NSF, 1994
30, Kentucky vs. Arizona, CH, 1997 (ot)
29, Arizona vs. North Carolina, NSF, 1997

FEWEST THREE-POINT FIELD GOALS ATTEMPTED
4, Indiana vs. UNLV, NSF, 1987
4, Kansas vs. Duke, NSF, 1988
4, Michigan vs. Kentucky, NSF, 1993 (ot)
6, Kansas vs. Oklahoma, CH, 1988
6, Connecticut vs. Ohio St., NSF, 1999

THREE-POINT FIELD-GOAL PERCENTAGE
(Minimum 7 3FGM)
66.7% (10-15), UNLV vs. Georgia Tech, NSF, 1990
63.6% (7-11), Indiana vs. Syracuse, CH, 1987
63.6% (7-11), Duke vs. Indiana, NSF, 1992
57.1% (8-14), UNLV vs. Duke, CH, 1990
55.0% (11-20), Kansas vs. North Carolina, NSF, 1993

LOWEST THREE-POINT FIELD-GOAL PERCENTAGE
(Minimum 5 3FGA)
9.1% (1-11), Duke vs. UNLV, CH, 1990
9.1% (1-11), Michigan vs. Duke, CH, 1992
13.0% (3-23), North Carolina vs. Utah, NSF, 1998
14.3% (2-14), Michigan St. vs. Wisconsin, NSF, 2000
14.3% (2-14), Michigan St. vs. Arizona, NSF, 2001

FREE THROWS MADE
37, *St. Joseph's vs. Utah, N3d, 1961 (4 ot)
37, Jacksonville vs. St. Bonaventure, NSF, 1970
34, DePaul vs. Pennsylvania, N3d, 1979
34, Virginia vs. LSU, N3d, 1981
34, Arizona vs. Kentucky, CH, 1997 (ot)

FEWEST FREE THROWS MADE
1, UNLV vs. North Carolina, NSF, 1977
2, Dartmouth vs. Utah, CH, 1944 (ot)
2, DePaul vs. Indiana St., NSF, 1979
2, North Carolina vs. Utah, NSF, 1998
3, Indiana vs. UCLA, NSF, 1973

FREE THROWS ATTEMPTED
45, Jacksonville vs. St. Bonaventure, NSF, 1970
44, Bradley vs. La Salle, CH, 1954
44, UCLA vs. Drake, NSF, 1969
44, North Carolina vs. Louisville, N3d, 1972
44, Syracuse vs. Providence, NSF, 1987

FEWEST FREE THROWS ATTEMPTED
5, Dartmouth vs. Stanford, CH, 1942
5, Dartmouth vs. Utah, CH, 1944 (ot)
5, UNLV vs. North Carolina, NSF, 1977
5, DePaul vs. Indiana St., NSF, 1979
6, Indiana vs. UCLA, NSF, 1973
6, Mississippi St. vs. Syracuse, NSF, 1996

FREE-THROW PERCENTAGE
(Minimum 15 FTM)
93.8% (15-16), Ohio St. vs. Cincinnati, CH, 1961 (ot)
92.0% (23-25), Marquette vs. North Carolina, CH, 1977
90.5% (19-21), Ohio St. vs. New York U., NSF, 1945 (ot)
90.5% (19-21), Duke vs. Louisville, CH, 1986
88.9% (16-18), *UCLA vs. Louisville, CH, 1980

LOWEST FREE-THROW PERCENTAGE
20.0% (1-5), UNLV vs. North Carolina, NSF, 1977
28.6% (2-7), North Carolina vs. Utah, NSF, 1998
33.3% (5-15), Oklahoma St. vs. New York U., CH, 1945
35.3% (6-17), Temple vs. Iowa, NSF, 1956
37.5% (6-16), Houston vs. UCLA, NSF, 1967

REBOUNDS
76, Houston vs. North Carolina, N3d, 1967
69, *Western Ky. vs. Villanova, NSF, 1971 (2 ot)
67, Kansas vs. Western Ky., N3d, 1971
65, Michigan St. vs. North Carolina, NSF, 1957 (3 ot)
65, Utah vs. St. Joseph's, N3d, 1961 (4 ot)

FEWEST REBOUNDS
17, Villanova vs. Georgetown, CH, 1985
17, Georgetown vs. Villanova, CH, 1985
20, Wisconsin vs. Michigan St., NSF, 2000
21, Memphis vs. UCLA, CH, 1973
21, DePaul vs. Indiana St., NSF, 1979

REBOUND MARGIN
25, Michigan St. (60) vs. San Francisco (35), N3d, 1957
24, Houston (76) vs. North Carolina (52), N3d, 1967
23, Seattle (56) vs. Kansas St. (33), NSF, 1958
23, New Mexico St. (57) vs. St. Bonaventure (34), N3d, 1970
22, Michigan St. (42) vs. Wisconsin (20), NSF, 2000

ASSISTS
26, Louisville vs. LSU, NSF, 1986
24, UNLV vs. Duke, CH, 1990
23, UNLV vs. Indiana, NSF, 1987
23, Michigan vs. Illinois, NSF, 1989
22, Arkansas vs. North Carolina, NSF, 1995
22, Kentucky vs. Syracuse, NSF, 1996

BLOCKED SHOTS
9, Kansas vs. Duke, NSF, 1988
8, Massachusetts vs. Kentucky, NSF, 1996
8, Arizona vs. North Carolina, NSF, 1997
7, Nine tied (most recent: three in 2001)

STEALS
16, UNLV vs. Duke, CH, 1990
15, Arkansas vs. UCLA, CH, 1995
14, Kentucky, vs. Minnesota, NSF, 1997
13, Duke vs. Louisville, CH, 1986
13, Oklahoma vs. Kansas, CH, 1988

PERSONAL FOULS
35, St. John's (N.Y.) vs. Kansas, CH, 1952
33, Providence vs. Syracuse, NSF, 1987
33, Indiana vs. Duke, NSF, 1992
32, Bradley vs. CCNY, CH, 1950
32, St. Bonaventure vs. Jacksonville, NSF, 1970

FEWEST PERSONAL FOULS
5, Stanford vs. Dartmouth, CH, 1942
6, Utah vs. Dartmouth, CH, 1944 (ot)
7, Dartmouth vs. Stanford, CH, 1942
8, Wisconsin vs. Pittsburgh, NSF, 1941
8, Washington St. vs. Wisconsin, CH, 1941

PLAYERS DISQUALIFIED
4, St. Bonaventure vs. Jacksonville, NSF, 1970
4, Syracuse vs. Louisville, N3d, 1975 (ot)
4, Pennsylvania vs. DePaul, N3d, 1979
4, Indiana vs. Duke, NSF, 1992
4, Kentucky vs. Arizona, CH, 1997 (ot)

Team and Two-Team Scoring by Halves

POINTS IN A HALF, TEAM
65, UCLA vs. Wichita St., NSF, 1965 (1st)
65, Princeton vs. Wichita St., N3d, 1965 (2nd)
62, Seton Hall vs. Duke, NSF, 1989 (2nd)
58, Memphis vs. Providence, NSF, 1973 (2nd)
58, Houston vs. Louisville, NSF, 1983 (2nd)

POINTS IN A HALF, BOTH TEAMS
111, Louisville (57) vs. North Carolina (54), N3d, 1972 (2nd)
108, Princeton (65) vs. Wichita St. (43), N3d, 1965 (2nd)
106, UCLA (57) vs. Rutgers (49), N3d, 1976 (1st)
105, Charlotte (55) vs. UNLV (50), N3d, 1977 (1st)
104, Notre Dame (57) vs. Duke (47), NSF, 1978 (2nd)

POINTS AT HALFTIME, TEAM
65, UCLA vs. Wichita St. (38), NSF, 1965
57, UCLA vs. Rutgers (49), N3d, 1976

FINAL FOUR GAME RECORDS—TEAM AND TWO-TEAM SCORING BY HALVES

55, Charlotte vs. UNLV (50), N3d, 1977
54, Drake vs. North Carolina (45), N3d, 1969
53, Six tied (most recent: Georgia Tech vs. UNLV [46], NSF, 1990)

POINTS AT HALFTIME, BOTH TEAMS
106, UCLA (57) vs. Rutgers (49), N3d, 1976
105, Charlotte (55) vs. UNLV (50), N3d, 1977
103, UCLA (65) vs. Wichita St. (38), NSF, 1965
102, Louisville (53) vs. Cincinnati (49) N3d, 1959
100, Indiana (53) vs. UNLV (47), NSF, 1987
100, Kansas (50) vs. Oklahoma (50), CH, 1988

FEWEST POINTS IN A HALF, TEAM
10, Villanova vs. Ohio St., NSF, 1939 (1st)
11, Oregon St. vs. Oklahoma St., NSF, 1949 (1st)
11, Kentucky vs. Georgetown, NSF, 1984 (2nd)
12, Pittsburgh vs. Wisconsin, NSF, 1941 (2nd)
13, Duquesne vs. Indiana, NSF, 1940 (1st)
13, Kentucky vs. Dartmouth, NSF, 1942 (1st)

FEWEST POINTS IN A HALF, BOTH TEAMS
31, Duquesne (17) vs. Indiana (14), NSF, 1940 (2nd)
32, Pittsburgh (18) vs. Wisconsin (14), NSF, 1941 (1st)
32, Oklahoma St. (21) vs. Oregon St. (11), NSF, 1949 (1st)
34, Wisconsin (22) vs. Pittsburgh (12), NSF, 1941 (2nd)
34, Wyoming (18) vs. Georgetown (16), CH, 1943 (1st)

FEWEST POINTS AT HALFTIME, TEAM
10, Villanova vs. Ohio St. (25), NSF, 1939
11, Oregon St. vs. Oklahoma St. (21), NSF, 1949
13, Duquesne vs. Indiana (25), NSF, 1940
13, Kentucky vs. Dartmouth (23), NSF, 1942
14, Wisconsin vs. Pittsburgh (18), NSF, 1941
14, Oklahoma St. vs. Kansas St. (37), NSF, 1951

FEWEST POINTS AT HALFTIME, BOTH TEAMS
32, Pittsburgh (18) vs. Wisconsin (14), NSF, 1941
32, Oklahoma St. (21) vs. Oregon St. (11), NSF, 1949
34, Wyoming (18) vs. Georgetown (16), CH, 1943
35, Ohio St. (25) vs. Villanova (10), NSF, 1939
35, Dartmouth (18) vs. Utah (17), CH, 1944

HALFTIME LEAD
33, Michigan St. (50) vs. Pennsylvania (17), NSF, 1979
27, UCLA (65) vs. Wichita St. (38), NSF, 1965
23, Kansas St. (37) vs. Oklahoma St. (14), NSF, 1951
23, Purdue (53) vs. North Carolina (30), NSF, 1969
22, UCLA (53) vs. Houston (31), NSF, 1968

HALFTIME DEFICIT OVERCOME
11, Temple vs. Kansas St., H: 28-39, F: 67-57, N3d, 1958
11, Duke vs. Maryland, H:38-49, F: 94-84, NSF, 2001
10, Kentucky vs. Utah, H: 41-31, F: 78-69, CH, 1998
9, Memphis vs. Providence, H: 40-49, F: 98-85, NSF, 1973
8, Loyola (Ill.) vs. Cincinnati, H: 21-29, F: 60-58 (ot), CH, 1963
8, Louisville vs. LSU, H: 36-44, F: 88-77, NSF, 1986

Two-Team Records

POINTS
247, *St. Joseph's (127) vs. Utah (120), N3d, 1961 (4 ot)
200, Princeton (118) vs. Wichita St. (82), N3d, 1965
200, UNLV (106) vs. Charlotte (94), N3d, 1977
198, UCLA (106) vs. Rutgers (92), N3d, 1976
197, UCLA (108) vs. Wichita St. (89), NSF, 1965

FEWEST POINTS
66, Wisconsin (36) vs. Pittsburgh (30), NSF, 1941
69, Indiana (39) vs. Duquesne (30), NSF, 1940
71, Utah (40) vs. Iowa St. (31), NSF, 1944
73, Wisconsin (39) vs. Washington St. (34) CH, 1941
75, Dartmouth (47) vs. Kentucky (28), NSF, 1942

FIELD GOALS
95, Utah (50) vs. *St. Joseph's (45), N3d, 1961 (4 ot)
83, UNLV (47) vs. Charlotte (36), N3d, 1977
82, UCLA (44) vs. Rutgers (38), N3d, 1976
80, UCLA (44) vs. Wichita St. (36), NSF, 1965
79, Memphis (41) vs. Providence (38), NSF, 1973

FIELD GOALS ATTEMPTED
204, Utah (103) vs. *St. Joseph's (101), N3d, 1961 (4 ot)
180, Rutgers (100) vs. UCLA (80), N3d, 1976
178, *Western Ky. (105) vs. *Villanova (73), NSF, 1971 (2 ot)
172, Houston (95) vs. Ohio St. (77), N3d, 1968
169, North Carolina (89) vs. Michigan St. (80), NSF, 1957 (3 ot)

THREE-POINT FIELD GOALS
22, Arkansas (12) vs. North Carolina (10), NSF, 1995
18, UNLV (10) vs. Georgia Tech (8), NSF, 1990
18, Kentucky (12) vs. Syracuse (6), CH, 1996
17, Michigan St. (11) vs. Florida (6), CH, 2000
16, Kansas (11) vs. North Carolina (5), NSF, 1993
16, Mississippi St. (11) vs. Syracuse (5) NSF, 1996
16, Kentucky (10) vs. Arizona (6), CH, 1997 (ot)
16, Stanford (11) vs. Kentucky (5), NSF, 1998 (ot)

THREE-POINT FIELD GOALS ATTEMPTED
62, Arkansas (34) vs. North Carolina (28), NSF, 1995
56, Arizona (32) vs. Arkansas (24), NSF, 1994
50, Arizona (29) vs. North Carolina (21), NSF, 1997
50, Florida (28) vs. North Carolina (22), NSF, 2000
49, Duke (27) vs. Arizona (22), CH, 2001

FREE THROWS MADE
60, North Carolina (33) vs. Louisville (27), N3d, 1972
57, *St. Joseph's (37) vs. Utah (20), N3d, 1961 (4 ot)
53, Indiana (30) vs. LSU (23), NSF, 1953
52, Jacksonville (37) vs. St. Bonaventure (15), NSF, 1970
51, Colorado (29) vs. Iowa (22), N3d, 1955

FREE THROWS ATTEMPTED
81, North Carolina (44) vs. Louisville (37), N3d, 1972
76, *St. Joseph's (42) vs. Utah (34), N3d, 1961 (4 ot)
70, Kentucky (38) vs. Syracuse (32), NSF, 1975
68, Bradley (44) vs. La Salle (24), CH, 1954
68, UCLA (44) vs. Drake (24), NSF, 1969
68, Florida St. (43) vs. North Carolina (25), NSF, 1972

REBOUNDS
128, Utah (65) vs. *St. Joseph's (63), N3d, 1961 (4 ot)
128, Houston (76) vs. North Carolina (52), N3d, 1967
123, *Western Ky. (69) vs. *Villanova (54), NSF, 1971 (2 ot)
123, Kansas (67) vs. *Western Ky. (56), N3d, 1971
119, Michigan St. (65) vs. North Carolina (54), NSF, 1957 (3 ot)

ASSISTS
39, Houston (20) vs. Georgetown (19), CH, 1984
39, Louisville (26) vs. LSU (13), NSF, 1986
39, UNLV (23) vs. Indiana (16), NSF, 1987
39, Kentucky (20) vs. Massachusetts (19), NSF, 1996
37, Three tied (most recent: Arkansas [22] vs. North Carolina [15], NSF, 1995)

BLOCKED SHOTS
14, Kansas (9) vs. Duke (5), NSF, 1988
14, Massachusetts (8) vs. Kentucky (6), NSF, 1996
12, Kentucky (7) vs. Stanford (5), NSF, 1998 (ot)
12, Arizona (7) vs. Duke (5), CH, 2001
11, Seton Hall (7) vs. Duke (4), NSF, 1989

STEALS
26, Arkansas (15) vs. UCLA (11), CH, 1995
24, Oklahoma (13) vs. Kansas (11), CH, 1988
21, UNLV (16) vs. Duke (5), CH, 1990
20, Kentucky (12) vs. Massachusetts (8), NSF, 1996
20, Kentucky (14) vs. Minnesota (6), NSF, 1997

PERSONAL FOULS
61, Kentucky (31) vs. Syracuse (30), NSF, 1975
57, Oklahoma St. (36) vs. Kentucky (21), CH, 1949
55, Louisville (31) vs. North Carolina (24), N3d, 1972
53, St. Bonaventure (32) vs. Jacksonville (21), NSF, 1970
53, Pennsylvania (31) vs. Michigan St. (22), NSF, 1979
53, Pennsylvania (31) vs. DePaul (22), N3d, 1979

PLAYERS DISQUALIFIED
6, CCNY (3) vs. North Carolina St. (3), NSF, 1950
6, Pennsylvania (4) vs. DePaul (2), N3d, 1979
6, LSU (4) vs. Virginia (2), N3d, 1981
5, Five tied (most recent: Kentucky [4] vs. Arizona [1], CH, 1997 [ot])

Championship Game Records

Record later vacated is indicated by (*).

Individual Records

POINTS
44, Bill Walton, UCLA vs. Memphis, 1973
42, Gail Goodrich, UCLA vs. Michigan, 1965
41, Jack Givens, Kentucky vs. Duke, 1978
37, Lew Alcindor, UCLA vs. Purdue, 1969
35, John Morton, Seton Hall vs. Michigan, 1989 (ot)

FIELD GOALS
21, Bill Walton, UCLA vs. Memphis, 1973
18, Jack Givens, Kentucky vs. Duke, 1978
15, Lew Alcindor, UCLA vs. North Carolina, 1968
15, Lew Alcindor, UCLA vs. Purdue, 1969
13, Four tied (most recent: Danny Manning, Kansas vs. Oklahoma, 1988)

FIELD GOALS ATTEMPTED
36, Rick Mount, Purdue vs. UCLA, 1969
32, Elgin Baylor, Seattle vs. Kentucky, 1958
30, Kevin Grevey, Kentucky vs. UCLA, 1975
29, Bill Spivey, Kentucky vs. Kansas St., 1951
29, Artis Gilmore, Jacksonville vs. UCLA, 1970

FIELD-GOAL PERCENTAGE
(Minimum 10 FGM)
95.5% (21-22), Bill Walton, UCLA vs. Memphis, 1973
83.3% (10-12), Udonis Haslam, Florida vs. Michigan St., 2000
76.5% (13-17), James Worthy, North Carolina vs. Georgetown, 1982
75.0% (15-20), Lew Alcindor, UCLA vs. Purdue, 1969
75.0% (12-16), Anderson Hunt, UNLV vs. Duke, 1990

THREE-POINT FIELD GOALS
7, Steve Alford, Indiana vs. Syracuse, 1987
7, Dave Sieger, Oklahoma vs. Kansas, 1988
7, Tony Delk, Kentucky vs. Syracuse, 1996
5, Glen Rice, Michigan vs. Seton Hall, 1989 (ot)
5, Donald Williams, North Carolina vs. Michigan, 1993
5, Trajan Langdon, Duke vs. Connecticut, 1999
5, Mike Dunleavy, Duke vs. Arizona, 2001

THREE-POINT FIELD GOALS ATTEMPTED
13, Dave Sieger, Oklahoma vs. Kansas, 1988
12, Glen Rice, Michigan vs. Seton Hall, 1989 (ot)
12, John Morton, Seton Hall vs. Michigan, 1989 (ot)
12, Tony Delk, Kentucky vs. Syracuse, 1996
12, Scott Padgett, Kentucky vs. Arizona, 1997 (ot)

THREE-POINT FIELD-GOAL PERCENTAGE
(Minimum 5 3FGM)
71.4% (5-7), Donald Williams, North Carolina vs. Michigan, 1993

The first reference to "Final Four" in an NCAA publication was in the 1975 Official Collegiate Basketball Guide. On page 5 in the National Preview-Review section written by Ed Chay of the Cleveland Plain Dealer, Chay writes "Outspoken Al McGuire of Marquette, whose team was one of the final four in Greensboro, was among several coaches who said it was good for college basketball that UCLA was finally beaten."

The first time Final Four was capitalized was in the 1978 basketball guide.

CHAMPIONSHIP GAME RECORDS—INDIVIDUAL

70.0% (7-10), Steve Alford, Indiana vs. Syracuse, 1987
58.3% (7-12), Tony Delk, Kentucky vs. Syracuse, 1996
55.6% (5-9), Mike Dunleavy, Duke vs. Arizona, 2001
53.8% (7-13), Dave Sieger, Oklahoma vs. Kansas, 1988

FREE THROWS MADE
18, Gail Goodrich, UCLA vs. Michigan, 1965
14, Miles Simon, Arizona vs. Kentucky, 1997 (ot)
12, Vern Hatton, Kentucky vs. Seattle, 1958
12, Christian Laettner, Duke vs. Kansas, 1991
11, Larry Finch, Memphis vs. UCLA, 1973
11, Wilt Chamberlain, Kansas vs. North Carolina, 1957 (3 ot)
11, Dick Estergard, Bradley vs. La Salle, 1954

FREE THROWS ATTEMPTED
20, Gail Goodrich, UCLA vs. Michigan, 1965
17, Bob Carney, Bradley vs. La Salle, 1954
17, Miles Simon, Arizona vs. Kentucky, 1997 (ot)
16, Wilt Chamberlain, Kansas vs. North Carolina, 1957 (3 ot)
15, Vern Hatton, Kentucky vs. Seattle, 1958

FREE-THROW PERCENTAGE
(Minimum 10 FTM)
100.0% (12-12), Christian Laettner, Duke vs. Kansas, 1991
91.7% (11-12), Dick Estergard, Bradley vs. La Salle, 1954
90.0% (18-20), Gail Goodrich, UCLA vs. Michigan, 1965
84.6% (11-13), Larry Finch, Memphis vs. UCLA, 1973
83.3% (10-12), Three tied (most recent: Eugene Banks, Duke vs. Kentucky, 1978)

REBOUNDS
27, Bill Russell, San Francisco vs. Iowa, 1956
21, Bill Spivey, Kentucky vs. Kansas St., 1951
20, Lew Alcindor, UCLA vs. Purdue, 1969
20, Bill Walton, UCLA vs. Florida St., 1972
19, Three tied (most recent: Derrick Coleman, Syracuse vs. Indiana, 1987)

ASSISTS
11, Rumeal Robinson, Michigan vs. Seton Hall, 1989 (ot)
9, Alvin Franklin, Houston vs. Georgetown, 1984
9, Michael Jackson, Georgetown vs. Villanova, 1985
9, Bobby Hurley, Duke vs. Kansas, 1991
8, Cameron Dollar, UCLA vs. Arkansas, 1995

BLOCKED SHOTS
4, Loren Woods, Arizona vs. Duke, 2001
3, Rony Seikaly, Syracuse vs. Indiana, 1987
3, Derrick Coleman, Syracuse vs. Indiana, 1987
3, Dean Garrett, Indiana vs. Syracuse, 1987
3, Terry Mills, Michigan vs. Seton Hall, 1989 (ot)
3, Chris Webber, Michigan vs. North Carolina, 1993
3, Grant Hill, Duke vs. Arkansas, 1994
3, Nazr Mohammed, Kentucky vs. Arizona, 1997 (ot)
3, Jamaal Magloire, Kentucky vs. Utah, 1998
3, Kevin Freeman, Connecticut vs. Duke, 1999

STEALS
7, Tommy Amaker, Duke vs. Louisville, 1986
7, Mookie Blaylock, Oklahoma vs. Kansas, 1988
5, Danny Manning, Kansas vs. Oklahoma, 1988
5, Greg Anthony, UNLV vs. Duke, 1990
4, Eight tied (most recent: two in 1996)

Team Records

POINTS
103, UNLV vs. Duke (73), 1990
98, UCLA vs. Duke (83), 1964
94, Kentucky vs. Duke (88), 1978
92, La Salle vs. Bradley (76), 1954
92, UCLA vs. Purdue (72), 1969
92, UCLA vs. Kentucky (85), 1975

FEWEST POINTS
33, Ohio St. vs. Oregon (46), 1939
34, Washington St. vs. Wisconsin (39), 1941
34, Georgetown vs. Wyoming (46), 1943
36, Oklahoma St. vs. Kentucky (46) 1949
38, Dartmouth vs. Stanford (53), 1942

WINNING MARGIN
30, UNLV (103) vs. Duke (73), 1990
23, UCLA (78) vs. North Carolina (55), 1968
21, UCLA (87) vs. Memphis (66), 1973
20, Ohio St. (75) vs. California (55), 1960
20, UCLA (92) vs. Purdue (72), 1969
20, Duke (71) vs. Michigan (51), 1992

SMALLEST WINNING MARGIN
1, Indiana (69) vs. Kansas (68), 1953
1, North Carolina (54) vs. Kansas (53), 1957 (3 ot)
1, California (71) vs. West Virginia (70), 1959
1, North Carolina (63) vs. Georgetown (62), 1982
1, Indiana (74) vs. Syracuse (73), 1987
1, Michigan (80) vs. Seton Hall (79), 1989 (ot)

POINTS BY LOSING TEAM
88, Duke vs. Kentucky (94), 1978
85, Kentucky vs. UCLA (92), 1975
83, Duke vs. UCLA (98), 1964
80, Michigan vs. UCLA (91), 1965
79, Oklahoma vs. Kansas (83), 1988
79, Seton Hall vs. Michigan (80), 1989 (ot)
79, Arizona vs. Arizona (84), 1997 (ot)

FIELD GOALS
41, UNLV vs. Duke, 1990
40, UCLA vs. Memphis, 1973
39, Kentucky vs. Duke, 1978
38, UCLA vs. Kentucky, 1975
37, La Salle vs. Bradley, 1954

FEWEST FIELD GOALS
9, Oklahoma St. vs. Kentucky, 1949
13, North Carolina vs. Oklahoma St., 1946
14, Ohio St. vs. Oregon, 1939
14, Washington St. vs. Wisconsin, 1941
14, Georgetown vs. Wyoming, 1943

FIELD GOALS ATTEMPTED
92, Purdue vs. UCLA, 1969
87, San Francisco vs. Iowa, 1956
86, Kentucky vs. UCLA, 1975
84, Loyola (Ill.) vs. Cincinnati, 1963 (ot)
80, Kansas St. vs. Kentucky, 1951
80, Jacksonville vs. UCLA, 1970

FEWEST FIELD GOALS ATTEMPTED
28, Villanova vs. Georgetown, 1985
41, Duke vs. Kansas, 1991
43, Michigan St. vs. Indiana St., 1979
46, Ohio St. vs. California, 1960
46, North Carolina St. vs. Marquette, 1974

FIELD-GOAL PERCENTAGE
78.6% (22-28), Villanova vs. Georgetown, 1985
67.4% (31-46), Ohio St. vs. California, 1960
64.5% (40-62), UCLA vs. Memphis, 1973
63.6% (35-55), Kansas vs. Oklahoma, 1988
61.2% (41-67), UNLV vs. Duke, 1990

LOWEST FIELD-GOAL PERCENTAGE
21.5% (14-65), Washington St. vs. Wisconsin, 1941
23.4% (15-64), Baylor vs. Kentucky, 1948
25.4% (16-63), Wisconsin vs. Washington St., 1941
27.4% (23-84), Loyola (Ill.) vs. Cincinnati, 1963 (ot)
28.8% (23-80), Kansas St. vs. Kentucky, 1951

THREE-POINT FIELD GOALS
12, Kentucky vs. Syracuse, 1996
11, Michigan St. vs. Florida, 2000
10, Oklahoma vs. Kansas, 1988
10, Arkansas vs. UCLA, 1995
10, Kentucky vs. Arizona, 1997 (ot)

FEWEST THREE-POINT FIELD GOALS
1, Duke vs. UNLV, 1990
1, Michigan vs. Duke, 1992
2, UCLA vs. Arkansas, 1995
3, Connecticut vs. Duke, 1999
4, Four tied (most recent: Arizona vs. Duke, 2001)

THREE-POINT FIELD GOALS ATTEMPTED
30, Kentucky vs. Arizona, 1997 (ot)
28, Arkansas vs. UCLA, 1995
27, Kentucky vs. Syracuse, 1996
27, Duke vs. Arizona, 2001
24, Oklahoma vs. Kansas, 1988

FEWEST THREE-POINT FIELD GOALS ATTEMPTED
6, Kansas vs. Oklahoma, 1988
7, UCLA vs. Arkansas, 1995
8, Connecticut vs. Duke, 1999
9, Duke vs. Michigan, 1992

10, Syracuse vs. Indiana, 1987
10, Duke vs. Kansas, 1991

THREE-POINT FIELD-GOAL PERCENTAGE
(Minimum 7 3FGM)
63.6% (7-11), Indiana vs. Syracuse, 1987
57.1% (8-14), UNLV vs. Duke, 1990
50.0% (11-22), Michigan St. vs. Florida, 2000
44.4% (12-27), Kentucky vs. Syracuse, 1996
41.7% (10-24), Oklahoma vs. Kansas, 1988

LOWEST THREE-POINT FIELD-GOAL PERCENTAGE
(Minimum 5 3FGA)
9.1% (1-11), Duke vs. UNLV, 1990
9.1% (1-11), Michigan vs. Duke, 1992
18.2% (4-22), Arizona vs. Duke, 2001
27.8% (5-18), Arkansas vs. Duke, 1994
28.6% (2-7), UCLA vs. Arkansas, 1995
28.6% (4-14), Utah vs. Kentucky, 1998

FREE THROWS MADE
34, Arizona vs. Kentucky, 1997 (ot)
32, Bradley vs. La Salle, 1954
30, Duke vs. Kentucky, 1978
28, UTEP vs. Kentucky, 1966
28, UCLA vs. Purdue, 1969

FEWEST FREE THROWS MADE
2, Dartmouth vs. Utah, 1944 (ot)
4, Dartmouth vs. Stanford, 1942
4, Kansas vs. Duke, 1991
5, Ohio St. vs. Oregon, 1939
5, Stanford vs. Dartmouth, 1942
5, Oklahoma St. vs. New York U., 1945

FREE THROWS ATTEMPTED
44, Bradley vs. La Salle, 1954
41, UCLA vs. Purdue, 1969
41, Arizona vs. Kentucky, 1997 (ot)
36, Kentucky vs. Seattle, 1958
35, CCNY vs. Bradley, 1950
35, UCLA vs. Jacksonville, 1970

FEWEST FREE THROWS ATTEMPTED
5, Dartmouth vs. Stanford, 1942
5, Dartmouth vs. Utah, 1944 (ot)
7, Michigan vs. North Carolina, 1993
8, Stanford vs. Dartmouth, 1942
8, Jacksonville vs. UCLA, 1970
8, Georgetown vs. Villanova, 1985
8, Kansas vs. Duke, 1991

FREE-THROW PERCENTAGE
(Minimum 15 FTM)
93.8% (15-16), Ohio St. vs. Cincinnati, 1961 (ot)
92.0% (23-25), Marquette vs. North Carolina, 1977
90.5% (19-21), Duke vs. Louisville, 1986
88.9% (16-18), *UCLA vs. Louisville, 1980
88.2% (30-34), Duke vs. Kentucky, 1978
88.2% (15-17), Kentucky vs. Utah, 1998

LOWEST FREE-THROW PERCENTAGE
33.3% (5-15), Oklahoma St. vs. New York U., 1945
40.0% (2-5), Dartmouth vs. Utah, 1944 (ot)
44.0% (11-25), UCLA vs. Dayton, 1967
45.5% (10-22), Indiana vs. Michigan St., 1979
46.2% (6-13), Georgetown vs. Wyoming, 1943

REBOUNDS
61, UCLA vs. Purdue, 1969
60, San Francisco vs. Iowa, 1956
55, Kentucky vs. Seattle, 1958
55, UCLA vs. Kentucky, 1975
54, UCLA vs. Dayton, 1967

FEWEST REBOUNDS
17, Villanova vs. Georgetown, 1985
17, Georgetown vs. Villanova, 1985
21, Memphis vs. UCLA, 1973
22, Georgetown vs. North Carolina, 1982
24, Kentucky vs. Utah, 1998

REBOUND MARGIN
19, UCLA (40) vs. Memphis (21), 1973
19, UCLA (50) vs. Arkansas (31), 1995
15, Kentucky (45) vs. Kansas St. (30), 1951
15, Utah (39) vs. Kentucky (24), 1998
14, North Carolina (42) vs. Kansas (28), 1957 (3 ot)

ASSISTS
24, UNLV vs. Duke, 1990
22, Kentucky vs. Syracuse, 1996

CHAMPIONSHIP GAME RECORDS—TEAM

21, UCLA vs. Arkansas, 1995
20, Houston vs. Georgetown, 1984
20, Indiana vs. Syracuse, 1987

BLOCKED SHOTS
7, Louisville vs. Duke, 1986
7, Syracuse vs. Indiana, 1987
7, North Carolina vs. Michigan, 1993
7, Duke vs. Arkansas, 1994
7, Kentucky vs. Arizona, 1997 (ot)
7, Arizona vs. Duke, 2001

STEALS
16, UNLV vs. Duke, 1990
15, Arkansas vs. UCLA, 1995
13, Duke vs. Louisville, 1986
13, Oklahoma vs. Kansas, 1988
11, Four tied (most recent: Kentucky vs. Syracuse, 1996)

PERSONAL FOULS
35, St. John's (N.Y.) vs. Kansas, 1952
32, Bradley vs. CCNY, 1950
30, Purdue vs. UCLA, 1969
29, Marquette vs. North Carolina St., 1974
29, Kentucky vs. Arizona, 1997 (ot)

FEWEST PERSONAL FOULS
5, Stanford vs. Dartmouth, 1942
6, Utah vs. Dartmouth, 1944 (ot)
7, Dartmouth vs. Stanford, 1942
8, Washington St. vs. Wisconsin, 1941
9, Oregon vs. Ohio St., 1939
9, UCLA vs. Villanova, 1971

PLAYERS DISQUALIFIED
4, Kentucky vs. Arizona, 1997 (ot)
4, Bradley vs. CCNY, 1950
3, Kentucky vs. Kansas St., 1951
3, Michigan vs. UCLA, 1965
3, Purdue vs. UCLA, 1969

Team and Two-Team Scoring by Halves

POINTS IN A HALF, TEAM
57, Indiana vs. Michigan, 1976 (2nd)
56, UNLV vs. Duke, 1990 (2nd)
50, Six tied (most recent: both Kansas and Oklahoma, 1988 [1st])

POINTS IN A HALF, BOTH TEAMS
100, Kansas (50) vs. Oklahoma (50), 1988 (1st)
99, Duke (50) vs. Kentucky (49), 1978 (2nd)
94, UCLA (49) vs. Kentucky (45), 1975 (2nd)
94, UNLV (56) vs. Duke (38), 1990 (2nd)

POINTS AT HALFTIME, TEAM
50, UCLA vs. Duke (38), 1964
50, UCLA vs. Purdue (41), 1969
50, UCLA vs. Florida St. (39), 1972
50, Kansas vs. Oklahoma (50), 1988
50, Oklahoma vs. Kansas (50), 1988

POINTS AT HALFTIME, BOTH TEAMS
100, Kansas (50) vs. Oklahoma (50), 1988
91, UCLA (50) vs. Purdue (41), 1969
89, UCLA (50) vs. Florida St. (39), 1972

FEWEST POINTS IN A HALF, TEAM
16, Ohio St. vs. Oregon, 1939 (1st)
16, Dartmouth vs. Stanford, 1942 (2nd)
16, Georgetown vs. Wyoming, 1943 (1st)
16, Oklahoma vs. Holy Cross, 1947 (2nd)

FEWEST POINTS IN A HALF, BOTH TEAMS
34, Wyoming (18) vs. Georgetown (16), 1943 (1st)
35, Dartmouth (18) vs. Utah (17), 1944 (1st)
37, Oregon (21) vs. Ohio St. (16), 1939 (1st)
37, Utah (19) vs. Dartmouth (18), 1944 (2nd)

FEWEST POINTS AT HALFTIME, TEAM
16, Ohio St. vs. Oregon (21), 1939
16, Georgetown vs. Wyoming (18), 1943
17, Utah vs. Dartmouth (18), 1944

FEWEST POINTS AT HALFTIME, BOTH TEAMS
34, Wyoming (18) vs. Georgetown (16), 1943
35, Dartmouth (18) vs. Utah (17), 1944
37, Oregon (21) vs. Ohio St. (16), 1939

HALFTIME LEAD
18, Ohio St. (37) vs. California (19), 1960
18, UCLA (38) vs. Dayton (20), 1967
14, Kansas (41) vs. St. John's (N.Y.) (27), 1952

HALFTIME DEFICIT OVERCOME
10, Kentucky vs. Utah, H: 31-41, F: 78-69, 1998
8, Loyola (Ill.) vs. Cincinnati, H: 21-29, F: 60-58 (ot), 1963
6, Indiana vs. Michigan, H: 29-35, F: 86-68, 1976

Overtime Games

OVERTIME PERIODS
3, North Carolina (54) vs. Kansas (53), 1957
1, Utah (42) vs. Dartmouth (40), 1944
1, Cincinnati (70) vs. Ohio St. (65), 1961
1, Loyola (Ill.) (60) vs. Cincinnati (58), 1963
1, Michigan (80) vs. Seton Hall (79), 1989
1, Arizona (84) vs. Kentucky (79), 1997

Two-Team Records

POINTS
182, Kentucky (94) vs. Duke (88), 1978
181, UCLA (98) vs. Duke (83), 1964
177, UCLA (92) vs. Kentucky (85), 1975
176, UNLV (103) vs. Duke (73), 1990
171, UCLA (91) vs. Michigan (80), 1965

FEWEST POINTS
73, Washington St. (34) vs. Wisconsin (39), 1941
79, Ohio St. (33) vs. Oregon (46), 1939
80, Georgetown (34) vs. Wyoming (46), 1943
82, Dartmouth (40) vs. Utah (42), 1944 (ot)
82, Oklahoma St. (36) vs. Kentucky (46), 1949

FIELD GOALS
71, UCLA (38) vs. Kentucky (33), 1975
68, UCLA (36) vs. Duke (32), 1964
68, Kentucky (39) vs. Duke (29), 1978
67, UCLA (36) vs. Florida St. (31), 1972
67, UNLV (41) vs. Duke (26), 1990

FIELD GOALS ATTEMPTED
167, San Francisco (87) vs. Iowa (80), 1956
164, Kentucky (86) vs. UCLA (78), 1975
151, San Francisco (83) vs. La Salle (68), 1955
150, Purdue (92) vs. UCLA (58), 1969
149, Kansas St. (80) vs. Kentucky (69), 1951

THREE-POINT FIELD GOALS
18, Kentucky (12) vs. Syracuse (6), 1996
17, Michigan St. (11) vs. Florida (6), 2000
16, Kentucky (10) vs. Arizona (6), 1997 (ot)
14, Oklahoma (10) vs. Kansas (4), 1988
13, Seton Hall (7) vs. Michigan (6), 1989 (ot)
13, Kansas (7) vs. Duke (6), 1991
13, Duke (9) vs. Arizona (4), 2001

THREE-POINT FIELD GOALS ATTEMPTED
49, Duke (27) vs. Arizona (22), 2001
43, Kentucky (30) vs. Arizona (13), 1997 (ot)
42, Kentucky (27) vs. Syracuse (15), 1996
40, Michigan St. (22) vs. Florida (18), 2000
39, Seton Hall (23) vs. Michigan (16), 1989 (ot)
38, Duke (20) vs. Arkansas (18), 1994

FREE THROWS MADE
50, Bradley (32) vs. La Salle (18), 1954
46, Kentucky (24) vs. Seattle (22), 1958
46, UCLA (28) vs. Purdue (18), 1969
46, Duke (30) vs. Kentucky (16), 1978
45, Kansas (26) vs. Indiana (19), 1953
45, UCLA (26) vs. Duke (19), 1964

FREE THROWS ATTEMPTED
68, Bradley (44) vs. La Salle (24), 1954
66, Kentucky (36) vs. Seattle (30), 1958
65, UCLA (41) vs. Purdue (24), 1969
61, Kansas (33) vs. Indiana (28), 1953
60, UCLA (32) vs. Duke (28), 1964

REBOUNDS
109, UCLA (61) vs. Purdue (48), 1969
108, San Francisco (60) vs. Iowa (48), 1956
105, UCLA (54) vs. Dayton (51), 1967
104, UCLA (55) vs. Kentucky (49), 1975
101, Kentucky (55) vs. Seattle (46), 1958

ASSISTS
39, Houston (20) vs. Georgetown (19), 1984
36, Oklahoma (19) vs. Kansas (17), 1988
36, UCLA (21) vs. Arkansas (15), 1995
35, UNLV (24) vs. Duke (11), 1990
34, Indiana (20) vs. Syracuse (14), 1987
34, Kentucky (22) vs. Syracuse (12), 1996

BLOCKED SHOTS
12, Arizona (7) vs. Duke (5), 2001
10, Syracuse (7) vs. Indiana (3), 1987
10, Duke (7) vs. Arkansas (3), 1994
10, Connecticut (6) vs. Duke (4), 1999
9, Kentucky (7) vs. Arizona (2), 1997 (ot)

STEALS
26, Arkansas (15) vs. UCLA (11), 1995
24, Oklahoma (13) vs. Kansas (11), 1988
21, UNLV (16) vs. Duke (5), 1990
18, Duke (13) vs. Louisville (5), 1986
17, Duke (9) vs. Michigan (8), 1992
17, Kentucky (11) vs. Syracuse (6), 1996

PERSONAL FOULS
57, Oklahoma St. (36) vs. Kentucky (21), 1949
49, Bradley (32) vs. CCNY (17), 1950
49, UCLA (25) vs. Duke (24), 1964
49, Purdue (30) vs. UCLA (19), 1969
48, Kentucky (26) vs. Duke (22), 1978

PLAYERS DISQUALIFIED
5, Kentucky (4) vs. Arizona (1), 1997 (ot)
4, Bradley (3) vs. CCNY (1), 1950
4, Kentucky (3) vs. Kansas St. (1), 1951
3, Seven tied (most recent: North Carolina [2] vs. Indiana [1], 1981)

Semifinals Game Records

Record later vacated is indicated by (*).

Individual Records

POINTS
39, Al Wood, North Carolina vs. Virginia, 1981
38, Jerry West, West Virginia vs. Louisville, 1959
38, Jerry Chambers, Utah vs. UTEP, 1966
38, Freddie Banks, UNLV vs. Indiana, 1987
36, Four tied (most recent: Rick Mount, Purdue vs. North Carolina, 1969)

FIELD GOALS
16, Don May, Dayton vs. North Carolina, 1967
16, Larry Bird, Indiana St. vs. DePaul, 1979
15, Ernie DiGregorio, Providence vs. Memphis, 1973
14, Eight tied (most recent: Armon Gilliam, UNLV vs. Indiana, 1987)

FIELD GOALS ATTEMPTED
42, Lennie Rosenbluth, North Carolina vs. Michigan St., 1957 (3 ot)
36, Ernie DiGregorio, Providence vs. Memphis, 1973
33, *Jerry Dunn, Western Ky. vs. Villanova, 1971 (2 ot)
31, Billy McGill, Utah vs. Cincinnati, 1961
31, Jerry Chambers, Utah vs. UTEP, 1966
31, Elvin Hayes, Houston vs. UCLA, 1967

FIELD-GOAL PERCENTAGE
(Minimum 10 FGM)
91.7% (11-12), Bill Walton, UCLA vs. Louisville, 1972
90.9% (10-11), Jerry Lucas, Ohio St. vs. St. Joseph's, 1961
90.9% (10-11), Billy Thompson, Louisville vs. LSU, 1986
84.2% (16-19), Larry Bird, Indiana St. vs. DePaul, 1979
83.3% (10-12), Sidney Wicks, UCLA vs. New Mexico St., 1970

THREE-POINT FIELD GOALS
10, Freddie Banks, UNLV vs. Indiana, 1987
7, Dennis Scott, Georgia Tech vs. UNLV, 1990
6, Bobby Hurley, Duke vs. Indiana, 1992
6, Darryl Wilson, Mississippi St. vs. Syracuse, 1996
6, Mike Bibby, Arizona vs. North Carolina, 1997

THE FINAL FOUR

SEMIFINALS GAME RECORDS—INDIVIDUAL

THREE-POINT FIELD GOALS ATTEMPTED
19, Freddie Banks, UNLV vs. Indiana, 1987
14, Dennis Scott, Georgia Tech vs. UNLV, 1990
13, Damon Stoudamire, Arizona vs. Arkansas, 1994
13, Darryl Wilson, Mississippi St. vs. Syracuse, 1996
12, Steve Kerr, Arizona vs. Oklahoma, 1988
12, Donald Williams, North Carolina vs. Arkansas, 1995

THREE-POINT FIELD-GOAL PERCENTAGE
(Minimum 5 3FGM)
71.4% (5-7), Adonis Jordan, Kansas vs. North Carolina, 1993
71.4% (5-7), Donald Williams, North Carolina vs. Kansas, 1993
66.7% (6-9), Bobby Hurley, Duke vs. Indiana, 1992
62.5% (5-8), Arthur Lee, Stanford vs. Kentucky, 1998 (ot)
55.6% (5-9), Anderson Hunt, UNLV vs. Georgia Tech, 1990
55.6% (5-9), Rex Walters, Kansas vs. North Carolina, 1993

FREE THROWS MADE
14, Jerry West, West Virginia vs. Louisville, 1959
13, Don Schlundt, Indiana vs. LSU, 1953
12, Jim Spanarkel, Duke vs. Notre Dame, 1978
12, Paul Hogue, Cincinnati vs. UCLA, 1962
11, Five tied (most recent: Steve Alford, Indiana vs. UNLV, 1987)

FREE THROWS ATTEMPTED
20, Jerry West, West Virginia vs. Louisville, 1959
18, Bob Pettit, LSU vs. Indiana, 1953
17, Don Schlundt, Indiana vs. LSU, 1953
17, Paul Hogue, Cincinnati vs. UCLA, 1962
16, Lew Alcindor, UCLA vs. Drake, 1969

FREE-THROW PERCENTAGE
(Minimum 10 FTM)
100.0% (12-12), Jim Spanarkel, Duke vs. Notre Dame, 1978
100.0% (10-10), Ron King, Florida St. vs. North Carolina, 1972
91.7% (11-12), Bill Walton, UCLA vs. Louisville, 1972
91.7% (11-12), Earvin "Magic" Johnson, Michigan St. vs. Pennsylvania, 1979
90.9% (10-11), Johnny Cox, Kentucky vs. Temple, 1958

REBOUNDS
24, Elvin Hayes, Houston vs. UCLA, 1967
23, Bill Russell, San Francisco vs. Southern Methodist, 1956
22, Elgin Baylor, Seattle vs. Kansas St., 1958
22, Tom Sanders, New York U. vs. Ohio St., 1960
22, Larry Kenon, Memphis vs. Providence, 1973
22, Akeem Olajuwon, Houston vs. Louisville, 1983

ASSISTS
18, Mark Wade, UNLV vs. Indiana, 1987
12, Rumeal Robinson, Michigan vs. Illinois, 1989
12, Edgar Padilla, Massachusetts vs. Kentucky, 1996
11, Michael Jackson, Georgetown vs. St. John's (N.Y.), 1985
11, Milt Wagner, Louisville vs. LSU, 1986

BLOCKED SHOTS
6, Danny Manning, Kansas vs. Duke, 1988
6, Marcus Camby, Massachusetts vs. Kentucky, 1996
4, Rasheed Wallace, North Carolina vs. Arkansas, 1995
4, A.J. Bramlett, Arizona vs. North Carolina, 1997
4, Andy Kowske, Wisconsin vs. Michigan St., 2000
4, Shane Battier, Duke vs. Maryland, 2001

STEALS
6, Gilbert Arenas, Arizona vs. Michigan St., 2001
5, Anthony Epps, Kentucky vs. Minnesota, 1997
5, Wayne Turner, Kentucky vs. Minnesota, 1997
4, 10 tied (most recent: Vince Carter, North Carolina vs. Arizona, 1997)

Team Records

POINTS
108, UCLA vs. Wichita St. (89), 1965
101, UCLA vs. Houston (69), 1968
101, Michigan St. vs. Pennsylvania (67), 1979
98, Memphis vs. Providence (85), 1973
97, Indiana vs. UNLV (93), 1987
97, Duke vs. Arkansas (83), 1990

FEWEST POINTS
28, Kentucky vs. Dartmouth (47), 1942
30, Duquesne vs. Indiana (39), 1940
30, Pittsburgh vs. Wisconsin (36), 1941
30, Oregon St. vs. Oklahoma St. (55), 1949
31, Iowa St. vs. Utah (40), 1944

WINNING MARGIN
34, Cincinnati (80) vs. Oregon St. (46), 1963
34, Michigan St. (101) vs. Pennsylvania (67), 1979
32, UCLA (101) vs. Houston (69), 1968
29, Kentucky (76) vs. Illinois (47), 1949
27, Oklahoma St. (68) vs. Arkansas (41), 1945
27, Purdue (92) vs. North Carolina (65), 1969

SMALLEST WINNING MARGIN
1, Kansas (43) vs. Southern California (42), 1940
1, Oklahoma (55) vs. Texas (54), 1947
1, Kentucky (61) vs. Temple (60), 1958
1, UCLA (75) vs. Louisville (74), 1975 (ot)
1, North Carolina (84) vs. UNLV (83), 1977
1, Kentucky (86) vs. Stanford (85), 1998 (ot)

POINTS BY LOSING TEAM
93, UNLV vs. Indiana (97), 1987
89, Wichita St. vs. UCLA (108), 1965
89, *Western Ky. vs. Villanova (92), 1971 (2 ot)
86, Notre Dame vs. Duke (90), 1978
85, Providence vs. Memphis (98), 1973
85, Stanford vs. Kentucky (86), 1998 (ot)

DEFICIT OVERCOME TO WIN
22, Duke vs. Maryland, 17-39 with 6:55 left in 1st half, F: 94-84, 2001

FIELD GOALS
44, UCLA vs. Wichita St., 1965
43, UCLA vs. Houston, 1968
41, Memphis vs. Providence, 1973
41, UNLV vs. North Carolina, 1977
39, *Western Ky. vs. Villanova, 1971 (2 ot)

FEWEST FIELD GOALS
10, Wisconsin vs. Pittsburgh, 1941
10, Kentucky vs. Dartmouth, 1942
11, Duquesne vs. Indiana, 1940
11, Oregon St. vs. Oklahoma St., 1949
13, Four tied (most recent: Kentucky vs. Georgetown, 1984)

FIELD GOALS ATTEMPTED
105, *Western Ky. vs. Villanova, 1971 (2 ot)
91, Kentucky vs. Illinois, 1951
89, North Carolina vs. Michigan St., 1957 (3 ot)
89, UCLA vs. Wichita St., 1965
83, UCLA vs. Houston, 1968
83, Drake vs. UCLA, 1969

FEWEST FIELD GOALS ATTEMPTED
38, Villanova vs. Memphis, 1985
41, Georgetown vs. Louisville, 1982
42, Houston vs. Virginia, 1984 (ot)
42, St. John's (N.Y.) vs. Georgetown, 1985
43, Charlotte vs. Marquette, 1977
43, Wisconsin vs. Michigan St., 2000

FIELD-GOAL PERCENTAGE
63.3% (38-60), Ohio St. vs. St. Joseph's, 1961
63.3% (38-60), Michigan St. vs. Pennsylvania, 1979
62.5% (35-56), Indiana vs. DePaul, 1979
61.7% (37-60), Indiana vs. UNLV, 1987
59.6% (34-57), Kansas vs. San Francisco, 1957

LOWEST FIELD-GOAL PERCENTAGE
24.5% (13-53), Kentucky vs. Georgetown, 1984
28.2% (22-78), Houston vs. UCLA, 1968
28.4% (21-74), New York U. vs. Ohio St., 1960
28.8% (23-80), Michigan St. vs. North Carolina, 1957 (3 ot)
28.8% (17-59), Oregon St. vs. Cincinnati, 1963

THREE-POINT FIELD GOALS
13, UNLV vs. Indiana, 1987
12, Arkansas vs. North Carolina, 1995
11, Kansas vs. North Carolina, 1993
11, Mississippi St. vs. Syracuse, 1996
11, Arizona vs. North Carolina, 1997
11, Stanford vs. Kentucky, 1998 (ot)

FEWEST THREE-POINT FIELD GOALS
0, Michigan vs. Kentucky, 1993 (ot)
1, Connecticut vs. Ohio St., 1999
2, Indiana vs. UNLV, 1987
2, Kansas vs. Duke, 1988
2, Illinois vs. Michigan, 1989
2, UCLA vs. Oklahoma St., 1995
2, Michigan St. vs. Wisconsin, 2000
2, Michigan St. vs. Arizona, 2001

THREE-POINT FIELD GOALS ATTEMPTED
35, UNLV vs. Indiana, 1987
34, Arkansas vs. North Carolina, 1995
32, Arizona vs. Arkansas, 1994
29, Arizona vs. North Carolina, 1997
28, Four tied (most recent: Florida vs. North Carolina, 2000)

FEWEST THREE-POINT FIELD GOALS ATTEMPTED
4, Indiana vs. UNLV, 1987
4, Kansas vs. Duke, 1988
4, Michigan vs. Kentucky, 1993 (ot)
6, Connecticut vs. Ohio St., 1999
7, North Carolina vs. Kansas, 1993
7, UCLA vs. Oklahoma St., 1995

THREE-POINT FIELD-GOAL PERCENTAGE
(Minimum 7 3FGM)
66.7% (10-15), UNLV vs. Georgia Tech, 1990
63.6% (7-11), Duke vs. Indiana, 1992
55.0% (11-20), Kansas vs. North Carolina, 1993
53.3% (8-15), Indiana vs. Duke, 1992
50.0% (7-14), Duke vs. Florida, 1994
50.0% (7-14), Arizona vs. Michigan St., 2001

LOWEST THREE-POINT FIELD-GOAL PERCENTAGE
(Minimum 5 3FGA)
13.0% (3-23), North Carolina vs. Utah, 1998
14.3% (2-14), Michigan St. vs. Wisconsin, 2000
14.3% (2-14), Michigan St. vs. Arizona, 2001
16.7% (3-18), North Carolina vs. Kansas, 1991
16.7% (1-6), Connecticut vs. Ohio St., 1999

FREE THROWS MADE
37, Jacksonville vs. St. Bonaventure, 1970
32, Duke vs. Notre Dame, 1978
30, Indiana vs. LSU, 1953
29, UCLA vs. Drake, 1969
29, Florida St. vs. North Carolina, 1972

FEWEST FREE THROWS MADE
1, UNLV vs. North Carolina, 1977
2, DePaul vs. Indiana St., 1979
2, North Carolina vs. Utah, 1998
3, Indiana vs. UCLA, 1973
5, Iowa St. vs. Utah, 1944
5, Marquette vs. Charlotte, 1977
5, Virginia vs. Houston, 1984 (ot)

FREE THROWS ATTEMPTED
45, Jacksonville vs. St. Bonaventure, 1970
44, UCLA vs. Drake, 1969
44, Syracuse vs. Providence, 1987
43, Florida St. vs. North Carolina, 1972
42, Duke vs. Indiana, 1992

FEWEST FREE THROWS ATTEMPTED
5, UNLV vs. North Carolina, 1977
5, DePaul vs. Indiana St., 1979
6, Indiana vs. UCLA, 1973
6, Mississippi St. vs. Syracuse, 1996
7, Four tied (most recent: North Carolina vs. Utah, 1998)

FREE-THROW PERCENTAGE
(Minimum 15 FTM)
90.5% (19-21), Ohio St. vs. New York U., 1945 (ot)
87.5% (21-24), Oklahoma St. vs. Oregon St., 1949
86.5% (32-37), Duke vs. Notre Dame, 1978
85.7% (18-21), Baylor vs. Bradley, 1950
85.7% (24-28), UCLA vs. Oklahoma St., 1995

LOWEST FREE-THROW PERCENTAGE
20.0% (1-5), UNLV vs. North Carolina, 1977
28.6% (2-7), North Carolina vs. Utah, 1998
35.3% (6-17), Temple vs. Iowa, 1956
37.5% (6-16), Houston vs. UCLA, 1967
40.0% (2-5), DePaul vs. Indiana St., 1979

REBOUNDS
69, *Western Ky. vs. Villanova, 1971 (2 ot)
65, Michigan St. vs. North Carolina, 1957 (3 ot)
57, UCLA vs. Houston, 1968

SEMIFINALS GAME RECORDS—TEAM

57, Kentucky vs. Syracuse, 1975
56, Seattle vs. Kansas St., 1958
56, California vs. Cincinnati, 1959

FEWEST REBOUNDS
20, Wisconsin vs. Michigan St., 2000
21, DePaul vs. Indiana St., 1979
21, Syracuse vs. Mississippi St., 1996
24, St. John's (N.Y.) vs. Georgetown, 1985
24, Kansas vs. North Carolina, 1993

REBOUND MARGIN
23, Seattle (56) vs. Kansas St. (33), 1958
22, Michigan St. (42) vs. Wisconsin (20), 2000
21, UCLA (55) vs. Wichita St. (34), 1965
20, Michigan (52) vs. Princeton (32), 1965
20, Mississippi St. (41) vs. Syracuse (21), 1996

ASSISTS
26, Louisville vs. LSU, 1986
23, UNLV vs. Indiana, 1987
23, Michigan vs. Illinois, 1989
22, Arkansas vs. North Carolina, 1995
21, Duke vs. UNLV, 1991

BLOCKED SHOTS
9, Kansas vs. Duke, 1988
8, Massachusetts vs. Kentucky, 1996
8, Arizona vs. North Carolina, 1997
7, Seton Hall vs. Duke, 1989
7, Kentucky vs. Stanford, 1998 (ot)
7, Arizona vs. Michigan St., 2001
7, Duke vs. Maryland, 2001

STEALS
14, Kentucky vs. Minnesota, 1997
12, Kentucky vs. Massachusetts, 1996
12, Arizona vs. Michigan St., 2001
11, Five tied (most recent: North Carolina vs. Arizona, 1997)

PERSONAL FOULS
33, Providence vs. Syracuse, 1987
33, Indiana vs. Duke, 1992
32, St. Bonaventure vs. Jacksonville, 1970
31, Kentucky vs. Syracuse, 1975
31, Pennsylvania vs. Michigan St., 1979

FEWEST PERSONAL FOULS
8, Wisconsin vs. Pittsburgh, 1941
9, Kansas vs. Southern California, 1940
9, Stanford vs. Colorado, 1942
9, Oklahoma St. vs. California, 1946
10, Three tied (most recent: Houston vs. Virginia, 1984 [ot])

PLAYERS DISQUALIFIED
4, St. Bonaventure vs. Jacksonville, 1970
4, Indiana vs. Duke, 1992
3, Eight tied (most recent: Kansas vs. Duke, 1986)

Team and Two-Team Scoring by Halves

POINTS IN A HALF, TEAM
65, UCLA vs. Wichita St., 1965 (1st)
62, Seton Hall vs. Duke, 1989 (2nd)
58, Memphis vs. Providence, 1973 (2nd)
58, Houston vs. Louisville, 1983 (2nd)

POINTS IN A HALF, BOTH TEAMS
104, Notre Dame (57) vs. Duke (47), 1978 (2nd)
103, UCLA (65) vs. Wichita St. (38), 1965 (1st)
103, UCLA (57) vs. Louisville (46), 1972 (2nd)

POINTS AT HALFTIME, TEAM
65, UCLA vs. Wichita St. (38), 1965
53, Four tied (most recent: Georgia Tech vs. UNLV [46], 1990)

POINTS AT HALFTIME, BOTH TEAMS
103, UCLA (65) vs. Wichita St. (38), 1965
100, Indiana (53) vs. UNLV (47), 1987
99, Georgia Tech (53) vs. UNLV (46), 1990

FEWEST POINTS IN A HALF, TEAM
10, Villanova vs. Ohio St., 1939 (1st)
11, Oregon St. vs. Oklahoma St., 1949 (1st)
11, Kentucky vs. Georgetown, 1984 (2nd)

FEWEST POINTS IN A HALF, BOTH TEAMS
31, Duquesne (17) vs. Indiana (14), 1940 (2nd)
32, Pittsburgh (18) vs. Wisconsin (14), 1941 (1st)
32, Oklahoma St. (21) vs. Oregon St. (11), 1949 (1st)

FEWEST POINTS AT HALFTIME, TEAM
10, Villanova vs. Ohio St. (25), 1939
11, Oregon St. vs. Oklahoma St. (21), 1949
13, Duquesne vs. Indiana (25), 1940
13, Kentucky vs. Dartmouth (23), 1942

FEWEST POINTS AT HALFTIME, BOTH TEAMS
32, Pittsburgh (18) vs. Wisconsin (14), 1941
32, Oklahoma St. (21) vs. Oregon St. (11), 1949
35, Ohio St. (25) vs. Villanova (10), 1939

HALFTIME LEAD
33, Michigan St. (50) vs. Pennsylvania (17), 1979
27, UCLA (65) vs. Wichita St. (38), 1965
23, Kansas St. (37) vs. Oklahoma St. (14), 1951
23, Purdue (53) vs. North Carolina (30), 1969

HALFTIME DEFICIT OVERCOME TO WIN
11, Duke vs. Maryland, H: 38-49, F: 95-84, 2001
9, Memphis vs. Providence, H: 40-49, F: 98-85, 1973
8, Louisville vs. LSU, H: 36-44, F: 88-77, 1986
7, Four tied (most recent: Duke vs. Florida, H: 32-39, F: 70-65, 1994)

Two-Team Records

POINTS
197, UCLA (108) vs. Wichita St. (89), 1965
190, Indiana (97) vs. UNLV (93), 1987
183, Memphis (98) vs. Providence (85), 1973
181, *Villanova (92) vs. *Western Ky. (89), 1971 (2 ot)
180, Duke (97) vs. Arkansas (83), 1990

FIELD GOALS
80, UCLA (44) vs. Wichita St. (36), 1965
79, Memphis (41) vs. Providence (38), 1973
75, *Western Ky. (39) vs. *Villanova (36), 1971 (2 ot)
74, UNLV (41) vs. North Carolina (33), 1977
73, Kansas St. (37) vs. UCLA (36), 1964
73, Houston (41) vs. Louisville (32), 1983

FIELD GOALS ATTEMPTED
178, *Western Ky. (105) vs. *Villanova (73), 1971 (2 ot)
169, North Carolina (89) vs. Michigan St. (80), 1957 (3 ot)
164, UCLA (89) vs. Wichita St. (75), 1965
162, Providence (82) vs. Memphis (80), 1973
161, Kentucky (91) vs. Illinois (70), 1951

THREE-POINT FIELD GOALS
22, Arkansas (12) vs. North Carolina (10), 1995
18, UNLV (10) vs. Georgia Tech (8), 1990
16, Kansas (11) vs. North Carolina (5), 1993
16, Mississippi St. (11) vs. Syracuse (5), 1996
16, Stanford (11) vs. Kentucky (5), 1998 (ot)

THREE-POINT FIELD GOALS ATTEMPTED
62, Arkansas (34) vs. North Carolina (28), 1995
56, Arizona (32) vs. Arkansas (24), 1994
50, Arizona (29) vs. North Carolina (21), 1997
50, Florida (28) vs. North Carolina (22), 2000
45, Duke (27) vs. Maryland (18), 2001

FREE THROWS MADE
53, Indiana (30) vs. LSU (23), 1953
52, Jacksonville (37) vs. St. Bonaventure (15), 1970
47, La Salle (24) vs. Iowa (23), 1955
47, UCLA (29) vs. Drake (18), 1969
47, Duke (28) vs. Arkansas (19), 1990

FREE THROWS ATTEMPTED
70, Kentucky (38) vs. Syracuse (32), 1975
68, UCLA (44) vs. Drake (24), 1969
68, Florida (43) vs. North Carolina (25), 1972
67, Jacksonville (45) vs. St. Bonaventure (22), 1970
65, Duke (39) vs. Arkansas (26), 1990

REBOUNDS
123, *Western Ky. (69) vs. *Villanova (54), 1971 (2 ot)
119, Michigan St. (65) vs. North Carolina (54), 1957 (3 ot)
111, UCLA (57) vs. Houston (54), 1968
103, North Carolina (54) vs. Ohio St. (49), 1968
102, UCLA (51) vs. Houston (51), 1967

ASSISTS
39, Louisville (26) vs. LSU (13), 1986
39, Kentucky (20) vs. Massachusetts (19), 1996
39, UNLV (23) vs. Indiana (16), 1987
37, Michigan (23) vs. Illinois (14), 1989
37, Arkansas (19) vs. Arizona (18), 1994
37, Arkansas (22) vs. North Carolina (15), 1995

BLOCKED SHOTS
14, Kansas (9) vs. Duke (5), 1988
14, Massachusetts (8) vs. Kentucky (6), 1996
12, Kentucky (7) vs. Stanford (5), 1998 (ot)
11, Seton Hall (7) vs. Duke (4), 1998
10, Arizona (8) vs. North Carolina (2), 1997
10, Arizona (7) vs. Michigan St. (3), 2001

STEALS
20, Kentucky (12) vs. Massachusetts (8), 1996
20, Kentucky (14) vs. Minnesota (6), 1997
19, Kentucky (11) vs. Michigan (8), 1993 (ot)
19, North Carolina (11) vs. Arizona (8), 1997
18, Providence (11) vs. Syracuse (7), 1987

PERSONAL FOULS
61, Kentucky (31) vs. Syracuse (30), 1975
53, St. Bonaventure (32) vs. Jacksonville (21), 1970
53, Pennsylvania (31) vs. Michigan St. (22), 1979
51, Five tied (most recent: Kentucky (27) vs. Michigan [24], 1993 [ot])

PLAYERS DISQUALIFIED
6, CCNY (3) vs. North Carolina St. (3), 1950
5, North Carolina (3) vs. Michigan St. (2), 1957 (3 ot)
5, Indiana (4) vs. Duke (1), 1992
4, Ohio St. (3) vs. New York U. (1), 1945 (ot)
4, St. Bonaventure (4) vs. Jacksonville (0), 1970
4, Syracuse (3) vs. Kentucky (1), 1975

Final Four Two-Game Records

Record later vacated is indicated by (*).

Individual Records

POINTS
87, Bill Bradley, Princeton, 1965
80, Hal Lear, Temple, 1956
70, Gail Goodrich, UCLA, 1965
70, Jerry Chambers, Utah, 1966
66, Clyde Lovellette, Kansas, 1952
66, Jerry West, West Virginia, 1959
65, Bob Pettit, LSU, 1953
64, Rick Mount, Purdue, 1969
64, Jack Givens, Kentucky, 1978
62, Lew Alcindor, UCLA, 1969

FIELD GOALS
34, Bill Bradley, Princeton, 1965
32, Hal Lear, Temple, 1956
28, Jack Givens, Kentucky, 1978
28, Bill Walton, UCLA, 1973
26, Rick Mount, Purdue, 1969

FIELD GOALS ATTEMPTED
64, Rick Mount, Purdue, 1969
58, Ernie DiGregorio, Providence, 1973
57, Lennie Rosenbluth, North Carolina, 1957
54, Billy McGill, Utah, 1961
54, Bill Bradley, Princeton, 1965
54, *Jim McDaniels, Western Ky., 1971

FIELD-GOAL PERCENTAGE
(Minimum 15 FGM)
84.2% (16-19), Billy Thompson, Louisville, 1986
82.4% (28-34), Bill Walton, UCLA, 1973
78.9% (15-19), Udonis Haslem, Florida, 2000
74.1% (20-27), James Worthy, North Carolina, 1982
71.4% (20-28), Jerry Lucas, Ohio St., 1961
71.4% (15-21), Sidney Wicks, UCLA, 1970

FINAL FOUR TWO-GAME RECORDS—INDIVIDUAL

In 1959, Oscar Robertson of Cincinnati set a record by sinking 24 free throws during the Final Four.

Photo by Rich Clarkson

THREE-POINT FIELD GOALS
10, Donald Williams, North Carolina, 1993
9, Steve Alford, Indiana, 1987
9, Anderson Hunt, UNLV, 1990
9, Mike Bibby, Arizona, 1997
8, Dave Sieger, Oklahoma, 1988
8, Tony Delk, Kentucky, 1996

THREE-POINT FIELD GOALS ATTEMPTED
20, Jason Williams, Duke, 2001
19, Dave Sieger, Oklahoma, 1988
18, Scott Padgett, Kentucky, 1997
17, Terry Brown, Kansas, 1991
16, Six tied (most recent: Morris Peterson, Michigan St., 2000)

**THREE-POINT FIELD-GOAL PERCENTAGE
(Minimum 7 3FGM)**
71.4% (10-14), Donald Williams, North Carolina, 1993
64.3% (9-14), Steve Alford, Indiana, 1987
58.3% (7-12), Bobby Hurley, Duke, 1992
56.3% (9-16), Anderson Hunt, UNLV, 1990
56.3% (9-16), Mike Bibby, Arizona, 1997

FREE THROWS MADE
24, Oscar Robertson, Cincinnati, 1959
24, Gail Goodrich, UCLA, 1965
22, Jerry West, West Virginia, 1959
21, Don Schlundt, Indiana, 1953
21, Christian Laettner, Duke, 1991

FREE THROWS ATTEMPTED
32, Jerry West, West Virginia, 1959
30, Oscar Robertson, Cincinnati, 1959
28, Bob Pettit, LSU, 1953
28, Don Schlundt, Indiana, 1953
28, Gail Goodrich, UCLA, 1965

**FREE-THROW PERCENTAGE
(Minimum 12 FTM)**
100.0% (15-15), Jeff Lamp, Virginia, 1981
100.0% (13-13), Ron King, Florida St., 1972
100.0% (12-12), *Kiki Vandeweghe, UCLA, 1980
95.0% (19-20), Bill Bradley, Princeton, 1965
94.4% (17-18), Jim Spanarkel, Duke, 1978

REBOUNDS
50, Bill Russell, San Francisco, 1956
41, Elgin Baylor, Seattle, 1958
41, Lew Alcindor, UCLA, 1969
41, Bill Walton, UCLA, 1972
40, Elvin Hayes, Houston, 1967
40, Akeem Olajuwon, Houston, 1983
38, Paul Hogue, Cincinnati, 1962
38, Lew Alcindor, UCLA, 1967
37, Bill Spivey, Kentucky, 1951
37, Artis Gilmore, Jacksonville, 1970

ASSISTS
23, Rumeal Robinson, Michigan, 1989
20, Michael Jackson, Georgetown, 1985
16, Alvin Franklin, Houston, 1985
16, Bobby Hurley, Duke, 1991
16, Lazarus Sims, Syracuse, 1996

BLOCKED SHOTS
8, Danny Manning, Kansas, 1988
7, Loren Woods, Arizona, 2001
6, A.J. Bramlett, Arizona, 1997
6, Shane Battier, Duke, 2001
5, Nine tied (most recent: two in 1998)

STEALS
10, Tommy Amaker, Duke, 1986
9, Mookie Blaylock, Oklahoma, 1988
9, Danny Manning, Kansas, 1988
8, Antoine Walker, Kentucky, 1996
7, Ed O'Bannon, UCLA, 1995
7, Anthony Epps, Kentucky, 1997
7, Gilbert Arenas, Arizona, 2001

Team Records

POINTS
199, UCLA, 1965
196, *St. Joseph's, 1961
194, Princeton, 1965
193, UNLV, 1990
189, UNLV, 1977
188, UCLA, 1964
187, Utah, 1961
186, Drake, 1969
180, Michigan, 1964
180, North Carolina, 1972
180, Kentucky, 1975

FIELD GOALS
88, UNLV, 1977
78, Princeton, 1965
77, Utah, 1961
77, UCLA, 1965
77, Drake, 1969

FIELD GOALS ATTEMPTED
181, *Western Ky., 1971
177, *St. Joseph's, 1961
176, Rutgers, 1976
176, Pennsylvania, 1979
175, UNLV, 1977

FIELD-GOAL PERCENTAGE
62.1% (64-103), Michigan St., 1979
61.7% (71-115), UCLA, 1973
57.6% (38-66), Villanova, 1985
57.3% (63-110), Ohio St., 1961
57.0% (61-107), Kansas, 1988

THREE-POINT FIELD GOALS
22, Arkansas, 1995
19, Kentucky, 1997
18, UNLV, 1990
17, Arizona, 1997
16, Duke, 2001

THREE-POINT FIELD GOALS ATTEMPTED
62, Arkansas, 1995
54, Duke, 2001
53, Kentucky, 1997
46, Florida, 2000
42, Arkansas, 1994
42, Arizona, 1997

**THREE-POINT FIELD-GOAL PERCENTAGE
(Minimum 9 3FGM)**
62.1% (18-29), UNLV, 1990
60.0% (9-15), Indiana, 1987
55.6% (10-18), Duke, 1991
55.6% (10-18), North Carolina, 1993
55.0% (11-20), Duke, 1992

FREE THROWS MADE
62, Duke, 1978
62, *St. Joseph's, 1961
57, UCLA, 1969
56, Bradley, 1954
51, Illinois, 1951
51, Colorado, 1955

FREE THROWS ATTEMPTED
85, UCLA, 1969
72, *St. Joseph's, 1961
71, Illinois, 1951
71, Duke, 1978
69, North Carolina, 1972

**FREE-THROW PERCENTAGE
(Minimum 20 FTM)**
88.7% (47-53), Virginia, 1981
87.5% (28-32), Marquette, 1977
87.3% (62-71), Duke, 1978
86.1% (62-72), *St. Joseph's, 1961
86.0% (37-43), *UCLA, 1980

REBOUNDS
127, Houston, 1967
125, Michigan St., 1957
125, *Western Ky., 1971
109, UCLA, 1969
108, Houston, 1968
107, Ohio St., 1968
106, Kentucky, 1975
105, UCLA, 1967
105, UCLA, 1968
104, Utah, 1961

ASSISTS
44, UNLV, 1990
42, Louisville, 1986
42, Michigan, 1989
42, Kentucky, 1996
37, Oklahoma, 1988
37, Arkansas, 1995

BLOCKED SHOTS
14, Arizona, 2001
13, Kansas, 1988
13, Duke, 1994
13, Kentucky, 1998
12, Kentucky, 1997
12, Duke, 2001

STEALS
24, Arkansas, 1995
23, Duke, 1986
23, Kentucky, 1996
23, Kentucky, 1997
22, UNLV, 1990

PERSONAL FOULS
62, Pennsylvania, 1979
59, Kentucky, 1975
57, St. John's (N.Y.), 1952
56, Oklahoma St., 1951
56, Syracuse, 1975

Final Four Cumulative Records

*does not include vacated years

Team Records

CHAMPIONSHIP TITLES
11, UCLA, 1964-95
7, Kentucky, 1948-98
5, Indiana, 1940-87
3, Duke, 1991-2001
3, North Carolina, 1957-93
2, Cincinnati, 1961-62
2, Kansas, 1952-88
2, Louisville, 1980-86
2, Michigan St., 1979-2000
2, North Carolina St., 1974-83
2, Oklahoma St., 1945-46
2, San Francisco, 1955-56

FINAL FOUR APPEARANCES
15, North Carolina, 1946-2000
14, *UCLA, 1962-95
13, Duke, 1963-2001
13, Kentucky, 1942-98
10, Kansas, 1940-93
9, Ohio St., 1939-99
7, Indiana, 1940-92
7, Louisville, 1959-86
6, Arkansas, 1945-95
6, Cincinnati, 1959-92
6, Michigan, 1964-93

CONSECUTIVE FINAL FOUR APPEARANCES
10, UCLA, 1967-76
5, Cincinnati, 1959-63
5, Duke, 1988-92
3, Houston, 1982-84
3, Kentucky, 1996-98
3, Michigan St., 1999-2001
3, North Carolina, 1967-69
3, Ohio St., 1944-46
3, Ohio St., 1960-62
3, San Francisco, 1955-57

FINAL FOUR GAMES
28, *UCLA, 1967-95
25, North Carolina, 1946-2000
24, Duke, 1963-2001
23, Kentucky, 1942-98
18, Kansas, 1940-93
15, Ohio St., 1939-99
13, Indiana, 1940-92
12, Louisville, 1959-86
12, Michigan, 1964-93
11, Cincinnati, 1959-92

FINAL FOUR WINS
24, *UCLA, 1962-95
17, Kentucky, 1942-98
14, Duke, 1963-2001
11, Indiana, 1940-92
11, North Carolina, 1946-2000
8, Kansas, 1940-93
7, Cincinnati, 1959-92
7, Michigan, 1964-93
7, Ohio St., 1939-99
5, Georgetown, 1943-85
5, Louisville, 1959-86
5, North Carolina St., 1950-83
5, Oklahoma St., 1945-95
5, San Francisco, 1955-57

FINAL FOUR WINNING PERCENTAGE
(Minimum 3 Games)
85.7% (24-4), *UCLA, 1962-95
84.6% (11-2), Indiana, 1940-92
83.3% (5-1), North Carolina St., 1950-83
83.3% (5-1), San Francisco, 1955-57
75.0% (3-1), Holy Cross, 1947-48
75.0% (3-1), La Salle, 1954-55
75.0% (3-1), Marquette, 1974-77
73.9% (17-6), Kentucky, 1942-98
66.7% (2-1), Stanford, 1942-98
66.7% (2-1), Villanova, 1939-85
66.7% (2-1), Wisconsin, 1941-2000

Most Outstanding Players and Their Final Four Statistics

Year	Player, Team	Cl.	G	FG-A	3FG-A	FT-A	Reb.	Ast.	Blk.	Stl.	PF	Pts.
1939	Jimmy Hull, Ohio St.	Sr.	2	15		10-12					3	40
1940	Marv Huffman, Indiana	Sr.	2	7		4						18
1941	John Kotz, Wisconsin	So.	2	8		6					3	22
1942	Howie Dallmar, Stanford	So.	2	8		4-6					0	20
1943	Ken Sailors, Wyoming	Jr.	2	10		8-11					5	28
1944	Arnie Ferrin, Utah	Fr.	2	11		6						28
1945	Bob Kurland, Oklahoma St.	Jr.	2	16		5					6	37
1946	Bob Kurland, Oklahoma St.	Sr.	2	21		10-15					8	52
1947	George Kaftan, Holy Cross	So.	2	18		12-17					6	48
1948	Alex Groza, Kentucky	Jr.	2	16		5						37
1949	Alex Groza, Kentucky	Sr.	2	19		14					9	52
1950	Irwin Dambrot, CCNY	Sr.	2	12-28		4-8					3	28
1951	Bill Spivey, Kentucky	Sr.	2	20-50		10-16	37				7	50
1952	Clyde Lovellette, Kansas	Sr.	2	24		18						66
1953	+ B.H. Born, Kansas	Jr.	2	17		17						51
1954	Tom Gola, La Salle	Jr.	2	12		14						38
1955	Bill Russell, San Francisco	Jr.	2	19		9						47
1956	† Hal Lear, Temple	Sr.	2	32		16						80
1957	+ Wilt Chamberlain, Kansas	So.	2	18-35		19-27	25				3	55
1958	+ Elgin Baylor, Seattle	Jr.	2	18-53		12-16	41				7	48
1959	+ Jerry West, West Virginia	Jr.	2	22-33		22-32	25				7	66
1960	Jerry Lucas, Ohio St.	So.	2	16-24		3-3	23				4	35
1961	+ Jerry Lucas, Ohio St.	Jr.	2	20-28		16-17	25				6	56
1962	Paul Hogue, Cincinnati	Sr.	2	23-36		12-19	38				5	58
1963	† Art Heyman, Duke	Sr.	2	18-44		15-22	19				8	51
1964	Walt Hazzard, UCLA	Sr.	2	11-20		8-12	10				7	30
1965	† Bill Bradley, Princeton	Sr.	2	34-54		19-20	24				9	87
1966	‡ Jerry Chambers, Utah	Sr.	2	25-47		20-24	35				6	70
1967	Lew Alcindor, UCLA	So.	2	14-23		11-24	38				1	39
1968	Lew Alcindor, UCLA	Jr.	2	22-35		9-10	34				6	53
1969	Lew Alcindor, UCLA	Sr.	2	23-34		16-25	41				5	62
1970	Sidney Wicks, UCLA	Jr.	2	15-21		9-15	34				6	39
1971	*+Howard Porter, Villanova	Sr.	2	20-41		7-9	24				5	47
1972	Bill Walton, UCLA	So.	2	20-29		17-23	41				6	57
1973	Bill Walton, UCLA	Jr.	2	28-34		2-5	30				8	58
1974	David Thompson, North Carolina St.	Jr.	2	19-37		11-14	17				6	49
1975	Richard Washington, UCLA	So.	2	23-42		8-11	20				8	54
1976	Kent Benson, Indiana	Jr.	2	17-34		7-11	18				7	41
1977	Butch Lee, Marquette	Jr.	2	11-32		8-8	6	2	1	1	4	30
1978	Jack Givens, Kentucky	Sr.	2	28-43		8-12	17	4	1	3	6	64
1979	Earvin "Magic" Johnson, Michigan St.	So.	2	17-25		19-22	17	3	0	2	5	53
1980	Darrell Griffith, Louisville	Sr.	2	23-37		11-16	7	15	0	2	4	57
1981	Isiah Thomas, Indiana	So.	2	14-25		9-11	4	9	3	4	8	37
1982	James Worthy, North Carolina	Jr.	2	20-27		2-7	8	9	0	4	6	42
1983	+ Akeem Olajuwon, Houston	So.	2	16-29		9-14	40	3	2	5	5	41

North Carolina forward James Worthy (52) battles for the ball against Houston's Akeem Olajuwon and Larry Micheaux (41) as Michael Jordan looks on. Worthy helped lead the Tar Heels to the NCAA title and earned him the Final Four's most outstanding player award.

Question... What Final Four most outstanding player hosted his own national network television talk show?

Answer... Magic Johnson

FINAL FOUR CUMULATIVE RECORDS—MOST OUTSTANDING PLAYERS AND THEIR STATISTICS

Year	Player, Team	Cl.	G	FG-A	3FG-A	FT-A	Reb.	Ast.	Blk.	Stl.	PF	Pts.
1984	Patrick Ewing, Georgetown	Jr.	2	8-14		2-2	18	1	15	1	7	18
1985	Ed Pinckney, Villanova	Sr.	2	8-14		12-16	15	6	3	0	6	28
1986	Pervis Ellison, Louisville	Fr.	2	15-25		6-8	24	2	3	1	7	36
1987	Keith Smart, Indiana	Jr.	2	14-22	0-1	7-9	7	7	0	2	7	35
1988	Danny Manning, Kansas	Sr.	2	25-45	0-1	6-9	17	4	8	9	6	56
1989	Glen Rice, Michigan	Sr.	2	24-49	7-16	4-4	16	1	0	3	3	59
1990	Anderson Hunt, UNLV	So.	2	19-31	9-16	2-4	4	9	1	1	1	49
1991	Christian Laettner, Duke	Jr.	2	12-22	1-1	21-23	17	2	1	2	5	46
1992	Bobby Hurley, Duke	Jr.	2	10-24	7-12	8-10	3	11	0	3	6	35
1993	Donald Williams, North Carolina	So.	2	15-23	10-14	10-10	4	1	0	2	2	50
1994	Corliss Williamson, Arkansas	So.	2	21-42	0-0	10-14	21	8	3	4	3	52
1995	Ed O'Bannon, UCLA	Sr.	2	16-35	3-8	10-13	25	3	1	7	3	45
1996	Tony Delk, Kentucky	Sr.	2	15-36	8-16	6-11	9	2	2	3	4	44
1997	Miles Simon, Arizona	Jr.	2	17-37	3-10	17-22	8	6	1	0	1	54
1998	Jeff Sheppard, Kentucky	Sr.	2	16-29	4-10	7-9	10	7	0	4	4	43
1999	Richard Hamilton, Connecticut	Jr.	2	20-39	3-7	8-11	12	4	1	2	4	51
2000	Mateen Cleaves, Michigan St.	Sr.	2	8-18	3-4	10-12	6	5	0	2	4	29
2001	Shane Battier, Duke	Sr.	2	13-26	5-12	12-17	19	8	6	2	4	43

+team finished second; †team finished third; ‡team finished fourth; *record later vacated

Larry Bird led Indiana State to the nation's No. 1 ranking in the Associated Press and the United Press International polls heading into the 1979 tournament. The Sycamores lost in the championship game to Michigan State, a team led by Magic Johnson and Greg Kelser, pictured guarding Bird.

Final Wire Service Polls No. 1 Teams

Year	AP Poll	UPI Poll	NCAA Champion	Champion's Final Ranking AP	UPI
1949	Kentucky	—	Kentucky	1	—
1950	Bradley	—	CCNY	NR	—
1951	Kentucky	Kentucky	Kentucky	1	1
1952	Kentucky	Kentucky	Kansas	8	3
1953	Indiana	Indiana	Indiana	1	1
1954	Kentucky	Indiana	La Salle	2	NR
1955	San Francisco	San Francisco	San Francisco	1	1
1956	San Francisco	San Francisco	San Francisco	1	1
1957	North Carolina	North Carolina	North Carolina	1	1
1958	West Virginia	West Virginia	Kentucky	9	NR
1959	Kansas St.	Kansas St.	California	NR	9
1960	Cincinnati	Cincinnati	Ohio St.	3	3
1961	Ohio St.	Ohio St.	Cincinnati	2	2
1962	Ohio St.	Ohio St.	Cincinnati	2	2
1963	Cincinnati	Cincinnati	Loyola (Ill.)	3	4
1964	UCLA	UCLA	UCLA	1	1
1965	Michigan	Michigan	UCLA	2	2
1966	Kentucky	Kentucky	UTEP	3	3
1967	UCLA	UCLA	UCLA	1	1
1968	Houston	Houston	UCLA	2	2
1969	UCLA	UCLA	UCLA	1	1
1970	Kentucky	Kentucky	UCLA	2	2
1971	UCLA	UCLA	UCLA	1	1
1972	UCLA	UCLA	UCLA	1	1
1973	UCLA	UCLA	UCLA	1	1
1974	North Carolina St.	North Carolina St.	North Carolina St.	1	1
1975	UCLA	Indiana	UCLA	1	2
1976	Indiana	Indiana	Indiana	1	1
1977	Michigan	Michigan	Marquette	7	14
1978	Kentucky	Kentucky	Kentucky	1	1
1979	Indiana St.	Indiana St.	Michigan St.	3	4
1980	DePaul	DePaul	Louisville	2	4
1981	DePaul	DePaul	Indiana	9	9
1982	North Carolina	North Carolina	North Carolina	1	1
1983	Houston	Houston	North Carolina St.	16	14
1984	North Carolina	North Carolina	Georgetown	2	2
1985	Georgetown	Georgetown	Villanova	NR	NR
1986	Duke	Duke	Louisville	7	7
1987	UNLV	UNLV	Indiana	3	3
1988	Temple	Temple	Kansas	NR	NR
1989	Arizona	Arizona	Michigan	10	10
1990	Oklahoma	Oklahoma	UNLV	3	3
1991	UNLV	UNLV	Duke	6	6
1992	Duke	Duke	Duke	1	1

Year	AP Poll	USA/NABC	NCAA Champion	AP	USA
1993	Indiana	Indiana	North Carolina	4	2
1994	North Carolina	Arkansas	Arkansas	2	1
1995	UCLA	UCLA	UCLA	1	1
1996	Massachusetts	Massachusetts	Kentucky	2	2
1997	Kansas	Kansas	Arizona	15	13
1998	North Carolina	North Carolina	Kentucky	5	6
1999	Duke	Duke	Connecticut	3	3
2000	Duke	Duke	Michigan St.	2	2
2001	Duke	Duke	Duke	1	1

NR—Not Ranked in Top 20 (Top 10 from 1949-67).
Note: Final poll rankings are released before the NCAA tournament.

Tournament trivia

Question...
Only three schools have to their credit a first-place finish in the Associated Press I-A football poll and a NCAA championship in basketball. Can you name those three schools?

Answer...
Michigan, Michigan State and Ohio State

FINAL FOUR CUMULATIVE RECORDS—SEEDS AT THE FINAL FOUR

Seeds at the Final Four

Year	Seeds	Teams
1979	1, 2, 2, 9 (14)	Indiana St., **Michigan St.**, DePaul, Pennsylvania
1980	2, 5, 6, 8 (21)	**Louisville**, Iowa, Purdue, UCLA
1981	1, 1, 2, 3 (7)	Virginia, LSU, North Carolina, **Indiana**
1982	1, 1, 3, 6 (11)	**North Carolina**, Georgetown, Louisville, Houston
1983	1, 1, 4, 6 (12)	Houston, Louisville, Georgia, **North Carolina St.**
1984	1, 1, 2, 7 (11)	Kentucky, **Georgetown**, Houston, Virginia
1985	1, 1, 2, 8 (12)	St. John's (N.Y.), Georgetown, Memphis, **Villanova**
1986	1, 1, 2, 11 (15)	Duke, Kansas, **Louisville**, LSU
1987	1, 1, 2, 6 (10)	UNLV, **Indiana**, Syracuse, Providence
1988	1, 1, 2, 6 (10)	Arizona, Oklahoma, Duke, **Kansas**
1989	1, 2, 3, 3 (9)	Illinois, Duke, Seton Hall, **Michigan**
1990	1, 3, 4, 4 (12)	**UNLV**, Duke, Georgia Tech, Arkansas
1991	1, 1, 2, 3 (7)	UNLV, North Carolina, **Duke**, Kansas
1992	1, 2, 4, 6 (13)	**Duke**, Indiana, Cincinnati, Michigan
1993	1, 1, 1, 2 (5)	**North Carolina**, Kentucky, Michigan, Kansas
1994	1, 2, 2, 3 (8)	**Arkansas**, Arizona, Duke, Florida
1995	1, 2, 2, 4 (9)	**UCLA**, Arkansas, North Carolina, Oklahoma St.
1996	1, 1, 4, 5 (11)	**Kentucky**, Massachusetts, Syracuse, Mississippi St.
1997	1, 1, 1, 4 (7)	Kentucky, Minnesota, North Carolina, **Arizona**
1998	1, 2, 3, 3 (9)	North Carolina, **Kentucky**, Stanford, Utah
1999	1, 1, 1, 4 (6)	**Connecticut**, Duke, Michigan St., Ohio St.
2000	1, 5, 8, 8 (22)	**Michigan St.**, Florida, North Carolina, Wisconsin
2001	1, 1, 2, 3 (7)	Arizona, **Duke**, Maryland, Michigan St.

Note: champion in bold

The Path to the Championship

Did the champion play the highest-seeded teams along the way?

Year	Team	Champion's Seed	1st	2nd	RSF	RF	NSF	CH
1979	Michigan St.	2		N(10)	Y(3)	Y(1)	N(9)	Y(1)
1980	Louisville	2		Y(7)	N(6)	Y(1)	N(5)	N(8)
1981	Indiana	3		Y(6)	N(7)	N(9)	Y(1)	N(2)
1982	North Carolina	1		N(9)	Y(4)	N(3)	N(6)	Y(1)
1983	North Carolina St.	6	(11)	Y(3)	N(10)	Y(1)	N(4)	Y(1)
1984	Georgetown	1		N(9)	N(5)	N(10)	Y(1)	N(2)
1985	Villanova	8	(9)	Y(1)	N(5)	Y(2)	N(2)	Y(1)
1986	Louisville	2	(15)	Y(7)	Y(3)	N(8)	N(11)	Y(1)
1987	Indiana	1	(16)	Y(8)	N(5)	N(10)	Y(1)	N(2)
1988	Kansas	6	(11)	N(14)	N(7)	N(4)	N(2)	Y(1)
1989	Michigan	3	(14)	N(11)	Y(2)	N(5)	Y(1)	N(3)
1990	UNLV	1	(16)	Y(8)	N(12)	N(11)	N(4)	N(3)
1991	Duke	2	(15)	Y(7)	N(11)	N(4)	Y(1)	N(3)
1992	Duke	1	(16)	N(9)	Y(4)	Y(2)	N(2)	N(6)
1993	North Carolina	1	(16)	Y(8)	Y(4)	Y(2)	N(2)	Y(1)
1994	Arkansas	1	(16)	N(9)	N(12)	N(3)	N(2)	N(2)
1995	UCLA	1	(16)	Y(8)	N(5)	Y(2)	N(4)	N(2)
1996	Kentucky	1	(16)	N(9)	Y(4)	Y(2)	Y(1)	N(4)
1997	Arizona	4	(13)	N(12)	Y(1)	N(10)	Y(1)	Y(1)
1998	Kentucky	2	(15)	N(10)	N(6)	Y(1)	N(3)	N(3)
1999	Connecticut	1	(16)	N(9)	N(5)	N(10)	N(4)	Y(1)
2000	Michigan St.	1	(16)	Y(8)	Y(4)	Y(2)	N(8)	N(5)
2001	Duke	1	(16)	N(9)	Y(4)	N(6)	N(3)	N(2)

Y—Yes; N—No; Opponent's seed in parentheses.

In 1953, Kansas center B.H. Born scored 51 points at the Final Four and became the first tournament most outstanding player not to play for the national champions.

All-Tournament Teams

(First player listed each year was the Most Outstanding Player.)

Final Four record later vacated is indicated by (*).

1939
Not chosen

1940
Marv Huffman, Indiana
Jay McCreary, Indiana
Bob Menke, Indiana
Howard Engleman, Kansas
Bob Allen, Kansas

1941-51
Not chosen

1952
Clyde Lovellette, Kansas
James Bredar, Illinois
John Kerr, Illinois
Dean Kelley, Kansas
Bob Zawoluk, St. John's (N.Y.)
Ron MacGilvray, St. John's (N.Y.)

1953
B.H. Born, Kansas
Bob Leonard, Indiana
Don Schlundt, Indiana
Dean Kelley, Kansas
Bob Houbregs, Washington

1954
Tom Gola, La Salle
Bob Carney, Bradley
Charlie Singley, La Salle
Jesse Arnelle, Penn St.
Roy Irvin, Southern California

1955
Bill Russell, San Francisco
Jim Ranglos, Colorado
Carl Cain, Iowa
Tom Gola, La Salle
K.C. Jones, San Francisco

1956
Hal Lear, Temple
Carl Cain, Iowa
Bill Logan, Iowa
Hal Perry, San Francisco
Bill Russell, San Francisco

1957
Wilt Chamberlain, Kansas
John Green, Michigan St.
Pete Brennan, North Carolina
Lennie Rosenbluth, North Carolina
Gene Brown, San Francisco

1958
Elgin Baylor, Seattle
Johnny Cox, Kentucky
Vern Hatton, Kentucky
Charley Brown, Seattle
Guy Rodgers, Temple

1959
Jerry West, West Virginia
Denny Fitzpatrick, California
Darrall Imhoff, California
Oscar Robertson, Cincinnati
Don Goldstein, Louisville

1960
Jerry Lucas, Ohio St.
Darrall Imhoff, California
Oscar Robertson, Cincinnati
Mel Nowell, Ohio St.
Tom Sanders, New York U.

1961
Jerry Lucas, Ohio St.
Carl Bouldin, Cincinnati
Bob Wiesenhahn, Cincinnati
Larry Siegfried, Ohio St.
*Jack Egan, St. Joseph's

1962
Paul Hogue, Cincinnati
Tom Thacker, Cincinnati
John Havlicek, Ohio St.
Jerry Lucas, Ohio St.
Len Chappell, Wake Forest

1963
Art Heyman, Duke

Ron Bonham, Cincinnati
Tom Thacker, Cincinnati
George Wilson, Cincinnati
Les Hunter, Loyola (Ill.)
1964
Walt Hazzard, UCLA
Jeff Mullins, Duke
Willie Murrell, Kansas St.
Bill Buntin, Michigan
Gail Goodrich, UCLA
1965
Bill Bradley, Princeton
Cazzie Russell, Michigan
Gail Goodrich, UCLA
Edgar Lacey, UCLA
Kenny Washington, UCLA
1966
Jerry Chambers, Utah
Jack Marin, Duke
Louie Dampier, Kentucky
Pat Riley, Kentucky
Bobby Joe Hill, UTEP
1967
Lew Alcindor, UCLA
Don May, Dayton
Elvin Hayes, Houston
Lucius Allen, UCLA
Mike Warren, UCLA
1968
Lew Alcindor, UCLA
Larry Miller, North Carolina
Lucius Allen, UCLA
Lynn Shackelford, UCLA
Mike Warren, UCLA
1969
Lew Alcindor, UCLA
Willie McCarter, Drake
Charlie Scott, North Carolina
Rick Mount, Purdue
John Vallely, UCLA
1970
Sidney Wicks, UCLA
Artis Gilmore, Jacksonville
Jimmy Collins, New Mexico St.
Curtis Rowe, UCLA
John Vallely, UCLA
1971
*Howard Porter, Villanova
*Hank Siemiontkowski, Villanova
*Jim McDaniels, Western Ky.
Steve Patterson, UCLA
Sidney Wicks, UCLA
1972
Bill Walton, UCLA
Ron King, Florida St.
Jim Price, Louisville
Bob McAdoo, North Carolina
Keith Wilkes, UCLA

1973
Bill Walton, UCLA
Steve Downing, Indiana
Larry Finch, Memphis
Larry Kenon, Memphis
Ernie DiGregorio, Providence
1974
David Thompson, North Carolina St.
Maurice Lucas, Marquette
Tom Burleson, North Carolina St.
Monte Towe, North Carolina St.
Bill Walton, UCLA
1975
Richard Washington, UCLA
Kevin Grevey, Kentucky
Allen Murphy, Louisville
Jim Lee, Syracuse
Dave Meyers, UCLA
1976
Kent Benson, Indiana
Tom Abernethy, Indiana
Scott May, Indiana
Rickey Green, Michigan
Marques Johnson, UCLA
1977
Butch Lee, Marquette
Bo Ellis, Marquette
Jerome Whitehead, Marquette
Walter Davis, North Carolina
Mike O'Koren, North Carolina
Cedric Maxwell, Charlotte
1978
Jack Givens, Kentucky
Ron Brewer, Arkansas
Mike Gminski, Duke
Jim Spanarkel, Duke
Rick Robey, Kentucky
1979
Earvin "Magic" Johnson, Michigan St.
Mark Aguirre, DePaul
Gary Garland, DePaul
Larry Bird, Indiana St.
Greg Kelser, Michigan St.
1980
Darrell Griffith, Louisville
Rodney McCray, Louisville
Joe Barry Carroll, Purdue
*Rod Foster, UCLA
*Kiki Vandeweghe, UCLA
1981
Isiah Thomas, Indiana
Jim Thomas, Indiana
Landon Turner, Indiana
Al Wood, North Carolina
Jeff Lamp, Virginia
1982
James Worthy, North Carolina
Patrick Ewing, Georgetown
Eric Floyd, Georgetown

Michael Jordan, North Carolina
Sam Perkins, North Carolina
1983
Akeem Olajuwon, Houston
Thurl Bailey, North Carolina St.
Sidney Lowe, North Carolina St.
Dereck Whittenburg, North Carolina St.
Milt Wagner, Louisville
1984
Patrick Ewing, Georgetown
Michael Graham, Georgetown
Alvin Franklin, Houston
Akeem Olajuwon, Houston
Michael Young, Houston
1985
Ed Pinckney, Villanova
Patrick Ewing, Georgetown
Harold Jensen, Villanova
Dwayne McClain, Villanova
Gary McLain, Villanova
1986
Pervis Ellison, Louisville
Mark Alarie, Duke
Tommy Amaker, Duke
Johnny Dawkins, Duke
Billy Thompson, Louisville
1987
Keith Smart, Indiana
Steve Alford, Indiana
Armon Gilliam, UNLV
Derrick Coleman, Syracuse
Sherman Douglas, Syracuse
1988
Danny Manning, Kansas
Sean Elliott, Arizona
Milt Newton, Kansas
Stacey King, Oklahoma
Dave Sieger, Oklahoma
1989
Glen Rice, Michigan
Danny Ferry, Duke
Rumeal Robinson, Michigan
Gerald Greene, Seton Hall
John Morton, Seton Hall
1990
Anderson Hunt, UNLV
Phil Henderson, Duke
Dennis Scott, Georgia Tech
Stacey Augmon, UNLV
Larry Johnson, UNLV
1991
Christian Laettner, Duke
Bobby Hurley, Duke
Bill McCaffrey, Duke
Mark Randall, Kansas
Anderson Hunt, UNLV
1992
Bobby Hurley, Duke
Grant Hill, Duke

Christian Laettner, Duke
Jalen Rose, Michigan
Chris Webber, Michigan
1993
Donald Williams, North Carolina
Jamal Mashburn, Kentucky
Chris Webber, Michigan
George Lynch, North Carolina
Eric Montross, North Carolina
1994
Corliss Williamson, Arkansas
Corey Beck, Arkansas
Scotty Thurman, Arkansas
Grant Hill, Duke
Antonio Lang, Duke
1995
Ed O'Bannon, UCLA
Clint McDaniel, Arkansas
Corliss Williamson, Arkansas
Bryant Reeves, Oklahoma St.
Toby Bailey, UCLA
1996
Tony Delk, Kentucky
Ron Mercer, Kentucky
*Marcus Camby, Massachusetts
Todd Burgan, Syracuse
John Wallace, Syracuse
1997
Miles Simon, Arizona
Mike Bibby, Arizona
Ron Mercer, Kentucky
Scott Padgett, Kentucky
Bobby Jackson, Minnesota
1998
Jeff Sheppard, Kentucky
Scott Padgett, Kentucky
Arthur Lee, Stanford
Michael Doleac, Utah
Andre Miller, Utah
1999
Richard Hamilton, Connecticut
Khalid El-Amin, Connecticut
Richard Moore, Connecticut
Elton Brand, Duke
Trajan Langdon, Duke
2000
Mateen Cleaves, Michigan St.
Udonis Haslem, Florida
Charlie Bell, Michigan St.
A.J. Granger, Michigan St.
Morris Peterson, Michigan St.
2001
Shane Battier, Duke
Mike Dunleavy, Duke
Jason Williams, Duke
Richard Jefferson, Arizona
Loren Woods, Arizona

All-Decade Teams

Note: All selections made before the 1988 tournament.

ALL-TIME TEAM
Lew Alcindor, UCLA (1967-68-69)
Larry Bird, Indiana St. (1979)
Wilt Chamberlain, Kansas (1957)
Earvin "Magic" Johnson, Michigan St. (1979)
Michael Jordan, North Carolina (1982)

1939-40s
Howie Dallmar, Stanford (1942)
Jim Pollard, Stanford (1942)
Kenny Sailors, Wyoming (1943)
Arnie Ferrin, Utah (1944)

Bob Kurland, Oklahoma St. (1945-46)
Gerald Tucker, Oklahoma (1947)
George Kaftan, Holy Cross (1947)
Ralph Beard, Kentucky (1948-49)
Alex Groza, Kentucky (1948-49)
Dwight Eddleman, Illinois (1949)

1950s
Clyde Lovellette, Kansas (1952)
Tom Gola, La Salle (1954)
K.C. Jones, San Francisco (1955)
Bill Russell, San Francisco (1955-56)
Wilt Chamberlain, Kansas (1957)
Lennie Rosenbluth, North Carolina (1957)
Elgin Baylor, Seattle (1958)
Guy Rodgers, Temple (1958)
Jerry West, West Virginia (1959)
Oscar Robertson, Cincinnati (1959-60)

1960s
Jerry Lucas, Ohio St. (1960-61)
John Havlicek, Ohio St. (1961-62)
Gail Goodrich, UCLA (1964-65)
Walt Hazzard, UCLA (1964)
Jeff Mullins, Duke (1964)
Bill Bradley, Princeton (1965)
Cazzie Russell, Michigan (1965)
Elvin Hayes, Houston (1967-68)
Lew Alcindor, UCLA (1967-68-69)
Charlie Scott, North Carolina (1968-69)

1970s
Sidney Wicks, UCLA (1969-70)
Bill Walton, UCLA (1972-73-74)
Keith Wilkes, UCLA (1972-73-74)
David Thompson, North Carolina St. (1974)

FINAL FOUR CUMULATIVE RECORDS—ALL-DECADE TEAMS

Marques Johnson, UCLA (1975-76)
Kent Benson, Indiana (1976)
Scott May, Indiana (1976)
Jack Givens, Kentucky (1978)
Larry Bird, Indiana St. (1979)
Earvin "Magic" Johnson, Michigan St. (1979)

1980-87
Darrell Griffith, Louisville (1980)
Rodney McCray, Louisville (1980)
Isiah Thomas, Indiana (1981)
Patrick Ewing, Georgetown (1982-84-85)
Michael Jordan, North Carolina (1982)
James Worthy, North Carolina (1982)
Akeem Olajuwon, Houston (1983-84)
Ed Pinckney, Villanova (1985)
Johnny Dawkins, Duke (1986)
Steve Alford, Indiana (1987)

SELECTION PANEL
Denny Crum, Louisville
Dean Smith, North Carolina
Joe B. Hall, Kentucky
Pete Newell, California
Vic Bubas, Sun Belt Conference
Dave Gavitt, Big East Conference
Jud Heathcote, Michigan St.
John Thompson, Georgetown
Henry Iba, Oklahoma St.
John Wooden, UCLA
Wayne Duke, Big Ten Conference

Consensus All-Americans in the Final Four

(Players who were consensus all-Americans the year their team played in the Final Four.)

Final Four record later vacated is indicated by (*). Injured in regional final game and did not play in Final Four is indicated by (#).

ARIZONA
Sean Elliott 1988

ARKANSAS
Johnny Adams 1941

BRADLEY
Paul Unruh 1950

CALIFORNIA
Darrall Imhoff 1960

CINCINNATI
Oscar Robertson 1959-1960
Ron Bonham 1963
Tom Thacker 1963

CONNECTICUT
Richard Hamilton 1999

DARTMOUTH
Audley Brindley 1944

DUKE
Art Heyman 1963
Johnny Dawkins 1986
Danny Ferry 89
Christian Laettner 1992

Grant Hill 1994
Elton Brand 1999
Shane Battier 2001
Jason Williams 2001

GEORGETOWN
Eric Floyd 1982
Patrick Ewing 1984-1985

HOUSTON
Elvin Hayes 1967-1968
Akeem Olajuwon 1984

ILLINOIS
Rod Fletcher 1952

INDIANA
Kent Benson 1976
Scott May 19 76
Isiah Thomas 1981
Steve Alford 1987

INDIANA ST.
Larry Bird 1979

KANSAS
Clyde Lovellette 1952
Wilt Chamberlain 1957
Danny Manning 1988

KANSAS ST.
Bob Boozer 1958

KENTUCKY
Ralph Beard 1948-1949
Alex Groza 1949
Bill Spivey 1951
Jamal Mashburn 1993
Tony Delk 1996
Ron Mercer 1997

LA SALLE
Tom Gola 1954-1955

LOUISVILLE
Darrell Griffith 1980

LOYOLA (ILL.)
Jerry Harkness 1963

MASSACHUSETTS
Marcus Camby 1996

MEMPHIS
*Keith Lee 1985

MICHIGAN
Cazzie Russell 1965
Chris Webber 1993

MICHIGAN ST.
Earvin "Magic" Johnson 1979
Mateen Cleaves 1999

UNLV
Larry Johnson 1990-1991

NORTH CAROLINA
Lennie Rosenbluth 1957
Larry Miller 1968
Bob McAdoo 1972
Phil Ford 1977
James Worthy 1982
Jerry Stackhouse 1995
Antawn Jamison 1998

NORTH CAROLINA ST.
David Thompson 1974

OHIO ST.
Jimmy Hull 1939
Jerry Lucas 1961-1962

OKLAHOMA
Gerald Tucker 1947

OKLAHOMA ST.
Bob Kurland 1945-1946

OREGON
Slim Wintermute 1939

PRINCETON
Bill Bradley 1965

PROVIDENCE
Ernie DiGregorio 1973

PURDUE
Rick Mount 1969
Joe Barry Carroll 1980

ST. BONAVENTURE
#Bob Lanier 1970

ST. JOHN'S (N.Y.)
Chris Mullin 1985

SAN FRANCISCO
Bill Russell 1955-1956

SEATTLE
Elgin Baylor 1958

SOUTHERN CALIFORNIA
Ralph Vaughn 1940

TEMPLE
Guy Rodgers 1958

UCLA
Walt Hazzard 1964
Gail Goodrich 1965
Lew Alcindor 1967, 1968-1969
Sidney Wicks 1971
Henry Bibby 1972
Bill Walton 1972-1974
Keith Wilkes 1973-1974
Dave Meyers 1975
Richard Washington 1976
Ed O'Bannon 1995

VIRGINIA
Ralph Sampson 1981

WAKE FOREST
Len Chappell 1962

WASHINGTON
Bob Houbregs 1953

WESTERN KY.
*Jim McDaniels 1971

WISCONSIN
Gene Englund 1941

WYOMING
Kenny Sailors 1943

Game Officials

Officiated the championship game is indicated by (#).

1939
Lyle Clarno#
John Getchell#

1940
Gil MacDonald#
Ted O'Sullivan#

1941
Wally Cameron#
Bill Haarlow#

1942
Glenn Adams#
Abb Curtis#

1943
Matty Begovich#
Pat Kennedy#

1944
Paul Menton#
James Osborne#

1945
Glenn Adams#
James Beiersdorfer
Edward Boyle
Abb Curtis#

1946
Jocko Collins#
Pat Kennedy#
John Nucatola
William Orwig

1947
Hagan Anderson#
Bill Haarlow

Pat Kennedy#
William Orwig

1948
Matty Begovich#
Bill Haarlow#
Gil MacDonald#
James Osborne

1949
Abb Curtis
Hal Lee#
Tim McCullough#
Cliff Ogden

1950
Lou Eisenstein#
Ronald Gibbs#
Remy Meyer
John Morrow

1951
No officials listed

1952
Lou Eisenstein#
Cliff Ogden#

1953
Joe Conway

Alex George
Al Lightner#
Cliff Ogden
Shaw#

1954
Hagan Anderson#
Dick Ball
Ross Dean#
Jim Enright

1955
Phil Fox
Mike Milner
Mohr
Cliff Ogden

FINAL FOUR CUMULATIVE RECORDS—GAME OFFICIALS

1956
No officials listed

1957
Hagan Anderson#
Joe Conway#
Al Lightner
Cliff Ogden

1958
Joe Conway
Al Mercer
Red Mihalik
John Morrow

1959
Tommy Bell#
Red Mihalik#

1960
Alex George#
Red Mihalik

1961
Curtis Filiberti#
Phil Fox#
Tom Glennon
Lenny Wirtz

1962
Charles Eckman#
Dan Elser
Rudy Marick#
Dan Watson

1963
Bill Bussenius#
Alex George#
Tom Glennon
Chuck Ovitz

1964
Charles Fouty
Tom Glennon#
Steve Honzo
Red Mihalik#

1965
Steve Honzo#
Bob Korte
Floyd Magnuson
Red Mihalik#

1966
Bill Bussenius
Steve Honzo
Thornton Jenkins#
Lenny Wirtz

1967
Lenny Wirtz#

1968
Bill Bussenius
Charles Fouty#
Steve Honzo#
Thornton Jenkins

1969
Irv Brown#
Michael DiTomasso#
Charles Fouty
John Overby

1970
Otis Allmond
Rudy Marich
Bobby Scott#
Art White
Lenny Wirtz#

1971
Jim Bain
Irv Brown#
Steve Honzo
Art White

1972
Irv Brown#
Reggie Copeland
Jim Hernjack
Bobby Scott#

1973
Jack Ditty
Jim Howell#
Joe Shosid#
Art White

1974
Irv Brown#
Paul Galvan
Jim Howell#
Rich Weiler

1975
Paul Galvan
Hank Nichols#
Lou Soriano
Bob Wortman#

1976
Jim Bain
Irv Brown#
Charles Fouty
Bob Wortman#

1977
Irv Brown
Reggie Copeland#
Charles Fouty
Paul Galvan#

1978
Jim Bain#
Roy Clymer#
Jim Howell
Dale Kelley

1979
Frank Buckiewicz
Gary Muncy#
Hank Nichols#
Jody Silvester
Rich Weiler
Lenny Wirtz#

1980
Robert Herrold
Larry Lembo#
Hank Nichols#
Bob Rhodes
Booker Turner
Rich Weiler

1981
Bobby Dibbler
Jim Howell
Dale Kelley
Ken Lauderdale#
Lou Moser#
Booker Turner

1982
John Dabrow#
Bobby Dibbler
Joe Forte
Hank Nichols#
Tom Rucker
Bob Wortman

1983
Joe Forte#
Paul Housman#
Larry Lembo
Hank Nichols#
Booker Turner
Rich Weiler

1984
Jim Clark
Hank Nichols
Dick Paparo
Ron Spitler#
Mike Tanco#
Booker Turner#

1985
Jim Burr
John Cloughery#
Bobby Dibbler#
Willis McJunkin
Don Rutledge#
Charles Vacca

1986
John Cloughery
Tom Fincken
Joe Forte
Paul Galvan
Hank Nichols#
Dick Paparo
Pete Pavia#
Don Rutledge#
Lenny Wirtz

1987
John Cloughery
Nolan Fine#
Joe Forte#
Paul Galvan
Luis Grillo
Rusty Herring
Dick Paparo
Don Rutledge
Jody Silvester#

1988
Jim Burr
John Cloughery#
Joe Forte
Luis Grillo
Tim Higgins#
Ed Hightower#
Paul Housman
Larry Lembo
Booker Turner

1989
John Cloughery#
Mickey Crowley#
Tom Harrington
Ed Hightower
Ted Hillary
David Jones
Larry Lembo
Tom Rucker#
Don Rutledge

1990
Jim Bain
Richie Ballesteros#
Frank Bosone
Jim Burr
Gerry Donaghy
Tim Higgins#
Ed Hightower#
Dick Paparo
Jim Stupin

1991
Jim Burr#
John Cloughery
Mickey Crowley#
Gerry Donaghy
Ed Hightower
Tom O'Neill

Pete Pavia
Charles Range#
Ted Valentine

1992
Jim Burr
John Cloughery
Gerry Donaghy#
Tom Harrington#
Tim Higgins
Ed Hightower
Dave Libbey#
Don Rutledge
Ted Valentine

1993
Jim Burr
John Cloughery
Gerry Donaghy
Tom Harrington#
Ed Hightower#
Dick Paparo
Larry Rose
Jim Stupin#
Ted Valentine

1994
Jim Burr#
Ted Hillary
Ed Hightower
Dave Libbey#
Tom Rucker
Mike Sanzere
Jody Silvester#
Jim Stupin
Ted Valentine#

1995
Jim Burr
John Cahill#
Tom Harrington
Tom Lopes
Gene Monje
Dick Paparo
Andre Pattillo
Charles Range
Ted Valentine#

1996
John Cloughery#
Ed Hightower
Michael Kitts
Dave Libbey#
Andre Pattillo
Tom Rucker
Mike Sanzere
Frank Scagliotta
Scott Thornley#

1997
Gerald Boudreaux
Jim Burr

John Cloughery
Tim Higgins
David Libbey#
Tom O'Neill#
Andre Pattillo
Frank Scagliotta
Ted Valentine#

1998
Jim Burr#
John Cloughery
Bob Donato
Donnee Gray#
Tim Higgins
Andre Pattillo
Larry Rose
Don Rutledge
Mike Sanzere#

1999
Gerald Boudreaux#
Jim Burr
John Cahill
Tim Higgins#
David Libbey
Larry Rose
Curtis Shaw
Scott Thornley#
Mark Whitehead

2000
Gerald Boudreaux#
Jim Burr#
John Cahill
John Cloughery
Donne Gray
David Hall#
Tim Higgins
Andre Patillo
Jody Silvester

2001
Gerald Boudreaux#
Ed Corbett#
Bob Donato
Tony Greene
Tim Higgins
Ted Hillary
David Libbey
Mark Reischling
Scott Thornley#

All-Time Participants

TEAM (Appearances-Players)

ARIZONA (4-36)
Gilbert Arenas 2001
Mike Bibby 1997
Joseph Blair 1994
A.J. Bramlett 1997
Andy Brown 1994
Jud Buechler 1988
Anthony Cook 1988
Bennett Davison 1997
Michael Dickerson 1997
Eugene Edgerson 1997, 2001
Sean Elliott 1988
Kevin Flanagan 1994
Jason Gardner 2001
Reggie Geary 1994

Donnell Harris 1997
Richard Jefferson 2001
Jarvis Kelley 1994
Steve Kerr 1988
Kenny Lofton 1988
Harvey Mason 1988
Joe McLean 1994
Craig McMillan 1988
Ray Owes 1994
Khalid Reeves 1994
Jason Richey 1994
Dylan Rigdon 1994
Miles Simon 1997
Damon Stoudamire 1994
Jason Terry 1997
Tom Tolbert 1988
Joe Turner 1988
Luke Walton 2001
Justin Wessel 2001
Corey Williams 1994
Loren Woods 2001
Michael Wright 2001

ARKANSAS (6-51)
Johnny Adams 1941
O'Neal Adams 1941
Corey Beck 1994-95
Chris Bennett 1978
Ken Biley 1994
Arlyn Bowers 1990
Ron Brewer 1978
Tony Byles 1945
Gordon Carpenter 1941
Jody Copeland 1945
Jim Counce 1978
Mario Credit 1990
Todd Day 1990
Marvin Delph 1978
Al Dillard 1994-95
Bill Flynt 1945
John Freiberger 1941
Reggie Garrett 1995
Darrell Hawkins 1990
Howard Hickey 1941
Lenzie Howell 1990

Ron Huery 1990
Charles Jolliff 1945
Kenneth Kearne 1945
George Kok 1945
Warren Linn 1990
Larry Marks 1990
Elmer Martin 1995
Lee Mayberry 1990
Clint McDaniel 1994-95
Oliver Miller 1990
Sidney Moncrief 1978
Ernie Murry 1990
R.C. Pitts 1941
Ulysses Reed 1978
Ocie Richie 1945
Davor Rimac 1994-95
Nobel Robbins 1941
Darnell Robinson 1994-95
Steve Schall 1978
Frank Schumchyk 1945
Mike Schumchyk 1945
Dwight Stewart 1994-95

FINAL FOUR CUMULATIVE RECORDS—ALL-TIME PARTICIPANTS

Scotty Thurman 1994-95
Paul Wheeler 1945
Cannon Whitby 1990
Landis Williams 1995
Corliss Williamson 1994-95
Lee Wilson 1994-95
Clayton Wynne 1941
Alan Zahn 1978

BAYLOR (2-15)
Gordon Carrington 1950
Gerald Cobb 1950
Bill DeWitt 1948, 50
W.A. Fleetwood 1950
William Harris 1950
Don Heathington 1948, 50
William Hickman 1948, 50
Edward Hovde 1950
Bill Johnson 1948, 50
Norman Mullins 1950
James Owens 1948
Odell Preston 1948, 50
Ralph Pulley 1948
Jackie Robinson 1948
William Srack 1948, 50

BRADLEY (2-22)
Harvey Babetch 1954
Elmer Behnke 1950
Bob Carney 1954
Mike Chianakas 1950
Dick Estergard 1954
Jack Gower 1954
Bud Grover 1950
Jim Kelly 1950
John Kent 1954
Barney Kilcullen 1954
Ed King 1954
Billy Mann 1950
Dino Melchiorre 1950
Gene Melchiorre 1950
Lee O'Connell 1954
Richard Petersen 1954
Aaron Preece 1950
John Riley 1954
Fred Schlictman 1950
Joe Stowell 1950
Paul Unruh 1950
Lee Utt 1954

CALIFORNIA (3-29)
Bill Alexander 1960
Bob Anderson 1946
Ned Averbuck 1960
Al Buch 1959
Bob Dalton 1959
Les Dean 1946
Dick Doughty 1959-60
Denny Fitzpatrick 1959
Tandy Gillis 1960
Jack Grout 1959
Bob Hogeboom 1946
Lowell Holcombe 1946
Darrall Imhoff 1959-60
Merv LaFaille 1946
Dick Larner 1946
Jerry Mann 1960
Bill McClintock 1959-60
Stan Morrison 1960
Art Mower 1946
Ed Pearson 1960
Cal Riemcke 1946
Earl Shultz 1960
Bernie Simpson 1959
James Smith 1946
Dave Stafford 1960
George Walker 1946
Bob Wendell 1960
Andy Wolfe 1946
Jim Wray 1946

CHARLOTTE (1-12)
Ken Angel 1977
Todd Crowley 1977
Jeff Gruber 1977
Mike Hester 1977
Chad Kinch 1977
Kevin King 1977
Lew Massey 1977
Cedric Maxwell 1977
Phil Scott 1977
Melvin Watkins 1977
Lee Whitfield 1977
Jerry Winston 1977

CINCINNATI (6-36)
Mark Altenau 1961
Corie Blount 1992
Ron Bonham 1962-63
Carl Bouldin 1959-61
John Bryant 1960
Anthony Buford 1992
Jim Calhoun 1961
Dick Cetrone 1959
Ken Cunningham 1963
Ralph Davis 1959-60
Fred Dierking 1960-61
Tarrance Gibson 1992
Dale Heidotting 1961, 63
Paul Hogue 1960-62
Allen Jackson 1992
Herb Jones 1992
Mel Landfried 1959
Erik Martin 1992
Fritz Meyer 1963
Ron Nall 1959
Terry Nelson 1992
Sandy Pomerantz 1960
Ron Reis 1960
Oscar Robertson 1959-60
Jeff Scott 1992
Larry Shingleton 1961, 63
Tom Sizer 1960-62
Gene Smith 1963
Dave Tenwick 1959
Tom Thacker 1961-63
Nick Van Exel 1992
Bill Whitaker 1959
Bob Wiesenhahn 1959-61
Larry Willey 1959-60
George Wilson 1962-63
Tony Yates 1961-63

CCNY (2-18)
Mason Benson 1947
Herb Cohen 1950
Irwin Dambrot 1947, 50
Phil Farbman 1947
Everett Finestone 1947
Joe Galiber 1947, 50
Sonny Jameson 1947
Floyd Layne 1950
Norman Mager 1950
Paul Malamed 1947
Lionel Malamed 1947
Ronald Nadell 1950
Edward Roman 1950
Alvin Roth 1950
Paul Schmones 1947
Hilpy Shapiro 1947
Sidney Trubowitz 1947
Edward Warner 1950

COLORADO (2-18)
Melvin Coffman 1955
Robert Doll 1942
Jim Grant 1955
Burdette Haldorson 1955
George Hamburg 1942
George Hannah 1955
Horace Huggins 1942
Bob Jeangerard 1955
Bob Kirchner 1942
Floyd Mansfield 1955
Leason McCloud 1942
Charlie Mock 1955
Heath Nuckolls 1942
Bill Peterson 1955
Donald Putnam 1942
Jim Ranglos 1955
Wilbert Walter 1955
Bob Yardley 1955

CONNECTICUT (1-11)
Khalid El-Amin 1999
Kevin Freeman 1999
Richard Hamilton 1999
E.J. Harrison 1999
Rashamel Jones 1999
Antric Klaiber 1999
Ricky Moore 1999
Albert Mouring 1999
Edmund Saunders 1999
Jake Voskuhl 1999
Souleymane Wane 1999

DARTMOUTH (2-20)
James Briggs 1942
Audley Brindley 1944
Robert Gale 1944
Vincent Goering 1944
Harry Leggat 1944
Richard McGuire 1944
Gordon McKernan 1942
Walter Mercer 1944
John Monahan 1944
George Munroe 1942
Franklin Murphy 1944
Robert Myers 1942
Everett Nordstrom 1944
William Parmer 1942
Charles Pearson 1942
Henry Pogue 1942
James Olsen 1942
Connor Shaw 1942
Stanley Skaug 1942
Joseph Vancisin 1944

DAYTON (1-12)
Tom Heckman 1967
Bob Hooper 1967
Dave Inderrieden 1967
Gene Klaus 1967
Don May 1967
Dan Obrovac 1967
Dan Sadlier 1967
John Samanich 1967
Ned Sharpenter 1967
Glinder Torain 1967
Jim Wannemacher 1967
Rudy Waterman 1967

DePAUL (2-15)
Mark Aguirre 1979
Clyde Bradshaw 1979
Jimmy Cominsky 1943
Mel Frailey 1943
Gary Garland 1979
John Jorgenson 1943
Tony Kelly 1943
William Madey 1979
Dennis McGuire 1979
George Mikan 1943
James Mitchem 1979
Chris Nikitas 1979
Bill Ryan 1943
Dick Starzyk 1943
Curtis Watkins 1979

DRAKE (1-12)
Don Draper 1969
Ron Gwin 1969
Bob Mast 1969
Willie McCarter 1969
Jim O'Dea 1969
Garry Odom 1969
Dolph Pulliam 1969
Dale Teeter 1969
Rick Wanamaker 1969
Al Williams 1969
Willie Wise 1969
Gary Zeller 1969

DUKE (13-81)
Alaa Abdelnaby 1988-90
Mark Alarie 1986
Tommy Amaker 1986
Christian Ast 1992
William Avery 1999
Eugene Banks 1978
Tony Barone 1966
Shane Battier 1999, 2001
Bob Bender 1978
Jay Bilas 1986
Kenny Blakeney 1992
Carlos Boozer 2001
Elton Brand 1999
Robert Brickey 1988-90
Clay Buckley 1989-90
Jay Buckley 1963-64
Andre Buckner 2001
Chris Burgess 1999
George Burgin 1989
Ron Burt 1992
Jeff Capel 1994
Chris Carrawell 1999
Warren Chapman 1966
Marty Clark 1992, 94
Chris Collins 1994
Joe Cook 1988, 90

Ray Cox 1963-64
Brian Davis 1989-92
Johnny Dawkins 1986
Kenny Dennard 1978
Chris Duhon 2001
Mike Dunleavy 2001
Dennis Ferguson 1963-64
Danny Ferry 1986, 88-89
Mike Gminski 1978
Scott Goetsch 1978
John Harrell 1978
Buzzy Harrison 1963-64
Frank Harscher 1964
David Henderson 1986
Phil Henderson 1988-90
Ron Herbster 1963-64
Art Heyman 1963
Grant Hill 1991-92, 94
Thomas Hill 1990-92
Bobby Hurley 1990-92
Nate James 1999, 2001
Bob Jamieson 1963
Joe Kennedy 1966
Billy King 1986
Brent Kitching 1963-64
Tim Kolodziej 1966
Greg Koubek 1988-91
Chris Laettner 1989-92
Antonio Lang 1991-92, 94
Trajan Langdon 1999
Mike Lewis 1966
Jim Liccardo 1966
Corey Maggette 1999
Ted Mann 1963-64
Jack Marin 1964, 66
Bill McCaffrey 1990-91
Erik Meek 1992, 94
Jeff Mullins 1963-64
Greg Newton 1994
Crawford Palmer 1989-91
Cherokee Parks 1992, 94
Bob Riedy 1966
Casey Sanders 2001
Fred Schmidt 1963
John Smith 1988-89
Quin Snyder 1988-89
Jim Spanarkel 1978
Kevin Strickland 1986
Jim Suddath 1978
Hack Tison 1963-64
Steve Vacendak 1964, 66
Bob Verga 1966
Ron Wendein 1966
Jason Williams 2001
Weldon Williams 1986

DUQUESNE (1-7)
Moe Becker 1940
Rudy Debnar 1940
Lou Kasperik 1940
Bill Lacey 1940
Melvin Milkovich 1940
George Reiber 1940
Paul Widowitz 1940

FLORIDA (2-19)
Jason Anderson 1994
Matt Bonner 2000
Craig Brown 1994
Dan Cross 1994
Andrew DeClercq 1994
Teddy Dupay 2000
Svein Dyrkolbotn 1994
Justin Hamilton 2000
Donnell Harvey 2000
Udonis Haslem 2000
Dametri Hill 1994
Martti Kuisma 1994
Mike Miller 2000
Brett Nelson 2000
Major Parker 2000
Brian Thompson 1994
Kenyan Weaks 2000
Greg Williams 1994
Brent Wright 2000

FLORIDA ST. (1-9)
Ottis Cole 1972
Rowland Garrett 1972
Larry Gay 1972
Ron Harris 1972
Ron King 1972
Lawrence McCray 1972

Otto Petty 1972
Reggie Royals 1972
Greg Samuel 1972

GEORGETOWN (4-30)
Horace Broadnax 1984-85
Fred Brown 1982, 84
Ralph Dalton 1984-85
Robert Duffey 1943
Patrick Ewing 1982, 84-85
William Feeney 1943
Frank Finnerty 1943
Eric Floyd 1982
Kevin Floyd 1985
Dan Gabbianelli 1943
Michael Graham 1984
Mike Hancock 1982
Bill Hassett 1943
Ron Highsmith 1985
Henry Hyde 1943
Michael Jackson 1984-85
Anthony Jones 1982
Daniel Kraus 1943
Tyrone Lockhart 1985
John Mahnken 1943
Bill Martin 1982, 84-85
Grady Mateen 1985
Perry McDonald 1985
Victor Morris 1984
Lloyd Potolicchio 1943
James Reilly 1943
Eric Smith 1982
Gene Smith 1982, 84
Ed Spriggs 1982
Reggie Williams 1984-85
David Wingate 1984-85

GEORGIA (1-8)
James Banks 1983
Richard Corhen 1983
Gerald Crosby 1983
Terry Fair 1983
Vern Fleming 1983
Derrick Floyd 1983
Donald Hartry 1983
Lamar Heard 1983

GEORGIA TECH (1-7)
Kenny Anderson 1990
Darryl Barnes 1990
Karl Brown 1990
Malcolm Mackey 1990
Johnny McNeil 1990
Brian Oliver 1990
Dennis Scott 1990

HOLY CROSS (2-14)
Charlie Bollinger 1947-48
Bob Cousy 1947-48
Bob Curran 1947-48
Bert Dolan 1948
Matthew Formon 1948
Charlie Graver 1947
Ken Haggerty 1947
George Kaftan 1947-48
Andy Laska 1947-48
Bob McMullan 1947-48
Joe Mullaney 1947-48
Dermie O'Connell 1947-48
Frank Oftring 1947-48
Jim Riley 1947

HOUSTON (5-37)
Marvin Alexander 1984
Benny Anders 1982-84
Greg Anderson 1984
Stacey Belcher 1984
Melvin Bell 1967-68
Andrew Benson 1967
Don Chaney 1967-68
Braxton Clark 1984
Larry Cooper 1968
Eric Davis 1982
Eric Dickens 1984
Clyde Drexler 1982-83
Alvin Franklin 1983-84
Reid Gettys 1983-84
Derek Giles 1983-84
Tom Gribben 1968
Gary Grider 1967
Neimer Hamood 1967-68
Elvin Hayes 1967-68
Don Kruse 1967

Theodis Lee 1967-68
Leary Lentz 1967
Vern Lewis 1967-68
Elliott McVey 1967
Larry Micheaux 1982-83
Akeem Olajuwon 1982-84
Gary Orsak 1984
David Rose 1983
Lynden Rose 1982
Ken Spain 1967-68
Kent Taylor 1968
Renaldo Thomas 1984
James Weaver 1984
Bryan Williams 1982-83
Rob Williams 1982
Rickie Winslow 1984
Michael Young 1982-84

ILLINOIS (4-33)
Nick Anderson 1989
Van Anderson 1949
Steve Bardo 1989
Kenny Battle 1989
Max Baumgardner 1951
Theodore Beach 1949, 51
Irving Bemoras 1951-52
James Bredar 1951-52
James Cottrell 1949
Dwight Eddleman 1949
William Erickson 1949
Rod Fletcher 1951-52
Richard Foley 1949
Clive Follmer 1951-52
Mack Follmer 1951
Roy Gatewood 1949
Herbert Gerecke 1951-52
Kendall Gill 1989
Fred Green 1949
Lowell Hamilton 1989
Max Hooper 1952
John Kerr 1952
Walter Kersulis 1949
Marcus Liberty 1989
James Marks 1949
John Marks 1951
Walter Osterkorn 1949
Robert Peterson 1951-52
Ervin Small 1989
Larry Smith 1989
Don Sunderlage 1949, 51
James Schuldt 1951
James Wright 1952

INDIANA (7-73)
Tom Abernethy 1973, 76
Steve Alford 1987
Eric Anderson 1992
Paul Armstrong 1940
Damon Bailey 1992
Kent Benson 1976
Quinn Buckner 1973, 76
Phil Byers 1953
Rick Calloway 1987
Goethe Chambers 1953
Calbert Cheaney 1992
Jim Crews 1973, 76
Jim DeaKyne 1953
Ralph Dorsey 1940
Steve Downing 1973
Bob Dro 1940
Dick Farley 1953
Chet Francis 1940
Chuck Franz 1981
Steve Eyl 1987
Dean Garrett 1987
Greg Graham 1992
Steve Green 1973
Jim Gridley 1940
Glen Grunwald 1981
Mark Haymore 1976
Alan Henderson 1992
Joe Hillman 1987
Marv Huffman 1940
Phil Isenbarger 1981
Ted Kitchel 1981
Charley Kraak 1953
Mike LaFave 1981
John Laskowski 1973
Todd Leary 1992
Bob Leonard 1953
Scott May 1976
Jay McCreary 1940

Jamal Meeks 1992
Jerry Memering 1973
Bill Menke 1940
Bob Menke 1940
Todd Meier 1987
Craig Morris 1973
Don Noort 1973
Matt Nover 1992
Paul Poff 1953
Wayne Radford 1976
Chris Reynolds 1992
Steve Risley 1981
John Ritter 1973
Herman Schaefer 1940
Don Schlundt 1953
Jim Schooley 1953
Burke Scott 1953
Keith Smart 1987
Kreigh Smith 1987
Trent Smock 1973
Ron Taylor 1953
Ray Tolbert 1981
Daryl Thomas 1987
Isiah Thomas 1981
Jim Thomas 1981
Landon Turner 1981
Rich Valavicius 1976
Dick White 1953
Bobby Wilkerson 1976
Frank Wilson 1973
Jim Wisman 1976
Randy Wittman 1981
Jack Wright 1953
Andy Zimmer 1940

INDIANA ST. (1-8)
Larry Bird 1979
Alex Gilbert 1979
Bob Heaton 1979
Brad Miley 1979
Rich Nemcek 1979
Carl Nicks 1979
Steve Reed 1979
Leroy Staley 1979

IOWA (3-22)
Mike Arens 1980
Kenny Arnold 1980
Kevin Boyle 1980
Vince Brookins 1980
Carl Cain 1955-56
Jon Darsee 1980
McKinley Davis 1955
Mark Gannon 1980
Bob George 1955-56
Tom Grogan 1980
Bob Hansen 1980
Mike Heller 1980
Mike Henry 1980
Steve Krafcisin 1980
Ronnie Lester 1980
Bill Logan 1955-56
Augie Martel 1955-56
Jim McConnell 1956
Sharm Scheuerman 1955-56
Bill Schoof 1955-56
Bill Seaberg 1955-56
Steve Waite 1980

IOWA ST. (1-7)
William Block 1944
Price Brookfield 1944
Roy Ewoldt 1944
James Myers 1944
Gene Oulman 1944
Robert Sauer 1944
Ray Wehde 1944

JACKSONVILLE (1-11)
Rusty Baldwin 1970
Mike Blevins 1970
Pembrook Burrows 1970
Chip Dublin 1970
Artis Gilmore 1970
Dan Hawkins 1970
Rod McIntyre 1970
Rex Morgan 1970
Gene Nelson 1970
Ken Selke 1970
Vaughn Wedeking 1970

KANSAS (10-93)
Jerry Alberts 1953
Robert Allen 1940
Scooter Barry 1988
Robert Billings 1957
B. H. Born 1952-53
Roger Brown 1971
Terry Brown 1991
Alton Campbell 1986
Randy Canfield 1971
Wilt Chamberlain 1957
Norman Cook 1974
Edwin Dater 1957
Larry Davenport 1952-53
Greg Douglas 1971
Greg Dreiling 1986
Donald Ebling 1940
Gene Elstun 1957
Howard Engleman 1940
Leland Green 1957
Dale Greenlee 1974
Jeff Gueldner 1988
Greg Gurley 1993
Darrin Hancock 1993
Dick Harp 1940
Keith Harris 1988
Arthur Heitholt 1952-53
Charlie Hoag 1952
William Hogben 1940
Blaine Hollinger 1957
Bill Hougland 1952
Rodney Hull 1986
Cedric Hunter 1986
Thomas Hunter 1940
Alonzo Jamison 1991
David Johanning 1991
Lewis Johnson 1957
Monte Johnson 1957
Wallace Johnson 1940
Adonis Jordan 1991, 93
John Keller 1952
Ron Kellogg 1986
Allen Kelly 1952-53
Dean Kelly 1952-53
Bob Kenney 1952
Lynn Kindred 1957
Maurice King 1957
Bob Kivisto 1971
Tom Kivisto 1974
John Kline 1940
Danny Knight 1974
Bill Lienhard 1952
Ron Loneski 1957
Clyde Lovellette 1952
Mike Maddox 1988, 91
Danny Manning 1986
Archie Marshall 1986
Mark Mathews 1971
Marvin Mattox 1988
Ralph Miller 1940
Lincoln Minor 1988
Roger Morningstar 1974
Aubrey Nash 1971
Milt Newton 1988
Clint Normore 1988
Greg Ostertag 1993
John Parker 1957
Harold Patterson 1953
Eric Pauley 1993
Sean Pearson 1993
Chris Piper 1953
Kevin Pritchard 1988
Mark Randall 1991
Calvin Rayford 1993
Gil Reich 1953
Patrick Richey 1991, 93
Dave Robisch 1971
Pierre Russell 1971
Jack Sands 1940
Richard Scott 1991, 93
Dean Smith 1953
Tommie Smith 1974
Bud Stallworth 1971
Rick Suttle 1974
Dave Taynor 1974
Calvin Thompson 1986
Sean Tunstall 1991
Mark Turgeon 1986
Donnie Von Moore 1974
Bruce Voran 1940
Kirk Wagner 1991

FINAL FOUR CUMULATIVE RECORDS—ALL-TIME PARTICIPANTS

Rex Walters 1993
Mark Williams 1971
Steve Woodbery 1991, 93

KANSAS ST. (4-45)
James Abbott 1958
Sonny Ballard 1958
Richard Barnard 1964
Ernie Barrett 1951
Clarence Brannum 1948
Bob Boozer 1958
Ward Clark 1948
John Dean 1948
Roy DeWitz 1958
Steve Douglas 1958
Larry Fischer 1958
Wally Frank 1958
John Gibson 1951
Joe Gottfrid 1964
Rick Harman 1948
Ed Head 1951
Lew Hitch 1951
James Hoffman 1964
Jim Holwerda 1958
Harold Howey 1948
James Iverson 1951
Dick Knostman 1951
Lloyd Krone 1948
Allan Langton 1948
Glen Long 1958
Kenneth Mahoney 1948
Don Matuszak 1958
Max Moss 1964
Willie Murrell 1964
David Nelson 1964
Ron Paradis 1964
Jack Parr 1958
Richard Peck 1951
Louis Poma 1964
Sammy Robinson 1964
Robert Rousey 1951
Dan Schuyler 1951
Howard Shannon 1948
Jeff Simons 1964
Jack Stone 1951
Roger Suttner 1964
Joe Thornton 1948
Don Upson 1951
David Weatherby 1948
Gary Williams 1964

KENTUCKY (13-103)
Marvin Akers 1942
Chuck Aleksinas 1978
Ermal Allen 1942
Derek Anderson 1996-97
Cliff Barker 1948-49
Dale Barnstable 1948-49
Dickie Beal 1984
Ralph Beard 1948-49
Bret Bearup 1984
Ed Beck 1958
Cliff Berger 1966
Winston Bennett 1984
James Blackmon 1984
Junior Braddy 1993
Michael Bradley 1998
Jeff Brassow 1993
Sam Bowie 1984
Melvin Brewer 1942
Dale Brown 1993
Dwane Casey 1978
Truman Claytor 1978
Lincoln Collinsworth 1958
Larry Conley 1966
Jimmy Dan Conner 1975
Scott Courts 1978
Fred Cowan 1978
Johnny Cox 1958
John Crigler 1958
Louie Dampier 1966
Tony Delk 1993, 96
Rodney Dent 1993
Allen Edwards 1996-98
Kenneth England 1942
Anthony Epps 1996-97
Heshimu Evans 1998
Mike Flynn 1975
Travis Ford 1993
Gary Gamble 1966
Chris Gettelfinger 1978
Jack Givens 1975, 78
Kevin Grevey 1975

Alex Groza 1948-49
Bob Guyette 1975
Cliff Hagan 1951
Jerry Hale 1975
Dan Hall 1975
Roger Harden 1984
Merion Haskins 1975
Vernon Hatton 1958
Walt Hirsch 1949
Joe Holland 1948
Thad Jaracz 1966
Larry Johnson 1975
Wallace Jones 1948-49
James King 1942
Tommy Kron 1966
James Lee 1975, 78
Jim LeMaster 1966
Jim Line 1948-49
Shelby Linville 1951
Kyle Macy 1978
Jamaal Magloire 1997-98
Gimel Martinez 1993
Jamal Mashburn 1993
Steve Masiello 1997
Jim Master 1984
Walter McCarty 1996
Ron Mercer 1996-97
Cameron Mills 1997-98
Don Mills 1958
Nazr Mohammed 1997-98
C.M. Newton 1951
Scott Padgett 1997-98
Mike Phillips 1975, 78
Mark Pope 1996
Jared Prickett 1993, 97
Frank Ramsey 1951
Lloyd Ramsey 1942
Rodrick Rhodes 1993
Andre Riddick 1993
Pat Riley 1966
Rick Robey 1975, 78
Kenneth Rollins 1948
Jay Shidler 1978
Jeff Sheppard 1996, 98
Adrian Smith 1958
G.J. Smith 1975
Saul Smith 1998
Carl Staker 1942
Tim Stephens 1978
Bill Spivey 1951
Bob Tallent 1966
Milton Ticco 1942
Lou Tsioropoulos 1951
Wayne Turner 1996-98
Melvin Turpin 1984
Antoine Walker 1996
Kenny Walker 1984
Reggie Warford 1975
Bobby Watson 1951
Lucian Whitaker 1951
Waller White 1942
LaVon Williams 1978

LA SALLE (2-10)
Frank Blatcher 1954-55
Walt Fredericks 1955
Tom Gola 1954-55
Chas Greensberg 1954-55
Al Lewis 1955
Bob Maples 1954-55
Frank O'Hara 1954
Fran O'Malley 1954-55
Charley Singley 1954-55
John Yodsnukis 1954

LSU (3-31)
Don Belcher 1953
Brian Bergeron 1981
Tyrone Black 1981
Ricky Blanton 1986
Kenneth Bridges 1953
Oliver Brown 1986
Howard Carter 1981
Ned Clark 1953
Ocie Conley 1986
Greg Cook 1981
Joe Costello 1981
Bob Freshley 1953
Johnny Jones 1981
Don Loughmiller 1953
Durand Macklin 1981
Norman Magee 1953
Ethan Martin 1981

Benny McArdle 1953
James McNeilly 1953
Leonard Mitchell 1981
Bob Pettit 1953
Don Redden 1986
Darrell Schultz 1953
Willie Sims 1981
Derrick Taylor 1986
John Tudor 1981
Jose Vargas 1986
John Williams 1986
Anthony Wilson 1986
Edwin Wilson 1986
Bernard Woodside 1986

LOUISVILLE (7-61)
Harley Andrews 1959
Harold Andrews 1959
Henry Bacon 1972
Ken Bradley 1972
Junior Bridgeman 1975
Phil Bond 1975
Tony Branch 1980
Danny Brown 1975
Wiley Brown 1980, 82
Bill Bunton 1972, 75
Roger Burkman 1980
George Burnette 1959
Larry Carter 1972
Daryl Cleveland 1980
Tim Cooper 1972
Wesley Cox 1975
Herbert Crook 1986
Greg Deuser 1980
Jerry Eaves 1980, 82
Pervis Ellison 1986
Ricky Gallon 1975
Bill Geiling 1959
Don Goldstein 1959
Lancaster Gordon 1982-83
Darrell Griffith 1980
Bryan Hall 1959
Jeff Hall 1983, 86
Billy Harmon 1975
Terry Howard 1975
Charles Jones 1982-83
Tony Kimbro 1986
Joe Kitchen 1959
Mike Lawhon 1972
Budd Leathers 1959
Alex Mantel 1959
Joe Meiman 1972
Rodney McCray 1980, 82-83
Scooter McCray 1982-83
Mark McSwain 1986
Allen Murphy 1975
Jim Price 1972
Paul Pry 1972
Marty Pulliam 1980
Ron Rubenstein 1959
Fred Sawyer 1959
Derek Smith 1980, 82
Howard Stacey 1959
Ron Stallings 1972
Roger Tieman 1959
Ron Thomas 1972
Billy Thompson 1983, 86
John Turner 1959
Robbie Valentine 1983
Al Vilcheck 1972
Milt Wagner 1982-83, 86
Kevin Walls 1986
Gerry Watkins 1959
Chris West 1983
Ike Whitfield 1975
Rick Wilson 1975
Poncho Wright 1980, 82

LOYOLA (ILL.) (1-9)
Dan Cannaughton 1963
John Egan 1963
Jerry Harkness 1963
Les Hunter 1963
Ron Miller 1963
Jim Reardon 1963
Rich Rochelle 1963
Vic Rouse 1963
Chuck Wood 1963

MARQUETTE (2-19)
Barry Brennan 1974
John Bryant 1974
Jim Boylan 1977

Rick Campbell 1974
Ed Daniels 1974
Dave Delsman 1974
Bo Ellis 1974, 77
Jerry Homan 1974
Greg Johnson 1974
Butch Lee 1977
Maurice Lucas 1974
Bill Neary 1977
Gary Rosenberger 1977
Earl Tatum 1974
Bernard Toone 1977
Paul Vollmer 1974
Lloyd Walton 1974
Marcus Washington 1974
Jerome Whitehead 1977

MARYLAND (1-10)
Lonny Baxter 2001
Steve Blake 2001
Juan Dixon 2001
Tahj Holden 2001
Mike Mardesich 2001
Danny Miller 2001
Terence Morris 2001
Byron Mouton 2001
Drew Nicholas 2001
Chris Wilcox 2001

MASSACHUSETTS (1-10)
Donta Bright 1996
Marcus Camby 1996
Charlton Clarke 1996
Dana Dingle 1996
Inus Norville 1996
Rigoberto Nunez 1996
Edgar Padilla 1996
Giddel Padilla 1996
Carmelo Travieso 1996
Tyrone Weeks 1996

MEMPHIS (2-21)
Ken Andrews 1973
Vincent Askew 1985
DeWayne Bailey 1985
Willie Becton 1985
William Bedford 1985
Dwight Boyd 1985
Bill Buford 1973
Bill Cook 1973
Larry Finch 1973
Baskerville Holmes 1985
Clarence Jones 1973
Larry Kenon 1973
Bill Laurie 1973
Keith Lee 1985
Jim Liss 1973
Doug McKinney 1973
Ron Robinson 1973
Jerry Tetzlaff 1973
Andre Turner 1985
Wes Westfall 1973
John Wilfong 1985

MICHIGAN (6-48)
Chip Armer 1992
Dennis Bankey 1965
Dave Baxter 1976
Tom Bergen 1976
Jason Bossard 1992
Wayman Britt 1976
Dan Brown 1965
Bill Buntin 1964-65
Demetrius Calip 1989
Bob Cantrell 1964
John Clawson 1964-65
Oliver Darden 1964-65
Craig Dill 1965
Rickey Green 1976
Mike Griffin 1989
Steve Grote 1976
Alan Hardy 1976
Doug Herner 1964
Sean Higgins 1989
Juwan Howard 1992-93
Phil Hubbard 1976
Mark Hughes 1989
Freddie Hunter 1992
Ray Jackson 1992-93
Bobby Jones 1976
Jimmy King 1992-93
Len Lillard 1976
Tom Ludwig 1965

THE FINAL FOUR

Terry Mills 1989
Jim Myers 1964-65
Rob Pelinka 1992-93
George Pomey 1964-65
Glen Rice 1989
Eric Riley 1992-93
John Robinson 1976
Rumeal Robinson 1989
Jalen Rose 1992-93
Cazzie Russell 1964-65
Lloyd Schinnerer 1976
Chris Seter 1992
Tom Staton 1976
Michael Talley 1992-93
Joel Thompson 1976
John Thompson 1965
Larry Tregoning 1964-65
Lou Vaught 1989
James Voskuil 1992-93
Chris Webber 1992-93

MICHIGAN ST. (5-41)
Aloysius Anagonye 2000-01
Bob Anderegg 1957
Jason Andreas 2001
Adam Ballinger 2000-01
Charlie Bell 1999-2001
Chuck Bencie 1957
Mike Brkovich 1979
Mike Chappell 2000-01
Ron Charles 1979
Steve Cherry 2000
Mateen Cleaves 1999-2000
Doug Davis 1999
Terry Donnelly 1979
George Ferguson 1957
Rob Gonzalez 1979
A.J. Granger 1999-2000
John Green 1957
Larry Hedden 1957
Jamie Huffman 1979
Andre Hutson 1999-2001
Mat Ishbia 2000-01
Earvin "Magic" Johnson 1979
Rick Kaye 1979
Thomas Kelley 1999
Gregory Kelser 1979
Jason Klein 1999
Greg Lloyd 1979
Mike Longaker 1979
Harry Lux 1957
Morris Peterson 1999-2000
Jack Quiggle 1957
Zach Randolph 2001
Jason Richardson 2000-01
David Scott 1957
Antonio Smith 1999
Brandon Smith 2000-01
Marcus Taylor 2001
David Thomas 2000-01
Jay Vincent 1979
Pat Wilson 1957
Adam Wolfe 2001

MINNESOTA (1-11)
Russ Archambault 1997
Eric Harris 1997
Bobby Jackson 1997
Sam Jacobson 1997
Courtney James 1997
Quincy Lewis 1997
Aaron Stauber 1997
Miles Tarver 1997
Charles Thomas 1997
John Thomas 1997
Trevor Winter 1997

MISSISSIPPI ST. (1-8)
Marcus Bullard 1996
Erick Dampier 1996
Whit Hughes 1996
Bart Hyche 1996
Dontae' Jones 1996
Russell Walters 1996
Tyrone Washington 1996
Darryl Wilson 1996

UNLV (4-32)
George Ackles 1991
Greg Anthony 1990-91
Stacey Augmon 1990-91
Freddie Banks 1987
Jarvis Basnight 1987

Travis Bice 1990
Lewis Brown 1977
David Butler 1990
Stacey Cvijanovich 1990
Armon Gilliam 1987
Glen Gondrezick 1977
Gary Graham 1987
Evric Gray 1991
Eldridge Hudson 1987
Anderson Hunt 1990-91
Chris Jeter 1990
Larry Johnson 1990-91
James Jones 1990
Larry Moffett 1977
Eddie Owens 1977
Gerald Paddio 1987
Dave Rice 1990
Rich Robinson 1987
Moses Scurry 1990
Robert Smith 1977
Sam Smith 1977
Tony Smith 1977
Elmore Spencer 1991
Reggie Theus 1977
Mark Wade 1987
David Willard 1987
Barry Young 1990

NEW MEXICO ST. (1-12)
John Burgess 1970
Jimmy Collins 1970
Charley Criss 1970
Rudy Franco 1970
Milton Horne 1970
Sam Lacey 1970
Lonnie Lefevre 1970
Tom McCarthy 1970
Bill Moore 1970
Roy Neal 1970
Chito Reyes 1970
Jeff Smith 1970

NEW YORK U. (2-21)
Al Barden 1960
Fred Benanti 1945
Russ Cunningham 1960
Mike DiNapoli 1960
Al Filardi 1960
Don Forman 1945
Marty Goldstein 1945
Al Grenert 1945
Rich Keith 1960
Art Loche 1960
Frank Mangiapane 1945
Bernie Mlodinoff 1960
Alvin Most 1945
Leo Murphy 1960
Ray Paprocky 1960
Bob Regan 1960
Jimmy Reiss 1960
Tom Sanders 1960
Dolph Schayes 1945
Sid Tanenbaum 1945
Herb Walsh 1945

NORTH CAROLINA (15-121)
Don Anderson 1946
Jimmy Black 1981-82
Jim Bostick 1967
Jimmy Braddock 1981-82
Dudley Bradley 1977
Pete Brennan 1957
Michael Brooker 2000
Joe Brown 1967-69
Chris Brust 1981-82
Bruce Buckley 1977
Pete Budko 1981
Bill Bunting 1967-69
Dante Calabria 1993-95
Jason Capel 2000
Craig Carson 1972
Vince Carter 1997-98
Dave Chadwick 1969
Bill Chamberlain 1972
Bill Chambers 1972
Scott Cherry 1991, 93
Pete Chilcutt 1991
Rusty Clark 1967-69
Dave Colescott 1977
Woody Coley 1977
Ed Cota 1997-98, 2000
Bob Cunningham 1957
Hubert Davis 1991

Larry Davis 1993
Walter Davis 1977
Lee Dedmon 1969
Jim Delany 1968-69
John Dillon 1946
Matt Doherty 1981-82
Ged Doughton 1977
Don Eggleston 1969
Jim Everett 2000
Ralph Fletcher 1967-68
Eddie Fogler 1968-69
Phil Ford 1977
Joseph Forte 2000
Rick Fox 1991
Jim Frye 1967-68
Tom Gauntlett 1967
Ed Geth 1993
Dale Gipple 1969
Dick Grubar 1967-68
Kenny Harris 1991
Brendan Haywood 1998, 2000
Jonathan Holmes 2000
Ray Hite 1972
Kim Huband 1972
Antawn Jamison 1997-98
Will Johnson 2000
Don Johnston 1972
Bobby Jones 1972
Jim Jordan 1946
Michael Jordon 1982
George Karl 1972
Tommy Kearns 1957
Eric Kenny 1981
Steve Krafcisin 1977
John Kuester 1977
Matt Laczkowski 2000
Pearce Landry 1995
Kris Lang 2000
Bob Lewis 1967
Danny Lotz 1957
George Lynch 1991, 93
Warren Martin 1982
Bob McAdoo 1972
Jeff McInnis 1995
Horace McKinney 1946
Charlie McNairy 1997
Orlando Melendez 2000
Larry Miller 1967-68
Donnie Moe 1967
Eric Montross 1991, 93
Terrence Newby 2000
Makhtar Ndiaye 1997-98
Mike O'Koren 1977
Ademola Okulaja 1997-98
Max Owens 2000
Bob Paxton 1946
Mike Pepper 1981
Julius Peppers 2000
Sam Perkins 1981-82
Buzz Peterson 1982
Derrick Phelps 1991, 93
Steve Previs 1972
Joe Quigg 1957
Brian Reese 1991, 93
King Rice 1991
Henrik Rodl 1991, 93
Lennie Rosenbluth 1957
Clifford Rozier 1991
Kevin Salvadori 1991, 93
Roger Scholbe 1946
Charlie Scott 1968-69
Roy Searcy 1957
Jerry Stackhouse 1995
Travis Stephenson 1993
Pat Sullivan 1991, 93, 95
Taylor Thorne 1946
Gerald Tuttle 1967-69
Richard Tuttle 1969
John Virgil 1977
Rasheed Wallace 1995
Matt Wenstrom 1991, 93
Jim White 1946
Kenny White 2000
Gra Whitehead 1968
Donald Williams 1993, 95
Shammond Williams 1995, 97-98
Jeff Wolf 1977
Al Wood 1981
James Worthy 1981-82
Dennis Wuycik 1972
Rich Yonakor 1977
Bob Young 1957

Tom Zaliagiris 1977
Serge Zwikker 1995, 97

NORTH CAROLINA ST. (3-25)
Thurl Bailey 1983
Alvin Battle 1983
Vic Bubas 1950
Tom Burleson 1974
Warren Cartier 1950
Lorenzo Charles 1983
Bob Cook 1950
Dick Dickey 1950
Terry Gannon 1983
Joe Harand 1950
Greg Hawkins 1974
Paul Horvath 1950
Sidney Lowe 1983
Cozell McQueen 1983
Mark Moeller 1974
Ernie Myers 1983
Sam Ranzino 1950
Moe Rivers 1974
Phil Spence 1974
Charlie Stine 1950
Tim Stoddard 1974
Lee Terrill 1950
David Thompson 1974
Monte Towe 1974
Dereck Whittenburg 1983

NOTRE DAME (1-10)
Dave Batton 1978
Rich Branning 1978
Bruce Flowers 1978
Bill Hanzlik 1978
Tracy Jackson 1978
Bill Laimbeer 1978
Kelly Tripucka 1978
Don Williams 1978
Stan Wilcox 1978
Orlando Woolridge 1978

OHIO ST. (9-70)
Warren Amling 1945-46
Dan Andreas 1968
Richard Baker 1939
Craig Barclay 1968
Dave Barker 1960
Richard Boughner 1939
Robert Bowen 1944, 46
Gary Bradds 1962
Brian Brown 1999
Rodney Caudill 1944-45
John Cedargren 1960
Neshaun Coleman 1999
Jack Dawson 1939
James Doughty 1962
John Dugger 1944-45
Clark Elliott 1946
Ollie Fink 1944
Jody Finney 1968
Donald Flatt 1962
Curtis Frazier 1962
Dick Furry 1960
Gary Gearhart 1960-62
Jim Geddes 1968
Donald Grate 1944-45
William Gunton 1944
John Havlicek 1960-62
Bill Hosket 1968
Steve Howell 1968
Richie Hoyt 1960-61
Jimmy Hull 1939
Paul Huston 1944-46
Ken Johnson 1999
Wilbur Johnston 1946
Bob Knight 1960-62
Charles Kuhn 1946
Jack Landes 1961
Kenneth Lee 1961
John Lovett 1946
Jerry Lucas 1960-62
Robert Lynch 1939
Charles Maag 1939
Doug McDonald 1961-62
Denny Meadors 1968
Jed Mees 1939
Gilbert Mickelson 1939
Nelson Miller 1961
Howard Nourse 1960
Mel Nowell 1960-62
Scoonie Penn 1999
Richard Reasbeck 1961-62

Michael Redd 1999
George Reese 1999
Arnold Risen 1944-45
Joe Roberts 1960
William Sattler 1939
Boban Savovic 1999
John Schick 1939
Bruce Schnabel 1968
Don Scott 1939
Larry Siegfried 1960-61
James Sims 1945
Jason Singleton 1999
Ed Smith 1968
Ray Snyder 1945-46
Dave Sorenson 1968
Robert Stafford 1939
Mike Swain 1968
Richard Taylor 1962
John Underman 1946
Wayne Wells 1946

OKLAHOMA (3-26)
Mookie Blaylock 1988
Garnett Corbin 1939
Paul Courty 1947
Harley Day 1947
Ricky Grace 1988
Harvey Grant 1988
Ben Kerr 1939
Stacey King 1988
Jack Landon 1947
Jim McNatt 1939
Paul Merchant 1947
Marvin Mesch 1939
Vernon Mullen 1939
Terrence Mullins 1988
Allie Paine 1947
Kenneth Pryor 1947
Dick Reich 1947
Gene Roop 1939
Herb Scheffler 1939
Dave Sieger 1988
Marvin Snodgrass 1939
Gerald Tucker 1947
Roscoe Walker 1939
Bill Waters 1947
Andre Wiley 1988
Matthew Zellner 1939

OKLAHOMA ST. (5-46)
Chad Alexander 1995
Frank Allen 1949
Louis Amaya 1951
Sam Aubrey 1946
Ben Baum 1995
Eugene Bell 1946
A.L. Bennett 1946
Joe Bradley 1946, 49
Terry Collins 1995
Pete Darcey 1951
Paul Geymann 1946
Joe Halbert 1945-46
Cecil Hankins 1945
Bob Harris 1949
Larry Hayes 1949
Jack Hobbs 1949
Tom Jacquet 1949
Don Johnson 1951
Weldon Kern 1945-46
Bob Kurland 1945-46
Emmett McAfee 1951
Gale McArthur 1949, 51
Kevin Miles 1995
John Miller 1951
John Nelson 1995
Andre Owens 1995
Bob Pager 1951
J.L. Parks 1945-46, 49
Doyle Parrack 1945
Scott Pierce 1995
Morman Pilgrim 1949
Bryant Reeves 1995
Chianti Roberts 1995
Gerald Rogers 1951
Randy Rutherford 1995
Kendall Sheets 1951
Jack Shelton 1949
Jason Skaer 1995
Keith Smith 1949, 51
Mark Steinmeyer 1946
Gerald Stockton 1951
Maurice Ward 1951

Blake Williams 1945-46
John Wylie 1945
Vernon Yates 1949

OREGON (1-9)
Bobby Anet 1939
John Dick 1939
Laddie Gale 1939
Bob Hardy 1939
Wally Johansen 1939
Ford Mullen 1939
Matt Pavalunas 1939
Ted Sarpola 1939
Slim Wintermute 1939

OREGON ST. (2-23)
Terry Baker 1963
Dick Ballantyne 1949
Rex Benner 1963
Tim Campbell 1963
Jim Catterall 1949
Mel Counts 1963
Cliff Crandall 1949
Ed Fleming 1949
Bill Harper 1949
Dave Hayward 1963
Tommy Holman 1949
Jim Jarvis 1963
Jim Kraus 1963
Steve Pauly 1963
Frank Peters 1963
Alex Petersen 1949
Len Rinearson 1949
Gary Rossi 1963
Paul Sliper 1949
Ray Snyder 1949
Ray Torgerson 1963
Dan Torrey 1949
Harvey Watt 1949

PENN ST. (1-9)
Jesse Arnelle 1954
Jim Blocker 1954
Jim Brewer 1954
Dave Edwards 1954
Earl Fields 1954
Ned Haag 1954
Robert Rohrland 1954
Jack Sherry 1954
Ron Weidenhammer 1954

PENNSYLVANIA (1-13)
Tom Condon 1979
Ted Flick 1979
Ken Hall 1979
David Jackson 1979
Ed Kuhl 1979
Tom Leifsen 1979
Tony Price 1979
Angelo Reynolds 1979
Vincent Ross 1979
James Salters 1979
Tim Smith 1979
Matt White 1979
Bobby Willis 1979

PITTSBURGH (1-11)
Bob Artman 1941
James Egan 1941
James Klein 1941
George Kocheran 1941
Clare Malarkey 1941
Sam Milanovich 1941
Melvin Port 1941
Larry Praffrath 1941
Ed Raymond 1941
Ed Straloski 1941
John Swacus 1941

PRINCETON (1-11)
Allen Adler 1965
Bill Bradley 1965
Robinson Brown 1965
Robert Haarlow 1965
Edward Hummer 1965
William Kingston 1965
William Koch 1965
Donald Neimann 1965
Donald Rodenbach 1965
Donald Roth 1965
Gary Walters 1965

PROVIDENCE (2-22)
Al Baker 1973

Marvin Barnes 1973
Gary Bello 1973
Delray Brooks 1987
Marty Conlon 1987
Fran Costello 1973
Charles Crawford 1973
Ernie DiGregorio 1973
Billy Donovan 1987
Jacek Duda 1987
Rich Dunphy 1973
Nehru King 1973
David Kipfer 1987
Ernie Lewis 1987
Mark McAndrew 1973
Dave Modest 1973
Carlton Screen 1987
David Sendeker 1987
Abdul Shamsid-Deen 1987
Kevin Stacom 1973
Darryl Wright 1987
Steve Wright 1987

PURDUE (2-24)
John Anthrop 1980
Roosevelt Barnes 1980
Tyrone Bedford 1969
Ted Benson 1980
Joe Barry Carroll 1980
Keith Edmonson 1980
George Faerber 1969
Herman Gilliam 1969
Arnette Hallman 1980
Jerry Johnson 1969
Frank Kaufman 1969
Bill Keller 1969
Jon Kitchel 1980
Steve Longfellow 1969
Drake Morris 1980
Rick Mount 1969
Ted Reasoner 1969
Kevin Stallings 1980
Mike Scearce 1980
Ralph Taylor 1969
Brian Walker 1980
Steve Walker 1980
Larry Weatherford 1969
Glenn Young 1969

RUTGERS (1-8)
Abdel Anderson 1976
Jim Bailey 1976
Mark Conlin 1976
Hollis Copeland 1976
Mike Dabney 1976
Steve Hefele 1976
Ed Jordan 1976
Phil Sellers 1976

ST. BONAVENTURE (1-10)
Tom Baldwin 1970
Gene Fahey 1970
Matt Gantt 1970
Greg Gary 1970
Paul Grys 1970
Paul Hoffman 1970
Bill Kalbaugh 1970
Mike Kull 1970
Dale Tepas 1970
Vic Thomas 1970

ST. JOHN'S (N.Y) (2-22)
Walter Berry 1985
Terry Bross 1985
Bob Cornegy 1985
Jim Davis 1952
Dick Duckett 1952
Frank Giancontieri 1952
Willie Glass 1985
Mark Jackson 1985
Shelton Jones 1985
Ron MacGilvray 1952
Jack McMahon 1952
Jim McMorrow 1952
Mike Moses 1985
Chris Mullin 1985
Carl Peterson 1952
Phil Sagona 1952
Ron Stewart 1985
Steve Shurina 1985
Solly Walker 1952
Jim Walsh 1952
Bill Wennington 1985
Bob Zawoluk 1952

ST. JOSEPH'S (1-11)
Harry Booth 1961
Dan Bugey 1961
Bob Dickey 1961
Jack Egan 1961
Bob Gormley 1961
Billy Hoy 1961
Vince Kempton 1961
Jim Lynam 1961
Frank Majewski 1961
Paul Westhead 1961
Tom Wynne 1961

SAN FRANCISCO (3-26)
Warren Baxter 1955-56
Carl Boldt 1956
Gene Brown 1956-57
Stan Buchanan 1955
Bill Bush 1955
Art Day 1957
Al Dunbar 1957
Mike Farmer 1956-57
K.C. Jones 1955
Jack King 1955-57
Gordon Kirby 1955
John Kolijian 1957
Dick Lawless 1955
Dave Lillevand 1957
Bill Mallen 1957
Ron Mancasola 1957
Jerry Mullen 1955
Tom Nelson 1956
Hal Perry 1955-56
Mike Preaseau 1956-57
Bob Radanovich 1957
Bill Russell 1955-56,
Charles Russell 1957
Bob Wiebusch 1955
Rudy Zannini 1955

SANTA CLARA (1-9)
Don Benedetti 1952
Dallas Brock 1952
Dick Garibaldi 1952
Gary Gatzert 1952
Bob Peters 1952
Herb Schoenstein 1952
Ken Sears 1952
Dick Soares 1952
Jim Young 1952

SEATTLE (1-14)
Elgin Baylor 1958
Charles Brown 1958
Jerry Frizzell 1958
Jim Harney 1958
Thornton Humphries 1958
John Kootnekoff 1958
Lloyd Murphy 1958
Don Ogorek 1958
Jude Petrie 1958
Don Piasecki 1958
Francis Saunders 1958
John Stepan 1958
Bob Swiewarga 1958
Bill Wall 1958

SETON HALL (1-15)
Anthony Avent 1989
Micheal Cooper 1989
Trevor Crowley 1989
Frantz Volcy 1989
Andrew Gaze 1989
Gerald Greene 1989
Nick Katsikis 1989
Khylem Long 1989
Rene Monteserin 1989
John Morton 1989
Ramon Ramos 1989
Jose Rebimbas 1989
Frantz Volcy 1989
Daryll Walker 1989
Pookey Wigington 1989

SOUTHERN CALIFORNIA (2-16)
Chester Carr 1954
Jack Dunne 1954
Richard Hammer 1954
Roy Irvin 1954
Keith Lambert 1940
Jack Lippert 1940
John Luber 1940
Alan Ludecke 1954

FINAL FOUR CUMULATIVE RECORDS—ALL-TIME PARTICIPANTS

THE FINAL FOUR

Tom McGarvin 1940
Jack Morrison 1940
Ralph Pausig 1954
Tony Psaltis 1954
Dale Sears 1940
Walter Thompson 1954
Ralph Vaughn 1940
Richard Welsh 1954

SOUTHERN METHODIST (1-8)
Rick Herrscher 1956
Jim Krebs 1956
Joel Krog 1956
Bob McGregor 1956
Buford Miller 1956
Bob Mills 1956
Ronnie Morris 1956
Larry Showalter 1956

STANFORD (2-22)
Don Burness 1942
Jarron Collins 1998
Bill Cowden 1942
Howie Dallmar 1942
Jack Dana 1942
John Eikelman 1942
Arthur Lee 1998
Fred Linari 1942
Bud Madden 1942
Mark Madsen 1998
Leo McCaffrey 1942
Michael McDonald 1998
Ryan Mendez 1998
David Moseley 1998
Fred Oliver 1942
Jim Pollard 1942
Peter Sauer 1998
Mark Seaton 1998
Pete Van Elswyk 1998
Ed Voss 1942
Kris Weems 1998
Tim Young 1998

SYRACUSE (3-28)
Derek Brower 1987
Todd Burgan 1996
Marty Byrnes 1975
Jason Cipolla 1996
Derrick Coleman 1987
Sherman Douglas 1987
Rudy Hackett 1975
Herman Harried 1987
Otis Hill 1996
Marius Janulis 1996
Larry Kelley 1975
Kevin King 1975
Ross Kindel 1975
Jim Lee 1975
Mark Meadors 1975
Greg Monroe 1987
Elimu Nelson 1996
Bob Parker 1975
J.B. Reafsnyder 1996
Chris Sease 1975
Earnie Seibert 1975
Rony Seikaly 1987
Steve Shaw 1975
Lazarus Sims 1996
Steve Thompson 1987
Howard Triche 1987
John Wallace 1996
Jim Williams 1975

TEMPLE (2-9)
Mel Brodsky 1958
Fred Cohen 1956
Dan Fleming 1956, 58
Bill Kennedy 1958
Hal Lear 1956
Jay Norman 1956, 58
Hal Reinfeld 1956
Guy Rodgers 1956, 58
Tink Van Patton 1956, 58

TEXAS (2-11)
Frank Brahaney 1943
Roy Cox 1943, 47
Jack Fitzgerald 1943
Tom Hamilton 1947
John Hargis 1943, 47
John Langdon 1943, 47
Al Madsen 1947
Slater Martin 1947

V. C. Overall 1943
Dan Wagner 1947
Dudley Wright 1943

UTEP (1-8)
Jerry Armstrong 1966
Orsten Artis 1966
Willie Cager 1966
Harry Flournoy 1966
Bobby Hill 1966
David Lattin 1966
Nevil Shed 1966
Willie Worsley 1966

UCLA (15-97)
Lew Alcindor 1967-69
Lucius Allen 1967-68
Darrell Allums 1980
Tony Anderson 1980
Toby Bailey 1995
Rick Betchley 1970-71
Henry Bibby 1970-72
Pete Blackman 1962
Kenny Booker 1970-71
Vince Carson 1972-73
Brice Chambers 1965
Jon Chapman 1970-72
Joe Chrisman 1967
Gary Cunningham 1962
Tommy Curtis 1972-74
Chuck Darrow 1964
Darren Daye 1980
Kevin Dempsey 1995
Cameron Dollar 1995
Ralph Drollinger 1974-76
John Ecker 1969-71
Tyus Edney 1995
Keith Erickson 1964-65
George Farmer 1969,
Larry Farmer 1971-73
Rod Foster 1980
Gary Franklin 1972-74
John Galbraith 1965
omm'A Givens 1995
Gail Goodrich 1964-65
Fred Goss 1965
John Green 1962
David Greenwood 1976
Roy Hamilton 1976
Walt Hazzard 1962, 64
Ken Heitz 1967-69
J. R. Henderson 1995
Bill Hicks 1962
Andy Hill 1970-72
Jack Hirsch 1964
Vaughn Hoffman 1964-65
Brad Holland 1976
Larry Hollyfield 1972-73
Michael Holton 1980
Mike Huggins 1964
Kris Johnson 1995
Marques Johnson 1974-76
Edgar Lacey 1965
Greg Lee 1972-74
Rich Levin 1964-65
Chris Lippert 1976
Dick Lynn 1967
Mike Lynn 1965, 68
John Lyons 1965
Andre McCarter 1974-76
Doug McIntosh 1964-65
Dave Meyers 1973-75
Jim Milhorn 1962
Bob Myers 1995
Swen Nater 1972-73
Jim Nielsen 1967-68
Ike Nwankwo 1995
Charles O'Bannon 1995
Ed O'Bannon 1995
Wilbert Olinde 1974-76
Steve Patterson 1969-71
Cliff Pruitt 1980
Curtis Rowe 1969-71
Don Saffer 1967
Mike Sanders 1980
Neville Saner 1967-68
Terry Schofield 1969-71
Bill Seibert 1969-70
Lynn Shackelford 1967-69
Gig Sims 1980
Fred Slaughter 1962, 64
Gavin Smith 1976

Jim Spillane 1974-76
Kim Stewart 1962, 64
Gene Sutherland 1967-68
Bill Sweek 1967-69
Ray Townsend 1976
Pete Trgovich 1974-75
John Vallely 1969-70
Kiki Vandeweghe 1980
Brett Vroman 1976
Bill Walton 1972-74
Mike Warren 1967-68
Kenny Washington 1964-65
Richard Washington 1974-76
Dave Waxman 1962
Bob Webb 1974
Sidney Wicks 1969-71
Keith Wilkes 1972-74
James Wilkes 1980
George Zidek 1995

UTAH (4-33)
Joe Aufterheide 1961
Leonard Black 1966
Trace Caton 1998
Jerry Chambers 1966
Bob Cozby 1961
Bo Crain 1961
Joe Day 1966
Michael Doleac 1998
Arnie Ferrin 1944
Drew Hansen 1998
David Jackson 1998
Merv Jackson 1966
Alex Jensen 1998
Neil Jenson 1961
Britton Johnsen 1998
Eugene Lake 1966
Bob Lewis 1944
Lyndon Mackay 1966
Billy McGill 1961
Jordie McTavish 1998
Andre Miller 1998
Wat Misaka 1944
Joe Morton 1961
Hanno Mottola 1998
Jeff Ockel 1966
Jim Rhead 1961
Ed Rowe 1961
Rich Ruffell 1961
Dick Smuin 1944
Fred Sheffield 1944
Rich Tate 1966
Jim Thomas 1961
Herb Wilkinson 1944

VILLANOVA (3-25)
Louis Dubino 1939
George Duzminski 1939
Chuck Everson 1985
Chris Ford 1971
John Fox 1971
Tom Ingelsby 1971
Harold Jensen 1985
John Krutulis 1939
Michael Lazorchak 1939
Dwayne McClain 1985
Joe McDowell 1971
Gary McLain 1985
James Montgomery 1939
Paul Nugent 1939
Ed Pinckney 1985
Mark Plansky 1985
Howard Porter 1971
Harold Pressley 1985
Lloyd Rice 1939
Ernest Robinson 1939
Hank Siemiontkowski 1971
William Sinnott 1939
Clarence Smith 1971
Dwight Wilbur 1985
Charles Yund 1939

VIRGINIA (2-16)
Rick Carlisle 1984
Louis Collins 1981
Kenton Edelin 1984
Terry Gates 1981
Jeff Jones 1981
Jeff Klein 1981
Jeff Lamp 1981
Lewis Lattimore 1981
Jim Miller 1984

Olden Polynice 1984
Lee Raker 1981
Craig Robinson 1981
Ralph Sampson 1981
Tom Sheehey 1984
Ricky Stokes 1981, 84
Othell Wilson 1981, 84

WAKE FOREST (1-12)
James Brooks 1962
Richard Carmichael 1962
Len Chappell 1962
Frank Christie 1962
Bryan Hassell 1962
Harry Hull 1962
Al Koehler 1962
Tommy McCoy 1962
Billy Packer 1962
Dave Wiedeman 1962
Bob Wollard 1962
Ted Zawacki 1962

WASHINGTON (1-10)
Don Apeland 1953
Joe Cipriano 1953
Will Elliott 1953
Roland Halle 1953
Bob Houbregs 1953
Charles Koon 1953
Doug McClary 1953
Mike McCutchen 1953
Dean Parsons 1953
Steve Roake 1953

WASHINGTON ST. (1-10)
Albert Akins 1941
Vern Butts 1941
Kirk Gebert 1941
Dale Gentry 1941
Marv Gilberg 1941
John Hooper 1941
Owen Hunt 1941
Paul Lindemann 1941
Ray Sundquist 1941
Jim Zimmerman 1941

WEST VIRGINIA (1-12)
Willie Akers 1959
Marvin Bolyard 1959
Robert Clousson 1959
Paul Goode 1959
Lee Patrone 1959
Joseph Posch 1959
Ronnie Retton 1959
James Ritchie 1959
Howard Schertzinger 1959
Bob Smith 1959
Nick Visnic 1959
Jerry West 1959

WESTERN KY. (1-9)
Rex Bailey 1971
Jerry Dunn 1971
Steve Eaton 1971
Clarence Glover 1971
Danny Johnson 1971
Jim McDaniels 1971
Jim Rose 1971
Gary Sundmacker 1971
Chuck Witt 1971

WICHITA ST. (1-11)
John Criss 1965
Gerald Davis 1965
Dave Leach 1965
Larry Nosich 1965
Kelly Pete 1965
Melvin Reed 1965
Gerard Reimond 1965
Vernon Smith 1965
Jamie Thompson 1965
Al Trope 1965
Manny Zafinos 1965

WISCONSIN (2-23)
Bob Alwin 1941
Roy Boone 2000
Jon Bryant 2000
Travon Davis 2000
Duany Duany 2000
Gene Englund 1941
Charles Epperson 1941
Erik Faust 2000
Mike Kelley 2000

FINAL FOUR CUMULATIVE RECORDS—ALL-TIME PARTICIPANTS

John Kotz 1941
Andy Kowske 2000
Maurice Linton 2000
Kirk Penney 2000
Fred Rehm 1941
Ed Scheiwe 1941

Warren Schrage 1941
Harlo Scott 1941
Robert Smith 2000
Ted Strain 1941
Julian Swartz 2000
Don Timmerman 1941

Mark Vershaw 2000
Charlie Willis 2000

WYOMING (1-8)
Jimmy Collins 1943
Milo Komenich 1943
Jim Reese 1943

Ted Roney 1943
Kenny Sailors 1943
Floyd Volker 1943
Don Waite 1943
Jim Weir 1943

NCAA Division I Men's Basketball Committee Chairs

Name	Affiliation	Years
Harold Olsen	Ohio St.	1940-46
Dutch Lonborg	Northwestern	1947-50
	Kansas	1951-60
Bernie Shively	Kentucky	1961-66
H.B. Lee	Kansas St.	1967-69
Tom Scott	Davidson	1970-75
Stan Watts	Brigham Young	1976-77
Wayne Duke	Big Ten Conference	1978-81
Dave Gavitt	Big East Conference	1982-84
Vic Bubas	Sun Belt Conference	1985
Dick Schultz	Virginia	1986-87
Arnie Ferrin	Utah	1988
Cedric Dempsey	Arizona	1989
Jim Delany	Big Ten Conference	1990-91
Tom Frericks	Dayton	1992
Roy Kramer	Southeastern Conference	1992
Tom Butters	Duke	1993-94
Bob Frederick	Kansas	1995-96
Terry Holland	Virginia	1997
C.M. Newton	Kentucky	1998-99
Craig Thompson	Mountain West Conference	2000
Mike Tranghese	Big East Conference	2001
Lee Fowler	North Carolina St.	2002-present

Former women's coach at Charlotte, Judy Rose is now the athletics director at the school and last year became the first woman to serve on the NCAA Division I Men's Basketball Committee.

Photo from Charlotte sports information

NCAA Division I Men's Basketball Committee Roster

Name	Affiliation	Years
Larry Albus	St. Louis	1975-76
	Metro Conference	1977-80
Phog Allen	Kansas	1940
Ladell Andersen	Utah St.	1978-82
Lewis Andreas	Syracuse	1943-44
	Syracuse	1954-58
Karl Benson	Western Athletic Conference	2002-present
McKinley Boston	Minnesota	1995-99
Bob Bowlsby	Iowa	2001-present
Hoyt Brawner	Denver	1966-71
Paul Brechler	Western Athletic Conference	1968
Bob Brown	West Virginia	1958-62
Vic Bubas	Sun Belt Conference	1980-85
John Bunn	Stanford	1940
Asa Bushnell	Eastern College Athletic Conference	1949-53
Tom Butters	Duke	1989-94
Ben Carnevale	Navy	1965-66
	New York U.	1967-70
Bernard Carnevale	William & Mary	1981
	James Madison	1982-83
Ernest Casale	Temple	1971-76
Willis Casey	North Carolina St.	1975-80
W.S. Chandler	Marquette	1940
John Conboy	La Salle	1977
Gene Corrigan	Notre Dame	1982-87
Jake Crouthamel	Syracuse	1991-96
Gary Cunningham	Fresno St.	1989-94
Rudy Davalos	Houston	1992
	New Mexico	1995-99
Everett Dean	Stanford	1947-50
Jim Delany	Ohio Valley Conference	1986-89
	Big Ten Conference	1990-91
Cedric Dempsey	Arizona	1984-89
DeLoss Dodds	Texas	1993-97
Wayne Duke	Big Ten Conference	1976-81
Joel Eaves	Georgia	1970-74
Hec Edmundson	Washington	1941-46
George Edwards	Missouri	1941-50
Doug Elgin	Missouri Valley Conference	1999-present

Name	Affiliation	Years
Bump Elliott	Iowa	1989-91
Arnie Ferrin	Utah	1983-88
Waldo Fisher	Northwestern	1962-67
Lee Fowler	Middle Tenn.	1998-2000
	North Carolina St.	2001-present
Bob Frederick	Kansas	1992-96
Kenneth Free	Mid-Eastern Athletic Conference	1988-92
Tom Frericks	Dayton	1988-92
Dave Gavitt	Providence	1980-82
	Big East Conference	1983-84
Andy Geiger	Pennsylvania	1978
	Stanford	1979-83
B.T. Grover	Ohio	1941
Wiles Hallock	Western Athletic Conference	1969-71
	Pacific-10 Conference	1972-75
Charles Harris	Arizona St.	1992-96
	Mid-Eastern Athletic Conference	1997-98
Dave Hart	Missouri	1981-86
Ed Hickox	Springfield	1945-46
Terry Holland	Davidson	1993-95
	Virginia	1996-98
Nat Holman	CCNY	1941
Ken Karr	San Diego St.	1976-80
	East Caro.	1981
Roy Keene	Oregon St.	1958-61
E.A. Kelleher	Fordham	1943
	Army	1944
Floyd Kerr	Southern U.	2002-present
Roy Kramer	Vanderbilt	1987-91
	Southeastern Conference	1992
Jack Kvancz	George Washington	1999-present
H.B. Lee	Kansas St.	1961-69
Jim Livengood	Arizona	2000-present
Dutch Lonborg	Northwestern	1947-50
	Kansas	1951-60
Dave Maggard	California	1990-91
Ernest McCoy	Penn St.	1960-65
Ralph McFillen	Metro Conference	1993-95
J.D. Morgan	UCLA	1969-74
Pete Newell	California	1963-68
C.M. Newton	Kentucky	1993-99
Albert Nixon	New York U.	1947-48
Nels Nordgen	Chicago	1942

FINAL FOUR CUMULATIVE RECORDS—DIVISION I COMMITTEE ROSTER

Name	Affiliation	Years
Harold Olsen	Ohio St.	1940-46
Reaves Peters	Big Seven	1948-57
Vadal Peterson	Utah	1953
Russ Potts	Southern Methodist	1980-81
Les Robinson	North Carolina St.	2000
	The Citadel	2001-present
Judy Rose	Charlotte	2000-present
James St. Clair	Southern Methodist	1941-45
H.H. Salmon	New York businessman	1940
Fred Schaus	West Virginia	1985-90
Dick Schultz	Virginia	1984-87
Tom Scott	Davidson	1967-75
Everett Shelton	Wyoming	1954-58
Bernie Shively	Kentucky	1959-66

Name	Affiliation	Years
Dick Shrider	Miami (Ohio)	1982-87
Gene Smith	Iowa St.	2000
Wilbur Smith	Tulane	1942
Neale Stoner	Illinois	1988
Fred Taylor	Ohio St.	1968-73
Craig Thompson	Sun Belt Conference	1996-98
	Mountain West Conference	1999-2000
Mike Tranghese	Big East Conference	1997-2001
Forrest Twogood	Southern California	1960-64
Stan Watts	Brigham Young	1974-77
Kevin Weiberg	Big 12 Conference	2001-present
Carroll Williams	Santa Clara	1997-2001
Frank Windegger	TCU	1982-88

Tournament Moments...

March 29, 1982, in the Louisiana Superdome in New Orleans – The picture says it all as North Carolina freshman Michael Jordan hits a 16-foot jumper for what turns out to be the last score of the game. Moments later, Georgetown's Fred Brown mistook North Carolina's James Worthy for teammate Sleepy Floyd and passed the ball to Worthy. The Tar Heels ran out the clock to take a 63-62 victory and give coach Dean Smith his first NCAA championship.

Photo by Allen Dean Steele

The Early Rounds

Regional Game Records 30
First- and Second-Rounds Game Records 31
East Region Game Records 33
South Region Game Records.................................... 35
Midwest Region Game Records 37
West Region Game Records..................................... 38
All-East Regional Teams 40
All-South/Southeast/Mideast Regional Teams 41
All-Midwest Regional Teams 43
All-West Regional Teams.. 44

Regional Game Records

A regional final game is indicated by (RF), a regional semifinal game by (RSF), a regional third-place game by (R3d), East region by (East), Southeast/Mideast region by (South), Midwest region by (MW), West/Far West region by (West) and record later vacated by (*).

Individual Records

POINTS
- 56, Oscar Robertson, Cincinnati vs. Arkansas, MW R3d, 1958
- 52, Austin Carr, Notre Dame vs. Kentucky, South RSF, 1970
- 47, Austin Carr, Notre Dame vs. Houston, MW R3d, 1971
- 46, Dave Corzine, DePaul vs. Louisville, MW RSF, 1978 (2 ot)
- 45, Bob Houbregs, Washington vs. Seattle, West RSF, 1953
- 45, Austin Carr, Notre Dame vs. Iowa, South R3d, 1970

FIELD GOALS
- 22, Austin Carr, Notre Dame vs. Kentucky, South RSF, 1970
- 21, Oscar Robertson, Cincinnati vs. Arkansas, MW R3d, 1958
- 21, Austin Carr, Notre Dame vs. Iowa, South R3d, 1970
- 20, Bob Houbregs, Washington vs. Seattle, West RSF, 1953
- 19, Oscar Robertson, Cincinnati vs. Kansas, MW RF, 1960
- 19, Jeff Mullins, Duke vs. Villanova, East RSF, 1964

FIELD GOALS ATTEMPTED
- 42, *Dwight Lamar, La.-Lafayette vs. Louisville, MW RSF, 1972
- 40, Austin Carr, Notre Dame vs. Houston, MW R3d, 1971
- 39, Austin Carr, Notre Dame vs. Iowa, South R3d, 1970
- 38, Bob Cousy, Holy Cross vs. North Carolina St., East RF, 1950
- 36, Oscar Robertson, Cincinnati vs. Arkansas, MW R3d, 1958

FIELD-GOAL PERCENTAGE
(Minimum 10 FGM)
- 100.0% (10-10), Marvin Barnes, Providence vs. Pennsylvania, East RSF, 1973
- 100.0% (10-10), Christian Laettner, Duke vs. Kentucky, East RF, 1992 (ot)
- 92.3% (12-13), Dennis Holman, Southern Methodist vs. Cincinnati, MW R3d, 1966
- 91.7% (11-12), Pembrook Burrows, Jacksonville vs. Iowa, South RSF, 1970
- 90.9% (10-11), Akeem Olajuwon, Houston vs. Villanova, MW RF, 1983
- 90.9% (10-11), Travis Ford, Kentucky vs. Wake Forest, South RSF, 1993

THREE-POINT FIELD GOALS
- 8, Glen Rice, Michigan vs. North Carolina, South RSF, 1989
- 8, Bo Kimble, Loyola Marymount vs. UNLV, West RF, 1990
- 8, Cuonzo Martin, Purdue vs. Kansas, South RSF, 1994
- 8, Dedric Willoughby, Iowa St. vs. UCLA, MW RSF, 1997
- 7, Five tied (most recent: Darryl Wilson, Mississippi St. vs. Connecticut, South RSF, 1996)

THREE-POINT FIELD GOALS ATTEMPTED
- 18, Darius Lane, Seton Hall vs. Oklahoma St., East RSF, 2000
- 17, Dedric Willoughby, Iowa St. vs. UCLA, MW RSF, 1997
- 16, Jeff Fryer, Loyola Marymount vs. UNLV, West RF, 1990
- 16, Darnell Burton, Cincinnati vs. Mississippi St., South RF, 1996
- 15, Mark Karcher, Temple vs. Duke, East RF, 1999

THREE-POINT FIELD-GOAL PERCENTAGE
(Minimum 5 3FGM)
- 100.0% (5-5), Hubert Davis, North Carolina vs. Eastern Mich., East RSF, 1991
- 100.0% (5-5), Jamal Mashburn, Kentucky vs. Wake Forest, South RSF, 1993
- 83.3% (5-6), Billy Donovan, Providence vs. Alabama, South RSF, 1987
- 83.3% (5-6), Dwayne Bryant, Georgetown vs. North Carolina St., East RSF, 1989
- 83.3% (5-6), Travis Ford, Kentucky vs. Wake Forest, South RSF, 1993
- 83.3% (5-6), Mike Bibby, Arizona vs. Maryland, West RSF, 1998
- 83.3% (5-6), Trajan Langdon, Duke vs. Temple, East RF, 1999

FREE THROWS MADE
- 23, Bob Carney, Bradley vs. Colorado, MW RSF, 1954
- 18, John O'Brien, Seattle vs. Wyoming, West R3d, 1953
- 17, Roger Newman, Kentucky vs. Ohio St., South RF, 1961
- 17, Barry Kramer, New York U. vs. West Virginia, East R3d, 1963
- 16, Five tied (most recent: Reggie Williams, Georgetown vs. Kansas, South RSF, 1987; Billy Donovan, Providence vs. Georgetown, South RF, 1987)

FREE THROWS ATTEMPTED
- 26, Bob Carney, Bradley vs. Colorado, MW RSF, 1954
- 24, Donnie Gaunce, Morehead St. vs. Iowa, South RSF, 1956
- 22, John O'Brien, Seattle vs. Wyoming, West R3d, 1953
- 22, Wilt Chamberlain, Kansas vs. Oklahoma City, MW RF, 1957
- 22, Roger Newman, Kentucky vs. Ohio St., South RF, 1961

FREE-THROW PERCENTAGE
(Minimum 12 FTM)
- 100.0% (13-13), Bill Bradley, Princeton vs. Providence, East RF, 1965
- 100.0% (13-13), Mike Maloy, Davidson vs. St. John's (N.Y.), East RSF, 1969
- 100.0% (12-12), Dan Issel, Kentucky vs. Miami (Ohio), South R3d, 1969
- 100.0% (12-12), Larry Finch, Memphis vs. Kansas St., MW RF, 1973
- 100.0% (12-12), Michael Jackson, Georgetown vs. UNLV, West RSF, 1984
- 100.0% (12-12), Michael Doleac, Utah vs. Stanford, West RSF, 1997

REBOUNDS
- 34, Fred Cohen, Temple vs. Connecticut, East RSF, 1956
- 31, Nate Thurmond, Bowling Green vs. Mississippi St., South R3d, 1963
- 30, Jerry Lucas, Ohio St. vs. Kentucky, South RF, 1961
- 28, Elvin Hayes, Houston vs. Pacific (Cal.), West R3d, 1966
- 27, John Green, Michigan St. vs. Notre Dame, South RSF, 1957

ASSISTS
- 13, Rumeal Robinson, Michigan vs. North Carolina, South RSF, 1989
- 13, Anderson Hunt, UNLV vs. Loyola Marymount, West RF, 1990
- 13, Andre Miller, Utah vs. Arizona, West RF, 1998
- 12, Six tied (most recent: Doug Gottlieb, Oklahoma St. vs. Seton Hall, East RSF, 2000)

BLOCKED SHOTS
- 9, David Robinson, Navy vs. Cleveland St., East RSF, 1986
- 8, Mark Strickland, Temple vs. Oklahoma St., East RSF, 1991 (ot)
- 8, Tim Duncan, Wake Forest vs. Oklahoma St., East RSF, 1995
- 7, Pervis Ellison, Louisville vs. Illinois, MW RSF, 1989
- 7, Tim Duncan, Wake Forest vs. Louisville, MW RSF, 1996
- 7, Ken Johnson, Ohio St. vs. St. John's (N.Y.), South RSF, 1999
- 7, Loren Woods, Arizona vs. Illinois, MW RF, 2001

STEALS
- 7, Ricky Grace, Oklahoma vs. Iowa, West RSF, 1987 (ot)
- 6, John Evans, Rhode Island vs. Duke, East RSF, 1988
- 6, Anderson Hunt, UNLV vs. Loyola Marymount, West RF, 1990
- 6, Jason Buchanan, St. John's (N.Y.) vs. Ohio St., MW RSF, 1991
- 6, George Lynch, North Carolina vs. Cincinnati, East RF, 1993
- 6, Damian Owens, West Virginia vs. Utah, West RSF, 1998
- 6, Pepe Sanchez, Temple vs. Purdue, East RSF, 1999

Team Records

POINTS
- 131, UNLV vs. Loyola Marymount (101), West RF, 1990
- 121, Iowa vs. Notre Dame (106), South R3d, 1970
- 119, Houston vs. Notre Dame (106), MW R3d, 1971
- 118, Notre Dame vs. Vanderbilt (88), South R3d, 1974
- 114, Arizona vs. UNLV (109), RSF, West 1976 (ot)

FEWEST POINTS
- 20, North Carolina vs. Pittsburgh (26), East RF, 1941
- 24, Springfield vs. Indiana (48), East RF, 1940
- 26, Pittsburgh vs. North Carolina (20), East RF, 1941
- 29, Western Ky. vs. Duquesne (30), East RF, 1940
- 29, Baylor vs. Oklahoma St. (44), West RF, 1946

WINNING MARGIN
- 49, UCLA (109) vs. Wyoming, (60), West RSF, 1967
- 47, Duke (101) vs. Connecticut (54), East RF, 1964
- 43, *Villanova (90) vs. Pennsylvania (47), East RF, 1971
- 40, Cincinnati (99) vs. DePaul (59), MW RSF, 1960
- 40, Princeton (109) vs. Providence (69), East RF, 1965
- 40, Louisville (93) vs. Kansas St. (53), MW R3d, 1968

POINTS BY LOSING TEAM
- 109, UNLV vs. Arizona (114), West RSF, 1976 (ot)
- 106, Notre Dame vs. Iowa (121), South R3d, 1970
- 106, Notre Dame vs. Houston (119), MW R3d, 1971
- 103, Iowa vs. Jacksonville (104), South RSF, 1970
- 103, Kentucky vs. Duke (104), East RF, 1992 (ot)

FIELD GOALS
- 52, Iowa vs. Notre Dame, South R3d, 1970
- 51, UCLA vs. Dayton, West RSF, 1974 (3 ot)
- 51, UNLV vs. Loyola Marymount, West RF, 1990
- 50, Kentucky vs. Austin Peay, South RSF, 1973 (ot)
- 49, Notre Dame vs. Vanderbilt, South R3d, 1974

FIELD GOALS ATTEMPTED
- 106, Indiana vs. Miami (Ohio), South R3d, 1958
- 103, St. Joseph's vs. West Virginia, East RSF, 1960
- 102, Notre Dame vs. Houston, MW R3d, 1971
- 100, Houston vs. Pacific (Cal.), West R3d, 1966
- 99, Brigham Young vs. Oklahoma City, West R3d, 1965
- 99, *Austin Peay vs. Kentucky, South RSF, 1973 (ot)

FIELD-GOAL PERCENTAGE
- 74.4% (29-39), Georgetown vs. Oregon St., West RF, 1982
- 68.8% (33-48), Providence vs. Alabama, South RSF, 1987
- 68.6% (35-51), Indiana vs. St. Joseph's, South RF, 1981
- 68.3% (41-60), Princeton vs. Providence, East RF, 1965
- 66.7% (30-45), Notre Dame vs. North Carolina, East RSF, 1977

LOWEST FIELD-GOAL PERCENTAGE
- 12.7% (8-63), Springfield vs. Indiana, East RSF, 1940
- 13.9% (10-72), Harvard vs. Ohio St., East RSF, 1946
- 19.4% (14-72), Creighton vs. Cincinnati, MW RSF, 1962
- 20.6% (13-63), Arkansas vs. Oregon St., West RSF, 1949
- 22.9% (16-70), St. John's (N.Y.) vs. Kentucky, East RSF, 1951

THREE-POINT FIELD GOALS
- 17, Loyola Marymount vs. UNLV, West RF, 1990
- 16, Kentucky vs. Wake Forest, South RSF, 1993
- 15, Purdue vs. Kansas, South RSF, 1994
- 14, Providence vs. Alabama, South RSF, 1987
- 13, Four tied (Most recent: Penn St. vs. Temple, South RSF, 2001)

REGIONAL GAME RECORDS—TEAM

THREE-POINT FIELD GOALS ATTEMPTED
- 41, Loyola Marymount vs. UNLV, West RF, 1990
- 36, Tulsa vs. Arkansas, MW RSF, 1994
- 36, Kentucky vs. North Carolina, South RF, 1995
- 34, Louisville vs. North Carolina, East RF, 1997
- 34, Seton Hall vs. Oklahoma St., East RF, 2000

THREE-POINT FIELD-GOAL PERCENTAGE
(Minimum 7 3FGM)
- 80.0% (8-10), Kansas St. vs. Purdue, MW RSF, 1988
- 72.7% (8-11), Duke vs. Indiana, MW RSF, 1987
- 72.7% (8-11), Kansas vs. California, MW RSF, 1993
- 70.0% (7-10), St. John's (N.Y.) vs. Duke, MW RF, 1991
- 69.2% (9-13), Maryland vs. Stanford, West RF, 2001

FREE THROWS MADE
- 43, Arizona vs. Illinois, MW RF, 2001
- 41, Utah vs. Santa Clara, West R3d, 1960
- 39, Seattle vs. Utah, West R3d, 1955
- 38, Bradley vs. Colorado, MW RSF, 1954
- 38, Loyola (Ill.) vs. Kentucky, South R3d, 1964

FREE THROWS ATTEMPTED
- 56, Arizona, vs. Illinois, MW RF, 2001
- 53, Morehead St. vs. Iowa, South RSF, 1956
- 52, Seattle vs. UCLA, West R3d, 1956
- 52, Iowa vs. Morehead St., South RSF, 1956
- 50, West Virginia vs. St. Joseph's, East RSF, 1959

FREE-THROW PERCENTAGE
(Minimum 15 FTM)
- 100.0% (22-22), Fordham vs. South Carolina, East R3d, 1971
- 100.0% (17-17), Villanova vs. Kentucky, South RSF, 1988
- 95.5% (21-22), Vanderbilt vs. Marquette, South RSF, 1974
- 95.2% (20-21), Notre Dame vs. Vanderbilt, South R3d, 1974
- 95.0% (19-20), North Carolina St. vs. St. John's (N.Y.), East R3d, 1951
- 95.0% (19-20), Iowa vs. Georgetown, East RF, 1980

REBOUNDS
- 76, Temple vs. Connecticut, East RSF, 1956
- 76, Houston vs. TCU, MW RF, 1968
- 76, UCLA vs. Weber St., West RSF, 1972
- 72, UCLA vs. Seattle, West R3d, 1956
- 72, Seattle vs. Utah St., West R3d, 1964

REBOUND MARGIN
- 33, Cincinnati (68) vs. Texas Tech (35), MW RSF, 1961
- 29, Utah (59) vs. Loyola Marymount (30), West RSF, 1961
- 28, Seattle (72) vs. Utah St. (44), West R3d, 1964
- 28, Indiana St. (50) vs. Oklahoma (22), MW RSF, 1979
- 27, Memphis (60) vs. South Carolina (33), MW RSF, 1973

ASSISTS
- 35, UNLV vs. Loyola Marymount, West RF, 1990
- 31, Arkansas vs. Tulsa, MW RSF, 1994
- 27, Kentucky vs. Arizona St., South RSF, 1995
- 26, Louisiana Tech vs. Oklahoma, MW RSF, 1985
- 25, Three tied (most recent: Oklahoma vs. Louisville, South RSF, 1988)

BLOCKED SHOTS
- 14, Kentucky vs. UCLA, South RSF, 1998
- 13, Louisville vs. Illinois, MW RSF, 1989
- 11, Duke vs. Temple, East RF, 1988
- 11, North Carolina vs. Georgetown, South RSF, 1995
- 10, Providence vs. Georgetown, South RF, 1987
- 10, Connecticut vs. Florida, East RSF, 1994
- 10, Kansas vs. Arizona, South RSF, 1997

STEALS
- 17, Duke vs. St. John's (N.Y.), MW RF, 1991
- 17, Duke vs. UCLA, East RSF, 2001
- 16, Massachusetts vs. Georgetown, East RF, 1996
- 15, Arkansas vs. Texas, MW RF, 1990
- 15, Syracuse vs. Duke, South RSF, 1998

PERSONAL FOULS
- 41, Dayton vs. Illinois, East RSF, 1952
- 36, UCLA vs. Seattle, West R3d, 1956
- 36, Illinois vs. Arizona, MW RF, 2001
- 35, Iowa vs. Morehead St., South RSF, 1956
- 35, DePaul vs. VMI, East RSF, 1976 (ot)
- 35, Texas Tech vs. Georgetown, East RSF, 1996

PLAYERS DISQUALIFIED
- 6, Illinois vs. Arizona, MW RF, 2001
- 5, Dayton vs. Illinois, East RSF, 1952
- 5, St. Joseph's vs. West Virginia, East RSF, 1959
- 5, DePaul vs. VMI, East RSF, 1976 (ot)
- 5, Syracuse vs. Virginia, East RSF, 1984
- 4, 12 tied (most recent: Texas Tech vs. Georgetown, East RSF, 1996)

Two-Team Records

POINTS
- 232, UNLV (131) vs. Loyola Marymount (101), West RF, 1990
- 227, Iowa (121) vs. Notre Dame (106), South R3d, 1970
- 225, Houston (119) vs. Notre Dame (106), MW R3d, 1971
- 223, Arizona (114) vs. UNLV (109), West RSF, 1976 (ot)
- 214, Oklahoma City (112) vs. Brigham Young (102), West R3d, 1965

FEWEST POINTS
- 46, Pittsburgh (26) vs. North Carolina (20), East RF, 1941
- 59, Duquesne (30) vs. Western Ky. (29), East RF, 1940
- 70, Southern California (38) vs. Colorado (32), West RF, 1940
- 72, Villanova (42) vs. Brown (30), East RF, 1939
- 72, Indiana (48) vs. Springfield (24), East RF, 1940

FIELD GOALS
- 97, Iowa (52) vs. Notre Dame (45), South R3d, 1970
- 96, Kentucky (50) vs. Austin Peay (46), South RSF, 1973 (ot)
- 91, UCLA (51) vs. Dayton (40), West RSF, 1974 (3 ot)
- 86, Six tied (most recent: UNLV (51) vs. Loyola Marymount (35), West RF, 1990)

FIELD GOALS ATTEMPTED
- 196, Austin Peay (99) vs. Kentucky (97), South RSF, 1973 (ot)
- 195, Iowa (98) vs. Notre Dame (97), South R3d, 1970
- 194, Indiana (106) vs. Miami (Ohio) (88), South R3d, 1958
- 194, Houston (100) vs. Pacific (Cal.) (94), West R3d, 1966
- 188, St. Joseph's (103) vs. West Virginia (85), East R3d, 1960

THREE-POINT FIELD GOALS
- 24, Loyola Marymount (17) vs. UNLV (7), West RF, 1990
- 23, Purdue (15) vs. Kansas (8), South RSF, 1994
- 22, Arkansas (12) vs. Memphis (10), MW RSF, 1995
- 21, Providence (14) vs. Alabama (7), South RSF, 1987
- 21, Purdue (21) vs. Temple (8), East RSF, 1999

THREE-POINT FIELD GOALS ATTEMPTED
- 59, Loyola Marymount (41) vs. UNLV (18), West RF, 1990
- 52, Tulsa (36) vs. Arkansas (16), MW RSF, 1994
- 52, Penn St. (33) vs. Temple (19), South RSF, 2001
- 51, Louisville (27) vs. Arizona (24), West RF, 1994
- 51, Kentucky (36) vs. North Carolina (15), South RF, 1995

FREE THROWS
- 68, Iowa (35) vs. Morehead St. (33), South RSF, 1956
- 68, Oklahoma City (35) vs. Kansas St. (33), MW RSF, 1956
- 64, Bradley (38) vs. Colorado (26), West RSF, 1954
- 63, Seattle (39) vs. Utah (24), West R3d, 1955
- 63, La Salle (35) vs. Canisius (28), East RF, 1955
- 63, Arizona (43) vs. Illinois (20), MW RF, 2001

FREE THROWS ATTEMPTED
- 105, Morehead St. (53) vs. Iowa (52), South RSF, 1956
- 92, Oklahoma City (48) vs. Kansas St. (44), MW RSF, 1956
- 92, Seattle (52) vs. UCLA (40), West R3d, 1956
- 89, New York U. (49) vs. St. Joseph's (40), East R3d, 1962
- 88, Seattle (51) vs. Utah (37), West R3d, 1955

REBOUNDS
- 132, Pacific (Cal.) (67) vs. Houston (65), West R3d, 1966
- 131, Houston (76) vs. TCU (55), MW RF, 1968
- 130, UCLA (76) vs. Weber St. (54), West RSF, 1972
- 128, UCLA (72) vs. Seattle (56), West R3d, 1956
- 126, Drake (66) vs. Notre Dame (60), MW RSF, 1971 (ot)

ASSISTS
- 58, UNLV (35) vs. Loyola Marymount (23), West RF, 1990
- 51, Arkansas (31) vs. Tulsa (20), MW RSF, 1994
- 47, North Carolina (25) vs. Louisville (22), West RSF, 1986
- 47, Kentucky (24) vs. Duke (23), East RF, 1992 (ot)
- 44, Connecticut (22) vs. Maryland (22), West RSF, 1995

BLOCKED SHOTS
- 20, Kentucky (14) vs. UCLA (6), South RSF, 1998
- 17, Duke (11) vs. Temple (6), East RF, 1988
- 16, Massachusetts (9) vs. Tulsa (7), East RSF, 1995
- 15, Louisville (13) vs. Illinois (2), MW RSF, 1989
- 15, North Carolina (11) vs. Georgetown (4), South RSF, 1995

STEALS
- 27, Loyola Marymount (14) vs. UNLV (13), West RF, 1990
- 27, Duke (17) vs. UCLA (10), East RSF, 2001
- 26, Duke (17), vs. St. John's (N.Y.) (9), MW RF, 1991
- 24, Massachusetts (16) vs. Georgetown (8), East RF, 1996
- 23, St. John's (N.Y.) (14) vs. Ohio St. (9), MW RSF, 1991
- 23, Syracuse (15) vs. Duke (8), South RSF, 1998
- 23, Florida (13) vs. Gonzaga (10), West RSF, 1999

PERSONAL FOULS
- 68, Iowa (35) vs. Morehead St. (33), South RSF, 1956
- 63, UNLV (34) vs. Arizona (29), West RSF, 1976
- 61, Colorado (34) vs. Bradley (27), West RSF, 1954
- 60, UCLA (36) vs. Seattle (24), R3d, 1956
- 60, Seattle (31) vs. UCLA (29), West RSF, 1964

First- and Second-Rounds Game Records

A second-round game is indicated by (2d), a first-round game by (1st), an opening-round game by (OR), East region by (East), Southeast/Mideast region by (South), Midwest region by (MW), West/Far West region by (West) and record later vacated by (*).

Individual Records

POINTS
- 61, Austin Carr, Notre Dame vs. Ohio, South 1st, 1970
- 52, Austin Carr, Notre Dame vs. TCU, MW 1st, 1971
- 50, David Robinson, Navy vs. Michigan, East 1st, 1987
- 49, Elvin Hayes, Houston vs. Loyola (Ill.), MW 1st, 1968
- 45, Bo Kimble, Loyola Marymount vs. New Mexico St., West 1st, 1990

FIELD GOALS
- 25, Austin Carr, Notre Dame vs. Ohio, South 1st, 1970
- 22, David Robinson, Navy vs. Michigan, East 1st, 1987
- 20, Elvin Hayes, Houston vs. Loyola (Ill.), MW 1st, 1968
- 20, Austin Carr, Notre Dame vs. TCU, MW 1st, 1971
- 18, Wally Szczerbiak, Miami (Ohio) vs. Washington, MW 1st, 1999

FIELD GOALS ATTEMPTED
- 44, Austin Carr, Notre Dame vs. Ohio, South 1st, 1970
- 37, David Robinson, Navy vs. Michigan, East 1st, 1987
- 37, Charles Jones, Long Island vs. Villanova, East 1st, 1997
- 36, Ronald "Popeye" Jones, Murray St. vs. Michigan St., South 1st, 1990 (ot)
- 35, Rich Laurel, Hofstra vs. Notre Dame, East 1st, 1977
- 35, Bo Kimble, Loyola Marymount vs. New Mexico St., West 1st, 1990

THE EARLY ROUNDS

FIRST- AND SECOND-ROUNDS GAME RECORDS—INDIVIDUAL

FIELD-GOAL PERCENTAGE
(Minimum 10 FGM)
- 100.0% (11-11), Kenny Walker, Kentucky vs. Western Ky., South 2d, 1986
- 92.3% (12-13), Quadre Lollis, Montana St. vs. Syracuse, West 1st, 1996
- 91.7% (11-12), Kenny Gregory, Kansas vs. DePaul, East 1st, 2000
- 90.9% (10-11), Dwayne McClain, Villanova vs. Marshall, South 1st, 1984
- 90.9% (10-11), Oliver Miller, Arkansas vs. Murray St., MW 1st, 1992

THREE-POINT FIELD GOALS
- 11, Jeff Fryer, Loyola Marymount vs. Michigan, West 2d, 1990
- 9, Garde Thompson, Michigan vs. Navy, East, 1st, 1987
- 9, Johnny Miller, Temple vs. Cincinnati, West 1st, 1995
- 9, Johnny Hemsley, Miami (Fla.) vs. Lafayette, East 1st, 1999
- 8, Eight tied (most recent: Rashod Johnson, Western Mich. vs. Clemson, MW 1st, 1998)

THREE-POINT FIELD GOALS ATTEMPTED
- 22, Jeff Fryer, Loyola Marymount vs. Arkansas, MW 1st, 1989
- 20, Chris Walker, Villanova vs. LSU, South 1st, 1990
- 19, Gerald Paddio, UNLV vs. Iowa, West 2d, 1988
- 19, Phillip Allen, N.C. A&T vs. Arkansas, MW 1st, 1994
- 18, Bobby Hurley, Duke vs. California, MW 2d, 1993
- 18, Jeff Boschee, Kansas vs. Kentucky, MW 2d, 1999

THREE-POINT FIELD-GOAL PERCENTAGE
(Minimum 5 3FGM)
- 100.0% (7-7), Sam Cassell, Florida St. vs. Tulane, South 2d, 1993
- 100.0% (6-6), Mike Buck, Middle Tenn. vs. Florida St., South 1st, 1989
- 100.0% (6-6), Migjen Bakalli, North Carolina St. vs. Southern Miss., East 1st, 1991
- 100.0% (6-6), Rex Walters, Kansas vs. Ball St., MW 1st, 1993
- 100.0% (5-5), Mitch Richmond, Kansas St. vs. Georgia, West 1st, 1987 (ot)
- 100.0% (5-5), Kwame Evans, George Washington vs. New Mexico, West 1st, 1993
- 100.0% (5-5), Dwayne Morton, Louisville vs. Minnesota, West 2d, 1994

FREE THROWS MADE
- 23, Travis Mays, Texas vs. Georgia, MW 1st, 1990
- 21, David Robinson, Navy vs. Syracuse, East 2d, 1986
- 19, Tom Hammonds, Georgia Tech vs. Iowa St., East 1st, 1988

- 18, Jon Rose, Connecticut vs. Boston U., East 1st, 1959
- 17, Tyrone Hill, Xavier vs. Kansas St., MW 1st, 1990
- 17, Steve Nash, Santa Clara vs. Maryland, West 1st, 1996

FREE THROWS ATTEMPTED
- 27, David Robinson, Navy vs. Syracuse, East 2d, 1986
- 27, Travis Mays, Texas vs. Georgia, MW 1st, 1990
- 21, Five tied (most recent: Brad Miller, Purdue vs. Rhode Island, South 1st, 1997)

FREE-THROW PERCENTAGE
(Minimum 12 FTM)
- 100.0% (16-16), Bill Bradley, Princeton vs. St. Joseph's, East 1st, 1963
- 100.0% (16-16), Fennis Dembo, Wyoming vs. UCLA, West 2d, 1987
- 100.0% (13-13), Al Gooden, Ball St. vs. Boston College, South 1st, 1981
- 100.0% (12-12), 10 tied (most recent: Dan Dickau, Gonzaga vs. Indiana St., South 2nd, 2001)

REBOUNDS
- 29, Toby Kimball, Connecticut vs. St. Joseph's, East 1st, 1965
- 27, Paul Silas, Creighton vs. Oklahoma City, MW 1st, 1964
- 27, Elvin Hayes, Houston vs. Loyola (Ill.), MW 1st, 1968
- 24, Paul Silas, Creighton vs. Memphis, MW 1st, 1962
- 24, Eddie Jackson, Oklahoma City vs. Creighton, MW 1st, 1964

ASSISTS
- 16, Sam Crawford, New Mexico St. vs. Nebraska, East 1st, 1993
- 16, Earl Watson, UCLA vs. Maryland, MW 2d, 2000
- 15, Kenny Patterson, DePaul vs. Syracuse, East 1st, 1985
- 15, Keith Smart, Indiana vs. Auburn, MW 2d, 1987
- 15, Pepe Sanchez, Temple vs. Oklahoma St., East 2d, 2000

BLOCKED SHOTS
- 11, Shaquille O'Neal, LSU vs. Brigham Young, West 1st, 1992
- 10, Shawn Bradley, Brigham Young vs. Virginia, West 1st, 1991
- 9, D'or Fischer, Northwestern St. vs. Winthrop, MW OR, 2001
- 8, Seven tied (most recent: Tarvis Williams, Hampton vs. Georgetown, West 2nd, 2001)

STEALS
- 8, Darrell Hawkins, Arkansas vs. Holy Cross, East 1st, 1993
- 8, Grant Hill, Duke vs. California, MW 2d, 1993
- 8, Duane Clemens, Ball St. vs. UCLA, MW 1st, 2000
- 7, Seven tied (most recent: Kawika Akina, Northern Ariz. vs. Cincinnati, West 1st, 1998)

Team Records

POINTS
- 149, Loyola Marymount vs. Michigan (115), West 2d, 1990
- 124, Oklahoma vs. Louisiana Tech (81), South 2d, 1989
- 123, North Carolina vs. Loyola Marymount (97), West 2d, 1988
- 121, UNLV vs. San Francisco (95), West 1st, 1977
- 120, Arkansas vs. Loyola Marymount (101), MW 1st, 1989

FEWEST POINTS
- 32, Wisconsin vs. Southwest Mo. St. (43), East 1st, 1999
- 35, Alabama St. vs. Michigan St. (69), South 1st, 2001
- 38, Ohio vs. Kansas (49), South 1st, 1985
- 38, Valparaiso vs. Michigan St. (65), MW 1st, 2000
- 39, Drexel vs. Temple (61), East 1st, 1994

WINNING MARGIN
- 69, Loyola (Ill.) (111) vs. Tennessee Tech (42), South 1st, 1963
- 58, Kansas (110) vs. Prairie View (52), MW 1st, 1998
- 49, Syracuse (101) vs. Brown (52), East 1st, 1986
- 47, DePaul (99) vs. Eastern Ky. (52), South 1st, 1965
- 46, Kentucky (113) vs. Mt. St. Mary's (67), South 1st, 1995

POINTS BY LOSING TEAM
- 115, Wyoming vs. Loyola Marymount (119), West 1st, 1988
- 115, Michigan vs. Loyola Marymount (149), West 2d, 1990
- 102, UCLA vs. Tulsa (112), MW 1st, 1994
- 101, Marshall vs. La.-Lafayette (112), MW 1st, 1972
- 101, Loyola Marymount vs. Arkansas (120), MW 1st, 1989

FIELD GOALS
- 50, Notre Dame vs. Austin Peay, South 1st, 1974
- 49, UNLV vs. San Francisco, West 1st, 1977
- 49, North Carolina vs. Loyola Marymount, West 2d, 1988
- 49, Loyola Marymount vs. Michigan, West 2d, 1990
- 48, Oklahoma vs. Louisiana Tech, South 2d, 1989

FIELD GOALS ATTEMPTED
- 112, Marshall vs. La.-Lafayette, MW 1st, 1972
- 103, Loyola Marymount vs. North Carolina, West 2d, 1988
- 101, Holy Cross vs. North Carolina St., East 1st, 1950
- 99, Oral Roberts vs. Louisville, MW 1st, 1974
- 98, Oklahoma vs. Louisiana Tech, South 2d, 1989
- 98, Arkansas vs. Loyola Marymount, MW 1st, 1989

FIELD-GOAL PERCENTAGE
- 80.0% (28-35), Oklahoma St. vs. Tulane, South 2d, 1992
- 79.0% (49-62), North Carolina vs. Loyola Marymount, West 2d, 1988
- 75.0% (33-44), Northeastern vs. Va. Commonwealth, East 1st, 1984
- 73.2% (30-41), North Carolina St. vs. UTEP, West 2d, 1985
- 72.7% (40-55), *Alabama vs. New Orleans, South 2d, 1987

LOWEST FIELD-GOAL PERCENTAGE
- 22.0% (18-82), Tennessee Tech vs. Loyola (Ill.), South 1st, 1963
- 23.3% (17-73), Prairie View vs. Kansas, MW 1st, 1998
- 25.0% (17-68), Massachusetts vs. New York U., East 1st, 1962
- 25.0% (16-64), Santa Clara vs. Kansas, West 2d, 1996
- 25.0% (12-48), Sanford vs. St. John's (N.Y.), South 1st, 1999
- 25.0% (13-52), Valparaiso vs. Michigan St., MW 1st, 2000
- 25% (14-56), Alabama St. vs. Michigan St., South 1st, 2001

THREE-POINT FIELD GOALS
- 21, Loyola Marymount vs. Michigan, West 2d, 1990
- 18, Duke vs. Monmouth, East 1st, 2001
- 16, Georgia Tech vs. Boston College, South 2d, 1996
- 15, Wisconsin vs. Missouri, West 2d, 1994
- 15, Southern Ill. vs. Syracuse, MW 1st, 1995
- 15, Cincinnati vs. Connecticut, West 2d, 1995
- 15, Arkansas vs. Siena, West 1st, 1999
- 15, Seton Hall vs. Temple, East 2d, 2000 (ot)

THREE-POINT FIELD GOALS ATTEMPTED
- 43, St. Joseph's vs. Boston College, West 2d, 1997 (ot)
- 42, Long Island vs. Villanova, East 1st, 1997
- 40, Loyola Marymount vs. Michigan, West 2d, 1990
- 39, Loyola Marymount vs. North Carolina, West 2d, 1988
- 39, Loyola Marymount vs. Arkansas, MW 1st, 1989
- 39, St. Louis vs. Wake Forest, East 2d, 1995

THREE-POINT FIELD-GOAL PERCENTAGE
(Minimum 7 3FGM)
- 88.9% (8-9), Kansas St. vs. Georgia, West 1st, 1987 (ot)
- 81.8% (9-11), *Alabama vs. N.C. A&T, South 1st, 1987
- 80.0% (8-10), Maryland vs. Massachusetts, MW 2d, 1994
- 77.8% (7-9), Colorado vs. Indiana, East 1st, 1997
- 76.9% (10-13), Kansas St. vs. DePaul, MW 2d, 1988

FREE THROWS MADE
- 41, Navy vs. Syracuse, East 2d, 1986
- 39, UTEP vs. Tulsa, West 1st, 1985
- 37, Morehead St. vs. Pittsburgh, South 1st, 1957
- 37, Xavier vs. Kansas St., MW 1st, 1990
- 36, Georgia Tech vs. Iowa St., East 1st, 1988
- 36, UCLA vs. Louisville, West 2d, 1992

In a first-round game against Brigham Young in 1992, LSU's Shaquille O'Neal blocked 11 shots to set the NCAA first- and second-round game record.

FIRST- AND SECOND-ROUNDS GAME RECORDS— TEAM

FREE THROWS ATTEMPTED
- 55, UTEP vs. Tulsa, West 1st, 1985
- 54, Morehead St. vs. Pittsburgh, South 1st, 1957
- 52, Weber St. vs. Hawaii, West 1st, 1972
- 52, Navy vs. Syracuse, East 2d, 1986
- 50, Notre Dame vs. Kansas, MW 1st, 1975

FREE-THROW PERCENTAGE (Minimum 15 FTM)
- 100.0% (17-17), Dayton vs. Villanova, South 1st, 1985
- 95.8% (23-24), Oklahoma St. vs. Loyola (La.), MW 1st, 1958
- 95.2% (20-21), Iowa vs. North Carolina St., East 2d, 1989 (2 ot)
- 95.0% (19-20), Oklahoma St. vs. Louisville, MW 2d, 1993
- 94.7% (18-19), UNLV vs. Kansas St., West 2d, 1987
- 94.7% (18-19), Utah vs. Charlotte, West 2d, 1997

REBOUNDS
- 86, Notre Dame vs. Tennessee Tech, South 1st, 1958
- 70, Western Ky. vs. Miami (Fla.), South 1st, 1960
- 68, Utah vs. Southern California, West 1st, 1960
- 68, Marshall vs. La.-Lafayette, MW 1st, 1972
- 66, Loyola (Ill.) vs. Tennessee Tech, South 1st, 1963
- 66, Arizona St. vs. Loyola Marymount, West 1st, 1980

REBOUND MARGIN
- 42, Notre Dame (86) vs. Tennessee Tech (44), South 1st, 1958
- 35, St. John's (N.Y.) (56) vs. Connecticut (21), East 1st, 1951
- 35, Kansas (64) vs. Prairie View (29), MW 1st, 1998
- 34, Kansas (61) vs. Jackson St. (27), South 1st, 1997
- 33, Kansas (56) vs. Syracuse (23), MW 2nd, 2001

ASSISTS
- 36, North Carolina vs. Loyola Marymount, West 2d, 1988
- 35, Kentucky vs. San Jose St., MW 1st, 1996
- 33, Loyola Marymount vs. Michigan, West 2d, 1990
- 33, Kansas vs. Chattanooga, South 1st, 1994
- 33, Kentucky vs. Mt. St. Mary's, South 1st, 1995

BLOCKED SHOTS
- 13, Brigham Young vs. Virginia, West 1st, 1991
- 13, Kansas vs. Jackson St., South 1st, 1997
- 12, Clemson vs. St. Mary's (Cal.), West 1st, 1989
- 12, LSU vs. Brigham Young, West 1st, 1992
- 12, Massachusetts vs. Stanford, East 2d, 1995

STEALS
- 19, Providence vs. Austin Peay, South 2d, 1987 (ot)
- 19, Connecticut vs. Boston U., East 1st, 1990
- 18, Xavier vs. Kansas, MW 1st, 1988
- 18, Arkansas vs. Holy Cross, East 1st, 1993
- 18, Louisville vs. Tulsa, MW 1st, 1996
- 18, Mississippi Val. vs. Georgetown, East 1st, 1996
- 18, Penn St. vs. North Carolina, South 2nd, 2001

PERSONAL FOULS
- 39, Kansas vs. Notre Dame, MW 1st, 1975
- 36, North Carolina vs. Texas A&M, MW 2d, 1980
- 35, Hawaii vs. Weber St., West 1st, 1972
- 35, DePaul vs. Boston College, MW 2d, 1982
- 34, Four tied (most recent: Northeastern vs. Purdue, East 1st, 1987; UTEP vs. Arizona, West 1st, 1987 [ot])

PLAYERS DISQUALIFIED
- 6, Kansas vs. Notre Dame, MW 1st, 1975
- 5, DePaul vs. Boston College, MW 2d, 1982
- 5, Wyoming vs. Loyola Marymount, West 1st, 1988
- 4, 13 tied (most recent: Florida St. vs. Iowa, West 1st, 1988)

Two-Team Records

POINTS
- 264, Loyola Marymount (149) vs. Michigan (115), West 2d, 1990
- 234, Loyola Marymount (119) vs. Wyoming (115), West 1st, 1988
- 221, Arkansas (120) vs. Loyola Marymount (101), MW 1st, 1989
- 220, North Carolina (123) vs. Loyola Marymount (97), West 2d, 1988
- 216, UNLV (121) vs. San Francisco (95), West 1st, 1977

FEWEST POINTS
- 73, Georgetown (37) vs. Southern Methodist (36), West 2d, 1984
- 75, Southwest Mo. St. (43) vs. Wisconsin (32), East 1st, 1999
- 84, Princeton (43) vs. UCLA (41), South 1st, 1996
- 87, Kansas (49) vs. Ohio (38), South 1st, 1985
- 90, Boston College (48) vs. Connecticut (42), East 1st, 1967

FIELD GOALS
- 94, Loyola Marymount (49) vs. Michigan (45), West 2d, 1990
- 89, Wyoming (47) vs. Loyola Marymount (42), West 1st, 1998
- 85, UNLV (49) vs. San Francisco (36), West 1st, 1997
- 84, La.-Lafayette (42) vs. Marshall (42), MW 1st, 1972
- 84, La Salle (42) vs. Villanova (42), East 1st, 1978

FIELD GOALS ATTEMPTED
- 192, Marshall (112) vs. La.-Lafayette (80), MW 1st, 1972
- 184, Ohio (94) vs. Notre Dame (90), South 1st, 1970
- 179, Loyola Marymount (98) vs. Arkansas (81), MW 1st, 1989
- 174, Kentucky (89) vs. Louisville (85), East 1st, 1951
- 174, Loyola Marymount (89) vs. Michigan (85), West 2d, 1990

THREE-POINT FIELD GOALS
- 28, Seton Hall (15) vs. Temple (13), East 2d, 2000
- 27, Wisconsin (15) vs. Missouri (12), West 2d, 1994
- 26, Temple (14) vs. Cincinnati (12), West 1st, 1995
- 25, Loyola Marymount (21) vs. Michigan (4), West 2d, 1990
- 25, Georgia Tech (16) vs. Boston College (9), South 2d, 1996

THREE-POINT FIELD GOALS ATTEMPTED
- 62, St. Joseph's (43) vs. Boston College (19), West 2d, 1997 (ot)
- 62, Temple (32) vs. Seton Hall (30), East 2d, 2000
- 61, Temple (32) vs. Lafayette (29), East 1st, 2000
- 61, Duke (38) vs. Monmouth (23), East 1st, 2001
- 59, N.C. A&T (31) vs. Arkansas (28), MW 1st, 1994

FREE THROWS MADE
- 69, Morehead St. (37) vs. Pittsburgh (32), South 1st, 1957
- 63, Manhattan (35) vs. West Virginia (28), East 1st, 1958
- 60, Purdue (31) vs. Northeastern (29), East 1st, 1987
- 56, UTEP (39) vs. Tulsa (17), West 1st, 1985
- 55, Boston College (29) vs. Maryland (26), East 1st, 1958
- 55, Iowa St. (34) vs. Kentucky (21), East 2d, 1992

FREE THROWS ATTEMPTED
- 97, Morehead St. (54) vs. Pittsburgh (43), South 1st, 1957
- 91, Manhattan (49) vs. West Virginia (42), East 1st, 1958
- 83, Purdue (45) vs. Northeastern (38), East 1st, 1987
- 80, Villanova (42) vs. Duke (38), East 1st, 1955
- 80, Maryland (42) vs. Boston College (38), East 1st, 1958

REBOUNDS
- 134, Marshall (68) vs. *La.-Lafayette (66), MW 1st, 1972
- 130, Notre Dame (86) vs. Tennessee Tech (44), South 1st, 1958
- 121, Utah (68) vs. Southern California (53), West 1st, 1960
- 119, Massachusetts (60) vs. New York U. (59), East 1st, 1962
- 119, Loyola Marymount (65) vs. Arkansas (54), MW 1st, 1989

ASSISTS
- 55, Michigan (30) vs. Florida (25), West 2d, 1988
- 54, Wyoming (33) vs. Michigan (21), West 2d, 1990
- 53, North Carolina (36) vs. Loyola Marymount (17), West 2d, 1988
- 52, Wyoming (29) vs. Loyola Marymount (23), West 1st, 1988
- 51, Wake Forest (27) vs. Alabama (24), South 2d, 1991
- 51, Kentucky (35) vs. San Jose St. (16), MW 1st, 1996

BLOCKED SHOTS
- 18, Iowa (10) vs. Duke (8), East 2d, 1992
- 18, Kansas (13) vs. Jackson St. (5), South 1st, 1997
- 17, Connecticut (10) vs. Colgate (7), South 1st, 1996
- 16, Oklahoma (9) vs. Louisiana Tech (7), South 2d, 1989
- 15, Four tied (most recent: Iona [8] vs. Mississippi [7], MW 1st, 2001)

STEALS
- 28, N.C. A&T (16) vs. Arkansas (12), MW 1st, 1994
- 28, Purdue (16) vs. Delaware (12), MW 1st, 1998
- 28, TCU (16) vs. Florida St. (12), MW 1st, 1998
- 26, Seven tied (most recent: Creighton [14] vs. Maryland [12], South 1st, 1999)

PERSONAL FOULS
- 61, West Virginia (32) vs. Manhattan (29), East 1st, 1958
- 59, Loyola Marymount (33) vs. Arkansas (26), MW 1st, 1989
- 59, Northeastern (34) vs. Purdue (25), East 1st, 1987
- 58, Tulsa (34) vs. UTEP (24), West 1st, 1985
- 56, Three tied (most recent: two in 1980)

East Region Game Records

A regional final game is indicated by (RF), a regional semifinal game by (RSF), a regional third-place game by (R3d), second-round game by (2d), first-round game by (1st), opening-round game by (OR) and record later vacated by (*).

Individual Records

POINTS
- 50, David Robinson, Navy vs. Michigan, 1st, 1987
- 44, Rod Thorn, West Virginia vs. St. Joseph's, RSF, 1963
- 43, Jeff Mullins, Duke vs. Villanova, RSF, 1964
- 43, Elijah Allen, Fairleigh Dickinson vs. Connecticut, 1st, 1998
- 42, John Clune, Navy vs. Connecticut, 1st, 1954

FIELD GOALS
- 22, David Robinson, Navy vs. Michigan, 1st, 1987
- 19, Jeff Mullins, Duke vs. Villanova, RSF, 1964
- 18, Hal Lear, Temple vs. Connecticut, RSF, 1956
- 18, Tom Rikers, South Carolina vs. Fordham, R3d, 1971
- 16, 10 tied (most recent: Antonio McDyess, Alabama vs. Pennsylvania, 1st, 1995 [ot])

FIELD GOALS ATTEMPTED
- 38, Bob Cousy, Holy Cross vs. North Carolina St., RF, 1950
- 37, David Robinson, Navy vs. Michigan, 1st, 1987
- 37, Charles Jones, Long Island vs. Villanova, 1st, 1997
- 35, Rich Laurel, Hofstra vs. Notre Dame, 1st, 1977
- 34, Reggie Lewis, Northeastern vs. Oklahoma, 1st, 1986

FIELD-GOAL PERCENTAGE (Minimum 10 FGM)
- 100.0% (10-10), Marvin Barnes, Providence vs. Pennsylvania, RSF, 1973
- 100.0% (10-10), Christian Laettner, Duke vs. Kentucky, RF, 1992 (ot)
- 91.7% (11-12), Kenny Gregory, Kansas vs. DePaul, 1st, 2000 (ot)
- 88.2% (15-17), Reggie Lewis, Northeastern vs. Va. Commonwealth, 1st, 1984
- 86.7% (13-15), Truman Claytor, Kentucky vs. VMI, RSF, 1977
- 86.7% (13-15), Erich Santifer, Syracuse vs. Villanova, 2d, 1980

THREE-POINT FIELD GOALS
- 9, Garde Thompson, Michigan vs. Navy, 1st, 1987
- 9, Johnny Hemsley, Miami (Fla.) vs. Lafayette, 1st, 1999
- 8, Anthony Parker, Bradley vs. Stanford, 1st, 1996

THE EARLY ROUNDS

33

8, Greg Francis, Fairfield vs. North Carolina, 1st, 1997
7, Chris Fleming, Richmond vs. Temple, 2d, 1991
7, Mark Mocnik, Campbell vs. Duke, 1st, 1992
7, Charles Jones, Long Island vs. Villanova, 1st, 1997
7, Ty Shine, Seton Hall vs. Temple, 2d, 2000 (ot)

THREE-POINT FIELD GOALS ATTEMPTED
18, Darius Lane, Seton Hall vs. Oklahoma St., RSF, 2000
16, Matt Maloney, Pennsylvania vs. Florida, 2d, 1994
16, Mark Karcher, Temple vs. Lafayette, 1st, 2000
15, Steve Henson, Kansas St. vs. Minnesota, 1st, 1989
15, Jeff Robinson, Siena vs. Minnesota, 2d, 1989
15, Randy Woods, La Salle vs. Seton Hall, 1st, 1992
15, Charles Jones, Long Island vs. Villanova, 1st, 1997
15, Mark Karcher, Temple vs. Duke, RF, 1999

THREE-POINT FIELD-GOAL PERCENTAGE
(Minimum 5 3FGM)
100.0% (6-6), Migjen Bakalli, North Carolina St. vs. Southern Miss., 1st, 1991
100.0% (5-5), Hubert Davis, North Carolina vs. Eastern Mich., RSF, 1991
85.7% (6-7), Elijah Allen, Fairleigh Dickinson vs. Connecticut, 1st, 1998
83.3% (5-6), Five tied (most recent: Frajan Langdon, Duke vs. Temple, RF, 1999)

FREE THROWS MADE
21, David Robinson, Navy vs. Syracuse, 2d, 1986
19, Tom Hammonds, Georgia Tech vs. Iowa St., 1st, 1988
18, Jon Rose, Connecticut vs. Boston U., 1st, 1959
17, Barry Kramer, New York U. vs. West Virginia, R3d, 1963
16, Bill Bradley, Princeton vs. St. Joseph's, 1st, 1963
16, Len Chappell, Wake Forest vs. St. Joseph's, RSF, 1962

FREE THROWS ATTEMPTED
27, David Robinson, Navy vs. Syracuse, 2d, 1986
21, Vernon Maxwell, Florida vs. North Carolina St., 1st, 1987
21, Tom Hammonds, Georgia Tech vs. Iowa St., 1st, 1988
20, Barry Kramer, New York U. vs. West Virginia, R3d, 1963
20, Len Chappell, Wake Forest vs. St. Joseph's, RSF, 1962

FREE-THROW PERCENTAGE
(Minimum 10 FTM)
100.0% (16-16), Bill Bradley, Princeton vs. St. Joseph's, 1st, 1963
100.0% (13-13), Bill Bradley, Princeton vs. Providence, RF, 1965
100.0% (13-13), Mike Maloy, Davidson vs. St. John's (N.Y.), RSF, 1969
100.0% (12-12), Calvin Duncan, Va. Commonwealth vs. La Salle, 1st, 1983
100.0% (11-11), Willie Burton, Minnesota vs. Kansas St., 1st, 1989

REBOUNDS
34, Fred Cohen, Temple vs. Connecticut, RSF, 1956
29, Toby Kimball, Connecticut vs. St. Joseph's, 1st, 1965
24, Tom Burleson, North Carolina St. vs. Providence, RSF, 1974
23, Cliff Anderson, St. Joseph's vs. North Carolina St., R3d, 1965
22, Tim Duncan, Wake Forest vs. Oklahoma St., RSF, 1995

ASSISTS
16, Sam Crawford, New Mexico St. vs. Nebraska, 1st, 1993
15, Kenny Patterson, DePaul vs. Syracuse, 1st, 1985
15, Pepe Sanchez, Temple vs. Lafayette, 1st, 2000
14, Tezale Archie, Pepperdine vs. Oklahoma St., 2nd, 2000
13, Sean Colson, Charlotte vs. Ill.-Chicago, 1st, 1998

BLOCKED SHOTS
9, David Robinson, Navy vs. Cleveland St., RSF, 1986
8, Tim Perry, Temple vs. Lehigh, 1st, 1988
8, Mark Strickland, Temple vs. Oklahoma St., RSF, 1991 (ot)

8, Acie Earl, Iowa vs. Duke, 2d, 1992
8, Tim Duncan, Wake Forest vs. Oklahoma St., RSF, 1995
8, Shane Battier, Duke vs. Kansas, 2d, 2000

STEALS
8, Darrell Hawkins, Arkansas vs. Holy Cross, 1st, 1993
7, Tommy Amaker, Duke vs. Old Dominion, 2d, 1986
7, Edgar Padilla, Massachusetts vs. UCF, 1st, 1996
6, 10 tied (most recent: Brandon Armstrong, Pepperdine vs. Indiana, 1st, 2000)

Team Records

POINTS
114, North Carolina St. vs. Southern Miss. (85), 1st, 1991
113, North Carolina vs. Pennsylvania (82), 1st, 1987
112, North Carolina vs. Rhode Island (67), 2d, 1993
110, North Carolina vs. Boston College (90), R3d, 1975
109, Princeton vs. Providence (69), RF, 1965
109, North Carolina vs. Michigan (97), 2d, 1987

FEWEST POINTS
20, North Carolina vs. Pittsburgh (26), RF, 1941
24, Springfield vs. Indiana (48), RF, 1940
26, Pittsburgh vs. North Carolina (20), RF, 1941
29, Western Ky. vs. Duquesne (30), RF, 1940
30, Brown vs. Villanova (43), RF, 1939
30, Duquesne vs. Western Ky. (29), RF, 1940

WINNING MARGIN
49, Syracuse (101) vs. Brown (52), 1st, 1986
47, Duke (101) vs. Connecticut (54), RF, 1964
45, North Carolina (112) vs. Rhode Island (67), 2d, 1993
43, *Villanova (90) vs. Pennsylvania (47), RF, 1971
43, Duke (95) vs. Monmouth (52), 1st, 2001

POINTS BY LOSING TEAM
103, Kentucky vs. Duke (104), RF, 1992 (ot)
100, St. Joseph's vs. West Virginia, (106), R3d, 1960
98, Iowa St. vs. Kentucky (106), 2d, 1992
97, La Salle vs. Villanova (103), 1st, 1978
97, Michigan vs. North Carolina (109), 2d, 1987

FIELD GOALS
44, Fordham vs. Furman, 1st, 1971
44, North Carolina vs. Boston College, R3d, 1975
43, Duke vs. Connecticut, RF, 1964
43, Providence vs. Maryland, R3d, 1973
42, Three tied (most recent: North Carolina vs. Rhode Island, 2d, 1993)

FIELD GOALS ATTEMPTED
103, St. Joseph's vs. West Virginia, R3d, 1960
101, Holy Cross vs. North Carolina St., 1st, 1950
95, Long Island vs. Villanova, 1st, 1997
94, Furman vs. Providence, R3d, 1974
92, West Virginia vs. St. Joseph's, RSF, 1959

FIELD-GOAL PERCENTAGE
75.0% (33-44), Northeastern vs. Va. Commonwealth, 1st, 1984
71.4% (25-35), Georgetown vs. Notre Dame, 2d, 1989
68.3% (41-60), Princeton vs. Providence, RF, 1965
67.3% (33-49), Pennsylvania vs. Providence, 1st, 1972
67.3% (33-49), Villanova vs. Houston, 1st, 1981

LOWEST FIELD-GOAL PERCENTAGE
12.7% (8-63), Springfield vs. Indiana, RSF, 1940
13.9% (10-72), Harvard vs. Ohio St., RSF, 1946
22.9% (16-70), St. John's (N.Y.) vs. Kentucky, RSF, 1951
24.4% (20-82), Holy Cross vs. Ohio St., R3d, 1950
25.0% (17-68), Massachusetts vs. New York U., 1st, 1962

THREE-POINT FIELD GOALS
18, Duke vs. Monmouth, 1st, 2001
15, Seton Hall vs. Temple, 2d, 2000 (ot)
14, Pennsylvania vs. Alabama, 1st, 1995 (ot)
14, Long Island vs. Villanova, 1st, 1997
13, Four tied (most recent: Kentucky vs. Iowa, 2d, 2001)

THREE-POINT FIELD GOALS ATTEMPTED
42, Long Island vs. Villanova, 1st, 1997
39, St. Louis vs. Wake Forest, 2d, 1995
38, Duke vs. Monmouth, 1st, 2001
37, Pennsylvania vs. Florida, 2d, 1994
35, La Salle vs. Clemson, 2d, 1990

THREE-POINT FIELD-GOAL PERCENTAGE
(Minimum 7 3FGM)
77.8% (7-9), Colorado vs. Indiana, 1st, 1997
70.0% (7-10), Rhode Island vs. Syracuse, 2d, 1988
66.7% (8-12), Minnesota vs. Kansas St., 1st, 1989
66.7% (8-12), Duke vs. Florida A&M, 1st 1999
64.3% (9-14), Purdue vs. Northeastern, 1st, 1987
64.3% (9-14), Iowa vs. Rutgers, 1st, 1989

FREE THROWS MADE
41, Navy vs. Syracuse, 2d, 1986
36, New York U. vs. St. Joseph's, R3d, 1962
36, Georgia Tech vs. Iowa St., 1st, 1988
35, La Salle vs. Canisius, RF, 1955
35, Manhattan vs. West Virginia, 1st, 1958

FREE THROWS ATTEMPTED
52, Navy vs. Syracuse, 2d, 1986
50, West Virginia vs. St. Joseph's, RSF, 1959
49, Manhattan vs. West Virginia, 1st, 1958
49, New York U. vs. St. Joseph's, R3d, 1962
46, West Virginia vs. St. Joseph's, R3d, 1960
46, Georgetown vs. Texas Tech, RSF, 1996

FREE-THROW PERCENTAGE
(Minimum 15 FTM)
100.0% (22-22), Fordham vs. South Carolina, R3d, 1971
95.2% (20-21), Iowa vs. North Carolina St., 2d, 1989 (2 ot)
95.0% (19-20), North Carolina St. vs. St. John's (N.Y.), R3d, 1951
95.0% (19-20), Iowa vs. Georgetown, RF, 1980
94.1% (16-17), Notre Dame vs. Georgetown, 2d, 1989

REBOUNDS
76, Temple vs. Connecticut, RSF, 1956
65, West Virginia vs. St. Joseph's, RSF, 1959
65, North Carolina vs. Princeton, RSF, 1967 (ot)
63, West Virginia vs. Dartmouth, 1st, 1959
63, West Virginia vs. St. Joseph's, R3d, 1960
63, Syracuse vs. Brown, 1st, 1986

REBOUND MARGIN
35, St. John's (N.Y.) (56) vs. Connecticut (21), 1st, 1951
29, West Virginia (63) vs. Dartmouth (34), 1st, 1959
26, North Carolina (60) vs. Pittsburgh (34), RF, 1974
24, Davidson (59) vs. Rhode Island (35), 1st, 1966
24, Syracuse (63) vs. Brown (39), 1st, 1986
24, North Carolina (57) vs. Navy (33), 1st, 1998
24, Michigan St. (39) vs. Princeton (15), 2nd, 1998

ASSISTS
31, Syracuse vs. Brown, 1st, 1986
30, North Carolina vs. Pennsylvania, 1st, 1987
28, North Carolina vs. Rhode Island, 2d, 1993
27, Richmond vs. Rider, OR, 1984
27, North Carolina vs. Villanova, 2d, 1991

BLOCKED SHOTS
12, Massachusetts vs. Stanford, 2d, 1995
11, Duke vs. Temple, RF, 1988
11, North Carolina St. vs. Iowa, 2d, 1989 (2 ot)
11, Villanova vs. Old Dominion, 1st, 1995 (3 ot)
10, Connecticut vs. Florida, RSF, 1994
10, Villanova vs. Long Island, 1st, 1997
10, Duke vs. Kansas, 2d, 2000

STEALS
19, Connecticut vs. Boston U., 1st, 1990
18, Arkansas vs. Holy Cross, 1st, 1993
18, Mississippi Val. vs. Georgetown, 1st, 1996
17, Duke vs. UCLA, RSF, 2001
16, Five tied (most recent: two in 1996)

PERSONAL FOULS
41, Dayton vs. Illinois, RSF, 1952
35, DePaul vs. VMI, RSF, 1976 (ot)
35, Texas Tech vs. Georgetown, RSF, 1996
34, Syracuse vs. Virginia, RSF, 1984

EAST REGION GAME RECORDS—TEAM

34, Syracuse vs. Navy, 2d, 1986
34, Northeastern vs. Purdue, 1st, 1987

PLAYERS DISQUALIFIED
5, Dayton vs. Illinois, RSF, 1952
5, St. Joseph's vs. West Virginia, RSF, 1959
5, DePaul vs. VMI, RSF, 1976 (ot)
5, Syracuse vs. Virginia, RSF, 1984
4, 12 tied (most recent: Texas Tech vs. Georgetown, RSF, 1996)

Two-Team Records

POINTS
207, Duke (104) vs. Kentucky (103), RF, 1992 (ot)
206, West Virginia (106) vs. St. Joseph's (100), R3d, 1960
206, North Carolina (109) vs. Michigan (97), 2d, 1987
204, Kentucky (106) vs. Iowa St. (98), 2d, 1992
200, North Carolina (110) vs. Boston College (90), R3d, 1975
200, Villanova (103) vs. La Salle (97), 1st, 1978

FEWEST POINTS
46, Pittsburgh (26) vs. North Carolina (20), RF, 1941
59, Duquesne (30) vs. Western Ky. (29), RF, 1940
72, Villanova (42) vs. Brown (30), RF, 1939
72, Indiana (48) vs. Springfield (24), RF, 1940
75, Southwest Mo. St. (43) vs. Wisconsin (32), 1st, 1999

FIELD GOALS
84, La Salle (42) vs. Villanova (42), 1st, 1978
83, Providence (43) vs. Maryland (40), RF, 1973
81, North Carolina (44) vs. Boston College (37), R3d, 1975
79, Boston College (42) vs. St. Bonaventure, 1st, 1968
78, Providence (41) vs. Furman (37), R3d, 1974

FIELD GOALS ATTEMPTED
188, St. Joseph's (103) vs. West Virginia (85), R3d, 1960
175, Furman (94) vs. Providence (81), R3d, 1974
174, Holy Cross (101) vs. North Carolina St. (73), RF, 1950
174, Kentucky (89) vs. Louisville (85), 1st, 1951
171, Miami (Ohio) (94) vs. DePaul (77), 1st, 1953

THREE-POINT FIELD GOALS
28, Seton Hall (15) vs. Temple (13), 2d, 2000 (ot)
24, Kentucky (13) vs. Iowa (11), 2d, 2001
23, Duke (18) vs. Monmouth (5), 1st, 2001
21, Pennsylvania (14) vs. Alabama (7), 1st, 1995 (ot)
21, Purdue (13) vs. Temple (8), RSF, 1999

THREE-POINT FIELD GOALS ATTEMPTED
62, Temple (32) vs. Seton Hall (30), 2d, 2000 (ot)
61, Temple (32) vs. Lafayette (29), 1st, 2000
61, Duke (38) vs. Monmouth (23), 1st, 2001
56, La Salle (33) vs. Southern Miss. (23), 1st, 1990
56, Long Island (42) vs. Villanova (14), 1st, 1997

FREE THROWS
63, La Salle (35) vs. Canisius (28), RF, 1955
63, Manhattan (35) vs. West Virginia (28), 1st, 1958
61, New York U. (36) vs. St. Joseph's (25), R3d, 1962
60, Purdue (31) vs. Northeastern (29), 1st, 1987
58, Villanova (29) vs. Canisius (29), RSF, 1955

FREE THROWS ATTEMPTED
91, Manhattan (49) vs. West Virginia (42), 1st, 1958
89, New York U. (49) vs. St. Joseph's (40), R3d, 1962
85, Marquette (44) vs. Iowa (41), RF, 1955
83, Purdue (45) vs. Northeastern (38), 1st, 1987
81, Georgetown (46) vs. Texas Tech (35), RSF, 1996

REBOUNDS
124, West Virginia (63) vs. St. Joseph's (61), R3d, 1960
120, West Virginia (65) vs. St. Joseph's (55), RSF, 1959
119, Manhattan (60) vs. Dartmouth (59), RSF, 1958
119, Massachusetts (60) vs. New York U. (59), 1st, 1962
118, North Carolina (65) vs. Princeton (53), 2d, 1967 (ot)

ASSISTS
47, Kentucky (24) vs. Duke (23), RF, 1992 (ot)
45, Florida (26) vs. Purdue (19), 2d, 1987
40, New Mexico St. (25) vs. Nebraska (15), 1st, 1993
40, Arkansas (21) vs. North Carolina (19), RSF, 1993
39, Pennsylvania (25) vs. Nebraska (14), 1st, 1994
39, North Carolina (22) vs. Fairfield (17), 1st, 1997
39, North Carolina (22) vs. Louisville (17), RF, 1997

BLOCKED SHOTS
18, Iowa (10) vs. Duke (8), 2d, 1992
17, Duke (11) vs. Temple (6), RF, 1988
16, Massachusetts (9) vs. Tulsa (7), RSF, 1995
15, Massachusetts (12) vs. Stanford (3), 2d, 1995
14, North Carolina (8) vs. Eastern Mich. (6), RSF, 1991
14, Massachusetts (9) vs. Oklahoma St. (5), RF, 1995

STEALS
27, Duke (17) vs. UCLA (10), RSF, 2001
26, Arkansas (18) vs. Holy Cross (8), 1st, 1993
26, Old Dominion (13) vs. Villanova (13), 1st, 1995 (3 ot)
25, South Carolina St. (13) vs. Duke (12), 1st, 1989
25, Mississippi Val. (18) vs. Georgetown (7), 1st, 1996

PERSONAL FOULS
61, West Virginia (32) vs. Manhattan (29), 1st, 1958
59, Northeastern (34) vs. Purdue (25), 1st, 1987
59, Texas Tech (35) vs. Georgetown (24), RSF, 1996
58, St. Joseph's (30) vs. New York U. (28), R3d, 1962
57, DePaul (35) vs. VMI (22), RSF, 1976

South Region Game Records

A regional final game is indicated by (RF), a regional semifinal game by (RSF), a regional third-place game by (R3d), second-round game by (2d), first-round game by (1st), opening-round game by (OR) and record later vacated by (*).

Individual Records

POINTS
61, Austin Carr, Notre Dame vs. Ohio, 1st, 1970
52, Austin Carr, Notre Dame vs. Kentucky, RSF, 1970
45, Austin Carr, Notre Dame vs. Iowa, R3d, 1970
44, Dan Issel, Kentucky vs. Notre Dame, RSF, 1970
44, Hersey Hawkins, Bradley vs. Auburn, 1st, 1988
44, Glenn Robinson, Purdue vs. Kansas, RSF, 1994

FIELD GOALS
25, Austin Carr, Notre Dame vs. Ohio, 1st, 1970
22, Austin Carr, Notre Dame vs. Kentucky, RSF, 1970
21, Austin Carr, Notre Dame vs. Iowa, R3d, 1970
17, Dan Issel, Kentucky vs. Notre Dame, RSF, 1970
17, Rickey Green, Michigan vs. Holy Cross, 1st, 1977

FIELD GOALS ATTEMPTED
44, Austin Carr, Notre Dame vs. Ohio, 1st, 1970
39, Austin Carr, Notre Dame vs. Iowa, R3d, 1970
36, Ronald "Popeye" Jones, Murray St. vs. Michigan St., 1st, 1990 (ot)
35, Austin Carr, Notre Dame vs. Kentucky, RSF, 1970
35, *Jim McDaniels, Western Ky. vs. Ohio St., RF, 1971 (ot)

FIELD-GOAL PERCENTAGE
(Minimum 10 FGM)
100.0% (11-11), Kenny Walker, Kentucky vs. Western Ky., 2d, 1986
91.7% (11-12), Pembrook Burrows, Jacksonville vs. Iowa, RSF, 1970
90.9% (10-11), Dwayne McClain, Villanova vs. Marshall, 1st, 1984
90.9% (10-11), Travis Ford, Kentucky vs. Wake Forest, RSF, 1993
86.7% (13-15), Brian Penny, Coastal Caro. vs. Indiana, 1st, 1991

THREE-POINT FIELD GOALS
8, Glen Rice, Michigan vs. North Carolina, RSF, 1989
8, Jamie Mercurio, Miami (Ohio) vs. North Carolina, 1st, 1992
8, Cuonzo Martin, Purdue vs. Kansas, RSF, 1994
8, Trent Pulliam, Jackson St. vs. Kansas, 1st, 1997
7, Six tied (most recent: two in 1996)

THREE-POINT FIELD GOALS ATTEMPTED
20, Chris Walker, Villanova vs. LSU, 1st, 1990
17, Shawn Respert, Michigan St. vs. Weber St., 1st, 1995
16, Carlos Sample, Southern U. vs. North Carolina, 1st, 1989
16, Darnell Burton, Cincinnati vs. Mississippi St., RF, 1996
16, Shawnta Rogers, George Washington vs. Indiana, 1st, 1999

THREE-POINT FIELD-GOAL PERCENTAGE
(Minimum 5 3FGM)
100.0% (7-7), Sam Cassell, Florida St. vs. Tulane, 2d, 1993
100.0% (6-6), Mike Buck, Middle Tenn. vs. Florida St., 1st, 1989
100.0% (5-5), Jamal Mashburn, Kentucky vs. Wake Forest, RSF, 1993
85.7% (6-7), Stephon Marbury, Georgia Tech vs. Boston College, 1st, 1996
83.3% (5-6), Five tied (most recent: Travis Ford, Kentucky vs. Wake Forest, RSF, 1993)

FREE THROWS
17, Roger Newman, Kentucky vs. Ohio St., RF, 1961
16, John Riser, Pittsburgh vs. Kentucky, RSF, 1957
16, Reggie Williams, Georgetown vs. Kansas, RSF, 1987
16, Billy Donovan, Providence vs. Georgetown, RF, 1987
16, Kiwane Garris, Illinois vs. Southern California, 1st, 1997

FREE THROWS ATTEMPTED
24, Donnie Gaunce, Morehead St. vs. Iowa, RSF, 1956
22, Roger Newman, Kentucky vs. Ohio St., RF, 1961
21, John Bagley, Boston College vs. Wake Forest, 2d, 1981
21, Brad Miller, Purdue vs. Rhode Island, 1st, 1997
20, Clarence Kea, Lamar vs. Detroit Mercy, 1st, 1979

FREE-THROW PERCENTAGE
(Minimum 11 FTM)
100.0% (15-15), Austin Croshere, Providence vs. Marquette, 1st, 1997
100.0% (13-13), Al Gooden, Ball St. vs. Boston College, 1st, 1981
100.0% (12-12), Dan Issel, Kentucky vs. Miami (Ohio), R3d, 1969
100.0% (12-12), Bryant Stith, Virginia vs. Middle Tenn., 2d, 1989
100.0% (12-12), Dan Dickau, Gonzaga vs. Indiana St., 2d, 2001

REBOUNDS
31, Nate Thurmond, Bowling Green vs. Mississippi St., R3d, 1963
30, Jerry Lucas, Ohio St. vs. Kentucky, RF, 1961
27, John Green, Michigan St. vs. Notre Dame, RSF, 1957
26, Howard Jolliff, Ohio vs. Georgia Tech, RSF, 1960
26, Phil Hubbard, Michigan vs. Detroit, RSF, 1977

ASSISTS
14, Dickey Beal, Kentucky vs. Brigham Young, 2d, 1984
14, John Crotty, Virginia vs. Middle Tenn., 2d, 1989
14, Pooh Richardson, UCLA vs. Iowa St., 1st, 1989
13, Rumeal Robinson, Michigan vs. North Carolina, RSF, 1989
12, Six tied (most recent: Doug Gottlieb, Oklahoma St. vs. Auburn, 2d 1999

BLOCKED SHOTS
8, Tim Duncan, Wake Forest vs. Col. of Charleston, 1st, 1994
7, Ken Johnson, Ohio St. vs. St. John's (N.Y.), RF, 1999
6, 11 tied (most recent: Ron Artest, St. John's (N.Y.) vs Maryland, RSF, 1999

STEALS
7, Delray Brooks, Providence vs. Austin Peay, 2d, 1987 (ot)
7, Ted Ellis, Manhattan vs. Oklahoma, 1st, 1995
6, Byron Dinkins, Charlotte vs. Brigham Young, 1st, 1988 (ot)
6, Vincent Rainey, Murray St. vs. North Carolina, 1st, 1995
6, Jason Hart, Syracuse vs. Iona, 1st, 1998
6, Cori Brandon, Creighton vs. Maryland, 2d, 1999

THE EARLY ROUNDS

Team Records

POINTS
- 124, Oklahoma vs. Louisiana Tech (81), 2d, 1989
- 121, Iowa vs. Notre Dame (106), R3d, 1970
- 118, Notre Dame vs. Vanderbilt (88), R3d, 1974
- 117, Arkansas vs. Georgia St. (76), 1st, 1991
- 113, Kentucky vs. Mt. St. Mary's (67), 1st, 1995

FEWEST POINTS
- 35, Alabama St. vs. Michigan St. (69), 1st, 2001
- 38, Ohio vs. Kansas (49), 1st, 1985
- 40, Ohio vs. Kentucky (57), 2d, 1983
- 41, Boston College vs. St. Joseph's (42), RSF, 1981
- 41, UCLA vs. Princeton (43), 1st, 1996
- 41, Winthrop vs. Auburn (80), 1st 1999

WINNING MARGIN
- 69, Loyola (Ill.) (111) vs. Tennessee Tech (42), 1st, 1963
- 47, DePaul (99) vs. Eastern Ky. (52), 1st, 1965
- 46, Kentucky (113) vs. Mt. St. Mary's (67), 1st, 1995
- 44, Kentucky (96) vs. Rider (52), 1st, 1993
- 43, Oklahoma (124) vs. Louisiana Tech (81), 2d, 1989

POINTS BY LOSING TEAM
- 106, Notre Dame vs. Iowa (121), R3d, 1970
- 103, Iowa vs. Jacksonville (104), RSF, 1970
- 100, Kentucky vs. Jacksonville (106), RF, 1970
- 100, *Austin Peay vs. Kentucky (106), RSF, 1973 (ot)
- 99, Notre Dame vs. Kentucky (109), RSF, 1970

FIELD GOALS
- 52, Iowa vs. Notre Dame, R3d, 1970
- 50, Kentucky vs. Austin Peay, RSF, 1973 (ot)
- 50, Notre Dame vs. Austin Peay, 1st, 1974
- 49, Notre Dame vs. Vanderbilt, R3d, 1974
- 48, Oklahoma vs. Louisiana Tech, 2d, 1989

FIELD GOALS ATTEMPTED
- 106, Indiana vs. Miami (Ohio), R3d, 1958
- 99, *Austin Peay vs. Kentucky, RSF, 1973 (ot)
- 98, Kentucky vs. Miami (Ohio), RSF, 1958
- 98, Iowa vs. Notre Dame, R3d, 1970
- 98, Oklahoma vs. Louisiana Tech, 2d, 1989

FIELD-GOAL PERCENTAGE
- 80.0% (28-35), Oklahoma St. vs. Tulane, 2d, 1992
- 72.7% (40-55), *Alabama vs. New Orleans, 2d, 1987
- 71.4% (30-42), Villanova vs. Marshall, 1st, 1984
- 68.8% (33-48), Providence vs. Alabama, RSF, 1987
- 68.6% (35-51), Indiana vs. St. Joseph's, RF, 1981

LOWEST FIELD-GOAL PERCENTAGE
- 22.0% (18-82), Tennessee Tech vs. Loyola (Ill.), 1st, 1963
- 25.0% (12-48), Samford vs. St. John's (N.Y.), 1st, 1999
- 25.0% (14-52), Alabama St. vs. Michigan St., 1st, 2001
- 25.5% (14-55), New Mexico vs. Syracuse, 2d, 1998
- 25.5% (14-55), Winthrop vs. Auburn, 1st, 1999

THREE-POINT FIELD GOALS
- 16, Kentucky vs. Wake Forest, RSF, 1993
- 16, Georgia Tech vs. Boston College, 2d, 1996
- 15, Purdue vs. Kansas, RSF, 1994
- 14, Providence vs. Alabama, RSF, 1987
- 14, Purdue vs. UCF, 1st, 1994

THREE-POINT FIELD GOALS ATTEMPTED
- 38, Kentucky vs. Marquette, 2d, 1994
- 36, Kentucky vs. North Carolina, RF, 1995
- 33, Samford vs. St. John's (N.Y.), 1st, 1999
- 32, Creighton vs. Maryland, 2d, 1999
- 31, East Tenn. St. vs. Michigan, 2d, 1992
- 31, George Washington vs. Indiana, 1st, 1999
- 31, Missouri vs. North Carolina, 1st, 2000

THREE-POINT FIELD-GOAL PERCENTAGE
(Minimum 7 3FGM)
- 81.8% (9-11), *Alabama vs. N.C. A&T, 1st, 1987
- 70.0% (7-10), Virginia vs. Providence, 1st, 1989
- 70.0% (7-10), Virginia vs. Middle Tenn., 2d, 1989
- 66.7% (16-24), Kentucky vs. Wake Forest, RSF, 1993
- 63.6% (14-22), Providence vs. Alabama, RSF, 1987
- 63.6% (7-11), *Alabama vs. New Orleans, 2d, 1987

FREE THROWS MADE
- 38, Loyola (Ill.) vs. Kentucky, R3d, 1964
- 37, Morehead St. vs. Pittsburgh, 1st, 1957
- 35, Iowa vs. Morehead St., RSF, 1956
- 35, UAB vs. Western Ky., 1st, 1981
- 34, Navy vs. LSU, 1st, 1985

FREE THROWS ATTEMPTED
- 54, Morehead St. vs. Pittsburgh, 1st, 1957
- 53, Morehead St. vs. Iowa, RSF, 1956
- 52, Iowa vs. Morehead St., RSF, 1956
- 48, Kentucky vs. Tennessee St., 1st, 1994
- 45, Purdue vs. Indiana, RSF, 1980

FREE-THROW PERCENTAGE
(Minimum 15 FTM)
- 100.0% (17-17), Dayton vs. Villanova, 1st, 1985
- 100.0% (17-17), Villanova vs. Kentucky, RSF, 1988
- 95.5% (21-22), Vanderbilt vs. Marquette, RSF, 1974
- 95.2% (20-21), Notre Dame vs. Vanderbilt, R3d, 1974
- 93.8% (15-16), Alabama vs. N.C. A&T, 1987
- 93.8% (15-16), Rutgers vs. Arizona St., 1st, 1991

REBOUNDS
- 86, Notre Dame vs. Tennessee Tech, 1st, 1958
- 70, Western Ky. vs. Miami (Fla.), 1st, 1960
- 66, Michigan St. vs. Notre Dame, RSF, 1957
- 66, Loyola (Ill.) vs. Tennessee Tech, 1st, 1963
- 66, Western Ky. vs. Dayton, R3d, 1966

REBOUND MARGIN
- 42, Notre Dame (86) vs. Tennessee Tech (44), 1st, 1958
- 34, Kansas (61) vs. Jackson St. (27), 1st, 1997
- 29, Indiana (52) vs. Robert Morris (23), 1st, 1982
- 27, Western Ky. (70) vs. Miami (Fla.) (43), 1st, 1960
- 26, Four tied (most recent: Ohio St. [51] vs. Detroit [25], 2d 1999)

ASSISTS
- 33, Kansas vs. Chattanooga, 1st, 1994
- 33, Kentucky vs. Mt. St. Mary's, 1st, 1995
- 32, Arkansas vs. Georgia St., 1st, 1991
- 32, Michigan vs. East Tenn. St., 2d, 1992
- 31, Oklahoma vs. Auburn, 2d, 1988

BLOCKED SHOTS
- 14, Kentucky vs. UCLA, RSF, 1998
- 13, Kansas vs. Jackson St., 1st, 1997
- 11, North Carolina vs. Georgetown, RSF, 1995
- 11, Kentucky vs. South Carolina St., 1st, 1998
- 10, Four tied (most recent: Kansas vs. Arizona, RSF, 1997

STEALS
- 19, Providence vs. Austin Peay, 2d, 1987 (ot)
- 18, Penn St. vs. North Carolina, 2d, 2001
- 17, Kentucky vs. Tennessee St., 1st, 1994
- 17, Duke vs. Michigan St., 2d, 1994
- 17, Duke vs. Radford, 1st, 1998

PERSONAL FOULS
- 35, Iowa vs. Morehead St., RSF, 1956
- 33, Indiana vs. Purdue, RSF, 1980
- 32, Kentucky vs. Florida St., 2d, 1980
- 32, LSU vs. Navy, 1st, 1985
- 31, Four tied (most recent: George Washington vs. Indiana, 1st, 1999)

PLAYERS DISQUALIFIED
- 4, Kentucky vs. Marquette, RSF, 1969
- 4, Kentucky vs. Jacksonville, RF, 1970
- 3, 23 tied (most recent: two in 1997)

Two-Team Records

POINTS
- 227, Iowa (121) vs. Notre Dame (106), R3d, 1970
- 208, Kentucky (109) vs. Notre Dame (99), RSF, 1970
- 207, Jacksonville (104) vs. Iowa (103), RSF, 1970
- 206, Four tied (most recent: Oklahoma [108] vs. Louisville [98], RSF, 1988)

FEWEST POINTS
- 83, St. Joseph's (42) vs. Boston College (41), RSF, 1981
- 84, Princeton (43) vs. UCLA (41), 1st, 1996
- 87, Kansas (49) vs. Ohio (38), 1st 1985
- 89, Villanova (46) vs. Maryland (43), RSF, 1985
- 94, Duke (52) vs. Pennsylvania (42), 2d, 1980
- 94, Middle Tenn. (50) vs. Kentucky (44), 1st, 1982

FIELD GOALS
- 97, Iowa (52) vs. Notre Dame (45), R3d, 1970
- 96, Kentucky (50) vs. Austin Peay (46), RSF, 1973 (ot)
- 86, Notre Dame (49) vs. Vanderbilt (37), R3d, 1974
- 85, Jacksonville (43) vs. Iowa (42), RSF, 1970
- 82, Notre Dame (46) vs. Ohio (36), 1st, 1970
- 82, Kentucky (43) vs. Notre Dame (39), RSF, 1970

FIELD GOALS ATTEMPTED
- 196, Austin Peay (99) vs. Kentucky (97), RSF, 1973 (ot)
- 195, Iowa (98) vs. Notre Dame (97), R3d, 1970
- 194, Indiana (106) vs. Miami (Ohio) (88), R3d, 1958
- 184, Ohio (94) vs. Notre Dame (90), 1st, 1970
- 180, Iowa (100) vs. Morehead St. (80), RSF, 1956

THREE-POINT FIELD GOALS
- 25, Georgia Tech (16) vs. Boston College (9), 2d, 1996
- 23, Purdue (15) vs. Kansas (8), RSF, 1994
- 21, Providence (14) vs. Alabama (7), RSF, 1987
- 21, Purdue (14) vs. UCF (7), 1st, 1994
- 21, Kentucky (13) vs. Mt. St. Mary's (8), 1st, 1995

THREE-POINT FIELD GOALS ATTEMPTED
- 54, Florida (29) vs. Temple (25), 2d, 2001
- 52, Tennessee (30) vs. La.-Lafayette (22), 1st, 2000
- 52, Penn St. (33) vs. Temple (19), RSF, 2001
- 51, Kentucky (38) vs. Marquette (13), 2d, 1994
- 51, Kentucky (36) vs. North Carolina (15), RF, 1995

FREE THROWS
- 69, Morehead St. (37) vs. Pittsburgh (32), 1st, 1957
- 68, Iowa (35) vs. Morehead St. (33), RSF, 1956
- 56, Kentucky (30) vs. Pittsburgh (26), RSF, 1957
- 52, Kentucky (33) vs. Tennessee St. (19), 1st, 1994
- 52, Seton Hall (28) vs. Michigan St. (24), 1st, 1994

FREE THROWS ATTEMPTED
- 105, Morehead St. (53) vs. Iowa (52), RSF, 1956
- 97, Morehead St. (54) vs. Pittsburgh (43), 1st, 1957
- 72, Kentucky (48) vs. Tennessee St. (24), 1st, 1994

Basketball facts

What two colleges met in the first basketball game between two schools? A good question with at least three answers, depending on how you look at it.

- On February 9, 1895, the first game was played between two college teams as the University of Minnesota School of Agriculture defeated Hamline, 9-3. However, nine players were allowed on the court at the same time for both teams. Also, the Agriculture School included students of both college and high-school age. So many people say that game doesn't count.

- The first college basketball game with five players on a side was played January 18, 1896, when the University of Chicago defeated the University of Iowa, 15-12, in Iowa City. Both teams' starting five played the entire game. However, Iowa's starters comprised a YMCA team who all were students at the university, so does this game count as a true college game?

- And finally, some basketball historians say that the first true collegiate men's game was played between Yale University and the University of Pennsylvania in February 1897. Yale defeated Pennsylvania, 32-10.

Remember, vote for only one.

MIDWEST REGION GAME RECORDS—TWO-TEAM

70, Kentucky (39) vs. Pittsburgh (31), RSF, 1957
70, Kentucky (39) vs. Ohio St. (31), RF, 1961

REBOUNDS
130, Notre Dame (86) vs. Tennessee Tech (44), 1st, 1958
122, Miami (Ohio) (65) vs. Indiana (57), R3d, 1958
118, Notre Dame (62) vs. Ohio (56), 1st, 1970
117, Jacksonville (59) vs. Western Ky. (58), 1st, 1971
116, Indiana (61) vs. Virginia Tech (55), 2d, 1967

ASSISTS
51, Wake Forest (27) vs. Alabama (24), 2d, 1991
50, Kentucky (33) vs. Mt. St. Mary's (17), 1st, 1995
48, Arkansas (32) vs. Georgia St. (16), 1st, 1991
47, Arkansas (24) vs. Arizona St. (23), 2d, 1991
47, Michigan (32) vs. East Tenn. St. (15), 2d, 1992

BLOCKED SHOTS
20, Kentucky (14) vs. UCLA (6), RSF, 1998
18, Kansas (13) vs. Jackson St. (5), 1st, 1997
17, Connecticut (10) vs. Colgate (7), 1st, 1996
16, Oklahoma (9) vs. Louisiana Tech (7), 2d, 1989
15, Arkansas (8) vs. Georgia St. (7), 1st, 1991
15, North Carolina (11) vs. Georgetown (4), RSF, 1995

STEALS
26, Providence (19) vs. Austin Peay (7), 2d, 1987 (ot)
26, Arkansas (16) vs. Georgia St. (10), 1st, 1991
26, Kentucky (17) vs. Tennessee St. (9), 1st, 1994
26, Duke (17) vs. Michigan St. (9), 2d, 1994
26, Creighton (14) vs. Maryland (12), 2d, 1999

PERSONAL FOULS
68, Iowa (35) vs. Morehead St. (33), RSF, 1956
56, Pittsburgh (31) vs. Morehead St. (25), 1st, 1957
56, Kentucky (32) vs. Florida St. (24), 2d, 1980
55, Providence (29) vs. Austin Peay (26), 2d, 1987 (ot)
53, Three tied (most recent: Illinois [27] vs. Southern California [26], 1st, 1997)

Midwest Region Game Records

A regional final game is indicated by (RF), a regional semifinal game by (RSF), a regional third-place game by (R3d), second-round game by (2d), first-round game by (1st), opening-round game by (OR) and record later vacated by (*).

Individual Records

POINTS
56, Oscar Robertson, Cincinnati vs. Arkansas, R3d, 1958
52, Austin Carr, Notre Dame vs. TCU, 1st, 1971
49, Elvin Hayes, Houston vs. Loyola (Ill.), 1st, 1968
47, Austin Carr, Notre Dame vs. Houston, R3d, 1971
46, Dave Corzine, DePaul vs. Louisville, RSF, 1978 (2 ot)

FIELD GOALS
21, Oscar Robertson, Cincinnati vs. Arkansas, R3d, 1958
20, Elvin Hayes, Houston vs. Loyola (Ill.), 1st, 1968
20, Austin Carr, Notre Dame vs. TCU, 1st, 1971
19, Oscar Robertson, Cincinnati vs. Kansas, RF, 1960
18, Willie Smith, Missouri vs. Michigan, RF, 1976
18, Dave Corzine, DePaul vs. Louisville, RSF, 1978 (2 ot)
18, Wally Szczerbiak, Miami (Ohio) vs. Washington, 1st, 1999

FIELD GOALS ATTEMPTED
42, *Dwight Lamar, La.-Lafayette vs. Louisville, RSF, 1972
40, Austin Carr, Notre Dame vs. Houston, R3d, 1971
36, Oscar Robertson, Cincinnati vs. Arkansas, R3d, 1958
35, Willie Smith, Missouri vs. Michigan, RF, 1976
34, Four tied (most recent: *Dwight Lamar, La.-Lafayette vs. Houston, 1st, 1973)

FIELD-GOAL PERCENTAGE (Minimum 10 FGM)
92.3% (12-13), Dennis Holman, Southern Methodist vs. Cincinnati, R3d, 1966
90.9% (10-11), Akeem Olajuwon, Houston vs. Villanova, RF, 1983
90.9% (10-11), Oliver Miller, Arkansas vs. Murray St., 1st, 1992
87.5% (14-16), Akeem Olajuwon, Houston vs. Wake Forest, RF, 1984
87.5% (14-16), Wayman Tisdale, Oklahoma vs. Illinois St., 2d, 1985

THREE-POINT FIELD GOALS
8, Brad Soucie, Eastern Mich. vs. Pittsburgh, 1st, 1988
8, Dedric Willoughby, Iowa St. vs. UCLA, RSF, 1997 (ot)
8, Rashod Johnson, Western Mich. vs. Clemson, 1st, 1998
7, Seven tied (most recent: Kyle Hill, Eastern Ill. vs. Arizona, 1st, 2001)

THREE-POINT FIELD GOALS ATTEMPTED
22, Jeff Fryer, Loyola Marymount vs. Arkansas, 1st, 1989
19, Phillip Allen, N.C. A&T vs. Arkansas, 1st, 1994
18, Bobby Hurley, Duke vs. California, 2d, 1993
18, Jeff Boschee, Kansas vs. Kentucky, 2d, 1999 (ot)
17, Damin Lopez, Pepperdine vs. Michigan, 1st, 1994
17, Dedric Willoughby, Iowa St. vs. UCLA, RSF, 1997 (ot)

THREE-POINT FIELD-GOAL PERCENTAGE (Minimum 5 3FGM)
100.0% (6-6), Rex Walters, Kansas vs. Ball St., 1st, 1993
87.5% (7-8), William Scott, Kansas St. vs. DePaul, 2d, 1988
87.5% (7-8), Shane Hawkins, Southern Ill. vs. Syracuse, 1st, 1995
85.7% (6-7), Bobby Hurley, Duke vs. Southern Ill., 1st, 1993
83.3% (5-6), Earl Watson, UCLA vs. Maryland, 2d, 2000

FREE THROWS MADE
23, Bob Carney, Bradley vs. Colorado, RSF, 1954
23, Travis Mays, Texas vs. Georgia, 1st, 1990
17, Tyrone Hill, Xavier vs. Kansas St., 1st, 1990
16, Byron Larkin, Xavier vs. Missouri, 1st, 1987
15, Jim Krebs, Southern Methodist vs. St. Louis, R3d, 1957
15, Adrian Dantley, Notre Dame vs. Kansas, 1st, 1975

FREE THROWS ATTEMPTED
27, Travis Mays, Texas vs. Georgia, 1st, 1990
26, Bob Carney, Bradley vs. Colorado, RSF, 1954
22, Wilt Chamberlain, Kansas vs. Oklahoma City, RF, 1957
21, Adrian Dantley, Notre Dame vs. Kansas, 1st, 1975
20, Byron Larkin, Xavier vs. Missouri, 1st, 1987

FREE-THROW PERCENTAGE (Minimum 11 FTM)
100.0% (12-12), Arlen Clark, Oklahoma St. vs. Loyola (Ill.), 1st, 1958
100.0% (12-12), Larry Finch, Memphis vs. Kansas St., RF, 1973
100.0% (12-12), Wesley Cox, Louisville vs. Oral Roberts, 1st, 1974
100.0% (11-11), Bob Hickman, Kansas vs. Texas, RSF, 1960
100.0% (11-11), Les Craft, Kansas St. vs. Northern Ill., 1st, 1982

REBOUNDS
27, Paul Silas, Creighton vs. Oklahoma City, 1st, 1964
27, Elvin Hayes, Houston vs. Loyola (Ill.), 1st, 1968
25, Elvin Hayes, Houston vs. TCU, RF, 1968
24, Five tied (most recent: Sam Lacey, New Mexico St. vs. Drake, RF, 1970)

ASSISTS
16, Earl Watson, UCLA vs. Maryland, 2d, 2000
15, Keith Smart, Indiana vs. Auburn, 2d, 1987
14, Jason Kidd, California vs. Duke, 2d, 1993
14, Mike Lloyd, Syracuse vs. Southern Ill., 1st, 1995
13, Rod Strickland, DePaul vs. Wichita St., 1st, 1988
13, Keith Jennings, East Tenn. St. vs. Iowa, 1st, 1991

BLOCKED SHOTS
9, D'or Fischer, Northwestern St. vs. Winthrop, MW OR, 2001
8, Kelvin Cato, Iowa St. vs. Illinois St., 1st, 1997
7, Tim Perry, Temple vs. Southern U., 1st, 1987
7, Pervis Ellison, Louisville vs. Illinois, RSF, 1989
7, Tim Duncan, Wake Forest vs. Louisville, RSF, 1996
7, Nakiea Miller, Iona vs. Mississippi, 1st, 2001
7, Loren Woods, Arizona vs. Illinois, RF, 2001

STEALS
8, Grant Hill, Duke vs. California, 2d, 1993
8, Duane Clemens, Ball St. vs. UCLA, 1st, 2000
7, Scott Burrell, Connecticut vs. Xavier, 2d, 1991
6, 10 tied (most recent: Brad Miller, Purdue vs. Delaware, 1st, 1998)

Team Records

POINTS
120, Arkansas vs. Loyola Marymount (101), 1st, 1989
119, Houston vs. Notre Dame (106), R3d, 1971
112, Tulsa vs. UCLA (102), 1st, 1994
112, *La.-Lafayette vs. Marshall (101), 1st, 1972
110, Kentucky vs. San Jose St. (72), 1st, 1996
110, Kansas vs. Prairie View (52), 1st, 1998

FEWEST POINTS
38, Valparaiso vs. Michigan St. (65), 1st, 2000
40, Mississippi vs. Temple (62), 1st, 1997
42, Loyola (La.) vs. Oklahoma St. (59), 1st, 1958
43, Temple vs. Kansas (65), 2d, 1986
43, Canisius vs. Utah, 1st, 1996
43, Miami (Ohio) vs. Kentucky (58), RSF, 1999

WINNING MARGIN
58, Kansas (110) vs. Prairie View (52), 1st, 1998
43, Indiana (97) vs. Wright St. (54), 1st, 1993
42, Illinois (96) vs. Northwestern St. (54), 1st, 2001
40, Cincinnati (99) vs. DePaul (59), RSF, 1960
40, Louisville (93) vs. Kansas St. (53), R3d, 1968

POINTS BY LOSING TEAM
106, Notre Dame vs. Houston (119), R3d, 1971
102, UCLA vs. Tulsa (112), 1st, 1994
101, Marshall vs. La.-Lafayette (112), 1st, 1972
101, Loyola Marymount vs. Arkansas (120), 1st, 1989
98, Notre Dame vs. Houston (99), 1st, 1965
98, Houston vs. Kansas St. (107), R3d, 1970

FIELD GOALS
47, Houston vs. Notre Dame, R3d, 1971
47, Kansas St. vs. Houston, R3d, 1970
47, Arkansas vs. Loyola Marymount, 1st, 1989
45, LSU vs. Lamar, 2d, 1981
44, New Mexico St. vs. Rice, 1st, 1970

FIELD GOALS ATTEMPTED
112, Marshall vs. La.-Lafayette, 1st, 1972
102, Notre Dame vs. Houston, R3d, 1971
99, Oral Roberts vs. Louisville, 1st, 1974
98, Arkansas vs. Loyola Marymount, 1st, 1989
94, Four tied (most recent: UCLA vs. Tulsa, 1st, 1994)

FIELD-GOAL PERCENTAGE
68.0% (34-50), Arkansas vs. Wake Forest, 1st, 1977
67.9% (38-56), Syracuse vs. Southern Ill., 1st, 1995
66.1% (41-62), Arkansas vs. Tulsa, RSF, 1994
66.0% (35-53), Oklahoma vs. Illinois St., 2d, 1985
65.5% (38-58), Houston vs. Alcorn St., 1st, 1982
65.5% (36-55), Maryland vs. Creighton, 1st, 1975

LOWEST FIELD-GOAL PERCENTAGE
19.4% (14-72), Creighton vs. Cincinnati, RSF, 1962
23.3% (17-73), Prairie View vs. Kansas, 1st, 1998
25.0% (13-52), Valparaiso vs. Michigan St., 1st, 2000
25.3% (22-87), Arkansas vs. Cincinnati, R3d, 1958
27.0% (20-74), Texas Southern vs. Georgetown, 1st, 1990

THREE-POINT FIELD GOALS
15, Southern Ill. vs. Syracuse, 1st, 1995
14, Duke vs. Southern Ill., 1st, 1993
14, UCLA vs. Maryland, 2d, 2000
13, Arkansas vs. Texas Southern, 1st, 1995
13, Oklahoma vs. Charlotte, 2d, 1999
13, Cal St. Northridge vs. Kansas, 1st, 2001

THREE-POINT FIELD GOALS ATTEMPTED
39, Loyola Marymount vs. Arkansas, 1st, 1989
36, Tulsa vs. Arkansas, RSF, 1995
33, Texas Southern vs. Georgetown, 1st, 1990
33, Arkansas vs. Texas Southern, 1st, 1995
32, St. Bonaventure vs. Kentucky, 1st, 2000
32, Creighton vs. Auburn, 1st, 2000

THREE-POINT FIELD-GOAL PERCENTAGE (Minimum 7 3FGM)
80.0% (8-10), Kansas St. vs. Purdue, RSF, 1988
80.0% (8-10), Maryland vs. Massachusetts, 2d, 1994
76.9% (10-13), Kansas St. vs. DePaul, 2d, 1988

THE EARLY ROUNDS

73.7% (14-19), Duke vs. Southern Ill., 1st, 1993
72.7% (8-11), Duke vs. Indiana, RSF, 1987
72.7% (8-11), Kansas vs. California, RSF, 1993

FREE THROWS MADE
43, Arizona vs. Illinois, RF, 2001
38, Bradley vs. Colorado, RSF, 1954
37, Xavier vs. Kansas St., 1st, 1990
35, Notre Dame vs. Kansas, 1st, 1975
35, Tulsa vs. UCLA, 1st, 1994

FREE THROWS ATTEMPTED
56, Arizona vs. Illinois, RF, 2001
50, Notre Dame vs. Kansas, 1st, 1975
48, Oklahoma City vs. Kansas St., RSF, 1956
48, Texas A&M vs. North Carolina, 2d, 1980
45, Three tied (most recent: Minnesota vs. Clemson, RSF, 1997 [2 ot])

FREE-THROW PERCENTAGE
(Minimum 15 FTM)
95.8% (23-24), Oklahoma St. vs. Loyola (La.), 1st, 1958
95.0% (19-20), Oklahoma St. vs. Louisville, 2d, 1993
94.4% (17-18), Michigan St. vs. Cincinnati, 2d, 1992
94.4% (17-18), Arizona vs. Butler, 2d, 2001
94.1% (16-17), Hawaii vs. Syracuse, 1st, 2001

REBOUNDS
76, Houston vs. TCU, RF, 1968
71, Kansas St. vs. Houston, R3d, 1970
68, Cincinnati vs. Texas Tech, RSF, 1961
68, Marshall vs. La.-Lafayette, 1st, 1972
67, Kansas St. vs. New Mexico St., RSF, 1970

REBOUND MARGIN
35, Kansas (64) vs. Prairie View (29), 1st, 1998
33, Cincinnati (68) vs. Texas Tech (35), RSF, 1961
33, Kansas (56) vs. Syracuse (23), 2d, 2001
30, Louisiana Tech (56) vs. Pittsburgh (26), 1st, 1985
30, Kansas (45) vs. Evansville (15), 1st, 1999

ASSISTS
35, Kentucky vs. San Jose St., 1st, 1996
32, Kansas vs. Howard, 1st, 1992
31, Arkansas vs. Tulsa, RSF, 1994
31, Purdue vs. Delaware, 1st, 1998
30, Four tied (most recent: Kansas vs. Prairie View, 1st, 1998)

BLOCKED SHOTS
13, Louisville vs. Illinois, RSF, 1989
10, Northwestern St. vs. Winthrop, OR, 2001
9, UTEP vs. Cincinnati, RSF, 1992
9, Rhode Island vs. Murray St., 1st, 1998
9, Arizona vs. Eastern Ill., 1st, 2001
9, Arizona vs. Illinois, RF, 2001

STEALS
18, Xavier vs. Kansas, 1st, 1988
18, Louisville vs. Tulsa, 1st, 1996
17, Duke vs. St. John's (N.Y.), RF, 1991
17, Kentucky vs. San Jose St., 1st, 1996
16, Five tied (most recent: two in 1998)

PERSONAL FOULS
39, Kansas vs. Notre Dame, 1st, 1975
36, North Carolina vs. Texas A&M, 2d, 1980
36, Illinois vs. Arizona, RF, 2001
35, DePaul vs. Boston College, 2d, 1982
33, Boston College vs. Houston, RF, 1982
33, Loyola Marymount vs. Arkansas, 1st, 1989

PLAYERS DISQUALIFIED
6, Kansas vs. Notre Dame, 1st, 1975
6, Illinois vs. Arizona, RF, 2001
5, DePaul vs. Boston College, 2d, 1982
4, Seven tied (most recent: Boston College vs. Houston, RF, 1982)

Two-Team Records

POINTS
225, Houston (119) vs. Notre Dame (106), R3d, 1971
221, Arkansas (120) vs. Loyola Marymount (101), 1st, 1989
214, Tulsa (112) vs. UCLA (102), 1st, 1994
213, La.-Lafayette (112) vs. Marshall (101), 1st, 1972
205, Kansas St. (107) vs. Houston (98), R3d, 1970

FEWEST POINTS
93, Utah (48) vs. St. Louis (45), 1st, 2000
97, Illinois St. (49) vs. Alabama (48), 1st, 1984

97, Purdue (49) vs. Wis.-Green Bay (48), 1st, 1995
100, Wichita St. (54) vs. Oklahoma St. (46), RF, 1965
100, Michigan St. (54) vs. Oklahoma (46), RSF, 1999

FIELD GOALS
86, Kansas St. (47) vs. Houston (39), R3d, 1970
86, Houston (47) vs. Notre Dame (39), R3d, 1971
84, La.-Lafayette (42) vs. Marshall (42), 1st, 1972
80, Notre Dame (40) vs. TCU (40), 1st, 1971
80, LSU (41) vs. Alcorn St. (39), 2d, 1980

FIELD GOALS ATTEMPTED
192, Marshall (112) vs. La.-Lafayette (80), 1st, 1972
186, Notre Dame (102) vs. Houston (84), R3d, 1971
184, Kansas St. (94) vs. Houston (90), R3d, 1970
180, TCU (91) vs. Houston (89), RF, 1968
179, Loyola Marymount (98) vs. Arkansas (81), 1st, 1989

THREE-POINT FIELD GOALS
23, Kansas (12) vs. Kentucky (11), 2d, 1999 (ot)
23, Creighton (12) vs. Auburn (11), 1st, 2000
22, Southern Ill. (15) vs. Syracuse (7), 1st, 1995
22, Arkansas (13) vs. Texas Southern (9), 1st, 1995
22, Arkansas (12) vs. Memphis (10), RSF, 1995
22, Cal St. Northridge (13) vs. Kansas (9), 1st, 2001

THREE-POINT FIELD GOALS ATTEMPTED
59, N.C. A&T (31) vs. Arkansas (28), 1st, 1994
58, Arkansas (33) vs. Texas Southern (25), 1st, 1995
57, Charlotte (30) vs. Illinois (27), 2d, 2001
55, Kansas (31) vs. Kentucky (24), 2d, 1999 (ot)
54, Temple (31) vs. Minnesota (23), 2d, 1997

FREE THROWS
68, Oklahoma City (35) vs. Kansas St. (33), RSF, 1956
63, Arizona (43) vs. Illinois (20), RF, 2001
59, Minnesota (34) vs. Clemson (25), RSF, 1997 (2 ot)
53, Kansas St. (27) vs. Cincinnati (26), RSF, 1958 (ot)
53, Xavier (37) vs. Kansas St. (16), 1st, 1990
53, Kansas St. (27) vs. Houston (26), RSF, 1961

FREE THROWS ATTEMPTED
92, Oklahoma City (48) vs. Kansas St. (44), RSF, 1956
81, Arizona (56) vs. Illinois (25), RF, 2001
80, Oklahoma City (40) vs. Texas (40), R3d, 1963
80, Minnesota (45) vs. Clemson (35), RSF, 1997 (2 ot)
78, Southern Methodist (46) vs. Houston (32), RSF, 1956
78, Kansas St. (40) vs. Cincinnati (38), RSF, 1958 (ot)

REBOUNDS
134, Marshall (68) vs. *La.-Lafayette (66), 1st, 1972
131, Houston (76) vs. TCU (55), RF, 1968
126, Drake (66) vs. Notre Dame (60), RSF, 1971 (ot)
124, Kansas St. (71) vs. Houston (53), R3d, 1970
121, Notre Dame (66) vs. Houston (55), R3d, 1971

ASSISTS
51, Arkansas (31) vs. Tulsa (20), RSF, 1994
51, Kentucky (35) vs. San Jose St. (16), 1st, 1996
50, Purdue (31) vs. Delaware (19), 1st, 1998
47, Georgia Tech (27) vs. Southern California (20), 2d, 1992
46, Kansas (32) vs. Howard (14), 1st, 1992
46, Syracuse (30) vs. Southern Ill. (16), 1st, 1995

BLOCKED SHOTS
15, Louisville (13) vs. Illinois (2), RSF, 1989
15, Georgia (8) vs. Texas (7), 1st, 1990
15, Iona (8) vs. Mississippi (7), 1st, 2001
14, Arizona (9) vs. Eastern Ill. (5), 1st, 2001
13, Six tied (most recent: Northwestern St. [10] vs. Winthrop [3], OR, 2001)

STEALS
28, N.C. A&T (16) vs. Arkansas (12), 1st, 1994
28, Purdue (16) vs. Delaware (12), 1st, 1998
28, TCU (16) vs. Florida St. (12), 1st, 1998
26, Duke (17) vs. St. John's (N.Y.) (9), RF, 1991
25, East Tenn. St. (14) vs. Iowa (11), 1st, 1991
25, Louisville (18) vs. Tulsa (7), 1st, 1996

PERSONAL FOULS
59, Loyola Marymount (33) vs. Arkansas (26), 1st, 1989
59, Illinois (36) vs. Arizona (23), RF 2001
57, Texas (30) vs. Oklahoma City (27), R3d, 1963
56, North Carolina (36) vs. Texas A&M (20), 2d, 1980
56, Clemson (32) vs. Minnesota (24), RSF, 1997 (2 ot)

West Region Game Records

A regional final game is indicated by (RF), a regional semifinal game by (RSF), a regional third-place game by (R3d), second-round game by (2d), first-round game by (1st), opening-round game by (OR) and record later vacated by (*).

Individual Records

POINTS
45, Bob Houbregs, Washington vs. Seattle, RSF, 1953
45, Bo Kimble, Loyola Marymount vs. New Mexico St., 1st, 1990
44, Clyde Lovellette, Kansas vs. St. Louis, RF, 1952
42, John O'Brien, Seattle vs. Idaho St., 1st, 1953
42, Bo Kimble, Loyola Marymount vs. UNLV, RF, 1990

FIELD GOALS
20, Bob Houbregs, Washington vs. Seattle, RSF, 1953
17, Seven tied (most recent: Bo Kimble, Loyola Marymount vs. New Mexico St., 1st, 1990)

FIELD GOALS ATTEMPTED
35, Bob Houbregs, Washington vs. Seattle, RSF, 1953
35, Marv Roberts, Utah St. vs. UCLA, RF, 1970
35, Bo Kimble, Loyola Marymount vs. New Mexico St., 1st, 1990
32, Chris Jackson, LSU vs. UTEP, 1st, 1989
32, Bo Kimble, Loyola Marymount vs. UNLV, RF, 1990

FIELD-GOAL PERCENTAGE
(Minimum 10 FGM)
92.3% (12-13), Quadre Lollis, Montana St. vs. Syracuse, 1st, 1996
88.2% (15-17), Dennis Awtrey, Santa Clara vs. Long Beach St., R3d, 1970
85.7% (12-14), Brad Daugherty, North Carolina vs. Utah, 1st, 1986
84.6% (11-13), Randy Reed, Kansas St. vs. San Francisco, 1st, 1981
84.6% (11-13), Kevin Gamble, Iowa vs. Oklahoma, RSF, 1987 (ot)

THREE-POINT FIELD GOALS
11, Jeff Fryer, Loyola Marymount vs. Michigan, 2d, 1990
9, Johnny Miller, Temple vs. Cincinnati, 1st, 1995
8, Gerald Paddio, UNLV vs. Iowa, 2d, 1988
8, Bo Kimble, Loyola Marymount vs. UNLV, RF, 1990
8, Bryce Drew, Valparaiso vs. Boston College, 1st, 1997

THREE-POINT FIELD GOALS ATTEMPTED
19, Gerald Paddio, UNLV vs. Iowa, 2d, 1988
17, Johnny Miller, Temple vs. Cincinnati, 1st, 1995
16, Jeff Fryer, Loyola Marymount vs. UNLV, RF, 1990
15, Four tied (most recent: two in 1995)

THREE-POINT FIELD-GOAL PERCENTAGE
(Minimum 5 3FGM)
100.0% (5-5), Mitch Richmond, Kansas St. vs. Georgia, 1st, 1987 (ot)
100.0% (5-5), Kwame Evans, George Washington vs. New Mexico, 1st, 1993
100.0% (5-5), Dwayne Morton, Louisville vs. Minnesota, 2d, 1994
83.3% (5-6), Paul O'Liney, Missouri vs. UCLA, 2d, 1995
83.3% (5-6), Mike Bibby, Arizona vs. Maryland, RSF, 1998

FREE THROWS MADE
18, John O'Brien, Seattle vs. Wyoming, R3d, 1953
17, Steve Nash, Santa Clara vs. Maryland, 1st, 1996
16, Conrad Wells, Idaho St. vs. Brigham Young, R3d, 1957
16, Fennis Dembo, Wyoming vs. UCLA, 2d, 1987
16, B.J. Armstrong, Iowa vs. Florida St., 1st, 1988

FREE THROWS ATTEMPTED
22, John O'Brien, Seattle vs. Wyoming, R3d, 1953
20, B.J. Armstrong, Iowa vs. Florida St., 1st, 1988
19, Roosevelt Chapman, Dayton vs. Oklahoma, 2d, 1984
19, Maurio Hanson, Chattanooga vs. Connecticut, 1st, 1995
18, Four tied (most recent: Steve Nash, Santa Clara vs. Maryland, 1st, 1996)

WEST REGION GAME RECORDS—INDIVIDUAL

FREE-THROW PERCENTAGE
(Minimum 12 FTM)
100.0% (16-16), Fennis Dembo, Wyoming vs. UCLA, 2d, 1987
100.0% (12-12), Willie Worsley, UTEP vs. Seattle, 1st, 1967
100.0% (12-12), Ken Owens, Idaho vs. Iowa, 2d, 1982 (ot)
100.0% (12-12), Wayman Tisdale, Oklahoma vs. Dayton, 2d, 1984
100.0% (12-12), Michael Jackson, Georgetown vs. UNLV, RSF, 1984
100.0% (12-12), John Morton, Seton Hall vs. UTEP, 1st, 1988
100.0% (12-12), Shaquille O'Neal, LSU vs. Indiana, 2d, 1992
100.0% (12-12) Michael Doleac, Utah vs. Stanford, RSF, 1997

REBOUNDS
28, Elvin Hayes, Houston vs. Pacific (Cal.), R3d, 1966
23, Keith Swagerty, Pacific (Cal.) vs. Houston, R3d, 1966
23, Lew Alcindor, UCLA vs. New Mexico St., RSF, 1968
23, Kresimir Cosic, Brigham Young vs. UCLA, RSF, 1971
22, James Ware, Oklahoma City vs. San Francisco, RSF, 1965
22, Tim Duncan, Wake Forest vs. St. Mary's (Cal.), 1st, 1997

ASSISTS
14, Carl Wright, Southern Methodist vs. Miami (Ohio), 1st, 1984
13, Mark Wade, UNLV vs. Kansas St., 2d, 1987
13, James Sanders, Alabama vs. Arizona, 2d, 1990
13, Anderson Hunt, UNLV vs. Loyola Marymount, RF, 1990
13, Reggie Geary, Arizona vs. Iowa, 2d, 1996
13, Andre Miller, Utah vs. Arizona, RF, 1998

BLOCKED SHOTS
11, Shaquille O'Neal, LSU vs. Brigham Young, 1st, 1992
10, Shawn Bradley, Brigham Young vs. Virginia, 1st, 1991
8, Erick Dampier, Mississippi St. vs. Utah, 2d, 1995
8, Tarvis Williams, Hampton vs. Georgetown, 2d, 2001
7, Anthony Cook, Arizona vs. UTEP, 1st, 1987 (ot)
7, Joe Smith, Maryland vs. Texas, 2d, 1995
7, Terrell Bell, Georgia vs. Purdue, 2d, 1996

STEALS
7, Reggie Miller, UCLA vs. Wyoming, 2d, 1987
7, Ricky Grace, Oklahoma vs. Iowa, RSF, 1987 (ot)
7, Kawika Akina, Northern Ariz. vs. Cincinnati, 1st, 1998
6, Nine tied (most recent: Mike Kelley, Wisconsin vs. Fresno St., 1st, 2000)

Team Records

POINTS
149, Loyola Marymount vs. Michigan (115), 2d, 1990
131, UNLV vs. Loyola Marymount (101), RF, 1990
123, North Carolina vs. Loyola Marymount (97), 2d, 1988
121, UNLV vs. San Francisco (95), 1st, 1977
119, Loyola Marymount vs. Wyoming (115), 1st, 1988

FEWEST POINTS
29, Baylor vs. Oklahoma St. (44), RF, 1946
32, Colorado vs. Southern California (38), RF, 1940
35, Missouri vs. Utah (45), RF, 1944
36, Southern Methodist vs. Georgetown (37), RSF, 1984
37, Utah vs. Oklahoma St. (62), RF, 1945
37, Georgetown vs. Southern Methodist (36), RSF, 1984

WINNING MARGIN
49, UCLA (109) vs. Wyoming, (60), RSF, 1967
40, Arizona (90) vs. Cornell (50), 1st, 1988
39, Indiana (94) vs. Eastern Ill. (55), 1st, 1992
39, Arizona (90) vs. Valparaiso (51), 1st, 1996
39, Arizona (99) vs. Nicholls St. (60), 1st, 1998

POINTS BY LOSING TEAM
115, Wyoming vs. Loyola Marymount (119), 1st, 1988
115, Michigan vs. Loyola Marymount (149), 2d, 1990
109, UNLV vs. Arizona (114), RSF, 1976 (ot)

102, Brigham Young vs. Oklahoma City (112), R3d, 1965
101, Loyola Marymount vs. UNLV (131), RF, 1990

FIELD GOALS
51, UCLA vs. Dayton, RSF, 1974 (3 ot)
51, UNLV vs. Loyola Marymount, RF, 1990
49, North Carolina vs. Loyola Marymount, 2d, 1988
49, UNLV vs. San Francisco, 1st, 1977
49, Loyola Marymount vs. Michigan, 2d, 1990

FIELD GOALS ATTEMPTED
103, Loyola Marymount vs. North Carolina, 2d, 1988
100, Houston vs. Pacific (Cal.), R3d, 1966
99, Brigham Young vs. Oklahoma City, R3d, 1965
97, UCLA vs. Dayton, RSF, 1974 (3 ot)
96, UNLV vs. Arizona, RSF, 1976 (ot)

FIELD-GOAL PERCENTAGE
79.0% (49-62), North Carolina vs. Loyola Marymount, 2d, 1988
74.4% (29-39), Georgetown vs. Oregon St., RF, 1982
73.2% (30-41), North Carolina St. vs. UTEP, 2d, 1985
70.5% (31-44), Washington vs. Duke, 2d, 1984
68.4% (39-57), San Francisco vs. Brigham Young, 2d, 1979

LOWEST FIELD-GOAL PERCENTAGE
20.6% (13-63), Arkansas vs. Oregon St., RSF, 1949
25.0% (16-64), Santa Clara vs. Kansas, 2d, 1996
26.1% (24-92), UCLA vs. Brigham Young, R3d, 1950
26.2% (17-65), Texas A&M vs. Washington, 1st, 1951
26.3% (15-57), Idaho St. vs. Brigham Young, R3d, 1957
26.3% (15-57), New Mexico vs. Connecticut, 2d, 1999

THREE-POINT FIELD GOALS
21, Loyola Marymount vs. Michigan, 2d, 1990
17, Loyola Marymount vs. UNLV, RF, 1990
15, Wisconsin vs. Missouri, 2d, 1994
15, Cincinnati vs. Connecticut, 2d, 1995
15, Arkansas vs. Siena, 1st, 1999

THREE-POINT FIELD GOALS ATTEMPTED
43, St. Joseph's vs. Boston College, 2d, 1997 (ot)
41, Loyola Marymount vs. UNLV, RF, 1990
40, Loyola Marymount vs. Michigan, 2d, 1990
39, Loyola Marymount vs. North Carolina, 2d, 1988
38, Chattanooga vs. Connecticut, 1st, 1995

THREE-POINT FIELD-GOAL PERCENTAGE
(Minimum 7 3FGM)
88.9% (8-9), Kansas St. vs. Georgia, 1st, 1987 (ot)
72.7% (8-11), Alabama vs. Colorado St., 1st, 1990
70.0% (7-10), Indiana vs. UTEP, 2d, 1989
69.2% (9-13), Maryland vs. Stanford, RF, 2001
63.6% (7-11), Indiana vs. Eastern Ill., 1st, 1992

FREE THROWS MADE
41, Utah vs. Santa Clara, R3d, 1960
39, Seattle vs. Utah, R3d, 1955
39, UTEP vs. Tulsa, 1st, 1985
36, UCLA vs. Louisville, 2d, 1992
34, Santa Clara vs. Maryland, 1st, 1996

FREE THROWS ATTEMPTED
55, UTEP vs. Tulsa, 1st, 1985
52, Seattle vs. UCLA, R3d, 1956
52, Weber St. vs. Hawaii, 1st, 1972
48, Utah vs. Santa Clara, R3d, 1960
46, Three tied (most recent: Utah vs. Michigan St., 2d, 1991 [2 ot])

FREE-THROW PERCENTAGE
(Minimum 15 FTM)
94.7% (18-19), Seattle vs. California, RF, 1958 (ot)
94.7% (18-19), UNLV vs. Kansas St., 2d, 1987
94.7% (18-19), Utah vs. Charlotte, 2d, 1997
91.7% (22-24), Arizona vs. Cornell, 1st, 1988
91.3% (21-23), DePaul vs. Air Force, 1st, 1960

REBOUNDS
76, UCLA vs. Weber St., RSF, 1972
72, UCLA vs. Seattle, R3d, 1956
72, Seattle vs. Utah St., R3d, 1964
70, Arizona St. vs. Southern California, RSF, 1961
68, Utah vs. Southern California, 1st, 1960

REBOUND MARGIN
29, Utah (59) vs. Loyola Marymount (30), RSF, 1961
28, Seattle (72) vs. Utah St. (44), R3d, 1964
27, New Mexico St. (62) vs. Brigham Young (35), 1st, 1969

24, Georgetown (51) vs Hampton (27), 2d, 2001
23, UNLV (57) vs. Boise St. (34), 1st, 1976
23, Arizona St. (66) vs. Loyola Marymount (43), 1st, 1980

ASSISTS
36, North Carolina vs. Loyola Marymount, 2d, 1988
35, UNLV vs. Loyola Marymount, RF, 1990
33, Loyola Marymount vs. Michigan, 2d, 1990
32, Kansas vs. South Carolina St., 1st, 1996
30, Michigan vs. Florida, 2d, 1988

BLOCKED SHOTS
13, Brigham Young vs. Virginia, 1st, 1991
12, Clemson vs. St. Mary's (Cal.), 1st, 1989
12, LSU vs. Brigham Young, 1st, 1992
11, Arizona vs. UTEP, 1st, 1987 (ot)
11, Syracuse vs. Wis.-Green Bay, 2d, 1994
11, Kentucky vs. Montana, 1st, 1997

STEALS
17, Seton Hall vs. Pepperdine, 1st, 1991
16, Loyola Marymount vs. Wyoming, 1st, 1988
15, Temple vs. Missouri, 1st, 1993
15, Florida vs. Weber St., 2d, 1999
14, Seven tied (most recent: Arizona vs. Nicholls St., 1st, 1998)

PERSONAL FOULS
36, UCLA vs. Seattle, R3d, 1956
35, Hawaii vs. Weber St., 1st, 1972
34, UNLV vs. Arizona, RSF, 1976 (ot)
34, Tulsa vs. UTEP, 1st, 1985
34, UTEP vs. Arizona, 1st, 1987 (ot)

PLAYERS DISQUALIFIED
5, Wyoming vs. Loyola Marymount, 1st, 1988
4, Five tied (most recent: Florida St. vs. Iowa, 1st, 1988)

Two-Team Records

POINTS
264, Loyola Marymount (149) vs. Michigan (115), 2d, 1990
234, Loyola Marymount (119) vs. Wyoming (115), 1st, 1988
232, UNLV (131) vs. Loyola Marymount (101), RF, 1990
223, Arizona (114) vs. UNLV (109), RSF, 1976 (ot)
220, North Carolina (123) vs. Loyola Marymount (97), 2d, 1988

FEWEST POINTS
70, Southern California (38) vs. Colorado (32), RF, 1940
73, Oklahoma St. (44) vs. Baylor (29), RF, 1946
73, Georgetown (37) vs. Southern Methodist (36), 2d, 1984

Carl Wright of Southern Methodist dished out 14 assists against Miami (Ohio) in a 1984 first-round game to set a West region record.

THE EARLY ROUNDS

79, Oklahoma St. (40) vs. Wyoming (39), RF, 1949
80, Utah (45) vs. Missouri (35), RF, 1944
FIELD GOALS
94, Loyola Marymount (49) vs. Michigan (45), 2d, 1990
91, UCLA (51) vs. Dayton (40), RSF, 1974 (3 ot)
89, Wyoming (47) vs. Loyola Marymount (42), 1st, 1988
86, Arizona (44) vs. UNLV (42), RSF, 1976
86, UNLV (51) vs. Loyola Marymount (35), RF, 1990
FIELD GOALS ATTEMPTED
194, Houston (100) vs. Pacific (Cal.) (94), R3d, 1966
183, Brigham Young (99) vs Oklahoma City (84), R3d, 1965
180, Loyola Marymount (94) vs. UNLV (86), RF, 1990
178, UCLA (100) vs. Seattle (78), R3d, 1956
174, UCLA (94) vs. Brigham Young (80), RSF, 1965
174, Loyola Marymount (89) vs. Michigan (85), 2d, 1990
THREE-POINT FIELD GOALS
27, Wisconsin (15) vs. Missouri (12), 2d, 1994
26, Temple (14) vs. Cincinnati (12), 1st, 1995
25, Loyola Marymount (21) vs. Michigan (4), 2d, 1990
24, Loyola Marymount (17) vs. UNLV (7), RF, 1990
23, Weber St. (14) vs. North Carolina (9), 1st, 1999
THREE-POINT FIELD GOALS ATTEMPTED
62, St. Joseph's (43) vs. Boston College (19), 2d, 1997 (ot)
59, Loyola Marymount (41) vs. UNLV (18), RF, 1990
56, Wisconsin (37) vs. Missouri (19), 2d, 1994

55, Oregon (33) vs. Texas (22), 1st, 1995
55, Arkansas (37) vs. Iowa (18), 2d, 1999
FREE THROWS
64, Bradley (38) vs. Colorado (26), RSF, 1954
63, Seattle (39) vs. Utah (24), R3d, 1955
58, Utah, (41) vs. Santa Clara (17), R3d, 1960
56, UTEP (39) vs. Tulsa (17), 1st, 1985
54, Three tied (most recent: Missouri [29] vs. Wisconsin [25], 2d, 1994)
FREE THROWS ATTEMPTED
92, Seattle (52) vs. UCLA (40), R3d, 1956
88, Seattle (51) vs. Utah (37), R3d, 1955
84, Seattle (45) vs. UCLA (39), RSF, 1964
83, Bradley (44) vs. Colorado (39), RSF, 1954
80, Seattle (42) vs. Wyoming (38), R3d, 1953
REBOUNDS
132, Pacific (Cal.) (67) vs. Houston (65), R3d, 1966
130, UCLA (76) vs. Weber St. (54), RSF, 1972
128, UCLA (72) vs. Seattle (56), R3d, 1956
124, UCLA (62) vs. Seattle (62), RSF, 1964
122, UCLA (66) vs. Brigham Young (56), RSF, 1965
ASSISTS
58, UNLV (35) vs. Loyola Marymount (23), RF, 1990
55, Michigan (30) vs. Florida (25), 2d, 1988
54, Loyola Marymount (33) vs. Michigan (21), 2d, 1990
53, North Carolina (36) vs. Loyola Marymount (17), 2d, 1988
52, Wyoming (29) vs. Loyola Marymount (23), 1st, 1988

BLOCKED SHOTS
14, UNLV (9) vs. Arizona (5), RSF, 1989
14, Brigham Young (13) vs. Virginia (1), 1st, 1991
14, UNLV (8) vs. Georgetown (6), 2d, 1991
14, Arizona (8) vs. Maryland (6), RSF, 1998
14, Connecticut (10) vs. Tex.-San Antonio (4), 1st, 1999
14, Hampton (9) vs. Georgetown (15), 2d, 2001
14, Maryland (7) vs. Georgetown (7), RSF, 2001
STEALS
28, Florida (15) vs. Weber St. (13), 2d, 1999
27, Loyola Marymount (14) vs. UNLV (13), RF, 1990
25, Arizona (14) vs. Nicholls St. (11), 1st, 1998
25, Arkansas (13) vs. Iowa (12), 2d, 1999
24, Wyoming (16) vs. Loyola Marymount (8), 1st, 1988
24, Seton Hall (17) vs. Pepperdine (7), 1st, 1991
PERSONAL FOULS
63, UNLV (34) vs. Arizona (29), RSF, 1976
61, Colorado (34) vs. Bradley (27), RSF, 1954
60, UCLA (36) vs. Seattle (24), R3d, 1956
60, Seattle (31) vs. UCLA (29), RSF, 1964
58, Tulsa (34) vs. UTEP (24), 1st, 1985

All-East Regional Teams

Most outstanding player is indicated by (#) and record later vacated by (*).

1950
Norman Mager, CCNY
Ed Roman, CCNY
Dick Dickey, North Carolina St.
Sam Ranzino, North Carolina St.
Dick Schnittker, Ohio St.
1951
Not available
1952
Cliff Hagan, Kentucky
Jesse Arnelle, Penn St.
Ron MacGilvray, St. John's (N.Y.)
Jack McMahon, St. John's (N.Y.)
Bob Zawoluk, St. John's (N.Y.)
1953
Earle Markey, Holy Cross
Togo Palazzi, Holy Cross
Howie Landa, Lebanon Valley
Bob Pettit, LSU
Dickie Hemric, Wake Forest
1954
#Tom Gola, La Salle
Lee Morton, Cornell
Don Lange, Navy
Vic Molodet, North Carolina St.
Mel Thompson, North Carolina St.
1955
Jim McCarthy, Canisius
Tom Gola, La Salle
Harold Haabestad, Princeton
John Devine, Villanova
Robert Schafer, Villanova
1956
Bob Kelly, Canisius
Hank Nowak, Canisius
Gordon Ruddy, Connecticut
Hal Lear, Temple
Guy Rodgers, Temple

1957
Hank Nowak, Canisius
Stu Murray, Lafayette
Pete Brennan, North Carolina
Tommy Kearns, North Carolina
Lennie Rosenbluth, North Carolina
Gary Clark, Syracuse
1958
Rudy LaRusso, Dartmouth
Nick Davis, Maryland
Bill Kennedy, Temple
Jay Norman, Temple
Guy Rodgers, Temple
1959
Bob Cumings, Boston U.
Jay Metzler, Navy
Jack Egan, St. Joseph's
Joe Spratt, St. Joseph's
Jerry West, West Virginia
1960
Russ Cunningham, New York U.
Tom Sanders, New York U.
Joe Gallo, St. Joseph's
Lee Patrone, West Virginia
Jerry West, West Virginia
1961
Peter Campbell, Princeton
Tom Stith, St. Bonaventure
*Jack Egan, St. Joseph's
*Jim Lynam, St. Joseph's
Len Chappell, Wake Forest
1962
#Len Chappell, Wake Forest
Tom Wynne, St. Joseph's
Wally Jones, Villanova
Hubie White, Villanova
Billy Packer, Wake Forest
1963
Art Heyman, Duke
Jeff Mullins, Duke
Barry Kramer, New York U.
Tom Wynne, St. Joseph's
Rod Thorn, West Virginia

1964
Thomas Kimball, Connecticut
Jeff Mullins, Duke
Steve Vacendak, Duke
Bill Bradley, Princeton
Wally Jones, Villanova
1965
Larry Lakins, North Carolina St.
Bill Bradley, Princeton
Robinson Brown, Princeton
Jim Walker, Providence
Cliff Anderson, St. Joseph's
1966
#Bob Verga, Duke
Jack Marin, Duke
Steve Vacendak, Duke
Matt Guokas, St. Joseph's
Dave Bing, Syracuse
1967
#Bob Lewis, North Carolina
Terry Driscoll, Boston College
Larry Miller, North Carolina
Chris Thomforde, Princeton
Rudy Bogad, St. John's (N.Y.)
1968
#Rusty Clark, North Carolina
Jim McMillian, Columbia
Mike Maloy, Davidson
Larry Miller, North Carolina
Charlie Scott, North Carolina
1969
#Charlie Scott, North Carolina
Doug Cook, Davidson
Mike Maloy, Davidson
Jarrett Durham, Duquesne
Bill Bunting, North Carolina
1970
#Bob Lanier, St. Bonaventure
Calvin Murphy, Niagara
Vann Williford, North Carolina St.
Matt Gantt, St. Bonaventure
Howard Porter, Villanova
1971
*#Howard Porter, Villanova
Charley Yelverton, Fordham

ALL-EAST REGIONAL TEAMS

Tom Riker, South Carolina
*Chris Ford, Villanova
*Hank Siemiontkowski, Villanova

1972
#Dennis Wuycik, North Carolina
George Karl, North Carolina
Bob McAdoo, North Carolina
Kevin Joyce, South Carolina
Hank Siemiontkowski, Villanova

1973
#Ernie DiGregorio, Providence
Tom McMillen, Maryland
Marvin Barnes, Providence
Kevin Stacom, Providence
Dennis Duval, Syracuse

1974
#Tom Burleson, North Carolina St.
#David Thompson, North Carolina St.
Bruce Grimm, Furman
Monte Towe, North Carolina St.
Bill Knight, Pittsburgh

1975
#Chuckie Williams, Kansas St.
Brad Hoffman, North Carolina
Mitch Kupchak, North Carolina
Rudy Hackett, Syracuse
Jim Lee, Syracuse

1976
#Ed Jordan, Rutgers
Tony Hanson, Connecticut
Al Weston, Connecticut
Mike Dabney, Rutgers
Ron Carter, VMI
Will Bynum, VMI

1977
#John Kuester, North Carolina
Jack Givens, Kentucky
Walter Davis, North Carolina
Toby Knight, Notre Dame
Ron Carter, VMI

1978
#Jim Spanarkel, Duke
Eugene Banks, Duke
Mike Gminski, Duke
Bobby Willis, Pennsylvania
Keith Herron, Villanova

1979
Tony Price, Pennsylvania
Tim Smith, Pennsylvania
Reggie Carter, St. John's (N.Y.)
Wayne McKoy, St. John's (N.Y.)
Ron Plair, St. John's (N.Y.)

1980
#Eric Floyd, Georgetown
Vince Brookins, Iowa
John Duren, Georgetown
Craig Shelton, Georgetown
Louis Orr, Syracuse

1981
#Jeff Lamp, Virginia
Danny Ainge, Brigham Young
Orlando Woolridge, Notre Dame
Lee Raker, Virginia
Ralph Sampson, Virginia

1982
#James Worthy, North Carolina
Jimmy Black, North Carolina
Sam Perkins, North Carolina
Ed Pinckney, Villanova
John Pinone, Villanova

1983
#James Banks, Georgia
Terry Fair, Georgia
Vern Fleming, Georgia
Michael Jordan, North Carolina
Chris Mullin, St. John's (N.Y.)

1984
#Jim Miller, Virginia
Steve Alford, Indiana
Uwe Blab, Indiana
Sam Perkins, North Carolina
Olden Polynice, Virginia

1985
#Patrick Ewing, Georgetown
David Wingate, Georgetown
Bruce Dalrymple, Georgia Tech
Mark Price, Georgia Tech
John Salley, Georgia Tech
Doug Altenberger, Illinois

1986
#Johnny Dawkins, Duke
Ken McFadden, Cleveland St.
Mark Alarie, Duke
David Robinson, Navy
Kylor Whitaker, Navy

1987
#Rony Seikaly, Syracuse
J.R. Reid, North Carolina
David Rivers, Notre Dame
Derrick Coleman, Syracuse
Sherman Douglas, Syracuse

1988
#Danny Ferry, Duke
Billy King, Duke
Kevin Strickland, Duke
Carlton Owens, Rhode Island
Tim Perry, Temple

1989
#Danny Ferry, Duke
Phil Henderson, Duke
Christian Laettner, Duke
Alonzo Mourning, Georgetown
Charles Smith, Georgetown

1990
#Christian Laettner, Duke
Alaa Abdelnaby, Duke
Phil Henderson, Duke
Tate George, Connecticut
Chris Smith, Connecticut

1991
#Mark Mason, Temple
Carl Thomas, Eastern Mich.
Hubert Davis, North Carolina
Rick Fox, North Carolina
Mik Kilgore, Temple

1992
#Christian Laettner, Duke
Bobby Hurley, Duke
Jamal Mashburn, Kentucky
Sean Woods, Kentucky
Gordon Winchester, Seton Hall

1993
#George Lynch, North Carolina
Erik Martin, Cincinnati
Nick Van Exel, Cincinnati
Eric Montross, North Carolina
Donald Williams, North Carolina

1994
#Craig Brown, Florida
Bill Curley, Boston College
Howard Eisley, Boston College
Dan Cross, Florida
Andrew DeClercq, Florida

1995
#Bryant Reeves, Oklahoma St.
Derek Kellogg, Massachusetts
Scott Pierce, Oklahoma St.
Randy Rutherford, Oklahoma St.
Tim Duncan, Wake Forest

1996
#Marcus Camby, Massachusetts
Allen Iverson, Georgetown
Donta Bright, Massachusetts
Carmelo Travieso, Massachusetts
Jason Sasser, Texas Tech

1997
#Shammond Williams, North Carolina
Alex Sanders, Louisville
Vince Carter, North Carolina
Ed Cota, North Carolina
Antawn Jamison, North Carolina

1998
#Antawn Jamison, North Carolina
Khalid El-Amin, Connecticut
Richard Hamilton, Connecticut
Vince Carter, North Carolina
Ed Cota, North Carolina
Shammond Williams, North Carolina

1999
#Trajan Langdon, Duke
William Avery, Duke
Elton Brand, Duke
Mark Karcher, Temple
Pepe Sanchez, Temple

2000
#Mike Miller, Florida
Brett Nelson, Florida
Udonis Haslem, Florida
Fredrik Jonzen, Oklahoma St.
Shane Battier, Duke

2001
#Jason Williams, Duke
Shane Battier, Duke
David Bluthenthal, Southern California
Sam Clancy, Southern California
Brian Scalabrine, Southern California

All-South/Southeast/Mideast Regional Teams

Most outstanding player is indicated by (#) and record later vacated by (*).

1953
Ron Feiereisel, DePaul
Bob Leonard, Indiana
Don Schlundt, Indiana
Rich Rosenthal, Notre Dame
Ernest Beck, Pennsylvania

1954
Bob Leonard, Indiana
Bob Pettit, LSU
Rich Rosenthal, Notre Dame
Jack Stephens, Notre Dame
Jesse Arnelle, Penn St.

1955
Not Available

1956
Carl Cain, Iowa
Milton Scheuerman, Iowa
Bill Seaberg, Iowa
Jerry Bird, Kentucky
Bob Burrow, Kentucky
Dan Swartz, Morehead St.

1957
Gerry Calvert, Kentucky
Johnny Cox, Kentucky
John Green, Michigan St.
Jack Quiggle, Michigan St.
John Riser, Pittsburgh

1958
Archie Dees, Indiana
Johnny Cox, Kentucky
Vern Hatton, Kentucky
Wayne Embry, Miami (Ohio)
Tom Hawkins, Notre Dame

1959
Bernie Coffman, Kentucky
Don Goldstein, Louisville
Don Kojis, Marquette
Bob Anderegg, Michigan St.
John Green, Michigan St.

THE EARLY ROUNDS

ALL-SOUTH/SOUTHEAST/MIDEAST REGIONAL TEAMS

1960
Roger Kaiser, Georgia Tech
Howard Jolliff, Ohio
John Havlicek, Ohio St.
Jerry Lucas, Ohio St.
Al Ellison, Western Ky.

1961
Bill Lickert, Kentucky
John Turner, Louisville
John Havlicek, Ohio St.
Jerry Lucas, Ohio St.
Larry Siegfried, Ohio St.

1962
#Jerry Lucas, Ohio St.
Cotton Nash, Kentucky
Larry Pursiful, Kentucky
John Havlicek, Ohio St.
Bobby Rascoe, Western Ky.

1963
#Jerry Harkness, Loyola (Ill.)
Howard Komives, Bowling Green
Nate Thurmond, Bowling Green
Dave Downey, Illinois
Leland Mitchell, Mississippi St.

1964
Les Hunter, Loyola (Ill.)
Bill Buntin, Michigan
Cazzie Russell, Michigan
Jerry Jackson, Ohio
Don Hilt, Ohio St.

1965
#Clyde Lee, Vanderbilt
Errol Palmer, DePaul
Bill Buntin, Michigan
Cazzie Russell, Michigan
Keith Thomas, Vanderbilt

1966
#Pat Riley, Kentucky
Henry Finkel, Dayton
Louie Dampier, Kentucky
Cazzie Russell, Michigan
Wayne Chapman, Western Ky.

1967
#Don May, Dayton
Bob Hooper, Dayton
Vernon Payne, Indiana
Ron Widby, Tennessee
Glen Combs, Virginia Tech

1968
#Dave Sorenson, Ohio St.
Mike Casey, Kentucky
Dan Issel, Kentucky
Brad Luchini, Marquette
Bill Hosket, Ohio St.

1969
#Rick Mount, Purdue
Dan Issel, Kentucky
Dean Meminger, Marquette
George Thompson, Marquette
Bill Keller, Purdue

1970
#Austin Carr, Notre Dame
Fred Brown, Iowa
Artis Gilmore, Jacksonville
Rex Morgan, Jacksonville
Dan Issel, Kentucky

1971
*#Jim McDaniels, Western Ky.
Jim Chones, Marquette
Dean Meminger, Marquette
Allan Hornyak, Ohio St.
Luther Witte, Ohio St.

1972
#Ron King, Florida St.
Jim Andrews, Kentucky
Bob Lackey, Marquette
*Jim Brewer, Minnesota
*Clyde Turner, Minnesota

1973
#Steve Downing, Indiana
*Howard Jackson, Austin Peay
Quinn Buckner, Indiana
Jim Andrews, Kentucky
Larry McNeill, Marquette

1974
#Campy Russell, Michigan
Bo Ellis, Marquette
Waymon Britt, Michigan
John Shumate, Notre Dame
Jeff Fosnes, Vanderbilt

1975
#Kent Benson, Indiana
Dan Roundfield, Central Mich.
Steve Green, Indiana
Jimmy Dan Conner, Kentucky
Mike Flynn, Kentucky

1976
#Scott May, Indiana
#Kent Benson, Indiana
Anthony Murray, Alabama
Earl Tatum, Marquette
Tom Cutter, Western Mich.

1977
#Cedric Maxwell, Charlotte
John Long, Detroit
Lew Massey, Charlotte
Rickey Green, Michigan
Phil Hubbard, Michigan

1978
#Kyle Macy, Kentucky
Jack Givens, Kentucky
Mike Phillips, Kentucky
Earvin "Magic" Johnson, Michigan St.
Greg Kelser, Michigan St.

1979
#Greg Kelser, Michigan St.
Earvin "Magic" Johnson, Michigan St.
Bill Hanzlik, Notre Dame
Kelly Tripucka, Notre Dame
Jim Swaney, Toledo

1980
#Joe Barry Carroll, Purdue
Mike Gminski, Duke
Isiah Thomas, Indiana
Fred Cowan, Kentucky
Drake Morris, Purdue

1981
#Isiah Thomas, Indiana
Glenn Marcus, UAB
Ray Tolbert, Indiana
Randy Wittman, Indiana
Brian Warwick, St. Joseph's

1982
#Oliver Robinson, UAB
Lancaster Gordon, Louisville
Charles Jones, Louisville
Derek Smith, Louisville
Ralph Sampson, Virginia

1983
#Lancaster Gordon, Louisville
Darrell Walker, Arkansas
Jim Master, Kentucky
Melvin Turpin, Kentucky
Scooter McCray, Louisville

1984
#Dickey Beal, Kentucky
Bruce Douglas, Illinois
Sam Bowie, Kentucky
Melvin Turpin, Kentucky
Lancaster Gordon, Louisville

1985
#Ed Pinckney, Villanova
Adrian Branch, Maryland
Brad Daugherty, North Carolina
Kenny Smith, North Carolina
Harold Pressley, Villanova

1986
#Don Redden, LSU
Mark Price, Georgia Tech
Winston Bennett, Kentucky
Kenny Walker, Kentucky
Ricky Blanton, LSU

1987
#Billy Donovan, Providence
Reggie Williams, Georgetown
Danny Manning, Kansas
Darryl Wright, Providence
Steve Wright, Providence

1988
#Stacey King, Oklahoma
*Rex Chapman, Kentucky
Harvey Grant, Oklahoma
Doug West, Villanova
Kenny Wilson, Villanova

1989
#Glen Rice, Michigan
Sean Higgins, Michigan
Rumeal Robinson, Michigan
J.R. Reid, North Carolina
John Crotty, Virginia

1990
#Kenny Anderson, Georgia Tech
Dennis Scott, Georgia Tech
Steve Smith, Michigan St.
Willie Burton, Minnesota
Melvin Newbern, Minnesota

1991
#Alonzo Jamison, Kansas
Todd Day, Arkansas
Oliver Miller, Arkansas
Terry Brown, Kansas
Adonis Jordan, Kansas

1992
#Jalen Rose, Michigan
Chris Webber, Michigan
Eric Montross, North Carolina
Lawrence Funderburke, Ohio St.
Jim Jackson, Ohio St.

1993
#Travis Ford, Kentucky
Rodney Dobard, Florida St.
Jamal Mashburn, Kentucky
Jared Prickett, Kentucky
Mark Bell, Western Ky.

1994
#Grant Hill, Duke
Jeff Capel, Duke
Cherokee Parks, Duke
Cuonzo Martin, Purdue
Glenn Robinson, Purdue

1995
#Jerry Stackhouse, North Carolina
Allen Iverson, Georgetown
Tony Delk, Kentucky
Rasheed Wallace, North Carolina
Donald Williams, North Carolina

1996
#Dontaé Jones, Mississippi St.
Darnell Burton, Cincinnati
Danny Fortson, Cincinnati
Erick Dampier, Mississippi St.
Darryl Wilson, Mississippi St.

1997
#Miles Simon, Arizona
Mike Bibby, Arizona
Paul Pierce, Kansas
God Shammgod, Providence
Jamel Thomas, Providence

1998
#Wayne Turner, Kentucky
Trajan Langdon, Duke
Roshown McLeod, Duke
Scott Padgett, Kentucky
Jeff Sheppard, Kentucky

1999
#Scoonie Penn, Ohio St.
Ken Johnson, Ohio St.

ALL-SOUTH/SOUTHEAST/MIDEAST REGIONAL TEAMS

Michael Redd, Ohio St.
Erick Barkley, St. John's (N.Y.)
Lavor Postell, St. John's (N.Y.)
2000
#Joseph Forte, North Carolina
Jason Capel, North Carolina
Ed Cota, North Carolina
Eric Coley, Tulsa
Brandon Kurtz, Tulsa
2001
#Charlie Bell, Michigan St.
Casey Calvary, Gonzaga
David Thomas, Michigan St.
Lynn Greer, Temple
Kevin Lyde, Temple

All-Midwest Regional Teams

Most outstanding player is indicated by (#) and record later vacated by (*).

1951
Bob Kenney, Kansas
Clyde Lovellette, Kansas
Bob Tackett, New Mexico St.
Lou McKenna, St. Louis
Ray Steiner, St. Louis
1952
Not Available
1953
#Dean Kelley, Kansas
B.H. Born, Kansas
Gil Reich, Kansas
Arnold Short, Oklahoma City
Bob Mattick, Oklahoma St.
1954
Bob Carney, Bradley
Dick Estergard, Bradley
Bob Mattick, Oklahoma St.
Don Lance, Rice
Gene Schwinger, Rice
1955
Stan Albeck, Bradley
Burdette Haldorson, Colorado
Tom Harrold, Colorado
Bob Jeangerard, Colorado
Bob Patterson, Tulsa
1956
Harry Wallace, Kansas St.
Hub Reed, Oklahoma City
Jim Krebs, Southern Methodist
Joel Krog, Southern Methodist
Bob Mills, Southern Methodist
1957
Wilt Chamberlain, Kansas
Maurice King, Kansas
Hub Reed, Oklahoma City
Harold Alcorn, St. Louis
Jim Krebs, Southern Methodist
1958
Oscar Robertson, Cincinnati
Bob Boozer, Kansas St.
Roy DeWitz, Kansas St.
Jack Parr, Kansas St.
Arlen Clark, Oklahoma St.
1959
Oscar Robertson, Cincinnati
Howie Carl, DePaul
Bob Boozer, Kansas St.
Don Matuszak, Kansas St.
H.E. Kirchner, TCU
1960
Paul Hogue, Cincinnati
Oscar Robertson, Cincinnati
Bill Bridges, Kansas

Wayne Hightower, Kansas
Jay Arnette, Texas
1961
#Bob Wiesenhahn, Cincinnati
#Larry Comley, Kansas St.
Tom Thacker, Cincinnati
Gary Phillips, Houston
Harold Hudgens, Texas Tech
1962
#Paul Hogue, Cincinnati
Tom Thacker, Cincinnati
George Wilson, Cincinnati
Ken Charlton, Colorado
Del Ray Mounts, Texas Tech
1963
#Ken Charlton, Colorado
Ron Bonham, Cincinnati
Tom Thacker, Cincinnati
George Wilson, Cincinnati
Bud Koper, Oklahoma City
1964
Paul Silas, Creighton
Willie Murrell, Kansas St.
Roger Suttner, Kansas St.
Bob Dibler, UTEP
Dave Stallworth, Wichita St.
1965
James King, Oklahoma St.
Carroll Hooser, Southern Methodist
Dave Leach, Wichita St.
Kelly Pete, Wichita St.
Vernon Smith, Wichita St.
1966
#Bobby Joe Hill, UTEP
Walter Wesley, Kansas
Dennis Holman, Southern Methodist
Carroll Hooser, Southern Methodist
David Lattin, UTEP
1967
#Elvin Hayes, Houston
Don Chaney, Houston
Joseph White, Kansas
Wes Unseld, Louisville
Dennis Holman, Southern Methodist
1968
#Elvin Hayes, Houston
Don Chaney, Houston
Theodis Lee, Houston
Butch Beard, Louisville
Wes Unseld, Louisville
1969
#Willie McCarter, Drake
Floyd Kerr, Colorado St.
Cliff Meely, Colorado
Dolph Pulliam, Drake
Willie Wise, Drake
1970
#Jimmy Collins, New Mexico St.
Al Williams, Drake
David Hall, Kansas St.
Jerry Venable, Kansas St.
Sam Lacey, New Mexico St.
1971
#Dave Robisch, Kansas
Jeff Halliburton, Drake
Poo Welch, Houston
Bud Stallworth, Kansas
Austin Carr, Notre Dame
1972
#Jim Price, Louisville
Dan Beard, Kansas St.
Ron Thomas, Louisville
*Dwight Lamar, La.-Lafayette
Larry Robinson, Texas
1973
#Larry Finch, Memphis
Larry Kenon, Memphis
Ron Robinson, Memphis

Alex English, South Carolina
*Dwight Lamar, La.-Lafayette
1974
#Sam McCants, Oral Roberts
Gene Harmon, Creighton
Danny Knight, Kansas
Roger Morningstar, Kansas
Allen Murphy, Louisville
1975
#Phil Bond, Louisville
Bob Miller, Cincinnati
Junior Bridgeman, Louisville
John Lucas, Maryland
Adrian Dantley, Notre Dame
1976
#Willie Smith, Missouri
Rickey Green, Michigan
Phil Hubbard, Michigan
Adrian Dantley, Notre Dame
Rick Bullock, Texas Tech
1977
#Butch Lee, Marquette
Bo Ellis, Marquette
Mike Glenn, Southern Ill.
Skip Brown, Wake Forest
Jerry Schellenberg, Wake Forest
1978
#Kelly Tripucka, Notre Dame
Dave Corzine, DePaul
Gary Garland, DePaul
Rick Wilson, Louisville
Rich Branning, Notre Dame
1979
#Larry Bird, Indiana St.
Sidney Moncrief, Arkansas
Steve Schall, Arkansas
Carl Nicks, Indiana St.
Raymond Whitley, Oklahoma
1980
#Darrell Griffith, Louisville
DeWayne Scales, LSU
Wiley Brown, Louisville
Mark Dressler, Missouri
David Britton, Texas A&M
1981
#Durand Macklin, LSU
Greg Cook, LSU
Ethan Martin, LSU
Cliff Levingston, Wichita St.
Randy Smithson, Wichita St.
1982
#Robert Williams, Houston
John Bagley, Boston College
John Garris, Boston College
Larry Micheaux, Houston
Ricky Frazier, Missouri
1983
#Akeem Olajuwon, Houston
Larry Micheaux, Houston
Michael Young, Houston
Greg Stokes, Iowa
John Pinone, Villanova
1984
#Akeem Olajuwon, Houston
Michael Young, Houston
*William Bedford, Memphis
Kenny Green, Wake Forest
Delaney Rudd, Wake Forest
1985
*#Andre Turner, Memphis
Karl Malone, Louisiana Tech
*William Bedford, Memphis
*Keith Lee, Memphis
Darryl Kennedy, Oklahoma
Wayman Tisdale, Oklahoma
1986
#Danny Manning, Kansas
Calvin Thompson, Kansas
Charles Shackleford, North Carolina St.
Chris Washburn, North Carolina St.
Scott Skiles, Michigan St.

THE EARLY ROUNDS

1987
#Nikita Wilson, LSU
Tommy Amaker, Duke
Steve Alford, Indiana
Rick Calloway, Indiana
Anthony Wilson, LSU

1988
#Danny Manning, Kansas
Milt Newton, Kansas
Kevin Pritchard, Kansas
Mitch Richmond, Kansas St.
William Scott, Kansas St.

1989
#Nick Anderson, Illinois
Kenny Battle, Illinois
Kendall Gill, Illinois
Sherman Douglas, Syracuse
Billy Owens, Syracuse

1990
#Lenzie Howell, Arkansas
Lee Mayberry, Arkansas
Oliver Miller, Arkansas
Lance Blanks, Texas
Travis Mays, Texas

1991
#Bobby Hurley, Duke
Thomas Hill, Duke
Christian Laettner, Duke
Jason Buchanan, St. John's (N.Y.)
Malik Sealy, St. John's (N.Y.)

1992
#Herb Jones, Cincinnati
Anthony Buford, Cincinnati
Nick Van Exel, Cincinnati
Jon Barry, Georgia Tech
Anfernee Hardaway, Memphis

1993
#Calbert Cheaney, Indiana
Greg Graham, Indiana
Adonis Jordan, Kansas
Richard Scott, Kansas
Rex Walters, Kansas

1994
#Juwan Howard, Michigan
Clint McDaniel, Arkansas
Scotty Thurman, Arkansas
Corliss Williamson, Arkansas
Gary Collier, Tulsa

1995
#Corliss Williamson, Arkansas
Scotty Thurman, Arkansas
Mingo Johnson, Memphis
Junior Burrough, Virginia
Harold Deane, Virginia

1996
#Tony Delk, Kentucky
Derek Anderson, Kentucky
Anthony Epps, Kentucky
Antoine Walker, Kentucky
Tim Duncan, Wake Forest

1997
#Bobby Jackson, Minnesota
Dedric Willoughby, Iowa St.
Sam Jacobson, Minnesota
Cameron Dollar, UCLA
Charles O'Bannon, UCLA

1998
#Arthur Lee, Stanford
Cuttino Mobley, Rhode Island
Tyson Wheeler, Rhode Island
Cameron Dollar, Stanford
Bryce Drew, Valparaiso

1999
#Morris Peterson, Michigan St.
Scott Padgett, Kentucky
Wally Szczerbiak, Miami (Ohio)
Mateen Cleaves, Michigan St.
A.J. Granger, Michigan St.

2000
#Morris Peterson, Michigan St.
Marcus Fizer, Iowa St.
Jamaal Tinsley, Iowa St.
Mateen Cleaves, Michigan St.
A.J. Granger, Michigan St.
Andre Hutson, Michigan St.

2001
#Gilbert Arenas, Arizona
Jason Gardner, Arizona
Richard Jefferson, Arizona
Loren Woods, Arizona
Robert Archibald, Illinois

All-West Regional Teams

Most outstanding player is indicated by (#) and record later vacated by (*).

1950
Don Heathington, Baylor
Gene Melchiorre, Bradley
Paul Unruh, Bradley
Joe Nelson, Brigham Young
George Stanich, UCLA

1951
Ed Head, Kansas St.
Jack Stone, Kansas St.
Don Johnson, Oklahoma St.
Gale McArthur, Oklahoma St.
Bob Houbregs, Washington

1952
Don Penwell, Oklahoma City
Arnold Short, Oklahoma City
Herb Schoenstein, Santa Clara
Ken Sears, Santa Clara
Ronnie Livingston, UCLA
George Radovich, Wyoming

1953
Ken Sears, Santa Clara
Johnny O'Brien, Seattle
Joe Cipriano, Washington
Bob Houbregs, Washington
Doug McClary, Washington

1954
Sam Beckham, Idaho St.
Ken Sears, Santa Clara
Jim Young, Santa Clara
Roy Irvin, Southern California
Tony Psaltis, Southern California

1955
Swede Halbrook, Oregon St.
K.C. Jones, San Francisco
Jerry Mullen, San Francisco
Bill Russell, San Francisco
Art Bunte, Utah

1956
Gene Brown, San Francisco
Bill Russell, San Francisco
Willie Naulls, UCLA
Art Bunte, Utah
Curtis Jensen, Utah

1957
John Benson, Brigham Young
Larry Friend, California
Earl Robinson, California
Gene Brown, San Francisco
Mike Farmer, San Francisco

1958
Don McIntosh, California
Earl Robinson, California
Gale Siemen, Idaho St.
Elgin Baylor, Seattle
Charles Brown, Seattle

1959
Al Buch, California
Denny Fitzpatrick, California
Darrall Imhoff, California
Jim Rodgers, Idaho St.
LaRoy Doss, St. Mary's (Cal.)

1960
Darrall Imhoff, California
Bill McClintock, California
Earl Shultz, California
Chuck Rask, Oregon
James Russi, Santa Clara

1961
Larry Armstrong, Arizona St.
Ed Bento, Loyola Marymount
John Rudometkin, Southern California
Billy McGill, Utah
Jim Rhead, Utah

1962
Terry Baker, Oregon St.
Bob Warlick, Pepperdine
Gary Cunningham, UCLA
John Green, UCLA
Walt Hazzard, UCLA
Cornell Green, Utah St.

1963
Art Becker, Arizona St.
Joe Caldwell, Arizona St.
Terry Baker, Oregon St.
Mel Counts, Oregon St.
Ollie Johnson, San Francisco

1964
#Walt Hazzard, UCLA
Ollie Johnson, San Francisco
John Tresvant, Seattle
Gail Goodrich, UCLA
Troy Collier, Utah St.

1965
#Ollie Johnson, San Francisco
Gary Gray, Oklahoma City
Joe Ellis, San Francisco
Keith Erickson, UCLA
Gail Goodrich, UCLA

1966
#Jerry Chambers, Utah
Elvin Hayes, Houston
Rick Whelan, Oregon St.
Charlie White, Oregon St.
Merv Jackson, Utah
Rich Tate, Utah

1967
#Lew Alcindor, UCLA
Dave Fox, Pacific (Cal.)
Lucius Allen, UCLA
Mike Warren, UCLA
David Lattin, UTEP

1968
#Lew Alcindor, UCLA
Ron Nelson, New Mexico
Bud Ogden, Santa Clara
Lucius Allen, UCLA
Mike Warren, UCLA

1969
#Lew Alcindor, UCLA
Jimmy Collins, New Mexico St.
Bud Ogden, Santa Clara
Ken Heitz, UCLA
John Vallely, UCLA
Justus Thigpen, Weber St.

1970
#Sidney Wicks, UCLA
Dennis Awtrey, Santa Clara
Henry Bibby, UCLA
Curtis Rowe, UCLA
Marvin Roberts, Utah St.
Nate Williams, Utah St.

1971
#Sidney Wicks, UCLA
*Ed Ratleff, Long Beach St.
*George Trapp, Long Beach St.

ALL-WEST REGIONAL TEAMS

John Gianelli, Pacific (Cal.)
Curtis Rowe, UCLA

1972
#Bill Walton, UCLA
*Ed Ratleff, Long Beach St.
Mike Quick, San Francisco
Henry Bibby, UCLA
Bob Davis, Weber St.

1973
#Bill Walton, UCLA
Mike Contreras, Arizona St.
Mike Quick, San Francisco
Phil Smith, San Francisco
Tommy Curtis, UCLA

1974
#Bill Walton, UCLA
Don Smith, Dayton
Mike Sylvester, Dayton
Dave Meyers, UCLA
Keith Wilkes, UCLA

1975
#Marques Johnson, UCLA
Lionel Hollins, Arizona St.
Eric Hays, Montana
Robert Smith, UNLV
Richard Washington, UCLA

1976
#Richard Washington, UCLA
Al Fleming, Arizona
Herman Harris, Arizona
Jim Rappis, Arizona
Marques Johnson, UCLA

1977
#Robert Smith, UNLV
#Eddie Owens, UNLV
Steve Hayes, Idaho St.
Ed Thompson, Idaho St.
Marques Johnson, UCLA
Jeff Jonas, Utah

1978
#Ron Brewer, Arkansas
Marvin Delph, Arkansas
Sidney Moncrief, Arkansas
Keith Anderson, Cal St. Fullerton
Greg Bunch, Cal St. Fullerton

1979
#Gary Garland, DePaul
Curtis Watkins, DePaul
Bill Cartwright, San Francisco
David Greenwood, UCLA
Roy Hamilton, UCLA

1980
*#Mike Sanders, UCLA
Larry Nance, Clemson
Kelvin Ransey, Ohio St.
*Rod Foster, UCLA
*Kiki Vandeweghe, UCLA

1981
#Al Wood, North Carolina
Sam Perkins, North Carolina
James Worthy, North Carolina
Rolando Blackman, Kansas St.
Ed Nealy, Kansas St.

1982
#Eric Floyd, Georgetown
Rod Higgins, Fresno St.
Patrick Ewing, Georgetown
*Lester Conner, Oregon St.
*Charlie Sitton, Oregon St.

1983
#Dereck Whittenburg, North Carolina St.
John Garris, Boston College
Thurl Bailey, North Carolina St.
Lorenzo Charles, North Carolina St.
Ralph Sampson, Virginia

1984
#Patrick Ewing, Georgetown
Roosevelt Chapman, Dayton
Ed Young, Dayton
Michael Jackson, Georgetown
Detlef Schrempf, Washington

1985
#Chris Mullin, St. John's (N.Y.)
Kenny Walker, Kentucky
Lorenzo Charles, North Carolina St.
Spud Webb, North Carolina St.
Walter Berry, St. John's (N.Y.)

1986
#Chuck Person, Auburn
Herbert Crook, Louisville
Pervis Ellison, Louisville
Billy Thompson, Louisville
Brad Daugherty, North Carolina

1987
#Armon Gilliam, UNLV
B.J. Armstrong, Iowa
Kevin Gamble, Iowa
Tim McCalister, Oklahoma
Fennis Dembo, Wyoming

1988
#Sean Elliott, Arizona
Steve Kerr, Arizona
Tom Tolbert, Arizona
Rumeal Robinson, Michigan
J.R. Reid, North Carolina

1989
#Andrew Gaze, Seton Hall
Sean Elliott, Arizona
David Butler, UNLV
Gerald Greene, Seton Hall
Daryll Walker, Seton Hall

1990
#Stacey Augmon, UNLV
Chandler Thompson, Ball St.
Bo Kimble, Loyola Marymount
Anderson Hunt, UNLV
Larry Johnson, UNLV

1991
#Larry Johnson, UNLV
Brian Williams, Arizona
Greg Anthony, UNLV
Stacey Augmon, UNLV
Terry Dehere, Seton Hall

1992
#Eric Anderson, Indiana
Damon Bailey, Indiana

Calbert Cheaney, Indiana
Alan Henderson, Indiana
Tracy Murray, UCLA

1993
#Chris Webber, Michigan
Juwan Howard, Michigan
Jalen Rose, Michigan
Eddie Jones, Temple
Aaron McKie, Temple

1994
#Khalid Reeves, Arizona
Damon Stoudamire, Arizona
Melvin Booker, Missouri
Adrian Autry, Syracuse
Lawrence Moten, Syracuse

1995
#Tyus Edney, UCLA
Ray Allen, Connecticut
Donny Marshall, Connecticut
Toby Bailey, UCLA
Ed O'Bannon, UCLA

1996
#John Wallace, Syracuse
Jacque Vaughn, Kansas
Pertha Robinson, Georgia
Shandon Anderson, Georgia
Otis Hill, Syracuse

1997
#Ron Mercer, Kentucky
Wayne Turner, Kentucky
Rashid Bey, St. Joseph's
Brevin Knight, Stanford
Keith Van Horn, Utah

1998
#Andre Miller, Utah
Mike Bibby, Arizona
Michael Doleac, Utah
Alex Jensen, Utah
Hanno Mottola, Utah

1999
#Richard Hamilton, Connecticut
Kevin Freeman, Connecticut
Richard Moore, Connecticut
Casey Calvary, Gonzaga
Quentin Hall, Gonzaga

2000
#Jon Bryant, Wisonsin
Brian Cardinal, Purdue
Carson Cunningham, Purdue
Mike Robinson, Purdue
Mike Kelley, Wisconsin
Andy Kowske, Wisconsin

2001
#Lonny Baxter, Maryland
Kenny Satterfield, Cincinnati
Juan Dixon, Maryland
Casey Jacobsen, Stanford
Ryan Mendez, Stanford

THE EARLY ROUNDS

45

Tournament Moments...

March 28, 1992, at the Spectrum in Philadelphia – With Duke down by a point in overtime, the Blue Devils inbounded the ball from under Kentucky's basket with 2.1 seconds left. The pass went from Grant Hill to Christian Laettner, who was standing at the top of the key just inside the three-point line. With his back to the basket, Laettner dribbled once to his left, then turned while putting up a successful jump shot. The celebration was on as the Blue Devils advanced to the Final Four with the 104-103 victory.

The Tournament

Tournament Records 48
Tournament History Facts 53
Conference Won-Lost Records 62
Televised College Basketball Games 67
Financial Analysis 68
Tournament Facts 69
Team-By-Team Won-Lost Records 71

Tournament Records

A national championship game is indicated by (CH), national semifinal game by (NSF), national third-place game by (N3d), regional final game by (RF), regional semifinal game by (RSF), regional third-place game by (R3d), second-round game by (2d), first-round game by (1st), opening-round game by (OR), East region by (East), Southeast/Mideast region by (South), Midwest region by (MW), West/Far West region by (West), and later vacated by (*).

Individual Game

POINTS
- 61, Austin Carr, Notre Dame vs. Ohio, South 1st, 1970
- 58, Bill Bradley, Princeton vs. Wichita St., N3d, 1965
- 56, Oscar Robertson, Cincinnati vs. Arkansas, MW R3d, 1958
- 52, Austin Carr, Notre Dame vs. Kentucky, South RSF, 1970
- 52, Austin Carr, Notre Dame vs. TCU, MW 1st, 1971
- 50, David Robinson, Navy vs. Michigan, East 1st, 1987
- 49, Elvin Hayes, Houston vs. Loyola (Ill.), MW 1st, 1968
- 48, Hal Lear, Temple vs. Southern Methodist, N3d, 1956
- 47, Austin Carr, Notre Dame vs. Houston, MW R3d, 1971
- 46, Dave Corzine, DePaul vs. Louisville, MW RSF, 1978 (2 ot)
- 45, Bob Houbregs, Washington vs. Seattle, West RSF, 1953
- 45, Austin Carr, Notre Dame vs. Iowa, South R3d, 1970
- 45, Bo Kimble, Loyola Marymount vs. New Mexico St., West 1st, 1990
- 44, Clyde Lovellette, Kansas vs. St. Louis, West RF, 1952
- 44, Rod Thorn, West Virginia vs. St. Joseph's, East RSF, 1963
- 44, Dan Issel, Kentucky vs. Notre Dame, South RSF, 1970
- 44, Bill Walton, UCLA vs. Memphis, CH, 1973
- 44, Hersey Hawkins, Bradley vs. Auburn, South 1st, 1988
- 44, Travis Mays, Texas vs. Georgia, MW 1st, 1990
- 44, Glenn Robinson, Purdue vs. Kansas, South RSF, 1994

POINTS BY TWO TEAMMATES
- 85, Austin Carr (61) and Collis Jones (24), Notre Dame vs. Ohio, South 1st, 1970
- 78, Austin Carr (52) and Collis Jones (26), Notre Dame vs. TCU, MW 1st, 1971
- 78, Jeff Fryer (41) and Bo Kimble (37), Loyola Marymount vs. Michigan, West 2d, 1990
- 74, Bill Bradley (58) and Don Rodenbach (16), Princeton vs. Wichita St., N3d, 1965
- 74, Austin Carr (52) and Collis Jones (22), Notre Dame vs. Kentucky, South RSF, 1970

POINTS BY TWO OPPOSING PLAYERS
- 96, Austin Carr (52), Notre Dame, and Dan Issel (44), Kentucky, South RSF, 1970
- 85, Austin Carr (61), Notre Dame, and John Canine (24), Ohio, South 1st, 1970
- 85, Austin Carr (47), Notre Dame, and Poo Welch (38), Houston, MW R3d, 1971
- 83, David Robinson (50), Navy, and Garde Thompson (33), Michigan, East 1st, 1987
- 77, Travis Mays (44), Texas, and Alec Kessler (33), Georgia, MW 1st, 1990

FIELD GOALS
- 25, Austin Carr, Notre Dame vs. Ohio, South 1st, 1970
- 22, Bill Bradley, Princeton vs. Wichita St., N3d, 1965
- 22, Austin Carr, Notre Dame vs. Kentucky, South RSF, 1970
- 22, David Robinson, Navy vs. Michigan, East 1st, 1987
- 21, Oscar Robertson, Cincinnati vs. Arkansas, MW R3d, 1958
- 21, Austin Carr, Notre Dame vs. Iowa, South R3d, 1970
- 21, Bill Walton, UCLA vs. Memphis, CH, 1973
- 20, Bob Houbregs, Washington vs. Seattle, West RSF, 1953
- 20, Elvin Hayes, Houston vs. Loyola (Ill.), MW 1st, 1968
- 20, Austin Carr, Notre Dame vs. TCU, MW 1st, 1971

FIELD GOALS ATTEMPTED
- 44, Austin Carr, Notre Dame vs. Ohio, South 1st, 1970
- 42, Lennie Rosenbluth, North Carolina vs. Michigan St., NSF, 1957 (3 ot)
- 42, *Dwight Lamar, La.-Lafayette vs. Louisville, MW RSF, 1972
- 40, Austin Carr, Notre Dame vs. Houston, MW R3d, 1971
- 39, Austin Carr, Notre Dame vs. Iowa, South R3d, 1970
- 38, Bob Cousy, Holy Cross vs. North Carolina St., East RF, 1950
- 37, David Robinson, Navy vs. Michigan, East 1st, 1987
- 37, Charles Jones, Long Island vs. Villanova, East 1st, 1997
- 36, Oscar Robertson, Cincinnati vs. Arkansas, MW R3d, 1958
- 36, Rick Mount, Purdue vs. UCLA, CH, 1969
- 36, Ernie DiGregorio, Providence vs. Memphis, NSF, 1973
- 36, Ronald "Popeye" Jones, Murray St. vs. Michigan St., South 1st, 1990 (ot)

FIELD-GOAL PERCENTAGE
(Minimum 10 FGM)
- 100.0% (11-11), Kenny Walker, Kentucky vs. Western Ky., South 2d, 1986
- 100.0% (10-10), Marvin Barnes, Providence vs. Pennsylvania, East RSF, 1973
- 100.0% (10-10), Christian Laettner, Duke vs. Kentucky, East RF, 1992 (ot)
- 95.5% (21-22), Bill Walton, UCLA vs. Memphis, CH, 1973
- 92.3% (12-13), Dennis Holman, Southern Methodist vs. Cincinnati, MW R3d, 1966
- 92.3% (12-13), Quadre Lollis, Montana St. vs. Syracuse, West 1st, 1996
- 91.7% (11-12), Pembrook Burrows, Jacksonville vs. Iowa, South RSF, 1970
- 91.7% (11-12), Kenny Gregory, Kansas vs. DePaul, East 1st, 2000
- 90.9% (10-11), Jerry Lucas, Ohio St. vs. St. Joseph's, NSF, 1961
- 90.9% (10-11), Akeem Olajuwon, Houston vs. Villanova, MW RF, 1983
- 90.9% (10-11), Dwayne McClain, Villanova vs. Marshall, South 1st, 1984
- 90.9% (10-11), Billy Thompson, Louisville vs. LSU, NSF, 1986
- 90.9% (10-11), Oliver Miller, Arkansas vs. Murray St., MW 1st, 1992
- 90.9% (10-11), Travis Ford, Kentucky vs. Wake Forest, South RSF, 1993

THREE-POINT FIELD GOALS
- 11, Jeff Fryer, Loyola Marymount vs. Michigan, West 2d, 1990
- 10, Freddie Banks, UNLV vs. Indiana, NSF, 1987
- 9, Garde Thompson, Michigan vs. Navy, East 1st, 1987
- 9, Johnny Miller, Temple vs. Cincinnati, West 1st, 1995
- 9, Johnny Hemsley, Miami (Fla.) vs. Lafayette, East 1st, 1999
- 8, 12 tied (most recent: Rashod Johnson, Western Mich. vs. Clemson, MW 1st, 1998)

THREE-POINT FIELD GOALS ATTEMPTED
- 22, Jeff Fryer, Loyola Marymount vs. Arkansas, MW 1st, 1989
- 20, Chris Walker, Villanova vs. LSU, South 1st, 1990
- 19, Freddie Banks, UNLV vs. Indiana, NSF, 1987
- 19, Gerald Paddio, UNLV vs. Iowa, West 2d, 1988
- 19, Phillip Allen, N.C. A&T vs. Arkansas, MW 1st, 1994
- 18, Bobby Hurley, Duke vs. California, MW 2d, 1993
- 18, Jeff Boschee, Kansas vs. Kentucky, MW 2d, 1999
- 17, Damin Lopez, Pepperdine vs. Michigan, MW 1st, 1994
- 17, Johnny Miller, Temple vs. Cincinnati, West 1st, 1995
- 17, Shawn Respert, Michigan St. vs. Weber St., South 1st, 1995
- 17, Dedric Willoughby, Iowa St. vs. UCLA, MW RSF, 1997 (ot)

THREE-POINT FIELD-GOAL PERCENTAGE
(Minimum 5 3FGM)
- 100.0% (7-7), Sam Cassell, Florida St. vs. Tulane, South 2d, 1993
- 100.0% (6-6), Mike Buck, Middle Tenn. St. vs. Florida St., South 1st, 1989
- 100.0% (6-6), Migjen Bakalli, North Carolina St. vs. Southern Miss., East 1st, 1991
- 100.0% (6-6), Rex Walters, Kansas vs. Ball St., MW 1st, 1993
- 100.0% (5-5), Mitch Richmond, Kansas St. vs. Georgia, West 1st, 1987 (ot)
- 100.0% (5-5), Hubert Davis, North Carolina vs. Eastern Mich., East RSF, 1991
- 100.0% (5-5), Kwame Evans, George Washington vs. New Mexico, West 1st, 1993
- 100.0% (5-5), Jamal Mashburn, Kentucky vs. Wake Forest, South RSF, 1993
- 100.0% (5-5), Dwayne Morton, Louisville vs. Minnesota, West 2d, 1994
- 87.5% (7-8), William Scott, Kansas St. vs. DePaul, MW 2d, 1988
- 87.5% (7-8), Shane Hawkins, Southern Ill. vs. Syracuse, MW 1st, 1995

FREE THROWS
- 23, Bob Carney, Bradley vs. Colorado, MW RSF, 1954
- 23, Travis Mays, Texas vs. Georgia, MW 1st, 1990
- 21, David Robinson, Navy vs. Syracuse, East 2d, 1986
- 19, Tom Hammonds, Georgia Tech vs. Iowa St., East 1st, 1988
- 18, John O'Brien, Seattle vs. Wyoming, West R3d, 1953
- 18, Jon Rose, Connecticut vs. Boston U., East 1st, 1959
- 18, Gail Goodrich, UCLA vs. Michigan, CH, 1965
- 17, Roger Newman, Kentucky vs. Ohio St., South RF, 1961
- 17, Barry Kramer, New York U. vs. West Virginia, East R3d, 1963
- 17, Tyrone Hill, Xavier vs. Kansas St., MW 1st, 1990
- 17, Steve Nash, Santa Clara vs. Maryland, West 1st, 1996

FREE THROWS ATTEMPTED
- 27, David Robinson, Navy vs. Syracuse, East 2d, 1986
- 27, Travis Mays, Texas vs. Georgia, MW 1st, 1990
- 26, Bob Carney, Bradley vs. Colorado, MW RSF, 1954
- 24, Donnie Gaunce, Morehead St. vs. Iowa, South RSF, 1956
- 22, John O'Brien, Seattle vs. Wyoming, West R3d, 1953
- 22, Wilt Chamberlain, Kansas vs. Oklahoma City, MW RF, 1957
- 22, Roger Newman, Kentucky vs. Ohio St., South RF, 1961
- 21, Adrian Dantley, Notre Dame vs. Kansas, MW 1st, 1975
- 21, John Bagley, Boston College vs. Wake Forest, South 2d, 1981
- 21, Vernon Maxwell, Florida vs. North Carolina St., East 1st, 1987
- 21, Tom Hammonds, Georgia Tech vs. Iowa St., East 1st, 1988
- 21, Brad Miller, Purdue vs. Rhode Island, South 1st, 1997

FREE-THROW PERCENTAGE
(Minimum 12 FTM)
- 100.0% (16-16), Bill Bradley, Princeton vs. St. Joseph's, East 1st, 1963
- 100.0% (16-16), Fennis Dembo, Wyoming vs. UCLA, West 2d, 1987
- 100.0% (15-15), Austin Croshere, Providence vs. Marquette, South 1st, 1997
- 100.0% (13-13), Bill Bradley, Princeton vs. Providence, East RF, 1965
- 100.0% (13-13), Mike Maloy, Davidson vs. St. John's (N.Y.), East RSF, 1969
- 100.0% (13-13), Al Gooden, Ball St. vs. Boston College, South 1st, 1981
- 100.0% (12-12), 16 tied (most recent: Dan Dickau, Gonzaga vs. Indiana St., South 2d, 2001)

REBOUNDS
- 34, Fred Cohen, Temple vs. Connecticut, East RSF, 1956

TOURNAMENT RECORDS—INDIVIDUAL GAME

31, Nate Thurmond, Bowling Green vs. Mississippi St., South R3d, 1963
30, Jerry Lucas, Ohio St. vs. Kentucky, South RF, 1961
29, Toby Kimball, Connecticut vs. St. Joseph's, East 1st, 1965
28, Elvin Hayes, Houston vs. Pacific (Cal.), West R3d, 1966
27, Bill Russell, San Francisco vs. Iowa, CH, 1956
27, John Green, Michigan St. vs. Notre Dame, South RSF, 1957
27, Paul Silas, Creighton vs. Oklahoma City, MW 1st, 1964
27, Elvin Hayes, Houston vs. Loyola (Ill.), MW 1st, 1968
26, Howard Jolliff, Ohio vs. Georgia Tech, South RSF, 1960
26, Phil Hubbard, Michigan vs. Detroit, South RSF, 1977
25, Jerry Lucas, Ohio St. vs. Western Ky., South RSF, 1960
25, Elvin Hayes, Houston vs. TCU, MW RF, 1968
24, K.E. Kirchner, TCU vs. DePaul, MW R3d, 1959
24, Paul Silas, Creighton vs. Memphis, MW 1st, 1962
24, Eddie Jackson, Oklahoma City vs. Creighton, MW 1st, 1964
24, Elvin Hayes, Houston vs. UCLA, NSF, 1967
24, Elvin Hayes, Houston vs. Louisville, MW RSF, 1968
24, Sam Lacey, New Mexico St. vs. Drake, MW RF, 1970
24, Tom Burleson, North Carolina St. vs. Providence, East RSF, 1974

ASSISTS
18, Mark Wade, UNLV vs. Indiana, NSF, 1987
16, Sam Crawford, New Mexico St. vs. Nebraska, East 1st, 1993
16, Earl Watson, UCLA vs. Maryland, MW 2d, 2000
15, Kenny Patterson, DePaul vs. Syracuse, East 1st, 1985
15, Keith Smart, Indiana vs. Auburn, MW 2d, 1987
15, Pepe Sanchez, Temple vs. Lafayette, East 1st, 2000
14, Dickey Beal, Kentucky vs. Brigham Young, South 2d, 1984
14, Carl Wright, Southern Methodist vs. Miami (Ohio), West 1st, 1984
14, John Crotty, Virginia vs. Middle Tenn., South 2d, 1989
14, Pooh Richardson, UCLA vs. Iowa St., South 1st, 1989
14, Jason Kidd, California vs. Duke, MW 2d, 1993
14, Mike Lloyd, Syracuse vs. Southern Ill., MW 1st, 1995
14, Tezale Archie, Pepperdine vs. Oklahoma St., East 2d, 2000

BLOCKED SHOTS
11, Shaquille O'Neal, LSU vs. Brigham Young, West 1st, 1992
10, Shawn Bradley, Brigham Young vs. Virginia, West 1st, 1991
9, David Robinson, Navy vs. Cleveland St., East RSF, 1986
9, D'or Fischer, Northwestern St. vs. Winthrop, MW OR, 2001
8, Tim Perry, Temple vs. Lehigh, East 1st, 1988
8, Mark Strickland, Temple vs. Oklahoma St., East RSF, 1991 (ot)
8, Acie Earl, Iowa vs. Duke, East 2d, 1992
8, Tim Duncan, Wake Forest vs. Col. of Charleston, South 1st, 1994
8, Erick Dampier, Mississippi St. vs. Utah, West 2d, 1995
8, Tim Duncan, Wake Forest vs. Oklahoma St., East RSF, 1995
8, Kelvin Cato, Iowa St. vs. Illinois St., MW 1st, 1997
8, Shane Battier, Duke vs. Kansas, East 2d, 2000
8, Tarvis Williams, Hampton vs. Georgetown, West 2d, 2001

STEALS
8, Darrell Hawkins, Arkansas vs. Holy Cross, East 1st, 1993
8, Grant Hill, Duke vs. California, MW 2d, 1993
8, Duane Clemens, Ball St. vs. UCLA, MW 1st, 2000
7, Tommy Amaker, Duke vs. Old Dominion, East 2d, 1986
7, Tommy Amaker, Duke vs. Louisville, CH, 1986
7, Reggie Miller, UCLA vs. Wyoming, West 2d, 1987
7, Delray Brooks, Providence vs. Austin Peay, South 2d, 1987 (ot)
7, Ricky Grace, Oklahoma vs. Iowa, West RSF, 1987 (ot)
7, Mookie Blaylock, Oklahoma vs. Kansas, CH, 1988
7, Scott Burrell, Connecticut vs. Xavier, MW 2d, 1991
7, Ted Ellis, Manhattan vs. Oklahoma, South 1st, 1995
7, Edgar Padilla, Massachusetts vs. UCF, East 1st, 1996
7, Kawika Akina, Northern Ariz. vs. Cincinnati, West 1st, 1998

Individual Series

(Three-Game Minimum for Averages and Percentages)

POINTS
184, Glen Rice, Michigan, 1989 (6 games)
177, Bill Bradley, Princeton, 1965 (5)
167, Elvin Hayes, Houston, 1968 (5)
163, Danny Manning, Kansas, 1988 (6)
160, Hal Lear, Temple, 1956 (5)
160, Jerry West, West Virginia, 1959 (5)
158, Austin Carr, Notre Dame, 1970 (3)
158, Joe Barry Carroll, Purdue, 1980 (6)
154, Jason Williams, Duke, 2001 (6)
153, Johnny Dawkins, Duke, 1986 (6)
153, Dennis Scott, Georgia Tech, 1990 (5)

SCORING AVERAGE
52.7 (158 points in 3 games), Austin Carr, Notre Dame, 1970
41.7 (125 in 3), Austin Carr, Notre Dame, 1971
35.8 (143 in 4), Jerry Chambers, Utah, 1966
35.8 (143 in 4), Bo Kimble, Loyola Marymount, 1990
35.4 (177 in 5), Bill Bradley, Princeton, 1965
35.3 (141 in 4), Clyde Lovellette, Kansas, 1952
35.0 (140 in 4), Gail Goodrich, UCLA, 1965
35.0 (105 in 3), Jerry West, West Virginia, 1960
34.8 (139 in 4), Bob Houbregs, Washington, 1953
33.4 (167 in 5), Elvin Hayes, Houston, 1968

FIELD GOALS
75, Glen Rice, Michigan, 1989 (6 games)
70, Elvin Hayes, Houston, 1968 (5)
69, Danny Manning, Kansas, 1988 (6)
68, Austin Carr, Notre Dame, 1970 (3)
66, Johnny Dawkins, Duke, 1986 (6)
65, Bill Bradley, Princeton, 1965 (5)
63, Hal Lear, Temple, 1956 (5)
63, Joe Barry Carroll, Purdue, 1980 (6)
63, Stacey King, Oklahoma, 1988 (6)
61, *Jim McDaniels, Western Ky., 1971 (5)

FIELD GOALS ATTEMPTED
138, *Jim McDaniels, Western Ky., 1971 (5 games)
137, Elvin Hayes, Houston, 1968 (5)
131, Glen Rice, Michigan, 1989 (6)
125, Danny Manning, Kansas, 1988 (6)
124, Lennie Rosenbluth, North Carolina, 1957 (5)
121, Ernie DiGregorio, Providence, 1973 (5)
121, Bo Kimble, Loyola Marymount, 1990 (4)
118, Austin Carr, Notre Dame, 1970 (3)
116, Rick Mount, Purdue, 1969 (4)
115, Dennis Scott, Georgia Tech, 1990 (5)

FIELD-GOAL PERCENTAGE
(Minimum 5 FGM Per Game)
78.8% (26-33), Christian Laettner, Duke, 1989 (5 games)
78.6% (22-28), Heyward Dotson, Columbia, 1968 (3)
78.3% (18-23), *Winston Bennett, Kentucky, 1988 (3)
78.0% (32-41), Kevin Gamble, Iowa, 1987 (4)
77.1% (27-35), Mark Dressler, Missouri, 1980 (3)
76.9% (20-26), Robert Werdann, St. John's (N.Y.), 1991 (4)
76.5% (26-34), Alex Gilbert, Indiana St., 1979 (5)
76.3% (29-38), Kelvin Johnson, Richmond, 1984 (3)
76.3% (45-59), Bill Walton, UCLA, 1973 (4)
76.2% (16-21), Dave Mills, DePaul, 1965 (3)

THREE-POINT FIELD GOALS
27, Glen Rice, Michigan, 1989 (6 games)
26, Freddie Banks, UNLV, 1987 (5)
24, Dennis Scott, Georgia Tech, 1990 (5)
23, Jeff Fryer, Loyola Marymount, 1990 (4)
23, Jason Williams, Duke, 2001 (6)
22, Donald Williams, North Carolina, 1993 (6)
21, Steve Alford, Indiana, 1987 (6)
21, William Scott, Kansas St., 1988 (4)
20, Carmelo Travieso, Massachusetts, 1996 (5)
19, Dave Sieger, Oklahoma, 1988 (6)
19, Darryl Wilson, Mississippi St., 1996 (5)

THREE-POINT FIELD GOALS ATTEMPTED
66, Jason Williams, Duke, 2001 (6 games)
65, Freddie Banks, UNLV, 1987 (5)
55, Jeff Fryer, Loyola Marymount, 1990 (4)
54, Dennis Scott, Georgia Tech, 1990 (5)
49, Glen Rice, Michigan, 1989 (6)
46, Dave Sieger, Oklahoma, 1988 (6)
46, Carmelo Travieso, Massachusetts, 1996 (5)
45, Terry Brown, Kansas, 1991 (5)
44, Phil Henderson, Duke, 1990 (6)
44, Donald Williams, North Carolina, 1993 (6)
44, Scotty Thurman, Arkansas, 1995 (6)

THREE-POINT FIELD-GOAL PERCENTAGE
(Minimum 1.5 3FGM Per Game)
100.0% (6-6), Ranzino Smith, North Carolina, 1987 (4 games)
85.7% (6-7), Mike Chappell, Duke, 1998 (4)
80.0% (8-10), John Crotty, Virginia, 1989 (4)
77.8% (7-9), Corey Williams, Oklahoma St., 1992 (3)
72.7% (8-11), A.J. Granger, Michigan St., 1999 (5)
71.4% (5-7), Ben Caton, Utah, 1996 (3)
70.6% (12-17), Sam Cassell, Florida St., 1993 (4)
68.4% (13-19), Ronnie McMahan, Vanderbilt, 1993 (3)
66.7% (6-9), Dwayne Bryant, Georgetown, 1989 (4)
66.7% (8-12), John Leahy, Seton Hall, 1992 (3)
64.3% (9-14), Greg Minor, Louisville, 1993 (3)

FREE THROWS
55, Bob Carney, Bradley, 1954 (5 games)
49, Don Schlundt, Indiana, 1953 (4)
49, Christian Laettner, Duke, 1991 (6)
47, Bill Bradley, Princeton, 1965 (5)
46, Jerry West, West Virginia, 1959 (5)
45, Cedric Maxwell, Charlotte, 1977 (5)
45, Michael Doleac, Utah, 1998 (6)
44, Len Chappell, Wake Forest, 1962 (5)
43, Travis Mays, Texas, 1990 (4)
42, Gail Goodrich, UCLA, 1965 (4)
42, Christian Laettner, Duke, 1990 (6)

FREE THROWS ATTEMPTED
71, Jerry West, West Virginia, 1959 (5 games)
70, Bob Carney, Bradley, 1954 (5)
63, Don Schlundt, Indiana, 1953 (4)
62, Len Chappell, Wake Forest, 1962 (5)
62, Wilt Chamberlain, Kansas, 1957 (4)
55, David Robinson, Navy, 1986 (4)
54, Christian Laettner, Duke, 1991 (6)
53, Cedric Maxwell, Charlotte, 1977 (5)
53, Ed Pinckney, Villanova, 1985 (6)
52, Christian Laettner, Duke, 1990 (6)
52, Miles Simon, Arizona, 1997 (6)

PERFECT FREE-THROW PERCENTAGE
(Minimum 2.5 FTM Per Game)
100.0% (35-35), Arthur Lee, Stanford, 1998 (5 games)
100.0% (23-23), Richard Morgan, Virginia, 1989 (4)
100.0% (21-21), Keith Van Horn, Utah, 1997 (4)
100.0% (20-20), Shammond Williams, North Carolina, 1998 (5)
100.0% (19-19), *Derrick McKey, Alabama, 1987 (3)
100.0% (18-18), Harley Swift, East Tenn. St., 1968 (3)
100.0% (18-18), Mike Vreeswyk, Temple, 1988 (4)
100.0% (17-17), Henry Bibby, UCLA, 1971 (4)
100.0% (17-17), Oliver Robinson, UAB, 1981 (3)
100.0% (15-15), John Pinone, Villanova, 1983 (3)
100.0% (15-15), LaBradford Smith, Louisville, 1988 (3)
100.0% (15-15), John Pelphrey, Kentucky, 1992 (4)

FREE-THROW PERCENTAGE
(Minimum 20 FTM)
100.0% (35-35), Arthur Lee, Stanford, 1998 (5 games)
100.0% (23-23), Richard Morgan, Virginia, 1989 (4)
100.0% (21-21), Keith Van Horn, Utah, 1997 (4)
100.0% (20-20), Shammond Williams, North Carolina, 1998 (5)
97.1% (33-34), Lynn Greer, Temple, 2001 (4)
96.3% (26-27), Sidney Moncrief, Arkansas, 1979 (3)
96.2% (25-26), Jeff Lamp, Virginia, 1981 (5)
96.2% (25-26), Michael Doleac, Utah, 1997 (4)
96.0% (24-25), Dwayne McClain, Villanova, 1985 (6)
95.5% (21-22), Steve Alford, Indiana, 1984 (3)

TOURNAMENT RECORDS—INDIVIDUAL SERIES

REBOUNDS
97, Elvin Hayes, Houston, 1968 (5 games)
93, Artis Gilmore, Jacksonville, 1970 (5)
91, Elgin Baylor, Seattle, 1958 (5)
90, Sam Lacey, New Mexico St., 1970 (5)
89, *Clarence Glover, Western Ky., 1971 (5)
86, Len Chappell, Wake Forest, 1962 (5)
83, Tom Sanders, New York U., 1960 (5)
82, Don May, Dayton, 1967 (5)
77, John Green, Michigan St., 1957 (4)
75, Elvin Hayes, Houston, 1967 (5)
75, Lew Alcindor, UCLA, 1968 (4)
75, Larry Johnson, UNLV, 1990 (6)

REBOUND AVERAGE
(Minimum 3 Games)
23.3 (70 rebounds in 3 games), Nate Thurmond, Bowling Green, 1963
21.3 (64 in 3), Howard Jolliff, Ohio, 1960
19.4 (97 in 5), Elvin Hayes, Houston, 1968
19.3 (77 in 4), John Green, Michigan St., 1957
19.0 (57 in 3), Paul Silas, Creighton, 1964
18.8 (75 in 4), Lew Alcindor, UCLA, 1968
18.6 (93 in 5), Artis Gilmore, Jacksonville, 1970
18.3 (73 in 4), Jerry Lucas, Ohio St., 1961
18.3 (55 in 3), James Ware, Oklahoma City, 1965
18.2 (91 in 5), Elgin Baylor, Seattle, 1958

ASSISTS
61, Mark Wade, UNLV, 1987 (5 games)
56, Rumeal Robinson, Michigan, 1989 (6)
49, Sherman Douglas, Syracuse, 1987 (6)
47, Bobby Hurley, Duke, 1992 (6)
46, Lazarus Sims, Syracuse, 1996 (6)
45, Michael Jackson, Georgetown, 1985 (6)
43, Bobby Hurley, Duke, 1991 (6)
42, Cedric Hunter, Kansas, 1986 (5)
42, Billy Donovan, Providence, 1987 (5)
42, Jamal Meeks, Indiana, 1992 (5)

BLOCKED SHOTS
24, Loren Woods, Arizona, 2001 (6 games)
23, David Robinson, Navy, 1986 (4)
21, Marcus Camby, Massachusetts, 1996 (5)
21, Ken Johnson, Ohio St., 1999 (5)
20, Tim Perry, Temple, 1988 (4)
19, Alonzo Mourning, Georgetown, 1989 (4)
18, Cherokee Parks, Duke, 1994 (6)
18, Marcus Camby, Massachusetts, 1995 (4)
18, Jamaal Magloire, Kentucky, 1998 (6)
17, Chris Webber, Michigan, 1992 (6)

STEALS
23, Mookie Blaylock, Oklahoma, 1988 (6 games)
19, Edgar Padilla, Massachusetts, 1996 (5)
18, Tommy Amaker, Duke, 1986 (6)
18, Mark Wade, UNLV, 1987 (5)
18, Lee Mayberry, Arkansas, 1990 (5)
17, Kendall Gill, Illinois, 1989 (5)
17, Antoine Walker, Kentucky, 1996 (6)
17, Jason Terry, Arizona, 1997 (6)
17, Wayne Turner, Kentucky, 1997 (6)
17, Gilbert Arenas, Arizona, 2001 (6)

Individual Career

(Two-Year Minimum for Averages and Percentages)

POINTS
407, Christian Laettner, Duke, 1989-92 (23 games)
358, Elvin Hayes, Houston, 1966-68 (13)
328, Danny Manning, Kansas, 1985-88 (16)
324, Oscar Robertson, Cincinnati, 1958-60 (10)
308, Glen Rice, Michigan, 1986-89 (13)
304, Lew Alcindor, UCLA, 1967-69 (12)
303, Bill Bradley, Princeton, 1963-65 (9)
303, Corliss Williamson, Arkansas, 1993-95 (15)
289, Austin Carr, Notre Dame, 1969-71 (7)
280, Juwan Howard, Michigan, 1992-94 (16)
279, Calbert Cheaney, Indiana, 1990-93 (13)
278, Shane Battier, Duke, 1998-2001 (19)
275, Jerry West, West Virginia, 1958-60 (9)
269, Danny Ferry, Duke, 1986-89 (19)
269, Grant Hill, Duke, 1991-94 (20)
266, Jerry Lucas, Ohio St., 1960-62 (12)
260, Reggie Williams, Georgetown, 1984-87 (17)

260, Miles Simon, Arizona, 1995-98 (14)
256, Patrick Ewing, Georgetown, 1982-85 (18)
254, Bill Walton, UCLA, 1972-74 (12)

SCORING AVERAGE
(Minimum 6 Games)
41.3 (289 points in 7 games), Austin Carr, Notre Dame, 1969-71
33.7 (303 in 9), Bill Bradley, Princeton, 1963-65
32.4 (324 in 10), Oscar Robertson, Cincinnati, 1958-60
30.6 (275 in 9), Jerry West, West Virginia, 1958-60
30.5 (183 in 6), Bob Pettit, LSU, 1953-54
29.3 (176 in 6), Dan Issel, Kentucky, 1968-70
29.3 (176 in 6), *Jim McDaniels, Western Ky., 1970-71
29.2 (175 in 6), *Dwight Lamar, La.-Lafayette, 1972-73
29.1 (204 in 7), Bo Kimble, Loyola Marymount, 1988-90
28.6 (200 in 7), David Robinson, Navy, 1985-87
27.6 (221 in 8), Len Chappell, Wake Forest, 1961-62
27.5 (358 in 13), Elvin Hayes, Houston, 1966-68
27.4 (192 in 7), Bob Houbregs, Washington, 1951, 53
27.0 (162 in 6), Don Schlundt, Indiana, 1953-54
25.7 (180 in 7), Kenny Anderson, Georgia Tech, 1990-91
25.4 (203 in 8), Adrian Dantley, Notre Dame, 1974-76
25.3 (304 in 12), Lew Alcindor, UCLA, 1967-69
25.2 (151 in 6), Barry Kramer, New York U., 1962-63
25.2 (151 in 6), Bob Lanier, St. Bonaventure, 1968, 70
25.1 (226 in 9), Cazzie Russell, Michigan, 1964-66

FIELD GOALS
152, Elvin Hayes, Houston, 1966-68 (13 games)
140, Danny Manning, Kansas, 1985-88 (16)
128, Glen Rice, Michigan, 1986-89 (13)
128, Christian Laettner, Duke, 1989-92 (23)
123, Corliss Williamson, Arkansas, 1993-95 (15)

FIELD GOALS ATTEMPTED
310, Elvin Hayes, Houston, 1966-68 (13 games)
257, Danny Manning, Kansas, 1985-88 (16)
235, Oscar Robertson, Cincinnati, 1958-60 (10)
225, Austin Carr, Notre Dame, 1969-71 (7)
224, Glen Rice, Michigan, 1986-89 (13)

FIELD-GOAL PERCENTAGE
(Minimum 70 FGM)
68.6% (109-159), Bill Walton, UCLA, 1972-74 (12 games)
68.4% (78-114), Stephen Thompson, Syracuse 1987-90 (15)
68.0% (70-103), Brad Daugherty, North Carolina, 1983-86 (12)
65.2% (86-132), Andre Huston, Michigan St., 1998-2001 (19)
65.1% (95-146), Akeem Olajuwon, Houston, 1982-84 (15)

THREE-POINT FIELD GOALS
42, Bobby Hurley, Duke, 1990-93 (20 games)
40, Tony Delk, Kentucky, 1993-96 (17)
38, Jeff Fryer, Loyola Marymount, 1988-90 (7)
38, Donald Williams, North Carolina, 1992-95 (15)
36, Scotty Thurman, Arkansas, 1993-95 (15)

THREE-POINT FIELD GOALS ATTEMPTED
103, Anderson Hunt, UNLV, 1989-91 (15 games)
97, Jeff Fryer, Loyola Marymount, 1988-90 (7)
96, Bobby Hurley, Duke, 1990-93 (20)
96, Tony Delk, Kentucky, 1993-96 (17)
92, Scotty Thurman, Arkansas, 1993-95 (15)

THREE-POINT FIELD-GOAL PERCENTAGE
(Minimum 20 FGM)
65.0% (26-40), William Scott, Kansas St., 1987-88 (5 games)
62.5% (20-32), Sam Cassell, Florida St., 1992-93 (7)
61.8% (21-34), Steve Alford, Indiana, 1984, 86-87 (10)
56.5% (35-62), Glen Rice, Michigan, 1986-89 (13)
55.3% (21-38), Rex Walters, Kansas, 1992-93 (7)

FREE THROWS
142, Christian Laettner, Duke, 1989-92 (23 games)
90, Oscar Robertson, Cincinnati, 1958-60 (10)
87, Bill Bradley, Princeton, 1963-65 (9)
83, Ed Pinckney, Villanova, 1982-85 (14)
82, Michael Doleac, Utah, 1995-98 (15)

FREE THROWS ATTEMPTED
167, Christian Laettner, Duke, 1989-92 (23 games)
119, Lew Alcindor, UCLA, 1967-69 (12)

116, Oscar Robertson, Cincinnati, 1958-60 (10)
115, Ed Pinckney, Villanova, 1982-85 (14)
114, Jerry West, West Virginia, 1958-60 (9)

FREE-THROW PERCENTAGE
(Minimum 30 FTM)
97.7% (42-43), Keith Van Horn, Utah, 1995-97 (8 games)
95.7% (45-47), LaBradford Smith, Louisville, 1988-90 (8)
94.9% (37-39), Phil Ford, North Carolina, 1975-78 (10)
94.3% (33-35), Lawrence Moten, Syracuse, 1992, 1994-95 (7)
93.5% (58-62), Arthur Lee, Stanford, 1996-99 (12) (12 games)

FREE-THROW PERCENTAGE
(Minimum 50 FTM)
93.5% (58-62), Arthur Lee, Stanford, 1996-99 (12) (12 games)
90.6% (87-96), Bill Bradley, Princeton, 1963-65 (9)
90.6% (58-64), Steve Alford, Indiana, 1984, 86-87 (10)
89.8% (53-59), Johnny Cox, Kentucky, 1957-59 (8)
85.4% (82-96), Michael Doleac, Utah, 1995-98 (15)

REBOUNDS
222, Elvin Hayes, Houston, 1966-68 (13 games)
201, Lew Alcindor, UCLA, 1967-69 (12)
197, Jerry Lucas, Ohio St., 1960-62 (12)
176, Bill Walton, UCLA, 1972-74 (12)
169, Christian Laettner, Duke, 1989-92 (23)
165, Tim Duncan, Wake Forest, 1994-97 (11)
160, Paul Hogue, Cincinnati, 1960-62 (12)
157, Sam Lacey, New Mexico St., 1968-70 (11)
155, Derrick Coleman, Syracuse, 1987-90 (14)
153, Akeem Olajuwon, Houston, 1982-84 (15)
144, Patrick Ewing, Georgetown, 1982-85 (18)
138, Marques Johnson, UCLA, 1974-77 (16)
138, George Lynch, North Carolina, 1990-93 (17)
137, Len Chappell, Wake Forest, 1961-62 (8)
135, Ed Pinckney, Villanova, 1982-85 (14)
135, Shane Battier, Duke, 1998-2001 (19)
134, Grant Hill, Duke, 1991-94 (20)
131, Oscar Robertson, Cincinnati, 1958-60 (10)
131, Curtis Rowe, UCLA, 1969-71 (12)
131, Danny Ferry, Duke, 1986-89 (19)

REBOUNDING AVERAGE
(Minimum 6 Games)
19.7 (118 rebounds in 6 games), John Green, Michigan St., 1957, 59
19.2 (115 in 6), Artis Gilmore, Jacksonville, 1970-71
18.5 (111 in 6), Paul Silas, Creighton, 1962-64
17.1 (137 in 8), Len Chappell, Wake Forest, 1961-62
17.1 (222 in 13), Elvin Hayes, Houston, 1966-68
16.8 (201 in 12), Lew Alcindor, UCLA, 1967-69
16.4 (197 in 12), Jerry Lucas, Ohio St., 1960-62
15.0 (165 in 11), Tim Duncan, Wake Forest, 1994-97
14.7 (176 in 12), Bill Walton, UCLA, 1972-74
14.3 (157 in 11), Sam Lacey, New Mexico St., 1968-70

ASSISTS
145, Bobby Hurley, Duke, 1990-93 (20 games)
106, Sherman Douglas, Syracuse, 1986-89 (14)
100, Greg Anthony, UNLV, 1989-91 (15)
93, Mark Wade, UNLV, 1986-87 (8)
93, Rumeal Robinson, Michigan, 1988-90 (11)
93, Jacque Vaughn, Kansas, 1994-97 (13)
93, Anthony Epps, Kentucky, 1994-97 (18)

BLOCKED SHOTS
50, Tim Duncan, Wake Forest, 1994-97 (11 games)
43, Marcus Camby, Massachusetts, 1994-96 (11)
42, Shane Battier, Duke, 1998-2001 (19)
37, Alonzo Mourning, Georgetown, 1989-92 (10)
35, Scot Pollard, Kansas, 1994-97 (13)

STEALS
39, Grant Hill, Duke, 1991-94 (20 games)
38, Wayne Turner, Kentucky, 1996-99 (21)
34, Anthony Epps, Kentucky, 1994-97 (18)
32, Mookie Blaylock, Oklahoma, 1988-89 (9)
32, Christian Laettner, Duke, 1989-92 (23)

GAMES PLAYED
23, Christian Laettner, Duke, 1989-92
22, Greg Koubek, Duke, 1988-91
22, Brian Davis, Duke, 1989-92
21, Wayne Turner, Kentucky, 1996-99
20, Thomas Hill, Duke, 1990-93
20, Bobby Hurley, Duke, 1990-93

TOURNAMENT RECORDS—INDIVIDUAL CAREER

20, Grant Hill, Duke, 1991-94
20, Antonio Lang, Duke, 1991-94

Team Game

POINTS
149, Loyola Marymount vs. Michigan (115), West 2d, 1990
131, UNLV vs. Loyola Marymount (101), West RF, 1990
127, *St. Joseph's vs. Utah (120), N3d, 1961 (4 ot)
124, Oklahoma, vs. Louisiana Tech (81), South 2d, 1989
123, North Carolina vs. Loyola Marymount (97), West 2d, 1988
121, Iowa vs. Notre Dame (106), South R3d, 1970
121, UNLV vs. San Francisco (95), West 1st, 1977
120, Utah vs. St. Joseph's (127), N3d, 1961 (4 ot)
120, Arkansas vs. Loyola Marymount (101), MW 1st, 1989
119, Houston vs. Notre Dame (106), MW R3d, 1971
119, Loyola Marymount vs. Wyoming (115), West 1st, 1988

FEWEST POINTS
20, North Carolina vs. Pittsburgh (26), East RF, 1941
24, Springfield vs. Indiana (48), East RF, 1940
26, Pittsburgh vs. North Carolina (20), East RF, 1941
28, Kentucky vs. Dartmouth (47), NSF, 1942
29, Western Ky. vs. Duquesne (30), East RF, 1940
29, Baylor vs. Oklahoma St. (44), West RF, 1946
30, Brown vs. Villanova (43), East RF, 1939
30, Duquesne vs. Western Ky. (29), East RF, 1940
30, Duquesne vs. Indiana (39), NSF, 1940
30, Pittsburgh vs. Wisconsin (36), NSF, 1941
30, Oregon St. vs. Oklahoma St. (55), NSF, 1949

WINNING MARGIN
69, Loyola (Ill.) (111) vs. Tennessee Tech (42), South 1st, 1963
58, Kansas (110) vs. Prairie View (52), MW 1st, 1998
49, UCLA (109) vs. Wyoming, (60), West RSF, 1967
49, Syracuse (101) vs. Brown (52), East 1st, 1986
47, Duke (101) vs. Connecticut (54), East RF, 1964
47, DePaul (99) vs. Eastern Ky. (52), South 1st, 1965
46, Kentucky (113) vs. Mt. St. Mary's (67), South 1st, 1995
45, North Carolina (112) vs. Rhode Island (67), East 2d, 1993
44, Kentucky (96) vs. Rider (52), South 1st, 1993
43, *Villanova (90) vs. Pennsylvania (47), East RF, 1971
43, Oklahoma (124) vs. Louisiana Tech (81), South 2d, 1989
43, Indiana (97) vs. Wright St. (54), MW 1st, 1993
43, Duke (95) vs. Monmouth (52), East 1st, 2001

SMALLEST WINNING MARGIN
1, 140 tied (most recent: three in 2001)

POINTS BY LOSING TEAM
120, Utah vs. St. Joseph's (127), N3d, 1961 (4 ot)
115, Wyoming vs. Loyola Marymount (119), West 1st, 1988
115, Michigan vs. Loyola Marymount (149), West 2d, 1990
109, UNLV vs. Arizona (114), West RSF, 1976 (ot)
106, Notre Dame vs. Iowa (121), South R3d, 1970
106, Notre Dame vs. Houston (119), MW R3d, 1971
103, Iowa vs. Jacksonville (104), South RSF, 1970
103, Kentucky vs. Duke (104), East RF, 1992 (ot)
102, Brigham Young vs. Oklahoma City (112), West R3d, 1965
102, UCLA vs. Tulsa (112), MW 1st, 1994

FIELD GOALS
52, Iowa vs. Notre Dame, South R3d, 1970
51, UCLA vs. Dayton, West RSF, 1974 (3 ot)
51, UNLV vs. Loyola Marymount, West RF, 1990
50, Utah vs. St. Joseph's, N3d, 1961 (4 ot)
50, Kentucky vs. Austin Peay, South RSF, 1973 (ot)
50, Notre Dame vs. Austin Peay, South 1st, 1974
49, Notre Dame vs. Vanderbilt, South R3d, 1974
49, UNLV vs. San Francisco, West 1st, 1977
49, North Carolina vs. Loyola Marymount, West 2d, 1988
49, Loyola Marymount vs. Michigan, West 2d, 1990

FEWEST FIELD GOALS
8, Springfield vs. Indiana, East 1st, 1940
9, Pittsburgh vs. North Carolina, East RSF, 1941
9, North Carolina vs. Pittsburgh, East RSF, 1941
9, Oklahoma St. vs. Kentucky, CH, 1949
10, Wisconsin vs. Pittsburgh, NSF, 1941
10, Kentucky vs. Dartmouth, NSF, 1942
10, Harvard vs. Ohio St., East 1st, 1946
11, Eight tied (most recent: Oregon St. vs. Oklahoma St., NSF, 1949)

FIELD GOALS ATTEMPTED
112, Marshall vs. La.-Lafayette, MW 1st, 1972
106, Indiana vs. Miami (Ohio), South R3d, 1958
105, *Western Ky. vs. Villanova, NSF, 1971 (2 ot)
103, St. Joseph's vs. West Virginia, East R3d, 1960
103, Utah vs. St. Joseph's, N3d, 1961 (4 ot)
103, Loyola Marymount vs. North Carolina, West 2d, 1988
102, Notre Dame vs. Houston, MW R3d, 1971
101, Holy Cross vs. North Carolina St., East 1st, 1950
101, *St. Joseph's vs. Utah, N3d, 1961 (4 ot)
100, Houston vs. Pacific (Cal.), West R3d, 1966
100, Rutgers vs. UCLA, N3d, 1976

FIELD-GOAL PERCENTAGE
80.0% (28-35), Oklahoma St. vs. Tulane, South 2d, 1992
79.0% (49-62), North Carolina vs. Loyola Marymount, West 2d, 1988
78.6% (22-28), Villanova vs. Georgetown, CH, 1985
75.0% (33-44), Northeastern vs. Va. Commonwealth, East 1st, 1984
74.4% (29-39), Georgetown vs. Oregon St., West RF, 1982
73.2% (30-41), North Carolina St. vs. UTEP, West 2d, 1985
72.7% (40-55), *Alabama vs. New Orleans, South 2d, 1987
71.4% (30-42), Villanova vs. Marshall, South 1st, 1984
71.4% (25-35), Georgetown vs. Notre Dame, East 2d, 1989
70.5% (31-44), Washington vs. Duke, West 2d, 1984

LOWEST FIELD-GOAL PERCENTAGE
12.7% (8-63), Springfield vs. Indiana, East RSF, 1940
13.9% (10-72), Harvard vs. Ohio St., East RSF, 1946
19.4% (14-72), Creighton vs. Cincinnati, MW RSF, 1962
19.5% (15-77), North Carolina St. vs. Baylor, N3d, 1950
20.6% (13-63), Arkansas vs. Oregon St., West RSF, 1949
21.5% (14-65), Washington St. vs. Wisconsin, CH, 1941
22.0% (18-82), Tennessee Tech vs. Loyola (Ill.), South 1st, 1963
22.9% (16-70), St. John's (N.Y.) vs. Kentucky, East RSF, 1951
23.3% (17-73), Prairie View vs. Kansas, MW 1st, 1998
23.4% (15-64), Baylor vs. Kentucky, CH, 1948

THREE-POINT FIELD GOALS
21, Loyola Marymount vs. Michigan, West 2d, 1990
18, Duke vs. Monmouth, East 1st, 2001
17, Loyola Marymount vs. UNLV, West RF, 1990
16, Kentucky vs. Wake Forest, South RSF, 1993
16, Georgia Tech vs. Boston College, South 2d, 1996
15, Wisconsin vs. Missouri, West 2d, 1994
15, Purdue vs. Kansas, South RSF, 1994
15, Southern Ill. vs. Syracuse, MW 1st, 1995
15, Cincinnati vs. Connecticut, West 2d, 1995
15, Arkansas vs. Siena, West 1st, 1999
15, Seton Hall vs. Temple, East 2d, 2000

THREE-POINT FIELD GOALS ATTEMPTED
43, St. Joseph's vs. Boston College, South 2d, 1997 (ot)
42, Long Island vs. Villanova, East 1st, 1997
41, Loyola Marymount vs. UNLV, West RF, 1990
40, Loyola Marymount vs. Michigan, West 2d, 1990
39, Loyola Marymount vs. North Carolina, West 2d, 1988
39, Loyola Marymount vs. Arkansas, MW 1st, 1989
39, St. Louis vs. Wake Forest, East 2d, 1995
38, Kentucky vs. Marquette, South 2d, 1994
38, Chattanooga vs. Connecticut, West 1st, 1995
38, Duke vs. Monmouth, East 1st, 2001
37, Wisconsin vs. Missouri, West 2d, 1994
37, Pennsylvania vs. Florida, East 2d, 1994
37, Arkansas vs. Iowa, West 2d, 1999

THREE-POINT FIELD-GOAL PERCENTAGE
(Minimum 7 3FGM)
88.9% (8-9), Kansas St. vs. Georgia, West 1st, 1987 (ot)
81.8% (9-11), *Alabama vs. N.C. A&T, South 1st, 1987
80.0% (8-10), Kansas St. vs. Purdue, MW RSF, 1988
80.0% (8-10), Maryland vs. Massachusetts, MW 2d, 1994
77.8% (7-9), Colorado vs. Indiana, East 1st, 1997
76.9% (10-13), Kansas St. vs. DePaul, MW 2d, 1988
73.7% (14-19), Duke vs. Southern Ill., MW 1st, 1993
72.7% (8-11), Duke vs. Indiana, MW RSF, 1987
72.7% (8-11), Alabama vs. Colorado St., West 1st, 1990
72.7% (8-11), Kansas vs. California, MW RSF, 1993

FREE THROWS
43, Arizona vs. Illinois, MW RF, 2001
41, Utah vs. Santa Clara, West R3d, 1960
41, Navy vs. Syracuse, East 2d, 1986
39, Seattle vs. Utah, West R3d, 1955
39, UTEP vs. Tulsa, West 1st, 1985
38, Bradley vs. Colorado, MW RSF, 1954
38, Loyola (Ill.) vs. Kentucky, South R3d, 1964
37, Morehead St. vs. Pittsburgh, South 1st, 1957
37, *St. Joseph's vs. Utah, N3d, 1961 (4 ot)
37, Jacksonville vs. St. Bonaventure, NSF, 1970
37, Xavier vs. Kansas St., MW 1st, 1990

FREE THROWS ATTEMPTED
56, Arizona vs. Illinois, MW RF, 2001
55, UTEP vs. Tulsa, West 1st, 1985
54, Morehead St. vs. Pittsburgh, South 1st, 1957
53, Morehead St. vs. Iowa, South RSF, 1956
52, Iowa vs. Morehead St., South RSF, 1956
52, Seattle vs. UCLA, West R3d, 1956
52, Weber St. vs. Hawaii, West 1st, 1972
52, Navy vs. Syracuse, East 2d, 1986
50, West Virginia vs. St. Joseph's, East RSF, 1959
50, Notre Dame vs. Kansas, MW 1st, 1975
49, Manhattan vs. West Virginia, East 1st, 1958
49, New York U. vs. St. Joseph's, East R3d, 1962

FREE-THROW PERCENTAGE
(Minimum 15 FTM)
100.0% (22-22), Fordham vs. South Carolina, East R3d, 1971
100.0% (17-17), Dayton vs. Villanova, South 1st, 1985
100.0% (17-17), Villanova vs. Kentucky, South RSF, 1988
95.8% (23-24), Oklahoma St. vs. Loyola (La.), MW 1st, 1958
95.5% (21-22), Vanderbilt vs. Marquette, South RSF, 1974
95.2% (20-21), Notre Dame vs. Vanderbilt, South R3d, 1974
95.2% (20-21), Iowa vs. North Carolina St., East 2d, 1989 (2 ot)
95.0% (19-20), North Carolina St. vs. St. John's (N.Y.), East R3d, 1951
95.0% (19-20), Iowa vs. Georgetown, East RF, 1980
95.0% (19-20), Oklahoma St. vs. Louisville, MW 2d, 1993

REBOUNDS
86, Notre Dame vs. Tennessee Tech, South 1st, 1958
76, Temple vs. Connecticut, East RSF, 1956
76, Houston vs. North Carolina, N3d, 1967
76, Houston vs. TCU, MW RF, 1968
76, UCLA vs. Weber St., West RSF, 1972
72, UCLA vs. Seattle, West R3d, 1956
72, Seattle vs. Utah St., West R3d, 1964
71, Kansas St. vs. Houston, MW R3d, 1970
70, Western Ky. vs. Miami (Fla.), South 1st, 1960
70, Arizona St. vs. Southern California, West RSF, 1961

REBOUND MARGIN
42, Notre Dame (86) vs. Tennessee Tech (44), South 1st, 1958
35, St. John's (N.Y.) (56) vs. Connecticut (21), East 1st, 1951
35, Kansas (64) vs. Prairie View (29), MW 1st, 1998
34, Kansas (61) vs. Jackson St. (27), South 1st, 1997
33, Cincinnati (68) vs. Texas Tech (35), MW RSF, 1961

33, Kansas (56) vs. Syracuse (23), MW 2d, 2001
30, Louisiana Tech (56) vs. Pittsburgh (26), MW 1st, 1985
30, Kansas (45) vs. Evansville (15), MW 1st, 1999
29, West Virginia (63) vs. Dartmouth (34), East 1st, 1959
29, Utah (59) vs. Loyola Marymount (30), West RSF, 1961
29, Indiana (52) vs. Robert Morris (23), South 1st, 1982

ASSISTS
36, North Carolina vs. Loyola Marymount, West 2d, 1988
35, UNLV vs. Loyola Marymount, West RF, 1990
35, Kentucky vs. San Jose St., MW 1st, 1996
33, Loyola Marymount vs. Michigan, West 2d, 1990
33, Kansas vs. Chattanooga, South 1st, 1994
33, Kentucky vs. Mt. St. Mary's, South 1st, 1995
32, Arkansas vs. Georgia St., South 1st, 1991
32, Kansas vs. Howard, MW 1st, 1992
32, Michigan vs. East Tenn. St., South 2d, 1992
32, Kansas vs. South Carolina St., West 1st, 1996

BLOCKED SHOTS
14, Kentucky vs. UCLA, South RSF, 1998
13, Louisville vs. Illinois, MW RSF, 1989
13, Brigham Young vs. Virginia, West 1st, 1991
13, Kansas vs. Jackson St., South 1st, 1997
12, Clemson vs. St. Mary's (Cal.), West 1st, 1989
12, LSU vs. Brigham Young, West 1st, 1992
12, Massachusetts vs. Stanford, East 2d, 1995
11, Eight tied (most recent: Kentucky vs. South Carolina, South 1st, 1998)

STEALS
19, Providence vs. Austin Peay, South 2d, 1987 (ot)
19, Connecticut vs. Boston U., East 1st, 1990
18, Xavier vs. Kansas, MW 1st, 1988
18, Arkansas vs. Holy Cross, East 1st, 1993
18, Louisville vs. Tulsa, MW 1st, 1996
18, Mississippi Val. vs. Georgetown, East 1st, 1996
18, Penn St. vs. North Carolina, South 2d, 2001
17, Seton Hall vs. Pepperdine, West 1st, 1991
17, Duke vs. St. John's (N.Y.), MW RF, 1991
17, Kentucky vs. Tennessee St., South 1st, 1994
17, Duke vs. Michigan St., South 2d, 1994
17, Kentucky vs. San Jose St., MW 1st, 1996
17, Duke vs. Radford, South 1st, 1998
17, Duke vs. UCLA, East RSF, 2001

PERSONAL FOULS
41, Dayton vs. Illinois, East RSF, 1952
39, Kansas vs. Notre Dame, MW 1st, 1975
36, UCLA vs. Seattle, West R3d, 1956
36, North Carolina vs. Texas A&M, MW 2d, 1980
36, Illinois vs. Arizona, MW RF, 2001
35, St. John's (N.Y.) vs. Kansas, CH, 1952
35, Iowa vs. Morehead St., South RSF, 1956
35, Hawaii vs. Weber St., West 1st, 1972
35, DePaul vs. VMI, East RSF, 1976 (ot)
35, DePaul vs. Boston College, MW 2d, 1982
35, Texas Tech vs. Georgetown, East RSF, 1996

PLAYERS DISQUALIFIED
6, Kansas vs. Notre Dame, MW 1st, 1975
6, Illinois vs. Arizona, MW RF, 2001
5, Dayton vs. Illinois, East RSF, 1952
5, St. Joseph's vs. West Virginia, East RSF, 1959
5, DePaul vs. VMI, East RSF, 1976 (ot)
5, DePaul vs. Boston College, MW 2d, 1982
5, Syracuse vs. Virginia, East RSF, 1984
5, Wyoming vs. Loyola Marymount, West 1st, 1988
4, 30 tied (most recent: Texas Tech vs. Georgetown, East RSF, 1996)

Two-Team Game

POINTS
264, Loyola Marymount (149) vs. Michigan (115), West 2d, 1990
247, *St. Joseph's (127) vs. Utah (120), N3d, 1961 (4 ot)
234, Loyola Marymount (119) vs. Wyoming (115), West 1st, 1988
232, UNLV (131) vs. Loyola Marymount (101), West RF, 1990
227, Iowa (121) vs. Notre Dame (106), South R3d, 1970
225, Houston (119) vs. Notre Dame (106), MW R3d, 1971
223, Arizona (114) vs. UNLV (109), West RSF, 1976 (ot)
221, Arkansas (120) vs. Loyola Marymount (101), MW 1st, 1989
220, North Carolina (123) vs. Loyola Marymount (97), West 2d, 1988
216, UNLV (121) vs. San Francisco (95), West 1st, 1977

FEWEST POINTS
46, Pittsburgh (26) vs. North Carolina (20), East RF, 1941
59, Duquesne (30) vs. Western Ky. (29), East RF, 1940
66, Wisconsin (36) vs. Pittsburgh (30), East NSF, 1941
69, Indiana (39) vs. Duquesne (30), NSF, 1940
70, Southern California (38) vs. Colorado (32), West RF, 1940
71, Utah (40) vs. Iowa St. (31), NSF, 1944
72, Villanova (42) vs. Brown (30), East RF, 1939
72, Indiana (48) vs. Springfield (24), East RF, 1946
73, Wisconsin (39) vs. Washington St. (34), CH, 1941
73, Oklahoma St. (44) vs. Baylor (29), West RF, 1946
73, Georgetown (37) vs. Southern Methodist (36), West RSF, 1984

FIELD GOALS
97, Iowa (52) vs. Notre Dame (45), South R3d, 1970
96, Kentucky (50) vs. Austin Peay (46), South RSF, 1973 (ot)
95, Utah (50) vs. *St. Joseph's (45), N3d, 1961 (4 ot)
94, Loyola Marymount (49) vs. Michigan (45), West 2d, 1990
91, UCLA (51) vs. Dayton (40), West RSF, 1974 (3 ot)

FIELD GOALS ATTEMPTED
204, Utah (103) vs. *St. Joseph's (101), N3d, 1961 (4 ot)
196, Austin Peay (99) vs. Kentucky (97), South RSF, 1973 (ot)
195, Iowa (98) vs. Notre Dame (97), South R3d, 1970
194, Indiana (106) vs. Miami (Ohio) (88), South R3d, 1958
194, Houston (100) vs. Pacific (Cal.) (94), West R3d, 1966

THREE-POINT FIELD GOALS
28, Seton Hall (15) vs. Temple (13), East 2d, 2000 (ot)
27, Wisconsin (15) vs. Missouri (12), West 2d, 1994
26, Temple (14) vs. Cincinnati (12), West 1st, 1995
25, Loyola Marymount (21) vs. Michigan (4), West 2d, 1990
25, Georgia Tech (16) vs. Boston College (9), South 2d, 1996

THREE-POINT FIELD GOALS ATTEMPTED
62, Arkansas (34) vs. North Carolina (28), NSF, 1995
62, St. Joseph's (43) vs. Boston College (19), West 2d, 1997 (ot)
62, Temple (32) vs. Seton Hall (30), East 2d, 2000 (ot)
61, Temple (32) vs. Lafayette (29), East 1st, 2000
61, Duke (38) vs. Monmouth (23), East 1st, 2001

FREE THROWS
69, Morehead St. (37) vs. Pittsburgh (32), South 1st, 1957
68, Iowa (35) vs. Morehead St. (33), South RSF, 1956
68, Oklahoma City (35) vs. Kansas St. (33), MW RSF, 1956
64, Bradley (38) vs. Colorado (26), West RSF, 1954
63, Four tied (most recent: Arizona [43] vs. Illinois [20], MW RF, 2001)

FREE THROWS ATTEMPTED
105, Morehead St. (53) vs. Iowa (52), South RSF, 1956
97, Morehead St. (54) vs. Pittsburgh (43), South 1st, 1957
92, Oklahoma City (48) vs. Kansas St. (44), MW RSF, 1956
92, Seattle (52) vs. UCLA (40), West R3d, 1956
91, Manhattan (49) vs. West Virginia (42), East 1st, 1958

REBOUNDS
134, Marshall (68) vs. *La.-Lafayette (66), MW 1st, 1972
132, Pacific (Cal.) (67) vs. Houston (65), West R3d, 1966
131, Houston (76) vs. TCU (55), MW RF, 1968
130, Notre Dame (86) vs. Tennessee Tech (44), South 1st, 1958
130, UCLA (76) vs. Weber St. (54), West RSF, 1972
128, UCLA (72) vs. Seattle (56), West R3d, 1956
128, Utah (65) vs. *St. Joseph's (63), N3d, 1961 (4 ot)
128, Houston (76) vs. North Carolina (52), N3d, 1967
126, Drake (66) vs. Notre Dame (60), MW RSF, 1971 (ot)
124, Three tied (most recent: Kansas St. [71] vs. Houston [53], MW R3d, 1970)

ASSISTS
58, UNLV (35) vs. Loyola Marymount (23), West RF, 1990
55, Michigan (30) vs. Florida (25), West 2d, 1988
54, Loyola Marymount (33) vs. Michigan (21), West 2d, 1990
53, North Carolina (36) vs. Loyola Marymount (17), West 2d, 1988
52, Wyoming (29) vs. Loyola Marymount (23), West 1st, 1988

BLOCKED SHOTS
18, Iowa (10) vs. Duke (8), East 2d, 1992
18, Kansas (13) vs. Jackson St. (5), South 1st, 1997
17, Duke (11) vs. Temple (6), East RF, 1988
17, Connecticut (10) vs. Colgate (7), South 1st, 1996
16, Oklahoma (9) vs. Louisiana Tech (7), South 2d, 1989
16, Massachusetts (9) vs. Tulsa (7), East RSF, 1995

STEALS
28, N.C. A&T (16) vs. Arkansas (12), MW 1st, 1994
28, Purdue (16) vs. Delaware (12), MW 1st, 1998
28, TCU (16) vs. Florida St. (12), MW 1st, 1998
28, Florida (15) vs. Weber St. (13), West 2d, 1999
27, Loyola Marymount (14) vs. UNLV (13), West RF, 1990
27, Duke (17) vs. UCLA (10), East RSF, 2001

PERSONAL FOULS
68, Iowa (35) vs. Morehead St. (33), South RSF, 1956
63, UNLV (34) vs. Arizona (29), West RSF, 1976
61, Colorado (34) vs. Bradley (27), West RSF, 1954
61, West Virginia (32) vs. Manhattan (29), East 1st, 1958
61, Kentucky (31) vs. Syracuse (30), NSF, 1975

Team Game—Overtimes

OVERTIME PERIODS
4, Canisius (79) vs. North Carolina St. (78), East 1st, 1956
4, *St. Joseph's (127) vs. Utah (120), N3d, 1961
3, North Carolina (54) vs. Kansas (53), CH, 1957
3, North Carolina (74) vs. Michigan St. (70), NSF, 1957
3, UCLA (111) vs. Dayton (100), West RSF, 1974
3, Villanova (76) vs. Northeastern (72), East 2d, 1982
3, Old Dominion (89) vs. Villanova (81), East 1st, 1995

POINTS IN OVERTIMES
38, *St. Joseph's vs. Utah, N3d, 1961 (4 ot)
31, Utah vs. St. Joseph's, N3d, 1961 (4 ot)
31, UCLA vs. Dayton, West RSF, 1974 (3 ot)
31, Old Dominion vs. Villanova, East 1st, 1995 (3 ot)
27, North Carolina St. vs. Iowa, East 2d, 1989 (2 ot)

POINTS IN OVERTIMES, BOTH TEAMS
69, *St. Joseph's (38) vs. Utah (31), N3d, 1961 (4 ot)
54, Old Dominion (31) vs. Villanova (23), East 1st, 1995 (3 ot)
51, UCLA (31) vs. Dayton (20), West RSF, 1974 (3 ot)
48, North Carolina St. (27) vs. Iowa (21), East 2d, 1989 (2 ot)
43, LSU (25) vs. Purdue (18), South 1st, 1986 (2 ot)

POINTS IN ONE OVERTIME PERIOD
25, Texas A&M vs. North Carolina, MW 2d, 1980 (2d ot)
24, Alabama vs. Pennsylvania, East 1st, 1995
22, Utah vs. Missouri, MW 1st, 1978
21, LSU vs. Purdue, South 1st, 1986 (2d ot)
19, Nine tied (most recent: North Carolina vs. Charlotte, East 2d, 1998)

TOURNAMENT RECORDS—TEAM GAME—OVERTIMES

POINTS IN ONE OVERTIME PERIOD, BOTH TEAMS
- 42, Alabama (24) vs. Pennsylvania (18), East 1st, 1995
- 37, Utah (22) vs. Missouri (15), MW 1st, 1978
- 35, LSU (21) vs. Purdue (14), South 1st, 1986 (2d ot)
- 34, Iowa (18) vs. Oklahoma (16), West RSF, 1987
- 33, Texas A&M (25) vs. North Carolina (8), MW 2d, 1980 (2d ot)

LEAST POINTS IN ONE OVERTIME PERIOD
- 0, Nine tied (most recent: Va. Commonwealth vs. Tennessee, East 2d, 1981)

LEAST POINTS IN ONE OVERTIME PERIOD, BOTH TEAMS
- 0, Canisius vs. North Carolina St., East 1st, 1956 (3rd ot)
- 0, North Carolina vs. Kansas, CH, 1957 (2d ot)
- 0, Texas A&M vs. North Carolina, MW 2d, 1980 (1st ot)
- 1, Southern California (1) vs. Santa Clara (0), West RF, 1956 (2d ot)
- 2, Tennessee (2) vs. Va. Commonwealth (0), East 2d, 1981 (1st ot)

LARGEST WINNING MARGIN IN AN OVERTIME GAME
- 17, Texas A&M (78) vs. North Carolina (61), MW 2d, 1980 (2 ot)
- 14, North Carolina St. (80) vs. Ark.-Little Rock (66), MW 2d, 1986 (2 ot)
- 12, UCLA (103) vs. Michigan (91), West 1st, 1975
- 12, Louisville (80) vs. Kentucky (68), South RF, 1983
- 11, Four tied (most recent: Charlotte [81] vs. Rhode Island [70], MW 1st, 1999)

OVERTIME GAMES BY ONE TEAM IN ONE TOURNAMENT
- 3, Syracuse, 1975
- 2, 12 tied (most recent: Arizona, 1997)

OVERTIME PERIODS BY ONE TEAM IN ONE TOURNAMENT
- 6, North Carolina, 1957 (2 games)
- 5, UCLA, 1974 (2 games)
- 3, 14 tied (most recent: Old Dominion, 1995 [2 games]; Villanova, 1995 [1 game])

Team Game — Miscellaneous

PLAYERS IN DOUBLE FIGURES, TEAM
- 7, Indiana vs. George Mason, West 1st, 1989
- 7, UNLV vs. Ark.-Little Rock, West 1st, 1990
- 6, 17 tied (most recent: two in 1995)

PLAYERS IN DOUBLE FIGURES, BOTH TEAMS
- 12, Notre Dame (6) vs. Houston (6), West 1st, 1965
- 11, Eight tied (most recent: Michigan [6] vs. Loyola Marymount [5], West 2d, 1990)

PLAYERS WITH 20-PLUS POINTS, TEAM
- 4, Fordham vs. South Carolina, East R3d, 1971
- 4, Syracuse vs. Western Ky., East 2d, 1987
- 4, Loyola Marymount vs. Michigan, West 2d, 1990
- 4, UNLV vs. Loyola Marymount, West RF, 1990

PLAYERS WITH 20-PLUS POINTS, BOTH TEAMS
- 6, 10 tied (most recent: two in 1990)

PLAYERS SCORED, TEAM
- 14, Iowa vs. Santa Clara, West 1st, 1987
- 13, Indiana vs. St. Joseph's, South RF, 1981
- 13, Indiana vs. Fairfield, MW 1st, 1987

PLAYERS SCORED, BOTH TEAMS
- 24, Brown (12) vs. Syracuse (12), East 1st, 1986
- 24, Iowa (14) vs. Santa Clara (10), West 1st, 1987
- 22, Duke (12) vs. Connecticut (10), East RF, 1964

FEWEST PLAYERS SCORED, TEAM
- 3, Utah St. vs. San Francisco, West RSF, 1964
- 4, 12 tied (most recent: Indiana vs. Syracuse, CH, 1987)

FEWEST PLAYERS SCORED, BOTH TEAMS
- 9, Connecticut (4) vs. Temple, East 1st, 1964
- 9, Michigan St. (4) vs. Washington (5), MW 1st, 1986
- 10, 13 tied (most recent: Indiana [4] vs. Syracuse [6], CH, 1987)

PLAYERS USED, TEAM
- 15, 14 tied (most recent: two in 1995)

PLAYERS USED, BOTH TEAMS
- 29, Arizona St. (15) vs. Loyola Marymount (14), West 1st, 1980
- 27, Eight tied (most recent: three in 1995)

FEWEST PLAYERS USED, TEAM
- 5, Nine tied (most recent: DePaul twice in 1979, vs. Southern California, West 2d, and vs. Indiana St., NSF)

FEWEST PLAYERS USED, BOTH TEAMS
- 12, Five tied (most recent: St. Joseph's [6] vs. DePaul [6], South 2d, 1981)

Team Series

(Three-Game Minimum for Averages and Percentages)

POINTS
- 571, UNLV, 1990 (6 games)
- 552, Oklahoma, 1988 (6)
- 540, Michigan, 1989 (6)
- 535, Indiana, 1987 (6)
- 535, Kentucky, 1996 (6)

SCORING AVERAGE
- 105.8, (423 points in 4 games), Loyola Marymount, 1990
- 105.7, (317 in 3), Notre Dame, 1970
- 101.0, (505 in 5), UNLV, 1977
- 100.0, (400 in 4), UCLA, 1965
- 98.7, (296 in 3), *La.-Lafayette, 1972

FIELD GOALS
- 218, UNLV, 1977 (5 games)
- 217, UNLV, 1990 (6)
- 217, Michigan, 1989 (6)
- 206, Oklahoma, 1988 (6)
- 203, Louisville, 1986 (6)

FIELD GOALS ATTEMPTED
- 442, *Western Ky., 1971 (5 games)
- 441, UNLV, 1977 (5)
- 418, Houston, 1968 (5)
- 412, Oklahoma, 1988 (6)
- 410, UNLV, 1990 (6)

FIELD-GOAL PERCENTAGE
- 60.4% (113-187), North Carolina, 1975 (3 games)
- 59.6% (96-161), Michigan, 1988 (3)
- 59.0% (92-156), Michigan St., 1978 (3)
- 58.6% (99-169), *Alabama, 1987 (3)
- 58.2% (85-146), Wake Forest, 1993 (3)

THREE-POINT FIELD GOALS
- 60, Arkansas, 1995 (6 games)
- 60, Duke, 2001 (6)
- 56, Loyola Marymount, 1990 (4)
- 49, Kentucky, 1993 (5)
- 47, Arkansas, 1994 (6)
- 45, Providence, 1987 (5)
- 45, Kentucky, 1997 (6)

THREE-POINT FIELD GOALS ATTEMPTED
- 175, Duke, 2001 (6 games)
- 165, Arkansas, 1995 (6)
- 137, Loyola Marymount, 1990 (4)
- 132, UNLV, 1987 (5)
- 120, Kentucky, 1997 (6)
- 120, Florida, 2000 (6)

THREE-POINT FIELD-GOAL PERCENTAGE (Minimum 12 3FGM)
- 60.9% (14-23), Indiana, 1989 (3 games)
- 59.3% (16-27), St. John's (N.Y.), 1991 (4)
- 54.0% (27-50), Virginia, 1989 (4)
- 53.5% (23-43), Miami (Ohio), 2000 (3)
- 52.5% (21-40), Indiana, 1987 (6)

THREE-POINT FIELD-GOAL PERCENTAGE (Minimum 30 3FGM)
- 51.9% (40-77), Kansas, 1993 (5 games)
- 50.8% (33-65), Kansas St., 1988 (4)
- 47.8% (43-90), Michigan, 1989 (6)
- 47.1% (49-104), Duke, 1999 (6)
- 47.1% (32-68), Vanderbilt, 1993 (3)

FREE THROWS
- 146, Bradley, 1954 (5 games)
- 136, *UCLA, 1980 (6)
- 136, Duke, 1990 (5)
- 136, Duke, 1992 (6)
- 130, Southern Methodist, 1956 (5)

FREE THROWS ATTEMPTED
- 194, Bradley, 1954 (5 games)
- 192, West Virginia, 1959 (5)
- 183, Duke, 1990 (5)
- 183, Duke, 1992 (6)
- 178, Purdue, 1980 (6)

FREE-THROW PERCENTAGE
- 87.0% (47-54), St. John's (N.Y.), 1969 (3 games)
- 85.7% (36-42), Utah, 1996 (3)
- 85.5% (47-55), Notre Dame, 1987 (3)
- 84.8% (50-59), *Alabama, 1987 (3)
- 84.4% (76-90), Temple, 1988 (4)

REBOUNDS
- 306, Houston, 1968 (5 games)
- 289, *Western Ky., 1971 (5)
- 268, New Mexico St., 1970 (5)
- 262, UNLV, 1990 (6)
- 246, Arizona, 1997 (6)

ASSISTS
- 143, Kentucky, 1996 (6 games)
- 140, UNLV, 1990 (6)
- 136, Oklahoma, 1988 (6)
- 125, Michigan, 1989 (6)
- 120, Louisville, 1986 (6)

BLOCKED SHOTS
- 48, Kentucky, 1998 (6 games)
- 42, Arizona, 2001 (6)
- 37, Massachusetts, 1995 (4)
- 35, Massachusetts, 1996 (5)
- 34, Duke, 1994 (6)

STEALS
- 72, Oklahoma, 1988 (6 games)
- 71, Kentucky, 1996 (6)
- 65, Arkansas, 1995 (6)
- 64, Kentucky, 1997 (6)
- 57, Arkansas, 1990 (5)
- 57, Massachusetts, 1996 (5)

PERSONAL FOULS
- 150, Pennsylvania, 1979 (6 games)
- 135, Providence, 1987 (5)
- 130, Arkansas, 1995 (6)
- 128, Kentucky, 1975 (5)
- 126, Kentucky, 1997 (6)

Tournament History Facts

Team Records

TOURNAMENT APPEARANCES
- 42, *Kentucky, 1942-2001
- 35, North Carolina, 1941-2001
- 35, *UCLA, 1950-2001
- 30, Indiana, 1940-2001
- 30, Kansas, 1940-2001
- 29, Louisville, 1951-2000
- 26, St. John's (N.Y.), 1951-2000
- 27, Syracuse, 1957-2001
- 26, Arkansas, 1945-2001
- 25, Duke, 1955-2001
- 25, Notre Dame, 1953-2001
- 25, Temple, 1944-2001

CONSECUTIVE TOURNAMENT APPEARANCES
- 27, North Carolina, 1975-2001
- 17, Arizona, 1985-2001
- 16, Indiana, 1986-2001
- 14, Georgetown, 1979-92
- 13, UCLA, 1967-79
- 13, UCLA, 1989-2001
- 11, Duke, 1984-94
- 12, Temple, 1990-2001
- 12, Kansas, 1990-2001
- 10, Cincinnati, 1992-2001
- 10, Kentucky, 1992-2001
- 10, LSU, 1984-93
- 10, Marquette, 1971-80
- 10, Syracuse, 1983-92

TOURNAMENT HISTORY FACTS—TEAM RECORDS

Only four times has the No. 15 seed won a NCAA tournament game, including last year when Tarvis Williams led Hampton to an upset win over No. 2 Iowa State.

CURRENT CONSECUTIVE TOURNAMENT APPEARANCES
27, North Carolina, 1975-2001
17, Arizona, 1985-2001
16, Indiana, 1986-2001
13, UCLA, 1989-2001
12, Kansas, 1990-2001
12, Temple, 1990-2001
10, Cincinnati, 1992-2001
10, Kentucky, 1992-2001
8, Maryland, 1994-2001
7, Oklahoma, 1995-2001
7, Stanford, 1995-2001

TOURNAMENT GAMES
124, *Kentucky, 1942-2001
116, North Carolina, 1941-2001
106, *UCLA, 1950-2001
95, Duke, 1955-2001
91, Kansas, 1940-2001
79, Louisville, 1951-2000
77, Indiana, 1940-2001
68, Syracuse, 1957-2001
65, Arkansas, 1945-2001
60, Michigan, 1948-98

TOURNAMENT WINS
87, *Kentucky, 1942-2001
81, North Carolina, 1941-2001
78, *UCLA, 1950-2001
73, Duke, 1955-2001
61, Kansas, 1940-2001
52, Indiana, 1940-2001
48, Louisville, 1951-2000
41, Michigan, 1948-98
40, Syracuse, 1957-2001
39, Arkansas, 1945-2001

TOURNAMENT WINNING PERCENTAGE
(Minimum 20 Games)
.768 (73-22), Duke, 1955-2001
.736 (78-28), *UCLA, 1950-2001
.702 (33-14), Michigan St., 1957-2001
.702 (87-37), *Kentucky, 1942-2001
.698 (81-35), North Carolina, 1941-2001
.698 (30-13), UNLV, 1975-2000
.683 (41-19), Michigan, 1948-98
.675 (52-25), Indiana, 1940-2001
.670 (61-30), Kansas, 1940-2001
.667 (14-7), Seton Hall, 1988-2000

* Does not include vacated years except for streaks

Farthest Seeds Have Advanced in the Tournament

(SINCE 1979)

Seed	Farthest Finish
# 1	CH—Arkansas 1994, Connecticut 1999, Duke 1992 & 2001, Georgetown 1984, Indiana 1987, Kentucky 1996, Michigan St. 2000, UNLV 1990, North Carolina 1982 & 1993, UCLA 1995
# 2	CH—Duke 1991, Kentucky 1998, Louisville 1980 & 1986, Michigan St. 1979
# 3	CH—Indiana 1981, Michigan 1989
# 4	CH—Arizona 1997
# 5	2d—Florida 2000
# 6	CH—Kansas 1988, North Carolina St. 1983
# 7	T3d—Virginia 1984
# 8	CH—Villanova 1985
# 9	4th—Pennsylvania 1979
#10	RR—Dayton 1984, Gonzaga 1999, LSU 1987, Providence 1997, St. John's (N.Y.) 1979, Texas 1990, Temple 1991
#11	T3d—LSU 1986
#12	RSF—Arkansas 1996, Ball St. 1990, DePaul 1986, Eastern Mich. 1991, George Washington 1993, Gonzaga 2001, Kentucky 1985, New Mexico St. 1992, Southwest Mo. St. 1999, Tulsa 1994, Wyoming 1987
#13	RSF—Oklahoma 1999, Richmond 1988, Valparaiso 1998
#14	RSF—Cleveland St. 1986, Chattanooga 1997
#15	2dR—Coppin St. 1997, Hampton 2001, Richmond 1991, Santa Clara 1993
#16	—

Won-Lost Records of Tournament Seeds

Year	#1	#2	#3	#4	#5	#6	#7	#8	#9	#10	#11	#12	#13	#14	#15	#16
1979	8-4	11-3	3-4	2-4	2-4	1-4	2-4	2-4	5-5	4-4						
1980	4-4	7-3	2-4	3-4	7-5	11-4	3-4	8-4	0-4	2-4	0-4	1-4				
1981	7-5	5-4	6-3	2-4	6-4	7-4	4-4	4-4	4-4	2-4	1-4	0-4				
1982	10-3	5-4	6-4	4-4	5-4	5-4	3-4	4-4	2-4	1-4	2-4	0-4				
1983	10-4	3-4	5-4	6-4	3-4	7-3	3-4	3-4	1-4	3-4	2-4	1-4		Opening Round		4-4
1984	10-3	6-4	2-4	4-4	5-4	5-4	5-4	3-4	1-4	4-4	1-4	1-4		Opening Round		5-5
1985	13-4	11-4	7-4	4-4	5-4	1-4	5-4	7-3	2-4	0-4	5-4	2-4	1-4	0-4	0-4	0-4
1986	13-4	10-3	3-4	5-4	5-4	5-4	6-4	5-4	1-4	1-4	4-4	2-4	0-4	3-4	0-4	0-4
1987	16-3	11-4	4-4	2-4	6-4	9-4	2-4	1-4	3-4	4-4	0-4	2-4	2-4	1-4	0-4	0-4
1988	14-4	10-4	4-4	5-4	6-4	10-3	4-4	3-4	1-4	1-4	2-4	0-4	2-4	1-4	0-4	0-4
1989	11-4	11-4	13-3	6-4	6-4	0-4	3-4	0-4	4-4	1-4	5-4	1-4	1-4	1-4	0-4	0-4
1990	12-3	5-4	7-4	10-4	3-4	6-4	5-4	3-4	2-4	3-4	3-4	3-4	0-4	1-4	0-4	0-4
1991	13-4	10-3	10-4	7-4	3-4	2-4	2-4	3-4	1-4	4-4		2-4	1-4	1-4	1-4	0-4
1992	13-3	10-4	5-4	8-4	3-4	10-4	3-4	1-4	4-4	2-4	0-4	2-4	1-4	1-4	0-4	0-4
1993	18-3	8-4	7-4	5-4	4-4	5-4	7-4	2-4	2-4	0-4	1-4	2-4	1-4	0-4	1-4	0-4
1994	13-3	12-4	10-4	6-4	3-4	4-4	2-4	0-4	6-4	3-4	1-4	3-4	0-4	0-4	0-4	0-4
1995	13-3	15-4	3-4	8-4	5-4	6-4	3-4	2-4	2-4	1-4	1-4	1-4	1-4	2-4	0-4	0-4
1996	13-3	12-4	7-4	8-4	5-4	4-4	2-4	2-4	3-4	2-4	1-4	1-4	0-4	0-4	0-4	0-4
1997	15-4	7-4	3-4	11-3	4-4	8-4	2-4	2-4	2-4	5-4	0-4	1-4	0-4	2-4	1-4	0-4
1998	11-4	12-3	10-4	5-4	4-4	3-4	1-4	5-4	1-4	4-4	3-4	1-4	2-4	1-4	0-4	0-4
1999	17-3	5-4	7-4	6-4	3-4	7-4	0-4	0-4	4-4	8-4	0-4	3-4	2-4	1-4	0-4	0-4
2000	10-3	6-4	6-4	7-4	8-4	7-4	4-4	10-4	0-4	4-4	1-4	0-4	0-4	0-4	0-4	0-4
2001	16-3	4-4	2-4	3-4	4-4	4-4	3-4	0-4	4-4	3-4	4-4	2-4	0-4	1-4	0-4	

Not Seeded: Opening Round 1-1 in 2001

Tournament trivia

Question...
What four No. 15 seeds upset No. 2 seeds to advance to the second round of the NCAA tournament?

Answer...
Richmond in 1991, Santa Clara in 1993, Coppin State in 1997 and Hampton in 2001

TOURNAMENT HISTORY FACTS—HOW THE SEEDS HAVE FARED

How the Seeds Have Fared

ROUND-BY-ROUND: 1985-99

	1st	2d	RSF	RF	NSF	CH	Total	
#1	68-0	59-9	48-11	30-18	16-14	10-6	231-58	10 CH, 6 2d, 14 T3d
#2	64-4	44-20	31-13	14-17	7-7	3-4	163-65	3 CH, 4 2d, 7 T3d
#3	55-13	30-25	15-15	8-7	5-3	1-4	114-67	CH, 4 2d, 3 T3d
#4	54-14	32-22	11-21	7-4	2-5	1-1	107-67	CH, 2d, 5 T3d
#5	48-20	22-26	3-19	2-1	1-1	0-1	76-68	2d, T3d
#6	47-21	27-20	11-16	3-8	2-1	1-1	91-67	CH, 2d, T3d
#7	40-28	11-29	3-8	0-3			54-68	
#8	29-39	7-22	5-2	3-2	1-2	1-0	46-67	CH, 2 T3d
#9	39-29	2-37	1-1	0-1			42-68	
#10	28-40	13-15	5-8	0-5			46-68	
#11	21-47	9-12	3-6	1-2	0-1		34-68	T3d
#12	20-48	11-9	0-11				31-68	
#13	14-54	3-11	0-3				17-68	
#14	13-55	2-11	0-2				15-68	
#15	4-64	0-4					4-68	
#16	0-68						0-68	
	544-544	272-272	136-136	68-68	34-34	17-17	1072-1072	

Not Seeded: Opening Round 1-1

1979-2000 TOTALS

Seed	W	L	Pct.	Final Four Finishes
# 1	280	81	.776	12 CH, 9 2d, 3d, 16 T3d, 4th
# 2	200	87	.697	5 CH, 6 2d, 3d, 7 T3d
# 3	138	90	.605	2 CH, 4 2d, 4 T3d
# 4	128	91	.584	CH, 2d, 6 T3d
# 5	104	93	.528	2d, T3d, 4th
# 6	127	90	.585	2 CH, 2d, 3d, 2 T3d
# 7	74	92	.446	T3d
# 8	70	91	.435	CH, 2d, 2 T3d
# 9	55	93	.372	4th
#10	62	92	.403	
#11	40	88	.313	T3d
#12	34	88	.279	
#13	17	68	.200	
#14	15	68	.181	
#15	4	68	.056	
#16	0	68	.000	
Not Seeded	1	1	.500	

Mel Counts of Oregon State led all scorers in the 1963 NCAA tournament with 123 points.

Individual Scoring Leaders

Note: On all percentages of the year-by-year leaders, a player must have played in at least 50 percent of the maximum tournament games. Thus, there is a two-game minimum from 1939-52 and a three-game minimum from 1953 to present.

Year	Player, Team	G	FG	FT	Pts.	Avg.
1939	Jim Hull, Ohio St.	3	22	14	58	19.3
1940	Howard Engleman, Kansas	3	18	3	39	13.0
1941	Johnny Adams, Arkansas	2	21	6	48	24.0
1942	Chet Palmer, Rice	2	19	5	43	21.5
	Jim Pollard, Stanford	2	20	3	43	21.5
1943	John Hargis, Texas	2	21	17	59	29.5
1944	Audley Brindley, Dartmouth	3	24	4	52	17.3
1945	Bob Kurland, Oklahoma St.	3	30	5	65	21.7
1946	Bob Kurland, Oklahoma St.	3	28	16	72	24.0
1947	George Kaftan, Holy Cross	3	25	13	63	21.0
1948	Alex Groza, Kentucky	3	23	8	54	18.0
1949	Alex Groza, Kentucky	3	31	20	82	27.3
1950	Sam Ranzino, North Carolina St.	3	25	25	75	25.0
1951	Don Sunderlage, Illinois	4	28	27	83	20.8
1952	Clyde Lovellette, Kansas	4	53	35	141	35.3
1953	Bob Houbregs, Washington	4	57	25	139	34.8
1954	Tom Gola, La Salle	5	38	38	114	22.8
1955	Bill Russell, San Francisco	5	49	20	118	23.6
1956	Hal Lear, Temple	5	63	34	160	32.0
1957	Lennie Rosenbluth, North Carolina	5	53	34	140	28.0
1958	Elgin Baylor, Seattle	5	48	39	135	27.0
1959	Jerry West, West Virginia	5	57	46	160	32.0
1960	Oscar Robertson, Cincinnati	4	47	28	122	30.5
1961	Billy McGill, Utah	4	49	21	119	29.8
1962	Len Chappell, Wake Forest	5	45	44	134	26.8
1963	Mel Counts, Oregon St.	5	50	23	123	24.6
1964	Jeff Mullins, Duke	4	50	16	116	29.0
1965	Bill Bradley, Princeton	5	65	47	177	35.4
1966	Jerry Chambers, Utah	4	55	33	143	35.8
1967	Elvin Hayes, Houston	5	57	14	128	25.6
1968	Elvin Hayes, Houston	5	70	27	167	33.4

Year	Player, Team	G	FG	FT	Pts.	Avg.
1969	Rick Mount, Purdue	4	49	24	122	30.5
1970	Austin Carr, Notre Dame	3	68	22	158	52.7
1971	*Jim McDaniels, Western Ky.	5	61	25	147	29.4
	Austin Carr, Notre Dame	3	48	29	125	41.7
1972	Jim Price, Louisville	4	41	21	103	25.8
1973	Ernie DiGregorio, Providence	5	59	10	128	25.6
1974	David Thompson, North Carolina St.	4	38	21	97	24.3
1975	Jim Lee, Syracuse	5	51	17	119	23.8
1976	Scott May, Indiana	5	45	23	113	22.6
1977	Cedric Maxwell, Charlotte	5	39	45	123	24.6
1978	Mike Gminski, Duke	5	45	19	109	21.8
1979	Tony Price, Pennsylvania	6	58	26	142	23.7
1980	Joe Barry Carroll, Purdue	6	63	32	158	26.3
1981	Al Wood, North Carolina	5	44	21	109	21.8
1982	Rob Williams, Houston	5	30	28	88	17.6
1983	Dereck Whittenburg, North Carolina St.	6	47	26	120	20.0
1984	Roosevelt Chapman, Dayton	4	35	35	105	26.3
1985	Chris Mullin, St. John's (N.Y.)	5	39	32	110	22.0
1986	Johnny Dawkins, Duke	6	66	21	153	25.5

Year	Player, Team	G	FG	3FG	FT	Pts.	Avg.
1987	Steve Alford, Indiana	6	42	21	33	138	23.0
	Rony Seikaly, Syracuse	6	53	0	32	138	23.0
1988	Danny Manning, Kansas	6	69	2	23	163	27.2
1989	Glen Rice, Michigan	6	75	7	27	184	30.7
1990	Dennis Scott, Georgia Tech	5	51	24	27	153	30.6
1991	Christian Laettner, Duke	6	37	2	49	125	20.8
1992	Christian Laettner, Duke	6	39	7	30	115	19.2
1993	Donald Williams, North Carolina	6	40	22	16	118	19.7
1994	Khalid Reeves, Arizona	5	45	8	39	137	27.4
1995	Corliss Williamson, Arkansas	6	49	0	27	125	20.8
1996	John Wallace, Syracuse	6	46	6	30	128	21.3
1997	Miles Simon, Arizona	6	42	10	38	132	22.0
1998	Michael Doleac, Utah	6	34	2	45	115	19.2
1999	Richard Hamilton, Connecticut	6	56	7	26	145	24.2
2000	Morris Peterson, Michigan St.	6	35	15	20	105	17.5
2001	Jason Williams, Duke	6	52	23	27	154	25.7

*later vacated

Highest Scoring Average

Year	Player, Team	G	FG	FT	Pts.	Avg.
1939	Jim Hull, Ohio St.	3	22	14	58	19.3
1940	Howard Engleman, Kansas	3	18	3	39	13.0
	Bob Kinney, Rice	2	12	2	26	13.0
1941	Johnny Adams, Arkansas	2	21	6	48	24.0
1942	Chet Palmer, Rice	2	19	5	43	21.5
	Jim Pollard, Stanford	2	20	3	43	21.5
1943	John Hargis, Texas	2	21	17	59	29.5
1944	Nick Bozolich, Pepperdine	2	17	11	45	22.5
1945	Dick Wilkins, Oregon	2	19	6	44	22.0
1946	Bob Kurland, Oklahoma St.	3	28	16	72	24.0
1947	George Kaftan, Holy Cross	3	25	13	63	21.0
1948	Jack Nichols, Washington	2	13	13	39	19.5
1949	Alex Groza, Kentucky	3	31	20	82	27.3
1950	Sam Ranzino, North Carolina St.	3	25	25	75	25.0
1951	Bill Kukoy, North Carolina St.	3	25	19	69	23.0
1952	Clyde Lovellette, Kansas	4	53	35	141	35.3
1953	Bob Houbregs, Washington	4	57	25	139	34.8
1954	John Clune, Navy	3	30	19	79	26.3
1955	Terry Rand, Marquette	3	31	11	73	24.3
1956	Hal Lear, Temple	5	63	34	160	32.0
1957	Wilt Chamberlain, Kansas	4	40	41	121	30.3
1958	Wayne Embry, Miami (Ohio)	3	32	19	83	27.7
1959	Jerry West, West Virginia	5	57	46	160	32.0
1960	Jerry West, West Virginia	3	35	35	105	35.0
1961	Billy McGill, Utah	4	49	21	119	29.8
1962	Len Chappell, Wake Forest	5	45	44	134	26.8
1963	Barry Kramer, New York U.	3	31	38	100	33.3
1964	Jeff Mullins, Duke	4	50	16	116	29.0
1965	Bill Bradley, Princeton	5	65	47	177	35.4
1966	Jerry Chambers, Utah	4	55	33	143	35.8
1967	Lew Alcindor, UCLA	4	39	28	106	26.5
1968	Elvin Hayes, Houston	5	70	27	167	33.4
1969	Rick Mount, Purdue	4	49	24	122	30.5
1970	Austin Carr, Notre Dame	3	68	22	158	52.7
1971	Austin Carr, Notre Dame	3	48	29	125	41.7
1972	*Dwight Lamar, La.-Lafayette	3	41	18	100	33.3
	Jim Price, Louisville	4	41	21	103	25.8
1973	Larry Finch, Memphis	4	34	39	107	26.8
1974	John Shumate, Notre Dame	3	35	16	86	28.7
1975	Adrian Dantley, Notre Dame	3	29	34	92	30.7
1976	Willie Smith, Missouri	3	38	18	94	31.3
1977	Cedric Maxwell, Charlotte	5	39	45	123	24.6
1978	Dave Corzine, DePaul	3	33	16	82	27.3
1979	Larry Bird, Indiana St.	5	52	32	136	27.2
1980	Joe Barry Carroll, Purdue	6	63	32	158	26.3
1981	Al Wood, North Carolina	5	44	21	109	21.8
1982	Oliver Robinson, UAB	3	27	12	66	22.0
1983	Greg Stokes, Iowa	3	24	13	61	20.3
1984	Roosevelt Chapman, Dayton	4	35	35	105	26.3
1985	Kenny Walker, Kentucky	3	28	19	75	25.0
1986	David Robinson, Navy	4	35	40	110	27.5

Year	Player, Team	G	FG	3FG	FT	Pts.	Avg.
1987	Fennis Dembo, Wyoming	3	25	11	23	84	28.0
1988	Danny Manning, Kansas	6	69	2	23	163	27.2
1989	Glen Rice, Michigan	6	75	7	27	184	30.7
1990	Bo Kimble, Loyola Marymount	4	51	15	26	143	35.8
1991	Terry Dehere, Seton Hall	4	34	12	17	97	24.3
1992	Jamal Mashburn, Kentucky	4	34	6	22	96	24.0
1993	Calbert Cheaney, Indiana	4	40	3	23	106	26.5
1994	Gary Collier, Tulsa	3	30	13	21	94	31.3
1995	Darryl Wilson, Mississippi St.	3	21	9	22	73	24.3
1996	Allen Iverson, Georgetown	4	38	12	23	111	27.8
1997	Dedric Willoughby, Iowa St.	3	24	14	12	74	24.7
1998	Khalid El-Amin, Connecticut	4	30	10	23	93	23.3
1999	Wally Szczerbiak, Miami (Ohio)	4	32	11	15	90	30.0
2000	Marcus Fizer, Iowa St.	4	32	2	14	80	20.0
2001	Jason Williams, Duke	6	52	23	27	154	25.7

*later vacated

Highest Field-Goal Percentage

(Minimum: 5 FGM Per Game)

Year	Player, Team	G	FGM	FGA	Pct.
1950	Dick Schnittker, Ohio St.	2	15	29	51.7
1951	Don Sunderlage, Illinois	4	28	62	45.2
1963	William Humphrey, Texas	3	16	22	72.7
1964	Jay Buckley, Duke	4	24	39	61.5
1965	Dave Mills, DePaul	3	16	21	76.2
1966	Henry Finkel, Dayton	3	37	61	60.7
1967	Ken Talley, Virginia Tech	3	20	30	66.7
1968	Heyward Dotson, Columbia	3	22	28	78.6
1969	Jarrett Durham, Duquesne	3	26	38	68.4
1970	Pembrook Burrows, Jacksonville	5	24	33	72.7
1971	Jim Chones, Marquette	3	29	48	60.4
1972	*Wilbert Loftin, La.-Lafayette	3	16	23	69.6
	Bill Walton, UCLA	4	28	41	68.3
1973	Bill Walton, UCLA	4	45	59	76.3
1974	John Shumate, Notre Dame	3	35	50	70.0
1975	Mitch Kupchak, North Carolina	3	29	40	72.5
1976	Ron Carter, VMI	3	22	37	59.5
1977	Rick Robey, Kentucky	3	16	22	72.7
1978	Greg Kelser, Michigan St.	3	29	40	72.5
1979	Alex Gilbert, Indiana St.	5	26	34	76.5
1980	Mark Dressler, Missouri	3	27	35	77.1
1981	Randy Reed, Kansas St.	4	22	33	66.7
1982	Larry Micheaux, Houston	5	29	45	64.4
1983	Ralph Sampson, Virginia	3	23	31	74.2
1984	Kelvin Johnson, Richmond	3	29	38	76.3
1985	Brad Daugherty, North Carolina	4	29	40	72.5
1986	Kenny Walker, Kentucky	4	35	50	70.0
1987	Kevin Gamble, Iowa	4	32	41	78.0
1988	*Winston Bennett, Kentucky	3	18	23	78.3
	Tim Perry, Temple	4	26	36	72.2
1989	Christian Laettner, Duke	5	26	33	78.8
1990	Alaa Abdelnaby, Duke	6	42	64	65.6
1991	Robert Werdann, St. John's (N.Y.)	4	20	26	76.9
1992	Eric Montross, North Carolina	3	24	32	75.0
1993	Corliss Williamson, Arkansas	3	19	25	76.0
1994	Keith Booth, Maryland	3	15	22	68.2
1995	Michael Wilson, Memphis	3	18	24	75.0
1996	Darvin Ham, Texas Tech	3	16	23	69.6
1997	Kelvin Cato, Iowa St.	3	18	27	66.7
1998	Brent Solheim, West Virginia	3	17	24	70.8
1999	Elton Brand, Duke	6	37	57	64.9
2000	Casey Calvary, Gonzaga	3	15	21	71.4
2001	Nick Collison, Kansas	3	23	32	71.9

*later vacated

Most Three-Point Field Goals

Year	Player, Team	G	3FGM
1987	Freddie Banks, UNLV	5	26
1988	William Scott, Kansas St.	4	21
1989	Glen Rice, Michigan	6	27
1990	Dennis Scott, Georgia Tech	5	24
1991	Terry Brown, Kansas	6	14
1992	Bobby Hurley, Duke	6	15
1993	Donald Williams, North Carolina	6	22
1994	Cuonzo Martin, Purdue	4	16
1995	Randy Rutherford, Oklahoma St.	5	17
	Scotty Thurman, Arkansas	6	17
1996	Carmelo Travieso, Massachusetts	5	20
1997	Mike Bibby, Arizona	6	18
1998	Richard Hamilton, Connecticut	4	14
1999	Trajan Langdon, Duke	5	17
2000	Jon Bryant, Wisconsin	5	18
2001	Jason Williams, Duke	6	23

Highest Three-Point Field-Goal Percentage

(Minimum: 1.5 3FGM Per Game)

Year	Player, Team	G	3FGM	3FGA	Pct.
1987	Ranzino Smith, North Carolina	4	6	6	100.0
1988	Glen Rice, Michigan	3	7	11	63.6
1989	John Crotty, Virginia	4	8	10	80.0
1990	Kevin Lynch, Minnesota	4	9	16	56.3
1991	Jason Buchanan, St. John's (N.Y.)	4	8	13	61.5
1992	Corey Williams, Oklahoma St.	3	7	9	77.8
1993	Sam Cassell, Florida St.	4	12	17	70.6
1994	Pat Graham, Indiana	3	5	8	62.5
1995	Donny Marshall, Connecticut	4	6	10	60.0
1996	Ben Caton, Utah	3	5	7	71.4
1997	Cameron Mills, Kentucky	6	17	27	63.0
1998	Mike Chappell, Duke	4	6	7	85.7
1999	A.J. Granger, Michigan St.	5	8	11	72.7
2000	Rimas Kaukenas, Seton Hall	3	8	14	57.1
2001	Casey Calvary, Gonzaga	3	5	7	71.4

TOURNAMENT HISTORY FACTS—HIGHEST FREE-THROW PERCENTAGE

Highest Free-Throw Percentage

(Minimum: 10 FTM and 2.5 FTM Per Game)

Year	Player, Team	G	FTM	FTA	Pct.
1941	Gene Englund, Wisconsin	3	16	19	84.2
1942	Charles Black, Kansas	2	10	14	71.4
1943	Bill Hassett, Georgetown	3	10	13	76.9
1945	Arnold Risen, Ohio St.	2	11	16	68.8
1946	Jack Underman, Ohio St.	3	18	21	85.7
1947	Gerald Tucker, Oklahoma	3	16	19	84.2
1948	Howard Shannon, Kansas St.	2	15	15	100.0
1949	Jack Shelton, Oklahoma	3	19	22	86.4
1950	Floyd Layne, CCNY	3	12	15	80.0
	Gene Melchiorre, Bradley	3	12	15	80.0
1951	Bill Kukoy, North Carolina St.	3	19	22	86.4
1952	Jim Young, Santa Clara	3	13	16	81.3
1953	Ron Perry, Holy Cross	3	18	20	90.0
1954	Jack Clune, Navy	3	19	22	86.4
1955	Tom Gola, La Salle	5	37	42	88.1
1956	Bob Mills, Southern Methodist	5	32	40	80.0
1957	John Riser, Pittsburgh	3	30	36	83.3
1958	Johnny Cox, Kentucky	4	21	23	91.3
1959	Howie Carl, DePaul	3	16	18	88.9
1960	Darrall Imhoff, California	5	22	24	91.7
1961	John Turner, Louisville	3	19	21	90.5
1962	Gary Cunningham, UCLA	4	17	19	89.5
	Mel Counts, Oregon St.	3	17	19	89.5
1963	Howard Komives, Bowling Green	3	29	32	90.6
1964	Wayne Estes, Utah St.	3	21	23	91.3
1965	Bill Bradley, Princeton	5	47	51	92.2
1966	Mike Lewis, Duke	4	17	18	94.4
1967	Steve Adelman, Boston College	3	14	16	87.5
1968	Harley Swift, East Tenn. St.	3	18	18	100.0
1969	Rick Mount, Purdue	4	24	27	88.9
1970	Chip Dublin, Jacksonville	5	19	20	95.0
1971	Henry Bibby, UCLA	4	17	17	100.0
1972	Larry McNeill, Marquette	3	11	12	91.7
1973	Ron Haigler, Pennsylvania	3	10	10	100.0
1974	Gene Harmon, Creighton	3	10	10	100.0
1975	Phil Ford, North Carolina	3	17	18	94.4
1976	Will Bynum, VMI	3	22	26	84.6
1977	Phil Ford, North Carolina	5	20	21	95.2
1978	Mike Gminski, Duke	5	19	21	90.5
1979	Sidney Moncrief, Arkansas	3	26	27	96.3
1980	*Cliff Pruitt, UCLA	6	14	15	93.3
	Eric Floyd, Georgetown	3	12	14	85.7
1981	Oliver Robinson, UAB	3	17	17	100.0
1982	Oliver Robinson, UAB	3	12	13	92.3
1983	John Pinone, Villanova	3	15	15	100.0
1984	Steve Alford, Indiana	3	21	22	95.5
1985	Dwayne McClain, Villanova	6	24	25	96.0
1986	Cliff Rees, Navy	4	10	10	100.0
1987	*Derrick McKey, Alabama	3	19	19	100.0
	*Jim Farmer, Alabama	3	14	14	100.0
	Reggie Williams, Georgetown	4	27	30	90.0
1988	Mike Vreeswyk, Temple	4	18	18	100.0
	LaBradford Smith, Louisville	3	15	15	100.0
	Tom Greis, Villanova	4	11	11	100.0
	Jeff Lebo, North Carolina	4	10	10	100.0
1989	Richard Morgan, Virginia	4	23	23	100.0
1990	Bo Kimble, Loyola Marymount	4	26	29	89.7
1991	Brian Davis, Duke	5	19	20	95.0
1992	John Pelphrey, Kentucky	4	15	15	100.0
1993	Greg Graham, Indiana	4	18	19	94.7
1994	Dwayne Morton, Louisville	3	18	19	94.7
1995	Kevin Ollie, Connecticut	4	12	13	92.3
1996	Miles Simon, Arizona	3	12	13	92.3
1997	Keith Van Horn, Utah	4	21	21	100.0
	Dedric Willoughby, Iowa St.	3	12	12	100.0
	Jacy Holloway, Iowa St.	3	11	11	100.0
	Mohamed Woni, Clemson	3	10	10	100.0
1998	Arthur Lee, Stanford	5	35	35	100.0
	Shammond Williams, North Carolina	5	20	20	100.0
1999	Richie Frahm, Gonzaga	4	17	18	94.4
2000	Joe Adkins, Oklahoma St.	4	13	13	100.0
2001	Lynn Greer, Temple	4	33	34	97.1

*later vacated

Individual Rebounding Leaders

Year	Player, Team	G	Reb.	Avg.
1951	Bill Spivey, Kentucky	4	65	16.3
1957	John Green, Michigan St.	4	77	19.3
1958	Elgin Baylor, Seattle	5	91	18.2
1959	Jerry West, West Virginia	5	73	14.6
1960	Tom Sanders, New York U.	5	83	16.6
1961	Jerry Lucas, Ohio St.	4	73	18.3
1962	Len Chappell, Wake Forest	5	86	17.2
1963	Nate Thurmond, Bowling Green	3	70	23.3
	Vic Rouse, Loyola (Ill.)	5	70	14.0
1964	Paul Silas, Creighton	3	57	19.0
1965	Bill Bradley, Princeton	5	57	11.4
1966	Jerry Chambers, Utah	4	56	14.0
1967	Don May, Dayton	5	82	16.4
1968	Elvin Hayes, Houston	5	97	19.4
1969	Lew Alcindor, UCLA	4	64	16.0
1970	Artis Gilmore, Jacksonville	5	93	18.6
1971	*Clarence Glover, Western Ky.	5	89	17.8
	Sidney Wicks, UCLA	4	52	13.0
1972	Bill Walton, UCLA	4	64	16.0
1973	Bill Walton, UCLA	4	58	14.5
1974	Tom Burleson, North Carolina St.	4	61	15.3
1975	Richard Washington, UCLA	5	60	12.0
1976	Phil Hubbard, Michigan	5	61	10.2
1977	Cedric Maxwell, Charlotte	5	64	12.8
1978	Eugene Banks, Duke	5	50	10.0
1979	Larry Bird, Indiana St.	5	67	13.4
1980	Mike Sanders, UCLA	6	60	10.0
1981	Cliff Levingston, Wichita St.	4	53	13.3
1982	Clyde Drexler, Houston	5	42	8.4
1983	Akeem Olajuwon, Houston	5	65	13.0
1984	Akeem Olajuwon, Houston	5	57	11.4
1985	Ed Pinckney, Villanova	6	48	8.0
1986	Pervis Ellison, Louisville	6	57	9.5
1987	Derrick Coleman, Syracuse	6	73	12.2
1988	Danny Manning, Kansas	6	56	9.3
1989	Daryll Walker, Seton Hall	6	58	9.7
1990	Larry Johnson, UNLV	6	75	12.5
1991	Larry Johnson, UNLV	5	51	10.2
1992	Chris Webber, Michigan	6	58	9.7
1993	Chris Webber, Michigan	6	68	11.3
1994	Cherokee Parks, Duke	6	55	9.2
1995	Ed O'Bannon, UCLA	6	54	9.0
1996	Tim Duncan, Wake Forest	4	52	13.0
1997	A.J. Bramlett, Arizona	6	62	10.3
1998	Antawn Jamison, North Carolina	5	63	12.6
1999	Elton Brand, Duke	6	55	9.2
2000	Brendan Haywood, North Carolina	5	48	9.6
2001	Shane Battier, Duke	6	61	10.2

*later vacated

Highest Rebounding Average

Year	Player, Team	G	Reb.	Avg.
1951	Bill Spivey, Kentucky	4	65	16.3
1957	John Green, Michigan St.	4	77	19.3
1958	Elgin Baylor, Seattle	5	91	18.2
1959	Oscar Robertson, Cincinnati	4	63	15.8
1960	Howard Jolliff, Ohio	3	64	21.3
1961	Jerry Lucas, Ohio St.	4	73	18.3
1962	Mel Counts, Oregon St.	3	53	17.7
1963	Nate Thurmond, Bowling Green	3	70	23.3
1964	Paul Silas, Creighton	3	57	19.0
1965	James Ware, Oklahoma City	3	55	18.3
1966	Elvin Hayes, Houston	3	50	16.7
1967	Don May, Dayton	5	82	16.4
1968	Elvin Hayes, Houston	5	97	19.4
1969	Lew Alcindor, UCLA	4	64	16.0
1970	Artis Gilmore, Jacksonville	5	93	18.6
1971	*Clarence Glover, Western Ky.	5	89	17.8
	Collis Jones, Notre Dame	3	49	16.3
1972	Bill Walton, UCLA	4	64	16.0
1973	Bill Walton, UCLA	4	58	14.5
1974	Marvin Barnes, Providence	3	51	17.0
1975	Mike Franklin, Cincinnati	3	49	16.3
1976	Al Fleming, Arizona	3	39	13.0
1977	Phil Hubbard, Michigan	3	45	15.0
1978	Greg Kelser, Michigan St.	3	37	12.3
1979	Larry Bird, Indiana St.	5	67	13.4
1980	Durand Macklin, LSU	3	31	10.3
1981	Cliff Levingston, Wichita St.	4	53	13.3
1982	Ed Pinckney, Villanova	3	30	10.0
1983	Akeem Olajuwon, Houston	5	65	13.0
1984	*Keith Lee, Memphis	3	37	12.3
	Akeem Olajuwon, Houston	5	57	11.4

Highest Rebounding Average

Year	Player, Team	G	Reb.	Avg.
1985	Karl Malone, Louisiana Tech	3	40	13.3
1986	David Robinson, Navy	4	47	11.8
1987	Derrick Coleman, Syracuse	6	73	12.2
1988	Pervis Ellison, Louisville	3	33	11.0
1989	Pervis Ellison, Louisville	3	31	10.3
	Stacey King, Oklahoma	3	31	10.3
1990	Dale Davis, Clemson	3	44	14.7
1991	Byron Houston, Oklahoma St.	3	36	12.0
	Perry Carter, Ohio St.	3	36	12.0
1992	Doug Edwards, Florida St.	3	32	10.7
1993	Chris Webber, Michigan	6	68	11.3
1994	Juwan Howard, Michigan	4	51	12.8
1995	Tim Duncan, Wake Forest	3	43	14.3
1996	Tim Duncan, Wake Forest	4	52	13.0
1997	Paul Pierce, Kansas	3	36	12.0
1998	Antawn Jamison, North Carolina	5	63	12.6
1999	Eduardo Najero, Oklahoma	3	35	11.7
2000	Eric Coley, Tulsa	4	43	10.8
2001	Dan Gadzuric, Gonzaga	3	36	12.0

*later vacated

Individual Assists Leaders

Year	Player, Team	G	Ast.
1984	Reid Gettys, Houston	5	36
1985	Michael Jackson, Georgetown	6	45
1986	Cedric Hunter, Kansas	5	42
1987	Mark Wade, UNLV	5	61
1988	Ricky Grace, Oklahoma	6	41
1989	Rumeal Robinson, Michigan	6	56
1990	Bobby Hurley, Duke	6	39
1991	Bobby Hurley, Duke	6	43
1992	Bobby Hurley, Duke	6	47
1993	Jason Kidd, California	3	31
1994	Grant Hill, Duke	6	34
1995	Tyus Edney, UCLA	6	38
1996	Lazarus Sims, Syracuse	6	46
1997	Ed Cota, North Carolina	5	36
1998	Andre Miller, Utah	6	41
1999	Mateen Cleaves, Michigan St.	5	38
2000	Ed Cota, North Carolina	5	37
2001	Jason Williams, Duke	6	31

Individual Blocked Shots Leaders

Year	Player, Team	G	Blk.
1986	David Robinson, Navy	4	23
1987	Derrick Coleman, Syracuse	6	16
1988	Tim Perry, Temple	4	20
1989	Alonzo Mourning, Georgetown	4	19
1990	Larry Johnson, UNLV	6	11
1991	Elmore Spencer, UNLV	5	15
1992	Chris Webber, Michigan	6	17
1993	Rodney Dobard, Florida St.	4	15
	Chris Webber, Michigan	6	15
1994	Cherokee Parks, Duke	6	18
1995	Marcus Camby, Massachusetts	4	18
1996	Marcus Camby, Massachusetts	5	21
1997	Kelvin Cato, Iowa St.	3	14
1998	Jamaal Magloire, Kentucky	6	18
1999	Ken Johnson, Ohio St.	5	21
2000	Brendan Haywood, North Carolina	5	15
2001	Loren Woods, Arizona	6	24

Individual Steals Leaders

Year	Player, Team	G	Stl.
1986	Tommy Amaker, Duke	6	18
1987	Mark Wade, UNLV	5	18
1988	Mookie Blaylock, Oklahoma	6	23
1989	Kendall Gill, Illinois	5	17
1990	Lee Mayberry, Arkansas	5	18
1991	Grant Hill, Duke	6	15
1992	John Pelphrey, Kentucky	4	13
	Christian Laettner, Duke	6	13
1993	Rick Brunson, Temple	4	14
1994	Dan Cross, Florida	5	12
1995	Cameron Dollar, UCLA	6	15
1996	Edgar Padilla, Massachusetts	5	19
1997	Jason Terry, Arizona	6	17
	Wayne Turner, Kentucky	6	17
1998	Wayne Turner, Kentucky	6	13
1999	Pepe Sanchez, Temple	4	14
2000	Mike Kelley, Wisconsin	5	19
2001	Gilbert Arenas, Arizona	6	17

Entering the NCAA Tournament, These Teams...

...WERE UNDEFEATED.

Year	Team (Coach)	Record	How It Did
1951	Columbia (Lou Rossini)	21-0	0-1
1956	San Francisco (Phil Woolpert)	25-0	4-0, CHAMPION
1957	North Carolina (Frank McGuire)	27-0	5-0, CHAMPION
1961	Ohio St. (Fred Taylor)	24-0	3-1, Final Four—2d
1964	UCLA (John Wooden)	26-0	4-0, CHAMPION
1967	UCLA (John Wooden)	26-0	4-0, CHAMPION
1968	Houston (Guy Lewis)	28-0	3-2, Final Four—4th
1968	St. Bonaventure (Larry Weise)	22-0	1-2
1971	Marquette (Al McGuire)	26-0	2-1, Regional 3rd
1971	Pennsylvania (Dick Harter)	26-0	2-1, Regional 2d
1972	UCLA (John Wooden)	26-0	4-0, CHAMPION
1973	UCLA (John Wooden)	26-0	4-0, CHAMPION
1975	Indiana (Bob Knight)	29-0	2-1, Regional 2d
1976	Indiana (Bob Knight)	27-0	5-0, CHAMPION
1976	Rutgers (Tom Young)	28-0	3-2, Final Four—4th
1979	Indiana St. (Bill Hodges)	29-0	4-1, Final Four—2d
1991	UNLV (Jerry Tarkanian)	30-0	4-1, Final Four—tie 3rd

...HAD ONE LOSS.

Year	Team (Coach)	Record	How It Did
1942	Colorado (Frosty Cox)	15-1	1-1, Final Four—tie 3rd
1944	Dartmouth (Earl Brown)	17-1	2-1, Final Four—2d
1946	Harvard (Floyd Stahl)	20-1	0-2, Regional 2d
1947	Navy (Ben Carnevale)	16-1	0-2, Regional 2d
1947	Texas (Jack Gray)	24-1	2-1, Final Four—3rd
1948	Columbia (Gordon Ridings)	20-1	0-2, Regional 2d
†1953	Lebanon Valley (George Marquette)	18-1	1-2
1953	LSU (Harry Rabenhorst)	20-1	2-2, Final Four—4th
1954	Seattle (Al Brightman)	26-1	0-1
1955	San Francisco (Phil Woolpert)	23-1	5-0, CHAMPION
†1955	Williams (Alex Shaw)	17-1	0-1
†1956	Wayne St. (Mich.) (Joel Mason)	17-1	1-2
1958	San Francisco (Phil Woolpert)	24-1	1-1
1958	West Virginia (Fred Schaus)	26-1	0-1
1959	Kansas St. (Tex Winter)	24-1	1-1, Regional 2d
1960	California (Pete Newell)	24-1	4-1, Final Four—2d
1960	Cincinnati (George Smith)	25-1	3-1, Final Four—3rd
1962	Ohio St. (Fred Taylor)	23-1	3-1, Final Four—2d
1963	Cincinnati (Ed Jucker)	23-1	3-1, Final Four—2d
1965	Providence (Joe Mullaney)	22-1	2-1, Regional 2d
1965	St. Joseph's (Jack Ramsay)	25-1	1-2
1966	Kentucky (Adolph Rupp)	24-1	3-1, Final Four—2d
1966	UTEP (Don Haskins)	23-1	5-0, CHAMPION
1967	Toledo (Bob Nichols)	23-1	0-1
1968	UCLA (John Wooden)	25-1	4-0, CHAMPION
1969	Santa Clara (Dick Garibaldi)	26-1	1-1, Regional 2d
1969	UCLA (John Wooden)	25-1	4-0, CHAMPION
1970	Jacksonville (Joe Williams)	23-1	4-1, Final Four—2d
1970	Kentucky (Adolph Rupp)	25-1	1-1, Regional 2d
1970	Pennsylvania (Dick Harter)	25-1	0-1
1970	St. Bonaventure (Larry Weise)	22-1	3-2, Final Four—4th
1971	Kansas (Ted Owens)	25-1	2-2, Final Four—4th
1971	UCLA (John Wooden)	25-1	4-0, CHAMPION
1974	North Carolina St. (Norm Sloan)	26-1	4-0, CHAMPION
1976	Marquette (Al McGuire)	25-1	2-1, Regional 2d
1976	UNLV (Jerry Tarkanian)	28-1	1-1
1977	Arkansas (Eddie Sutton)	26-1	0-1
1977	San Francisco (Bob Gaillard)	29-1	0-1
1980	Alcorn St. (Davey L. Whitney)	27-1	1-1
1980	DePaul (Ray Meyer)	26-1	0-1
1981	DePaul (Ray Meyer)	27-1	0-1
1981	Oregon St. (Ralph Miller)	26-1	0-1
1982	DePaul (Ray Meyer)	26-1	0-1
1987	UNLV (Jerry Tarkanian)	33-1	4-1, Final Four—tie 3rd
1988	Temple (John Chaney)	29-1	3-1, Regional 2d
1990	La Salle (Speedy Morris)	29-1	1-1
1996	Massachusetts (John Calipari)	31-1	4-1, Final Four—tie 3rd
1996	Texas Tech (James Dickey)	28-1	2-1
1997	Kansas (Roy Williams)	32-1	2-1
1998	Princeton (Bill Carmody)	26-1	1-1
1999	Duke (Mike Krzyzewski)	32-1	5-1, Final Four—2d

†Before the advent of the College Division (now Division II), the tournament committee had the option of selecting teams below Division I.

TOURNAMENT HISTORY FACTS—TEAMS WITH TWO LOSSES

...HAD TWO LOSSES.

Year	Team (Coach)	Record	How It Did
1940	Colorado (Frosty Cox)	17-2	0-2, Regional 2d
1940	Duquesne (Chick Davies)	19-2	1-1, Final Four—tie 3rd
1940	Rice (Buster Brannon)	21-2	1-1, Regional 2d
1940	Southern California (Sam Barry)	19-2	1-1, Final Four—tie 3rd
1940	Springfield (Ed Hickox)	16-2	0-1, Regional 2d
1941	Arkansas (Glen Rose)	19-2	1-1, Final Four—tie 3rd
1942	Penn St. (John Lawther)	17-2	1-1, Regional 2d
1943	Dartmouth (Ozzie Cowles)	19-2	1-1, Regional 2d
1943	Wyoming (Everett Shelton)	28-2	3-0, CHAMPION
1945	Utah (Vadal Peterson)	17-2	0-2, Regional 2d
1946	New York U. (Howard Cann)	18-2	1-1, Regional 2d
1946	Oklahoma St. (Henry Iba)	28-2	3-0, CHAMPION
1948	Kentucky (Adolph Rupp)	31-2	3-0, CHAMPION
1949	Kentucky (Adolph Rupp)	29-2	3-0, CHAMPION
1950	Holy Cross (Buster Sheary)	27-2	0-2, Regional 2d
1951	Kentucky (Adolph Rupp)	28-2	4-0, CHAMPION
1952	Kansas (Phog Allen)	22-2	4-0, CHAMPION
1952	Kentucky (Adolph Rupp)	28-2	1-1, Regional 2d
1953	Washington (Tippy Dye)	25-2	3-1, Final Four—3rd
1954	Connecticut (Hugh Greer)	23-2	0-1
1954	George Washington (Bill Reinhart)	23-2	0-1
1954	Notre Dame (John Jordan)	20-2	2-1, Regional 2d
1955	Kentucky (Adolph Rupp)	22-2	1-1
1955	Marquette (Jack Nagle)	22-2	2-1, Regional 2d
1956	Southern Methodist (Doc Hayes)	22-2	3-2, Final Four—4th
1957	Kansas (Dick Harp)	21-2	3-1, Final Four—2d
1957	Idaho St. (John Grayson)	24-2	1-2
1958	Temple (Harry Litwack)	24-2	3-1, Final Four—3rd
1958	Cincinnati (George Smith)	24-2	1-1
1959	Kentucky (Adolph Rupp)	23-2	1-1
1960	Utah (Jack Gardner)	24-2	2-1
1962	Cincinnati (Ed Jucker)	25-2	4-0, CHAMPION
1962	Kentucky (Adolph Rupp)	22-2	1-1, Regional 2d
1963	Loyola (Ill.) (George Ireland)	24-2	5-0, CHAMPION
1963	Duke (Vic Bubas)	24-2	3-1, Final Four—3rd
1963	Arizona St. (Ned Wulk)	24-2	2-1, Regional 2d
1964	UTEP (Don Haskins)	23-2	2-1
1965	UCLA (John Wooden)	24-2	4-0, CHAMPION
1965	Connecticut (Fred Shabel)	23-2	0-1
1966	Western Ky. (Johnny Oldham)	23-2	2-1
1966	Loyola (Ill.) (George Ireland)	22-2	0-1
1967	Princeton (Butch van Breda Kolff)	23-2	2-1
1967	Western Ky. (Johnny Oldham)	23-2	0-1
1967	Boston College (Bob Cousy)	19-2	2-1, Regional 2d
1969	Davidson (Lefty Driesell)	25-2	2-1, Regional 2d
1969	Weber St. (Phil Johnson)	25-2	2-1
1970	UCLA (John Wooden)	24-2	4-0, CHAMPION
1970	New Mexico St. (Lou Henson)	23-2	4-1, Final Four—3rd
1970	Western Ky. (Johnny Oldham)	22-2	0-1
1971	Fordham (Digger Phelps)	24-2	2-1
1972	Hawaii (Red Rocha)	24-2	0-1
1972	Marquette (Al McGuire)	24-2	1-2
1972	Pennsylvania (Chuck Daly)	23-2	2-1, Regional 2d
1973	Long Beach St. (Jerry Tarkanian)	24-2	2-1
1973	Providence (Dave Gavitt)	24-2	3-2, Final Four—4th
1974	Notre Dame (Digger Phelps)	24-2	2-1
1975	Louisville (Denny Crum)	24-2	4-1, Final Four—3rd
1976	Western Mich. (Eldon Miller)	24-2	1-1
1977	UNLV (Jerry Tarkanian)	25-2	4-1, Final Four—3rd
1977	Detroit (Dick Vitale)	25-2	1-1
1978	Kentucky (Joe B. Hall)	25-2	5-0, CHAMPION
1978	DePaul (Ray Meyer)	25-2	2-1, Regional 2d
1978	UCLA (Gary Cunningham)	24-2	1-1
1980	Weber St. (Neil McCarthy)	26-2	0-1
1982	North Carolina (Dean Smith)	27-2	5-0, CHAMPION
1982	Fresno St. (Boyd Grant)	26-2	1-1
1982	Idaho (Don Monson)	26-2	1-1
1983	Houston (Guy Lewis)	27-2	4-1, Final Four—2d
1983	UNLV (Jerry Tarkanian)	28-2	0-1
1984	DePaul (Ray Meyer)	26-2	1-1
1984	North Carolina (Dean Smith)	27-2	1-1
1985	Georgetown (John Thompson)	30-2	5-1, Final Four—2d
1985	Louisiana Tech (Andy Russo)	27-2	2-1
1986	Duke (Mike Krzyzewski)	32-2	5-1, Final Four—2d
1986	Bradley (Dick Versace)	31-2	1-1
1987	DePaul (Joey Meyer)	26-2	2-1
1988	Arizona (Lute Olson)	31-2	4-1, Final Four—tie 3rd
1988	N.C. A&T (Don Corbett)	26-2	0-1
1989	Ball St. (Rick Majerus)	28-2	1-1
1991	Princeton (Pete Carril)	24-2	0-1
1992	Duke (Mike Krzyzewski)	28-2	6-0, CHAMPION
1994	Pennsylvania (Fran Dunphy)	24-2	1-1
1995	UCLA (Jim Harrick)	25-2	6-0, CHAMPION

Providence had a 24-2 record entering the 1973 NCAA tournament and reached the Final Four under coach Dave Gavitt.

Notre Dame entered the 1974 NCAA tournament with a 24-2 record but fell short of the Final Four. Coach Digger Phelps led the Fighting Irish into the tournament 14 times during his career.

TOURNAMENT HISTORY FACTS—TEAMS WITH TWO LOSSES

Year	Team (Coach)	Record	How It Did
1996	Connecticut (Jim Calhoun)	30-2	2-1
1996	Kentucky (Rick Pitino)	28-2	6-0, CHAMPION
1997	Col. of Charleston (John Kresse)	28-2	1-1
1999	Col. of Charleston (John Kresse)	28-2	0-1
1999	Connecticut (Jim Calhoun)	28-2	6-0, CHAMPION
2001	Stanford (Mike Montgomery)	28-2	3-1, Regional 2d

...HAD A .500 RECORD.

Year	Team (Coach)	Record	How It Qualified	How It Did
1958	Wyoming (Everett Shelton)	13-13	Skyline Conference champion at 10-4	0-1
1965	West Virginia (George King)	14-14	won Southern Conference tournament	0-1
1972	East Caro. (Tom Quinn)	14-14	won Southern Conference tournament	0-1
1985	Pennsylvania (Craig Littlepage)	13-13	Ivy Group champion at 10-4	0-1
1987	Fairfield (Mitch Buonaguro)	15-15	won Metro Atlantic Conference tournament	0-1
1987	Idaho St. (Jim Boutin)	15-15	won Big Sky Conference tournament	0-1
2000	Lamar (Mike Deane)	15-15	won Southland Conference tournament	0-1

...HAD A LOSING RECORD.

Year	Team (Coach)	Record	How It Qualified	How It Did
1955	Bradley (Bob Vanatta)	7-19	‡Independent	2-1, Regional 2d
1955	Oklahoma City (Doyle Parrack)	9-17	‡Independent	0-1
1961	George Washington (Bill Reinhart)	9-16	won Southern Conference tournament	0-1
1974	Texas (Leon Black)	12-14	Southwest Conference champion at 11-3	0-1
1978	Missouri (Norm Stewart)	14-15	won Big Eight Conference tournament	0-1
1985	Lehigh (Tom Schneider)	12-18	won East Coast Conference tournament	0-1
1986	Montana St. (Stu Starner)	14-16	won Big Sky Conference tournament	0-1
1993	East Caro. (Eddie Payne)	13-16	won Colonial Conference tournament	0-1
1995	Florida Int'l (Bob Weltlich)	11-18	won Trans America Conference tournament	0-1
1996	San Jose St. (Stan Morrison)	13-16	won Big West Conference tournament	0-1
1996	UCF (Kirk Speraw)	11-18	won Trans America Conference tournament	0-1
1997	Jackson St. (Andy Stoglin)	14-15	won Southwestern Athletic Conference tournament	0-1
1997	Fairfield (Paul Cormier)	11-18	won Metro Atlantic Conference tournament	0-1
1998	Prairie View (Elwood Plummer)	13-16	won Southwestern Conference tournament	0-1
1999	Florida A&M (Mickey Clayton)	12-18	won Mid-Eastern Athletic Conference tournament	0-1

‡*District 5 committee restricted to District 5 independents (only two in the district) to fill out bracket; this rule was changed for the 1956 tournament.*

...HAD A LOSING CONFERENCE RECORD AS AT-LARGE SELECTIONS.

Year	Team (Coach)	Overall Record	Conference	Conference Record	Conference Finish	How It Did
1960	Southern Calif. (Forrest Twogood)	16-10	AAWU	5-7	3d	0-1
1983	Alabama (Wimp Sanderson)	20-11	Southeastern	8-10	T8th	0-1
1984	Virginia (Terry Holland)	17-11	Atlantic Coast	6-8	T5th	4-1, T3d
1985	Boston College (Gary Williams)	18-10	Big East	7-9	6th	2-1
1986	Maryland (Lefty Driesell)	18-13	Atlantic Coast	6-8	6th	1-1
1987	LSU (Dale Brown)	21-14	Southeastern	8-10	T6th	3-1, RR
1988	Iowa St. (Johnny Orr)	20-11	Big Eight	6-8	5th	0-1
1988	Maryland (Bob Wade)	17-12	Atlantic Coast	6-8	5th	1-1
1989	Providence (Rick Barnes)	18-10	Big East	7-9	T5th	0-1
1990	Indiana (Bob Knight)	18-10	Big Ten	8-10	7th	0-1
1990	Virginia (Terry Holland)	19-11	Atlantic Coast	6-8	T5th	1-1
1991	Georgia Tech (Bobby Cremins)	16-12	Atlantic Coast	6-8	T5th	1-1
1991	Villanova (Rollie Massimino)	16-14	Big East	7-9	T7th	1-1
1991	Virginia (Jeff Jones)	21-11	Atlantic Coast	6-8	T5th	0-1
1992	Iowa St. (Johnny Orr)	20-12	Big Eight	5-9	T6th	1-1
1992	Wake Forest (Dave Odom)	17-11	Atlantic Coast	7-9	5th	1-1
1994	Seton Hall (P.J. Carlesimo)	17-12	Big East	8-10	7th	0-1
1994	Wisconsin (Stu Jackson)	17-10	Big Ten	8-10	7th	1-1
1995	Iowa St. (Tim Floyd)	22-10	Big Eight	6-8	5th	1-1
1996	Clemson (Rick Barnes)	18-10	Atlantic Coast	7-9	6th	0-1
1997	Virginia (Jeff Jones)	18-12	Atlantic Coast	7-9	6th	0-1
1998	Clemson (Rick Barnes)	18-13	Atlantic Coast	7-9	T4th	0-1
1998	Florida St. (Steve Robinson)	17-13	Atlantic Coast	6-10	T6th	1-1
1999	Purdue (Gene Keady)	19-12	Big Ten	7-9	7th	2-1
2001	Penn St. (Jerry Dunn)	19-11	Big Ten	7-9	T6th	2-1

Photo from College of Charleston sports information

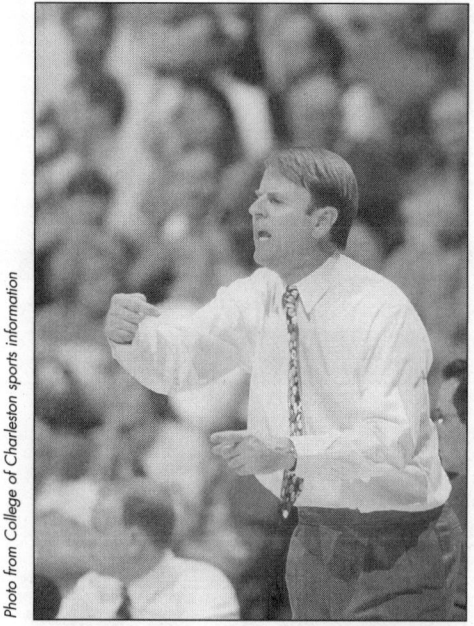

Coach John Kresse has led the College of Charleston into the NCAA tournament four times, including 1997 and 1999. The Cougars finished both regular seasons 28-2.

Tournament trivia

Question...
What are the only two teams with 13 or more losses to advance to the Final Four?

Answer...
Both North Carolina and Wisconsin were 22-13 at the start of the 2000 Final Four.

At-Large Selections History

LOSSES FOR AT-LARGE TEAMS (SINCE 1985)

Teams	Year	Won	Lost	Pct.
Villanova	1991	16	14	.533
Georgia	2001	16	14	.533
Kansas St.	1990	17	14	.548
Villanova	1990	18	14	.563
LSU	1987	21	14	.600
LSU	1988	16	13	.552
Michigan	1995	17	13	.567
Florida St.	1998	17	13	.567
Maryland	1986	18	13	.581
Clemson	1998	18	13	.581
North Carolina	2000	18	13	.581
Wisconsin	2000	18	13	.581

FEWEST WINS FOR AT-LARGE TEAMS (SINCE 1985)

Teams	Year	Won	Lost	Pct.
Villanova	1991	16	14	.533
Georgia	2001	16	14	.533
LSU	1988	16	13	.552
Georgia Tech	1991	16	12	.571
Notre Dame	1990	16	12	.571
Ohio St.	1990	16	12	.571

TOURNAMENT HISTORY FACTS—AT-LARGE SELECTIONS HISTORY

Teams	Year	Won	Lost	Pct.
Georgia Tech	1987	16	12	.571
DePaul	1986	16	12	.571
Kentucky	1985	16	12	.571
Texas	1997	16	11	.593
Maryland	1994	16	11	.593

LOWEST WINNING PERCENTAGE FOR AT-LARGE TEAMS (SINCE 1985)

Teams	Year	Won	Lost	Pct.
Villanova	1991	16	14	.533
Georgia	2001	16	14	.533
Kansas St.	1990	17	14	.548
LSU	1988	16	13	.552
Villanova	1990	18	14	.563
Michigan	1995	17	13	.567
Florida St.	1998	17	13	.567
Notre Dame	1990	16	12	.571
Ohio St.	1990	16	12	.571
Georgia Tech	1991	16	12	.571
Georgia Tech	1987	16	12	.571
DePaul	1986	16	12	.571
Kentucky	1985	16	12	.571

FEWEST LOSSES FOR TEAMS NOT TO MAKE THE TOURNAMENT (SINCE 1985)

Teams	Year	Won	Lost	Pct.
#UNLV	1992	26	2	.929
Col. of Charleston	1996	24	3	.889
Davidson	1996	25	4	.862
Wis.-Green Bay	1992	25	4	.862
UC Irvine	2001	25	4	.862
Wis.-Milwaukee	1993	23	4	.852
Howard	1987	26	5	.839
Southern U.	1990	25	5	.833
Holy Cross	1990	24	5	.828
Ga. Southern	1985	24	5	.828
Col. of Charleston	1995	23	5	.821
Long Beach St.	2000	24	5	.828

#ineligible for postseason play

MOST WINS FOR TEAMS NOT TO MAKE THE TOURNAMENT (SINCE 1985)

Teams	Year	Won	Lost	Pct.
#UNLV	1992	26	2	.929
Howard	1987	26	5	.839
Southern Ill.	1990	26	7	.788
Davidson	1996	25	4	.862
Wis.-Green Bay	1992	25	4	.862
UC Irvine	2001	25	4	.862
Southern U.	1990	25	5	.833
New Mexico	1987	25	9	.735

16 tied with 24

#ineligible for postseason play

By the Numbers

(Year-by-year numbers: AA—Teams in Division I men's basketball. BB—Number of automatic qualifiers for the NCAA tournament. CC—Teams entered into the NCAA tournament. DD—Tournament games played. EE—Overtime tournament games. FF—One-point wins in tournament play. GG—Two-point wins in tournament play. HH—Three-point wins in tournament play. JJ—Close games (overtime games plus any regulation games won by three points or less). KK—number of times 100 points scored in a game.)

Year	AA	BB	CC	DD	EE	FF	GG	HH	JJ	KK
1939			8	8	0	0	1	0	1	0
1940			8	8	1	2	0	0	3	0
1941			8	9	0	3	0	0	3	0
1942			8	9	0	0	3	0	3	0
1943			8	9	0	0	1	1	2	0
1944			8	9	1	0	1	0	1	0
1945			8	9	1	0	0	2	3	0
1946			8	10	1	0	0	2	2	0
1947			8	10	0	2	2	0	4	0
1948	160		8	10	0	0	1	0	1	0
1949	148		8	10	0	1	0	1	0	0
1950	145		8	10	0	2	1	1	4	0
1951	153	10	16	18	0	0	2	0	2	0
1952	156	10	16	20	0	0	2	2	4	0
1953	158	14	22	26	0	1	3	0	4	0
1954	160	15	24	28	3	2	5	0	7	0
1955	162	15	24	28	0	3	2	1	6	1
1956	166	17	25	29	2	2	2	0	6	1
1957	167	16	23	27	3	3	1	0	6	0
1958	173	16	24	28	2	1	1	1	4	0
1959	174	16	23	27	0	3	1	1	5	1
1960	175	14	25	29	1	1	1	1	3	3
1961	173	15	24	28	2	1	4	0	7	2
1962	178	15	25	29	4	2	5	2	11	0
1963	178	15	25	29	3	2	1	2	6	1
1964	179	15	25	29	0	0	2	0	2	4
1965	182	15	23	27	2	2	4	0	8	8

In the first Final Four held in Atlanta 25 years ago, teams led by Dean Smith (right) of North Carolina and Al McGuire of Marquette squared off in the championship game, which was won by Marquette and turned out to be McGuire's last game. Combined, these two men coached in 121 tournament games, which contributed greatly to the "By the Numbers" chart.

Photo by Rich Clarkson

Tournament trivia

Question... On the "By the Numbers" chart, a close game is considered one that goes into overtime or is won by three or fewer points. The most close games in one NCAA tournament is 24. What year was it?

Answer... 1990

TOURNAMENT HISTORY FACTS—BY NUMBERS

Year	AA	BB	CC	DD	EE	FF	GG	HH	JJ	KK
1966	182	14	22	26	2	2	3	1	6	2
1967	185	15	23	27	3	3	4	0	9	1
1968	189	14	23	27	1	2	1	0	3	4
1969	193	15	25	29	2	2	5	3	11	1
1970	196	15	25	29	0	2	0	1	3	13
1971	203	15	25	29	3	2	4	4	11	6
1972	210	16	25	29	1	0	2	0	3	4
1973	216	16	25	29	1	3	1	1	6	5
1974	233	16	25	29	4	1	1	5	9	5
1975	235	20	32	36	6	2	3	3	13	2
1976	235	21	32	32	4	3	2	0	8	4
1977	245	21	32	32	2	3	2	1	8	3
1978	254	21	32	32	4	5	2	4	12	2
1979	257	23	40	40	2	1	6	3	11	1
1980	261	23	48	48	5	3	2	4	11	0
1981	264	26	48	48	2	7	5	3	15	0
1982	273	28	48	47	2	7	2	2	12	1
1983	274	28	52	51	2	5	7	4	17	0
1984	276	29	53	52	3	7	8	2	17	1
1985	282	29	64	63	3	5	8	5	18	0
1986	283	29	64	63	5	2	7	2	15	1
1987	290	28	64	63	5	6	4	5	17	7
1988	290	30	64	63	2	1	0	9	12	10
1989	293	30	64	63	3	4	3	4	13	9
1990	292	30	64	63	5	7	10	6	24	9
1991	295	29	64	63	4	1	3	5	11	4
1992	298	30	64	63	4	2	4	2	11	7
1993	298	30	64	63	4	0	3	6	10	4
1994	301	30	64	63	3	0	2	3	8	5
1995	302	29	64	63	7	3	4	2	14	3
1996	305	30	64	63	2	2	5	3	8	3
1997	305	30	64	63	7	4	0	4	14	2
1998	306	30	64	63	5	7	4	5	19	1
1999	310	30	64	63	3	3	3	3	12	1
2000	318	29	64	63	5	3	3	2	10	1
2001	318	31	65	64	2	3	3	4	11	1

Column EE of this chart is overtime games. There were five such games in the 1980 NCAA tournament, including an 87-84 Missouri win over Notre Dame in which Tom Dore played for the Tigers.

Photo from Missouri sports information

Basketball facts

The three-point field goal was "officially" introduced in college basketball during the 1986-87 season, having been previously used on an experimental basis. But when was it first used as an experiment in a college game? Most people would say the few years before the 1986-87 season because several conferences experimented with the rule during that time. But the first college game in which the three-point goal was used was in 1945.

On February 7, 1945, Columbia defeated Fordham, 73-58, in a game that featured several rule revisions designed to eliminate the zone defense and reduce the effectiveness of a tall center. The innovations were suggested by Columbia graduate Julian Rice and Oregon coach Howard Hobson, who led the Ducks to the first NCAA championship in 1939. One change was to widen the foul lane from six to 12 feet. The other revision was to award three points for goals scored from beyond an arc 21 feet away from the basket. Also, a fouled player had the option of shooting a free throw for one point from the regular 15-foot distance or shooting for two points from the 21-foot line. During the game, the two teams combined for 20 "long goals" and eight "long fouls," and at half time, the crowd voted its approval of the rule changes. Eleven years later, the wider lane was adopted as rule, but it took 41 years for the three-point field goal to be implemented.

Conference Won-Lost Records— Through 2000

Using Current Conference Membership

Conference	Teams	App.	Won	Lost	Pct.	CH	2d	3d	4th	FF	RR
America East	2	12	5	12	.294	0	0	0	0	0	1
Atlantic 10	12	117	107	124	.463	1	2	3	1	7	12
Atlantic Coast	9	151	283	147	.658	8	11	16	2	37	25
Atlantic Sun	6	14	5	14	.263	0	1	0	0	1	0
Big 12	12	173	198	185	.517	4	9	9	7	29	29
Big East	14	226	268	236	.532	3	8	4	4	19	34
Big Sky	5	32	15	36	.294	0	0	0	0	0	1
Big South	5	8	0	8	.000	0	0	0	0	0	0
Big Ten	10	164	265	160	.624	10	9	18	3	40	23
Big West	7	31	13	35	.271	0	0	0	0	0	4
Colonial	9	35	10	35	.222	0	0	0	0	0	0
Conference USA	14	156	186	168	.525	5	5	10	4	24	11
Horizon	7	22	18	21	.462	1	0	0	0	1	0
Ivy	8	58	38	68	.358	0	2	1	1	4	9
Metro Atlantic	10	28	10	30	.250	0	0	0	0	0	2
Mid-American	12	60	23	64	.264	0	0	0	0	0	1
Mid-Continent	3	8	4	8	.333	0	0	0	0	0	1
Mid-Eastern	6	20	2	20	.091	0	0	0	0	0	0
Missouri Valley	10	54	42	56	.429	0	3	1	1	5	6
Mountain West	8	90	90	102	.469	3	1	3	2	9	13
Northeast	7	17	1	17	.056	0	0	0	0	0	0
Ohio Valley	8	30	6	31	.162	0	0	0	0	0	0
Pacific Ten	10	128	189	125	.602	15	3	7	5	30	22
Patriot	6	29	15	31	.326	1	0	1	0	2	5
Southeastern	12	153	212	154	.579	8	5	11	2	26	23
Southern	10	40	15	43	.259	0	0	0	0	0	3
Southland	7	20	6	20	.231	0	0	0	0	0	0
Southwestern	7	21	4	21	.160	0	0	0	0	0	0
Sun Belt	10	56	24	59	.289	0	0	0	0	1	1
West Coast	8	54	50	55	.476	2	0	1	1	4	12
Western Athletic	10	62	42	64	.396	1	0	0	1	2	4
Others	17	45	33	56	.371	1	2	0	2	5	7

CONFERENCE WON-LOST RECORDS—USING CURRENT CONFERENCE MEMBERSHIP

Conference	Teams	App.	Won	Lost	Pct.	CH	2d	3d	4th	FF	RR
Vacated	30	50	78	52	.600	0	2	4	0	6	3
TOTAL	280	2164	2257	2257	.500	63	63	90	36	252	252

Notes: Third-place games were played from 1946 through 1981. Results from the other years are treated as third-place ties. The "Teams" column represent the number of teams in that conference that have appeared in the NCAA tournament.

App.-Appearances; Pct.-Winning percentage; CH-Champion; 2d-Second place; 3d-Third place; 4th-Fourth place; FF-Final; Four appearances; RR-Regional Runner-up.

Using Actual Conference Membership for Each Season

Conference, Former Names, Years	App.	Won	Lost	Pct.	CH	2d	3d	4th	FF	RR
America East; North Atlantic; ECAC North, ECAC North Atlantic, 1980-2001	22	5	22	.185	0	0	0	0	0	0
American South, 1987-91	3	1	3	.250	0	0	0	0	0	0
Atlantic Coast, 1954-2001	137	269	132	.671	8	9	15	2	34	21
Atlantic Sun, Trans America, 1981-2001	21	3	21	.125	0	0	0	0	0	0
Atlantic 10; Eastern Collegiate, Eastern Eight, 1977-2001	59	55	59	.482	0	0	0	0	0	8
Big East, 1980-2001	104	167	101	.623	3	5	2	0	10	17
Big Eight; Big Seven; Big Six, 1939-96	103	134	108	.554	2	7	5	6	20	18
Big Sky, 1968-2001	34	10	36	.217	0	0	0	0	0	1
Big South, 1991-2001	10	0	10	.000	0	0	0	0	0	0
Big Ten; Big Nine; Western, 1939-2001	158	258	152	.629	10	9	17	2	38	22
Big 12, 1997-2001	26	25	26	.490	0	0	0	0	0	2
Big West; Pacific Coast Athl. Assn., 1970-2001	36	29	36	.446	1	0	2	0	3	3
Border, 1951-62	12	2	13	.133	0	0	0	0	0	1
Colonial; ECAC South, 1983-2001	20	12	20	.375	0	0	0	0	0	1
Conference USA, 1996-2001	21	20	21	.488	0	0	0	0	0	2
East Coast; Middle Atlantic, 1959-95	32	9	36	.200	0	0	0	0	0	2
Florida Intercollegiate, 1960	1	0	1	.000	0	0	0	0	0	0
Great Midwest, 1992-95	13	16	13	.552	0	0	1	0	1	2
Horizon, Midwestern, 1982-2001	26	12	26	.316	0	0	0	0	0	0
Indiana Collegiate, 1962	1	2	1	.667	0	0	0	0	0	0
Ivy Group; Eastern Intercollegiate, 1941-2001	56	38	65	.369	0	2	1	1	4	7
Kentucky Intercollegiate, 1940	1	0	1	.000	0	0	0	0	0	1
Little Three (New England), 1955	1	0	1	.000	0	0	0	0	0	0
Metro, 1976-95	39	39	37	.513	2	0	2	0	4	0
Metro Atlantic, 1984-2001	19	2	19	.095	0	0	0	0	0	0
Mid-American, 1953-2001	54	23	58	.284	0	0	0	0	0	1
Mid-Continent, 1986-2001	17	7	17	.292	0	0	0	0	0	0
Mid-Eastern, 1981-2001	20	2	20	.091	0	0	0	0	0	0
Missouri Valley, 1941-2001	72	74	76	.493	4	5	4	3	16	8
Mountain West, 2001	3	1	3	.250	0	0	0	0	0	0
Northeast; ECAC Metro, 1982-2001	20	1	20	.048	0	0	0	0	0	0
Ohio Valley, 1953-2001	46	15	49	.234	0	0	0	0	0	0
Pacific-10; Pacific-8, AAWU, Pacific Coast, 1939-2001	113	173	108	.616	15	3	7	4	29	17
Patriot, 1992-2001	10	0	10	.000	0	0	0	0	0	0
Presidents Athletic, 1956	1	1	2	.333	0	0	0	0	0	0
Rocky Mountain, 1951-60	9	6	11	.353	0	0	0	0	0	0
Skyline Eight; Mountain States, 1939-62	24	20	34	.370	2	0	1	1	4	12
Southeastern, 1942-2001	132	188	131	.589	8	5	7	2	22	21
Southern, 1939-2001	54	28	58	.326	0	2	1	0	3	6
Southland, 1969-2001	24	9	24	.273	0	0	0	0	0	0
Southwest, 1939-96	77	73	88	.453	0	3	7	2	12	10
Southwestern, 1980-2001	21	4	21	.160	0	0	0	0	0	0
Sun Belt, 1977-2001	38	21	39	.350	0	0	0	1	1	1
West Coast; California Basketball Assn., 1953-2001	55	52	55	.486	2	0	1	0	3	11
Western Athletic, 1963-2001	72	59	78	.431	0	1	0	1	2	6
Western New York Little Three, 1955-57	3	6	3	.667	0	0	0	0	0	2
Yankee, 1951-67	15	4	16	.200	0	0	0	0	0	1
Independents, 1939-91	279	304	324	.484	6	10	12	11	39	45
Vacated	50	78	52	.600	0	2	5	0	7	3
TOTAL	2164	2257	2257	.500	63	63	90	36	252	252

Note: Third-place games were played from 1946 through 1981. Results from the other years are treated as third-place ties.

The Pacific Coast Conference (now known as the Pacific-10) and the Big Ten Conference were represented in the first NCAA championship game in 1939. Oregon defeated Ohio State, 46-33.

Number of Conference Teams in the Tournament

1939-49

Conference	1939	1940	1941	1942	1943	1944	1945	1946	1947	1948	1949	TOTAL
Big Eight	1:1-1	1:2-1	0	1:1-1	1:1-1	2:2-2	0	0	1:2-1	1:1-2	0	8:10-9
Big Ten	1:2-1	1:3-0	1:3-0	1:0-2	0	1:1-1	1:2-1	1:2-1	1:1-1	1:1-1	1:2-1	10:16-9
Ivy	—	—	1:1-1	1:2-1	1:1-1	1:2-1	0	0	0	1:0-2	1:0-2	6:6-8
Ky. Intercollegiate	—	1:0-1	—	—	—	—	—	—	—	—	—	1:0-1
Missouri Valley	—	—	1:1-1	0	0	1:3-0	1:3-0	0	0	1:2-1		4:9-2
Pacific-10	1:3-0	1:1-1	1:2-1	1:3-0	1:0-2	0	1:1-1	1:2-1	1:1-1	1:1-1	1:1-2	10:14-11
Skyline Eight	1:1-1	1:0-2	1:0-2	1:1-1	1:3-0	1:3-0	1:0-2	1:1-1	1:0-2	1:0-2	1:0-2	11:9-15
Southeastern	—	—	—	1:1-1	0	0	1:1-1	0	0	1:3-0	1:3-0	4:8-2
Southern	1:0-1	0	1:0-2	0	0	0	1:2-1	0	0	0	0	3:2-4

Question... What is the only school from the Big Ten Conference not to have earned a trip to the Final Four?

Answer... Northwestern

CONFERENCE WON-LOST RECORDS—TEAMS IN THE TOURNAMENT

Before entering the Pacific-10 Conference for the 1978-79 season, Arizona represented the Western Athletic Conference in the 1976 and 1977 NCAA tournaments, where the Wildcats were led by center Bob Elliott.

Photo from Arizona sports information

Tournament trivia

Question...

Match the following NCAA tournament teams with the "unofficial" team nickname it was known by:

Team
1. Houston 1983
2. Illinois 1942
3. Indiana 1940
4. Kentucky 1948
5. Kentucky 1958
6. Kentucky 1966
7. Louisville 1980
8. Michigan 1992-93
9. Oregon 1939
10. Texas 1947
11. UCLA 1972-73-74
12. Utah 1944

Nickname
A. The Blitz Kids
B. The Doctors of Dunk
C. The Fab Five
D. The Fabulous Five
E. The Fiddlin' Five
F. The Hurryin' Hoosiers
G. The Mighty Mice
H. Phi Slama Jama
J. Rupp's Runts
K. The Tall Firs
L. The Walton Gang
M. The Whiz Kids

Answer...

1-H, 2-M, 3-F, 4-D, 5-E, 6-J, 7-B, 8-C, 9-K, 10-G, 11-L, 12-A

Conference	1939	1940	1941	1942	1943	1944	1945	1946	1947	1948	1949	TOTAL
Southwest	1:0-2	1:1-1	1:1-1	1:0-2	1:1-1	0	1:1-1	1:0-2	1:2-1	1:2-1	1:1-1	10:9-13
Independents	2:1-2	2:1-2	1:1-1	1:1-1	3:3-3	3:1-5	2:2-3	2:1-3	3:4-4	1:2-1	1:1-1	21:18-27
TOTALS	8:8-8	8:8-8	8:9-9	8:9-9	8:9-9	8:9-9	8:9-9	8:10-10	8:10-10	8:10-10	8:10-10	88: 101-101

1950-59

Conference	1950	1951	1952	1953	1954	1955	1956	1957	1958	1959	TOTAL
Atlantic Coast	—	—	—	0	1:2-1	1:0-1	1:0-1	1:5-0	1:2-1	1:0-1	6:9-5
Big Eight	0	1:3-1	1:4-0	1:3-1	1:0-2	1:3-1	1:1-1	1:3-1	1:2-2	1:1-1	9:20-10
Big Ten	1:1-1	1:3-1	1:3-1	1:4-0	1:1-1	1:2-2	1:3-1	1:2-2	1:1-1	1:1-1	10:21-11
Border	—	1:0-1	1:0-2	1:0-1	1:0-1	1:0-1	1:0-1	1:0-1	1:0-1	1:0-1	9:0-10
East Coast	—	—	—	—	—	—	—	—	—	1:0-2	1:0-2
Ivy	0	1:0-1	1:0-2	1:1-1	1:0-2	1:0-2	1:2-1	1:0-1	1:2-1	1:0-1	9:5-12
Little Three	—	—	—	—	—	1:0-1	—	—	—	—	1:0-1
Mid-American	—	—	—	1:0-1	1:0-1	1:0-1	1:0-1	1:0-1	1:1-2	1:0-1	7:1-8
Missouri Valley	1:2-1	1:2-2	1:1-1	1:1-1	1:1-1	1:1-1	1:0-2	1:2-1	1:1-1	1:3-1	10:12-13
Ohio Valley	—	—	—	1:0-1	0	0	1:2-1	1:0-1	1:0-1	1:3-1	5:2-5
Pacific-10	1:0-2	1:2-1	1:0-2	1:3-1	1:2-2	1:1-1	1:1-1	1:1-1	1:1-1	1:4-0	10:15-12
Presidents Athletic	—	—	—	—	—	—	1:1-2	—	—	—	1:1-2
Rocky Mountain	—	1:0-1	0	1:0-1	1:0-1	1:0-1	1:0-1	1:1-2	1:0-1	1:0-1	8:6-10
Skyline Eight	1:1-1	1:1-2	1:1-1	1:0-2	1:0-2	1:1-1	1:1-1	1:1-1	1:0-1	1:0-2	10:6-14
Southeastern	0	1:4-0	1:1-1	1:2-2	1:0-2	1:1-1	1:1-1	1:1-1	1:4-0	1:1-1	9:15-9
Southern	1:2-1	1:1-2	1:1-1	1:1-1	1:0-1	1:0-1	1:0-1	1:0-1	1:0-1	1:4-1	10:9-11
Southwest	1:1-2	1:0-1	1:1-1	1:1-1	1:1-1	1:0-2	1:3-2	1:1-1	1:0-2	1:1-1	10:9-14
West Coast	—	—	—	1:2-1	1:2-1	1:5-0	1:4-0	1:3-1	—	1:1-1	7:18-5
W'ern N.Y. Little Three	—	—	—	—	—	1:2-1	1:2-1	1:2-1	—	—	3:6-3
Yankee	—	1:0-1	0	0	1:0-1	0	1:1-2	1:0-1	1:0-1	1:0-1	6:1-7
Independents	2:3-2	4:2-4	6:8-8	8:8-11	9:17-8	8:12-10	7:7-8	6:7-8	8:12-9	6:9-9	64:85-77
TOTAL	8:10-10	16:18-18	16:20-20	22:26-26	24:28-28	24:29-29	25:29-29	23:27-27	24:28-28	23:27-27	205:241-241

1960-69

Conference	1960	1961	1962	1963	1964	1965	1966	1967	1968	1969	TOTAL
Atlantic Coast	1:2-1	1:2-1	1:4-1	1:3-1	1:3-1	1:1-1	1:3-1	1:2-1	1:3-1	1:2-2	10:25-12
Big Eight	1:1-1	1:1-1	1:1-1	1:1-1	1:2-2	1:1-1	1:1-1	1:1-1	1:0-2	1:1-1	10:10-12
Big Sky	—	—	—	—	—	—	—	1:0-1	1:2-1	2:2-2
Big Ten	1:4-0	1:3-1	1:3-1	—	1:3-1	1:3-1	1:1-1	1:1-1	1:3-1	1:3-1	10:25-9
Border	1:0-1	1:2-1	1:0-1	—	—	—	—	—	—	—	3:2-3
East Coast	1:0-2	1:3-1	1:0-2	1:2-1	1:0-1	1:1-2	1:2-1	1:0-1	1:0-1	1:0-1	10:8-13
Florida Intercollegiate	1:0-1	—	—	—	—	—	—	—	—	—	1:0-1
Indiana Collegiate	—	—	1:2-1	—	—	—	—	—	—	—	1:2-1
Ivy	1:0-1	1:1-2	1:0-1	1:0-1	1:1-2	1:4-1	0	1:2-1	1:2-1	1:0-1	9:10-11
Mid-American	1:1-2	1:0-1	1:0-1	1:1-2	1:2-1	1:0-1	1:0-1	1:0-1	1:0-1	1:1-2	10:5-13
Missouri Valley	1:3-1	1:4-0	1:4-0	1:3-1	1:1-1	1:2-2	1:0-2	1:0-2	1:1-1	1:3-1	10:21-11
Ohio Valley	1:2-1	1:1-2	1:1-2	1:0-1	1:0-1	1:0-1	1:2-1	1:0-1	1:1-2	1:0-1	10:7-13
Pacific-10	2:4-2	1:1-2	1:2-2	1:0-2	1:4-0	1:4-0	1:1-1	1:4-0	1:4-0	1:4-0	11:28-9
Rocky Mountain	1:0-1	—	—	—	—	—	—	—	—	—	1:0-1
Skyline Eight	1:2-1	1:2-2	1:1-2	—	—	—	—	—	—	—	3:5-5
Southeastern	1:1-1	1:1-1	1:1-1	1:1-1	1:0-2	1:1-1	1:3-1	1:0-2	1:1-1	1:1-1	10:10-12
Southern	1:2-1	1:0-1	1:0-1	1:2-1	1:0-1	1:0-1	1:1-2	1:0-1	1:2-1	1:2-1	10:9-11
Southland	—	—	—	—	—	—	—	—	1:0-1	—	1:0-1
Southwest	1:0-2	1:1-1	1:1-2	1:2-1	1:0-1	1:1-1	1:1-1	1:1-1	1:1-1	1:1-2	10:9-13
West Coast	1:0-2	1:1-1	1:1-1	1:1-1	1:1-1	1:1-1	1:0-2	1:1-1	1:1-1	1:1-1	10:8-12
Western Athletic	—	—	—	1:2-1	1:0-1	1:0-2	1:2-2	1:0-2	1:0-2	1:0-1	7:4-11
Yankee	1:0-1	1:0-1	1:0-1	1:0-1	1:2-1	1:0-1	1:0-1	1:0-1	—	—	8:2-8
Independents	6:7-7	8:5-9	8:8-8	10:10-12	10:10-12	8:8-10	8:9-8	8:15-9	8:8-10	9:8-11	83:88-96
TOTAL	25:29-29	24:28-28	25:29-29	25:29-29	25:29-29	23:27-27	22:26-26	23:27-27	23:27-27	25:29-29	240:280-280

1970-79

Conference	1970	1971	1972	1973	1974	1975	1976	1977	1978	1979	TOTAL
Atlantic Coast	1:1-1	1:0-2	1:3-1	1:1-1	1:4-0	2:4-2	2:0-2	2:6-2	2:4-2	2:0-2	15:23-15
Atlantic 10	—	—	—	—	—	—	1:0-1	1:2-1	1:1-1	—	3:3-3
Big Eight	1:1-1	1:2-2	1:1-1	1:1-1	1:2-2	2:2-2	1:2-1	1:1-1	2:0-2	1:1-1	12:13-14
Big Sky	1:0-1	1:0-1	1:1-2	1:0-1	1:0-1	1:1-2	1:0-1	1:2-1	1:0-1	1:1-1	10:5-12
Big Ten	1:1-1	1:1-1	1:1-1	1:3-1	1:1-1	2:2-2	2:9-1	2:2-2	2:3-2	2:5-1	15:28-13
Big West	1:1-2	1:2-1	1:2-1	1:2-1	1:0-1	1:0-1	1:0-1	1:0-1	1:2-1	2:0-2	11:9-12
Colonial	—	—	—	—	0	0	0	0	0	0	0:0-0
East Coast	1:0-1	1:0-1	1:0-1	1:0-1	1:0-1	1:0-1	1:0-1	1:0-1	1:0-1	1:0-1	10:0-10
Ivy	1:0-1	1:2-1	1:2-1	1:1-2	1:0-1	1:0-1	1:0-1	1:0-1	1:1-1	1:4-2	10:10-12
Metro	—	—	—	—	—	2:0-2	2:0-2	2:1-2	2:2-2	—	8:3-8
Mid-American	1:0-1	1:0-1	1:0-1	1:0-1	1:0-1	1:2-1	1:1-1	1:0-1	1:1-1	1:1-1	10:5-10
Missouri Valley	1:1-1	1:1-1	1:2-2	1:3-1	1:0-2	2:4-2	1:0-1	1:1-1	1:0-1	2:4-2	12:16-14
Ohio Valley	1:0-1	1:4-1	1:0-1	1:1-2	1:0-1	1:0-1	1:0-1	1:1-1	1:0-1	1:0-1	10:6-11
Pacific-10	1:4-0	1:4-0	1:4-0	1:4-0	1:3-1	2:6-2	2:4-2	1:1-1	1:1-1	2:3-2	13:34-9
Southeastern	1:1-1	1:0-2	1:1-1	1:1-1	1:0-2	2:4-2	2:1-2	2:2-2	1:5-0	2:2-2	14:17-15
Southern	1:0-1	1:0-1	1:0-1	1:0-1	1:1-2	1:0-1	1:2-1	1:1-1	1:0-1	1:0-1	10:4-11
Southland	0	0	1:2-1	1:1-2	0	0	0	0	1:1-1	—	3:4-4
Southwest	1:0-1	1:0-1	1:1-2	1:0-1	1:0-1	1:0-1	1:0-1	1:1-1	1:0-1	2:4-2	12:8-13
Sun Belt	—	—	—	—	—	—	—	1:3-2	0	2:0-2	3:3-4
West Coast	1:1-1	1:1-1	1:1-1	1:1-1	1:1-1	1:2-1	1:1-1	1:0-1	1:1-1	2:2-2	11:11-11

CONFERENCE WON-LOST RECORDS—TEAMS IN THE TOURNAMENT

Conference	1970	1971	1972	1973	1974	1975	1976	1977	1978	1979	TOTAL
Western Athletic	1:0-1	1:1-2	1:0-1	1:1-2	1:2-1	2:2-2	1:2-1	2:1-2	2:1-2	2:0-2	14:10-16
Yankee	0	0	0	0	0	0	1:1-1	—	—	—	1:1-1
Independents	9:18-13	9:11-10	8:8-10	8:9-9	9:5-10	9:7-12	9:8-10	8:12-7	8:5-9	9:11-9	86:104-99
TOTAL	25:29-29	25:29-29	25:29-29	25:29-29	25:29-29	32:36-36	32:32-32	32:32-32	32:32-32	40:40-40	293:317-317

1980-89

Conference	1980	1981	1982	1983	1984	1985	1986	1987	1988	1989	TOTAL
American East	1:0-1	1:1-1	1:1-1	1:0-1	1:1-1	1:0-1	1:0-1	1:0-1	1:0-1	1:1-1	10:4-10
American South	—	—	—	—	—	—	0	0	1:1-1	1:1-1	1:1-1
Atlantic Coast	5:6-5	4:9-4	4:7-3	4:11-3	5:8-5	5:12-5	6:13-6	6:5-6	5:9-5	6:12-6	50:92-48
Atlantic Sun	—	1:0-1	1:0-1	1:0-1	1:0-1	1:0-1	1:1-1	1:0-1	1:0-1	1:0-1	9:1-9
Atlantic 10	1:1-1	1:1-1	2:1-2	2:1-2	2:2-2	1:1-1	3:2-3	2:1-2	2:5-2	2:1-2	18:16-18
Big East	3:3-3	3:3-3	4:10-4	5:6-5	4:7-3	6:18-5	4:4-4	5:14-5	6:7-6	5:11-5	45:83-43
Big Eight	2:3-2	3:5-3	2:3-2	3:1-3	2:1-2	3:4-3	5:7-5	4:5-4	5:14-4	4:4-4	33:47-32
Big Sky	1:0-1	1:0-1	1:1-1	1:0-1	1:0-1	1:0-1	1:0-1	1:0-1	1:0-1	1:0-1	10:1-10
Big South	—	—	—	—	—	—	0	0	0	0	0:0-0
Big Ten	4:11-5	3:6-2	4:3-4	5:5-5	3:4-3	6:4-6	6:4-6	6:12-5	5:7-5	5:15-4	47:71-45
Big West	2:0-2	1:0-1	1:1-1	2:0-2	2:2-2	1:1-1	1:2-1	1:4-1	3:1-3	1:3-1	15:14-15
Colonial	0	0	0	1:1-1	1:2-1	1:1-1	2:3-2	1:0-1	1:2-1	1:0-1	8:9-8
East Coast	1:0-1	1:3-1	1:0-1	1:1-1	1:0-1	1:0-1	1:0-1	1:0-1	1:0-1	1:0-1	10:4-10
Horizon	—	—	1:0-1	1:0-1	1:0-1	1:2-1	1:0-1	1:1-1	1:0-1	2:1-2	9:4-9
Ivy	1:1-1	1:1-1	1:0-1	1:2-1	1:1-1	1:0-1	1:0-1	1:0-1	1:0-1	1:0-1	10:6-10
Metro	3:7-2	1:0-1	2:4-2	2:4-2	2:4-2	2:4-2	3:7-2	0	3:3-3	4:2-4	22:35-20
Metro Atlantic	—	—	—	—	1:0-1	1:0-1	1:0-1	1:0-1	1:0-1	1:0-1	6:0-6
Mid-American	1:0-1	1:0-1	1:0-1	1:1-1	1:0-1	2:0-2	2:0-2	1:0-1	1:0-1	1:1-1	12:2-12
Mid-Continent	—	—	—	—	—	—	1:2-1	1:1-1	1:0-1	1:0-1	4:3-4
Mid-Eastern	—	1:0-1	1:0-1	1:0-1	1:0-1	1:0-1	1:0-1	1:0-1	1:0-1	1:0-1	9:0-9
Missouri Valley	1:0-1	2:3-2	1:0-1	1:0-1	2:1-2	3:1-3	2:1-2	2:0-2	2:0-2	1:0-1	17:6-17
Northeast	—	—	1:0-1	1:1-1	1:0-1	1:0-1	1:0-1	1:0-1	1:0-1	1:01	8:1-8
Ohio Valley	1:0-1	1:0-1	1:1-1	1:0-1	1:1-1	1:0-1	1:0-1	2:1-2	1:1-1	1:1-1	11:5-11
Pacific-10	4:6-4	3:0-3	2:2-2	2:1-2	2:2-2	4:0-4	2:0-2	2:1-2	2:4-2	4:3-4	27:19-27
Southeastern	3:4-3	4:4-5	3:2-3	4:6-4	4:3-4	5:7-5	4:12-4	6:8-6	5:6-5	5:0-5	43:52-44
Southern	1:0-1	1:0-1	1:1-1	1:0-1	1:0-1	1:0-1	1:0-1	1:0-1	1:0-1	1:0-1	10:1-10
Southland	1:2-1	1:1-1	1:0-1	1:1-1	1:1-1	1:2-1	1:0-1	1:0-1	1:0-1	1:0-1	10:7-10
Southwest	2:2-2	2:2-2	2:2-2	2:4-2	2:5-2	3:5-3	3:2-3	1:0-1	3:1-3	3:1-3	23:24-23
Southwestern	1:1-1	1:0-1	1:0-1	1:1-1	1:1-1	1:0-1	1:0-1	1:0-1	1:0-1	1:0-1	10:3-10
Sun Belt	2:0-2	2:3-2	1:2-1	2:1-2	2:1-2	3:2-3	4:3-4	2:1-2	1:0-1	1:1-1	20:14-20
West Coast	1:0-1	1:0-1	2:1-2	1:0-1	1:0-1	1:0-1	1:0-1	2:0-2	1:1-1	2:0-2	13:2-13
Western Athletic	1:0-1	3:5-3	1:1-1	1:2-1	2:1-2	2:1-2	2:0-2	3:3-3	3:1-3	2:2-2	20:16-20
Independents	5:1-5	4:2-4	4:2-4	2:0-2	2:4-2	3:1-3	2:2-2	3:5-3	2:1-2	2:2-2	29:20-29
TOTAL	48:48-48	48:48-48	48:47-47	52:51-51	53:52-52	64:63-63	64:63-63	64:63-63	64:63-63	64:63-63	569:561-561

1990-99

Conference	1990	1991	1992	1993	1994	1995	1996	1997	1998	1999	TOTAL
America East	1: 0-1	1: 0-1	1: 0-1	1: 0-1	1: 0-1	1: 0-1	1: 1-1	1: 0-1	1: 0-1	1: 0-1	10: 1-10
American South	0	2: 0-2	—	—	—	—	—	—	—	—	2: 0-2
American West	—	—	—	—	0	0	—	—	—	—	0: 0-0
Atlantic Coast	5: 14-5	6: 13-5	5: 12-4	6: 14-5	5: 10-5	4: 11-4	6: 6-6	6: 8-6	5: 10-5	3: 7-3	51: 105-48
Atlantic Sun	1: 0-1	1: 0-1	1: 0-1	0	2: 0-2	1: 0-1	1: 0-1	1: 1-1	1: 0-1	1: 0-1	10: 1-10
Atlantic 10	1: 0-1	3: 4-3	3: 2-3	4: 7-4	3: 3-3	2: 3-2	4: 6-4	5: 4-5	5: 3-5	3: 3-3	33: 35-33
Big East	6: 7-6	7: 11-7	5: 5-5	3: 2-3	6: 8-6	4: 6-4	5: 12-5	4: 5-4	5: 7-5	5: 10-4	50: 73-49
Big Eight	4: 2-4	3: 7-3	6: 5-6	6: 5-6	4: 6-4	5: 8-5	4: 4-4	—	—	—	32: 37-32
Big Sky	1: 0-1	1: 0-1	1: 0-1	1: 0-1	1: 0-1	1: 1-1	1: 0-1	1: 0-1	1: 0-1	1: 1-1	10: 2-10
Big South	0	1: 0-1	1: 0-1	1: 0-1	1: 0-1	0	1: 0-1	1: 0-1	1: 0-1	1: 0-1	8: 0-8
Big Ten	7: 8-7	5: 6-5	5: 14-5	5: 10-5	7: 11-7	6: 1-6	5: 2-5	6: 7-6	5: 7-5	7: 13-7	58: 79-58
Big 12	—	—	—	—	—	—	—	5: 7-5	4: 2-4	5: 4-5	14: 13-14
Big West	3: 7-2	2: 4-2	1: 2-1	2: 1-2	1: 0-1	1: 0-1	1: 0-1	1: 0-1	1: 0-1	1: 0-1	14: 14-13
Colonial	1: 0-1	1: 1-1	1: 0-1	1: 0-1	1: 0-1	1: 1-1	1: 0-1	1: 1-1	1: 0-1	1: 0-1	10: 3-10
Conference USA	—	—	—	—	—	—	4: 6-4	4: 5-4	3: 3-3	4: 2-4	15: 16-15
East Coast	1: 0-1	1: 0-1	0	—	0	—	—	—	—	—	2: 0-2
Great Midwest	—	—	3: 7-3	3: 3-3	4: 2-4	3: 4-3	—	—	—	—	13: 16-13
Horizon	2: 3-2	1: 1-1	1: 0-1	2: 1-2	0	2: 0-2	2: 0-2	1: 0-1	3: 1-3	1: 1-1	15: 7-15
Ivy	1: 0-1	1: 0-1	1: 0-1	1: 0-1	1: 1-1	1: 0-1	1: 1-1	1: 1-1	1: 0-1	1: 0-1	10: 3-10
Metro	2: 1-2	2: 1-2	2: 4-2	2: 3-2	1: 2-1	3: 1-3	—	—	—	—	14: 10-14
Metro Atlantic	1: 1-1	1: 0-1	1: 0-1	1: 0-1	1: 0-1	2: 1-2	1: 0-1	1: 0-1	1: 0-1	1: 0-1	11: 2-11
Mid-American	1: 2-1	1: 2-1	1: 0-1	1: 0-1	1: 0-1	2: 1-2	1: 1-1	1: 0-1	2: 1-2	2: 2-2	13: 9-13
Mid-Continent	2: 1-2	2: 0-2	1: 0-1	1: 0-1	1: 1-1	0	1: 0-1	1: 0-1	1: 2-1	1: 0-1	11: 4-11
Mid-Eastern	1: 0-1	0	1: 0-1	1: 0-1	1: 0-1	1: 0-1	1: 1-1	1: 0-1	1: 0-1	1: 0-1	9: 1-9
Missouri Valley	1: 0-1	1: 1-1	1: 0-1	1: 0-1	1: 0-1	2: 2-2	2: 2-2	2: 0-2	1: 1-1	3: 3-3	15: 9-15
Northeast	1: 0-1	1: 0-1	1: 0-1	1: 0-1	1: 0-1	1: 0-1	1: 0-1	1: 0-1	1: 0-1	1: 0-1	10: 0-10
Ohio Valley	1: 0-1	1: 0-1	1: 0-1	1: 0-1	1: 0-1	1: 0-1	1: 0-1	1: 0-1	1: 0-1	1: 0-1	10: 0-10
Pacific-10	4: 4-4	4: 3-4	4: 4-4	3: 3-3	4: 4-4	5: 9-4	4: 3-4	5: 13-4	4: 11-4	4: 1-4	41: 55-39
Patriot	—	0	1: 0-1	1: 0-1	1: 0-1	1: 0-1	1: 0-1	1: 0-1	1: 0-1	1: 0-1	8: 0-8
Southeastern	3: 3-3	5: 2-5	4: 6-4	4: 8-4	4: 12-3	5: 11-5	4: 14-3	5: 5-5	5: 7-4	6: 10-6	45: 78-42
Southern	1: 0-1	1: 0-1	1: 1-1	1: 0-1	1: 0-1	1: 0-1	1: 0-1	1: 2-1	1: 0-1	1: 0-1	10: 3-10
Southland	1: 0-1	1: 0-1	1: 0-1	1: 0-1	1: 0-1	1: 0-1	1: 0-1	1: 0-1	1: 0-1	1: 0-1	10: 0-10
Southwest	3: 7-3	2: 4-2	2: 0-2	2: 0-2	1: 1-1	1: 1-1	2: 3-2	—	—	—	13: 16-13
Southwestern	1: 0-1	0	1: 0-1	1: 1-1	1: 0-1	1: 0-1	1: 0-1	1: 0-1	1: 0-1	1: 0-1	9: 1-9
Sun Belt	2: 0-2	1: 0-1	1: 1-1	2: 2-2	2: 0-2	1: 0-1	1: 0-1	1: 0-1	1: 0-1	1: 0-1	13: 4-13
West Coast	1: 3-1	1: 0-1	1: 0-1	1: 0-1	1: 0-1	1: 0-1	2: 0-2	1: 2-1	1: 0-1	3: 3-1	12: 8-12
Western Athletic	3: 0-3	3: 3-3	2: 2-2	3: 2-3	2: 0-2	2: 1-2	2: 0-2	3: 2-3	3: 5-3	4: 6-4	27: 25-27
Independents	1: 0-1	1: 0-1	0	—	0	0	0	0	—	0	2: 0-2
TOTAL	64: 63-63	64: 63-63	64: 63-63	64: 63-63	64: 63-63	64: 63-63	64: 63-63	64: 63-63	64: 63-63	64: 63-63	640: 630-630

In the 1980s, Big Ten Conference teams made 47 appearances in the NCAA tournament. Clark Kellogg started for Ohio State in two of those years, 1980 and 1982.

Photo from Ohio State sports information

Question...

Match the following NCAA tournament players with their nickname:

Team
1. Nate Archibald
2. Wilt Chamberlain
3. Clyde Drexler
4. Pervis Ellison
5. Eric Floyd
6. Jack Givens
7. Anfernee Hardaway
8. John Havlicek
9. Earvin Johnson
10. Bob Kurland
11. Bryant Reeves
12. David Robinson
13. Oscar Robertson
14. Bill Russell
15. Jerry West

Nickname
A. The Admiral
B. Big Country
C. The Big O
D. Foothills
E. The Glide
F. Goose
G. Hondo
H. Magic
J. Never Nervous
K. Penny
L. The Secretary of Defense
M. Sleepy
N. The Stilt
P. Tiny
Q. Zeke from Cabin Creek

Answer...

1-P, 2-N, 3-E, 4-J, 5-M, 6-F, 7-K, 8-G, 9-H, 10-D, 11-B, 12-A, 13-C, 14-L, 15-Q

THE TOURNAMENT

Tournament trivia

Conference Teams in the Tournament

1939-99

	1939-40s	1950s	1960s	1970s	1980s	1990s	1900s TOTAL
America East				0	10: 4-10	10: 1-10	20: 5-20
American South					1: 1-1	2: 0-2	3: 1-3
Atlantic Coast		6: 9-5	10: 25-12	15: 23-15	50: 92-48	51: 105-48	132: 254-128
Atlantic Sun					9: 1-9	10: 1-10	19: 2-19
Atlantic 10				3: 3-3	18: 16-18	33: 35-33	54: 54-54
Big East					45: 83-43	50: 73-49	95: 156-92
Big Eight	8: 10-9	9: 20-10	10: 10-12	12: 13-14	33: 47-32	32: 37-32	104: 137-109
Big Sky			2: 2-2	10: 5-12	10: 1-10	10: 2-10	32: 10-34
Big South					0	8: 0-8	8: 0-8
Big Ten	10: 16-9	10: 21-11	10: 25-9	15: 28-13	47: 71-45	58: 79-58	150: 240-145
Big 12						14: 13-14	14: 13-14
Big West				11: 9-12	15: 14-15	14: 14-13	40: 37-40
Border		9: 0-10	3: 2-3				12: 2-13
Colonial				0	8: 9-8	10: 3-10	18: 12-18
Conference USA						15: 16-15	15: 16-15
East Coast		1: 0-2	10: 8-13	10: 0-10	10: 4-10	2: 0-2	33: 12-37
Florida Intercollegiate			1: 0-1				1: 0-1
Great Midwest						13: 16-13	13: 16-13
Horizon					9: 4-9	15: 7-15	24: 11-24
Indiana Collegiate			1: 2-1				1: 2-1
Ivy	6: 6-8	9: 5-12	9: 10-11	10: 10-12	10: 4-10	10: 3-10	54: 38-63
Ky. Intercollegiate	1: 0-1						1: 0-1
Little Three		1: 0-1					1: 0-1
Metro				8: 3-8	22: 35-20	14: 10-14	44: 48-42
Metro Atlantic					6: 0-6	11: 2-11	17: 2-17
Mid-American		7: 1-8	10: 5-13	10: 5-10	12: 2-12	13: 9-13	52: 22-56
Mid-Continent					4: 3-4	11: 4-11	15: 7-15
Mid-Eastern					9: 0-9	9: 1-9	18: 1-18
Missouri Valley	4: 9-2	10: 12-13	10: 21-11	12: 16-14	17: 6-17	15: 9-15	68: 73-72
Northeast				0	8: 1-8	10: 0-10	18: 1-18
Ohio Valley		5: 2-5	10: 7-13	10: 6-11	11: 5-11	10: 0-10	46: 20-50
Pacific-10	10: 14-11	10: 15-12	11: 28-9	13: 34-9	27: 19-27	41: 55-39	112: 165-107
Patriot						8: 0-8	8: 0-8
Presidents Athletic		1: 1-2					1: 1-2
Rocky Mountain		8: 6-10	1: 0-1				9: 6-11
Skyline Eight	11: 9-15	10: 6-14	3: 5-5				24: 20-34
Southeastern	4: 8-2	9: 15-9	10: 10-12	14: 17-15	43: 52-44	45: 78-42	125: 180-124
Southern	3: 2-4	10: 9-11	10: 9-11	10: 4-11	10: 1-10	10: 3-10	53: 28-57
Southland			1: 0-1	3: 4-4	10: 7-10	10: 0-10	24: 11-25
Southwest	10: 9-13	10: 9-14	10: 9-13	12: 8-13	23: 24-23	13: 16-13	78: 75-89
Southwestern					10: 3-10	9: 1-9	19: 4-19
Sun Belt				3: 3-4	20: 14-20	13: 4-13	36: 21-37
West Coast		7: 18-5	10: 8-12	11: 11-11	13: 2-13	12: 8-12	53: 47-53
Western Athletic			7: 4-11	14: 10-16	20: 16-20	27: 25-27	68: 55-74
W'ern N.Y. Little Three		3: 6-3					3: 6-3
Yankee		6: 1-7	8: 2-8	1: 1-1			15: 4-16
Independents	21: 18-27	64: 85-77	83: 88-96	86: 104-99	29: 20-29	2: 0-2	285: 315-330
TOTAL	88:101-101	205:241-241	240:280-280	293:317-317	569:561-561	640:630-630	2035: 2130-2130

1939-2001

Year	2000	2001	2000s TOTAL	1900s TOTAL	ALL-TIME TOTAL
America East	1: 0-1	1: 0-1	2: 0-2	20: 5-20	22: 5-22
Atlantic Coast	3: 7-3	6: 11-5	9: 18-8	132: 254-128	141: 272-136
Atlantic Sun	1: 0-1	1: 1-1	2: 1-2	19: 2-19	21: 3-21
Atlantic 10	3: 1-3	3: 4-3	6: 5-6	54: 54-54	60: 59-60
Big East	5: 8-5	5: 5-5	10: 13-10	95: 156-92	105: 169-102
Big Sky	1: 0-1	1: 0-1	2: 0-2	32: 10-34	34: 10-36
Big South	1: 0-1	1: 0-1	2: 0-2	8: 0-8	10: 0-10
Big Ten	6: 15-5	7: 10-7	13: 25-12	150: 240-145	163: 265-157
Big 12	6: 9-6	6: 3-6	12: 12-12	14: 13-14	26: 25-26
Big West	1: 0-1	1: 1-1	2: 1-2	40: 37-40	42: 38-42
Colonial	1: 0-1	1: 0-1	2: 0-2	18: 12-18	20: 12-20
Conference USA	4: 1-4	2: 3-2	6: 4-6	15: 16-15	21: 20-21
Horizon	1: 0-1	1: 1-1	2: 1-2	24: 11-24	26: 12-26
Ivy	1: 0-1	1: 0-1	2: 0-2	54: 38-63	56: 38-65
Metro Atlantic	1: 0-1	1: 0-1	2: 0-2	17: 2-17	19: 2-19
Mid-American	1: 0-1	1: 1-1	2: 1-2	52: 22-56	54: 23-58
Mid-Continent	1: 0-1	1: 0-1	2: 0-2	15: 7-15	17: 7-17
Mid—Eastern	1: 0-1	1: 1-1	2: 1-2	18: 1-18	20: 2-20
Missouri Valley	2: 0-2	2: 1-2	4: 1-4	68: 73-72	72: 74-76
Mountain West	2: 1-2	1: 0-1	3: 1-3	—	3: 1-3
Northeast	1: 0-1	1: 0-1	2: 0-2	18: 1-18	20: 1-20
Ohio Valley	1: 0-1	1: 0-1	2: 0-2	46: 20-50	48: 20-52
Pacific1-10	4: 4-4	5: 13-5	9: 17-9	112: 165-107	121: 182-116
Patriot	1: 0-1	1: 0-1	2: 0-2	8: 0-8	10: 0-10
Southeastern	6: 11-6	6: 5-6	12: 16-12	125: 180-124	137: 196-136
Southern	1: 0-1	1: 0-1	2: 0-2	53: 28-57	55: 28-59
Southland	1: 0-1	1: 1-1	2: 1-2	24: 11-25	26: 12-27
Southwestern	1: 0-1	1: 0-1	2: 0-2	19: 4-19	21: 4-21
Sun Belt	1: 0-1	1: 0-1	2: 0-2	36: 21-37	38: 21-39
West Coast	2: 3-2	1: 2-1	3: 5-3	53: 47-53	56: 52-56
Western Athletic	2: 3-2	2: 1-2	4: 4-4	68: 55-74	72: 59-78

From 1939-99, the Big Ten led all conferences in NCAA tournament appearances with 150. Ted Kitchell helped Indiana to land three of those tournament spots from 1980-82.

Photo from Indiana sports information

Tournament trivia

Question... What state has produced the most NCAA Division I basketball champions?

Answer... California with 15. The rest of the list: Kentucky, nine; North Carolina, eight; Indiana, five; Michigan and Ohio, three; Kansas, Oklahoma, Pennsylvania and Wisconsin, two; and Arizona, Arkansas, Connecticut, Illinois, Massachusetts, Nevada, New York, Oregon, Texas, Utah and Wyoming, one. One team from the District of Columbia has won.

Year	2000	2001	2000s TOTAL	1900s TOTAL	ALL-TIME TOTAL
Independents	0: 0-0	0: 0-0	0: 0-0	285: 315-330	285: 315-330
TOTAL	64: 63-63	65: 64-64	129: 127-127	2035: 2130-2130	2164: 2257-2257

Tournament Field by State

Most Schools From One State In One Tournament

- 6 California, 1997 (California, Pacific, St. Mary's, Southern California, Stanford, UCLA)
- 6 California, 2001 (California, Cal St. Northridge, Fresno St., Southern California, Stanford, UCLA)
- 6 Indiana, 2000 (Ball St., Butler, Indiana, Indiana St., Purdue, Valparaiso)
- 5 California, 1979 (Pacific, Pepperdine, San Francisco, Southern California, UCLA)
- 5 California, 1996 (California, San Jose St., Santa Clara, Stanford, UCLA)
- 5 Louisiana, 1993 (La.-Monroe, LSU, New Orleans, Southern U., Tulane)
- 5 Michigan, 1998 (Detroit, Eastern Mich., Michigan, Michigan St., Western Mich.)
- 5 New York, 2000 (Hofstra, Iona, St. Bonaventure, St. John's, Syracuse)
- 5 North Carolina, 1986 (Davidson, Duke, North Carolina, N.C. A&T, North Carolina St.)
- 5 North Carolina, 1988 (Duke, North Carolina, N.C. A&T, North Carolina St., Charlotte)
- 5 North Carolina, 1992 (Campbell, Duke, North Carolina, Charlotte, Wake Forest)
- 5 North Carolina, 1996 (Duke, North Carolina, UNC Greensboro, Wake Forest, Western Caro.)
- 5 Pennsylvania, 1982 (Pennsylvania, Pittsburgh, Robert Morris, St. Joseph's, Villanova)
- 5 Pennsylvania, 1988 (La Salle, Lehigh, Pittsburgh, Temple, Villanova)
- 5 Pennsylvania, 1991 (Penn St., Pittsburgh, St. Francis, Temple, Villanova)
- 5 Tennessee, 1989 (East Tenn. St., Memphis, Middle Tenn., Tennessee, Vanderbilt)
- 5 Texas, 1988 (Baylor, North Texas, Southern Methodist, Tex.-San Antonio, UTEP)
- 4 48 times

The duo of Jim Nantz and Billy Packer has covered the Final Four for CBS since 1991.

Most Schools From One State All-Time

17	California	4	Connecticut
17	Texas	4	District of Columbia
16	New York	4	Iowa
14	Pennsylvania	4	Missouri
13	North Carolina	4	Washington
12	Ohio	3	Arizona
11	Virginia	3	Arkansas
10	Illinois	3	Colorado
10	Louisiana	3	Idaho
9	Massachusetts	3	Kansas
9	Tennessee	3	Oregon
8	Florida	3	Rhode Island
8	South Carolina	3	Wisconsin
7	Indiana	2	Montana
7	New Jersey	2	Nebraska
6	Alabama	2	Nevada
6	Maryland	2	New Mexico
6	Michigan	2	West Virginia
6	Mississippi	1	Delaware
5	Georgia	1	Hawaii
5	Kentucky	1	Minnesota
5	Oklahoma	1	New Hampshire
5	Utah	1	Wyoming

Televised College Basketball Games

Highest-Rated

	Date	Game	Round	Network	Rating/Share	Homes
1.	3/26/1979	Michigan St. vs. Indiana St.	CH	NBC	24.1/38	17,950,000
2.	4/1/1985	Georgetown vs. Villanova	CH	CBS	23.3/33	19,780,000
3.	4/6/1992	Duke vs. Michigan	CH	CBS	22.7/35	20,910,000
4.	4/4/1983	North Carolina St. vs. Houston	CH	CBS	22.3/32	18,580,000
5.	4/5/1993	North Carolina vs. Michigan	CH	CBS	22.2/34	20,670,000
6.	4/4/1994	Arkansas vs. Duke	CH	CBS	21.6/33	20,350,000
6.	3/29/1982	North Carolina vs. Georgetown	CH	CBS	21.6/31	17,600,000
8.	4/3/1989	Michigan vs. Seton Hall	CH	CBS	21.3/33	19,260,000
8.	3/31/1975	UCLA vs. Kentucky	CH	NBC	21.3/33	14,590,000
10.	3/31/1986	Louisville vs. Duke	CH	CBS	20.7/31	17,780,000
10.	3/30/1981	Indiana vs. North Carolina	CH	NBC	20.7/29	16,100,000
12.	3/26/1973	UCLA vs. Memphis	CH	NBC	20.5/32	13,280,000
13.	3/29/1976	Indiana vs. Michigan	CH	NBC	20.4/31	14,200,000
14.	4/2/1990	UNLV vs. Duke	CH	CBS	20.0/31	18,420,000

TELEVISED COLLEGE BASKETBALL GAMES—HIGHEST RATED

The freshman Fab Five of Michigan lost to Duke in the championship game in 1992 as almost 21 million homes watched on television. That set the record for most homes tuned into a college basketball game. The Fab Five were (from right) Chris Webber, Juwon Howard, Jalen Rose, Ray Jackson and Jimmy King.

	Date	Game	Round	Network	Rating/Share	Homes
15.	3/27/1978	Kentucky vs. Duke	CH	NBC	19.9/31	14,510,000
15.	3/25/1974	North Carolina St. vs. Marquette	CH	NBC	19.9/30	13,170,000
17.	3/24/1980	Louisville vs. UCLA	CH	NBC	19.8/30	15,110,000
18.	4/2/1984	Georgetown vs. Houston	CH	CBS	19.7/29	16,510,000
19.	3/30/1987	Syracuse vs. Indiana	CH	CBS	19.6/28	17,130,000
20.	4/1/1991	Duke vs. Kansas	CH	CBS	19.4/30	18,060,000
21.	4/3/1995	UCLA vs. Arkansas	CH	CBS	19.3/30	18,410,000
21.	3/28/1977	Marquette vs. North Carolina	CH	NBC	19.3/29	13,740,000
23.	3/31/1997	Arizona vs. Kentucky	CH	CBS	18.9/31	18,290,000
24.	4/4/1988	Kansas vs. Oklahoma	CH	CBS	18.8/30	16,660,000
25.	4/1/1996	Kentucky vs. Syracuse	CH	CBS	18.3/29	17,540,000

CH—national championship game; NSF—national semifinal game.

Most-Watched Telecasts (By Homes)

	Date	Game	Round	Network	Rating/Share	Homes
1.	4/6/1992	Duke vs. Michigan	CH	CBS	22.7/35	20,910,000
2.	4/5/1993	North Carolina vs. Michigan	CH	CBS	22.2/34	20,670,000
3.	4/4/1994	Arkansas vs. Duke	CH	CBS	21.6/33	20,350,000
4.	4/1/1985	Georgetown vs. Villanova	CH	CBS	23.3/33	19,780,000
5.	4/3/1989	Michigan vs. Seton Hall	CH	CBS	21.3/33	19,260,000
6.	4/4/1983	North Carolina St. vs. Houston	CH	CBS	22.3/32	18,580,000
7.	4/2/1990	UNLV vs. Duke	CH	CBS	20.0/31	18,420,000
8.	4/3/1995	UCLA vs. Arkansas	CH	CBS	19.3/30	18,410,000
9.	3/31/1997	Arizona vs. Kentucky	CH	CBS	18.9/31	18,290,000
10.	4/1/1991	Duke vs. Kansas	CH	CBS	19.4/30	18,060,000
11.	3/26/1979	Michigan St. vs. Indiana St.	CH	NBC	24.1/38	17,950,000
12.	3/31/1986	Louisville vs. Duke	CH	CBS	20.7/31	17,780,000
13.	3/29/1982	North Carolina vs. Georgetown	CH	CBS	21.6/31	17,600,000
14.	4/1/1996	Kentucky vs. Syracuse	CH	CBS	18.3/29	17,540,000
15.	3/30/1998	Kentucky vs. Utah	CH	CBS	17.8/28	17,490,000
16.	3/29/1999	Connecticut vs. Duke	CH	CBS	17.2/27	17,139,000
17.	3/30/1987	Syracuse vs. Indiana	CH	CBS	19.6/28	17,130,000
18.	4/4/1988	Kansas vs. Oklahoma	CH	CBS	18.8/30	16,660,000
19.	4/2/1984	Georgetown vs. Houston	CH	CBS	19.7/29	16,510,000
20.	3/30/1981	Indiana vs. North Carolina	CH	NBC	20.7/29	16,100,000
21.	4/2/2001	Duke vs. Arizona	CH	CBS	15.6/24	15,992,000
22.	4/4/1992	Duke vs. Indiana	NSF	CBS	16.8/30	15,473,000
23.	3/24/1980	Louisville vs. UCLA	CH	NBC	19.8/30	15,110,000
24.	4/3/1993	Michigan vs. Kentucky	NSF	CBS	16.0/29	14,912,000
25.	4/2/1983	Houston vs. Louisville	NSF	CBS	17.8/35	14,827,000

CH—national championship game; NSF—national semifinal game.

Financial Analysis

Division I Men's Basketball, 1970-98

Year	Teams	Dates	Total Paid Attendance	Average Attendance	Ticket Sales	Avg. Per Ticket	Television Revenue	Other Revenue	Gross Receipts
1970	25	16	146,794	9,175			$550,000		$1,374,976
1971	25	16	207,200	12,950			726,500		1,937,009
1972	25	16	147,304	9,207			743,500		1,741,442
1973	25	16	163,160	10,198			1,165,755		2,301,205
1974	25	16	154,112	9,632			1,240,999		2,314,236
1975	32	18	183,857	10,214			2,530,000		3,972,859
1976	32	18	202,502	11,250			2,590,000		4,286,456
1977	32	18	241,610	13,423	$1,880,190	$7.78	4,041,063	191,788	6,113,041
1978	32	18	227,149	12,619	1,805,399	7.95	4,690,684	133,394	6,629,477
1979	40	22	262,101	11,914	2,482,528	9.47	5,159,473	267,533	7,909,534
1980	48	26	321,260	12,356	3,113,214	9.69	8,856,948	186,840	12,157,002
1981	48	26	347,414	13,362	3,769,732	10.85	10,317,521	332,233	14,419,486
1982	48	26	427,251	16,433	4,987,948	11.67	14,630,849	487,333	20,106,130
1983	52	28	364,356	13,013	4,482,242	12.30	16,878,979	395,065	21,756,286
1984	53	28	397,481	14,196	5,666,841	14.26	20,137,980	1,079,361	26,884,182
1985	64	34	422,519	12,427	5,846,704	13.84	28,327,009	654,100	34,827,813
1986	64	34	499,704	14,697	7,382,986	14.77	33,031,128	746,021	41,160,135
1987	64	34	654,744	19,257	10,623,809	16.23	36,635,300	1,833,096	49,092,205
1988	64	34	558,998	16,441	9,157,202	16.38	57,789,600	1,283,711	68,230,513
1989	64	34	613,242	18,037	10,916,138	17.80	57,161,500	2,336,767	70,414,405
1990	64	34	537,138	15,798	9,845,904	18.33	63,505,000	2,827,888	76,178,792
1991	64	34	665,707	19,580	14,401,237	21.63	112,437,757	3,278,202	17,679,439
1992	64	34	580,462	17,072	12,367,201	21.31	120,060,000	2,983,944	15,351,145
1993	64	34	707,719	20,815	15,819,943	22.35	129,060,000	3,093,886	18,913,829
1994	64	34	578,007	17,000	13,847,926	23.96	137,060,000	4,000,648	17,848,574
1995	64	34	540,101	15,885	14,114,931	26.13	166,200,000	4,331,481	18,446,412
1996	64	34	631,834	18,583	17,464,818	27.64	178,300,000	4,819,262	22,284,080

FINANCIAL ANALYSIS

Year	Teams	Dates	Total Paid Attendance	Average Attendance	Ticket Sales	Avg. Per Ticket	Television Revenue	Other Revenue	Gross Receipts
1997	64	34	646,531	19,016	21,463,044	33.20	188,400,000	1,566,609	23,029,653
1998	64	34	663,876	19,526	24,693,678	37.20	200,900,000	760,508	25,454,186
1999	64	34	720,685	21,197	26,671,587	37.01	213,800,000	476,158	27,147,745
2000	64	34	624,777	18,375	25,079,444	40.14	227,700,000	500,250	25,579,694
2001	65	35	612,089	17,488	27,502,995	44.93	242,100,000	379,337	27,882,332

Year	Game Expense	Team Expense	Net Receipts	NCAA Share	Teams Share	Final Four	Reg. Finals	Reg. Semis	Second Round	First Round
1970	$209,106	$99,978	$1,065,892	$532,946	$532,946	$49,576	$24,788	$24,788	$8,263	$8,263
1971	268,863	112,668	1,555,478	777,739	777,739	72,348	36,174	36,174	12,058	12,058
1972	218,767	136,664	1,386,011	693,005	693,006	64,466	32,233	32,233	10,744	10,744
1973	231,646	147,192	1,922,367	961,183	961,184	81,961	44,706	44,706	14,902	14,902
1974	239,892	158,182	1,916,162	958,081	958,081	89,124	44,561	44,561	14,854	14,854
1975	334,256	259,617	3,378,986	1,689,493	1,689,493	133,381	66,691	66,691	22,230	22,230
1976	424,704	222,449	3,639,303	1,819,651	1,819,652	143,657	71,828	71,828	23,943	23,943
1977	499,204	235,011	5,378,826	2,689,413	2,689,413	212,322	106,161	106,161	35,387	35,387
1978	437,921	242,526	6,088,955	3,044,477	3,044,478	240,354	120,177	120,177	40,059	40,059
1979	699,696	329,319	7,209,838	3,604,919	3,604,919	235,103	117,552	117,552	39,184	39,184
1980	808,278	500,673	11,348,725	4,984,363	6,364,362	326,378	203,986	203,986	81,594	81,594
1981	1,266,445	725,067	13,153,041	5,686,520	7,466,521	382,899	239,312	239,312	95,725	95,725
1982	1,725,260	614,630	17,766,240	7,106,496	10,659,744	507,607	380,705	380,705	126,902	126,902
1983	1,520,645	766,462	19,469,179	7,787,671	11,681,508	530,979	398,234	398,234	132,744	132,744
1984	1,925,396	905,432	24,053,354	9,621,324	14,432,030	648,630	486,472	486,472	162,158	162,158
1985	2,087,762	1,661,560	31,078,491	12,431,387	18,647,104	751,899	601,519	451,139	300,760	150,380
1986	2,673,609	1,577,259	36,909,267	14,763,703	22,145,564	892,966	714,373	535,780	357,187	178,593
1987	3,734,260	1,708,844	43,649,101	17,459,645	26,189,456	1,056,027	844,821	633,616	422,411	211,205
1988	3,747,664	2,031,293	55,651,556	22,260,617	33,390,939	1,198,173	958,539	718,904	479,269	239,635
1989	5,453,219	2,015,964	62,945,222	25,178,085	37,767,137	1,274,224	1,099,379	824,534	549,689	274,845
1990	6,862,405	2,169,996	66,992,571	26,858,547	40,287,844	1,472,339	1,177,871	883,404	588,936	294,468
1991	7,063,956	6,473,207	4,142,276	4,142,276						
1992	6,058,532	6,643,559	2,649,054	2,649,054						
1993	6,632,633	7,320,543	4,704,975	4,704,975						
1994	6,410,471	6,343,571	5,094,532	5,094,532						
1995	7,195,540	6,588,754	4,662,118	4,662,118						
1996	9,395,653	6,944,240	5,944,187	5,944,187						
1997	9,087,577	7,286,912	6,655,164	6,655,164						
1998	9,599,287	7,571,589	8,283,310	8,283,310						
1999	10,118,441	4,635,722	9,536,502	9,536,502						
2000	10,241,330	8,322,281	7,016,083	7,016,083						
2001	10,860,377	10,059,371	6,962,584	6,962,584						

Note: Beginning in 1991, in accordance with the revenue-distribution plan adopted by the then-NCAA Executive Committee, television rights fees were no longer included in the gross receipts. Moneys are distributed to conferences and independent institutions for their tournament participation, based upon a rolling six-year average.

Tournament Facts

Game Milestones

Game No.

1 Villanova defeated Brown, 42-30, on March 17, 1939, in Philadelphia. In the second game of the double-header, Ohio State defeated Wake Forest, 64-52.

50 Dartmouth defeated Ohio State, 60-53, in the Eastern regional final on March 28, 1944, in New York.

100 Illinois defeated Oregon State, 57-53, in the national third-place game in March 1949 in Seattle.

200 Bradley defeated Southern California, 74-72, in the national semifinal game on March 19, 1954, in Kansas City, Missouri.

300 Temple defeated Maryland, 71-67, in the fifth of eight regional semifinal games on March 14, 1958. The East region game took place in Charlotte, North Carolina.

400 Wake Forest defeated Yale, 92-82 in overtime, in the first game of the 1962 tournament. The East region game took place in Philadelphia and was the first of seven first-round games played on March 12.

500 Providence defeated St. Joseph's, 81-73 in overtime, in an East region semifinal game in College Park, Maryland, on March 12, 1965. The game was the fifth of eight regional semifinal games played that day.

600 New Mexico State defeated Brigham Young, 74-62, on March 8, 1969, in Las Cruces, New Mexico. The West region game was the seventh of nine first-round games played that day.

700 Louisiana-Lafayette defeated Texas, 100-70, in Ames, Iowa, in a regional third-place game on March 1, 1972. The Midwest region game was the third of four regional third-place games played that day, along with four regional finals.

800 Kentucky defeated Syracuse, 95-79, in the national semifinal game on March 29, 1975, played in San Diego.

900 St. John's (New York) defeated Temple, 75-70, on March 9 in the first game of the 1979 tournament. The East region game took place in Raleigh, North Carolina.

1,000 Villanova defeated Houston, 90-72, on March 13, 1981, in Charlotte, North Carolina. The East region game was the fifth of eight first-round games played that day.

1,100 Iowa defeated Utah State, 64-59, on March 18, 1983, in Louisville, Kentucky. The Midwest region game was the sixth of eight first-round games played that day.

1,200 Illinois State defeated Southern California, 58-55, on March 14, 1985, in Tulsa, Oklahoma. The Midwest region game was the 15th of 16 first-round games played that day.

1,300 Louisville defeated North Carolina, 94-79, on March 20, 1986, in Houston. The West region semifinal game was the fourth of four games played that day.

1,400 Maryland defeated UC Santa Barbara, 92-82, on March 18, 1988, in Cincinnati. The Southeast region game was the 10th of 16 first-round games played that day.

1,500 Michigan defeated Seton Hall, 80-79 in overtime, for the national championship on April 3, 1989, in Seattle. It was the first time in tournament history that a first-year head coach—Steve Fisher—won the national title.

1,600 Temple defeated Richmond, 77-64, on March 16, 1991, in East Rutherford, New Jersey. The East region game was the fifth of eight second-round games played that day.

1,700 In one of the biggest upsets in tournament history, Santa Clara defeated Arizona, 64-61, on March 18, 1993, in Salt Lake City. The West region game was the 11th of 16 first-round games played that day. It was the second time in tournament history that a No. 15 seed defeated a No. 2 seed.

1,800 In the game to decide the final team to make the 1994 "Sweet Sixteen," Louisville defeated Minnesota, 60-55, on March 20 in Sacramento, California. The West region game was the final game of the second round and the fourth game in the tournament played that day.

1,900 Iowa State defeated California, 74-64, on March 14, 1996, in Dallas. The Midwest region game was the 12th of 16 first-round games played that day.

2,000 In the game to decide the final team to make the 1997 Final Four, Arizona defeated Providence, 96-92, in overtime, on March 23 in Birmingham, Alabama. The Southeast regional final was the second and final game played in the tournament that day. Arizona went on to win its first national championship in basketball.

2,100 In the first game of the 1999 season round, St. John's (N.Y.) defeated Indiana, 86-61, on March 13 in the South regioin in Orlando, Florida.

2,200 In the seventh game of the 2001 first round, Final Four-bound Maryland just got by George Mason, 83-80, on March 15 in the West region in Boise, Idaho.

Tournament History

1939 The first National Collegiate men's basketball tournament was held. For the first 12 years, district playoffs often were held with the winner entering an eight-team field for the championship. The district games were not considered a part of the tournament. The winners of the East and West regionals were the only two teams to advance to the final site.

1940 The National Association of Basketball Coaches held its annual convention at the site of the national finals for the first time. It has been held in conjunction with the tournament ever since.

1946 The championship game was televised locally for the first time in New York City by WCBS-TV as Oklahoma State defeated North Carolina, 43-40. The initial viewing audience was estimated to be 500,000.

This was the first time four teams advanced to the final site. With only East and West regionals, the two regional champions played for the national title while the regional runners-up played for third place.

1950 CCNY became the only team that has ever won both national postseason tournaments: the NCAA tournament and the National Invitational Tournament (NIT).

1951 The field was expanded to 16 teams, with 10 conference champions qualifying automatically for the first time. Those 10 conferences were: Big Seven (Big Eight), Big Ten, Border, Eastern (Ivy), Missouri Valley, Mountain States (also known as Skyline), Pacific Coast (Pacific-10), Southeastern, Southern and Southwest.

1952 Tournament games were televised regionally for the first time.

The number of regional sites changed from two to four, with the four winners advancing to the finals.

1953 The bracket expanded from 16 teams to 22 and fluctuated between 22 and 25 teams until 1974.

Teams are limited to one national postseason tournament. No longer can teams play in both the NCAA tournament and the National Invitational Tournament (NIT).

1954 The Tuesday-Wednesday format for semifinals and the final game was changed to Friday-Saturday.

The championship game was televised nationally for the first time as La Salle defeated Bradley, 94-76, in Kansas City, Missouri.

1957 The largest media group to date assembled for the finals in Kansas City, Missouri. Coverage included an 11-station television network, 64 newspaper writers and live radio broadcasts on 73 stations in 11 states.

1963 A contract to run through 1968 was worked out with Sports Network for the championship game to be televised nationally. Television rights totaled $140,000.

For the first time, sites for the tournament competition were selected two years in advance.

1966 Net income for the entire tournament exceeded $500,000 for the first time.

A television-blackout provision requiring a 48-hour advance sellout was adopted.

1969 The Friday-Saturday format for semifinals and the final game changed to Thursday-Saturday.

NBC was selected to televise the championship at television rights totaling $547,500, exceeding $500,000 for the first time. The tournament's net income of $1,032,915 was the first time above the million-dollar mark.

1971 NBC recorded the largest audience ever for a basketball network telecast during the semifinals as 9,320,000 homes saw the game.

1973 The Thursday-Saturday format for semifinals and the final game changed to Saturday-Monday.

Television rights totaled $1,165,755, exceeding $1 million for the first time. NBC reported that the championship game was the highest-rated basketball telecast of all time. The contest received a rating of 20.5 and was seen by 13,580,000 television households reaching a total audience of 39 million persons. Also for the first time, the championship game was televised in prime time.

TVS, with the approval of NBC, agreed to televise those games not carried by NBC for a two-year period at the rights fee of $65,000 per year.

First-round byes were determined on the basis of an evaluation of the conference's won-lost record over the past 10 years in National Collegiate Championship play.

The first public draw to fill oversubscribed orders for Final Four game tickets was administered by the committee for the 1974 championship.

1974 The bracket rotation was changed for the first time, eliminating East versus West bracketing in effect since 1939. East played West and Mideast played Midwest in the national semifinals.

The Eastern Collegiate Athletic Conference was divided to receive multiple automatic-qualification berths in the tournament.

1975 A 32-team bracket was adopted and teams other than the conference champion could be chosen at large from the same conference for the first time.

Dressing rooms opened to media representatives after a 10-minute cooling-off period.

1976 The rights for the NCAA Radio Network were awarded to Host Communications, Inc., of Lexington, Kentucky.

Regional third-place games were eliminated.

For the first time, two teams from the same conference (Big Ten) played in the national championship game, with Indiana defeating Michigan.

1977 NBC televised 23 hours and 18 minutes of tournament programming.

1978 A seeding process was used for the first time for individual teams. A maximum of four automatic-qualifying conference teams were seeded in each of the four regional brackets. These teams were seeded based on their respective conferences' won-lost percentages in tournament play during the past five years. At-large seeding in each region was based on current won-lost records, strength of schedule and eligibility status of student-athletes for postseason competition.

NBC televised the four regional championship games and a first-round doubleheader on Saturday and Sunday.

NCAA Productions began producing first/second round and selected regional semifinal games and airing them in the regions of the participating teams.

Complimentary tickets for all NCAA championships were eliminated.

1979 The bracket was expanded to 40 teams and all teams were seeded for the first time.

NBC received a record one-game rating with a 24.1 in Michigan State's national championship victory over Indiana State. The 38 share and the 18 million homes viewing were both records at the time.

The Division I Men's Basketball Committee assigned three-man officiating crews for all tournament games.

A public lottery for the drawing of Final Four game tickets was first held.

1980 The bracket was expanded to 48 teams, which included 24 automatic qualifiers and 24 at-large teams. The top 16 seeds received byes to the second round.

The limit of two teams from the same conference being allowed in the tournament was lifted. This gave the committee maximum flexibility to balance the bracket as well as to select the best possible at-large entrants.

ESPN began telecasting nationally the games that were being produced by NCAA Productions. ESPN continued its coverage of early-round games through the 1990 tournament.

1981 Principles for the seeding and placement of teams to develop a balanced tournament bracket were implemented. They included establishing 12 levels that transcended each of the four regions; dividing each region into three sections with four levels each; only one conference team could be placed in each regional section; and placing teams in their geographical area or on their home court if the first three principles are not compromised.

A computer ranking system was used as an aid in evaluating teams in the preparation for making at-large selections.

It became policy that "no more than 50 percent of the tournament berths shall be filled by automatic qualifiers."

Virginia defeated LSU in the last third-place game conducted at the Final Four site.

1982 CBS was awarded the television rights for 16 exposures to the championship for three years.

The selection show was shown on live national television for the first time.

North Carolina's national championship win against Georgetown received a 21.6 rating and was the 11th-ranked prime time program for that week. CBS also achieved second-round record ratings with an 11.8 rating and 27 share on Saturday, and an 11.3 rating and 28 share on Sunday.

Host Communications, Inc., and the CBS Radio Network coproduced the NCAA Radio Network.

1983 An opening round was added that required the representatives of eight automatic-qualifying conferences to compete for four positions in the 52-team tournament bracket. This concept permitted the committee to retain a 48-team bracket evenly balanced with 24 automatic qualifiers and 24 at-large selections, yet award automatic qualification to each of the 28 conferences that received it the year before. The 16 top-seeded teams received byes to the second round of the tournament.

The current format was established that begins the tournament the third weekend in March, regional championships on the fourth Saturday and Sunday, and the national semifinals and final the following Saturday and Monday.

North Carolina State's national championship victory over Houston attracted what then was a record 18.6 million homes to the CBS telecast. The game had a 22.3 rating (third best) and a 32 share. It was the fifth-ranked prime time television program for that week.

A national semifinal record also was set in Houston's victory over Louisville. The game had a 17.8 rating and 35 share and was viewed by 14,800,000 homes on CBS.

The committee determined that a facility in which the final session is held must have a minimum of 17,000 seats.

1984 One additional opening-round game was established, requiring 10 automatic-qualifying conferences to compete for five positions in the 53-team bracket that included 24 automatic qualifiers and 24 at-large selections.

For the first time, awards were presented to all participating teams in the championship.

1985 The tournament bracket was expanded to include 64 teams, which eliminated all first-round byes.

TOURNAMENT FACTS—TOURNAMENT HISTORY

The committee realigned each region and renamed the Mideast region the Southeast region. Specifically, the Southern and Mid-Eastern conferences were moved from the East to the Southeast region; the Big Ten, Mid-American and Southwestern conferences moved from the Southeast to the Midwest; the Metro and Trans America conferences were moved from the Midwest to the Southeast, and the Southland and Southwest conferences were moved from the Midwest to the West region.

The number of automatic qualifiers was capped at 30 for a five-year period (1986-90).

CBS had a record 19.8 million homes view Villanova's national championship victory over Georgetown. The game attracted a 23.3 rating (second best) and a 33 share, and was the second-rated prime time program on television for that week.

The East regional championship game (Georgetown defeated Georgia Tech) set television records for that level of tournament competition with a 12.6 rating, a 32 share and 10.7 million homes tuned to CBS.

The NCAA Radio Network reached an all-time high radio audience for any sports event when the Villanova-Georgetown game attracted 21 million listeners.

CBS began a second three-year contract that included 19 exposures.

1986 CBS televised 40 hours, 51 minutes of tournament programming.

The NCAA Radio Network included a record 426 stations, including 92 of the top 100 markets.

It became policy that all regional competition will be played at neutral sites. If an institution selected to host this level of competition is a participant in the tournament, it will be bracketed in another region.

Three separate three-man officiating crews were assigned to the two national semifinals and the championship final.

1987 The National Association of Basketball Coaches reaffirmed its endorsement of the policy that permits an institution to participate on its home court in the first and second rounds of competition.

Championship team members were awarded 10-karat gold rings, while the other three teams in the Final Four received silver rings.

All 64 teams selected for the championship were subject to drug testing for the first time.

1988 CBS began a third three-year contract. All regional semifinal games were televised in prime time.

Separate three-man officiating crews were assigned to all competition at regional and national championship sites.

1989 The NCAA Executive Committee expanded a moratorium enacted in 1984 limiting the bracket to 30 automatic-qualifying conference champions and 34 at-large teams through the 1998 championship.

NCAA Executive Regulation 1-6-(b)-1 was amended to strengthen criteria governing automatic qualification for conferences.

Bracket rotation was established, with East vs. West, Midwest vs. Southeast in 1989; Southeast vs. West, East vs. Midwest in 1990, and West vs. Midwest, Southeast vs. East in 1991.

Awards for the national runner-up were presented in the dressing room immediately after the championship game.

Host Communications, Inc., began a three-year contract for rights to the NCAA Radio Network and programs for all sites.

Neutral courts were used in all rounds of the championship for the first time.

After determining that three of the next four Final Four host facilities should have a minimum capacity of 30,000, the committee selected Charlotte, Seattle, The Meadowlands and Indianapolis to host in 1994, 1995, 1996 and 1997.

1990 General public was limited to purchasing two tickets to future Final Fours.

The basketball committee defined "home court" as an arena in which a team has played no more than 50 percent of its regular-season schedule, excluding conference tournament games.

The NCAA Executive Committee approved "play-in" concept to identify the 30 automatic-qualifying conferences in December 1989. The Ratings Percentage Index (RPI) administered by the NCAA was computed for the nonconference schedules of all eligible conferences. Those with the lowest ranking competed for the available automatic-qualifying positions. The play-in was implemented in 1991 with 33 eligible conferences. Six conference representatives played for three automatic-qualifying berths in the 64-team bracket.

1991 CBS Sports began a seven-year contract for $1 billion, which included live coverage of all sessions of the championship.

The definition of "home court" was amended to include playing no more than three games of a regular-season schedule, excluding conference tournaments, in one arena.

A play-in was conducted between the six lowest-rated conferences from the previous year's RPI since 33 conferences were eligible for automatic qualification. Game results were as follows: St. Francis (Pennsylvania) (Northeast Conference) defeated Fordham (Patriot League), 70-64; Louisiana-Monroe (Southland) defeated Florida A&M (Mid-Eastern), 87-63; and Coastal Carolina (Big South) defeated Jackson State (Southwestern), 86-75.

1992 Duke won its second consecutive national championship, the first team to successfully defend its title since UCLA in 1973.

1993 A minimum facility seating capacity of 12,000 for first and second rounds and regionals was established.

The basketball committee selected San Antonio; St. Petersburg, Florida; Indianapolis; Minneapolis; and Atlanta to host the Final Four in 1998 through 2002. All the facilities had capacities in excess of 30,000.

1994 For the first time, all 100 of the top 100 markets in the country received the radio play-by-play broadcast of the Final Four. This included a record 488 stations.

President Bill Clinton became the first sitting president to attend the tournament, when he was present at the Midwest regional championship game in Dallas and the national semifinals and final in Charlotte, North Carolina.

The use of combined shots clocks/game clocks was required at all sites.

The weighing of the three factors comprising the Ratings Percentage Index (RPI)—Division I winning percentage, opponents' winning percentage and opponents' opponent's winning percentage—was adjusted from 20-40-40 to 25-50-25. A second RPI, adjusted based upon a team's "good" wins, "bad" losses and non-conference scheduling, was provided.

1995 The existing CBS Sports contract was replaced with a new agreement for $1.725 billion extending through the 2002 championship.

1996 The NCAA created the first online computer page for the men's Final Four.

Pool reporters permitted under specified conditions to interview game officials after games.

Participating institutions' seating locations moved closer to mid-court and nearer to the playing floor.

1997 Bracketing policies were changed so that once the highest-seeded team from a conference is assigned to a region, only the eighth team selected from that conference may be placed in that region.

The NCAA's on-line computer page expanded to include preliminary rounds.

1998 Competition at all three sites within each region began being conducted on the same days of the week and tournament hosts' teams permitted to play on the days they are hosting.

The name of the Southeast Region was changed to the South Region.

The basketball committee continued selecting Final Four host facilities with a minimum seating capacity of 30,000 when it picked New Orleans, San Antonio, St. Louis, Indianapolis and Atlanta to host in 2003-2007.

1999 Bracketing policies were changed so that, once the highest-seeded team from a conference is assigned to a region, only the sixth team from that conference may be placed in that region.

The NCAA signed a new 11-year agreement with CBS Sports, commencing with the 2003 championship. The agreement, which is for a minimum of $6 billion, includes rights to television (over-the-air, cable, satellite, digital and home video), marketing, game programs, radio, Internet, fan festivals and licensing (excluding concessionaire agreements).

In its continuing effort to combat the effects of gambling, the committee began conducting background checks on game officials. The NCAA checked 50 officials randomly selected from among the 96 who worked the previous year's tournament.

2001 Inasmuch as 31 conferences were eligible for automatic qualification, the committee agreed to conduct an opening-round game the Tuesday before the first/second rounds, pitting teams seeded Nos. 64 and 65.

2002 Championship-, first- and second-round sites will no longer be assigned to specific regions. Rather, the committee will have flexibility to assign four-team pods to sites near the teams' natural geographic areas, if possible.

Team-By-Team Won-Lost Records

By Coach, 1939-2000

(280 Teams)

	Yrs.	Won	Lost	CH	2D	3d%	4th	RR
AIR FORCE								
Bob Spear (DePauw 1941) 1960, 62	2	0	2	0	0	0	0	0
TOTAL	2	0	2	0	0	0	0	0
AKRON								
Bob Huggins (West Virginia 1977) 1986	1	0	1	0	0	0	0	0
TOTAL	1	0	1	0	0	0	0	0
ALABAMA*								
C.M. Newton (Kentucky 1952) 1975, 76	2	1	2	0	0	0	0	0
Wimp Sanderson (North Ala. 1959) 1982, 83,84, 85, 86, 87, 89, 90, 91,92	10	12	10	0	0	0	0	0
David Hobbs (Va. Commonwealth 1971) 1994,95	2	2	2	0	0	0	0	0
TOTAL	14	15	14	0	0	0	0	0

TEAM-BY-TEAM WON-LOST RECORDS—BY COACH

	Yrs.	Won	Lost	CH	2D	3d%	4th	RR
ALABAMA ST.								
Rob Spivery (Ashland 1972) 2001	1	0	1	0	0	0	0	0
TOTAL	1	0	1	0	0	0	0	0
UAB								
Gene Bartow (Truman 1953) 1981, 82RR, 83,84, 85, 86, 87, 90, 94	9	6	9	0	0	0	0	1
Murry Bartow (UAB 1985) 1999	1	0	1	0	0	0	0	0
TOTAL	10	6	10	0	0	0	0	1
ALCORN ST.								
Davey L. Whitney (Kentucky St. 1953) 1980, 82, 83, 84, 99	5	3	5	0	0	0	0	0
TOTAL	5	3	5	0	0	0	0	0
APPALACHIAN ST.								
Bobby Cremins (South Carolina 1970) 1979	1	0	1	0	0	0	0	0
Buzz Peterson (North Carolina 1986) 2000	1	0	1	0	0	0	0	0
TOTAL	2	0	2	0	0	0	0	0
ARIZONA *								
Fred Enke (Minnesota 1921) 1951	1	0	1	0	0	0	0	0
Fred Snowden [Wayne St. (Mich.) 1958] 1976RR, 77	2	2	2	2	0	0	0	1
Luther "Lute" Olson (Augsburg 1957) 1985, 86, 87, 88-T3d, 89, 90, 91, 92, 93, 94-T3d, 95, 96, 97-CH, 98RR, 99, 2000, 01-2d	17	30	16	1	1	2	0	1
TOTAL	20	32	19	1	1	2	0	2
ARIZONA ST. *								
Ned Wulk (Wis.-La Crosse 1942) 1958, 61RR, 62, 63RR, 64, 73, 75RR, 80, 81	9	8	10	0	0	0	0	3
Bill Frieder (Michigan 1964) 1991, 95	2	3	2	0	0	0	0	0
TOTAL	11	11	12	0	0	0	0	3
ARKANSAS								
Eugene Lambert (Arkansas 1929) 1945-T3d, 49RR	2	2	2	0	0	1	0	1
Glen Rose (Arkansas 1928) 1941-T3d, 58	2	1	3	0	0	1	0	0
Eddie Sutton (Oklahoma St. 1958) 1977, 78-3d, 79RR,80, 81, 82, 83, 84, 85	9	10	9	0	0	1	0	1
Nolan Richardson (UTEP 1965) 1988, 89, 90-T3d, 91RR, 92, 93, 94-CH, 95-2d, 96, 98, 99, 2000, 01	13	26	13	1	1	1	0	1
TOTAL	26	39	26	1	1	4	0	3
ARKANSAS ST.								
Dickey Nutt (Oklahoma St. 1982) 1999	1	0	1	0	0	0	0	0
TOTAL	1	0	1	0	0	0	0	0
ARK.-LITTLE ROCK								
Mike Newell (Sam Houston St. 1973) 1986, 89, 90	3	1	3	0	0	0	0	0
TOTAL	3	1	3	0	0	0	0	0
AUBURN								
Sonny Smith (Milligan 1958) 1984, 85, 86RR, 87, 88	5	7	5	0	0	0	0	1
Cliff Ellis (Florida St. 1968) 1999, 2000	2	3	2	0	0	0	0	0
TOTAL	7	10	7	0	0	0	0	1
AUSTIN PEAY*								
Lake Kelly (Ga. Tech 1956) 1973, 74, 87	3	2	4	0	0	0	0	0
Dave Loos (Memphis 1970) 1996	1	0	1	0	0	0	0	0
TOTAL	4	2	5	0	0	0	0	0
BALL ST.								
Steve Yoder (Ill. Wesleyan 1962) 1981	1	0	1	0	0	0	0	0
Al Brown (Purdue 1964) 1986	1	0	1	0	0	0	0	0
Rich Majerus (Marquette 1989) 1989	1	1	1	0	0	0	0	0
Dick Hunsaker (Weber St. 1977) 1990, 93	2	2	2	0	0	0	0	0
Ray McCallum (Ball St. 1983) 1995, 2000	2	0	2	0	0	0	0	0
TOTAL	7	3	7	0	0	0	0	0
BAYLOR								
R.E. "Bill" Henderson (Howard Payne 1925) 1946RR, 48-2d, 50-4th	3	3	5	0	1	0	1	1
Gene Iba (Tulsa 1963) 1988	1	0	1	0	0	0	0	0
TOTAL	4	3	6	0	1	0	1	1
BOISE ST.								
Doran "Bus" Connor (Idaho St. 1955) 1976	1	0	1	0	0	0	0	0
Bob Dye (Idaho St. 1962) 1988, 93, 94	3	0	3	0	0	0	0	0
TOTAL	4	0	4	0	0	0	0	0
BOSTON COLLEGE								
Donald Martin (Georgetown 1941) 1958	1	0	1	0	0	0	0	0
Bob Cousy (Holy Cross 1948) 1967RR, 68	2	2	2	0	0	0	0	1
Bob Zuffelato (Central Conn. St. 1959) 1975	1	1	2	0	0	0	0	0
Tom Davis (Wis.-Platteville 1960) 1981, 82RR	2	5	2	0	0	0	0	1
Gary Williams (Maryland 1967) 1983, 85	2	3	2	0	0	0	0	0
Jim O'Brien (Boston College 1971) 1994RR, 96, 97	3	5	3	0	0	0	0	1
Al Skinner (Massachusetts 1974) 2001	1	1	1	0	0	0	0	0
TOTAL	12	17	13	0	0	0	0	3
BOSTON U.								
Matt Zunic (George Washington 1942) 1959RR	1	2	1	0	0	0	0	1
Rick Pitino (Massachusetts 1974) 1983	1	0	1	0	0	0	0	0
Mike Jarvis (Northeastern 1968) 1988, 90	2	0	2	0	0	0	0	0
Dennis Wolff (Connecticut 1978) 1997	1	0	1	0	0	0	0	0
TOTAL	5	2	5	0	0	0	0	1
BOWLING GREEN								
Harold Anderson (Otterbein 1924) 1959, 62, 63	3	1	4	0	0	0	0	0
Bill Fitch (Coe 1954) 1968	1	0	1	0	0	0	0	0
TOTAL	4	1	5	0	0	0	0	0
BRADLEY								
Forrest "Forddy" Anderson (Stanford 1942) 1950-2d, 54-2d	2	6	2	0	2	0	0	0
Bob Vanatta (Central Methodist 1945) 1955RR	1	2	1	0	0	0	0	1
Dick Versace (Wisconsin 1964) 1980, 86	2	1	2	0	0	0	0	0
Stan Albeck (Bradley 1955) 1988	1	0	1	0	0	0	0	0
Jim Molinari (Ill. Wesleyan 1977) 1996	1	0	1	0	0	0	0	0
TOTAL	7	9	7	0	2	0	0	1
BRIGHAM YOUNG								
Stan Watts (Brigham Young 1938) 1950RR, 51RR, 57, 65, 69, 71, 72	7	4	10	0	0	0	0	2
Frank Arnold (Idaho St. 1956) 1979, 80, 81RR	3	3	3	0	0	0	0	1
Ladell Andersen (Utah St. 1951) 1984, 87, 88	3	2	3	0	0	0	0	0
Roger Reid (Weber St. 1967) 1990, 91, 92, 93, 95	5	2	5	0	0	0	0	0
Steve Cleveland (UC Irvine 1976) 2001	1	0	1	0	0	0	0	0
TOTAL	19	11	22	0	0	0	0	3
BROWN								
George Allen (West Virginia 1935) 1939RR	1	0	1	0	0	0	0	1
Mike Cingiser (Brown 1962) 1986	1	0	1	0	0	0	0	0
TOTAL	2	0	2	0	0	0	0	1
BUCKNELL								
Charles Woollum (William & Mary 1962) 1987, 89	2	0	2	0	0	0	0	0
TOTAL	2	0	2	0	0	0	0	0
BUTLER								
Paul "Tony" Hinkle (Chicago 1921) 1962	1	2	1	0	0	0	0	0
Barry Collier (Butler 1976) 1997, 98, 2000	3	0	3	0	0	0	0	0
Thad Matta (1990) 2001	1	1	1	0	0	0	0	0
TOTAL	5	3	5	0	0	0	0	0
CALIFORNIA*								
Clarence "Nibs" Price (California 1914) 1946-4th	1	1	2	0	0	0	1	0
Pete Newell (Loyola Marymount 1940) 1957RR, 58RR, 59-CH, 60-2d	4	10	3	1	1	0	0	2
Lou Campanelli (Montclair St. 1960) 1990	1	1	1	0	0	0	0	0
Todd Bozeman (Rhode Island 1986) 1993, 94, 96	3	2	3	0	0	0	0	0
Ben Braun (Wisconsin 1975) 1997, 2001	2	2	2	0	0	0	0	0
TOTAL	11	16	11	1	1	0	1	2
UC SANTA BARB.								
Jerry Pimm (Southern California 1961) 1988, 90	2	1	2	0	0	0	0	0
TOTAL	2	1	2	0	0	0	0	0
CAL ST. FULLERTON								
Bob Dye (Idaho St. 1962) 1978RR	1	2	1	0	0	0	0	1
TOTAL	1	2	1	0	0	0	0	1
CAL ST. LOS ANGELES								
Bob Miller (Occidental 1953) 1974	1	0	1	0	0	0	0	0
TOTAL	1	0	1	0	0	0	0	0
CAL ST. NORTHRIDGE								
Bobby Braswell (Cal St. Northridge 1984) 2001	1	0	1	0	0	0	0	0
TOTAL	1	0	1	0	0	0	0	0
CAMPBELL								
Billy Lee (Barton 1971) 1992	1	0	1	0	0	0	0	0
TOTAL	1	0	1	0	0	0	0	0

TEAM-BY-TEAM WON-LOST RECORDS—BY COACH

	Yrs.	Won	Lost	CH	2D	3d%	4th	RR
CANISIUS								
Joseph Curran (Canisius 1943) 1955RR, 56RR, 57	3	6	3	0	0	0	0	2
John Beilein (Wheeling Jesuit 1975) 1996	1	0	1	0	0	0	0	0
TOTAL	4	6	4	0	0	0	0	2
CATHOLIC								
John Long (Catholic 1928) 1944RR	1	0	2	0	0	0	0	1
TOTAL	1	0	2	0	0	0	0	1
CENTRAL CONN. ST.								
Howie Dickenmann (Central Conn. St. 1970) 2000	1	0	1	0	0	0	0	0
TOTAL	1	0	1	0	0	0	0	0
UCF								
Kirk Speraw (Iowa 1980) 1994, 96	2	0	2	0	0	0	0	0
TOTAL	2	0	2	0	0	0	0	0
CENTRAL MICH.								
Dick Parfitt (Central Mich. 1953) 1975, 77	2	2	2	0	0	0	0	0
Charlie Coles [Miami (Ohio) 1965] 1987	1	0	1	0	0	0	0	0
TOTAL	3	2	3	0	0	0	0	0
COL. OF CHARLESTON								
John Kresse [St. John's (N.Y.) 1964] 1994, 97, 98, 99	4	1	4	0	0	0	0	0
TOTAL	4	1	4	0	0	0	0	0
CHARLESTON SO.								
Tom Conrad (Old Dominion 1979) 1997	1	0	1	0	0	0	0	0
TOTAL	1	0	1	0	0	0	0	0
CHARLOTTE								
Lee Rose (Transylvania 1958) 1977-4th	1	3	2	0	0	0	1	0
Jeff Mullins (Duke 1964) 1988, 92, 95	3	0	3	0	0	0	0	0
Melvin Watkins (Charlotte 1977) 1997, 98	2	2	2	0	0	0	0	0
Bob Lutz (Charlotte 1980) 1999, 2001	2	2	2	0	0	0	0	0
TOTAL	8	7	9	0	0	0	1	0
CHATTANOOGA								
Murray Arnold (American 1960) 1981, 82, 83	3	1	3	0	0	0	0	0
Mack McCarthy (Virginia Tech 1974) 1988, 93, 94, 95, 97	5	2	5	0	0	0	0	0
TOTAL	8	3	8	0	0	0	0	0
CINCINNATI								
George Smith (Cincinnati 1935) 1958, 59-3d, 60-3d	3	7	3	0	0	2	0	0
Ed Jucker (Cincinnati 1940) 1961-CH, 62-CH, 63-2d	3	11	1	2	1	0	0	0
Tay Baker (Cincinnati 1950) 1966	1	0	2	0	0	0	0	0
Gale Catlett (West Virginia 1963) 1975, 76, 77	3	2	3	0	0	0	0	0
Bob Huggins (West Virginia 1977) 1992-T3d, 93RR, 94, 95,96RR, 97, 98, 99, 2000, 01	10	17	10	0	0	1	0	2
TOTAL	20	37	19	2	1	3	0	2
CCNY								
Nat Holman (Savage School of Phys. Ed. 1917) 1947-4th, 50-CH	2	4	2	1	0	0	1	0
TOTAL	2	4	2	1	0	0	1	0
CLEMSON*								
Bill C. Foster (Carson-Newman 1958) 1980RR	1	3	1	0	0	0	0	1
Cliff Ellis (Florida St. 1968) 1987, 89, 90	3	3	3	0	0	0	0	0
Rick Barnes (Lenoir-Rhyne 1977) 1996, 97, 98	3	2	3	0	0	0	0	0
TOTAL	7	8	7	0	0	0	0	1
CLEVELAND ST.								
Kevin Mackey (St. Anselm 1967) 1986	1	2	1	0	0	0	0	0
TOTAL	1	2	1	0	0	0	0	0
COASTAL CARO.								
Russ Bergman (LSU 1970) 1991, 93	2	0	2	0	0	0	0	0
TOTAL	2	0	2	0	0	0	0	0
COLGATE								
Jack Bruen (Catholic 1972) 1995, 96	2	0	2	0	0	0	0	0
TOTAL	2	0	2	0	0	0	0	0
COLORADO								
Forrest "Frosty" Cox (Kansas 1930) 1940RR, 42-T3d, 46RR	3	2	4	0	0	1	0	2
Horace "Bebe" Lee (Stanford 1938) 1954, 55-3d	2	3	3	0	0	1	0	0
Russell "Sox" Walseth (Colorado 1948) 1962RR, 63RR, 69	3	3	3	0	0	0	0	2
Ricardo Patton (Belmont 1980) 1997	1	1	1	0	0	0	0	0
TOTAL	9	9	11	0	0	2	0	4

	Yrs.	Won	Lost	CH	2D	3d%	4th	RR
COLORADO ST.								
Bill Strannigan (Wyoming 1941) 1954	1	0	2	0	0	0	0	0
Jim Williams (Utah St. 1947) 1963, 65, 66, 69RR	4	2	4	0	0	0	0	1
Boyd Grant (Colorado St. 1957) 1989, 90	2	1	2	0	0	0	0	0
TOTAL	7	3	8	0	0	0	0	1
COLUMBIA								
Gordon Ridings (Oregon 1929) 1948RR	1	0	2	0	0	0	0	1
Lou Rossini (Columbia 1948) 1951	1	0	1	0	0	0	0	0
John "Jack" Rohan (Columbia 1953) 1968	1	2	1	0	0	0	0	0
TOTAL	3	2	4	0	0	0	0	1
CONNECTICUT*								
Hugh Greer (Connecticut 1926) 1951, 54, 56, 57, 58, 59, 60	7	1	8	0	0	0	0	0
George Wigton (Ohio St. 1956) 1963	1	0	1	0	0	0	0	0
Fred Shabel (Duke 1954) 1964RR, 65, 67	3	2	3	0	0	0	0	1
Donald "Dee" Rowe (Middlebury 1952) 1976	1	1	1	0	0	0	0	0
Dom Perno (Connecticut 1964) 1979	1	0	1	0	0	0	0	0
Jim Calhoun (American Int'l 1968) 1990RR, 91, 92, 94,95RR, 96, 98RR, 99-CH, 2000	9	23	8	1	0	0	0	3
TOTAL	22	27	22	1	0	0	0	4
COPPIN ST.								
Ron Mitchell (Edison 1984) 1990, 93, 97	3	1	3	0	0	0	0	0
TOTAL	3	1	3	0	0	0	0	0
CORNELL								
Royner Greene (Illinois 1929) 1954	1	0	2	0	0	0	0	0
Mike Dement (East Caro. 1976) 1988	1	0	1	0	0	0	0	0
TOTAL	2	0	3	0	0	0	0	0
CREIGHTON								
Eddie Hickey (Creighton 1927) 1941RR	1	1	1	0	0	0	0	1
John "Red" McManus (St. Ambrose 1949) 1962, 64	2	3	3	0	0	0	0	0
Eddie Sutton (Oklahoma St. 1958) 1974	1	2	1	0	0	0	0	0
Tom Apke (Creighton 1965) 1975, 78, 81	3	0	3	0	0	0	0	0
Tony Barone (Duke 1968) 1989, 91	2	1	2	0	0	0	0	0
Dana Altman (Eastern N.M. 1980) 1999, 2000, 01	3	1	3	0	0	0	0	0
TOTAL	12	8	13	0	0	0	0	1
DARTMOUTH								
Osborne "Ozzie" Cowles (Carleton 1922) 1941RR, 42-2d, 43RR	3	4	3	0	1	0	0	2
Earl Brown (Notre Dame 1939) 1944-2d	1	2	1	0	1	0	0	0
Alvin "Doggie" Julian (Bucknell 1923) 1956, 58RR, 59	3	4	3	0	0	0	0	1
TOTAL	7	10	7	0	2	0	0	3
DAVIDSON								
Charles "Lefty" Driesell (Duke 1954) 1966, 68RR, 69RR	3	5	4	0	0	0	0	2
Terry Holland (Davidson 1964) 1970	1	0	1	0	0	0	0	0
Bobby Hussey (Appalachian St. 1962) 1986	1	0	1	0	0	0	0	0
Bob McKillop (Hofstra 1972) 1998	1	0	1	0	0	0	0	0
TOTAL	6	5	7	0	0	0	0	2
DAYTON								
Tom Blackburn [Wilmington (Ohio) 1931] 1952	1	1	1	0	0	0	0	0
Don Donoher (Dayton 1954) 1965, 66, 67-2d, 69, 70, 74, 84RR, 85	8	11	10	0	1	0	0	1
Jim O'Brien (St. Joseph's 1974) 1990	1	0	1	0	0	0	0	0
Oliver Purnell (Old Dominion 1975) 2000	1	1	1	0	0	0	0	0
TOTAL	11	13	13	0	1	0	0	1
DELAWARE								
Steve Steinwedel (Mississippi St. 1975) 1992, 93	2	0	2	0	0	0	0	0
Mike Brey (George Washington 1982) 1998, 99	2	0	2	0	0	0	0	0
TOTAL	4	0	4	0	0	0	0	0
DePAUL*								
Ray Meyer (Notre Dame 1938) 1943-T3d, 53, 56, 59, 60, 65, 76, 78RR, 79-3d, 80, 81, 82, 84	13	14	16	0	0	2	0	1
Joey Meyer (DePaul 1971) 1985, 86, 87, 88, 89, 91, 92	7	6	7	0	0	0	0	0
Pat Kennedy [King's (Pa.) 1976] 2000	1	0	1	0	0	0	0	0
TOTAL	21	20	24	0	0	2	0	1
DETROIT								
Robert Calihan (Detroit 1940) 1962	1	0	1	0	0	0	0	0
Dick Vitale (Seton Hall 1962) 1977	1	1	1	0	0	0	0	0

TEAM-BY-TEAM WON-LOST RECORDS—BY COACH

	Yrs.	Won	Lost	CH	2D	3d%	4th	RR
Dave "Smokey" Gaines (LeMoyne-Owen 1963) 1979	1	0	1	0	0	0	0	0
Perry Watson (Eastern Mich. 1972) 1998, 99	2	2	2	0	0	0	0	0
TOTAL	5	3	5	0	0	0	0	0
DRAKE								
Maurice John (Central Mo. St. 1941) 1969-3d, 70RR, 71RR	3	5	3	0	0	1	0	2
TOTAL	3	5	3	0	0	1	0	2
DREXEL								
Eddie Burke (La Salle 1967) 1986	1	0	1	0	0	0	0	0
Bill Herrion (Merrimack 1981) 1994, 95, 96	3	1	3	0	0	0	0	0
TOTAL	4	1	4	0	0	0	0	0
DUKE								
Harold Bradley (Hartwick 1934) 1955	1	0	1	0	0	0	0	0
Vic Bubas (North Carolina St. 1951) 1960RR, 63-3d, 64-2d, 66-3d	4	11	4	0	1	2	0	1
W.E. "Bill" Foster (Elizabethtown 1954) 1978-2d, 79, 80RR	3	6	3	0	1	0	0	1
Mike Krzyzewski (Army 1969) 1984, 85, 86-2d, 87, 88-T3d, 89-T3d, 90-2d, 91-CH, 92-CH, 93, 94-2d, 96, 97, 98RR, 99-2d, 2000, 01-CH	17	56	14	3	4	2	0	1
TOTAL	25	73	22	3	6	4	0	3
DUQUESNE								
Charles "Chick" Davies (Duquesne 1934) 1940-T3d	1	1	1	0	0	1	0	0
Donald "Dudey" Moore (Duquesne 1934) 1952RR	1	1	1	0	0	0	0	1
John "Red" Manning (Duquesne 1951) 1969, 71	2	2	2	0	0	0	0	0
John Cinicola (Duquesne 1955) 1977	1	0	1	0	0	0	0	0
TOTAL	5	4	5	0	0	1	0	1
EAST CARO.								
Tom Quinn (Marshall 1954) 1972	1	0	1	0	0	0	0	0
Eddie Payne (Wake Forest 1973) 1993	1	0	1	0	0	0	0	0
TOTAL	2	0	2	0	0	0	0	0
EAST TENN. ST.								
J. Madison Brooks (Louisiana Tech 1937) 1968	1	1	2	0	0	0	0	0
Les Robinson (North Carolina St. 1964) 1989, 90	2	0	2	0	0	0	0	0
Alan LeForce (Cumberland 1957) 1991, 92	2	1	2	0	0	0	0	0
TOTAL	5	2	6	0	0	0	0	0
EASTERN ILL.								
Rick Samuels (Chadron St. 1971) 1992, 2001	2	0	2	0	0	0	0	0
TOTAL	2	0	2	0	0	0	0	0
EASTERN KY.								
Paul McBrayer (Kentucky 1930) 1953, 59	2	0	2	0	0	0	0	0
Jim Baechtold (Eastern Ky. 1952) 1965	1	0	1	0	0	0	0	0
Guy Strong (Eastern Ky. 1955) 1972	1	0	1	0	0	0	0	0
Ed Byhre [Augustana (S.D.) 1966] 1979	1	0	1	0	0	0	0	0
TOTAL	5	0	5	0	0	0	0	0
EASTERN MICH.								
Ben Braun (Wisconsin 1975) 1988, 91, 96	3	3	3	0	0	0	0	0
Milton Barnes (Albion 1979) 1998	1	0	1	0	0	0	0	0
TOTAL	4	3	4	0	0	0	0	0
EVANSVILLE								
Dick Walters (Illinois St. 1969) 1982	1	0	1	0	0	0	0	0
Jim Crews (Indiana 1976) 1989, 92, 93, 99	4	1	4	0	0	0	0	0
TOTAL	5	1	5	0	0	0	0	0
FAIRFIELD								
Mitch Buonaguro (Boston College 1975) 1986, 87	2	0	2	0	0	0	0	0
Paul Cormier (New Hampshire 1973) 1997	1	0	1	0	0	0	0	0
TOTAL	3	0	3	0	0	0	0	0
FDU-TEANECK								
Tom Green (Syracuse 1971) 1985, 88, 98	3	0	3	0	0	0	0	0
TOTAL	3	0	3	0	0	0	0	0
FLORIDA*								
Norm Sloan (North Carolina St. 1951) 1987, 88, 89	3	3	3	0	0	0	0	0
Lon Kruger (Kansas St. 1974) 1994-T3d, 95	2	4	2	0	0	1	0	0

	Yrs.	Won	Lost	CH	2D	3d%	4th	RR
Billy Donovan (Providence 1987) 1999, 2000-2d, 01	3	8	3	0	1	0	0	0
TOTAL	8	15	8	0	1	1	0	0
FLORIDA A&M								
Mickey Clayton (Florida A&M 1975) 1999	1	0	1	0	0	0	0	0
TOTAL	1	0	1	0	0	0	0	0
FLORIDA INT'L								
Bob Weltlich (Ohio St. 1967) 1995	1	0	1	0	0	0	0	0
TOTAL	1	0	1	0	0	0	0	0
FLORIDA ST.								
Hugh Durham (Florida St. 1959) 1968, 72-2d, 78	3	4	3	0	1	0	0	0
Joe Williams (Southern Methodist 1956) 1980	1	1	1	0	0	0	0	0
Pat Kennedy [King's (Pa.) 1976] 1988, 89, 91, 92, 93RR	5	6	5	0	0	0	0	1
Steve Robinson (Radford 1981) 1998	1	1	1	0	0	0	0	0
TOTAL	10	12	10	0	1	0	0	1
FORDHAM								
John Bach (Fordham 1948) 1953, 54	2	0	2	0	0	0	0	0
Richard "Digger" Phelps (Rider 1963) 1971	1	2	1	0	0	0	0	0
Nick Macarchuk (Fairfield 1963) 1992	1	0	1	0	0	0	0	0
TOTAL	4	2	4	0	0	0	0	0
FRESNO ST.								
Boyd Grant (Colorado St. 1961) 1981, 82, 84	3	1	3	0	0	0	0	0
Jerry Tarkanian (Fresno St. 1956) 2000, 01	2	1	2	0	0	0	0	0
TOTAL	5	2	5	0	0	0	0	0
FURMAN								
Joe Williams (Southern Methodist 1956) 1971, 73, 74, 75, 78	5	1	6	0	0	0	0	0
Eddie Holbrook (Lenoir-Rhyne 1962) 1980	1	0	1	0	0	0	0	0
TOTAL	6	1	7	0	0	0	0	0
GEORGE MASON								
Ernie Nestor (Alderson-Broaddus 1968) 1989	1	0	1	0	0	0	0	0
Jim Larranaga (Providence 1971) 1999, 2001	2	0	2	0	0	0	0	0
TOTAL	3	0	3	0	0	0	0	0
GEORGE WASHINGTON								
Bill Reinhart (Oregon 1923) 1954, 61	2	0	2	0	0	0	0	0
Mike Jarvis (Northeastern 1968) 1993, 94, 96, 98	4	3	4	0	0	0	0	0
Tom Penders (Connecticut 1967) 1999	1	0	1	0	0	0	0	0
TOTAL	7	3	7	0	0	0	0	0
GEORGETOWN								
Elmer Ripley (No college) 1943-2d	1	2	1	0	1	0	0	0
John Thompson (Providence 1964) 1975, 76, 79, 80RR, 81, 82-2d, 83, 84-CH, 85-2d, 86, 87RR, 88, 89RR, 90, 91, 92, 94, 95, 96RR, 97	20	34	19	1	2	0	0	4
Craig Esherick (Georgetown 1978) 2001	1	2	1	0	0	0	0	0
TOTAL	22	38	21	1	3	0	0	4
GEORGIA*								
Hugh Durham (Florida St. 1959) 1983-T3d, 85, 87, 90, 91	5	4	5	0	0	1	0	0
Tubby Smith (High Point 1973) 1996, 97	2	2	2	0	0	0	0	0
Jim Harrick [Charleston (W.Va.) 1960] 2001	1	0	1	0	0	0	0	0
TOTAL	8	6	8	0	0	1	0	0
GA. SOUTHERN								
Frank Kerns (Alabama 1957) 1983, 87, 92	3	0	3	0	0	0	0	0
TOTAL	3	0	3	0	0	0	0	0
GEORGIA ST.								
Bob Reinhart (Indiana 1961) 1991	1	0	1	0	0	0	0	0
Charles "Lefty" Driesell (Duke 1954) 2001	1	1	1	0	0	0	0	0
TOTAL	2	1	2	0	0	0	0	0
GEORGIA TECH								
John "Whack" Hyder (Georgia Tech 1937) 1960RR	1	1	1	0	0	0	0	1
Bobby Cremins (South Carolina 1970) 1985RR, 86, 87, 88, 89, 90-T3d, 91, 92, 93, 96	10	15	10	0	0	1	0	1
Paul Hewitt (St. John Fisher 1985) 2001	1	0	1	0	0	0	0	0
TOTAL	12	16	12	0	0	1	0	2
GONZAGA								
Dan Fitzgerald (Cal St. Los Angeles 1965) 1995	1	0	1	0	0	0	0	0

TEAM-BY-TEAM WON-LOST RECORDS—BY COACH

	Yrs.	Won	Lost	CH	2D	3d%	4th	RR
Dan Monson (Idaho 1985) 1999RR........	1	3	1	0	0	0	0	1
Mark Few (Oregon 1987) 2000, 01	2	4	2	0	0	0	0	0
TOTAL	4	7	4	0	0	0	0	1
HAMPTON								
Steve Merfeld (Wis.-LaCrosse 1984) 2001	1	1	1	0	0	0	0	0
TOTAL	1	1	1	0	0	0	0	0
HARDIN-SIMMONS								
Bill Scott (Hardin-Simmons 1947) 1953, 57	2	0	2	0	0	0	0	0
TOTAL	2	0	2	0	0	0	0	0
HARVARD								
Floyd Stahl (Illinois 1926) 1946RR	1	0	2	0	0	0	0	1
TOTAL	1	0	2	0	0	0	0	1
HAWAII								
Ephraim "Red" Rocha (Oregon St. 1950) 1972	1	0	1	0	0	0	0	0
Riley Wallace [Centenary (La.) 1964] 1994, 2001	2	0	2	0	0	0	0	0
TOTAL	3	0	3	0	0	0	0	0
HOFSTRA								
Roger Gaeckler (Gettysburg 1965) 1976, 77	2	0	2	0	0	0	0	0
Jay Wright (Bucknell 1983) 2000, 01	2	0	2	0	0	0	0	0
TOTAL	4	0	4	0	0	0	0	0
HOLY CROSS								
Alvin "Doggie" Julian (Bucknell 1923) 1947-CH, 48-3d	2	5	1	1	0	1	0	0
Lester "Buster" Sheary (Catholic 1933) 1950RR, 53RR	2	2	3	0	0	0	0	2
Roy Leenig [Trinity (Conn.) 1942] 1956..	1	0	1	0	0	0	0	0
George Blaney (Holy Cross 1961) 1977, 80, 93	3	0	3	0	0	0	0	0
Ralph Willard (Holy Cross 1967) 2001 ..	1	0	1	0	0	0	0	0
TOTAL	9	7	9	1	0	1	0	2
HOUSTON								
Alden Pasche (Rice 1932) 1956	1	0	2	0	0	0	0	0
Guy Lewis (Houston 1947) 1961, 65, 66, 67-3d, 68-4th, 70, 71, 72, 73, 78, 81, 82-T3d, 83-2d, 84-2d	14	26	18	0	2	2	1	0
Pat Foster (Arkansas 1961) 1987, 90, 92	3	0	3	0	0	0	0	0
TOTAL	18	26	23	0	2	2	1	0
HOUSTON BAPTIST								
Gene Iba (Tulsa 1963) 1984	1	0	1	0	0	0	0	0
TOTAL	1	0	1	0	0	0	0	0
HOWARD								
A.B. Williamson (N.C. A&T 1968) 19811	0	1	0	0	0	0	0	
Alfred "Butch" Beard (Louisville 1972) 1992	1	0	1	0	0	0	0	0
TOTAL	2	0	2	0	0	0	0	0
IDAHO								
Don Monson (Idaho 1955) 1981, 82	2	1	2	0	0	0	0	0
Kermit Davis Jr. (Mississippi St. 1982) 1989, 90	2	0	2	0	0	0	0	0
TOTAL	4	1	4	0	0	0	0	0
IDAHO ST.								
Steve Belko (Idaho 1939) 1953, 54, 55, 56	4	2	4	0	0	0	0	0
John Grayson (Oklahoma 1938) 1957, 58, 59	3	4	5	0	0	0	0	0
John Evans (Idaho 1948) 1960	1	0	1	0	0	0	0	0
Jim Killingsworth (Northeastern Okla. St. 1948) 1974, 77RR	2	2	2	0	0	0	0	1
Jim Boutin (Lewis & Clark 1964) 1987	1	0	1	0	0	0	0	0
TOTAL	11	8	13	0	0	0	0	1
ILLINOIS								
Doug Mills (Illinois 1930) 1942RR	1	0	2	0	0	0	0	1
Harry Combes (Illinois 1937) 1949-3d, 51-3d, 52-3d, 63RR	4	9	4	0	0	3	0	1
Lou Henson (New Mexico St. 1955) 1981, 83, 84RR, 85, 86, 87, 88, 89-T3d, 90, 93, 94, 95	12	12	12	0	0	1	0	1
Lon Kruger (Kansas St. 1974) 1997, 98 2000	3	3	3	0	0	0	0	0
Bill Self (Oklahoma St. 1985) 2001RR....	1	3	1	0	0	0	0	1
TOTAL	21	27	22	0	0	4	0	4
ILLINOIS ST.								
Bob Donewald (Hanover 1964) 1983, 84, 85	3	2	3	0	0	0	0	0
Bob Bender (Duke 1980) 1990	1	0	1	0	0	0	0	0
Kevin Stallings (Purdue 1982) 1997, 98	2	1	2	0	0	0	0	0
TOTAL	6	3	6	0	0	0	0	0

In two seasons as coach, Mark Few has led Gonzaga to two NCAA tournament appearances and four tournament victories.

	Yrs.	Won	Lost	CH	2D	3d%	4th	RR
ILL.-CHICAGO								
Jimmy Collins (New Mexico St. 1970) 1998	1	0	1	0	0	0	0	0
TOTAL	1	0	1	0	0	0	0	0
INDIANA								
Branch McCracken (Indiana 1930) 1940-CH, 53-CH, 54, 58	4	9	2	2	0	0	0	0
Lou Watson (Indiana 1950) 1967	1	1	1	0	0	0	0	0
Bob Knight (Ohio St. 1962) 1973-3d, 75RR, 76-CH, 78, 80, 81-CH, 82, 83, 84RR, 86, 87-CH, 88, 89, 90, 91, 92-T3d, 93RR, 94, 95, 96, 97, 98, 99, 2000	24	42	21	3	0	2	0	3
Mike Davis (Alabama 1983) 2001	1	0	1	0	0	0	0	0
TOTAL	30	52	25	5	0	2	0	3
INDIANA ST.								
Bill Hodges (Marian 1970) 1979-2d	1	4	1	0	1	0	0	0
Royce Waltman (Slippery Rock 1964) 2000	1	0	0	0	0	0	0	0
Royce Waltman (Slippery Rock 1964) 2000, 01	2	1	2	0	0	0	0	0
TOTAL	3	5	3	0	1	0	0	0
IONA*								
Jim Valvano (Rutgers 1967) 1979, 80	2	1	2	0	0	0	0	0
Pat Kennedy [King's (Pa.) 1976] 1984, 85	2	0	2	0	0	0	0	0
Tim Welsh (Potsdam St. 1984) 1998	1	0	1	0	0	0	0	0
Jeff Ruland (Iona 1991) 2000, 01	2	0	2	0	0	0	0	0
TOTAL	7	1	7	0	0	0	0	0
IOWA								
Frank "Bucky" O'Connor (Drake 1938) 1955-4th, 56-2d	2	5	3	0	1	0	1	0
Ralph Miller (Kansas 1942) 1970	1	1	1	0	0	0	0	0
Luther "Lute" Olson (Augsburg 1957) 1979, 80-4th, 81, 82, 83	5	7	6	0	0	0	1	0
George Raveling (Villanova 1960) 1985, 86	2	0	2	0	0	0	0	0
Tom Davis (Wis.-Platteville 1960) 1987RR, 88, 89, 91, 92, 93, 96, 97, 99	9	13	9	0	0	0	0	1
Steve Alford (Indiana 1987) 2001	1	1	1	0	0	0	0	0
TOTAL	20	27	22	0	1	0	2	1
IOWA ST.								
Louis Menze (Central Mo. St. 1928) 1944-T3d	1	1	1	0	0	1	0	0
Johnny Orr (Beloit 1949) 1985, 86, 88, 89, 92, 93	6	3	6	0	0	0	0	0
Tim Floyd (Louisiana Tech 1977) 1995, 96, 97	3	4	3	0	0	0	0	0

… TEAM-BY-TEAM WON-LOST RECORDS—BY COACH

	Yrs.	Won	Lost	CH	2D	3d%	4th	RR
Larry Eustachy (Long Beach St. 1979) 2000RR, 01	2	3	2	0	0	0	0	1
TOTAL	12	11	12	0	0	1	0	0

JACKSON ST.

	Yrs.	Won	Lost	CH	2D	3d%	4th	RR
Andy Stoglin (UTEP 1965) 1997, 2000	2	0	2	0	0	0	0	0
TOTAL	2	0	2	0	0	0	0	0

JACKSONVILLE

	Yrs.	Won	Lost	CH	2D	3d%	4th	RR
Joe Williams (Southern Methodist 1956) 1970-2d	1	4	1	0	1	0	0	0
Tom Wasdin (Florida 1957) 1971, 73	2	0	2	0	0	0	0	0
Tates Locke (Ohio Wesleyan 1959) 1979	1	0	1	0	0	0	0	0
Bob Wenzel (Rutgers 1971) 1986	1	0	1	0	0	0	0	0
TOTAL	5	4	5	0	1	0	0	0

JAMES MADISON

	Yrs.	Won	Lost	CH	2D	3d%	4th	RR
Lou Campanelli (Montclair St. 1960) 1981, 82, 83	3	3	3	0	0	0	0	0
Charles "Lefty" Driesell (Duke 1954) 1994	1	0	1	0	0	0	0	0
TOTAL	4	3	4	0	0	0	0	0

KANSAS

	Yrs.	Won	Lost	CH	2D	3d%	4th	RR
Forrest C. "Phog" Allen (Kansas 1906) 1940-2d, 42RR, 52-CH, 53-2d	4	10	3	1	2	0	0	1
Dick Harp (Kansas 1940) 1957-2d, 60RR	2	4	2	0	1	0	0	1
Ted Owens (Oklahoma 1951) 1966RR, 67, 71-4th, 74-4th, 75, 78, 81	7	8	9	0	0	0	2	1
Larry Brown (North Carolina 1963) 1984, 85, 86-T3d, 87, 88-CH	5	14	4	1	0	1	0	0
Roy Williams (North Carolina 1972) 1990, 91-2d, 92, 93-T3d, 94, 95, 96RR, 97, 98, 99, 2000, 01	12	25	12	0	1	1	0	1
TOTAL	30	61	30	2	4	2	2	4

KANSAS ST.

	Yrs.	Won	Lost	CH	2D	3d%	4th	RR
Jack Gardner (Southern California 1932) 1948-4th, 51-2d	2	4	3	0	1	0	1	0
Fred "Tex" Winter (Southern California 1947) 1956, 58-4th, 59RR, 61RR, 64-4th, 68	6	7	9	0	0	0	2	2
Lowell "Cotton" Fitzsimmons (Midwestern St. 1955) 1970	1	1	1	0	0	0	0	0
Jack Hartman (Oklahoma St. 1949) 1972RR, 73RR, 75RR, 77, 80, 81RR, 82	7	11	7	0	0	0	0	4
Lon Kruger (Kansas St. 1974) 1987, 88RR, 89, 90	4	4	4	0	0	0	0	1
Dana Altman (Eastern N.M. 1980) 1993	1	0	1	0	0	0	0	0
Tom Asbury (Wyoming 1967) 1996	1	0	1	0	0	0	0	0
TOTAL	22	27	26	0	1	0	3	7

KENT ST.

	Yrs.	Won	Lost	CH	2D	3d%	4th	RR
Gary Waters (Ferris St. 1975) 1999, 2001	2	1	2	0	0	0	0	0
TOTAL	2	1	2	0	0	0	0	0

KENTUCKY*

	Yrs.	Won	Lost	CH	2D	3d%	4th	RR
Adolph Rupp (Kansas 1923) 1942-T3d, 45RR, 48-CH,49-CH, 51-CH, 52RR, 55, 56RR, 57RR, 58-CH, 59,61RR, 62RR, 64, 66-2d, 68RR, 69, 70RR, 71, 72RR	20	30	18	4	1	1	0	9
Joe B. Hall (Sewanee 1951) 1973RR, 75-2d, 77RR, 78-CH, 80, 81, 82, 83RR, 84-T3d, 85	10	20	9	1	1	1	0	3
Eddie Sutton (Oklahoma St. 1958) 1986RR, 87, 88	3	5	3	0	0	0	0	1
Rick Pitino (Massachusetts 1974) 1992RR, 93-T3d, 94, 95RR 96-CH, 97-2d	6	22	5	1	1	1	0	2
Tubby Smith (High Point 1973) 1998-CH, 99RR, 2000, 01	4	12	3	1	0	0	0	1
TOTAL	43	89	38	7	3	3	0	16

LA SALLE

	Yrs.	Won	Lost	CH	2D	3d%	4th	RR
Ken Loeffler (Penn St. 1924) 1954-CH, 55-2d	2	9	1	1	1	0	0	0
Jim Harding (Iowa 1949) 1968	1	0	1	0	0	0	0	0
Paul Westhead (St. Joseph's 1961) 1975, 78	2	0	2	0	0	0	0	0
Dave "Lefty" Ervin (La Salle 1968) 1980, 83	2	1	2	0	0	0	0	0
Bill "Speedy" Morris (St. Joseph's 1973) 1988, 89, 90, 92	4	1	4	0	0	0	0	0
TOTAL	11	11	10	1	1	0	0	0

LAFAYETTE

	Yrs.	Won	Lost	CH	2D	3d%	4th	RR
George Davidson (Lafayette 1951) 1957	1	0	2	0	0	0	0	0
Fran O'Hanlon (Villanova 1970) 1999, 2000	2	0	2	0	0	0	0	0
TOTAL	3	0	4	0	0	0	0	0

LAMAR

	Yrs.	Won	Lost	CH	2D	3d%	4th	RR
Billy Tubbs (Lamar 1958) 1979, 80	2	3	2	0	0	0	0	0
Pat Foster (Arkansas 1961) 1981, 83	2	2	2	0	0	0	0	0

	Yrs.	Won	Lost	CH	2D	3d%	4th	RR
Mike Deane (Potsdam St. 1974) 2000	1	0	1	0	0	0	0	0
TOTAL	5	5	5	0	0	0	0	0

LEBANON VALLEY

	Yrs.	Won	Lost	CH	2D	3d%	4th	RR
George "Rinso" Marquette (Lebanon Valley 1948) 1953	1	1	2	0	0	0	0	0
TOTAL	1	1	2	0	0	0	0	0

LEHIGH

	Yrs.	Won	Lost	CH	2D	3d%	4th	RR
Tom Schneider (Bucknell 1969) 1985	1	0	1	0	0	0	0	0
Fran McCaffery (Pennsylvania 1982) 1988	1	0	1	0	0	0	0	0
TOTAL	2	0	2	0	0	0	0	0

LIBERTY

	Yrs.	Won	Lost	CH	2D	3d%	4th	RR
Jeff Meyer (Taylor 1976) 1994	1	0	1	0	0	0	0	0
TOTAL	1	0	1	0	0	0	0	0

LONG BEACH ST.*

	Yrs.	Won	Lost	CH	2D	3d%	4th	RR
Jerry Tarkanian (Fresno St. 1956) 1970, 71RR, 72RR, 73	4	7	5	0	0	0	0	2
Dwight Jones (Pepperdine 1965) 1977	1	0	1	0	0	0	0	0
Seth Greenberg (FDU-Teaneck 1978) 1993, 95	2	0	2	0	0	0	0	0
TOTAL	7	7	8	0	0	0	0	2

LONG ISLAND

	Yrs.	Won	Lost	CH	2D	3d%	4th	RR
Paul Lizzo (Northwest Mo. St. 1963) 1981, 84	2	0	2	0	0	0	0	0
Ray Haskins (Shaw 1972) 1997	1	0	1	0	0	0	0	0
TOTAL	3	0	3	0	0	0	0	0

LSU

	Yrs.	Won	Lost	CH	2D	3d%	4th	RR
Harry Rabenhorst (Wake Forest 1921) 1953-4th, 54	2	2	4	0	0	0	1	0
Dale Brown (Minot St. 1957) 1979, 80RR, 81-4th, 84, 85, 86-T3d, 87RR, 88, 89, 90, 91, 92, 93	13	15	14	0	0	1	1	2
John Brady (Belhaven 1976) 2000	1	2	1	0	0	0	0	0
TOTAL	16	19	19	0	0	1	2	2

LOUISIANA TECH

	Yrs.	Won	Lost	CH	2D	3d%	4th	RR
Andy Russo (Lake Forest 1970) 1984, 85	2	3	2	0	0	0	0	0
Tommy Joe Eagles (Louisiana Tech 1971) 1987, 89	2	1	2	0	0	0	0	0
Jerry Loyd (LeTourneau 1976) 1991	1	0	1	0	0	0	0	0
TOTAL	5	4	5	0	0	0	0	0

LA.-LAFAYETTE*

	Yrs.	Won	Lost	CH	2D	3d%	4th	RR
Beryl Shipley (Delta St. 1951) 1972, 73	2	3	3	0	0	0	0	0
Bobby Paschal (Stetson 1964) 1982, 83	2	0	2	0	0	0	0	0
Marty Fletcher (Maryland 1973) 1992, 94	2	1	2	0	0	0	0	0
Jessie Evans (Eastern Mich. 1972) 2000	1	0	1	0	0	0	0	0
TOTAL	7	4	8	0	0	0	0	0

LA.-MONROE

	Yrs.	Won	Lost	CH	2D	3d%	4th	RR
Mike Vining (La.-Monroe 1967) 1982, 86, 90, 91, 92, 93, 96	7	0	7	0	0	0	0	0
TOTAL	7	0	7	0	0	0	0	0

LOUISVILLE

	Yrs.	Won	Lost	CH	2D	3d%	4th	RR
Bernard "Peck" Hickman (Western Ky. 1935) 1951, 59-4th, 61, 64, 67	5	5	7	0	0	0	1	0
John Dromo (John Carroll 1939) 1968	1	1	1	0	0	0	0	0
Denny Crum (UCLA 1959) 1972-4th, 74, 75-3d, 77, 78, 79, 80-CH, 81, 82-T3d, 83-T3d, 84, 86-CH, 88, 89, 90, 92, 93, 94, 95, 96, 97RR, 99, 2000	23	42	23	2	0	3	1	1
TOTAL	29	48	31	2	0	3	2	1

LOYOLA MARYMOUNT*

	Yrs.	Won	Lost	CH	2D	3d%	4th	RR
William Donovan (Loyola Marymount 1950) 1961	1	1	2	0	0	0	0	0
Ron Jacobs (Southern California 1964) 1980	1	0	1	0	0	0	0	0
Paul Westhead (St. Joseph's 1961) 1988, 89, 90RR	3	4	3	0	0	0	0	1
TOTAL	5	5	5	0	0	0	0	1

LOYOLA (ILL.)

	Yrs.	Won	Lost	CH	2D	3d%	4th	RR
George Ireland (Notre Dame 1936) 1963-CH, 64, 66, 68	4	7	3	1	0	0	0	0
Gene Sullivan (Notre Dame 1953) 1985	1	2	1	0	0	0	0	0
TOTAL	5	9	4	1	0	0	0	0

LOYOLA (LA.)

	Yrs.	Won	Lost	CH	2D	3d%	4th	RR
Jim McCafferty [Loyola (La.) 1942] 1954, 57	2	0	2	0	0	0	0	0
Jim Harding (Iowa 1949) 1958	1	0	1	0	0	0	0	0
TOTAL	3	0	3	0	0	0	0	0

LOYOLA (MD.)

	Yrs.	Won	Lost	CH	2D	3d%	4th	RR
Skip Prosser (Merchant Marine 1972) 1994	1	0	1	0	0	0	0	0
TOTAL	1	0	1	0	0	0	0	0

TEAM-BY-TEAM WON-LOST RECORDS—BY COACH 77

	Yrs.	Won	Lost	CH	2D	3d%	4th	RR
MANHATTAN								
Ken Norton (Long Island 1939) 1956, 58	2	1	3	0	0	0	0	0
Fran Fraschilla (Brooklyn 1980) 1993, 95	2	1	2	0	0	0	0	0
TOTAL	4	2	5	0	0	0	0	0
MARIST								
Matt Furjanic (Point Park 1973) 1986	1	0	1	0	0	0	0	0
Dave Magarity (St. Francis (Pa.) 1974) 1987	1	0	1	0	0	0	0	0
TOTAL	2	0	2	0	0	0	0	0
MARQUETTE								
Jack Nagle (Marquette 1940) 1955RR	1	2	1	0	0	0	0	1
Eddie Hickey (Creighton 1927) 1959, 61	2	1	3	0	0	0	0	0
Al McGuire [St. John's (N.Y.) 1951] 1968, 69RR, 71, 72, 73, 74-2d, 75, 76RR, 77-CH	9	20	9	1	1	0	0	2
Hank Raymonds (St. Louis 1948) 1978, 79, 80, 82, 83	5	2	5	0	0	0	0	0
Kevin O'Neill (McGill 1979) 1993, 94	2	2	2	0	0	0	0	0
Mike Deane (Potsdam St. 1974) 1996, 97	2	1	2	0	0	0	0	0
TOTAL	21	28	22	1	1	0	0	3
MARSHALL*								
Jule Rivlin (Marshall 1940) 1956	1	0	1	0	0	0	0	0
Carl Tacy (Davis & Elkins 1956) 1972	1	0	1	0	0	0	0	0
Rick Huckabay (Louisiana Tech 1967) 1984, 85, 87	3	0	3	0	0	0	0	0
TOTAL	5	0	5	0	0	0	0	0
MARYLAND*								
H.A. "Bud" Millikan (Oklahoma St. 1942) 1958	1	2	1	0	0	0	0	0
Charles "Lefty" Driesell (Duke 1954) 1973RR, 75RR, 80, 81, 83, 84, 85, 86	8	10	8	0	0	0	0	2
Bob Wade (Morgan St. 1967) 1988	1	1	1	0	0	0	0	0
Gary Williams (Maryland 1967) 1994, 95, 96, 97, 98, 99, 2000, 01-T3d	8	13	8	0	0	1	0	0
TOTAL	18	26	18	0	0	1	0	2
MASSACHUSETTS*								
Matt Zunic (George Washington 1942) 1962	1	0	1	0	0	0	0	0
John Calipari (Clarion 1982) 1992, 93, 94, 95RR, 96-T3d	5	11	5	0	0	1	0	1
James Flint (St. Joseph's 1987) 1997, 98	2	0	2	0	0	0	0	0
TOTAL	8	11	8	0	0	1	0	1
McNEESE ST.								
Steve Welch (Southeastern La. 1971) 1989	1	0	1	0	0	0	0	0
TOTAL	1	0	1	0	0	0	0	0
MEMPHIS*								
Eugene Lambert (Arkansas 1929) 1955, 56	2	0	2	0	0	0	0	0
Bob Vanatta (Central Methodist 1945) 1962	1	0	1	0	0	0	0	0
Gene Bartow (Truman 1953) 1973-2d..1	3	1	0	1	0	0	0	0
Wayne Yates (Memphis 1961) 1976	1	0	1	0	0	0	0	0
Dana Kirk (Marshall 1960) 1982, 83, 84, 85-T3d, 86	5	9	5	0	0	1	0	0
Larry Finch (Memphis 1973) 1988, 89, 92RR, 93, 95, 96	6	6	6	0	0	0	0	1
TOTAL	16	18	16	0	1	1	0	1
MERCER								
Bill Bibb (Ky. Wesleyan 1957) 1981, 85	2	0	2	0	0	0	0	0
TOTAL	2	0	2	0	0	0	0	0
MIAMI (FLA.)								
Bruce Hale (Santa Clara 1941) 1960	1	0	1	0	0	0	0	0
Leonard Hamilton (Tenn.-Martin 1971) 1998, 99, 2000	3	3	3	0	0	0	0	0
TOTAL	4	3	4	0	0	0	0	0
MIAMI (OHIO)								
Bill Rohr (Ohio Wesleyan 1940) 1953, 55, 57	3	0	3	0	0	0	0	0
Dick Shrider (Ohio 1948) 1958, 66	2	1	3	0	0	0	0	0
Tates Locke (Ohio Wesleyan 1959) 1969	1	1	2	0	0	0	0	0
Darrell Hedric [Miami (Ohio) 1955] 1971, 73, 78, 84	4	1	4	0	0	0	0	0
Jerry Peirson [Miami (Ohio) 1966] 1985, 86	2	0	2	0	0	0	0	0
Joby Wright (Indiana 1972) 1992	1	0	1	0	0	0	0	0
Herb Sendek (Carnegie Mellon 1985) 1995	1	1	1	0	0	0	0	0
Charlie Coles [Miami (Ohio) 1965] 1997, 99	2	2	2	0	0	0	0	0
TOTAL	16	6	18	0	0	0	0	0

	Yrs.	Won	Lost	CH	2D	3d%	4th	RR
MICHIGAN#								
Osborne "Ozzie" Cowles (Carleton 1922) 1948RR	1	1	1	0	0	0	0	1
Dave Strack (Michigan 1946) 1964-3d, 65-2d, 66RR	3	7	3	0	1	1	0	1
Johnny Orr (Beloit 1949) 1974RR, 75, 76-2d, 77RR	4	7	4	0	1	0	0	2
Bill Frieder (Michigan 1964) 1985, 86, 87, 88	4	5	4	0	0	0	0	0
Steve Fisher (Illinois St. 1967) 1989-CH, 90, 92-2d, 93-2d, 94RR, 95, 96	7	20	6	1	2	0	0	1
Brian Ellerbe (Rutgers 1985) 1998	1	1	1	0	0	0	0	0
TOTAL	20	41	19	1	4	1	0	5
MICHIGAN ST.								
Forrest "Forddy" Anderson (Stanford 1942) 1957-4th, 59RR	2	3	3	0	0	0	1	1
George "Jud" Heathcote (Washington St. 1950) 1978RR, 79-CH, 85, 86, 90, 91, 92, 94, 95	9	14	8	1	0	0	0	1
Tom Izzo (Northern Mich. 1977) 1998, 99-T3d, 2000-CH, 01-T3d	4	16	3	1	0	2	0	0
TOTAL	15	33	14	2	0	2	1	2
MIDDLE TENN.								
Jimmy Earle (Middle Tenn. 1959) 1975, 77	2	0	2	0	0	0	0	0
Stan Simpson (Ga. Southern 1961) 1982	1	1	1	0	0	0	0	0
Bruce Stewart (Jacksonville St. 1975) 1985, 87, 89	3	1	3	0	0	0	0	0
TOTAL	6	2	6	0	0	0	0	0
MINNESOTA*								
Bill Musselman (Wittenberg 1961) 1972	1	1	1	0	0	0	0	0
Jim Dutcher (Michigan 1955) 1982	1	1	1	0	0	0	0	0
Clem Haskins (Western Ky. 1967) 1989, 90RR, 94, 95, 97-T3d, 99	6	10	6	0	0	1	0	1
TOTAL	8	12	8	0	0	1	0	1
MISSISSIPPI								
Bob Weltlich (Ohio St. 1967) 1981	1	0	1	0	0	0	0	0
Rob Evans (New Mexico St. 1968) 1997, 98	2	0	2	0	0	0	0	0
Roderick Barnes (Mississippi 1988) 1999, 2001	2	3	2	0	0	0	0	0
TOTAL	5	3	5	0	0	0	0	0
MISSISSIPPI ST.								
James "Babe" McCarthy (Mississippi St. 1949) 1963	1	1	1	0	0	0	0	0
Richard Williams (Mississippi St. 1967) 1991, 95, 96-T3d	3	6	3	0	0	1	0	0
TOTAL	4	7	4	0	0	1	0	0
MISSISSIPPI VAL.								
Lafayette Stribling (Miss. Industrial 1957) 1986, 92, 96	3	0	3	0	0	0	0	0
TOTAL	3	0	3	0	0	0	0	0
MISSOURI#								
George Edwards (Missouri 1913) 1944RR	1	1	1	0	0	0	0	1
Norm Stewart (Missouri 1956) 1976RR, 78, 80, 81, 82 83, 86, 87, 88, 89, 90, 92, 93, 94RR, 95, 99	16	12	16	0	0	0	0	2
Quin Snyder (Duke 1989) 2000, 01	2	1	2	0	0	0	0	0
TOTAL	19	14	19	0	0	0	0	3
MONMOUTH								
Wayne Szoke (Maryland 1963) 1996	1	0	1	0	0	0	0	0
Dave Calloway [Monmouth 1991] 2001	1	0	1	0	0	0	0	0
TOTAL	2	0	2	0	0	0	0	0
MONTANA								
George "Jud" Heathcote (Washington St. 1950) 1975	1	1	2	0	0	0	0	0
Stew Morrill (Gonzaga 1974) 1991	1	0	1	0	0	0	0	0
Blaine Taylor (Montana 1982) 1992, 97	2	0	2	0	0	0	0	0
TOTAL	4	1	5	0	0	0	0	0
MONTANA ST.								
John Breeden (Montana St. 1929) 1951	1	0	1	0	0	0	0	0
Stu Starner (Minn.-Morris 1965) 1986	1	0	1	0	0	0	0	0
Mike Durham (Montana St. 1979) 1996	1	0	1	0	0	0	0	0
TOTAL	3	0	3	0	0	0	0	0
MOREHEAD ST.								
Robert Laughlin (Morehead St. 1937) 1956, 57, 61	3	3	4	0	0	0	0	0
Wayne Martin (Morehead St. 1968) 1983, 84	2	1	2	0	0	0	0	0
TOTAL	5	4	6	0	0	0	0	0

THE TOURNAMENT

TEAM-BY-TEAM WON-LOST RECORDS—BY COACH

	Yrs.	Won	Lost	CH	2D	3d%	4th	RR
MT. ST. MARY'S								
James Phelan (La Salle 1951) 1995, 99	2	0	2	0	0	0	0	0
TOTAL	2	0	2	0	0	0	0	0
MURRAY ST.								
Cal Luther (Valparaiso 1951) 1964, 69..	2	0	2	0	0	0	0	0
Steve Newton (Indiana St. 1963) 1988, 90, 91	3	1	3	0	0	0	0	0
Scott Edgar (Pitt.-Johnstown 1978) 1992, 95	2	0	2	0	0	0	0	0
Mark Gottfried (Alabama 1987) 1997, 98	2	0	2	0	0	0	0	0
Tevester Anderson (Ark.-Pine Bluff 1962) 1999	1	0	1	0	0	0	0	0
TOTAL	10	1	10	0	0	0	0	0
NAVY								
Ben Carnevale (New York U. 1938) 1947RR, 53, 54RR, 59, 60	5	4	6	0	0	0	0	2
Paul Evans (Ithaca 1967) 1985, 86RR	2	4	2	0	0	0	0	1
Pete Herrmann (Geneseo St. 1970) 1987	1	0	1	0	0	0	0	0
Don DeVoe (Ohio St. 1964) 1994, 97, 98	3	0	3	0	0	0	0	0
TOTAL	11	8	12	0	0	0	0	3
NEBRASKA								
Moe Iba (Oklahoma St. 1962) 1986	1	0	1	0	0	0	0	0
Danny Nee (St. Marys of the Plains 1971) 1991, 92, 93, 94, 98	5	0	5	0	0	0	0	0
TOTAL	6	0	6	0	0	0	0	0
UNLV								
Jerry Tarkanian (Fresno St. 1956) 1975, 76, 77-3d, 83, 84, 85, 86, 87-T3d, 88, 89RR, 90-CH, 91-T3d	12	30	11	1	0	3	0	1
Bill Bayno (Sacred Heart 1985) 1998, 2000	2	0	2	0	0	0	0	0
TOTAL	14	30	13	1	0	3	0	1
NEVADA								
Sonny Allen (Marshall 1959) 1984, 85 ..	2	0	2	0	0	0	0	0
TOTAL	2	0	2	0	0	0	0	0
NEW MEXICO								
Bob King (Iowa 1947) 1968	1	0	2	0	0	0	0	0
Norm Ellenberger (Butler 1955) 1974, 78	2	2	2	0	0	0	0	0
Dave Bliss (Cornell 1965) 1991, 93, 94, 96, 97, 98, 99	7	4	7	0	0	0	0	0
TOTAL	10	6	11	0	0	0	0	0
NEW MEXICO ST.*								
George McCarty (New Mexico St. 1950) 1952	1	0	2	0	0	0	0	0
Presley Askew (Southeastern Okla. 1930) 1959, 60	2	0	2	0	0	0	0	0
Ken Hayes (Northeastern St. 1956) 1979	1	0	1	0	0	0	0	0
Neil McCarthy (Sacramento St. 1965) 1990, 91, 92, 93, 94	5	3	5	0	0	0	0	0
Lou Henson (New Mexico St. 1955) 1967, 68, 69, 70-3d, 71, 75, 99	7	7	8	0	0	1	0	0
TOTAL	16	10	18	0	0	1	0	0
NEW ORLEANS								
Benny Dees (Wyoming 1958) 1987	1	1	1	0	0	0	0	0
Tim Floyd (Louisiana Tech 1977) 1991, 93	2	0	2	0	0	0	0	0
Tic Price (Virginia Tech 1979) 1996	1	0	1	0	0	0	0	0
TOTAL	4	1	4	0	0	0	0	0
NEW YORK U.								
Howard Cann (New York U. 1920) 1943RR, 45-2d, 46RR	3	3	4	0	1	0	0	2
Lou Rossini (Columbia 1948) 1960-4th, 62, 63	3	6	5	0	0	0	1	0
TOTAL	6	9	9	0	1	0	1	2
NIAGARA								
Frank Layden (Niagara 1955) 1970	1	1	2	0	0	0	0	0
TOTAL	1	1	2	0	0	0	0	0
NICHOLLS ST.								
Rickey Broussard (La.-Lafayette 1970) 1995, 98	2	0	2	0	0	0	0	0
TOTAL	2	0	2	0	0	0	0	0
NORTH CAROLINA								
Bill Lange (Wittenberg 1921) 1941RR	1	0	2	0	0	0	0	1
Ben Carnevale (New York U. 1938) 1946-2d	1	2	1	0	1	0	0	0
Frank McGuire [St. John's (N.Y.) 1936] 1957-CH, 59	2	5	1	1	0	0	0	0
Dean Smith (Kansas 1953) 1967-4th, 68-2d, 69-4th, 72-3d, 75 76, 77-2d, 78, 79, 80, 81-2d, 82-CH, 83RR, 84, 85RR 86, 87RR, 88RR, 89, 90, 91-T3d, 92, 93-CH, 94, 95-T3d, 96, 97-T3d	27	65	27	2	3	4	2	4
Bill Guthridge (Kansas St. 1963) 1998-T3d, 99, 2000-T3d	3	8	3	0	0	2	0	0
Matt Doherty (North Carolina 1984) 2001	1	1	1	0	0	0	0	0
TOTAL	35	81	35	3	4	6	2	5
N.C. A&T								
Don Corbett [Lincoln (Mo.) 1965] 1982, 83, 84, 85, 86, 87, 88	7	0	7	0	0	0	0	0
Jeff Capel (Fayetteville St. 1977) 1994	1	0	1	0	0	0	0	0
Roy Thomas (Baylor 1974) 1995	1	0	1	0	0	0	0	0
TOTAL	9	0	9	0	0	0	0	0
UNC GREENSBORO								
Randy Peele (Va. Wesleyan 1980) 1996	1	0	1	0	0	0	0	0
Fran McCaffery (Pennsylvania 1982) 2001	1	0	1	0	0	0	0	0
TOTAL	2	0	2	0	0	0	0	0
UNC WILMINGTON								
Jerry Wainwright (Colorado Col. 1968) 2000	1	0	1	0	0	0	0	0
TOTAL	1	0	1	0	0	0	0	0
NORTH CAROLINA ST.*								
Everett Case (Wisconsin 1923) 1950-3d, 51RR, 52, 54, 56	5	6	6	0	0	1	0	1
Press Maravich (Davis & Elkins 1941) 1965	1	1	1	0	0	0	0	0
Norm Sloan (North Carolina St. 1951) 1970, 74-CH, 80	3	5	2	1	0	0	0	0
Jim Valvano (Rutgers 1967) 1982, 83-CH, 85RR, 86RR 87, 88, 89	7	14	6	1	0	0	0	2
Les Robinson (North Carolina St. 1964) 1991	1	1	1	0	0	0	0	0
TOTAL	17	27	16	2	0	1	0	3
NORTH TEXAS								
Jimmy Gales (Alcorn St. 1963) 1988	1	0	1	0	0	0	0	0
TOTAL	1	0	1	0	0	0	0	0
NORTHEASTERN								
Jim Calhoun (American Int'l 1966) 1981, 82, 84, 85, 86	5	3	5	0	0	0	0	0
Karl Fogel (Colby 1968) 1987, 91	2	0	2	0	0	0	0	0
TOTAL	7	3	7	0	0	0	0	0
NORTHERN ARIZ.								
Ben Howland (Weber St. 1980) 1998	1	0	1	0	0	0	0	0
Mike Adras (UC Santa Barb. 1983) 2000	1	0	1	0	0	0	0	0
TOTAL	2	0	2	0	0	0	0	0
NORTHERN ILL.								
John McDougal (Evansville 1950) 1982	1	0	1	0	0	0	0	0
Jim Molinari (Ill. Wesleyan 1977) 1991	1	0	1	0	0	0	0	0
Brian Hammel (Bentley 1975) 1996	1	0	1	0	0	0	0	0
TOTAL	3	0	3	0	0	0	0	0
NORTHERN IOWA								
Eldon Miller (Wittenberg 1961) 1990	1	1	1	0	0	0	0	0
TOTAL	1	1	1	0	0	0	0	0
NORTHWESTERN ST.								
Mike McConathy (Louisiana Tech 1977) 2001	1	1	1	0	0	0	0	0
TOTAL	1	1	1	0	0	0	0	0
NOTRE DAME								
John Jordan (Notre Dame 1935) 1953RR, 54RR, 57, 58RR, 60, 63	6	8	6	0	0	0	0	3
Johnny Dee (Notre Dame 1946) 1965, 69, 70, 71	4	2	6	0	0	0	0	0
Richard "Digger" Phelps (Rider 1963) 1974,75, 76, 77, 78-4th, 79RR, 80, 81, 85, 86, 87, 88, 89, 90	14	15	16	0	0	0	1	1
Mike Brey (George Washington 1982) 2001	1	1	1	0	0	0	0	0
TOTAL	25	26	29	0	0	0	1	4
OHIO								
James Snyder (Ohio 1941) 1960, 61, 64RR, 65, 70, 72, 74	7	3	8	0	0	0	0	1
Danny Nee (St. Mary of the Plains 1971) 1983, 85	2	1	2	0	0	0	0	0
Larry Hunter (Ohio 1971) 1994	1	0	1	0	0	0	0	0
TOTAL	10	4	11	0	0	0	0	1
OHIO ST.								
Harold Olsen (Wisconsin 1917) 1939-2d, 44-T3d, 45-T3d, 46-3d	4	6	4	0	1	3	0	0
William "Tippy" Dye (Ohio St. 1937) 1950RR	1	1	1	0	0	0	0	0
Fred Taylor (Ohio St. 1950) 1960-CH, 61-2d, 62-2d, 68-3d, 71RR	5	14	4	1	2	1	0	1
Eldon Miller (Wittenberg 1961) 1980, 82, 83, 85	4	3	4	0	0	0	0	0

TEAM-BY-TEAM WON-LOST RECORDS—BY COACH

	Yrs.	Won	Lost	CH	2D	3d%	4th	RR
Gary Williams (Maryland 1967) 1987 ...	1	1	1	0	0	0	0	0
Randy Ayers [Miami (Ohio) 1978] 1990, 91, 92RR	3	6	3	0	0	0	0	1
Jim O'Brien (Boston College 1971) 1999-T3d, 2000, 01	3	5	3	0	0	1	0	0
TOTAL	21	36	20	1	3	5	0	3
OKLAHOMA								
Bruce Drake (Oklahoma 1929) 1939-T3d, 43RR, 47-2d	3	4	3	0	1	1	0	1
Dave Bliss (Cornell 1965) 1979	1	1	1	0	0	0	0	0
Billy Tubbs (Lamar 1958) 1983, 84, 85RR, 86, 87, 88-2d, 89, 90, 92	9	15	9	0	1	0	0	1
Kelvin Sampson (UNC Pembroke 1978) 1995, 96, 97, 98, 99, 2000, 01	7	3	7	0	0	0	0	0
TOTAL	20	23	20	0	2	1	0	2
OKLAHOMA CITY								
Doyle Parrack (Oklahoma St. 1945) 1952, 53, 54, 55	4	1	5	0	0	0	0	0
A.E. "Abe" Lemons (Oklahoma City 1949) 1956RR, 57RR, 63, 64, 65, 66, 73	7	7	8	0	0	0	0	2
TOTAL	11	8	13	0	0	0	0	2
OKLAHOMA ST.								
Henry Iba [Westminster (Mo.) 1928] 1945-CH, 46-CH, 49-2d, 51-4th, 53-RR, 54-RR, 58RR, 65RR	8	15	7	2	1	0	1	4
Paul Hansen (Oklahoma City 1950) 1983	1	0	1	0	0	0	0	0
Eddie Sutton (Oklahoma St. 1958) 1991, 92, 93, 94, 95-T3d, 98, 99, 2000RR, 01	9	15	9	0	0	1	0	1
TOTAL	18	30	17	2	1	1	1	5
OLD DOMINION								
Paul Webb (William & Mary 1951) 1980, 82, 85	3	0	3	0	0	0	0	0
Tom Young (Maryland 1958) 1986	1	1	1	0	0	0	0	0
Oliver Purnell (Old Dominion 1975) 1992	1	0	1	0	0	0	0	0
Jeff Capel (Fayetteville St. 1977) 1995, 97	2	1	2	0	0	0	0	0
TOTAL	7	2	7	0	0	0	0	0
ORAL ROBERTS								
Ken Trickey (Middle Tenn. 1954) 1974RR	1	2	1	0	0	0	0	1
Dick Acres (UC Santa Barb.) 1984	1	0	1	0	0	0	0	0
TOTAL	2	2	2	0	0	0	0	1
OREGON								
Howard Hobson (Oregon 1926) 1939-CH	1	3	0	1	0	0	0	0
John Warren (Oregon 1928) 1945RR	1	1	1	0	0	0	0	1
Steve Belko (Idaho 1939) 1960RR, 61	2	2	2	0	0	0	0	1
Jerry Green (Appalachian St. 1968) 1995	1	0	1	0	0	0	0	0
Ernie Kent (Oregon 1977) 2000	1	0	1	0	0	0	0	0
TOTAL	6	6	5	1	0	0	0	2
OREGON ST.*								
Amory "Slats" Gill (Oregon St. 1925) 1947RR, 49-4th,55RR, 62RR, 63-4th, 64	6	8	8	0	0	0	2	3
Paul Valenti (Oregon St. 1942) 1966RR	1	1	1	0	0	0	0	1
Ralph Miller (Kansas 1942) 1975, 80, 81, 82RR, 84, 85, 88, 89	8	3	9	0	0	0	0	1
Jim Anderson (Oregon St. 1959) 1990	1	0	1	0	0	0	0	0
TOTAL	16	12	19	0	0	0	2	5
PACIFIC (CAL.)								
Dick Edwards (Culver-Stockton 1952) 1966, 67RR, 71	3	2	4	0	0	0	0	1
Stan Morrison (California 1962) 1979	1	0	1	0	0	0	0	0
Bob Thomason [Pacific (Cal.) 1971] 1997	1	0	1	0	0	0	0	0
TOTAL	5	2	6	0	0	0	0	1
PENN ST.								
John Lawther [Westminster (Pa.) 1919] 1942RR	1	1	1	0	0	0	0	1
Elmer Gross (Penn St. 1942) 1952, 54-3d	2	4	3	0	0	1	0	0
John Egli (Penn St. 1947) 1955, 65	2	1	3	0	0	0	0	0
Bruce Parkhill (Lock Haven 1971) 1991	1	1	1	0	0	0	0	0
Jerry Dunn (George Mason 1980) 1996, 2001	2	2	2	0	0	0	0	0
TOTAL	8	9	10	0	0	1	0	1
PENNSYLVANIA								
Howard "Howie" Dallmar (Stanford 1948) 1953	1	1	1	0	0	0	0	0
Dick Harter (Pennsylvania 1953) 1970, 71RR	2	2	2	0	0	0	0	1

	Yrs.	Won	Lost	CH	2D	3d%	4th	RR
Chuck Daly (Bloomsburg 1953) 1972RR, 73, 74, 75	4	3	5	0	0	0	0	1
Bob Weinhauer (Cortland St. 1961) 1978, 79-4th, 80, 82	4	6	5	0	0	0	1	0
Craig Littlepage (Pennsylvania 1973) 1985	1	0	1	0	0	0	0	0
Tom Schneider (Bucknell 1969) 1987	1	0	1	0	0	0	0	0
Fran Dunphy (La Salle 1970) 1993, 94, 95, 99, 2000	5	1	5	0	0	0	0	0
TOTAL	18	13	20	0	0	0	1	2
PEPPERDINE								
Al Duer (Emporia St. 1929) 1944RR	1	0	2	0	0	0	0	1
R.L. "Duck" Dowell (Northwest Mo. St. 1933) 1962	1	1	1	0	0	0	0	0
Gary Colson (David Lipscomb 1956) 1976, 79	2	2	2	0	0	0	0	0
Jim Harrick [Charleston (W.Va.) 1960] 1982, 83, 85, 86	4	1	4	0	0	0	0	0
Tom Asbury (Wyoming 1967) 1991, 92, 94	3	0	3	0	0	0	0	0
Jan van Breda Kolff (Vanderbilt 1974) 2000	1	1	1	0	0	0	0	0
TOTAL	12	5	13	0	0	0	0	1
PITTSBURGH								
Henry Carlson (Pittsburgh 1917) 1941-T3d	1	1	1	0	0	1	0	0
Bob Timmons (Pittsburgh 1933) 1957, 58, 63	3	1	4	0	0	0	0	0
Charles "Buzz" Ridl [Westminster (Pa.) 1942] 1974RR	1	2	1	0	0	0	0	1
Roy Chipman (Maine 1961) 1981, 82, 85	3	1	3	0	0	0	0	0
Paul Evans (Ithaca 1967) 1987, 88, 89, 91, 93	5	3	5	0	0	0	0	0
TOTAL	13	8	14	0	0	1	0	1
PORTLAND								
Al Negratti (Seton Hall 1943) 1959	1	0	1	0	0	0	0	0
Rob Chavez (Mesa St. 1980) 1996	1	0	1	0	0	0	0	0
TOTAL	2	0	2	0	0	0	0	0
PRAIRIE VIEW								
Elwood Plummer (Jackson St. 1966) 1998	1	0	1	0	0	0	0	0
TOTAL	1	0	1	0	0	0	0	0
PRINCETON#								
Franklin Cappon (Michigan 1924) 1952, 55, 60	3	0	5	0	0	0	0	0
J.L. "Jake" McCandless (Princeton 1951) 1961	1	1	2	0	0	0	0	0
Butch van Breda Kolff (Princeton 1947) 1963, 64, 65-3d, 67	4	7	5	0	0	1	0	0
Pete Carril (Lafayette 1952) 1969, 76, 77, 81, 83, 84, 89, 90, 91, 92, 96	11	4	11	0	0	0	0	0
Bill Carmody (Union 1975) 1997, 98	2	1	2	0	0	0	0	0
John Thompson III (Princeton 1989) 2001	1	0	1	0	0	0	0	0
TOTAL	22	13	26	0	0	1	0	0
PROVIDENCE								
Joe Mullaney (Holy Cross 1949) 1964, 65RR, 66	3	2	3	0	0	0	0	1
Dave Gavitt (Dartmouth 1959) 1972, 73-4th, 74, 77, 78	5	5	6	0	0	1	0	0
Rick Pitino (Massachusetts 1974) 1987 tie-3d	1	4	1	0	0	1	0	0
Rick Barnes (Lenior-Rhyne 1977) 1989, 90, 94	3	0	3	0	0	0	0	0
Pete Gillen (Fairfield 1968) 1997RR	1	3	1	0	0	0	0	1
Tim Welsh (Potsdam St. 1984) 2001	1	0	1	0	0	0	0	0
TOTAL	14	14	15	0	0	1	1	2
PURDUE								
George King [Charleston (W.Va.) 1950] 1969-2d	1	3	1	0	1	0	0	0
Fred Schaus (West Virginia 1949) 1977	1	0	1	0	0	0	0	0
Lee Rose (Transylvania 1958) 1980-3d	1	5	1	0	0	1	0	0
Gene Keady (Kansas St. 1958) 1983, 84, 85, 86, 87, 88, 90, 91, 93, 94RR, 95, 96, 97, 98, 99, 2000RR	16	18	16	0	0	0	0	2
TOTAL	19	26	19	0	1	1	0	2
RADFORD								
Ron Bradley (Eastern Nazarene 1973) 1998	1	0	1	0	0	0	0	0
TOTAL	1	0	1	0	0	0	0	0
RHODE ISLAND								
Ernie Calverley (Rhode Island 1946) 1961, 66	2	0	2	0	0	0	0	0
Jack Kraft (St. Joseph's 1942) 1978	1	0	1	0	0	0	0	0
Tom Penders (Connecticut 1967) 1988	1	2	1	0	0	0	0	0
Al Skinner (Massachusetts 1974) 1993, 97	2	1	2	0	0	0	0	0

THE TOURNAMENT

	Yrs.	Won	Lost	CH	2D	3d%	4th	RR
Jim Harrick [Charleston (W.Va.) 1960] 1998, 99	2	3	2	0	0	0	0	1
TOTAL	8	6	8	0	0	0	0	1

RICE
	Yrs.	Won	Lost	CH	2D	3d%	4th	RR
Byron "Buster" Brannon (TCU 1933) 1940RR, 42RR	2	1	3	0	0	0	0	2
Don Suman (Rice 1944) 1954	1	1	1	0	0	0	0	0
Don Knodel [Miami (Ohio) 1953] 1970	1	0	1	0	0	0	0	0
TOTAL	4	2	5	0	0	0	0	2

RICHMOND
	Yrs.	Won	Lost	CH	2D	3d%	4th	RR
Dick Tarrant (Fordham 1951) 1984, 86, 88, 90, 91	5	5	5	0	0	0	0	0
John Beilein (Wheeling Jesuit 1975) 1998	1	1	1	0	0	0	0	0
TOTAL	6	6	6	0	0	0	0	0

RIDER
	Yrs.	Won	Lost	CH	2D	3d%	4th	RR
John Carpenter (Penn St. 1958) 1984	1	0	1	0	0	0	0	0
Kevin Bannon (St. Peter's 1979) 1993, 94	2	0	2	0	0	0	0	0
TOTAL	3	0	3	0	0	0	0	0

ROBERT MORRIS
	Yrs.	Won	Lost	CH	2D	3d%	4th	RR
Matt Furjanic (Point Park 1973) 1982, 83	2	1	2	0	0	0	0	0
Jarrett Durham (Duquesne 1971) 1989, 90, 92	3	0	3	0	0	0	0	0
TOTAL	5	1	5	0	0	0	0	0

RUTGERS
	Yrs.	Won	Lost	CH	2D	3d%	4th	RR
Tom Young (Maryland 1958) 1975, 76-4th, 79, 83	4	5	5	0	0	0	1	0
Bob Wenzel (Rutgers 1971) 1989, 91	2	0	2	0	0	0	0	0
TOTAL	6	5	7	0	0	0	1	0

ST. BONAVENTURE
	Yrs.	Won	Lost	CH	2D	3d%	4th	RR
Eddie Donovan (St. Bonaventure 1950) 1961	1	2	1	0	0	0	0	0
Larry Weise (St. Bonaventure 1958) 1968, 70-4th	2	4	4	0	0	0	1	0
Jim Satalin (St. Bonaventure 1969) 1978	1	0	1	0	0	0	0	0
Jim Baron (St. Bonaventure 1977) 2000	1	0	1	0	0	0	0	0
TOTAL	5	6	7	0	0	0	1	0

ST. FRANCIS (PA.)
	Yrs.	Won	Lost	CH	2D	3d%	4th	RR
Jim Baron (St. Bonaventure 1977) 1991	1	0	1	0	0	0	0	0
TOTAL	1	0	1	0	0	0	0	0

ST. JOHN'S (N.Y.)
	Yrs.	Won	Lost	CH	2D	3d%	4th	RR
Frank McGuire [St. John's (N.Y.) 1936] 1951RR, 52-2d	2	5	2	0	1	0	0	1
Joe Lapchick (No college) 1961	1	0	1	0	0	0	0	0
Frank Mulzoff [St. John's (N.Y.) 1951] 1973	1	0	1	0	0	0	0	0
Lou Carnesecca [St. John's (N.Y.) 1946] 1967, 68, 69, 76, 77, 78, 79RR, 80, 82, 83, 84, 85-T3d, 86, 87, 88, 90, 91RR, 92	18	17	20	0	0	1	0	2
Brian Mahoney (Manhattan 1971) 1993	1	1	1	0	0	0	0	0
Fran Fraschilla (Brooklyn 1980) 1998	1	0	1	0	0	0	0	0
Mike Jarvis (Northeastern 1968) 1999RR, 2000	2	4	2	0	0	0	0	1
TOTAL	26	27	28	0	1	1	0	4

ST. JOSEPH'S*
	Yrs.	Won	Lost	CH	2D	3d%	4th	RR
John "Jack" Ramsay (St. Joseph's 1949) 1959, 60, 61-3d, 62, 63RR, 65, 66	7	8	11	0	0	1	0	1
John "Jack" McKinney (St. Joseph's 1957) 1969, 71, 73, 74	4	0	4	0	0	0	0	0
Jim Lynam (St. Joseph's 1964) 1981RR	1	3	1	0	0	0	0	1
Jim Boyle (St. Joseph's 1964) 1982, 86	2	1	2	0	0	0	0	0
Phil Martelli (Widener 1976) 1997, 2001	2	3	2	0	0	0	0	0
TOTAL	16	15	20	0	0	1	0	2

ST. LOUIS
	Yrs.	Won	Lost	CH	2D	3d%	4th	RR
Eddie Hickey (Creighton 1927) 1952RR, 57	2	1	3	0	0	0	0	1
Charlie Spoonhour (School of Ozarks 1961) 1994, 95, 98	3	2	3	0	0	0	0	0
Lorenzo Romar (Washington 1980) 2000	1	0	1	0	0	0	0	0
TOTAL	6	3	7	0	0	0	0	1

ST. MARY'S (CAL.)
	Yrs.	Won	Lost	CH	2D	3d%	4th	RR
James Weaver (DePaul 1947) 1959RR	1	1	1	0	0	0	0	1
Lynn Nance (Washington 1965) 1989	1	0	1	0	0	0	0	0
Ernie Kent (Oregon 1977) 1997	1	0	1	0	0	0	0	0
TOTAL	3	1	3	0	0	0	0	1

ST. PETER'S
	Yrs.	Won	Lost	CH	2D	3d%	4th	RR
Ted Fiore (Seton Hall 1962) 1991, 95	2	0	2	0	0	0	0	0
TOTAL	2	0	2	0	0	0	0	0

SAMFORD
	Yrs.	Won	Lost	CH	2D	3d%	4th	RR
Jimmy Tillette (Our Lady of Holy Cross 1975) 1999, 2000	2	0	2	0	0	0	0	0
TOTAL	2	0	2	0	0	0	0	0

SAN DIEGO
	Yrs.	Won	Lost	CH	2D	3d%	4th	RR
Jim Brovelli (San Francisco 1964) 1984	1	0	1	0	0	0	0	0
Hank Egan (Navy 1960) 1987	1	0	1	0	0	0	0	0
TOTAL	2	0	2	0	0	0	0	0

SAN DIEGO ST.
	Yrs.	Won	Lost	CH	2D	3d%	4th	RR
Tim Vezie (Denver 1967) 1975, 76	2	0	2	0	0	0	0	0
Dave "Smokey" Gaines (LeMoyne-Owen 1963) 1985	1	0	1	0	0	0	0	0
TOTAL	3	0	3	0	0	0	0	0

SAN FRANCISCO
	Yrs.	Won	Lost	CH	2D	3d%	4th	RR
Phil Woolpert (Loyola Marymount 1940) 1955-CH, 56-CH, 57-3d, 58	4	13	2	2	0	1	0	0
Peter Peletta (Sacramento St. 1950) 1963, 64RR, 65RR	3	3	3	0	0	0	0	2
Bob Gaillard (San Francisco 1962) 1972, 73RR, 74RR, 77, 78	5	4	5	0	0	0	0	2
Dan Belluomini (San Francisco 1964) 1979	1	1	1	0	0	0	0	0
Peter Barry (San Francisco 1970) 1981, 82	2	0	2	0	0	0	0	0
Phil Mathews (UC Irvine 1972) 1998	1	0	1	0	0	0	0	0
TOTAL	16	21	14	2	0	1	0	4

SAN JOSE ST.
	Yrs.	Won	Lost	CH	2D	3d%	4th	RR
Walter McPherson (San Jose St. 1940) 1951	1	0	1	0	0	0	0	0
Bill Berry (Michigan St. 1965) 1980	1	0	1	0	0	0	0	0
Stan Morrison (California 1962) 1996	1	0	1	0	0	0	0	0
TOTAL	3	0	3	0	0	0	0	0

SANTA CLARA
	Yrs.	Won	Lost	CH	2D	3d%	4th	RR
Bob Feerick (Santa Clara 1941) 1952-4th, 53RR, 54RR, 60	4	6	6	0	0	0	1	2
Dick Garibaldi (Santa Clara 1957) 1968RR, 69RR, 70	3	3	3	0	0	0	0	2
Carroll Williams (San Jose St. 1955) 1987	1	0	1	0	0	0	0	0
Dick Davey [Pacific (Cal.) 1964] 1993, 95, 96	3	2	3	0	0	0	0	0
TOTAL	11	11	13	0	0	0	1	4

SEATTLE#
	Yrs.	Won	Lost	CH	2D	3d%	4th	RR
Al Brightman [Charleston (W.Va.)] 1953, 54, 55, 56	4	4	6	0	0	0	0	0
John Castellani (Notre Dame 1952) 1958-2d	1	4	1	0	1	0	0	0
Vince Cazzetta (Arnold 1950) 1961, 62	2	0	2	0	0	0	0	0
Clair Markey (Seattle 1963) 1963	1	0	1	0	0	0	0	0
Bob Boyd (Southern California 1953) 1964	1	2	1	0	0	0	0	0
Lionel Purcell (UC Santa Barb. 1952) 1967	1	0	1	0	0	0	0	0
Morris Buckwalter (Utah 1956) 1969	1	0	1	0	0	0	0	0
TOTAL	11	10	13	0	1	0	0	0

SETON HALL
	Yrs.	Won	Lost	CH	2D	3d%	4th	RR
P. J. Carlesimo (Fordham 1971) 1988, 89-2d, 91RR, 92, 93, 94	6	12	6	0	1	0	0	1
Tommy Amaker (Duke 1987) 2000	1	2	1	0	0	0	0	0
TOTAL	7	14	7	0	1	0	0	1

SIENA
	Yrs.	Won	Lost	CH	2D	3d%	4th	RR
Mike Deane (Potsdam St. 1974) 1989	1	1	1	0	0	0	0	0
Paul Hewitt (St. John Fisher 1985) 1999	1	0	1	0	0	0	0	0
TOTAL	2	1	2	0	0	0	0	0

SOUTH ALA.
	Yrs.	Won	Lost	CH	2D	3d%	4th	RR
Cliff Ellis (Florida St. 1968) 1979, 80	2	0	2	0	0	0	0	0
Ronnie Arrow (Southwest Tex. St. 1969) 1989, 91	2	1	2	0	0	0	0	0
Bill Musselman (Wittenberg 1962) 1997	1	0	1	0	0	0	0	0
Bob Weltlich (Ohio St. 1967) 1998	1	0	1	0	0	0	0	0
TOTAL	6	1	6	0	0	0	0	0

SOUTH CAROLINA
	Yrs.	Won	Lost	CH	2D	3d%	4th	RR
Frank McGuire [St. John's (N.Y.) 1936] 1971, 72, 73, 74	4	4	5	0	0	0	0	0
George Felton (South Carolina 1975) 1989	1	0	1	0	0	0	0	0
Eddie Fogler (North Carolina 1970) 1997, 98	2	0	2	0	0	0	0	0
TOTAL	7	4	8	0	0	0	0	0

SOUTH CAROLINA ST.
	Yrs.	Won	Lost	CH	2D	3d%	4th	RR
Cy Alexander (Catawba 1975) 1989, 96, 98, 2000	4	0	4	0	0	0	0	0
TOTAL	4	0	4	0	0	0	0	0

SOUTH FLA.
	Yrs.	Won	Lost	CH	2D	3d%	4th	RR
Bobby Paschal (Stetson 1964) 1990, 92	2	0	2	0	0	0	0	0
TOTAL	2	0	2	0	0	0	0	0

SOUTHEAST MO. ST.
	Yrs.	Won	Lost	CH	2D	3d%	4th	RR
Gary Garner (Missouri 1965) 2000	1	0	1	0	0	0	0	0
TOTAL	1	0	1	0	0	0	0	0

SOUTHERN U.
	Yrs.	Won	Lost	CH	2D	3d%	4th	RR
Carl Stewart (Grambling 1954) 1981	1	0	1	0	0	0	0	0

TEAM-BY-TEAM WON-LOST RECORDS—BY COACH

	Yrs.	Won	Lost	CH	2D	3d%	4th	RR
Robert Hopkins (Grambling 1956) 1985	1	0	1	0	0	0	0	0
Ben Jobe (Fisk 1956) 1987, 88, 89, 93	4	1	4	0	0	0	0	0
TOTAL	6	1	6	0	0	0	0	0

SOUTHERN CALIFORNIA
Justin "Sam" Barry (Lawrence 13) 1940-T3d	1	1	1	0	0	1	0	0
Forrest Twogood (Iowa 1929) 1954-4th, 60, 61	3	3	5	0	0	0	1	0
Bob Boyd (Southern California 1953) 1979	1	1	1	0	0	0	0	0
Stan Morrison (California 1962) 1982, 85	2	0	2	0	0	0	0	0
George Raveling (Villanova 1960) 1991, 92	2	1	2	0	0	0	0	0
Henry Bibby (UCLA 1972) 1997, 2001RR	2	3	2	0	0	0	0	1
TOTAL	11	9	13	0	0	1	1	1

SOUTHERN ILL.
Paul Lambert (William Jewell 1956) 1977	1	1	1	0	0	0	0	0
Rich Herrin (McKendree 1956) 1993, 94, 95	3	0	3	0	0	0	0	0
TOTAL	4	1	4	0	0	0	0	0

SOUTHERN METHODIST
E.O. "Doc" Hayes (North Texas 1927) 1955, 56-4th, 57, 65, 66, 67RR	6	7	8	0	0	0	1	1
Dave Bliss (Cornell 1965) 1984, 85, 88	3	3	3	0	0	0	0	0
John Shumate (Notre Dame 1974) 1993	1	0	1	0	0	0	0	0
TOTAL	10	10	12	0	0	0	1	1

SOUTHERN MISS.
M.K. Turk (Livingston 1964) 1990, 91	2	0	2	0	0	0	0	0
TOTAL	2	0	2	0	0	0	0	0

SOUTHERN UTAH
Bill Evans (Southern Utah 1972) 2001	1	0	1	0	0	0	0	0
TOTAL	1	0	1	0	0	0	0	0

SOUTHWEST MO. ST.
Charlie Spoonhour (School of Ozarks 1961) 1987, 88, 89, 90, 92	5	1	5	0	0	0	0	0
Steve Alford (Indiana 1987) 1999	1	2	1	0	0	0	0	0
TOTAL	6	3	6	0	0	0	0	0

SOUTHWEST TEX. ST.
Jim Wooldridge (Louisiana Tech 1977) 1994	1	0	1	0	0	0	0	0
Mike Miller (Tex. A&M-Commerce 1987) 1997	1	0	1	0	0	0	0	0
TOTAL	2	0	2	0	0	0	0	0

SPRINGFIELD
Ed Hickox (Ohio Wesleyan 1905) 1940RR	1	0	1	0	0	0	0	1
TOTAL	1	0	1	0	0	0	0	1

STANFORD
Everett Dean (Indiana 1921) 1942-CH	1	3	0	1	0	0	0	0
Mike Montgomery (Long Beach St. 1968) 1989, 92, 95, 96, 97, 98-T3d, 99, 2000, 01RR	9	13	9	0	0	1	0	0
TOTAL	10	16	9	1	0	1	0	0

SYRACUSE
Marc Guley (Syracuse 1936) 1957RR	1	2	1	0	0	0	0	1
Fred Lewis (Eastern Ky. 1946) 1966RR	1	1	1	0	0	0	0	1
Roy Danforth (Southern Miss. 1962) 1973, 74, 75-4th, 76	4	5	5	0	0	0	1	0
Jim Boeheim (Syracuse 1966) 1977, 78, 79, 80, 83, 84, 85, 86, 87-2d, 89RR, 90, 91, 92, 94, 95, 96-2d, 98, 99, 2000, 01	21	32	21	0	2	0	0	1
TOTAL	27	40	28	0	2	0	1	3

TEMPLE
Josh Cody (Vanderbilt 1920) 1944RR	1	1	1	0	0	0	0	1
Harry Litwack (Temple 1930) 1956-3d, 58-3d, 64, 67, 70, 72	6	7	6	0	0	2	0	0
Don Casey (Temple 1970) 1979	1	0	1	0	0	0	0	0
John Chaney (Bethune-Cookman 1955) 1984, 85, 86, 87, 88RR, 90, 91RR, 92, 93RR, 94, 95, 96, 97, 98, 99RR, 2000, 01RR	17	23	17	0	0	0	0	5
TOTAL	25	31	25	0	0	2	0	6

TENNESSEE
Ramon "Ray" Mears [Miami (Ohio) 1949] 1967, 76, 77	3	0	4	0	0	0	0	0
Don DeVoe (Ohio St. 1964) 1979, 80, 81, 82, 83, 89	6	5	6	0	0	0	0	0
Jerry Green (Appalachian St. 1968) 1998, 99, 2000, 01	4	3	4	0	0	0	0	0
TOTAL	13	8	14	0	0	0	0	0

TENNESSEE ST.
Frankie Allen (Roanoke 1971) 1993, 94	2	0	2	0	0	0	0	0
TOTAL	2	0	2	0	0	0	0	0

TENNESSEE TECH
Johnny Oldham (Western Ky. 1948) 1958, 63	2	0	2	0	0	0	0	0
TOTAL	2	0	2	0	0	0	0	0

TEXAS
H.C. "Bully" Gilstrap (Texas 1922) 1943-T3d	1	1	1	0	0	1	0	0
Jack Gray (Texas 1935) 1939RR, 47-3d	2	2	3	0	0	1	0	1
Harold Bradley (Hartwick 1934) 1960, 63	2	2	3	0	0	0	0	0
Leon Black (Texas 1953) 1972, 74	2	1	3	0	0	0	0	0
A.E. "Abe" Lemons (Oklahoma City 1949) 1979	1	0	1	0	0	0	0	0
Tom Penders (Connecticut 1967) 1989, 90RR, 91, 92, 94, 95, 96, 97	8	10	8	0	0	0	0	1
Rick Barnes (Lenoir-Rhyne 1977) 1999, 2000, 01	3	1	3	0	0	0	0	0
TOTAL	19	17	22	0	0	2	0	2

TEXAS A&M
John Floyd (Oklahoma St. 1941) 1951	1	0	1	0	0	0	0	0
Shelby Metcalf (Tex. A&M-Commerce 1953) 1964, 69, 75, 80, 87	5	3	6	0	0	0	0	0
TOTAL	6	3	7	0	0	0	0	0

TCU
Byron "Buster" Brannon (TCU 1933) 1952, 53, 59	3	3	3	0	0	0	0	0
Johnny Swaim (TCU 1953) 1968RR, 71	2	1	2	0	0	0	0	1
Jim Killingsworth (Northeastern Okla. St. 1948) 1987	1	1	1	0	0	0	0	0
Billy Tubbs (Lamar 1958) 1998	1	0	1	0	0	0	0	0
TOTAL	7	5	7	0	0	0	0	1

TEXAS-SAN ANTONIO
Ken Burmeister [St. Mary's (Tex.) 1971] 1988	1	0	1	0	0	0	0	0
Tim Carter (Kansas 1979) 1999	1	0	1	0	0	0	0	0
TOTAL	2	0	2	0	0	0	0	0

TEXAS SOUTHERN
Robert Moreland (Tougaloo 1962) 1990, 94, 95	3	0	3	0	0	0	0	0
TOTAL	3	0	3	0	0	0	0	0

TEXAS TECH
Polk Robison (Texas Tech 1935) 1954, 56, 61	3	1	3	0	0	0	0	0
Gene Gibson (Texas Tech 1950) 1962	1	1	2	0	0	0	0	0
Gerald Myers (Texas Tech 1959) 1973, 76, 85, 86	4	1	4	0	0	0	0	0
James Dickey (Central Ark. 1976) 1993, 96	2	2	2	0	0	0	0	0
TOTAL	10	5	11	0	0	0	0	0

TOLEDO
Jerry Bush [St. John's (N.Y.) 1938] 1954	1	0	1	0	0	0	0	0
Bob Nichols (Toledo 1953) 1967, 79, 80	3	1	3	0	0	0	0	0
TOTAL	4	1	4	0	0	0	0	0

TOWSON
Terry Truax (Maryland 1968) 1990, 91	2	0	2	0	0	0	0	0
TOTAL	2	0	2	0	0	0	0	0

TRINITY (TEX.)
Bob Polk (Evansville 1939) 1969	1	0	1	0	0	0	0	0
TOTAL	1	0	1	0	0	0	0	0

TUFTS
Richard Cochran (Tufts 1934) 1945RR	1	0	2	0	0	0	0	1
TOTAL	1	0	2	0	0	0	0	1

TULANE
Perry Clark (Gettysburg 1974) 1992, 93, 95	3	3	3	0	0	0	0	0
TOTAL	3	3	3	0	0	0	0	0

TULSA
Clarence Iba (Panhandle St. 1936) 1955	1	1	1	0	0	0	0	0
Nolan Richardson (UTEP 1965) 1982, 84, 85	3	0	3	0	0	0	0	0
J.D. Barnett (Winona St. 1966) 1986, 87	2	0	2	0	0	0	0	0
Tubby Smith (High Point 1973) 1994, 95	2	4	2	0	0	0	0	0
Steve Robinson (Radford 1981) 1996, 97	2	1	2	0	0	0	0	0
Bill Self (Oklahoma St. 1985) 1999, 2000RR	2	4	2	0	0	0	0	1
TOTAL	12	10	12	0	0	0	0	1

UCLA*
John Wooden (Purdue 1932) 1950RR, 52, 56, 62-4th, 63, 64-CH, 65-CH, 67-CH, 68-CH, 69-CH, 70-CH, 71-CH, 72-CH, 73-CH, 74-3d, 75-CH	16	47	10	10	0	1	1	1
Gene Bartow (Truman 1953) 1976-3d, 77	2	5	2	0	0	1	0	0
Gary Cunningham (UCLA 1962) 1978, 79RR	2	3	2	0	0	0	0	1
Larry Brown (North Carolina 1963) 1980-2d, 81	2	5	2	0	1	0	0	0

	Yrs.	Won	Lost	CH	2D	3d%	4th	RR
Larry Farmer (UCLA 1973) 1983	1	0	1	0	0	0	0	0
Walt Hazzard (UCLA 1964) 1987	1	1	1	0	0	0	0	0
Jim Harrick [Charleston (W.Va.) 1960] 1989, 90, 91, 92RR, 93, 94, 95-CH, 96	8	13	7	1	0	0	0	1
Steve Lavin (Chapman 1988) 1997RR, 98, 99, 2000, 01	5	9	5	0	0	0	0	1
TOTAL	37	83	30	11	1	2	1	4

UTAH
	Yrs.	Won	Lost	CH	2D	3d%	4th	RR
Vadal Petersen (Utah 1920) 1944-CH, 45RR	2	3	2	1	0	0	0	1
Jack Gardner (Southern California 1932) 1955, 56RR, 59, 60, 61-4th, 66-4th	6	8	9	0	0	0	2	1
Jerry Pimm (Southern California 1960) 1977, 78, 79, 81, 83	5	5	5	0	0	0	0	0
Lynn Archibald (Fresno St. 1968) 1986	1	0	1	0	0	0	0	0
Rick Majerus (Marquette 1970) 1991, 93, 95, 96, 97RR, 98-2d, 99, 2000	8	16	8	0	1	0	0	1
TOTAL	22	32	25	1	1	0	2	3

UTAH ST.
	Yrs.	Won	Lost	CH	2D	3d%	4th	RR
E.L. "Dick" Romney (Utah 1917) 1939RR	1	1	0	0	0	0	0	1
Ladell Andersen (Utah St. 1951) 1962, 63, 64, 70RR, 71	5	4	7	0	0	0	0	1
Gordon "Dutch" Belnap (Utah St. 1958) 1975, 79	2	0	2	0	0	0	0	0
Rod Tueller (Utah St. 1959) 1980, 83, 88	3	0	3	0	0	0	0	0
Larry Eustachy (Long Beach St. 1979) 1998	1	0	1	0	0	0	0	0
Steve Morrill (Gonzaga 1974) 2000, 01	2	1	2	0	0	0	0	0
TOTAL	14	6	16	0	0	0	0	2

UTEP
	Yrs.	Won	Lost	CH	2D	3d%	4th	RR
Don Haskins (Oklahoma St. 1953) 1963, 64, 66-CH, 67, 70, 75, 84, 85, 86, 87, 88, 89, 90, 92	14	14	13	1	0	0	0	0
TOTAL	14	14	13	1	0	0	0	0

VALPARAISO
	Yrs.	Won	Lost	CH	2D	3d%	4th	RR
Homer Drew (William Jewell 1966) 1996, 97, 98, 99, 2000	5	2	5	0	0	0	0	0
TOTAL	5	2	5	0	0	0	0	0

VANDERBILT
	Yrs.	Won	Lost	CH	2D	3d%	4th	RR
Roy Skinner (Presbyterian 1952) 1965RR, 74	2	1	3	0	0	0	0	1
C.M. Newton (Kentucky 1952) 1988, 89	2	2	2	0	0	0	0	0
Eddie Fogler (North Carolina 1970) 1991, 93	2	2	2	0	0	0	0	0
Jan van Breda Kolff (Vanderbilt 1974) 1997	1	0	1	0	0	0	0	0
TOTAL	7	5	8	0	0	0	0	1

VILLANOVA*
	Yrs.	Won	Lost	CH	2D	3d%	4th	RR
Alex Severance (Villanova 1929) 1939-T3d, 49RR, 51, 55	4	4	4	0	0	1	0	1
Jack Kraft (St. Joseph's 1942) 1962RR, 64, 69, 70RR, 71-2d, 72	6	11	7	0	1	0	0	2
Rollie Massimino (Vermont 1956) 1978RR, 80, 81, 82RR, 83RR, 84, 85-CH, 86, 88RR, 90, 91	11	20	10	1	0	0	0	4
Steve Lappas (CCNY 1977) 1995, 96, 97, 99	4	2	4	0	0	0	0	0
TOTAL	25	37	25	1	1	1	0	7

VIRGINIA
	Yrs.	Won	Lost	CH	2D	3d%	4th	RR
Terry Holland (Davidson 1964) 1976, 81-3d, 82, 83RR, 84-T3d, 86, 87, 89RR, 90	9	15	9	0	0	2	0	2
Jeff Jones (Virginia 1982) 1991, 93, 94, 95RR, 97	5	6	5	0	0	0	0	1
Pete Gillen (Fairfield 1968) 2001	1	0	1	0	0	0	0	0
TOTAL	15	21	15	0	0	2	0	3

VA. COMMONWEALTH
	Yrs.	Won	Lost	CH	2D	3d%	4th	RR
J.D. Barnett (Winona St. 1966) 1980, 81, 83, 84, 85	5	4	5	0	0	0	0	0
Sonny Smith (Milligan 1958) 1996	1	0	1	0	0	0	0	0
TOTAL	6	4	6	0	0	0	0	0

VMI
	Yrs.	Won	Lost	CH	2D	3d%	4th	RR
Louis "Weenie" Miller (Richmond 1947) 1964	1	0	1	0	0	0	0	0
Bill Blair (VMI 1964) 1976RR	1	2	1	0	0	0	0	1
Charlie Schmaus (VMI 1966) 1977	1	1	1	0	0	0	0	0
TOTAL	3	3	3	0	0	0	0	1

VIRGINIA TECH
	Yrs.	Won	Lost	CH	2D	3d%	4th	RR
Howard Shannon (Kansas St. 1948) 1967RR	1	2	1	0	0	0	0	1
Don DeVoe (Ohio St. 1964) 1976	1	0	1	0	0	0	0	0
Charles Moir (Appalachian St. 1952) 1979, 80, 85, 86	4	2	4	0	0	0	0	0

	Yrs.	Won	Lost	CH	2D	3d%	4th	RR
Bill C. Foster (Carson-Newman 1958) 1996	1	1	1	0	0	0	0	0
TOTAL	7	5	7	0	0	0	0	1

WAKE FOREST
	Yrs.	Won	Lost	CH	2D	3d%	4th	RR
Murray Greason (Wake Forest 1926) 1939RR, 53	2	1	2	0	0	0	0	1
Horace "Bones" McKinney (North Carolina 1946) 1961RR, 62-3d	2	6	2	0	0	1	0	1
Carl Tacy (Davis & Elkins 1956) 1977RR, 81, 82, 84RR	4	5	4	0	0	0	0	2
Dave Odom (Guilford 1965) 1991, 92, 93, 94, 95, 96RR, 97, 2001	8	10	8	0	0	0	0	1
TOTAL	16	22	16	0	0	1	0	5

WASHINGTON
	Yrs.	Won	Lost	CH	2D	3d%	4th	RR
Clarence "Hec" Edmundson (Idaho 1909) 1943RR	1	0	1	0	0	0	0	1
Art McLarney (Washington St. 1932) 1948RR	1	1	1	0	0	0	0	1
William "Tippy" Dye (Ohio St. 1937) 1951RR, 53-3d	2	5	2	0	0	1	0	1
Marv Harshman (Pacific Lutheran 1942) 1976, 84, 85	3	2	3	0	0	0	0	0
Andy Russo (Lake Forest 1970) 1986	1	0	1	0	0	0	0	0
Bob Bender (Duke 1980) 1998, 99	2	2	2	0	0	0	0	0
TOTAL	10	10	11	0	0	1	0	3

WASHINGTON ST.
	Yrs.	Won	Lost	CH	2D	3d%	4th	RR
Jack Friel (Washington St. 1923) 1941-2d	1	2	1	0	1	0	0	0
George Raveling (Villanova 1960) 1980, 83	2	1	2	0	0	0	0	0
Kelvin Sampson (UNC Pembroke 1978) 1994	1	0	1	0	0	0	0	0
TOTAL	4	3	4	0	1	0	0	0

WAYNE ST. (MICH.)
	Yrs.	Won	Lost	CH	2D	3d%	4th	RR
Joel Mason (Western Mich. 1936) 1956	1	1	2	0	0	0	0	0
TOTAL	1	1	2	0	0	0	0	0

WEBER ST.
	Yrs.	Won	Lost	CH	2D	3d%	4th	RR
Dick Motta (Utah St. 1953) 1968	1	0	1	0	0	0	0	0
Phil Johnson (Utah St. 1953) 1969, 70, 71	3	2	3	0	0	0	0	0
Gene Visscher (Weber St. 1966) 1972, 73	2	1	3	0	0	0	0	0
Neil McCarthy (Sacramento St. 1965) 1978, 79, 80, 83	4	1	4	0	0	0	0	0
Ron Abegglen (Brigham Young 1962) 1995, 99	2	2	2	0	0	0	0	0
TOTAL	12	6	13	0	0	0	0	0

WEST TEXAS A&M
	Yrs.	Won	Lost	CH	2D	3d%	4th	RR
W.A. "Gus" Miller (West Texas A&M 1927) 1955	1	0	1	0	0	0	0	0
TOTAL	1	0	1	0	0	0	0	0

WEST VIRGINIA
	Yrs.	Won	Lost	CH	2D	3d%	4th	RR
Fred Schaus (West Virginia 1949) 1955, 56, 57, 58, 59-2d, 60	6	6	6	0	1	0	0	0
George King [Charleston (W.Va.) 1950] 1962, 63, 65	3	2	3	0	0	0	0	0
Raymond "Bucky" Waters (North Carolina St. 1957) 1967	1	0	1	0	0	0	0	0
Gale Catlett (West Virginia 1963) 1982, 83, 84, 86, 87, 89, 92, 98	8	5	8	0	0	0	0	0
TOTAL	18	13	18	0	1	0	0	0

WESTERN CARO.
	Yrs.	Won	Lost	CH	2D	3d%	4th	RR
Phil Hopkins (Gardner-Webb 1972) 1996	1	0	1	0	0	0	0	0
TOTAL	1	0	1	0	0	0	0	0

WESTERN KY.*
	Yrs.	Won	Lost	CH	2D	3d%	4th	RR
Ed Diddle (Centre 1921) 1940RR, 60, 62	3	3	4	0	0	0	0	1
Johnny Oldham (Western Ky. 1948) 1966, 67, 70, 71-3d	4	6	4	0	0	1	0	0
Jim Richards (Western Ky. 1959) 1976, 78	2	1	2	0	0	0	0	0
Gene Keady (Kansas St. 1958) 1980	1	0	1	0	0	0	0	0
Clem Haskins (Western Ky. 1967) 1981, 86	2	1	2	0	0	0	0	0
Murray Arnold (American 1960) 1987	1	1	1	0	0	0	0	0
Ralph Willard (Holy Cross 1967) 1993, 94	2	2	2	0	0	0	0	0
Matt Kilcullen (Lehman 1976) 1995	1	1	1	0	0	0	0	0
Dennis Felton (Howard 1985) 2001	1	0	1	0	0	0	0	0
TOTAL	17	15	18	0	0	1	0	1

WESTERN MICH.
	Yrs.	Won	Lost	CH	2D	3d%	4th	RR
Eldon Miller (Wittenberg 1961) 1976	1	1	1	0	0	0	0	0
Bob Donewald (Hanover 1964) 1998	1	1	1	0	0	0	0	0
TOTAL	2	2	2	0	0	0	0	0

TEAM-BY-TEAM WON-LOST RECORDS—BY COACH

	Yrs.	Won	Lost	CH	2D	3d%	4th	RR
WICHITA ST.								
Ralph Miller (Kansas 1942) 1964RR	1	1	1	0	0	0	0	1
Gary Thompson (Wichita St. 1954) 1965-4th	1	2	2	0	0	0	1	0
Harry Miller (Eastern N.M. 1951) 1976	1	0	1	0	0	0	0	0
Gene Smithson (North Central 1961) 1981RR, 85	2	3	2	0	0	0	0	1
Eddie Fogler (North Carolina 1970) 1987, 88	2	0	2	0	0	0	0	0
TOTAL	7	6	8	0	0	0	1	2
WILLIAMS								
Alex Shaw (Michigan 1932) 1955	1	0	1	0	0	0	0	0
TOTAL	1	0	1	0	0	0	0	0
WINTHROP								
Gregg Marshall (Randolph-Macon 1985) 1999, 2000, 01	3	0	3	0	0	0	0	0
TOTAL	3	0	3	0	0	0	0	0
WISCONSIN								
Harold "Bud" Foster (Wisconsin 1930) 1941-CH, 47RR	2	4	1	1	0	0	0	1
Stu Jackson (Seattle 1978) 1994	1	1	1	0	0	0	0	0
Dick Bennett (Ripon 1965) 1997, 99, 2000-T-3d	3	4	3	0	0	1	0	0
Brad Soderberg (Wis.-Stevens Point 1985) 2001	1	0	1	0	0	0	0	0
TOTAL	7	9	6	1	0	1	0	1
WIS.-GREEN BAY								
Dick Bennett (Ripon 1965) 1991, 94, 95	3	1	3	0	0	0	0	0
Mike Heideman (Wis.-La Crosse 1971) 1996	1	0	1	0	0	0	0	0
TOTAL	4	1	4	0	0	0	0	0
WRIGHT ST.								
Ralph Underhill (Tennessee Tech 1964) 1993	1	0	1	0	0	0	0	0
TOTAL	1	0	1	0	0	0	0	0

	Yrs.	Won	Lost	CH	2D	3d%	4th	RR
WYOMING								
Everett Shelton (Phillips 1923) 1941RR, 43-CH, 47RR, 48RR, 49RR, 52RR, 53, 58	8	4	12	1	0	0	0	5
Bill Strannigan (Wyoming 1941) 1967	1	0	2	0	0	0	0	0
Jim Brandenburg (Colorado St. 1958) 1981, 82, 87	3	4	3	0	0	0	0	0
Benny Dees (Wyoming 1958) 1988	1	0	1	0	0	0	0	0
TOTAL	13	8	18	1	0	0	0	5
XAVIER								
Jim McCafferty [Loyola (La.) 1942] 1961	1	0	1	0	0	0	0	0
Bob Staak (Connecticut 1971) 1983	1	0	1	0	0	0	0	0
Pete Gillen (Fairfield 1968) 1986, 87, 88, 89, 90, 91, 93	7	5	7	0	0	0	0	0
Skip Prosser (Merchant Marine 1972) 1995, 97, 98, 2001	4	1	4	0	0	0	0	0
TOTAL	13	6	13	0	0	0	0	0
YALE								
Howard Hobson (Oregon 1926) 1949RR	1	0	2	0	0	0	0	1
Joe Vancisin (Dartmouth 1944) 1957, 62	2	0	2	0	0	0	0	0
TOTAL	3	0	4	0	0	0	0	1

%National 3d-place games did not start until 1946 and ended with 1981; in other years, two teams tied for third and both listed this column. RR Regional runner-up, or one victory from Final Four, thus in the top eight.

NOTES ON TEAMS AND COACHES:
MICHIGAN: Steve Fisher coached Michigan in the 1989 tournament; Bill Freider was the coach during the regular season.
MISSOURI: Rich Daly coached Missouri in the 1989 tournament due to Norm Stewart's illness; Missouri credits the entire 1989 season to Stewart.
PRINCETON: J.L. McCandless coached Princeton in the 1961 tournament; Franklin Cappon suffered a heart attack 11 games into the season; Princeton credits the 1961 regular season to Cappon and the postseason to McCandless.
SEATTLE: Clair Markey coached Seattle in the 1963 tournament due to Vince Cazetta's resignation.

* TEAMS VACATING NCAA TOURNAMENT ACTION

Teams	Years	Record	Placing	Conference
Alabama	1987	2-1		Southeastern
Arizona	1999	0-1		Pacific 10
Arizona St.	1995	2-1		Pacific 10
Austin Peay	1973	1-2		Ohio Valley
California	1996	0-1		Pacific 10
Clemson	1990	2-1		Atlantic Coast
Connecticut	1996	2-1		Big East
DePaul	1986-89	6-4		Independent
Florida	1987-88	3-2		Southeastern
Georgia	1985	1-1		Southeastern
Iona	1980	1-1		Independent
Kentucky	1988	2-1		Southeastern
Long Beach St.	1971-73	6-3	2 RR	Pacific Coast
La.-Lafayette	1972-73	3-3		Southland
Loyola Marymount	1980	0-1		West Coast
Marshall	1987	0-1		Southern
Maryland	1988	1-1		Atlantic Coast
Massachusetts	1996	4-1	3d	Atlantic 10
Memphis	1982-86	9-5	3d	Metro
Minnesota	1972, 94-95, 97	6-4	3d	Big Ten
Missouri	1994	3-1	RR	Big Eight
New Mexico	1992-94	3-3		Big West
North Carolina St.	1987-88	0-2		Atlantic Coast
Oregon St.	1980-82	2-3	RR	Pacific 10
Purdue	1996	1-1		Big Ten
St. Joseph's	1961	3-1	3d	Middle Atlantic
Texas Tech	1996	2-1		Southwest
UCLA	1980, 99	5-2	2d	Pacific 10
Villanova	1971	4-1	2d	Independent
Western Ky.	1971	4-1	3d	Ohio Valley
30 schools	50 years	78-52	2 2d, 5 3d, 4 RR	

Official NCAA Records	Yrs	Won	Lost	CH	2d	3d	4th	RR
Alabama	13	13	13	0	0	0	0	2
Arizona	19	32	18	1	1	2	0	2
Arizona St.	10	9	11	0	0	0	0	3
Austin Peay	3	1	3	0	0	0	0	0
California	10	16	10	1	1	0	1	2
Clemson	6	6	6	0	0	0	0	1
Connecticut	21	25	21	1	0	0	0	4
DePaul	17	14	20	0	0	2	0	1
Florida	6	12	6	0	0	1	0	0
Georgia	7	5	7	0	0	1	0	0
Iona	6	0	6	0	0	0	0	0
Kentucky	42	87	37	7	3	3	0	16
Long Beach St.	4	1	5	0	0	0	0	0
La.-Lafayette	5	1	5	0	0	0	0	0
Loyola Marymount	4	5	4	0	0	0	0	0
Marshall	4	0	4	0	0	0	0	0
Maryland	17	25	17	0	0	1	0	2
Massachusetts	7	7	7	0	0	0	0	1
Memphis	11	9	11	0	1	0	0	1
Minnesota	4	6	4	0	0	0	0	1
Missouri	17	10	17	0	0	0	0	2
New Mexico St.	13	7	15	0	0	0	1	0
North Carolina St.	15	27	14	2	0	1	0	3
Oregon St.	13	10	16	0	0	0	2	4
Purdue	18	25	18	0	1	1	0	2
St. Joseph's	15	12	19	0	0	0	0	0
Texas Tech	9	3	10	0	0	0	0	0
UCLA	35	78	28	11	0	2	1	4
Villanova	24	33	24	1	0	1	0	7
Western Ky.	16	11	17	0	0	0	0	1

Tournament Moments...

Photo by Paul Jones

March 23, 1962, national semifinal game in the Freedom Hall in Louisville, Kentucky – Tom Thacker scored the game-winnner as Cincinnati defeated UCLA, 72-70. The Bearcats beat Ohio State in the championship game to earn their second consecutive title.

The Coaches

Coaches Records 86
Coaches with Accomplished Records..................... 87
Coaches Who Have Played and Coached
   in the Final Four and Tournament 88
Coaches of All-Time 90

Coaches Records

Won-Lost Records of Champions

Year	Champion	Coach	W-L	Pct.
1939	Oregon	Howard Hobson	29-5	.853
1940	Indiana	Branch McCracken	20-3	.870
1941	Wisconsin	Harold Foster	20-3	.870
1942	Stanford	Everett Dean	28-4	.875
1943	Wyoming	Everett Shelton	31-2	.939
1944	Utah	Vadal Peterson	21-4	.840
1945	Oklahoma St.	Henry Iba	27-4	.871
1946	Oklahoma St.	Henry Iba	31-2	.939
1947	Holy Cross	Doggie Julian	27-3	.900
1948	Kentucky	Adolph Rupp	36-3	.923
1949	Kentucky	Adolph Rupp	32-2	.941
1950	CCNY	Nat Holman	24-5	.828
1951	Kentucky	Adolph Rupp	32-2	.941
1952	Kansas	Phog Allen	28-3	.903
1953	Indiana	Branch McCracken	23-3	.885
1954	La Salle	Ken Loeffler	26-4	.867
1955	San Francisco	Phil Woolpert	28-1	.966
1956	San Francisco	Phil Woolpert	29-0	1.000
1957	North Carolina	Frank McGuire	32-0	1.000
1958	Kentucky	Adolph Rupp	23-6	.793
1959	California	Pete Newell	25-4	.862
1960	Ohio St.	Fred Taylor	25-3	.893
1961	Cincinnati	Ed Jucker	27-3	.900
1962	Cincinnati	Ed Jucker	29-2	.935
1963	Loyola (Ill.)	George Ireland	29-2	.935
1964	UCLA	John Wooden	30-0	1.000
1965	UCLA	John Wooden	28-2	.933
1966	UTEP	Don Haskins	28-1	.966
1967	UCLA	John Wooden	30-0	1.000
1968	UCLA	John Wooden	29-1	.967
1969	UCLA	John Wooden	29-1	.967
1970	UCLA	John Wooden	28-2	.933
1971	UCLA	John Wooden	29-1	.967
1972	UCLA	John Wooden	30-0	1.000
1973	UCLA	John Wooden	30-0	1.000
1974	North Carolina St.	Norm Sloan	30-1	.968
1975	UCLA	John Wooden	28-3	.903
1976	Indiana	Bob Knight	32-0	1.000
1977	Marquette	Al McGuire	25-7	.781
1978	Kentucky	Joe B. Hall	30-2	.938
1979	Michigan St.	Jud Heathcote	26-6	.813
1980	Louisville	Denny Crum	33-3	.917
1981	Indiana	Bob Knight	26-9	.743
1982	North Carolina	Dean Smith	32-2	.941
1983	North Carolina St.	Jim Valvano	26-10	.722
1984	Georgetown	John Thompson	34-3	.919
1985	Villanova	Rollie Massimino	25-10	.714
1986	Louisville	Denny Crum	32-7	.821
1987	Indiana	Bob Knight	30-4	.882
1988	Kansas	Larry Brown	27-11	.711
1989	Michigan	Steve Fisher	30-7	.811
1990	UNLV	Jerry Tarkanian	35-5	.875
1991	Duke	Mike Krzyzewski	32-7	.821
1992	Duke	Mike Krzyzewski	34-2	.944
1993	North Carolina	Dean Smith	34-4	.895
1994	Arkansas	Nolan Richardson	31-3	.912
1995	UCLA	Jim Harrick	31-2	.939
1996	Kentucky	Rick Pitino	34-2	.944
1997	Arizona	Lute Olson	25-9	.735
1998	Kentucky	Tubby Smith	35-4	.897
1999	Connecticut	Jim Calhoun	34-2	.944
2000	Michigan St.	Tom Izzo	32-7	.821
2001	Duke	Mike Krzyzewski	35-4	.897

Final Four Records

Note: Records adjusted for vacated games.

NCAA CHAMPIONSHIPS
- 10, John Wooden, UCLA, 1964-75
- 4, Adolph Rupp, Kentucky, 1948-58
- 3, Bob Knight, Indiana, 1976-87
- 3, Mike Krzyzewski, Duke, 1991-2001
- 2, Denny Crum, Louisville, 1980-86
- 2, Henry Iba, Oklahoma St., 1945-46
- 2, Ed Jucker, Cincinnati, 1961-62
- 2, Branch McCracken, Indiana, 1940-53
- 2, Dean Smith, North Carolina, 1982-93
- 2, Phil Woolpert, San Francisco, 1955-56

FINAL FOUR APPEARANCES
- 12, John Wooden, UCLA, 1962-75
- 11, Dean Smith, North Carolina, 1967-97
- 9, Mike Krzyzewski, Duke, 1986-2001
- 6, Denny Crum, Louisville, 1972-86
- 6, Adolph Rupp, Kentucky, 1942-66
- 5, Bob Knight, Indiana, 1973-92
- 5, Guy Lewis, Houston, 1967-84
- 5, Lute Olson, Iowa and Arizona, 1980-2001
- 4, Jack Gardner, Kansas St. and Utah, 1948-66
- 4, Henry Iba, Oklahoma St., 1945-51
- 4, Harold Olsen, Ohio St., 1939-46
- 4, Jerry Tarkanian, UNLV, 1977-91
- 4, Fred Taylor, Ohio St., 1960-68

Tournament trivia

Question...
What three coaches ended their college coaching careers by winning the NCAA championship?

Answer...
John Wooden (UCLA 1975), Al McGuire (Marquette 1977) and Larry Brown (Kansas 1988).

CONSECUTIVE FINAL FOUR APPEARANCES
- 9, John Wooden, UCLA, 1967-75
- 5, Mike Krzyzewski, Duke, 1988-92
- 3, Tom Izzo, Michgan St., 1999-2001
- 3, Ed Jucker, Cincinnati, 1961-63
- 3, Guy Lewis, Houston, 1982-84
- 3, Harold Olsen, Ohio St., 1944-46
- 3, Dean Smith, North Carolina, 1967-69
- 3, Fred Taylor, Ohio St., 1960-62
- 3, Phil Woolpert, San Francisco, 1955-57
- 2, 18 tied

FINAL FOUR WINS
- 21, John Wooden, UCLA, 1962-75
- 10, Mike Krzyzewski, Duke, 1988-2001
- 9, Adolph Rupp, Kentucky, 1942-66
- 8, Dean Smith, North Carolina, 1967-97
- 7, Bob Knight, Indiana, 1973-87
- 5, Denny Crum, Louisville, 1972-86
- 5, Henry Iba, Oklahoma St., 1945-51
- 5, Ed Jucker, Cincinnati, 1961-63
- 5, Fred Taylor, Ohio St., 1960-68
- 5, Phil Woolpert, San Francisco, 1955-57

FINAL FOUR WINNING PERCENTAGE
(Minimum 3 games)
- 1.000 (4-0), Branch McCracken, Indiana, 1940-53
- .875 (21-3), John Wooden, UCLA, 1962-75
- .833 (5-1), Ed Jucker, Cincinnati, 1961-63
- .833 (5-1), Phil Woolpert, San Francisco, 1955-57
- .818 (9-2), Adolph Rupp, Kentucky, 1942-66
- .778 (7-2), Bob Knight, Indiana, 1973-92
- .750 (3-1), Doggie Julian, Holy Cross, 1947-48
- .750 (3-1), Ken Loeffler, La Salle, 1954-55
- .750 (3-1), Al McGuire, Marquette, 1974-77
- .750 (3-1), Frank McGuire, St. John's (N.Y.) and North Carolina, 1952-57
- .750 (3-1), Pete Newell, California, 1959-60

Tournament Records

TOURNAMENT APPEARANCES
- 27, Dean Smith, North Carolina, 1967-97
- 24, Bob Knight, Indiana, 1973-2000
- 23, Denny Crum, Louisville, 1972-2000
- 21, Jim Boeheim, Syracuse, 1977-2001
- 21, Lute Olson, Iowa and Arizona, 1979-2001
- 21, Eddie Sutton, Creighton, Arkansas, Kentucky and Oklahoma St., 1974-2001
- 20, John Thompson, Georgetown, 1975-97
- 20, Adolph Rupp, Kentucky, 1942-72
- 19, Lou Henson, Illinois and New Mexico St., 1967-99
- 18, Lou Carnesecca, St. John's (N.Y.), 1967-92

CONSECUTIVE TOURNAMENT APPEARANCES
- 23, Dean Smith, North Carolina, 1975-97
- 17, Lute Olson, Arizona, 1985-2001
- 15, Bob Knight, Indiana, 1986-2000
- 14, John Thompson, Georgetown, 1979-92
- 12, John Chaney, Temple, 1990-2001
- 12, Roy Williams, Kansas, 1990-2001
- 11, Mike Krzyzewski, Duke, 1984-94
- 11, Eddie Sutton, Arkansas and Kentucky, 1977-87
- 10, Jim Boeheim, Syracuse, 1983-92
- 10, Dale Brown, LSU, 1984-93
- 10, Bob Huggins, Cincinnati, 1992-2001

TOURNAMENT WINS
- 65, Dean Smith, North Carolina, 1967-97
- 56, Mike Krzyzewski, Duke, 1984-2001
- 47, John Wooden, UCLA, 1950-75
- 42, Denny Crum, Louisville, 1972-2000
- 42, Bob Knight, Indiana, 1973-2000
- 37, Lute Olson, Iowa and Arizona, 1979-2001
- 34, John Thompson, Georgetown, 1975-97
- 32, Jim Boeheim, Syracuse, 1977-2001
- 32, Jerry Tarkanian, Long Beach St. and UNLV and Fresno St. 1970-2001
- 30, Adolph Rupp, Kentucky, 1942-72
- 30, Eddie Sutton, Creighton, Arkansas, Kentucky and Oklahoma St., 1974-2001

TOURNAMENT WINNING PERCENTAGE
(Minimum 10 games)
- .917 (11-1), Ed Jucker, Cincinnati, 1961-63
- .900 (9-1), Ken Loeffler, La Salle, 1954-55
- .867 (13-2), Phil Woolpert, San Francisco, 1955-58
- .842 (16-3), Tom Izzo, Michigan St., 1998-2001
- .825 (47-10), John Wooden, UCLA, 1950-75
- .818 (9-2), Branch McCracken, Indiana, 1940-58
- .800 (56-14), Mike Krzyzewski, Duke, 1984-2001
- .788 (26-7), Rick Pitino, Boston U., Providence and Kentucky, 1983-97

COACHES RECORDS—TOURNAMENT RECORDS

.778 (14-4), Fred Taylor, Ohio St., 1960-71
.769 (20-6), Steve Fisher, Michigan, 1989-96
.769 (10-3), Phog Allen, Kansas, 1940-53
.769 (10-3), Pete Newell, California, 1957-60

Tournament Records—Active Coaches

MOST TOURNAMENT APPEARANCES
21, Jim Boeheim, Syracuse, 1977-2001
21, Lute Olson, Iowa and Arizona, 1979-2001
21, Eddie Sutton, Creighton, Arkansas, Kentucky, and Oklahoma St., 1974-2001
19, Lou Henson, Illinois and New Mexico St., 1967-99
17, John Chaney, Temple, 1984-2001
17, Mike Krzyzewski, Duke, 1984-2001
16, Gene Keady, Western Ky. and Purdue, 1980-2000
16, Nolan Richardson, Tulsa and Arkansas, 1982-2001
15, Jim Harrick, Pepperdine, UCLA, Rhode Island and Georgia, 1982-2001
15, Jerry Tarkanian, Long Beach St., UNLV and Fresno St., 1970-2001
13, Jim Calhoun, Northeastern and Connecticut, 1981-2000
13, Lefty Driesell, Davidson, Maryland, James Madison and Georgia St., 1966-2001

MOST CONSECUTIVE TOURNAMENT APPEARANCES
17, Lute Olson, Arizona, 1985-2001
12, John Chaney, Temple, 1990-2001
12, Roy Williams, Kansas, 1990-2001
11, Mike Krzyzewski, Duke, 1984-94
11, Eddie Sutton, Arkansas and Kentucky, 1977-87
10, Jim Boeheim, Syracuse, 1983-92
10, Bob Huggins, Cincinnati, 1992-2001
9, Nolan Richardson, Arkansas, 1988-96
9, Jerry Tarkanian, UNLV, 1983-91
8, Jim Harrick, UCLA, 1989-96
8, Lou Henson, Illinois, 1983-90
8, Gene Keady, Purdue, 1993-2000
8, Kelvin Sampson, Washington St. and Oklahoma, 1994-2001
8, Tubby Smith, Tulsa, Georgia and Kentucky, 1994-2001
8, Gary Williams, Maryland, 1994-2001

CURRENT CONSECUTIVE TOURNAMENT APPEARANCES
17, Lute Olson, Arizona, 1985-2001
12, John Chaney, Temple, 1990-2001
12, Roy Williams, Kansas, 1990-2001
10, Bob Huggins, Cincinnati, 1992-2001
8, Kelvin Sampson, Washington St. and Oklahoma, 1994-2001
8, Tubby Smith, Tulsa, Georgia and Kentucky, 1994-2001
8, Gary Williams, Maryland, 1994-2001
7, Mike Montgomery, Stanford, 1995-2001
6, Mike Krzyzewski, Duke, 1996-2001
5, Steve Lavin, UCLA, 1997-2001

MOST TOURNAMENT WINS
56, Mike Krzyzewski, Duke, 1984-2001
37, Lute Olson, Iowa and Arizona, 1979-2001
32, Jim Boeheim, Syracuse, 1976-2001
32, Jerry Tarkanian, Long Beach St., UNLV and Fresno St., 1970-2001
30, Eddie Sutton, Creighton, Arkansas, Kentucky and Oklahoma St., 1974-2001
26, Nolan Richardson, Tulsa and Arkansas, 1982-2001
25, Roy Williams, Kansas, 1990-2001
24, Jim Calhoun, Northeastern and Connecticut, 1981-2000
23, John Chaney, Temple, 1984-2001
20, Steve Fisher, Michigan, 1989-96
20, Rollie Massimino, Villanova, 1978-91

HIGHEST TOURNAMENT WINNING PERCENTAGE (Minimum 10 games)
.842 (16-3), Tom Izzo, Michigan St., 1998-2001
.800 (56-14), Mike Krzyzewski, Duke, 1984-2001
.788 (26-7), Rick Pitino, Boston U., Providence and Kentucky, 1983-97
.769 (20-6), Steve Fisher, Michigan, 1989-96
.727 (8-3), Billy Donovan, Florida, 1999-2001
.720 (18-7), Tubby Smith, Tulsa, Georgia and Kentucky, 1994-2001
.700 (7-3), Bill Self, Tulsa and Illinois, 1999-2001
.692 (9-4), Steve Lavin, UCLA, 1997-2001
.681 (32-15), Jerry Tarkanian, Long Beach St., UNLV and Fresno St., 1970-2001
.676 (25-12), Roy Williams, Kansas, 1990-2001

Note: Records adjusted for vacated games except for streaks.

Coaches with Accomplished Records

Two Different Teams Taken to the Final Four

Coach	First Team	Second Team
Forddy Anderson	Bradley	Michigan St.
Gene Bartow	Memphis	UCLA
Larry Brown	UCLA	Kansas
† Hugh Durham	Florida St.	Georgia
Jack Gardner	Kansas St.	Utah
Lou Henson	New Mexico St.	Illinois
Frank McGuire	St. John's (N.Y.)	North Carolina
† Lute Olson	Iowa	Arizona
† Rick Pitino	Providence	Kentucky
Lee Rose	Charlotte	Purdue
† Eddie Sutton	Arkansas	Oklahoma St.

Four Different Teams Taken to the Tournament

Coach	First Team	Second Team	Third Team	Fourth Team
† Lefty Driesell	Davidson	Maryland	James Madison	Georgia St.
† Jim Harrick	Pepperdine	UCLA	Rhode Island	Georgia
† Eddie Sutton	Creighton	Arkansas	Kentucky	Oklahoma St.

Three Different Teams Taken to the Tournament

Coach	First Team	Second Team	Third Team
†Rick Barnes	Providence	Clemson	Texas
Gene Bartow	Memphis	UCLA	UAB
† Dave Bliss	Oklahoma	Southern Methodist	New Mexico
†Mike Deane	Siena	Marquette	Lamar
† Don DeVoe	Virginia Tech	Tennessee	Navy
†Cliff Ellis	South Ala.	Clemson	Auburn
† Eddie Fogler	Wichita St.	Vanderbilt	South Carolina
†Pete Gillen	Xavier	Providence	Virginia
Eddie Hickey	Creighton	St. Louis	Marquette
†Mike Jarvis	Boston U.	George Washington	St. John's (N.Y.)
†Pat Kennedy	Iona	Florida St.	DePaul
Lon Kruger	Kansas St.	Florida	Illinois
Frank McGuire	St. John's (N.Y.)	North Carolina	South Carolina
Eldon Miller	Western Mich.	Ohio St.	Northern Iowa
Ralph Miller	Wichita St.	Iowa	Oregon St.
† Stan Morrison	Pacific (Cal.)	Southern California	San Jose St.
Tom Penders	Rhode Island	Texas	George Washington
† Rick Pitino	Boston U.	Providence	Kentucky
George Raveling	Washington St.	Iowa	Southern California
† Tubby Smith	Tulsa	Georgia	Kentucky
†Jerry Tarkanian	Long Beach St.	UNLV	Fresno St.
† Billy Tubbs	Lamar	Oklahoma	TCU
† Bob Weltlich	Mississippi	Florida Int'l	South Ala.
† Gary Williams	Boston College	Ohio St.	Maryland
Joe Williams	Jacksonville	Furman	Florida St.

Two Different Teams Taken to the Tournament

Coach	First Team	Second Team
†Steve Alford	Southwest Mo. St.	Iowa
†Dana Altman	Kansas St.	Creighton
Ladell Andersen	Utah St.	Brigham Young
Forddy Anderson	Bradley	Michigan St.
Murray Arnold	Chattanooga	Western Ky.
Tom Asbury	Pepperdine	Kansas St.
† J.D. Barnett	Va. Commonwealth	Tulsa
†Jim Baron	St. Francis (Pa.)	St. Bonaventure
† John Beilein	Canisius	Richmond
Steve Belko	Idaho St.	Oregon
† Bob Bender	Illinois St.	Washington
† Dick Bennett	Wis.-Green Bay	Wisconsin
Bob Boyd	Seattle	Southern California
Harold Bradley	Duke	Texas
Buster Brannon	Rice	TCU
† Ben Braun	Eastern Wash.	California
†Mike Brey	Delaware	Notre Dame
Larry Brown	UCLA	Kansas
† Jim Calhoun	Northeastern	Connecticut
Lou Campanelli	James Madison	California

COACHES WITH ACCOMPLISHED RECORDS—TWO DIFFERENT TEAMS TAKEN TO THE TOURNAMENT

Coach	First Team	Second Team
Jeff Capel	N.C. A&T	Old Dominion
Ben Carnevale	North Carolina	Navy
† Gale Catlett	Cincinnati	West Virginia
† Charlie Coles	Central Mich.	Miami (Ohio)
Ozzie Cowles	Dartmouth	Michigan
Bobby Cremins	Appalachian St.	Georgia Tech
† Tom Davis	Boston College	Iowa
Benny Dees	New Orleans	Wyoming
Bob Donewald	Illinois St.	Western Mich.
† Hugh Durham	Florida St.	Georgia
Bob Dye	Cal St. Fullerton	Boise St.
Tippy Dye	Ohio St.	Washington
† Larry Eustachy	Utah St.	Iowa St.
Paul Evans	Navy	Pittsburgh
Tim Floyd	New Orleans	Iowa St.
† Bill C. Foster	Clemson	Virginia Tech
† Pat Foster	Lamar	Houston
Fran Fraschilla	Manhattan	St. John's (N.Y.)
Bill Frieder	Michigan	Arizona St.
Matt Furjanic	Robert Morris	Marist
Smokey Gaines	Detroit	San Diego St.
Jack Gardner	Kansas St.	Utah
Boyd Grant	Fresno St.	Colorado St.
† Jerry Green	Oregon	Tennessee
Jim Harding	Loyola (La.)	La Salle
† Clem Haskins	Western Ky.	Minnesota
Jud Heathcote	Montana	Michigan St.
† Lou Henson	New Mexico St.	Illinois
† Paul Hewitt	Siena	Georgia Tech
Howard Hobson	Oregon	Yale
Terry Holland	Davidson	Virginia
† Bob Huggins	Akron	Cincinnati
† Gene Iba	Houston Baptist	Baylor
Doggie Julian	Holy Cross	Dartmouth
† Gene Keady	Western Ky.	Purdue
† Ernie Kent	St. Mary's (Cal.)	Oregon
Jim Killingsworth	Idaho St.	TCU
George King	West Virginia	Purdue
Jack Kraft	Villanova	Rhode Island
Eugene Lambert	Arkansas	Memphis
Abe Lemons	Oklahoma City	Texas
Tates Locke	Miami (Ohio)	Jacksonville
† Rick Majerus	Ball St.	Utah
Jim McCafferty	Loyola (La.)	Xavier
† Fran McCaffery	Lehigh	UNC Greensboro
Neil McCarthy	Weber St.	New Mexico St.
† Jim Molinari	Northern Ill.	Bradley
† Steve Morrill	Montana	Utah St.
Bill Musselman	Minnesota	South Ala.
† Danny Nee	Ohio	Nebraska
C.M. Newton	Alabama	Vanderbilt
†Jim O'Brien	Boston College	Ohio St.
Johnny Oldham	Tennessee Tech	Western Ky.
† Lute Olson	Iowa	Arizona
Johnny Orr	Michigan	Iowa St.

Coach	First Team	Second Team
Bobby Paschal	La.-Lafayette	South Fla.
Digger Phelps	Fordham	Notre Dame
Jerry Pimm	Utah	UC Santa Barb.
† Skip Prosser	Loyola (Md.)	Xavier
† Oliver Purnell	Old Dominion	Dayton
† Nolan Richardson	Tulsa	Arkansas
Les Robinson	East Tenn. St.	North Carolina St.
† Steve Robinson	Tulsa	Florida St.
Lee Rose	Charlotte	Purdue
Lou Rossini	Columbia	New York U.
Andy Russo	Louisiana Tech	Washington
† Kelvin Sampson	Washington St.	Oklahoma
Fred Schaus	West Virginia	Purdue
Tom Schneider	Lehigh	Pennsylvania
† Bill Self	Tulsa	Illinois
† Al Skinner	Rhode Island	Boston College
Norm Sloan	North Carolina St.	Florida
Sonny Smith	Auburn	Va. Commonwealth
† Charlie Spoonhour	Southwest Mo. St.	St. Louis
Bill Strannigan	Colorado St.	Wyoming
Carl Tacy	Marshall	Wake Forest
Jim Valvano	Iona	North Carolina St.
† Jan van Breda Kolff	Vanderbilt	Pepperdine
Bob Vanatta	Bradley	Memphis
† Tim Welsh	Iona	Providence
† Bob Wenzel	Jacksonville	Rutgers
† Paul Westhead	La Salle	Loyola Marymount
† Ralph Willard	Western Ky.	Holy Cross
Tom Young	Rutgers	Old Dominion
Matt Zunic	Boston U.	Massachusetts

†active

Coaches Who Have Played and Coached in the Final Four and Tournament

Final Four

	Player	Coach
Vic Bubas	North Carolina St.: 1950-3d	Duke: 1963-3d, 64-2d, 66-3d
Billy Donovan	Providence: 1987-3d	Florida: 2000-2d
Dick Harp	Kansas: 1940-2d	Kansas: 1957-2d
Bob Knight	Ohio St.: 1960-CH, 61-2d, 62-2d	Indiana: 1973-3d, 76-CH, 81-CH, 87-CH, 92-T3d
Bones McKinney	North Carolina: 1946-2d	Wake Forest: 1962-3d
Dean Smith	Kansas: 1952-CH, 53-2d	North Carolina: 1967-4th, 68-2d, 69-4th, 72-3d, 77-2d, 81-2d, 82-CH, 91-T3d, 93-CH, 95-T3d, 97-T3d

Tournament

Coach	Played in NCAA Team-Years	G	FG-A	3FG-A	FT-A	RB	Pts.	Team W-L+	Finish
Stan Albeck	Bradley 1955	3	13		15		41	2-1	55-RR
Steve Alford	Indiana 1984, 86-87	10	67-133	21-34	58-64	26	213	8-2	84-RR, 87-CH
Tommy Amaker	Duke 1984-87	12	42-95	6-8	33-43	29	123	8-4	86-2d
Tom Apke	Creighton 1964	3	0-6		0-1	9	0	1-2	
Frank Arnold	Idaho St. 1955	1	0		0	0	0	0-1	
Tom Asbury	Wyoming 1967	2	11-28		4-7	16	26	0-2	
Randy Ayers	Miami (Ohio) 1978	2	16-24		6-7	18	38	1-1	
Tony Barone	Duke 1966	2	1-2		0-0	1	2	1-1	66-3d
Murry Bartow	UAB 1984-85	3	0-2		0	2	0	1-2	
Butch Beard	Louisville 1967-68	4	31-68		11-20	27	73	1-3	
Dan Belluomini	San Francisco 1964	1	0-0		0-0	1	0	0-1	
Bob Bender	Indiana 1976, Duke 78, 80	10	9-22		17-24	12	35	8-2	76-CH, 78-2d, 80-RR
Henry Bibby	UCLA 1970-72	12	70-154		42-47	53	182	12-0	70-CH, 71-CH, 72-CH
Bill Blair	VMI 1964	1	6-20		8-12	4	20	0-1	
Jim Boeheim	Syracuse 1966	2	13-19		3-4	4	29	1-1	66-RR
Jim Boyle	St. Joseph's 1962-63	5	26-60		16-19	35	68	2-3	63-RR
Jim Brovelli	San Francisco 1963-64	4	16-30		7-8	9	39	2-2	64-RR
Vic Bubas	North Carolina St. 1950	3	4-12		6-8		14	2-1	50-3d
Morris Buckwalter	Utah 1955-56	4	8		19		35	2-2	56-RR
Mitch Buonaguro	Boston College 1975	1	2-2		0-1	1	4	0-1	
P.J. Carlesimo	Fordham 1971	3	0-0		0-0	0	0	2-1	
Gale Catlett	West Virginia 1962-63	4	11-29		4-5	11	26	2-2	

Randy Ayers coached Ohio State from 1990-97. Ayers played in the NCAA tournament for Miami (Ohio) in 1978.

COACHES WHO HAVE PLAYED AND COACHED IN THE FINAL FOUR AND TOURNAMENT—TOURNAMENT

Coach	Played in NCAA Team-Years	G	FG-A	3FG-A	FT-A	RB	Pts.	Team W-L+	Finish
Jimmy Collins	New Mexico St. 1968-70	11	91-199		37-51	42	219	7-4	70-3d
Bus Connor	Idaho St. 1953-55	5	15		20		50	2-3	
Bob Cousy	Holy Cross 1947-48	6	17		12		46	5-1	47-CH, 48-3d
Jim Crews	Indiana 1973, 75-76	8	13-30		4-6	15	30	7-1	73-3d, 75-RR, 76-CH
Gary Cunningham	UCLA 1962	4	26-58		17-19	38	69	2-2	62-4th
Howie Dallmar	Stanford 1942	3	11		4-6		26	3-0	42-CH
Mike Davis	Alabama 1982-83	3	10-28		2-5	3	22	1-2	
Matt Doherty	North Carolina 1981-84	15	43-90		49-62	49	135	12-3	81-2d, 82-CH, 83-RR
Don Donoher	Dayton 1952	2	2		1		5	1-1	
Billy Donovan	Providence 1987	5	32-58	14-22	36-43	15	114	4-1	87-T3d
Fran Dunphy	La Salle 1968	1	1-2		0-2	2	2	0-1	
Jarrett Durham	Duquesne 1969, 71	4	29-49		16-21	22	74	2-2	
Hank Egan	Navy 1959-60	3	4-9		2-4	3	10	1-2	
John Egli	Penn St. 1942	2	6		4-6		16	1-1	
Brian Ellerbe	Rutgers 1983	2	4-8		3-4	4	11	1-1	
Lefty Ervin	La Salle 1968	1	1-2		0-0	0	2	0-1	
Craig Esherick	Georgetown 1975-76	2	0-2		0-0	0	0	0-2	
Rob Evans	New Mexico St. 1967-68	4	16-39		13-18	16	45	2-2	68-RR
Larry Farmer	UCLA 1971-73	11	36-84		11-20	43	83	11-0	71-CH, 72-CH, 73-CH
Larry Finch	Memphis 1973	4	34-64		39-44	10	107	3-1	73-2d
James Flint	St. Joseph's 1986	2	1-4		0-0	1	2	1-1	
Eddie Fogler	North Carolina 1968-69	8	15-41		7-11	9	37	5-3	68-2d, 69-4th
Dave Gavitt	Dartmouth 1958-59	4	5-19		1-2	12	11	2-2	58-RR
Mark Gottfried	Alabama 1985-87	9	28-57	10-18	8-10	15	74	6-3	
Elmer Gross	Penn St. 1942	2	3		7-9		13	1-1	
Bill Guthridge	Kansas St. 1959	2	3-7		1-2	3	7	1-1	57-RR
Dick Harp	Kansas 1940	3	11		5-8		27	2-1	40-2d
Clem Haskins	Western Ky. 1966-67	4	26-65		16-23	45	68	2-2	
Don Haskins	Oklahoma St. 1953	1	0		0		0	1-1	53-RR
Walt Hazzard	UCLA 1962-64	10	57-123		48-61	57	162	6-4	62-4th, 64-CH
Darrell Hedric	Miami (Ohio) 1953, 55	2	2		0	4	4	0-2	
Ben Howland	Weber St. 1978-79	3	12-23		8-10	5	22	2-2	
Larry Hunter	Ohio 1970	1	1-3		0-0	3	2	0-1	
Jeff Jones	Virginia 1981-82	7	27-46		15-19	16	69	5-2	81-3d
Bob Knight	Ohio St. 1960-62	11	14-36		2-3	14	30	9-2	60-CH, 61-2d, 62-2d
Don Knodel	Miami (Ohio) 1953	2	4		1		9	0-1	
Lon Kruger	Kansas St. 1972-73	4	19-40		18-22	21	56	2-2	
Craig Littlepage	Pennsylvania 1971-73	9	10-24		12-21	26	32	5-4	71-RR, 72-RR
Jim Lynam	St. Joseph's 1962-63	5	25-44		13-20	13	63	2-3	63-RR
Fran McCaffery	Pennsylvania 1982	1	1-4		0-1	0	2	0-1	
Ray McCallum	Ball St. 1981	1	13-19		0-0	2	26	0-1	
Al McGuire	St. John's (N.Y.) 1951	3	6-15		9-17	12	21	2-1	51-RR
Bones McKinney	North Carolina 1946	3	10		5-10		25	2-1	46-2d
Ralph Miller	Kansas 1940, 42	5	11		12-23		34	3-2	40-2d
Stan Morrison	California 1960	3	2		1		5	2-1	60-2d
Joe Mullaney	Holy Cross 1947-48	6	14		4		32	5-1	47-CH, 48-3d
Jeff Mullins	Duke 1963-64	8	84-156		32-40	63	200	6-2	63-3d, 64-2d
Frank Mulzoff	St. John's (N.Y.) 1951	3	2-15		2-2	9	6	2-1	51-RR
C.M. Newton	Kentucky 1951	2	0-0		0-0	0	0	2-0	51-CH
Jim O'Brien	St. Joseph's 1973-74	2	4-15		2-3	3	10	0-2	
Fran O'Hanlon	Villanova 1969-70	4	23-56		12-16	21	58	2-2	70-RR
Doyle Parrack	Oklahoma St. 1945	3	12		2		26	3-0	45-CH
Jerry Peirson	Miami (Ohio) 1966	1	4-7		1-2	4	9	0-1	
Tom Penders	Connecticut 1965, 67	2	4-9		3-6	4	11	0-2	
Dom Perno	Connecticut 1963-64	4	10-44		13-19	11	33	2-2	64-RR
Buzz Peterson	North Carolina 1982, 84-85	11	7-25		5-8	10	19	9-2	82-CH, 84-RR
Jerry Pimm	Southern California 1960	1	6-20		4-5	7	16	0-1	
Tic Price	Virginia Tech 1979	2	2-7		0-0	3	4	1-1	
Roger Reid	Weber St. 1968	1	2-4		0-0	1	4	0-1	
Nolan Richardson	UTEP 1963	1	2-7		0-1	2	4	0-1	
Red Rocha	Oregon St. 1947	2	8		5		21	1-1	
Jack Rohan	Columbia 1951	1	0-1		0-0	0	0	0-1	
Jeff Ruland	Iona 1979-80	3	21-31		9-16	31	51	1-2	
Jim Satalin	St. Bonaventure 1968	3	9-35		6-7	11	24	1-2	
Charlie Schmaus	VMI 1964	1	2-7		1-1	5	5	0-1	
Bill Self	Oklahoma St. 1985	1	3-4		2-4	4	8	0-1	
Howard Shannon	Kansas St. 1948	3	11		15		37	1-2	48-4th
John Shumate	Notre Dame 1974	3	35-50		16-18	34	86	2-1	
Dean Smith	Kansas 1952-53	7	1		2		4	6-1	52-CH, 53-2d
Quin Synder	Duke 1986-89	16	22-62	6-26	13-27	40	63	13-3	86-2d, 88-T3d, 89-T3d
Kevin Stallings	Purdue 1980	6	2-7		2-3	2	6	5-1	80-3d
Andy Stoglin	UTEP 1964	3	12-34		10-11	21	34	2-1	
Bill Strannigan	Wyoming 1941	2	11		2-5		24	0-2	
Gene Sullivan	Notre Dame 1953	3	3		2	8	8	2-1	53-RR
Eddie Sutton	Oklahoma St. 1958	3	8-13		4-4	11	20	2-1	58-RR
Johnny Swaim	TCU 1952-53	4	8		3		19	2-2	
Fred Taylor	Ohio St. 1950	2	9-26		0-3	18	18	1-1	
Bob Thomason	Pacific (Cal.) 1971	2	11-32		8-11	5	30	1-1	
John Thompson	Providence 1964	1	7-13		4-8	3	18	0-1	
Ralph Underhill	Tennessee Tech 1964	1	0-1		0-0	1	0	0-1	
Jan van Breda Kolff	Vanderbilt 1974	2	4-11		6-6	15	14	0-2	
Joe Vancisin	Dartmouth 1944	3	5		0-0		10	2-1	44-2d
Sox Walseth	Colorado 1946	2	7		4-4		18	1-1	
Melvin Watkins	Charlotte 1977	5	24-41		10-15	20	58	3-2	77-4th
Paul Westhead	St. Joseph's 1960-61	5	3-15		4-6	11	10	2-3	61-3d*
Tom Young	Maryland 1958	3	9		20		38	2-1	

+W-L for games played in only (blanks above mean those figures were not listed in available box scores).
*later vacated

Kansas coach Dick Harp shakes Wilt Chamberlain's hand after a Final Four semifinal win in 1957. Harp is the only man to play for and later coach his alma mater to the Final Four.

Photo by Rich Clarkson

Tournament trivia

Question...

Match the following NCAA tournament coaches with their nicknames:

Coach
1. Denny Crum
2. Don Haskins
3. Bob Knight
4. Mike Krzyzewski
5. Adolph Rupp
6. Dean Smith
7. Norm Stewart
8. Jerry Tarkanian
9. Jim Valvano
10. John Wooden

Nickname
A. The Baron of the Bluegrass
B. The Bear
C. Coach K
D. Cool Hand Luke
E. The Dean of College Basketball
F. The General
G. The Shark
H. Stormin' Norman
J. Jimmy V
K. The Wizard of Westwood

Answer...

1-D, 2-B, 3-F, 4-C, 5-A, 6-E, 7-H, 8-G, 9-J, 10-K

THE COACHES

Coaches of All-Time

Final Four Appearances

Coach	Tournament Team: Year-Finish	W-L	Pct.
12 Times			
John Wooden	UCLA: 1962-4th, 64-CH, 65-CH, 67-CH, 68-CH, 69-CH, 70-CH, 71-CH, 72-CH, 73-CH, 74-3d, 75-CH	21-3	.875
11 Times			
Dean Smith	North Carolina: 1967-4th, 68-2d, 69-4th, 72-3d, 77-2d, 81-2d, 82-CH, 91-T3d, 93-CH, 95-T3d, 97-T3d	8-11	.421
9 Times			
+Mike Krzyzewski	Duke: 1986-2d, 88-T3d, 89-T3d, 90-2d, 91-CH, 92-CH, 94-2d, 99-2d, 2001-CH	10-6	.625
6 Times			
Denny Crum	Louisville: 1972-4th, 75-3d, 80-CH, 82-T3d, 83-T3d, 86-CH	5-5	.500
Adolph Rupp	Kentucky: 42-T3d, 48-CH, 49-CH, 51-CH, 58-CH, 66-2d	9-2	.818
5 Times			
+Bob Knight	Indiana: 1973-3d, 76-CH, 81-CH, 87-CH, 92-T3d	7-2	.778
Guy Lewis	Houston: 67-3d, 68-4th, 82-T3d, 83-2d, 84-2d	3-6	.333
+Lute Olson	Iowa: 1980-4th; Arizona: 88-T3d, 94-T3d, 97-CH, 2001-2d	3-5	.375
4 Times			
Jack Gardner	Kansas St.: 1948-4th, 51-2d; Utah: 61-4th, 66-4th	1-7	.125
Henry Iba	Oklahoma St.: 1945-CH, 46-CH, 49-2d, 51-4th	5-3	.625
Harold Olsen	Ohio St.: 1939-2d, 44-T3d, 45-T3d, 46-3d	2-4	.333
+Rick Pitino	Providence: 1987-T3d; Kentucky: 93-T3d, 96-CH, 97-2d	3-3	.500
+Jerry Tarkanian	UNLV: 1977-3d, 87-T3d, 90-CH, 91-T3d	3-3	.500
Fred Taylor	Ohio St.: 1960-CH, 61-2d, 62-2d, 68-3d	5-3	.625
3 Times			
Phog Allen	Kansas: 1940-2d, 52-CH, 53-2d	4-2	.667
Forddy Anderson	Bradley: 1950-2d, 54-2d; Michigan St.: 57-4th	2-4	.333
Larry Brown	*UCLA: 1980-2d; Kansas: 86-T3d, 88-CH	3-2	.600
Vic Bubas	Duke: 1963-3d, 64-2d, 66-3d	3-3	.500
Harry Combes	Illinois: 1949-3d, 51-3d, 52-3d	3-3	.500
+Steve Fisher	Michigan: 1989-CH, 92-2d, 93-2d	4-2	.667
Joe B. Hall	Kentucky: 1975-2d, 78-CH, 84-T3d	3-2	.600
+Tom Izzo	Michigan St.: 1999-T3d, 2000-CH, 01-T3d	2-2	.500
Ed Jucker	Cincinnati: 1961-CH, 62-CH, 63-2d	5-1	.833
+Nolan Richardson	Arkansas: 1990-T3d, 94-CH, 95-2d	3-2	.600
John Thompson	Georgetown: 1982-2d, 84-CH, 85-2d	4-2	.667
Phil Woolpert	San Francisco: 1955-CH, 56-CH, 57-3d	5-1	.833
2 Times			
Gene Bartow	Memphis: 1973-2d; UCLA: 76-3d	2-2	.500
+Jim Boeheim	Syracuse: 1987-2d, 96-2d	2-2	.500
Dale Brown	LSU: 1981-4th, 86-T3d	0-3	.000
Bruce Drake	Oklahoma: 1939-T3d, 47-2d	1-2	.333
+Hugh Durham	Florida St.: 1972-2d; Georgia: 83-T3d	1-2	.333
Slats Gill	Oregon St.: 1949-4th, 63-4th	0-4	.000
+Bill Guthridge	North Carolina: 1998-T3d, 2000-T3d	0-2	.000
Bill Henderson	Baylor: 1948-2d, 50-4th	1-3	.250
+Lou Henson	New Mexico St.: 1970-3d; Illinois: 89-T3d	1-2	.333
Terry Holland	Virginia: 1981-3d, 84-T3d	1-2	.333
Nat Holman	CCNY: 1947-4th, 50-CH	2-2	.500
Doggie Julian	Holy Cross: 1947-CH, 48-3d	3-1	.750
Harry Litwack	Temple: 1956-3d, 58-3d	2-2	.500
Ken Loeffler	La Salle: 1954-CH, 55-2d	3-1	.750
Branch McCracken	Indiana: 1940-CH, 53-CH	4-0	1.000
Al McGuire	Marquette: 1974-2d, 77-CH	3-1	.750
Frank McGuire	St. John's (N.Y.): 1952-2d; North Carolina: 57-CH	3-1	.750
Ray Meyer	DePaul: 1943-T3d, 79-3d	1-2	.333
Pete Newell	California: 1959-CH, 60-2d	3-1	.750
Bucky O'Connor	Iowa: 1955-4th, 56-2d	1-3	.250
Ted Owens	Kansas: 1971-4th, 74-4th	0-4	.000
Lee Rose	Charlotte: 1977-4th; Purdue: 80-3d	1-3	.250
George Smith	Cincinnati: 1959-3d, 60-3d	2-2	.500
Dave Strack	Michigan: 1964-3d, 65-2d	2-2	.500
+Eddie Sutton	Arkansas: 1978-3d; Oklahoma St.: 95-T3d	1-2	.333
+Roy Williams	Kansas: 1991-2d, 93-T3d	1-2	.333
Tex Winter	Kansas St.: 1958-4th, 64-4th	0-4	.000
1 Time			
Sam Barry	Southern California: 1940-T3d	0-1	.000
+Dick Bennett	Wisconsin: 2000-T3d	0-1	.000
Earl Brown	Dartmouth: 1944-2d	1-1	.500
+Jim Calhoun	Connecticut: 1999-CH	2-0	1.000
+John Calipari	Massachusetts: 1996-T3d	0-1	.000
Howard Cann	New York U.: 1945-2d	1-1	.500
P.J. Carlesimo	Seton Hall: 1989-2d	1-1	.500
Harold Carlson	Pittsburgh: 1941-T3d	0-1	.000
Lou Carnesecca	St. John's (N.Y.): 1985-T3d	0-1	.000
Ben Carnevale	North Carolina: 1946-2d	1-1	.500
Everett Case	North Carolina St.: 1950-3d	1-1	.500
John Castellani	Seattle: 1958-2d	1-1	.500
Ozzie Cowles	Dartmouth: 1942-2d	1-1	.500

Photo from Purdue sports information

Coach John Wooden became a living legend after leading UCLA to the Final Four 12 times from 1962 to 1975, winning the championship 10 times.

Tournament trivia

Question...
Of the 11 coaches who have taken two different schools to the Final Four, which coach has the most Final Four appearances?

Answer...
Lute Olson with five (one with Iowa and four with Arizona)

COACHES OF ALL-TIME—FINAL FOUR APPEARANCES

Coach	Tournament Team: Year-Finish	W-L	Pct.
Frosty Cox	Colorado: 1942-T3d	0-1	.000
+Bobby Cremins	Georgia Tech: 1990-T3d	0-1	.000
Roy Danforth	Syracuse: 1975-4th	0-2	.000
Chick Davies	Duquesne: 1940-T3d	0-1	.000
Everett Dean	Stanford: 1942-CH	2-0	1.000
Don Donoher	Dayton: 1967-2d	1-1	.500
Tippy Dye	Washington: 1953-3d	1-1	.500
+Billy Donovan	Florida: 2000-2d	1-1	.500
Bob Feerick	Santa Clara: 1952-4th	0-2	.000
Bill E. Foster	Duke: 1978-2d	1-1	.500
Bud Foster	Wisconsin: 1941-CH	2-0	1.000
Jack Friel	Washington St.: 1941-2d	1-1	.500
Dave Gavitt	Providence: 1973-4th	0-2	.000
Bully Gilstrap	Texas: 1943-T3d	0-1	.000
Jack Gray	Texas: 1947-3d	1-1	.500
Elmer Gross	Penn St.: 1954-3d	1-1	.500
Dick Harp	Kansas: 1957-2d	1-1	.500
+Jim Harrick	UCLA: 1995-CH	2-0	1.000
Clem Haskins	*Minnesota: 1997-T3d	0-1	.000
Don Haskins	UTEP: 1966-CH	2-0	1.000
Doc Hayes	Southern Methodist: 1956-4th	0-2	.000
Jud Heathcote	Michigan St.: 1979-CH	2-0	1.000
Peck Hickman	Louisville: 1959-4th	0-2	.000
Howard Hobson	Oregon: 1939-CH	2-0	1.000
Bill Hodges	Indiana St.: 1979-2d	1-1	.500
+Bob Huggins	Cincinnati: 1992-T3d	0-1	.000
George Ireland	Loyola (Ill.): 1963-CH	2-0	1.000
Maurice John	Drake: 1969-3d	1-1	.500
George King	Purdue: 1969-2d	1-1	.500
Dana Kirk	*Memphis: 1985-T3d	0-1	.000
Jack Kraft	*Villanova: 1971-2d	1-1	.500
+Lon Kruger	Florida: 1994-T3d	0-1	.000
Eugene Lambert	Arkansas: 1945-T3d	0-1	.000
Bebe Lee	Colorado: 1955-3d	1-1	.500
+Rick Majerus	Utah: 1998-2d	1-1	.500
+Rollie Massimino	Villanova: 1985-CH	2-0	1.000
Bones McKinney	Wake Forest: 1962-3d	1-1	.500
Louis Menze	Iowa St.: 1944-T3d	0-1	.000
+Mike Montgomery	Stanford: 1998-T3d	0-1	.000
+Jim O'Brien	Ohio St.: 1999-T3d	0-1	.000
Johnny Oldham	*Western Ky.: 1971-3d	1-1	.500
Johnny Orr	Michigan: 1976-2d	1-1	.500
Vadal Peterson	Utah: 1944-CH	2-0	1.000
Digger Phelps	Notre Dame: 1978-4th	0-2	.000
Nibs Price	California: 1946-4th	0-2	.000
Harry Rabenhorst	LSU: 1953-4th	0-2	.000
Jack Ramsay	*St. Joseph's: 1961-3d	1-1	.500
Elmer Ripley	Georgetown: 1943-2d	1-1	.500
Glen Rose	Arkansas: 1941-3d	0-1	.000
Lou Rossini	New York U.: 1960-4th	0-2	.000
Fred Schaus	West Virginia: 1959-2d	1-1	.500
Alex Severance	Villanova: 1939-T3d	0-1	.000
Everett Shelton	Wyoming: 1943-CH	2-0	1.000
Norm Sloan	North Carolina St.: 1974-CH	2-0	1.000
+Tubby Smith	Kentucky: 1998-CH	2-0	1.000
Gary Thompson	Wichita St.: 1965-4th	0-2	.000
+Billy Tubbs	Oklahoma: 1988-2d	1-1	.500
Forrest Twogood	Southern California: 1954-4th	0-2	.000
Jim Valvano	North Carolina St.: 1983-CH	2-0	1.000
Butch van Breda Kolff	Princeton: 1965-3d	1-1	.500
Bob Weinhauer	Pennsylvania: 1979-4th	0-2	.000
Larry Weise	St. Bonaventure: 1970-4th	0-2	.000
+Gary Williams	Maryland: 2001-T3d	0-1	.000
Joe Williams	Jacksonville: 1970-2d	1-1	.500
+Richard Williams	Mississippi St.: 1996-T3d	0-1	.000
Tom Young	Rutgers: 1976-4th	0-2	.000

+Active. *Final Four records later vacated.

In 1940, 31-year-old Branch McCracken (right) accepted the game ball from Phog Allen of Kansas after winning the 1940 NCAA championship. McCracken is the youngest coach ever to win the NCAA title. Twelve years later in 1952, the 66-year-old Allen became the oldest coach to win the NCAA championship, leading the Jayhawks to the title.

Championship Coaches' Age

Coaches' age the day his team won the championship.

YOUNGEST

Rk.	Coach	School	Championship Year	Yrs	Ms	Ds
1.	Branch McCracken	Indiana	1940	31	9	21
2.	Harold Foster	Wisconsin	1941	34	9	29
3.	Fred Taylor	Ohio St.	1960	35	3	16
4.	Bob Knight	Indiana	1976	35	5	4
5.	Howard Hobson	Oregon	1939	35	8	23
6.	Don Haskins	UTEP	1966	36	0	5
7.	Jim Valvano	North Carolina St.	1983	37	0	24
8.	Phil Woolpert	San Francisco	1955	39	2	0
9.	Phil Woolpert	San Francisco	1956	40	2	5
10.	Frank McGuire	North Carolina	1957	40	4	15

Tournament facts

All the head coaches in the 1998 Final Four were making their first appearance as a Final Four head coach. That was the seventh time this had happened and the first since 1959. The other five times were the first five tournaments from 1939-43.

COACHES OF ALL-TIME—CHAMPIONSHIP COACHES' AGE

OLDEST

Rk.	Coach	School	Championship Year	Yrs	Ms	Ds
1.	Phog Allen	Kansas	1952	66	4	8
2.	John Wooden	UCLA	1975	64	5	17
3.	Lute Olson	Arizona	1997	62	6	9
4.	John Wooden	UCLA	1973	62	5	12
5.	Dean Smith	North Carolina	1993	62	1	7
6.	John Wooden	UCLA	1972	61	5	11
7.	John Wooden	UCLA	1971	60	5	13
8.	Jerry Tarkanian	UNLV	1990	59	7	24
9.	John Wooden	UCLA	1970	59	5	7
10.	John Wooden	UCLA	1969	58	5	8

ACTIVE YOUNGEST TO OLDEST

Rk.	Coach	School	Championship Year	Yrs	Ms	Ds
1.	Bob Knight	Indiana	1976	35	5	4
2.	Bob Knight	Indiana	1981	40	5	5
3.	Steve Fisher	Michigan	1989	44	0	9
4.	Mike Krzyzewski	Duke	1991	44	1	18
5.	Mike Krzyzewski	Duke	1992	45	1	23
6.	Tom Izzo	Michigan St.	2000	45	2	3
7.	Bob Knight	Indiana	1987	46	5	5
8.	Tubby Smith	Kentucky	1998	46	9	0
9.	Rollie Massimino	Villanova	1985	50	4	18
10.	Nolan Richardson	Arkansas	1994	52	3	7
11.	Mike Krzyzewski	Duke	2001	54	1	19
12.	Jim Harrick	UCLA	1995	56	8	8
13.	Jim Calhoun	Connecticut	1999	56	9	11
14.	Jerry Tarkanian	UNLV	1990	59	7	24
15.	Lute Olson	Arizona	1997	62	6	9

Pete Carril coached for 30 years, compiled 525 wins and took Princeton to the NCAA tournament 11 times.

Photo from Princeton sports information

Tournament Coaches

Coach (Alma Mater) Career Record, Tourney Teams and Years in Tourney	Yrs	W	L	Pct.	Last Year of Career
Ron Abegglen (Brigham Young 1962) 13: 260-129; Weber St.: 1995, 99	2	2	2	.500	1999
Dick Acres (UC Santa Barb.) 3: 47-34; Oral Roberts: 1984	1	0	1	.000	1985
Mike Adras (UC Santa Barb. 1983) Northern Ariz.: 2000	1	0	1	.000	Active
Stan Albeck (Bradley 1955) 19: 284-188; Bradley: 1988	1	0	1	.000	1991
Cy Alexander (Catawba 1975) South Carolina St.: 1989, 96, 98, 2000	4	0	4	.000	Active
Steve Alford (Indiana 1987) 1 at Southwest Mo. St.: 1999; 1 at Iowa: 2001	2	3	2	.600	Active
Frankie Allen (Roanoke 1971) Tennessee St.: 1993, 94	2	0	2	.000	Active
George Allen (West Virginia 1935) 3: 39-20; Brown: 1939-RR	1	0	1	.000	1941
Phog Allen (Kansas 1906) 46: 770-233; Kansas: 1940-2nd, 42-RR, 52-CH, 53-2nd	4	10	3	.769	1956
Sonny Allen (Marshall 1959) 22: 356-260; Nevada: 1984, 85	2	0	2	.000	1987
Dana Altman (Eastern N. M. 1980) 1 at Kansas St.: 1993; 3 at Creighton: 99, 2000, 01	4	1	4	.200	Active
Tommy Amaker (Duke 1987) Seton Hall: 2000	1	2	1	.667	Active
Ladell Andersen (Utah St. 1951) 16: 286-168; 5 at Utah St.: 1962, 63, 64, 70-RR, 71; 3 at Brigham Young: 84, 87, 88	8	6	10	.375	1989
Forddy Anderson (Stanford 1942) 24: 368-234; 2 at Bradley: 1950-2nd, 54-2nd; 2 at Michigan St.: 57-4th, 59-RR	4	9	5	.643	1970
Harold Anderson (Otterbein 1924) 29: 504-226; Bowling Green: 1959, 62, 63	3	1	4	.200	1963
Jim Anderson (Oregon St. 1959) 6: 79-90; Oregon St.: 1990	1	0	1	.000	1995
Tevester Anderson (Ark.-Pine Bluff 1962) Murray St.: 1999	1	0	1	.000	Active
Tom Apke (Creighton 1965) 22: 328-292; Creighton: 1975, 78, 81	3	0	3	.000	1996
Lynn Archibald (Fresno St. 1968) 11: 163-152; Utah: 1986	1	0	1	.000	1989
Frank Arnold (Idaho St. 1956) 10: 148-139; Brigham Young: 1979, 80, 81-RR	3	3	3	.500	1987
Murray Arnold (American 1960) 22: 407-221; 3 at Chattanooga: 1981, 82, 83; 1 at Western Ky.: 87	4	2	4	.333	2001
Ronnie Arrow (Southwest Tex. St. 1969) 8: 122-108; South Ala.: 1989, 91	2	1	2	.333	1995
Tom Asbury (Wyoming 1967) 12: 210-147; 3 at Pepperdine: 1991, 92, 94; 1 at Kansas St.: 96	4	0	4	.000	2000
Presley Askew (Southeastern Okla. 1930) 15: 179-181; New Mexico St.: 1959, 60	2	0	2	.000	1965
Randy Ayers (Miami [Ohio] 1978) 8: 124-108; Ohio St.: 1990, 91, 92-RR	3	6	3	.667	1997
John Bach (Fordham 1948) 28: 384-314; Fordham: 1953, 54	2	0	2	.000	1978
Jim Baechtold (Eastern Ky. 1952) 6: 70-57; Eastern Ky.: 1965	1	0	1	.000	1967
Tay Baker (Cincinnati 1950) 13: 195-149; Cincinnati: 1966	1	0	2	.000	1979
Kevin Bannon (St. Peter's 1979) 19: 335-211; Rider: 1993, 94	2	0	2	.000	2001
Milton Barnes (Albion 1979) 4: 62-53; Eastern Wash.: 1998	1	0	1	.000	2000
Rick Barnes (Lenoir-Rhyne 1977) 3 at Providence: 1989, 90, 94; 3 at Clemson: 96, 97, 98; 3 at Texas: 99, 2000, 01	9	3	9	.250	Active
Roderick Barnes (Mississippi 1988) Mississippi: 1999, 2001	2	3	2	.600	Active
J.D. Barnett (Winona St. 1966) 21: 345-254; 5 at Va. Commonwealth: 1980, 81, 83, 84, 85; 2 at Tulsa: 86, 87	7	4	7	.364	1999
Jim Baron (St. Bonaventure 1977) 1 at St. Francis (Pa.): 1991; 1 at St. Bonaventure: 2000	2	0	2	.000	Active
Tony Barone (Duke 1968) 13: 178-202; Creighton: 1989, 91	2	1	2	.333	1998
Peter Barry (San Francisco 1970) 2: 49-13; San Francisco: 1981, 82	2	0	2	.000	1982
Sam Barry (Wisconsin 1916) 28: 365-217; Southern California: 1940-T3rd	1	1	1	.500	1950
Gene Bartow (Truman 1953) 34: 647-353; 1 at Memphis: 1973-2nd; 2 at UCLA: 76-3rd, 77; 9 at UAB: 81, 82-RR, 83, 84, 85, 86, 87, 90, 94	12	14	12	.538	1996
Murry Bartow (UAB 1985) UAB: 1999	1	0	1	.000	Active
Bill Bayno (Sacred Heart 1985) 6: 94-64; UNLV: 1998, 2000	2	0	2	.000	2001
Butch Beard (Louisville 1972) Howard: 1992	1	0	1	.000	Active
John Beilein (Wheeling Jesuit 1975) 1 at Canisius: 1996; 1 at Richmond: 98	2	1	2	.333	Active

Tournament trivia

Question...
Who is the only player to play for two schools in two different Final Four championship games?

Answer...
Bob Bender, currently the head coach at Washington, played in the 1976 title game for Indiana's title-winning team, and two years later scored seven points for Duke in a losing cause to Kentucky in the season's final game. Steve Krafcisin is the only other player to play in two Final Fours for two different schools. Krafcisin played for North Carolina in 1977 and Iowa in 1980.

COACHES OF ALL-TIME—TOURNAMENT COACHES

Coach (Alma Mater)	Career Record, Tourney Teams and Years in Tourney	Tournament Yrs	W	L	Pct.	Last Year of Career
Steve Belko (Idaho 1939) 26: 287-263; 4 at Idaho St.: 1953, 54, 55, 56; 2 at Oregon: 60-RR, 61		6	4	6	.400	1971
Dan Belluomini (San Francisco 1964) 2: 44-14; San Francisco: 1979		1	1	1	.500	1980
Dutch Belnap (Utah St. 1958) 6: 108-56; Utah St.: 1975, 79		2	0	2	.000	1979
Bob Bender (Duke 1980) 1 at Illinois St.: 1990; 2 at Washington: 98, 99		3	2	3	.400	Active
Dick Bennett (Ripon 1965) 25: 455-256; 3 at Wis.-Green Bay: 1991, 94, 95; 3 at Wisconsin: 97, 99, 2000-T3rd		6	5	6	.455	2001
Russ Bergman (LSU 1970) 19: 306-246; Coastal Caro.: 1991, 93		2	0	2	.000	1994
Bill Berry (Michigan St. 1965) 10: 142-144; San Jose St.: 1980		1	0	1	.000	1989
Bill Bibb (Ky. Wesleyan 1957) 15: 222-194; Mercer: 1981, 85		2	0	2	.000	1989
Henry Bibby (UCLA 1972) Southern California: 1997, 2001-RR		2	3	2	.600	Active
Leon Black (Texas 1953) 9: 106-121; Texas: 1972, 74		2	1	3	.250	1976
Tom Blackburn (Wilmington [Ohio] 1931) 17: 352-141; Dayton: 1952		1	1	1	.500	1964
Bill Blair (VMI 1964) 9: 114-130; VMI: 1976-RR		1	2	1	.667	1981
George Blaney (Holy Cross 1961) 30: 459-382; Holy Cross: 1977, 80, 93		3	0	3	.000	1997
Dave Bliss (Cornell 1965) 1 at Oklahoma: 1979; 3 at Southern Methodist: 84, 85, 88; 7 at New Mexico: 91, 93, 94, 96, 97, 98, 99		11	8	11	.421	Active
Jim Boeheim (Syracuse 1966) Syracuse: 1977, 78, 79, 80, 83, 84, 85, 86, 87-2nd, 88, 89-RR, 90, 91, 92, 94, 95, 96-2nd, 98, 99, 2000, 01		21	32	21	.604	Active
Jim Boutin (Lewis & Clark 1964) 23: 397-253; Idaho St.: 1987		1	0	1	.000	1990
Bob Boyd (Southern California 1953) 20: 312-231; 1 at Seattle: 1964; 1 at Southern California: 79		2	3	2	.600	1986
Jim Boyle (St. Joseph's 1964) 9: 151-114; St. Joseph's: 1982, 86		2	1	2	.333	1990
Todd Bozeman* (Rhode Island 1986) 4: 63-35; California: 1993, 94, 96		3	2	3	.400	1996
John Brady (Belhaven 1976) LSU: 2000		1	2	1	.667	Active
Harold Bradley (Hartwick 1934) 20: 337-169; 1 at Duke: 1955; 2 at Texas: 60, 63		3	2	4	.333	1967
Ron Bradley (Eastern Nazarene 1973) Radford: 1998		1	0	1	.000	Active
Jim Brandenburg (Colorado St. 1958) 16: 267-199; Wyoming: 1981, 82, 87		3	4	3	.571	1992
Buster Brannon (TCU 1933) 24: 285-290; 2 at Rice: 1940-RR, 42-RR; 3 at TCU: 52, 53, 59		5	4	6	.400	1967
Bobby Braswell (Cal St. Northridge 1984) Cal St. Northridge: 2001		1	0	1	.000	Active
Ben Braun (Wisconsin 1975) 3 at Eastern Mich.: 1988, 91, 96; 2 at California: 97, 2001		5	5	5	.500	Active
John Breeden (Montana St. 1929) 17: 283-198; Montana St.: 1951		1	0	1	.000	1954
Mike Brey (George Washington 1982) Delaware: 1998, 99, 2001		3	1	3	.250	Active
Al Brightman (Charleston [W.Va.]) 8: 174-67; Seattle: 1953, 54, 55, 56		4	4	6	.400	1956
J. Madison Brooks (Louisiana Tech 1937) 25: 370-267; East Tenn. St.: 1968		1	1	2	.333	1973
Rickey Broussard (La.-Lafayette 1970) Nicholls St.: 1995, 98		2	0	2	.000	Active
Jim Brovelli (San Francisco 1964) 21: 289-288; San Diego: 1984		1	0	1	.000	1995
Al Brown (Purdue 1964) 5: 68-75; Ball St.: 1986		1	0	1	.000	1987
Dale Brown (Minot St. 1957) 25: 448-301; LSU: 1979, 80-RR, 81-4th, 84, 85, 86-T3rd, 87-RR, 88, 89, 90, 91, 92, 93		13	15	14	.517	1997
Earl Brown (Notre Dame 1939) 1: 19-2; Dartmouth: 1944-RR		1	2	1	.667	1944
Larry Brown* (North Carolina 1963) 7: 172-60; 2 at UCLA: 1980-2nd, 81; 5 at Kansas: 84, 85, 86-T3rd, 87, 88-CH		7	19	6	.760	1988
Jack Bruen (Catholic 1972) 16: 226-214; Colgate: 1995, 96		2	0	2	.000	1998
Vic Bubas (North Carolina St. 1951) 10: 213-67; Duke: 1960-RR, 63-3rd, 64-2nd, 66-3rd		4	11	4	.733	1969
Morris Buckwalter (Utah 1956) 5: 78-54; Seattle: 1969		1	0	1	.000	1972
Mitch Buonaguro (Boston College 1975) 6: 72-103; Fairfield: 1986, 87		2	0	2	.000	1991
Eddie Burke (La Salle 1967) 14: 205-189; Drexel: 1986		1	0	1	.000	1991
Ken Burmeister (St. Mary's [Tex.] 1971) 8: 112-115; Texas-San Antonio: 1988		1	0	1	.000	1998
Jerry Bush (St. John's [N.Y.] 1938) 16: 209-190; Toledo: 1954		1	0	1	.000	1963
Ed Byhre (Augustana [S.D.] 1966) 5: 69-63; Eastern Ky.: 1979		1	0	1	.000	1981
Jim Calhoun* (American Int'l 1966) 5 at Northeastern: 1981, 82, 84, 85, 86; 9 at Connecticut: 90-RR, 91, 92, 94, 95-RR, 96, 98-RR, 99-CH, 2000		14	26	13	.667	Active
Robert Calihan (Detroit 1940) 21: 299-242; Detroit: 1962		1	0	1	.000	1969
John Calipari* (Clarion St. 1982) Massachusetts: 1992, 93, 94, 95-RR, 96-T3rd		5	11	5	.688	Active
Dave Calloway (Monmouth 1991) Monmouth: 2001		1	0	1	.000	Active
Ernie Calverley (Rhode Island 1946) 11: 154-125; Rhode Island: 1961, 66		2	0	2	.000	1968
Lou Campanelli (Montclair St. 1960) 21: 361-226; 3 at James Madison: 1981, 82, 83; 1 at California: 90		4	4	4	.500	1993
Howard Cann (New York U. 1920) 35: 409-232; New York U.: 1943-RR, 45-2nd, 46-RR		3	3	4	.429	1958
Jeff Capel (Fayetteville St. 1977) 12: 201-162; 1 at N.C. A&T: 1994; 2 at Old Dominion: 95, 97		3	1	3	.250	2001
Franklin Cappon# (Michigan 1924) 28: 361-257; Princeton: 1952, 55, 60		3	0	5	.000	1961
P.J. Carlesimo (Fordham 1971) 19: 291-272; Seton Hall: 1988, 89-2nd, 91-RR, 92, 93, 94		6	12	6	.667	1994
Henry Carlson (Pittsburgh 1917) 31: 367-248; Pittsburgh: 1941-T3rd		1	1	1	.500	1953
Bill Carmody (Union 1975) Princeton: 1997, 98		2	1	2	.333	Active
Lou Carnesecca (St. John's [N.Y.] 1946) 24: 526-200; St. John's (N.Y.): 1967, 68, 69, 76, 77, 78, 79-RR, 80, 82, 83, 84, 85-T3rd, 86, 87, 88, 90, 91-RR, 92		18	17	20	.459	1992
Ben Carnevale (New York U. 1938) 22: 309-171; 1 at North Carolina: 1946-2nd; 5 at Navy: 47-RR, 53, 54, 59, 60		6	6	7	.462	1966
John Carpenter (Penn St. 1958) 23: 292-328; Rider: 1984		1	0	1	.000	1989
Pete Carril (Lafayette 1952) 30: 525-273; Princeton: 1969, 76, 77, 81, 83, 84, 89, 90, 91, 92, 96		11	4	11	.267	1996
Tim Carter (Kansas 1979) Texas-San Antonio: 1999		1	0	1	.000	Active
Everett Case (Wisconsin 1923) 18: 377-134; North Carolina St.: 1950-3rd, 51-RR, 52, 54, 56		5	6	6	.500	1964
Don Casey (Temple 1970) 9: 151-94; Temple: 1979		1	0	1	.000	1982
John Castellani (Notre Dame 1952) 2: 45-9; Seattle: 1958-2nd		1	4	1	.800	1958
Gale Catlett (West Virginia 1963) 3 at Cincinnati: 1975, 76, 77; 8 at West Virginia: 82, 83, 84, 86, 87, 89, 92, 98		11	7	11	.389	Active
Vince Cazzetta# (Arnold 1950) 5: 94-39; Seattle: 1961, 62		2	0	2	.000	1963
John Chaney (Bethune-Cookman 1955) Temple: 1984, 85, 86, 87, 88-RR, 90, 91-RR, 92, 93-RR, 94, 95, 96, 97, 98, 99-RR, 2000, 01-RR		17	23	17	.575	Active
Rob Chavez (Mesa St. 1980) 9: 121-130; Portland: 1996		1	0	1	.000	2001

P.J. Carlesimo (left) coached Seton Hall to its only Final Four appearance in 1989. Brent Musburger of CBS prepares to interview Carlesimo after the Pirates defeated Duke, 95-78, to advance to the championship game.

Question... Who is the only bearded head coach to take his team to the Final Four?

Answer... P.J. Carlesimo with Seton Hall in 1989

COACHES OF ALL-TIME—TOURNAMENT COACHES

With 675 wins, including 42 in the NCAA tournament, Denny Crum retired from Louisville after the 2001 season with 23 NCAA tournament appearances in 30 years of coaching.

Tournament trivia

Question...

Before first-year coach Steve Fisher led Michigan to the 1989 NCAA championship, when was the last time a coach won the title in his first tournament appearance?

Answer...

In 1963, George Ireland coached Loyola (Illinois) to the national title in his first tournament appearance.

Coach (Alma Mater) Career Record, Tourney Teams and Years in Tourney	Yrs	W	L	Pct.	Last Year of Career
Roy Chipman (Maine 1961) 18: 326-160; Pittsburgh: 1981, 82, 85	3	1	3	.250	1986
Mike Cingiser (Brown 1962) 10: 93-170; Brown: 1986	1	0	1	.000	1991
John Cinicola (Duquesne 1955) 4: 52-56; Duquesne: 1977	1	0	1	.000	1978
Perry Clark (Gettysburg 1974) Tulane: 1992, 93, 95	3	3	3	.500	Active
Mickey Clayton (Florida A&M 1975) 6: 48-105; Florida A&M: 1999	1	0	1	.000	2001
Steve Cleveland (UC Irvine 1976) Brigham Young: 2001	1	0	1	.000	Active
Richard Cochran (Tufts 1934) 2: 17-17; Tufts: 1945-RR	1	0	2	.000	1946
Josh Cody (Vanderbilt 1920) 24: 259-243; Temple: 1944-RR	1	1	1	.500	1952
Charlie Coles (Miami [Ohio] 1965) 1 at Central Mich.: 1987; 2 at Miami (Ohio): 97, 99	3	2	3	.400	Active
Barry Collier (Butler 1976) Butler: 1997, 98, 2000	3	0	3	.000	Active
Jimmy Collins (New Mexico St. 1970) Ill.-Chicago: 1998	1	0	1	.000	Active
Gary Colson (David Lipscomb 1956) 34: 563-385; Pepperdine: 1976, 79	2	2	2	.500	1995
Harry Combes (Illinois 1937) 20: 316-150; Illinois: 1949-3rd, 51-3rd, 52-3rd, 63-RR	4	9	4	.692	1967
Bus Connor (Idaho St. 1955) 8: 93-106; Boise St.: 1976	1	0	1	.000	1980
Tom Conrad (Old Dominion 1979) 4: 42-72; Charleston So.: 1997	1	0	1	.000	2000
Don Corbett (Lincoln [Mo.] 1965) 22: 413-204; N.C. A&T: 1982, 83, 84, 85, 86, 87, 88	7	0	7	.000	1993
Paul Cormier (New Hampshire 1973) 14: 173-206; Fairfield: 1997	1	0	1	.000	1998
Bob Cousy (Holy Cross 1948) 6: 114-38; Boston College: 1967-RR, 68	2	2	2	.500	1969
Ozzie Cowles (Carleton 1922) 31: 421-198; 3 at Dartmouth: 1941-RR, 42-2nd, 43-RR; 1 at Michigan: 48-RR	4	5	4	.556	1959
Frosty Cox (Kansas 1930) 18: 203-151; Colorado: 1940-RR, 42-T3rd, 46-RR	3	2	4	.333	1960
Bobby Cremins (South Carolina 1970) 25: 454-307; 1 at Appalachian St.: 1979; 10 at Georgia Tech: 85-RR, 86, 87, 88, 89, 90-T3rd, 91, 92, 93, 96	11	15	11	.577	2000
Jim Crews (Indiana 1976) Evansville: 1989, 92, 93, 99	4	1	4	.200	Active
Denny Crum (UCLA 1959) 30: 675-295; Louisville: 1972-4th, 74, 75-3rd, 77, 78, 79, 80-CH, 81, 82-T3rd, 83-T3rd, 84, 86-CH, 88, 89, 90, 92, 93, 94, 95, 96, 97-RR, 99, 2000	23	42	23	.646	2001
Gary Cunningham (UCLA 1962) 2: 50-8; UCLA: 1978, 79-RR	2	3	2	.600	1979
Joseph Curran (Canisius 1943) 6: 76-66; Canisius: 1955-RR, 56-RR, 57	3	6	3	.667	1959
Howie Dallmar (Stanford 1948) 27: 363-315; Pennsylvania: 1953	1	1	1	.500	1975
Chuck Daly (Bloomsburg 1953) 8: 151-62; Pennsylvania: 1972-RR, 73, 74, 75	4	3	5	.375	1977
Roy Danforth (Southern Miss. 1962) 13: 193-161; Syracuse: 1973, 74, 75-4th, 76..	4	5	5	.500	1981
Dick Davey (Pacific [Cal.] 1964) Santa Clara: 1993, 95, 96	3	2	3	.400	Active
George Davidson (Lafayette 1951) 12: 170-116; Lafayette: 1957	1	0	2	.000	1967
Chick Davies (Duquesne 1934) 21: 314-106; Duquesne: 1940-T3rd	1	1	1	.500	1948
Kermit Davis Jr. (Mississippi St. 1982) 4: 71-50; Idaho: 1989, 90	2	0	2	.000	1997
Mike Davis (Alabama 1983) Indiana: 2001	1	0	1	.000	Active
Tom Davis (Wis.-Platteville 1960) 28: 543-290; 2 at Boston College: 1981, 82-RR; 9 at Iowa: 87-RR, 88, 89, 91, 92, 93, 96, 97, 99	11	18	11	.621	1999
Everett Dean (Indiana 1921) 28: 374-215; Stanford: 1942-CH	1	3	0	1.000	1951
Mike Deane (Potsdam St. 1974) 1 at Siena: 1989; 2 at Marquette: 96, 97; 1 at Lamar: 2000	4	2	4	.333	Active
Johnny Dee (Notre Dame 1946) 11: 184-105; Notre Dame: 1965, 69, 70, 71	4	2	6	.250	1971
Benny Dees (Wyoming 1958) 12: 197-144; 1 at New Orleans: 1987; 1 at Wyoming: 88	2	1	2	.333	1995
Mike Dement (East Caro. 1976) Cornell: 1988	1	0	1	.000	Active
Don DeVoe (Ohio St. 1964) 1 at Virginia Tech: 1976; 6 at Tennessee: 79, 80, 81, 82, 83, 89; 3 at Navy: 94, 97, 98	10	5	10	.333	Active
Howie Dickenman (Central Conn. St. 1970) Central Conn. St.: 2000	1	0	1	.000	Active
James Dickey* (Central Ark. 1976) 10: 166-124; Texas Tech: 1993, 96	2	2	2	.500	2001
Ed Diddle (Centre 1921) 42: 759-302; Western Ky.: 1940-RR, 60, 62	3	3	4	.429	1964
Matt Doherty (North Carolina 1984) North Carolina: 2001	1	1	1	.500	Active
Bob Donewald (Hanover 1964) 22: 358-277; 3 at Illinois St.: 1983, 84, 85; 1 at Western Mich.: 98	4	3	4	.429	2000
Don Donoher (Dayton 1954) 25: 437-275; Dayton: 1965, 66, 67-2nd, 69, 70, 74, 84-RR, 85	8	11	10	.524	1989
Billy Donovan (Providence 1987) Florida: 1999, 2000-2nd, 01	3	8	3	.727	Active
Eddie Donovan (St. Bonaventure 1950) 8: 139-57; St. Bonaventure: 1961	1	2	1	.667	1961
William Donovan (Loyola Marymount 1950) 8: 107-101; Loyola Marymount: 1961	1	1	1	.500	1961
Duck Dowell (Westminster [Mo.] 1933) 20: 263-263; Pepperdine: 1962	1	1	1	.500	1968
Bruce Drake (Oklahoma 1929) 17: 200-181; Oklahoma: 1939-T3rd, 43-RR, 47-2nd	3	4	3	.571	1955
Homer Drew (William Jewell 1966) Valparaiso: 1996, 97, 98, 99, 2000	5	2	5	.286	Active
Lefty Driesell (Duke 1954) 3 at Davidson: 1966, 68-RR, 69-RR; 8 at Maryland: 73-RR, 75-RR, 80, 81, 83, 84, 85, 86; 1 at James Madison: 94; 1 at Georgia St.: 2001	13	16	14	.533	Active
John Dromo (John Carroll 1939) 4: 80-31; Louisville: 1968	1	1	1	.500	1971
Al Duer (Emporia St. 1929) 9: 176-95; Pepperdine: 1944-RR	1	0	2	.000	1948
Jerry Dunn (George Mason 1980) Penn St.: 1996, 2001	2	2	2	.500	Active
Fran Dunphy (La Salle 1970) Pennsylvania: 1993, 94, 95, 99, 2000	5	1	5	.167	Active
Hugh Durham* (Florida St. 1959) 3 at Florida St.: 1968, 72-2nd, 78; 5 at Georgia: 83-T3rd, 85, 87, 90, 91	8	8	8	.500	Active
Jarrett Durham (Duquesne 1971) 12: 157-183; Robert Morris: 1989, 90, 92	3	0	3	.000	1996
Mick Durham (Montana St. 1979) Montana St.: 1996	1	0	1	.000	Active
Jim Dutcher (Michigan 1955) 17: 290-196; Minnesota: 1982	1	1	1	.500	1986
Bob Dye (Idaho St. 1962) 21: 373-221; 1 at Cal St. Fullerton: 1978-RR; 3 at Boise St.: 88, 93, 94	4	2	4	.333	1995
Tippy Dye (Ohio St. 1937) 14: 225-132; 1 at Ohio St.: 1950-RR; 2 at Washington: 51-RR, 53-3rd	3	6	3	.667	1959
Tommy Joe Eagles (Louisiana Tech 1971) 9: 151-118; Louisiana Tech: 1987, 89	2	1	2	.333	1994
Jimmy Earle (Middle Tenn. 1959) 10: 164-103; Middle Tenn.: 1975, 77	2	0	2	.000	1979
Scott Edgar (Pitt.-Johnstown 1978) 7: 108-95; Murray St.: 1992, 95	2	0	2	.000	1998
Hec Edmundson (Idaho 1909) 29: 497-201; Washington: 1943-RR	1	0	2	.000	1947
Dick Edwards (Culver-Stockton 1952) 15: 241-157; Pacific (Cal.): 1966, 67-RR, 71..	3	2	4	.333	1978
George Edwards (Missouri 1913) 20: 181-172; Missouri: 1944-RR	1	1	1	.500	1946
Hank Egan (Navy 1960) 23: 303-312; San Diego: 1987	1	0	1	.000	1994
John Egli (Penn St. 1947) 14: 187-135; Penn St.: 1955, 65	2	1	3	.250	1968
Norm Ellenberger (Butler 1955) 10: 164-98; New Mexico: 1974, 78	2	2	2	.500	1979

COACHES OF ALL-TIME—TOURNAMENT COACHES 95

Coach (Alma Mater)	Career Record, Tourney Teams and Years in Tourney	Tournament Yrs	W	L	Pct.	Last Year of Career
Brian Ellerbe (Rutgers 1985) 7: 96-107; Michigan: 1998		1	1	1	.500	2001
Cliff Ellis* (Florida St. 1968) 2 at South Ala.: 1979, 80; 3 at Clemson: 87, 89, 90; 2 at Auburn: 99, 2000		7	6	7	.462	Active
Fred Enke (Minnesota 1921) 38: 522-344; Arizona: 1951		1	0	1	.000	1961
Lefty Ervin (La Salle 1968) 7: 119-87; La Salle: 1980, 83		2	1	2	.333	1986
Craig Esherick (Georgetown 1978) Georgetown: 2001		1	2	1	.667	Active
Larry Eustachy (Long Beach St. 1979) 1 at Utah St.: 1998; 2 at Iowa St.: 2000-RR, 01		3	3	3	.500	Active
Bill Evans (Southern Utah 1972) Southern Utah: 2001		1	0	1	.000	Active
Jesse Evans (Eastern Mich. 1972) La.-Lafayette: 2000		1	0	1	.000	Active
John Evans (Idaho 1948) 4: 60-41; Idaho St.: 1960		1	0	1	.000	1963
Paul Evans (Ithaca 1967) 21: 392-208; 2 at Navy: 1985, 86-RR; 5 at Pittsburgh: 87, 88, 89, 91, 93		7	7	7	.500	1994
Rob Evans (New Mexico St. 1968) Mississippi: 1997, 98		2	0	2	.000	Active
Larry Farmer (UCLA 1973) UCLA: 1983		1	0	1	.000	Active
Bob Feerick (Santa Clara 1941) 12: 186-120; Santa Clara: 1952-4th, 53-RR, 54-RR, 60		4	6	6	.500	1962
Dennis Felton (Howard 1985) Western Ky.: 2001		1	0	1	.000	Active
George Felton (South Carolina 1975) 5: 87-62; South Carolina: 1989		1	0	1	.000	1991
Mark Few (Oregon 1987) Gonzaga: 2000, 01		2	4	2	.667	Active
Larry Finch (Memphis 1973) 11: 220-130; Memphis: 1988, 89, 92-RR, 93, 95, 96.		6	6	6	.500	1997
Ted Fiore (Seton Hall 1962) 9: 151-110; St. Peter's: 1991, 95		2	0	2	.000	1995
Steve Fisher# (Illinois St. 1967) Michigan: 1989-CH, 90, 92-2nd, 93-2nd, 94-RR, 95, 96		7	20	6	.769	Active
Bill Fitch (Coe 1954) 12: 185-114; Bowling Green: 1968		1	0	1	.000	1970
Dan Fitzgerald (Cal St. Los Angeles 1965) 15: 251-171; Gonzaga: 1995		1	0	1	.000	1997
Cotton Fitzsimmons (Midwestern St. 1955) 2: 34-20; Kansas St.: 1970		1	1	1	.500	1970
Marty Fletcher (Maryland 1973) 19: 246-298; La.-Lafayette: 1992, 94		2	1	2	.333	2001
Bruiser Flint (St. Joseph's 1987) Massachusetts: 1997, 98		2	0	2	.000	Active
John Floyd (Oklahoma St. 1941) 5: 38-82; Texas A&M: 1951		1	0	1	.000	1955
Tim Floyd (Louisiana Tech 1977) 12: 243-130; 2 at New Orleans: 1991, 93; 3 at Iowa St.: 95, 96, 97		5	4	5	.444	1998
Karl Fogel (Colby 1968) Northeastern: 1987, 91		2	0	2	.000	Active
Eddie Fogler (North Carolina 1970) 15: 265-197; 2 at Wichita St.: 1987, 88; 2 at Vanderbilt: 91, 93; 2 at South Carolina: 97, 98		6	2	6	.250	2001
Bill C. Foster (Carson-Newman 1958) 30: 532-325; 1 at Clemson: 1980-RR; 1 at Virginia Tech: 96		2	4	2	.667	1997
Bill E. Foster (Elizabethtown 1954) 33: 467-409; Duke: 1978-2nd, 79, 80-RR		3	6	3	.667	1993
Bud Foster (Wisconsin 1930) 25: 265-267; Wisconsin: 1941-CH, 47-RR		2	4	1	.800	1959
Pat Foster (Arkansas 1961) 19: 366-203; 2 at Lamar: 1981, 83; 3 at Houston: 87, 90, 92		5	2	5	.286	1999
Fran Fraschilla (Brooklyn Col. 1980) 2 at Manhattan: 1993, 95; 1 at St. John's (N.Y.): 98		3	1	3	.250	Active
Bill Frieder* (Michigan 1964) 17: 321-197; 4 at Michigan: 1985, 86, 87, 88; 2 at Arizona St.: 91, 95		6	8	6	.571	1997
Jack Friel (Washington St. 1923) 30: 494-377; Washington St.: 1941-2nd		1	2	1	.667	1958
Matt Furjanic (Point Park 1973) 7: 109-95; 2 at Robert Morris: 1982, 83; 1 at Marist: 86		3	1	3	.250	1986
Gary Garner (Missouri 1965) Southeast Mo. St.: 2000		1	0	1	.000	Active
Roger Gaeckler (Gettysburg 1965) 10: 131-124; Hofstra: 1976, 77		2	0	2	.000	1979
Bob Gaillard (San Francisco 1962) 8: 165-57; San Francisco: 1972, 73-RR, 74-RR, 77, 78		5	4	5	.444	1978
Smokey Gaines (LeMoyne-Owen 1963) 10: 159-127; 1 at Detroit: 1979; 1 at San Diego St.: 85		2	0	2	.000	1987
Jimmy Gales (Alcorn St. 1963) 7: 84-116; North Texas: 1988		1	0	1	.000	1993
Jack Gardner (Southern California 1932) 28: 486-235; 2 at Kansas St.: 1948-4th, 51-2nd; 6 at Utah: 55, 56-RR, 59, 60, 61-4th, 66-4th		8	12	12	.500	1971
Dick Garibaldi (Santa Clara 1957) 8: 137-79; Santa Clara: 1968-RR, 69-RR, 70		3	3	3	.500	1970
Dave Gavitt (Dartmouth 1959) 12: 227-117; Providence: 1972, 73-4th, 74, 77, 78.		5	5	6	.455	1979
Gene Gibson (Texas Tech 1950) 8: 100-92; Texas Tech: 1962		1	1	2	.333	1969
Slats Gill (Oregon St. 1925) 36: 599-392; Oregon St.: 1947-RR, 49-4th, 55-RR, 62-RR, 63-4th, 64		6	8	8	.500	1964
Pete Gillen (Fairfield 1968) 7 at Xavier: 1986, 87, 88, 89, 90, 91, 93; 1 at Providence: 97-RR; 1 at Virginia: 2001		9	8	9	.471	Active
Bully Gilstrap (Texas 1922) 3: 43-28; Texas: 1943-T3rd		1	1	1	.500	1945
Mark Gottfried (Alabama 1987) Murray St.: 1997, 98		2	0	2	.000	Active
Boyd Grant (Colorado St. 1961) 13: 275-120; 3 at Fresno St.: 1981, 82, 84; 2 at Colorado St.: 89, 90		5	2	5	.286	1991
Jack Gray (Texas 1935) 12: 194-97; Texas: 1939-RR, 47-3rd		2	2	3	.400	1951
John Grayson (Oklahoma 1938) 9: 165-82; Idaho St.: 1957, 58, 59		3	4	5	.444	1963
Murray Greason (Wake Forest 1926) 23: 285-244; Wake Forest: 1939-RR, 53		2	1	2	.333	1957
Jerry Green (Appalachian St. 1968) 18: 312-213; 1 at Oregon: 1995; 4 at Tennessee: 98, 99, 2000, 01		5	3	5	.375	2001
Tom Green (Syracuse 1971) Fairleigh Dickinson: 1985, 88, 98		3	0	3	.000	Active
Seth Greenberg (Fairleigh Dickinson 1978) Long Beach St.: 1993, 95		2	0	2	.000	Active
Royner Greene (Illinois 1929) 20: 236-216; Cornell: 1954		1	0	1	.000	1967
Hugh Greer (Connecticut 1926) 17: 286-112; Connecticut: 1951, 54, 56, 57, 58, 59, 60		7	1	8	.111	1963
Elmer Gross (Penn St. 1942) 5: 80-40; Penn St.: 1952, 54-3rd		2	4	3	.571	1954
Marc Guley (Syracuse 1936) 12: 136-129; Syracuse: 1957-RR		1	2	1	.667	1962
Bill Guthridge (Kansas St. 1963) 3: 80-28; North Carolina: 1998-T3rd, 99, 2000-T3rd		3	8	3	.727	2000
Bruce Hale (Santa Clara 1941) 16: 246-164; Miami (Fla.): 1960		1	0	1	.000	1973
Joe Hall (Sewanee 1951) 19: 373-156; Kentucky: 1973-RR, 75-2nd, 77-RR, 78-CH, 80, 81, 82, 83-RR, 84-T3rd, 85		10	20	9	.690	1985
Leonard Hamilton (Tenn.-Martin 1971) 14: 200-210; Miami (Fla.): 1998, 99, 2000.		3	3	3	.500	2000
Brian Hammel (Bentley 1975) 16: 208-208; Northern Ill.: 1996		1	0	1	.000	2001
Paul Hansen (Oklahoma City 1950) 13: 189-168; Oklahoma St.: 1983		1	0	1	.000	1986
Jim Harding (Iowa 1949) 9: 147-71; 1 at Loyola (La.): 1958; 1 at La Salle: 68		2	0	2	.000	1973

As a player, Larry Farmer (right) won three NCAA titles with UCLA from 1971-73. Farmer has coached at UCLA and Weber State, and now coaches at Loyola (Illinois). His only NCAA tournament coaching appearance came with his alma mater.

Tournament facts

Elmer Gross was the first NCAA tournament player to later coach a team into the tournament. Gross played for Penn State in the 1942 and coached his alma mater to tournament appearances in 1952 and 1954.

THE COACHES

COACHES OF ALL-TIME—TOURNAMENT COACHES

Henry Iba was the first coach to lead his team to back-to-back NCAA championships. Oklahoma State (then Oklahoma A&M) won the titles in 1945 and 1946.

Photo by Rich Clarkson

Coach (Alma Mater)	Career Record, Tourney Teams and Years in Tourney	Yrs	W	L	Pct.	Last Year of Career
Dick Harp (Kansas 1940) 10: 141-105; Kansas: 1957-2nd, 60-RR		2	4	2	.667	1964
Jim Harrick (Charleston [W.Va.] 1960) 4 at Pepperdine: 1982, 83, 85, 86; 8 at UCLA: 89, 90, 91, 92-RR, 93, 94, 95-CH, 96; 2 at Rhode Island: 98, 99; 1 at Georgia: 2001		15	17	14	.548	Active
Marv Harshman (Pacific Lutheran 1942) 40: 642-448; Washington: 1976, 84, 85		3	2	3	.400	1986
Dick Harter (Pennsylvania 1953) 18: 296-195; Pennsylvania: 1970, 71-RR		2	2	2	.500	1983
Jack Hartman (Oklahoma St. 1949) 24: 439-233; Kansas St.: 1972-RR, 73-RR, 75-RR, 77, 80, 81-RR, 82		7	11	7	.611	1986
Clem Haskins* (Western Ky. 1967) 19: 341-238; 2 at Western Ky.: 1981, 86; 6 at Minnesota: 89, 90-RR, 94, 95; 97-T3rd, 99		8	11	8	.579	1999
Don Haskins (Oklahoma St. 1953) 38: 719-353; UTEP: 1963, 64, 66-CH, 67, 70, 75, 84, 85, 86, 87, 88, 89, 90, 92		14	14	13	.519	1999
Ray Haskins (Shaw 1972) 4: 60-56; Long Island: 1997		1	0	1	.000	1998
Doc Hayes (North Texas 1927) 20: 298-191; Southern Methodist: 1955, 56-4th, 57, 65, 66, 67-RR		6	7	8	.467	1967
Ken Hayes (Northeastern St. 1956) 15: 236-158; New Mexico St.: 1979		1	0	1	.000	1983
Walt Hazzard (UCLA 1964) 6: 120-61; UCLA: 1987		1	1	1	.500	1988
Jud Heathcote (Washington St. 1950) 24: 417-275; 1 at Montana: 1975; 9 at Michigan St.: 78-RR, 79-CH, 85, 86, 90, 91, 92, 94, 95		10	15	10	.600	1995
Darrell Hedric (Miami [Ohio] 1955) 14: 216-157; Miami (Ohio): 1971, 73, 78, 84		4	1	4	.200	1984
Mike Heideman (Wis.-La Crosse 1971) Wis.-Green Bay: 1996		1	0	1	.000	Active
Bill Henderson (Howard Payne 1925) 18: 201-232; Baylor: 1946-RR, 48-2nd, 50-4th 1961		3	3	5	.375	
Lou Henson (New Mexico St. 1955) 12 at Illinois: 81, 83, 84-RR, 85, 86, 87, 88, 89-T3rd, 90, 93, 94, 95; 7 at New Mexico St.: 1967, 68, 69, 70-3rd, 71, 75, 99		19	19	20	.487	Active
Rich Herrin (McKendree 1956) 13: 225-176; Southern Ill.: 1993, 94, 95		3	0	3	.000	1998
Bill Herrion (Merrimack 1981) Drexel: 1994, 95, 96		3	1	3	.250	Active
Pete Herrmann (Geneseo St. 1970) 6: 63-110; Navy: 1987		1	0	1	.000	1992
Paul Hewitt (St. John Fisher 1985) 1 at Siena: 1999; 1 at Georgia Tech: 2001		2	0	2	.000	Active
Eddie Hickey (Creighton 1927) 26: 435-231; 1 at Creighton: 1941-RR; 2 at St. Louis: 52-RR, 57; 2 at Marquette: 59, 61		5	3	7	.300	1964
Peck Hickman (Western Ky. 1935) 23: 443-183; Louisville: 1951, 59-4th, 61, 64, 67 1967		5	5	7	.417	
Ed Hickox (Ohio Wesleyan 1905) 18: 241-100; Springfield: 1940-RR		1	0	1	.000	1947
Tony Hinkle (Chicago 1921) 41: 560-392; Butler: 1962		1	2	1	.667	1970
David Hobbs (Va. Commonwealth 1971) 6: 110-76; Alabama: 1994, 95		2	2	2	.500	1998
Howard Hobson (Oregon 1926) 23: 400-257; 1 at Oregon: 1939-CH, 1 at Yale: 49-RR		2	3	2	.600	1956
Bill Hodges (Marian 1970) 15: 239-208; Indiana St.: 1979-2nd		1	4	1	.800	1997
Eddie Holbrook (Lenoir-Rhyne 1962) 13: 283-89; Furman: 1980		1	0	1	.000	1982
Terry Holland (Davidson 1964) 21: 418-216; 1 at Davidson: 1970; 9 at Virginia: 76, 81-3rd, 82, 83-RR, 84-T3rd, 86, 87, 89-RR, 90		10	15	10	.600	1990
Nat Holman (Savage School of Phys. Ed. 1917) 37: 423-190; CCNY: 1947-4th, 50-CH		2	4	2	.667	1960
Phil Hopkins (Gardner-Webb 1972) 5: 65-76; Western Caro.: 1996		1	0	1	.000	2000
Robert Hopkins (Grambling 1956) 16: 256-166; Southern U.: 1985		1	0	1	.000	1992
Ben Howland (Weber St. 1980) Northern Ariz.: 1998		1	0	1	.000	Active
Ricky Huckabay* (Louisiana Tech 1967) 6: 129-59; Marshall: 1984, 85, 87		3	0	3	.000	1989
Bob Huggins (West Virginia 1977) 1 at Akron: 1986; 10 at Cincinnati: 92-T3rd, 93-RR, 94, 95, 96-RR, 97, 98, 99, 2000, 01		11	17	11	.607	Active
Dick Hunsaker (Weber St. 1977) 8: 166-73; Ball St.: 1990, 93		2	2	2	.500	2001
Larry Hunter (Ohio 1971) 25: 509-224; Ohio: 1994		1	0	1	.000	2001
Bobby Hussey (Appalachian St. 1962) 20: 311-269; Davidson: 1986		1	0	1	.000	1999
Whack Hyder (Georgia Tech 1937) 22: 292-271; Georgia Tech: 1960-RR		1	1	1	.500	1973
Clarence Iba (Panhandle St. 1936) 11: 137-147; Tulsa: 1955		1	1	1	.500	1960
Gene Iba (Tulsa 1963) 1 at Houston Baptist: 1984; 1 at Baylor: 88		2	0	2	.000	Active
Henry Iba (Westminster [Mo.] 1931) 41: 767-338; Oklahoma St.: 1945-CH, 46-CH, 49-2nd, 51-4th, 53-RR, 54-RR, 58-RR, 65-RR		8	15	7	.682	1970
Moe Iba (Oklahoma St. 1962) 17: 239-244; Nebraska: 1986		1	0	1	.000	1994
George Ireland (Notre Dame 1936) 24: 318-255; Loyola (Ill.): 1963-CH, 64, 66, 68		4	7	3	.700	1975
Tom Izzo (Northern Mich. 1977) Michigan St.: 1998, 99-T3rd, 2000-CH, 01-T3d		4	16	3	.842	Active
Stu Jackson (Seattle 1978) 2: 32-25; Wisconsin: 1994		1	1	1	.500	1994
Ron Jacobs* (Southern California 1964) 1: 14-13; Loyola Marymount: 1980		1	0	1	.000	1980
Mike Jarvis (Northeastern 1968) 2 at Boston U.: 1988, 90; 4 at George Washington: 93, 94, 96, 98; 2 at St. John's (N.Y.): 99-RR, 2000		8	7	8	.467	Active
Ben Jobe (Fisk 1956) Southern U.: 1987, 88, 89, 93		4	1	4	.200	Active
Maurice John (Central Mo. St. 1941) 16: 243-156; Drake: 1969-3rd, 70-RR, 71-RR		3	5	3	.625	1974
Phil Johnson (Utah St. 1953) 3: 68-16; Weber St.: 1969, 70, 71		3	2	3	.400	1971
Dwight Jones (Pepperdine 1965) 4: 70-40; Long Beach St.: 1977		1	0	1	.000	1978
Jeff Jones (Virginia 1982) Virginia: 1991, 93, 94, 95-RR, 97		5	6	5	.545	Active
John Jordan (Notre Dame 1935) 14: 214-145; Notre Dame: 1953-RR, 54-RR, 57, 58-RR, 60, 63		6	8	6	.571	1964
Ed Jucker (Cincinnati 1940) 17: 266-109; Cincinnati: 1961-CH, 62-CH, 63-2nd		3	11	1	.917	1977
Doggie Julian (Bucknell 1923) 32: 388-358; 2 at Holy Cross: 1947-CH, 48-3rd; 3 at Dartmouth: 56, 58-RR, 59		5	9	4	.692	1967
Gene Keady* (Kansas St. 1958) 1 at Western Ky.: 1980; 16 at Purdue: 83, 84, 85, 86, 87, 88, 90, 91, 93, 94-RR, 95, 96, 97, 98, 99, 2000-RR		17	18	17	.514	Active
Lake Kelly* (Georgia Tech 1956) 13: 218-144; Austin Peay: 1973, 74, 87		3	2	4	.333	1990
Pat Kennedy (King's [Pa.] 1976) 2 at Iona: 1984, 85; 5 at Florida St.: 88, 89, 91, 92, 93-RR; 1 at DePaul: 2000		8	6	8	.429	Active
Ernie Kent (Oregon 1977) 1 at St. Mary's (Cal.): 1997; 1 at Oregon: 2000		2	0	2	.000	Active
Frank Kerns (Alabama 1957) 22: 381-210; Ga. Southern: 1983, 87, 92		3	0	3	.000	1995
Matt Kilcullen (Lehman 1976) 10: 121-146; Western Ky.: 1995		1	1	1	.500	1998
Jim Killingsworth (Northeastern Okla. St. 1948) 16: 261-191; 2 at Idaho St.: 1974, 77-RR; 1 at TCU: 87		3	3	3	.500	1987
Bob King (Iowa 1947) 13: 236-113; New Mexico: 1968		1	0	1	.000	1978
George King (Charleston [W.Va.] 1950) 13: 223-119; 3 at West Virginia: 1962, 63, 65; 1 at Purdue: 69-2nd		4	5	4	.556	1972
Dana Kirk* (Marshall 1960) 15: 281-131; Memphis: 1982, 83, 84, 85-T3rd, 86		5	9	5	.643	1986

Tournament trivia

Question...
What were the three schools from the state of Georgia to make the NCAA tournament last season (2001) and who were their coaches?

Answer...
Georgia- Jim Harrick, Georgia State-Lefty Driesell and Georgia Tech-Paul Hewitt

COACHES OF ALL-TIME—TOURNAMENT COACHES 97

Coach (Alma Mater)	Career Record, Tourney Teams and Years in Tourney	Tournament Yrs	W	L	Pct.	Last Year of Career
Bob Knight (Ohio St. 1962) Indiana: 1973-3rd, 75-RR, 76-CH, 78, 80, 81-CH, 82, 83, 84-RR, 86, 87-CH, 88, 89, 90, 91, 92-T3rd, 93-RR, 94, 95, 96, 97, 98, 99, 2000		24	42	21	.667	Active
Don Knodel (Miami [Ohio] 1953) 8: 77-126; Rice: 1970		1	0	1	.000	1974
Jack Kraft* (St. Joseph's 1942) 20: 361-191; 6 at Villanova: 1962-RR, 64, 69, 70-RR, 71-2nd, 72; 1 at Rhode Island: 78		7	11	8	.579	1981
John Kresse (St. John's [N.Y.] 1964) Col. of Charleston: 1994, 97, 98, 99		4	1	4	.200	Active
Lon Kruger (Kansas St. 1974) 18: 316-233; 4 at Kansas St.: 1987, 88-RR, 89, 90; 2 at Florida: 94-T3rd, 95; 3 at Illinois: 97, 98, 2000		9	11	9	.550	2000
Mike Krzyzewski (Army 1969) Duke: 1984, 85, 86-2nd, 87, 88-T3rd, 89-T3rd, 90-2nd, 91-CH, 92-CH, 93, 94-2nd, 96, 97, 98-RR, 99-2nd, 2000, 01-CH		17	56	14	.800	Active
Eugene Lambert (Arkansas 1929) 18: 264-190; 2 at Arkansas: 1945-T3rd, 49-RR; 2 at Memphis: 55, 56		4	2	4	.333	1960
Paul Lambert (William Jewell 1956) 15: 227-160; Southern Ill.: 1977		1	1	1	.500	1978
Bill Lange (Wittenberg 1921) 18: 219-134; North Carolina: 1941-RR		1	0	2	.000	1944
Joe Lapchick (No College) 20: 335-129; St. John's (N.Y.): 1961		1	0	1	.000	1965
Steve Lappas (CCNY 1977) Villanova: 1995, 96, 97, 99		4	2	4	.333	Active
Jim Larranaga (Providence 1971) George Mason: 1999, 2001		2	0	2	.000	Active
Robert Laughlin (Morehead St. 1937) 12: 166-119; Morehead St.: 1956, 57, 61		3	3	4	.429	1965
Steve Lavin* (Chapman 1988) UCLA: 1997-RR, 98, 99, 2000, 01		5	9	5	.643	Active
John Lawther (Westminster [Pa.] 1919) 13: 153-93; Penn St.: 1942-RR		1	1	1	.500	1949
Frank Layden (Niagara 1955) 10: 135-121; Niagara: 1970		1	1	2	.333	1976
Bebe Lee (Stanford 1938) 9: 92-119; Colorado: 1954, 55-3rd		2	3	3	.500	1956
Billy Lee (Barton 1971) Campbell: 1992		1	0	1	.000	Active
Roy Leenig (Trinity [Conn.] 1942) 6: 104-48; Holy Cross: 1956		1	0	1	.000	1961
Alan LeForce (Cumberland 1957) 15: 238-160; East Tenn.: 1991, 92		2	1	2	.333	1996
Abe Lemons (Oklahoma City 1949) 34: 597-344; 7 at Oklahoma City: 1956-RR, 57-RR, 63, 64, 65, 66, 73; 1 at Texas: 79		8	7	9	.438	1990
Fred Lewis (Eastern Ky. 1946) 13: 208-125; Syracuse: 1966-RR		1	1	1	.500	1985
Guy Lewis (Houston 1947) 30: 592-279; Houston: 1961, 65, 66, 67-3rd, 68-4th, 70, 71, 72, 73, 78, 81, 82-T3rd, 83-2nd, 84-2nd		14	26	18	.591	1986
Craig Littlepage (Pennsylvania 1973) 6: 63-102; Pennsylvania: 1985		1	0	1	.000	1988
Harry Litwack (Temple 1930) 21: 373-193; Temple: 1956-3rd, 58-3rd, 64, 67, 70, 72		6	7	6	.538	1973
Paul Lizzo (Northwest Mo. St. 1963) 24: 296-353; Long Island: 1981, 84		2	0	2	.000	1995
Tates Locke (Ohio Wesleyan 1959) 19: 255-254; 1 at Miami (Ohio): 1969; 1 at Jacksonville: 79		2	1	3	.250	1994
Ken Loeffler (Penn St. 1924) 22: 310-198; La Salle: 1954-CH, 55-2nd		2	9	1	.900	1957
John Long (Catholic 1928) 1: 17-7; Catholic: 1944-RR		1	0	2	.000	1944
Dave Loos (Memphis 1970) Austin Peay: 1996		1	0	1	.000	Active
Jerry Loyd (LeTourneau 1976) 5: 72-73; Louisiana Tech: 1991		1	0	1	.000	1994
Cal Luther (Valparaiso 1951) 38: 494-462; Murray St.: 1964, 69		2	0	2	.000	1999
Bob Lutz (Charlotte 1980) Charlotte: 1999, 2001		2	2	2	.500	Active
Jim Lynam (St. Joseph's 1964) 10: 158-118; St. Joseph's: 1981-RR		1	3	1	.750	1981
Nick Macarchuk (Fairfield 1963) Fordham: 1992		1	0	1	.000	Active
Kevin Mackey (St. Anselm 1967) 7: 144-67; Cleveland St.: 1986		1	2	1	.667	1990
Dave Magarity (St. Francis [Pa.] 1974) Marist: 1987		1	0	1	.000	Active
Brian Mahoney (Manhattan 1971) 7: 72-120; St. John's (N.Y.): 1993		1	1	1	.500	1996
Rick Majerus (Marquette 1970) 1 at Ball St.: 1989; 8 at Utah: 91, 93, 95, 96, 97-RR, 98-2nd, 99, 2000		9	17	9	.654	Active
Red Manning (Duquesne 1951) 16: 247-138; Duquesne: 1969, 71		2	2	2	.500	1974
Press Maravich (Davis & Elkins 1941) 20: 232-279; North Carolina St.: 1965		1	1	1	.500	1975
Clair Markey# (Seattle 1963) 1: 0-1; Seattle: 1963		1	0	1	.000	1963
Rinso Marquette (Lebanon Valley 1948) 8: 98-74; Lebanon Valley: 1953		1	1	2	.333	1960
Gregg Marshall (Randolph-Macon 1985) Winthrop: 1999, 2000, 01		3	0	3	.000	Active
Phil Martelli (Widener 1976) St. Joseph's: 1997, 2001		2	3	2	.600	Active
Donald Martin (Georgetown 1941) 9: 109-102; Boston College: 1958		1	0	1	.000	1962
Wayne Martin (Morehead St. 1968) 13: 216-153; Morehead St.: 1983, 84		2	1	2	.333	1987
Joel Mason (Western Mich. 1936) 18: 186-173; Wayne St. (Mich.): 1956		1	1	2	.333	1966
Rollie Massimino (Vermont 1956) Villanova: 1978-RR, 80, 81, 82-RR, 83-RR, 84, 85-CH, 86, 88-RR, 90, 91		11	20	10	.667	Active
Phil Mathews (UC Irvine 1972) San Francisco: 1998		1	0	1	.000	Active
Thad Matta (Butler 1990) Butler: 2001		1	1	1	.500	Active
Paul McBrayer (Kentucky 1930) 16: 212-141; Eastern Ky.: 1953, 59		2	0	2	.000	1962
Jim McCafferty (Loyola [La.] 1942) 10: 132-117; 2 at Loyola (La.): 1954, 57; 1 at Xavier: 61		3	0	3	.000	1962
Fran McCaffery (Pennsylvania 1982) 3: 49-39; 1 at Lehigh: 1988; 1 at UNC Greensboro: 2001		2	0	2	.000	1988
Ray McCallum (Ball St. 1983) Ball St.: 1995, 2000		2	0	2	.000	Active
Jake McCandless# (Princeton 1951) 1: 13-10; Princeton: 1961		1	1	2	.333	1962
Babe McCarthy (Mississippi St. 1949) 11: 175-103; Mississippi St.: 1963		1	1	1	.500	1967
Mack McCarthy (Virginia Tech 1974) Chattanooga: 1988, 93, 94, 95, 97		5	2	5	.286	Active
Neil McCarthy* (Sacramento St. 1965) 22: 448-221; 4 at Weber St.: 1978, 79, 80, 83; 5 at New Mexico St.: 90, 91, 92, 93, 94		9	4	9	.308	1997
George McCarty (New Mexico St. 1950) 4: 60-51; New Mexico St.: 1952		1	0	2	.000	1953
Mike McConathy (Louisiana Tech 1977) Northwestern St.: 2001		1	1	1	.500	Active
Branch McCracken (Indiana 1930) 32: 450-231; Indiana: 1940-CH, 53-CH, 54, 58		4	9	2	.818	1965
John McDougal (Evansville 1950) 10: 136-141; Northern Ill.: 1982		1	0	1	.000	1986
Al McGuire (St. John's [N.Y.] 1951) 20: 405-143; Marquette: 1968, 69-RR, 71, 72, 73, 74-2nd, 75, 76-RR, 77-CH		9	20	9	.690	1977
Frank McGuire (St. John's [N.Y.] 1936) 30: 550-235; 2 at St. John's (N.Y.): 1951-RR, 52-2nd; 2 at North Carolina: 57-CH, 59; 4 at South Carolina: 1971, 72, 73, 74		8	14	8	.636	1980
Bob McKillop (Hofstra 1972) Davidson: 98		1	0	1	.000	Active
Bones McKinney (North Carolina 1946) 8: 122-94; Wake Forest: 1961-RR, 62-3rd		2	6	2	.750	1965
Jack McKinney (St. Joseph's 1957) 9: 164-83; St. Joseph's: 1969, 71, 73, 74		4	0	4	.000	1974
Art McLarney (Washington St. 1932) 3: 53-36; Washington: 1948-RR		1	1	1	.500	1950
Red McManus (St. Ambrose 1949) 10: 138-118; Creighton: 1962, 64		2	3	3	.500	1969

Rick Majerus has nine tournament appearances with 17 wins while coaching Ball State and Utah. In 1998, he led the Utes to the Final Four.

Photo from Utah sports information

Question...
Who are the only two active coaches who have won more than one NCAA championship?

Answer...
Mike Krzyzewski of Duke and Bob Knight of Texas Tech (who won his titles with Indiana), with three each.

Tournament trivia

THE COACHES

COACHES OF ALL-TIME—TOURNAMENT COACHES

From 1980 to 1992, George Raveling coached Washington State, Iowa and Southern California to two NCAA tournaments apiece.

Coach (Alma Mater) Career Record, Tourney Teams and Years in Tourney	Yrs	W	L	Pct.	Last Year of Career
Walter McPherson (San Jose St. 1940) 17: 252-197; San Jose St.: 1951	1	0	1	.000	1960
Ray Mears (Miami [Ohio] 1949) 21: 399-135; Tennessee: 1967, 76, 77	3	0	4	.000	1977
Louis Menze (Central Mo. St. 1928) 19: 166-153; Iowa St.: 1944-T3rd	1	1	1	.500	1947
Steve Merfeld (Wis.-LaCrosse 1984) Hampton: 2001	1	1	1	.500	Active
Shelby Metcalf (Tex. A&M-Commerce 1953) 27: 443-313; Texas A&M: 1964, 69, 75, 80, 87	5	3	6	.333	1990
Jeff Meyer (Taylor 1976) 16: 259-206; Liberty: 1994	1	0	1	.000	1997
Joey Meyer* (DePaul 1971) 13: 226-147; DePaul: 1985, 86, 87, 88, 89, 91, 92	7	6	7	.462	1997
Ray Meyer (Notre Dame 1938) 42: 724-354; DePaul: 1943-T3rd, 53, 56, 59, 60, 65, 76, 78-RR, 79-3rd, 80, 81, 82, 84	13	14	16	.467	1984
Bob Miller (Occidental 1953) 9: 124-112; Cal St. Los Angeles: 1974	1	0	1	.000	1978
Eldon Miller (Wittenberg 1961) 36: 568-419; 1 at Western Mich.: 1976; 4 at Ohio St.: 80, 82, 83, 85; 1 at Northern Iowa: 90	6	5	6	.455	1998
Gus Miller (West Tex. St. 1927) 22: 377-168; West Tex. St.: 1955	1	0	1	.000	1957
Harry Miller (Eastern N. M. 1951) 34: 534-374; Wichita St.: 1976	1	0	1	.000	1988
Mike Miller (East Texas St. 1987) 6: 87-79; Southwest Tex. St.: 1997	1	0	1	.000	2000
Ralph Miller* (Kansas 1942) 38: 657-382; 1 at Wichita St.: 1964-RR; 1 at Iowa: 70; 8 at Oregon St.: 75, 80, 81, 82-RR, 84, 85, 88, 89	10	5	11	.313	1989
Weenie Miller (Richmond 1947) 9: 79-123; VMI: 1964	1	0	1	.000	1964
Bud Millikan (Oklahoma St. 1942) 17: 243-182; Maryland: 1958	1	2	1	.667	1967
Doug Mills (Illinois 1930) 11: 151-66; Illinois: 1942-RR	1	0	2	.000	1947
Ron Mitchell (Edison 1984) Coppin St.: 1990, 93, 97	3	1	3	.250	Active
Charles Moir (Appalachian St. 1952) 20: 392-196; Virginia Tech: 1979, 80, 85, 86	4	2	4	.333	1987
Jim Molinari (Ill. Wesleyan 1977) 1 at Northern Ill.: 1991; 1 at Bradley: 96	2	0	2	.000	Active
Dan Monson (Idaho 1985) Gonzaga: 1999	1	3	1	.750	Active
Don Monson (Idaho 1955) 14: 216-186; Idaho: 1981, 82	2	1	2	.333	1992
Mike Montgomery (Long Beach St. 1968) Stanford: 1989, 92, 95, 96, 97, 98-T3rd, 99, 2000, 01-RR	9	13	9	.591	Active
Dudey Moore (Duquesne 1934) 15: 270-107; Duquesne: 1952-RR	1	1	1	.500	1963
Robert Moreland (Tougaloo 1962) 26: 399-351; Texas Southern: 1990, 94, 95	3	0	3	.000	2001
Stew Morrill (Gonzaga 1974) 1 at Montana: 1991; 2 at Utah St.: 2000, 01	3	1	3	.250	Active
Speedy Morris (St. Joseph's 1973) 15: 238-203; La Salle: 1988, 89, 90, 92	4	1	4	.200	2001
Stan Morrison (California 1962) 23: 275-355; 1 at Pacific (Cal.): 1979; 2 at Southern California: 82, 85; 1 at San Jose St.: 96	4	0	4	.000	1998
Dick Motta (Utah St. 1953) 6: 120-33; Weber St.: 1968	1	0	1	.000	1968
Joe Mullaney (Holy Cross 1949) 22: 366-218; Providence: 1964, 65-RR, 66	3	2	3	.400	1985
Jeff Mullins (Duke 1964) 11: 182-142; Charlotte: 1988, 92, 95	3	0	3	.000	1996
Frank Mulzoff (St. John's [N.Y.] 1951) 3: 56-27; St. John's (N.Y.): 1973	1	0	1	.000	1986
Bill Musselman* (Wittenberg 1961) 12: 232-85; 1 at Minnesota: 1972; 1 at South Ala.: 97	2	1	2	.333	1997
Gerald Myers (Texas Tech 1959) 24: 357-305; Texas Tech: 1973, 76, 85, 86	4	1	4	.200	1991
Jack Nagle (Marquette 1940) 8: 108-70; Marquette: 1955-RR	1	2	1	.667	1958
Lynn Nance (Washington 1965) 16: 269-188; St. Mary's (Cal.): 1989	1	0	1	.000	1993
Danny Nee (St. Mary of the Plains 1971) 2 at Ohio: 1983, 85; 5 at Nebraska: 91, 92, 93, 94, 98	7	1	7	.125	Active
Al Negratti (Seton Hall 1943) 12: 163-156; Portland: 1959	1	0	1	.000	1967
Ernie Nestor (Alderson-Broaddus 1968) 5: 68-81; George Mason: 1989	1	0	1	.000	1993
Mike Newell (Sam Houston St. 1973) 9: 175-104; Ark.-Little Rock: 1986, 89, 90	3	1	3	.250	1993
Pete Newell (Loyola Marymount 1940) 14: 234-123; California: 1957-RR, 58-RR, 59-CH, 60-2nd	4	10	3	.769	1960
C.M. Newton (Kentucky 1952) 32: 509-375; 2 at Alabama: 1975, 76; 2 at Vanderbilt: 88, 89	4	3	4	.429	1989
Steve Newton (Indiana St. 1963) 8: 136-100; Murray St.: 1988, 90, 91	3	1	3	.250	1993
Bob Nichols (Toledo 1953) 22: 377-211; Toledo: 1967, 79, 80	3	1	3	.250	1987
Ken Norton (Long Island 1939) 22: 310-205; Manhattan: 1956, 58	2	1	3	.250	1968
Dickey Nutt (Oklahoma St. 1982) Arkansas St.: 1999	1	0	1	.000	Active
Jim O'Brien (Boston College 1971) 3 at Boston College: 1994-RR, 96, 97; 3 at Ohio St.: 99-T3rd, 2000, 01	6	10	6	.625	Active
Jim O'Brien (St. Joseph's 1974) 10: 135-156; Dayton: 1990	1	1	1	.500	1994
Bucky O'Connor (Drake 1938) 7: 108-54; Iowa: 1955-4th, 56-2nd	2	5	3	.625	1958
Dave Odom (Guilford 1965) Wake Forest: 1991, 92, 93, 94, 95, 96, 97, 2001	8	10	8	.556	Active
Fran O'Hanlon (Villanova 1970) Lafayette: 1999, 2000	2	0	2	.000	Active
Johnny Oldham* (Western Ky. 1948) 16: 260-123; 2 at Tennessee Tech: 1958, 63; 4 at Western Ky.: 66, 67, 70, 71-3rd	6	6	6	.500	1971
Harold Olsen (Wisconsin 1917) 30: 306-234; Ohio St.: 1939-2nd, 44-T3rd, 45-T3rd, 46-3rd	4	6	4	.600	1952
Lute Olson* (Augsburg 1957) 26: 586-213; 5 at Iowa: 1979, 80-4th, 81, 82, 83; 17 at Arizona: 85, 86, 87, 88-T3rd, 89, 90, 91, 92, 93, 94-T3rd, 95, 96, 97-CH, 98-RR, 99, 2000, 01-2nd	22	37	22	.627	Active
Kevin O'Neill (McGill 1979) 12: 169-179; Marquette: 1993, 94	2	2	2	.500	2000
Johnny Orr (Beloit 1949) 29: 466-346; 4 at Michigan: 1974-RR, 75, 76-2nd, 77-RR; 6 at Iowa St.: 85, 86, 88, 89, 92, 93	10	10	10	.500	1994
Ted Owens (Oklahoma 1951) 21: 369-217; Kansas: 1966-RR, 67, 71-4th, 74-4th, 75, 78, 81	7	8	9	.471	1987
Dick Parfitt (Central Mich. 1953) 14: 193-179; Central Mich.: 1975, 77	2	2	2	.500	1985
Bruce Parkhill (Lock Haven 1971) 18: 270-244; Penn St.: 1991	1	1	1	.500	1995
Doyle Parrack (Oklahoma St. 1945) 15: 208-178; Oklahoma City: 1952, 53, 54, 55	4	1	5	.167	1962
Bobby Paschal (Stetson 1964) 18: 280-244; 2 at La.-Lafayette: 1982, 83; 2 at South Fla.: 90, 92	4	0	4	.000	1996
Alden Pasche (Rice 1932) 11: 135-116; Houston: 1956	1	0	2	.000	1956
Ricardo Patton (Belmont 1980) Colorado: 1997	1	1	1	.500	Active
Eddie Payne (Wake Forest 1973) East Caro.: 1993	1	0	1	.000	Active
Randy Peele (Va. Wesleyan 1980) 4: 46-69; UNC Greensboro: 1996	1	0	1	.000	1999
Jerry Peirson (Miami [Ohio] 1966) 6: 94-80; Miami (Ohio): 1985, 86	2	0	2	.000	1990
Peter Peletta (Sacramento St. 1950) 6: 114-51; San Francisco: 1963, 64-RR, 65-RR	3	3	3	.500	1966
Tom Penders (Connecticut 1967) 30: 527-361; 1 at Rhode Island: 1988; 8 at Texas: 89, 90-RR, 91, 92, 94, 95, 96, 97; 1 at George Washington: 99	10	12	10	.545	2001

Tournament trivia

Question...
Who are the only three head coaches to win the NCAA championship during their first year at a new school?

Answer...
Ed Jucker with Cincinnati in 1961, Steve Fisher with Michigan in 1989 and Tubby Smith with Kentucky in 1998

COACHES OF ALL-TIME—TOURNAMENT COACHES

Coach (Alma Mater) Career Record, Tourney Teams and Years in Tourney	Yrs	W	L	Pct.	Last Year of Career
Dom Perno (Connecticut 1964) 9: 139-114; Connecticut: 1979	1	0	1	.000	1986
Buzz Peterson (North Carolina 1986) Appalachian St.: 2000	1	0	1	.000	Active
Vadal Peterson (Utah 1920) 26: 384-224; Utah: 1944-CH, 45-RR	2	3	2	.600	1953
Jim Phelan (La Salle 1951) Mt. St. Mary's (Md.): 1995, 99	2	0	2	.000	Active
Digger Phelps (Rider 1963) 21: 419-200; 1 at Fordham: 1971; 14 at Notre Dame: 74, 75, 76, 77, 78-4th, 79-RR, 80, 81, 85, 86, 87, 88, 89, 90	15	17	17	.500	1991
Jerry Pimm (Southern California 1960) 24: 395-288; 5 at Utah: 1977, 78, 79, 81, 83; 2 at UC Santa Barb.: 88, 90	7	6	7	.462	1998
Rick Pitino (Massachusetts 1974) 1 at Boston U.: 1983; 1 at Providence: 87-T3rd; 6 at Kentucky: 92-RR, 93-T3rd, 94, 95-RR, 96-CH; 97-2nd	8	26	7	.788	Active
Elwood Plummer (Jackson St. 1966) Prairie View: 1998	1	0	1	.000	Active
Bob Polk (Evansville 1939) 25: 355-257; Trinity (Tex.): 1969	1	0	1	.000	1977
Tic Price (Virginia Tech 1979) New Orleans: 1996	1	0	1	.000	Active
Nibs Price (California 1914) 31: 463-298; California: 1946-4th	1	1	2	.333	1954
Skip Prosser (Merchant Marine 1972) 1 at Loyola (Md.): 1994; 4 at Xavier: 95, 97, 98, 2001	5	1	5	.167	Active
Lionel Purcell (UC Santa Barb. 1952) 2: 24-18; Seattle: 1967	1	0	1	.000	1967
Oliver Purnell (Old Dominion 1975) 1 at Old Dominion: 1992; 1 at Dayton: 2000	2	0	2	.000	Active
Tom Quinn (Marshall 1954) 16: 258-175; East Caro.: 1972	1	0	1	.000	1974
Harry Rabenhorst (Wake Forest 1921) 29: 340-264; LSU: 1953-4th, 54	2	2	4	.333	1957
Jack Ramsay* (St. Joseph's 1949) 11: 231-71; St. Joseph's: 1959, 60, 61-3rd, 62, 63-RR, 65, 66	7	8	11	.421	1966
George Raveling (Villanova 1960) 22: 336-292; 2 at Washington St.: 1980, 83; 2 at Iowa: 85, 86; 2 at Southern California: 91, 92	6	2	6	.250	1994
Hank Raymonds (St. Louis 1948) 12: 237-97; Marquette: 1978, 79, 80, 82, 83	5	2	5	.286	1983
Roger Reid (Weber St. 1967) 8: 152-77; Brigham Young: 1990, 91, 92, 93, 95	5	2	5	.286	1997
Bob Reinhart (Indiana 1961) 9: 107-148; Georgia St.: 1991	1	0	1	.000	1994
Bill Reinhart (Oregon 1923) 36: 464-331; George Washington: 1954, 61	2	0	2	.000	1966
Jim Richards (Western Ky. 1959) 7: 102-84; Western Ky.: 1976, 78	2	1	2	.333	1978
Nolan Richardson (UTEP 1965) 3 at Tulsa: 1982, 84, 85; 13 at Arkansas: 88, 89, 90-T3rd, 91-RR, 92, 93, 94-CH, 95-2nd, 96, 98, 99, 2000, 01	16	26	15	.634	Active
Gordon Ridings (Oregon 1929) 4: 70-21; Columbia: 1948-RR	1	0	2	.000	1950
Buzz Ridl (Westminster [Pa.] 1942) 19: 312-174; Pittsburgh: 1974-RR	1	2	1	.667	1975
Elmer Ripley (No college) 10: 133-82; Georgetown: 1943-2nd	1	2	1	.667	1949
Jule Rivlin (Marshall 1940) 8: 100-88; Marshall: 1956	1	0	1	.000	1963
Les Robinson (North Carolina St. 1964) 22: 291-330; 2 at East Tenn. St.: 1989, 90; 1 at North Carolina St.: 91	3	1	3	.250	1996
Steve Robinson (Radford 1981) 2 at Tulsa: 1996, 97; 1 at Florida St.: 98	3	2	3	.400	Active
Polk Robison (Texas Tech 1935) 18: 253-196; Texas Tech: 1954, 56, 61	3	1	3	.250	1961
Red Rocha (Oregon St. 1950) 10: 110-135; Hawaii: 1972	1	0	1	.000	1973
Jack Rohan (Columbia 1953) 18: 197-248; Columbia: 1968	1	2	1	.667	1995
Bill Rohr (Ohio Wesleyan 1940) 12: 157-117; Miami (Ohio): 1953, 55, 57	3	0	3	.000	1963
Lorenzo Romar (Washington 1980) St. Louis: 2000	1	0	1	.000	Active
Dick Romney (Utah 1917) 22: 224-160; Utah St.: 1939-RR	1	1	1	.500	1941
Glen Rose (Arkansas 1928) 27: 383-233; Arkansas: 1941-T3rd, 58	2	1	3	.250	1966
Lee Rose (Transylvania 1958) 19: 388-162; 1 at Charlotte: 1977-4th; 1 at Purdue: 80-3rd	2	8	3	.727	1986
Lou Rossini (Columbia 1948) 25: 359-256; 1 at Columbia: 1951; 3 at New York U.: 60-4th, 62, 63	4	6	6	.500	1979
Dee Rowe (Middlebury 1952) 8: 120-88; Connecticut: 1976	1	1	1	.500	1977
Jeff Ruland (Iona 1991) Iona: 2000, 01	2	0	2	.000	Active
Adolph Rupp (Kansas 1923) 41: 875-190; Kentucky: 1942-T3rd, 45-RR, 48-CH, 49-CH, 51-CH, 52-RR, 55, 56-RR, 57-RR, 58-CH, 59, 61-RR, 62-RR, 64, 66-2nd, 68-RR, 69, 70-RR, 71, 72-RR	20	30	18	.625	1972
Andy Russo (Lake Forest 1970) 10: 183-117; 2 at Louisiana Tech: 1984, 85; 1 at Washington: 86	3	3	3	.500	1989
Kelvin Sampson (UNC Pembroke 1978) 1 at Washington St.: 1994; 7 at Oklahoma: 95, 96, 97, 98, 99, 2000, 01	8	3	8	.273	Active
Rick Samuels (Chadron St. 1971) Eastern Ill.: 1992, 2001	2	0	2	.000	Active
Wimp Sanderson* (North Ala. 1959) 17: 350-176; Alabama: 1982, 83, 84, 85, 86, 87, 89, 90, 91, 92	10	12	10	.545	1999
Jim Satalin (St. Bonaventure 1969) 16: 240-213; St. Bonaventure: 1978	1	0	1	.000	1989
Fred Schaus (West Virginia 1949) 12: 251-96; 6 at West Virginia: 1955, 56, 57, 58, 59-2nd, 60; 1 at Purdue: 77	7	6	7	.462	1978
Charlie Schmaus (VMI 1966) 6: 75-90; VMI: 1977	1	1	1	.500	1982
Tom Schneider (Bucknell 1969) 9: 97-150; 1 at Lehigh: 1985; 1 at Pennsylvania: 87	2	0	2	.000	1992
Bill Scott (Hardin-Simmons 1947) 11: 129-161; Hardin-Simmons: 1953, 57	2	0	2	.000	1962
Bill Self (Oklahoma St. 1985) 2 at Tulsa: 1999, 2000, 1 at Illinois: 2001-RR	3	7	3	.700	Active
Herb Sendek (Carnegie Mellon 1985) Miami (Ohio): 1995	1	1	1	.500	Active
Alex Severance (Villanova 1929) 25: 413-201; Villanova: 1939-T3rd, 49-RR, 51, 55	4	4	4	.500	1961
Fred Shabel (Duke 1954) 4: 72-29; Connecticut: 64-RR, 65, 67	3	2	3	.400	1967
Howard Shannon (Kansas St. 1948) 7: 104-68; Virginia Tech: 1967-RR	1	2	1	.667	1971
Alex Shaw (Michigan 1932) 24: 299-169; Williams: 1955	1	0	1	.000	1973
Buster Sheary (Catholic 1933) 7: 155-36; Holy Cross: 1950-RR, 53-RR	2	2	3	.400	1955
Everett Shelton (Phillips 1923) 31: 494-347; Wyoming: 1941-RR, 43-CH, 47-RR, 48-RR, 49-RR, 52-RR, 53, 58	8	4	12	.250	1968
Beryl Shipley* (Delta St. 1951) 16: 293-126; La.-Lafayette: 1972, 73	2	3	3	.500	1973
Dick Shrider (Ohio 1948) 9: 126-96; Miami (Ohio): 1958, 66	2	1	3	.250	1966
John Shumate (Notre Dame 1974) 10: 136-151; Southern Methodist: 1993	1	0	1	.000	1995
Stan Simpson (Ga. Southern 1961) 5: 71-66; Middle Tenn.: 1982	1	1	1	.500	1984
Al Skinner (Massachusetts 1974) 2 at Rhode Island: 1993, 97; 1 at Boston College: 2001	3	2	3	.400	Active
Roy Skinner (Presbyterian 1952) 16: 278-135; Vanderbilt: 1965-RR, 74	2	1	3	.250	1976
Norm Sloan* (North Carolina St. 1951) 37: 627-395; 3 at North Carolina St.: 1970, 74-CH, 80; 3 at Florida: 87, 88, 89	6	8	5	.615	1989
Dean Smith (Kansas 1953) 36: 879-254; North Carolina: 1967-4th, 68-2nd, 69-4th, 72-3rd, 75, 76, 77-2nd, 78, 79, 80, 81-2nd, 82-CH, 83-RR, 84, 85-RR, 86, 87-RR, 88-RR, 89, 90, 91-T3rd, 92, 93-CH, 94, 95-T3rd, 96, 97-T3rd	27	65	27	.707	1997

Tubby Smith coached Tulsa, Georgia and Kentucky to NCAA tournament appearances in the 1990s, including the 1998 championship year with the Wildcats.

Question...

Match the following nicknamed NCAA tournament coaches with their real first name:

Coach
1. Phog Allen
2. Lefty Driesell
3. Hec Edmundson
4. Slats Gill
5. Jud Heathcote
6. Tony Hinkle
7. Doggie Julian
8. Bones McKinney
9. Digger Phelps
10. Wimp Sanderson
11. Tubby Smith
12. Tex Winter

Nickname
A. Alvin
B. Amory
C. Charles
D. Clarance
E. Forrest
F. Fred
G. George
H. Horace
J. Orlando
K. Paul
L. Richard
M. Winfrey

Answer...

1-E, 2-C, 3-D, 4-B, 5-G, 6-K, 7-A, 8-H, 9-L, 10-M, 11-J, 12-F.

COACHES OF ALL-TIME—TOURNAMENT COACHES

Ohio State coach Fred Taylor led the Buckeyes to the championship in 1960 and runner-up spots in 1961 and 1962.
Photo by Rich Clarkson

Coach (Alma Mater) Career Record, Tourney Teams and Years in Tourney	Yrs	W	L	Pct.	Last Year of Career
George Smith (Cincinnati 1935) 8: 154-56; Cincinnati: 1958, 59-3rd, 60-3rd	3	7	3	.700	1960
Sonny Smith (Milligan 1958) 22: 339-304; 5 at Auburn: 1984, 85, 86-RR, 87, 88; 1 at Va. Commonwealth: 96	6	7	6	.538	1998
Tubby Smith (High Point 1973) 2 at Tulsa: 1994, 95; 2 at Georgia: 96, 97; 4 at Kentucky: 98-CH, 99-RR, 2000, 01	8	18	7	.720	Active
Gene Smithson (North Central 1961) 11: 221-99; Wichita St.: 1981-RR, 85	2	3	2	.600	1986
Fred Snowden (Wayne St. [Mich.] 1958) 10: 167-108; Arizona: 1976-RR, 77	2	2	2	.500	1982
James Snyder (Ohio 1941) Ohio: 1960, 61, 64-RR, 65, 70, 72, 74	7	3	8	.273	1974
Quin Snyder (Duke 1989) Missouri: 2000, 01	2	1	2	.333	Active
Brad Soderberg (Wis.-Stevens Point 1985) 8: 131-73; Wisconsin: 2001	1	0	1	.000	2001
Bob Spear (DePauw 1941) 15: 177-176; Air Force: 1960, 62	2	0	2	.000	1971
Kirk Speraw (Iowa 1980) Central Fla.: 1994, 96	2	0	2	.000	Active
Rob Spivery (Ashland 1972) Alabama St.: 2001	1	0	1	.000	Active
Charlie Spoonhour (School of Ozarks 1961) 5 at Southwest Mo. St.: 1987, 88, 89, 90, 92; 3 at St. Louis: 94, 95, 98	8	3	8	.273	Active
Bob Staak (Connecticut 1971) 10: 133-155; Xavier: 1983	1	0	1	.000	1989
Floyd Stahl (Illinois 1926) 11: 107-120; Harvard: 1946-RR	1	0	2	.000	1958
Kevin Stallings (Purdue 1982) Illinois St.: 1997, 98	2	1	2	.333	Active
Stu Starner (Minn.-Morris 1965) 12: 194-153; Montana St.: 1986	1	0	1	.000	1995
Steve Steinwedel (Mississippi St. 1975) 10: 163-121; Delaware: 1992, 93	2	0	2	.000	1995
Bruce Stewart (Jacksonville St. 1975) 9: 205-84; Middle Tenn.: 1985, 87, 89	3	1	3	.250	1991
Carl Stewart (Grambling 1954) 10: 153-119; Southern U.: 1981	1	0	1	.000	1982
Norm Stewart#* (Missouri 1956) Missouri: 1976-RR, 78, 80, 81, 82, 83, 86, 87, 88, 89, 90, 92, 93, 94-RR, 95, 99	16	12	16	.429	1999
Andy Stoglin (UTEP 1965) 12: 186-166; Jackson St.: 1997, 2000	2	0	2	.000	Active
Dave Strack (Michigan 1946) 9: 124-104; Michigan: 1964-3rd, 65-2nd, 66-RR	3	7	3	.700	1968
Bill Strannigan (Wyoming 1941) 23: 308-289; 1 at Colorado St.: 1954; 1 at Wyoming: 67	2	0	4	.000	1973
Lafayette Stribling (Mississippi Industrial 1957) Mississippi Val.: 1986, 92, 96	3	0	3	.000	Active
Guy Strong (Eastern Ky. 1955) 14: 191-161; Eastern Ky.: 1972	1	0	1	.000	1977
Gene Sullivan (Notre Dame 1953) 9: 149-114; Loyola (Ill.): 1985	1	2	1	.667	1989
Don Suman (Rice 1944) 10: 132-105; Rice: 1954	1	1	1	.500	1959
Eddie Sutton* (Oklahoma St. 1958) 1 at Creighton: 1974; 9 at Arkansas: 77, 78-3rd, 79-RR, 80, 81, 82, 83, 84, 85; 3 at Kentucky: 86-RR, 87, 88; 9 at Oklahoma St.: 91, 92, 93, 94, 95-T3rd, 98, 99, 2000, 01	22	32	22	.593	Active
Johnny Swaim (TCU 1953) 10: 102-151; TCU: 1968-RR, 71	2	1	2	.333	1977
Wayne Szoke (Maryland 1963) 14: 205-174; Monmouth: 1996	1	0	1	.000	1998
Carl Tacy (Davis & Elkins 1956) 14: 245-153; 1 at Marshall: 1972; 4 at Wake Forest: 77-RR, 81, 82, 84-RR	5	5	5	.500	1985
Jerry Tarkanian* (Fresno St. 1956) 4 at Long Beach St.: 1970, 71-RR, 72-RR, 73; 12 at UNLV: 75, 76, 77-3rd, 83, 84, 85, 86, 87-T3rd, 88, 89-RR, 90-CH, 91-T3rd; 2 at Fresno St.: 2000, 01	18	38	18	.679	Active
Dick Tarrant (Fordham 1951) 12: 239-126; Richmond: 1984, 86, 88, 90, 91	5	5	5	.500	1993
Blaine Taylor (Montana 1982) 7: 141-66; Montana: 1992, 97	2	0	2	.000	1998
Fred Taylor (Ohio St. 1950) 18: 297-158; Ohio St.: 1960-CH, 61-2nd, 62-2nd, 68-3rd, 71-RR	5	14	4	.778	1976
Roy Thomas (Baylor 1974) 5: 61-79; N.C. A&T: 1995	1	0	1	.000	1999
Bob Thomason (Pacific [Cal.] 1971) Pacific (Cal.): 1997	1	0	1	.000	Active
Gary Thompson (Wichita St. 1954) 7: 93-94; Wichita St.: 1965-4th	1	2	2	.500	1971
John Thompson (Providence 1964) 27: 596-239; Georgetown: 1975, 76, 79, 80-RR, 81, 82-2nd, 83, 84-CH, 85-2nd, 86, 87-RR, 88, 89-RR, 90, 91, 92, 94, 95, 96-RR, 97	20	34	19	.642	1999
John Thompson III (Princeton 1989) Princeton: 2001	1	0	1	.000	Active
Jimmy Tillette (Our Lady of Holy Cross 1975) Samford: 1999, 2000	2	0	2	.000	Active
Bob Timmons (Pittsburgh 1933) 15: 174-189; Pittsburgh: 1957, 58, 63	3	1	4	.200	1968
Ken Trickey (Middle Tenn. 1954) 15: 217-173; Oral Roberts: 1974-RR	1	2	1	.667	1989
Terry Truax (Maryland 1968) 14: 202-203; Towson: 1990, 91	2	0	2	.000	1997
Billy Tubbs (Lamar 1958) 2 at Lamar: 1979, 80; 9 at Oklahoma: 83, 84, 85-RR, 86, 87, 88-2nd, 89, 90, 92; 1 at TCU: 98	12	18	12	.600	Active
Rod Tueller (Utah St. 1959) 9: 139-120; Utah St.: 1980, 83, 88	3	0	3	.000	1988
M.K. Turk (Livingston 1964) 20: 300-267; Southern Miss.: 1990, 91	2	0	2	.000	1996
Forrest Twogood (Iowa 1929) 21: 321-256; Southern California: 1954-4th, 60, 61	3	3	5	.375	1966
Ralph Underhill (Tennessee Tech 1964) 18: 356-162; Wright St.: 1993	1	0	1	.000	1996
Paul Valenti (Oregon St. 1942) 7: 91-82; Oregon St.: 1966-RR	1	1	1	.500	1970
Jim Valvano* (Rutgers 1967) 19: 345-211; 2 at Iona: 1979, 80; 7 at North Carolina St.: 82, 83-CH, 85-RR, 86-RR, 87, 88, 89	9	15	8	.652	1990
Bob Vanatta (Central Methodist 1945) 22: 349-199; 1 at Bradley: 1955-RR; 1 at Memphis: 62	2	2	2	.500	1973
Butch van Breda Kolff (Princeton 1947) 28: 482-272; Princeton: 1963, 64, 65-3rd, 67	4	7	5	.583	1994
Jan van Breda Kolff (Vanderbilt 1974) 1 at Vanderbilt: 1997; 1 at Pepperdine: 2000	2	1	2	.333	Active
Joe Vancisin (Dartmouth 1944) 19: 206-242; Yale: 1957, 62	2	0	2	.000	1975
Dick Versace (Wisconsin 1964) 8: 156-88; Bradley: 1980, 86	2	1	2	.333	1986
Tim Vezie (Denver 1967) 7: 103-86; San Diego St.: 1975, 76	2	0	2	.000	1979
Mike Vining (La.-Monroe 1967) La.-Monroe: 1982, 86, 90, 91, 92, 93, 96	7	0	7	.000	Active
Gene Visscher (Weber St. 1966) 6: 74-74; Weber St.: 1972, 73	2	1	3	.250	1983
Dick Vitale (Seton Hall 1962) 4: 78-30; Detroit: 1977	1	1	1	.500	1977
Bob Wade* (Morgan St. 1967) 3: 36-50; Maryland: 1988	1	1	1	.500	1989
Jerry Wainwright (Colorado Col. 1968) UNC Wilmington: 2000	1	0	1	.000	Active
Riley Wallace (Centenary [La.] 1964) Hawaii: 1994, 2001	2	0	2	.000	Active
Sox Walseth (Colorado 1948) 22: 292-263; Colorado: 1962-RR, 63-RR, 69	3	3	3	.500	1976
Dick Walters (Illinois St. 1969) 7: 114-87; Evansville: 1982	1	0	1	.000	1985
Royce Waltman (Slippery Rock 1964) Indiana St.: 2000, 01	2	1	2	.333	Active
John Warren (Oregon 1928) 5: 87-74; Oregon: 1945-RR	1	1	1	.500	1951
Tom Wasdin (Florida 1957) 3: 63-18; Jacksonville: 1971, 73	2	0	2	.000	1973
Bucky Waters (North Carolina St. 1957) 8: 132-86; West Virginia: 1967	1	0	1	.000	1973
Gary Waters (Ferris St. 1975) Kent St.: 1999, 2001	2	1	2	.333	Active

Tournament trivia

Question...
Who are the only three coaches to lead four different teams into the NCAA tournament?

Answer...
Lefty Driesell, Jim Harrick and Eddie Sutton

COACHES OF ALL-TIME—TOURNAMENT COACHES

Coach (Alma Mater)	Career Record, Tourney Teams and Years in Tourney	Yrs	W	L	Pct.	Last Year of Career
Lou Watson (Indiana 1950) 5: 62-60; Indiana: 1967		1	1	1	.500	1971
Melvin Watkins (Charlotte 1977) Charlotte: 1997, 98		2	2	2	.500	Active
Perry Watson (Eastern Mich. 1972) Detroit: 1998, 99		2	2	2	.500	Active
Stan Watts (Brigham Young 1938) 23: 371-254; Brigham Young: 1950-RR, 51-RR, 57, 65, 69, 71, 72		7	4	10	.286	1972
James Weaver (DePaul 1947) 7: 110-69; St. Mary's (Cal.): 1959-RR		1	1	1	.500	1962
Paul Webb (William & Mary 1951) 29: 511-257; Old Dominion: 1980, 82, 85		3	0	3	.000	1985
Bob Weinhauer (Cortland St. 1961) 8: 143-90; Pennsylvania: 1978, 79-4th, 80, 82		4	6	5	.545	1985
Larry Weise (St. Bonaventure 1958) 12: 202-90; St. Bonaventure: 1968, 70-4th		2	4	4	.500	1973
Steve Welch (Southeastern La. 1971) 7: 75-121; McNeese St.: 1989		1	0	1	.000	1994
Tim Welsh (Potsdam St. 1984) 1 at Iona: 1998; 1 at Providence: 2001		2	0	2	.000	Active
Bob Weltlich (Ohio St. 1967) 1 at Mississippi: 1981; 1 at Florida Int'l: 95; 1 at South Ala.: 98		3	0	3	.000	Active
Bob Wenzel (Rutgers 1971) 15: 216-221; 1 at Jacksonville: 1986; 2 at Rutgers: 89, 91		3	0	3	.000	1997
Paul Westhead (St. Joseph's 1961) 18: 285-223; 2 at La Salle: 1975, 78; 3 at Loyola Marymount: 88, 89, 90-RR		5	4	5	.444	1997
Davey L. Whitney (Kentucky St. 1953) Alcorn St.: 1980, 82, 83, 84, 99		5	3	5	.375	Active
George Wigton (Ohio St. 1956) 21: 175-275; Connecticut: 1963		1	0	1	.000	1986
Ralph Willard (Holy Cross 1967) 2 at Western Ky.: 1993, 94; 1 at Holy Cross: 2001		3	2	3	.400	Active
Carroll Williams (San Jose St. 1955) 22: 341-277; Santa Clara: 1987		1	0	1	.000	1992
Gary Williams (Maryland 1967) 2 at Boston College: 1983, 85; 1 at Ohio St.: 87; 8 at Maryland: 94, 95, 96, 97, 98, 99, 2000, 01-T3d		11	17	11	.607	Active
Jim Williams (Utah St. 1947) 26: 352-293; Colorado St.: 1963, 65, 66, 69-RR		4	2	4	.333	1980
Joe Williams (Southern Methodist 1956) 22: 363-253; 1 at Jacksonville: 1970-2nd; 5 at Furman: 71, 73, 74, 75, 78; 1 at Florida St.: 80		7	6	8	.429	1986
Richard Williams (Mississippi St. 1967) 12: 191-163; Mississippi St.: 1991, 95, 96-T3rd		3	6	3	.667	1998
Roy Williams (North Carolina 1972) Kansas: 1990, 91-2nd, 92, 93-T3rd, 94, 95, 96-T9, 97, 98, 99, 2000, 01		12	25	12	.676	Active
A.B. Williamson (N.C. A&T 1968) 15: 241-182; Howard: 1981		1	0	1	.000	1990
Tex Winter (Southern California 1947) 30: 454-333; Kansas St.: 1956, 58-4th, 59-RR, 61-RR, 64-4th, 68		6	7	9	.438	1983
Dennis Wolff (Connecticut 1978) Boston U.: 1997		1	0	1	.000	Active
John Wooden (Purdue 1932) 29: 664-162; UCLA: 1950-RR, 52, 56, 62-4th, 63, 64-CH, 65-CH, 67-CH, 68-CH, 69-CH, 70-CH, 71-CH, 72-CH, 73-CH, 74-3rd, 75-CH		16	47	10	.825	1975
Jim Wooldridge (Louisiana Tech 1977) Southwest Tex. St.: 1994		1	0	1	.000	Active
Charles Woollum (William & Mary 1962) 25: 387-315; Bucknell: 1987, 89		2	0	2	.000	2000
Phil Woolpert (Loyola Marymount 1940) 16: 239-164; San Francisco: 1955-CH, 56-CH, 57-3rd, 58		4	13	2	.867	1969
Jay Wright (Bucknell 1983) Hofstra: 2000, 01		2	0	2	.000	Active
Joby Wright (Indiana 1972) 7: 114-89; Miami (Ohio): 1992		1	0	1	.000	1997
Ned Wulk (Wis.-La Crosse 1942) 31: 495-342; Arizona St.: 1958, 61-RR, 62, 63-RR, 64, 73, 75-RR, 80, 81		9	8	10	.444	1982
Wayne Yates (Memphis 1961) 10: 141-141; Memphis: 1976		1	0	1	.000	1985
Steve Yoder (Ill. Wesleyan 1962) 15: 205-227; Ball St.: 1981		1	0	1	.000	1992
Tom Young (Maryland 1958) 31: 524-328; 4 at Rutgers: 1975, 76-4th, 79, 83; 1 at Old Dominion: 86		5	6	6	.500	1991
Bob Zuffelato (Central Conn. St. 1959) 10: 154-121; Boston College: 1975		1	1	2	.333	1983
Matt Zunic (George Washington 1942) 15: 213-135; 1 at Boston U.: 1959-RR; 1 at Massachusetts: 62		2	2	2	.500	1976

In 1977, Terry Tyler led Detroit to an NCAA tournament win under coach Dick Vitale.

*Official NCAA Tournament Records

	Yrs.	Won	Lost	Pct.
Todd Bozeman	2	2	2	.500
Larry Brown	6	14	5	.737
Jim Calhoun	13	24	12	.667
John Calipari	4	7	4	.636
James Dickey	1	0	1	.000
Hugh Durham	7	7	7	.500
Cliff Ellis	6	4	6	.400
Bill Frieder	5	6	5	.545
Clem Haskins	5	5	5	.500
Ricky Huckabay	2	0	2	.000
Ron Jacobs	0	0	0	.000
Gene Keady	16	17	16	.515
Lake Kelly	2	1	2	.333
Dana Kirk	0	0	0	.000
Jack Kraft	6	7	7	.500
Steve Lavin	4	9	4	.692
Neil McCarthy	6	1	6	.143
Joey Meyer	3	0	3	.000
Ralph Miller	7	3	8	.273
Bill Musselman	1	0	1	.000
Johnny Oldham	5	2	5	.286
Lute Olson	21	37	21	.638
Jack Ramsay	6	5	10	.333
Wimp Sanderson	9	10	9	.526
Berly Shipley	0	0	0	.000
Norm Sloan	4	5	3	.625
Norm Stewart	15	9	15	.375
Eddie Sutton	21	30	21	.588
Jerry Tarkanian	15	32	15	.681
Jim Valvano	6	14	5	.737
Bob Wade	0	0	0	.000

Tournament Moments...

Photo by Sam Riche

Photo by Sam Riche

Photo by Sam Riche

March 13, 1998, Midwest first-round game in the Myriad Convention Center in Oklahoma City – With 2.5 seconds remaining and Valparaiso down two to Mississippi and a length-of-the-court play needed to tie or win, coach Homer Drew called a play called "The Pacer." Jamie Sykes, who also played baseball, tossed a perfect pass beyond mid-court to Bill Jenkins, who outjumped two Ole Miss defenders to make the catch and flip the ball to the coach's son Bryce, who swished a 23-foot jumper for a 70-69 victory.

Attendance and Sites

Attendance History 104
Attendance Records 105
All-Time Site and Arena History 106
Tournament Game Arenas By Site 107
Future Dates and Sites 114

Attendance History

By Tournament

Year	Final Date	Final Crowd	*Total Atten.	Sess.	Avg. Atten.	Final Site	Final Facility	No. of Teams
1939	3-27	5,500	15,025	5	3,005	Evanston, IL	Patten Gymnasium	8
1940	3-30	10,000	36,880	5	7,376	Kansas City, MO	Municipal Auditorium	8
1941	3-29	7,219	48,055	5	9,611	Kansas City, MO	Municipal Auditorium	8
1942	3-28	6,500	24,372	5	4,874	Kansas City, MO	Municipal Auditorium	8
1943	3-30	13,300	56,876	5	11,375	New York	Madison Square Garden	8
1944	3-28	15,000	59,369	5	11,874	New York	Madison Square Garden	8
1945	3-27	18,035	67,780	5	13,556	New York	Madison Square Garden	8
1946	3-26	18,479	73,116	5	14,623	New York	Madison Square Garden	8
1947	3-25	18,445	72,959	5	14,592	New York	Madison Square Garden	8
1948	3-23	16,174	72,523	5	14,505	New York	Madison Square Garden	8
1949	3-26	10,600	66,077	5	13,215	Seattle	Edmundson Pavilion	8
1950	3-28	18,142	75,464	5	15,093	New York	Madison Square Garden	8
1951	3-27	15,348	110,645	9	12,294	Minneapolis	Williams Arena	16
1952	3-26	10,700	115,712	10	11,571	Seattle	Edmundson Pavilion	16
1953	3-18	10,500	127,149	14	9,082	Kansas City, MO	Municipal Auditorium	22
1954	3-20	10,500	115,391	15	7,693	Kansas City, MO	Municipal Auditorium	24
1955	3-19	10,500	116,983	15	7,799	Kansas City, MO	Municipal Auditorium	24
1956	3-23	10,600	132,513	15	8,834	Evanston, IL	McGaw Hall	25
1957	3-23	10,500	108,891	14	7,778	Kansas City, MO	Municipal Auditorium	23
1958	3-22	18,803	176,878	14	12,634	Louisville, KY	Freedom Hall	24
1959	3-21	18,498	161,809	14	11,558	Louisville, KY	Freedom Hall	23
1960	3-19	14,500	155,491	16	9,718	San Francisco	Cow Palace	25
1961	3-25	10,700	169,520	14	12,109	Kansas City, MO	Municipal Auditorium	24
1962	3-24	18,469	177,469	14	12,676	Louisville, KY	Freedom Hall	25
1963	3-23	19,153	153,065	14	10,933	Louisville, KY	Freedom Hall	25
1964	3-21	10,864	140,790	14	10,056	Kansas City, MO	Municipal Auditorium	25
1965	3-20	13,204	140,673	13	10,821	Portland, OR	Memorial Coliseum	23
1966	3-19	14,253	140,925	13	10,840	College Park, MD	Cole Fieldhouse	22
1967	3-25	18,892	159,570	14	11,398	Louisville, KY	Freedom Hall	23
1968	3-23	14,438	160,888	14	11,492	Los Angeles	Sports Arena	23
1969	3-22	18,669	165,712	15	11,047	Louisville, KY	Freedom Hall	25
1970	3-21	14,380	146,794	16	9,175	College Park, MD	Cole Fieldhouse	25
1971	3-27	31,765	207,200	16	12,950	Houston	Astrodome	25
1972	3-25	15,063	147,304	16	9,207	Los Angeles	Sports Arena	25
1973	3-26	19,301	163,160	16	10,198	St. Louis	St. Louis Arena	25
1974	3-25	15,742	154,112	16	9,632	Greensboro, NC	Greensboro Coliseum	25
1975	3-31	15,151	183,857	18	10,214	San Diego	Sports Arena	32
1976	3-29	17,540	202,502	18	11,250	Philadelphia	Spectrum	32
1977	3-28	16,086	241,610	18	13,423	Atlanta	Omni	32
1978	3-27	18,721	227,149	18	12,619	St. Louis	Checkerdome	32
1979	3-26	15,410	262,101	22	11,914	Salt Lake City	Special Events Center	40
1980	3-24	16,637	321,260	26	12,356	Indianapolis	Market Square Arena	48
1981	3-30	18,276	347,414	26	13,362	Philadelphia	Spectrum	48
1982	3-29	61,612	427,251	26	16,433	New Orleans	Louisiana Superdome	48
1983	4-4	17,327	364,356	28	13,013	Albuquerque, NM	U. of New Mexico Pit	52
1984	4-2	38,471	397,481	28	14,196	Seattle	Kingdome	53
1985	4-1	23,124	422,519	34	12,427	Lexington, KY	Rupp Arena	64
1986	3-31	16,493	499,704	34	14,697	Dallas	Reunion Arena	64
1987	3-30	64,959	654,744	34	19,257	New Orleans	Louisiana Superdome	64
1988	4-4	16,392	558,998	34	16,441	Kansas City, MO	Kemper Arena	64
1989	4-3	39,187	613,242	34	18,037	Seattle	Kingdome	64
1990	4-2	17,765	537,138	34	15,798	Denver	McNichols Arena	64
1991	4-1	47,100	665,707	34	19,580	Indianapolis	RCA Dome	64
1992	4-6	50,379	580,462	34	17,072	Minneapolis	Humphrey Metrodome	64
1993	4-5	64,151	707,719	34	20,815	New Orleans	Louisiana Superdome	64
1994	4-4	23,674	578,007	34	17,000	Charlotte, NC	Charlotte Coliseum	64
1995	4-3	38,540	540,101	34	15,885	Seattle	Kingdome	64
1996	4-1	19,229	631,834	34	18,583	East Rutherford, NJ	Continental Airlines Arena	64
1997	3-31	47,028	646,531	34	19,016	Indianapolis	RCA Dome	64
1998	3-30	40,509	663,876	34	19,526	San Antonio	Alamodome	64
1999	3-29	41,340	720,685	34	21,197	St. Petersburg, FL	Tropicana Field	64
2000	4-3	43,116	624,777	34	18,375	Indianapolis	RCA Dome	64
2001	4-2	45,994	612,089	35	17,488	Minneapolis	Humphrey Metrodome	65
2002	4-1					Atlanta	Georgia Dome	
2003	4-7					New Orleans	Louisiana Superdome	
2004	4-5					San Antonio	Alamodome	
2005	4-4					St. Louis	Trans World Dome	
2006	4-3					Indianapolis	RCA Dome	
2007	4-2					Atlanta	Georgia Dome	

Championship Game...

Years	Final Session	*Total Atten.	Avg. Atten.
1939-49	11	139,252	12,659
1950-59	10	134,091	13,409
1960-69	10	153,142	15,314
1970-79	10	179,159	17,916
1980-89	10	312,478	31,248
1990-99	10	389,715	38,972
2000-01	2	89,110	44,555
All Time	63	1,396,947	174,073

Tournament History...

Years	All Sessions	*Total Atten.	*Avg. Atten.
1939-49	55	593,032	10,782
1950-59	125	1,241,435	9,931
1960-69	141	1,564,103	11,093
1970-79	174	1,935,789	11,125
1980-89	304	4,606,969	15,155
1990-99	340	6,272,060	18,447
2000-01	69	1,236,866	17,926
All Time	1,208	17,450,254	94,459

*Total attendance: 1939-69; paid attendance: 1970-present.

Twenty-five years ago, UNLV's Reggie Theus towered over North Carolina's Phil Ford in the semifinal game at the Omni during the first Final Four held in Atlanta in 1977, a one-point Tar Heels win.

Photo by Rich Clarkson

Tournament trivia

Question...
Has a school ever won the title game while playing in its home city?

Answer...
Yes, three times. CCNY won the title in New York City in 1950 and UCLA won in 1968 and 1972 in Los Angeles.

# Attendance Records

HIGHEST TOTAL FOR TOURNAMENT
- 720,685, 1999 (34 sessions)
- 707,719, 1993 (34)
- 665,707, 1991 (34)
- 663,876, 1998 (34)
- 654,744, 1987 (34)
- 646,531, 1997 (34)
- 631,834, 1996 (34)
- 624,777, 2000 (34)
- 613,242, 1989 (34)
- 612,089, 2001 (35)

HIGHEST AVERAGE PER GAME OR SESSION FOR TOURNAMENT
- 21,197, 1999 (720,685 in 34 sessions)
- 20,815, 1993 (707,719 in 34)
- 19,580, 1991 (665,707 in 34)
- 19,526, 1998 (663,876 in 34)
- 19,257, 1987 (654,744 in 34)
- 19,016, 1997 (646,531 in 34)
- 18,583, 1996 (631,834 in 34)
- 18,375, 2000 (624,777 in 34)
- 18,037, 1989 (613,242 in 34)
- 17,488, 2001 (612,089 in 35)

HIGHEST GAME OR SESSION—TOURNAMENT
- 64,959, Louisiana Superdome, New Orleans, 1987, CH, Indiana (74) vs. Syracuse (73); NSF, Indiana (97) vs. UNLV (93) and Syracuse vs. Providence (63)
- 64,151, Louisiana Superdome, New Orleans, 1993, CH, North Carolina (77) vs. Michigan (71); NSF, North Carolina (78) vs. Kansas (68) and Michigan (81) vs. Kentucky (78) (ot)
- 61,612, Louisiana Superdome, New Orleans, 1982, CH, North Carolina (63) vs. Georgetown (62); NSF, North Carolina (68) vs. Houston (63) and Georgetown (50) vs. Louisville (46)
- 50,379, Hubert H. Humphrey Metrodome, Minneapolis, 1992, CH, Duke (71) vs. Michigan (51); NSF, Duke (81) vs. Indiana (78) and Michigan (76) vs. Cincinnati (72)
- 47,100, RCA Dome, Indianapolis, 1991, CH, Duke (72) vs. Kansas (65); NSF, Duke (79) vs. UNLV (77) and Kansas (79) vs. North Carolina (73)
- 47,028, RCA Dome, Indianapolis, 1997, CH, Arizona (84) vs. Kentucky (79) (ot); NSF, Arizona (66) vs. North Carolina (58) and Kentucky (78) vs. Minnesota (69)
- 43,116, RCA Dome, Indianapolis, 2000, CH, Michigan St. (89) vs. Florida (76); NSF, Michigan St. (53) vs. Wisconsin (41) and Florida (71) vs. North Carolina (59)
- 45,994, Hubert H. Humphrey Metrodome, Minneapolis, 2001, CH, Duke (82) vs. Arizona (72) (45,406 in semifinals)
- 42,519, Trans World Dome, St. Louis, 1999, MW RF, Michigan St. (73) vs. Kentucky (66)
- 42,440, Trans World Dome, St. Louis, 1999, MW RSF, Michigan St. (54) vs. Oklahoma (46) and Kentucky (58) vs. Miami (Ohio) (43)

[Note: Figures are paid attendance. For Final Four games, media are included.]

HIGHEST SINGLE GAME OR SESSION—FINAL FOUR
- 64,959, Louisiana Superdome, New Orleans, 1987, CH, Indiana (74) vs. Syracuse (73); NSF, Indiana (97) vs. UNLV (93) and Syracuse (77) vs. Providence (63)
- 64,151, Louisiana Superdome, New Orleans, 1993, CH, North Carolina (77) vs. Michigan (71); NSF, North Carolina (78) vs. Kansas (68) and Michigan (81) vs. Kentucky (78) (ot)
- 61,612, Louisiana Superdome, New Orleans, 1982, CH, North Carolina (63) vs. Georgetown (62); NSF, North Carolina (68) vs. Houston (63) and Georgetown (50) vs. Louisville (46)
- 50,379, Hubert H. Humphrey Metrodome, Minneapolis, 1992, CH, Duke (71) vs. Michigan (51); NSF, Duke (81) vs. Indiana (78) and Michigan (76) vs. Cincinnati (72)
- 47,100, RCA Dome, Indianapolis, 1991, CH, Duke (72) vs. Kansas (65); NSF, Duke (79) vs. UNLV (77) and Kansas (79) vs. North Carolina (73)
- 47,028, RCA Dome, Indianapolis, 1997, CH, Arizona (84) vs. Kentucky (79) (ot); NSF, Arizona (66) vs. North Carolina (58) and Kentucky (78) vs. Minnesota (69)
- 45,994, Hubert H. Humphrey Metrodome, Minneapolis, 2001, CH, Duke (82) vs. Arizona (72) (45,406 in semifinals)
- 43,116, RCA Dome, Indianapolis, 2000, CH, Michigan St. (89) vs. Florida (76); NSF, Michigan St. (53) vs. Wisconsin (41) and Florida (71) vs. North Carolina (59)
- 41,340, Tropicana Field, St. Petersburg, Florida, 1999, CH, Connecticut (77) vs. Duke (74); NSF, Connecticut (64) vs. Ohio St. (58) and Duke (68) vs. Michigan St. (62)
- 40,509, Alamodome, San Antonio, 1998, CH, Kentucky (78) vs. Utah (69); NSF, Utah (69) vs. North Carolina (65) and Kentucky (86) vs. Stanford (85) (ot)

[Note: Figures are paid attendance. For Final Four games, media are included.]

HIGHEST SINGLE GAME— NATIONAL CHAMPIONSHIP
- 64,959, Louisiana Superdome, New Orleans, 1987, Indiana (74) vs. Syracuse (73)
- 64,151, Louisiana Superdome, New Orleans, 1993, North Carolina (77) vs. Michigan (71)
- 61,612, Louisiana Superdome, New Orleans, 1982, North Carolina (63) vs. Georgetown (62)
- 50,379, Hubert H. Humphrey Metrodome, Minneapolis, 1992, Duke (71) vs. Michigan (51)
- 47,100, RCA Dome, Indianapolis, 1991, Duke (72) vs. Kansas (65)

HIGHEST SINGLE GAME—REGIONALS FINAL
- 42,519, Trans World Dome, St. Louis, 1999, MW RF, Michigan St. (73) vs. Kentucky (66)
- 40,589, Tropicana Field, St. Petersburg, Florida, 1998, South, Kentucky (96) vs. UCLA (68) and Duke (80) vs. Syracuse (67)
- 33,560, Hubert H. Humphrey Metrodome, Minneapolis, 1989, MW, Illinois (89) vs. Syracuse (86)
- 32,747, Louisiana Superdome, New Orleans, 1981, MW, LSU (96) vs. Wichita St. (85)
- 32,328, Georgia Dome, Atlanta, 1996, East, Massachusetts (86) vs. Georgetown (62)

HIGHEST SINGLE SESSION— REGIONALS SEMIFINAL
- 42,440, Trans World Dome, St. Louis, 1999, MW RSF, Michigan St. (54) vs. Oklahoma (46) and Kentucky (58) vs. Miami (Ohio) (43)
- 40,589, Tropicana Field, St. Petersburg, Florida, 1998, South, Kentucky (96) vs. UCLA (68) and Duke (80) vs. Syracuse (67)
- 34,614, Georgia Dome, Atlanta, 1996, East, Massachusetts (79) vs. Arkansas (63) and Georgetown (98) vs. Texas Tech (90)
- 34,036, Louisiana Superdome, New Orleans, 1981, MW, Wichita St. (66) vs. Kansas (65) and LSU (72) vs. Arkansas (56)
- 33,560, Hubert H. Humphrey Metrodome, Minneapolis, 1989, MW, Illinois (83) vs. Louisville (69) and Syracuse (83) vs. Missouri (80)

HIGHEST SINGLE SESSION—SECOND ROUND
- 37,842, RCA Dome, Indianapolis, 1990, MW, Texas (73) vs. Purdue (72) and Xavier (74) vs. Georgetown (71)
- 37,444, RCA Dome, Indianapolis, 1989, MW, Illinois (72) vs. Ball St. (60) and Louisville (93) vs. Arkansas (84)
- 37,411, RCA Dome, Indianapolis, 1993, MW, Louisville (78) vs. Oklahoma St. (63) and Indiana (107) vs. Xavier (70)
- 34,576, RCA Dome, Indianapolis, 1987, MW, Duke (65) vs. Xavier (60) and Indiana (107) vs. Auburn (90)
- 32,758, RCA Dome, Indianapolis, 1999, South, Ohio St. (75) vs. Detroit (44) and Auburn (81) vs. Oklahoma St. (74)

HIGHEST SINGLE SESSION—FIRST ROUND
- 39,940, RCA Dome, Indianapolis, 1990, MW (2nd session), Texas (100) vs. Georgia (88) and Purdue (75) vs. Northeast La. (63)
- 39,417, RCA Dome, Indianapolis, 1990, MW (1st session), Georgetown (70) vs. Texas Southern (52) and Xavier (87) vs. Kansas St. (79)
- 38,387, RCA Dome, Indianapolis, 1993, MW (2nd session), Xavier (73) vs. New Orleans (55) and Indiana (97) vs. Wright St. (54)
- 38,343, RCA Dome, Indianapolis, 1993, MW (1st session), Oklahoma St. (74) vs. Marquette (62) and Louisville (76) vs. Delaware (70)
- 36,823, RCA Dome, Indianapolis, 1989, MW (2nd session), Illinois (77) vs. McNeese St. (71) and Ball St. (68) vs. Pittsburgh (64)

HIGHEST SINGLE GAME OR SESSION—EAST
- 34,614, Georgia Dome, Atlanta, 1996, RSF, Massachusetts (79) vs. Arkansas (63) and Georgetown (98) vs. Texas Tech (90)
- 32,328, Georgia Dome, Atlanta, 1996, RF, Massachusetts (86) vs. Georgetown (62)
- 30,617, Carrier Dome, Syracuse, N.Y., 1997, RSF, North Carolina (63) vs. California (57) and Louisville (78) vs. Texas (63)
- 30,388, Carrier Dome, Syracuse, N.Y., 2000, RF, Florida (77) vs. Oklahoma St. (65)
- 30,230, Carrier Dome, Syracuse, N.Y., 1997, RF, North Carolina (97) vs. Louisville (74)

HIGHEST SINGLE GAME OR SESSION—SOUTH
- 40,589, Tropicana Field, St. Petersburg, Florida, 1998, RF, Kentucky (86) vs. Duke (84); RSF Kentucky (96) vs. UCLA (68) and Duke (80) vs. Syracuse (67)
- 32,758, RCA Dome, Indianapolis, 1999, 2d, Ohio St. (75) vs. Detroit (44) and Auburn (81) vs. Oklahoma St. (74)
- 32,293, RCA Dome, Indianapolis, 1996, 2nd, Connecticut (95) vs. Eastern Mich. (81) and Mississippi St. (63) vs. Princeton (41)
- 31,373, RCA Dome, Indianapolis, 1996, 1st (1st session), Connecticut (68) vs. Colgate (59) and Eastern Mich. (75) vs. Duke (60)
- 31,569, RCA Dome, Indianapolis, 1996, 1st (2nd session), Mississippi St. (58) vs. Va. Commonwealth (51) and Princeton (43) vs. UCLA (41)

HIGHEST SINGLE GAME OR SESSION— MIDWEST
- 42,519, Trans World Dome, St. Louis, 1999, RF, Michigan St. (73) vs. Kentucky (66)
- 42,440, Trans World Dome, St. Louis, 1999, RSF, Michigan St. (54) vs. Oklahoma (46) and Kentucky (58) vs. Miami (Ohio) (43)
- 39,940, RCA Dome, Indianapolis, 1990, 1st (2nd session), Texas (100) vs. Georgia (88) and Purdue (75) vs. Northeast La. (63)
- 39,417, RCA Dome, Indianapolis, 1990, 1st (1st session), Georgetown (70) vs. Texas Southern (52) and Xavier (87) vs. Kansas St. (79)
- 38,387, RCA Dome, Indianapolis, 1993, 1st (2nd session), Xavier (73) vs. New Orleans (55) and Indiana (97) vs. Wright St. (54)

HIGHEST SINGLE GAME OR SESSION—WEST
- 24,196, Kingdome, Seattle, 1993, RF, Michigan (77) vs. Temple (72)
- 24,021, Kingdome, Seattle, 1993, RSF, Michigan (72) vs. George Washington (64) and Temple (67) vs. Vanderbilt (59)
- 23,666, Kingdome, Seattle, 1991, RF, UNLV (77) vs. Seton Hall (65)
- 23,229, Kingdome, Seattle, 1988, RSF, Arizona (99) vs. Iowa (79) and North Carolina (78) vs. Michigan (69)
- 23,035, Kingdome, Seattle, 1987, RSF, Iowa (93) vs. Oklahoma (91) (ot) and UNLV (92) vs. Wyoming (78)

Capacity Percentages for Preliminary-Round Games

	1st-2nd Round			Regionals			Non-Dome Total			Preliminary-Round Total		
	Capacity	Sold	Pct.	Capacity	Sold	Pct.	Capacity	Sold	Pct.	Capacity	Sold	Pct.
1989	425,625	359,064	84.4	186,834	176,390	94.4	421,734	357,653	84.8	612,459	535,454	87.4
1990	451,818	370,362	82.0	141,000	133,383	94.6	431,093	365,208	84.7	592,818	503,745	85.0
1991	449,275	379,708	84.5	234,666	191,759	81.7	357,375	336,994	94.3	683,941	571,467	83.7
1992	356,354	334,644	93.9	145,598	145,352	99.8	501,952	479,996	95.6	501,952	479,996	95.6
1993	495,390	415,274	83.8	181,400	168,141	92.7	399,290	375,443	94.0	676,790	583,415	86.2
1994	403,941	395,092	97.8	140,036	137,623	98.3	467,477	457,846	97.9	543,977	532,715	97.9
1995	339,921	329,521	96.9	134,520	133,658	99.4	474,441	463,179	97.6	474,441	463,179	97.6
1996	440,491	389,453	88.4	215,374	203,921	94.7	396,604	372,669	94.0	655,865	593,374	90.5
1997	419,198	359,994	85.9	217,000	192,553	88.7	489,098	429,765	87.9	636,198	552,547	86.9
1998	431,050	377,075	87.5	204,900	204,365	99.7	475,250	448,033	94.3	635,950	581,440	91.4
1999	486,603	428,373	88.0	208,114	207,456	99.7	450,817	426,988	94.7	694,717	635,829	91.5
2000	403,152	375,949	93.9	168,318	164,318	97.6	433,260	413,561	95.5	571,470	540,199	94.5
2001	396,150	317,827	80.2	216,500	184,546	85.2	412,650	359,392	87.1	612,650	502,373	82.0

More NCAA tournament games have been played in North Carolina than in any other state. Len Elmore and Maryland played in two of them in the Charlotte Coliseum in 1973.

All-Time Site and Arena History

TOURNAMENT GAMES BY ARENA
- 83, Municipal Auditorium, Kansas City, Mo., 1940-64
- 71, Madison Square Garden, New York, 1943-61
- 69, Jon M. Huntsman Center, Salt Lake City, 1971-2000
- 62, University of Dayton Arena, Dayton, Ohio, 1970-2001
- 55, Omni, Atlanta, 1977-92
- 53, Charlotte Coliseum I, Charlotte, N.C., 1958-93
- 51, Palestra, Philadelphia, 1939-84
- 50, Freedom Hall, Louisville, Ky., 1958-91
- 47, McKale Center, Tucson, Ariz., 1974-2000
- 45, Greensboro Coliseum, Greensboro, 1974-2001
- 45, RCA Dome, Indianapolis, 1987-2000

REGIONAL CHAMPIONSHIP GAMES BY ARENA
- 13, Municipal Auditorium, Kansas City, Mo., 1940-52
- 9, Continental Airlines Arena, East Rutherford, N.J., 1984-99
- 9, Madison Square Garden, New York, 1943-51
- 8, Allen Field House, Lawrence, Kan., 1956-78
- 8, Gill Coliseum, Corvallis, Ore., 1952-67
- 8, William Neal Reynolds Coliseum, Raleigh, N.C., 1952-82
- 6, Ahearn Field House, Manhattan, Kan., 1953-69
- 6, Cole Field House, College Park, Md., 1962-77
- 6, Palestra, Philadelphia, 1939-80
- 6, Rupp Arena, Lexington, Ky., 1977-96

NATIONAL CHAMPIONSHIP GAMES BY ARENA
- 9, Municipal Auditorium, Kansas City, Mo., 1940-64
- 7, Madison Square Garden, New York, 1943-50
- 6, Freedom Hall, Louisville, Ky., 1958-69
- 3, Kingdome, Seattle, 1984-95
- 3, Louisiana Superdome, New Orleans, 1982-93
- 3, RCA Dome, Indianapolis, 1991-2000
- 2, Cole Field House, College Park, Md., 1966-70
- 2, Hubert H. Humphrey Metrodome, 1992-2001
- 2, L.A. Sports Arena, Los Angeles, 1968-72
- 2, St. Louis Arena, St. Louis, 1973-78
- 2, Spectrum, Philadelphia, 1976-81

TOURNAMENT GAMES BY CITY
- 110, Kansas City, Mo., 1940-2001
- 76, New York, 1943-74
- 71, Charlotte, N.C., 1958-99
- 71, Salt Lake City, 1968-2000
- 67, Atlanta, 1977-2001
- 65, Philadelphia, 1939-2001
- 62, Dayton, Ohio, 1970-2001
- 61, Indianapolis, 1940-2000
- 61, Lexington, Ky., 1955-98
- 50, Louisville, Ky., 1958-91

REGIONAL CHAMPIONSHIPS BY CITY
- 17, Kansas City, Mo., 1940-95
- 10, Lexington, Ky., 1957-96
- 9, East Rutherford, N.J., 1986-99
- 9, New York, 1943-51
- 8, Corvallis, Ore., 1952-67
- 8, Lawrence, Kan., 1956-78
- 8, Raleigh, N.C., 1951-82
- 7, Charlotte, N.C., 1958-93
- 7, Philadelphia, 1939-2001
- 7, Provo, Utah, 1962-82

NATIONAL CHAMPIONSHIP GAMES BY CITY
- 10, Kansas City, Mo., 1940-88
- 7, New York, 1943-50
- 6, Louisville, Ky., 1958-69
- 5, Seattle, 1949-95
- 4, Indianapolis, 1980-2000
- 3, Minneapolis, 1951-2001
- 3, New Orleans, 1982-93
- 2, College Park, Md., 1966-70
- 2, Evanston, Ill., 1939-56
- 2, Los Angeles, 1968-72
- 2, Philadelphia, 1976-81
- 2, St. Louis, 1973-78

TOURNAMENT GAMES BY STATE
- 182, North Carolina, 1951-2001
- 139, New York, 1943-2001
- 133, Missouri, 1940-2001
- 126, Utah, 1960-2000
- 119, Texas, 1957-2001
- 117, Kentucky, 1955-98
- 114, California, 1939-2001
- 100, Indiana, 1940-2000
- 96, Ohio, 1957-2001
- 91, Kansas, 1953-94

REGIONAL CHAMPIONSHIPS BY STATE
- 22, Missouri, 1940-99
- 18, North Carolina, 1952-98
- 17, Kansas, 1953-78
- 14, California, 1939-2001
- 14, Kentucky, 1957-96
- 12, New York, 1943-2000
- 11, Texas, 1957-2001
- 10, Oregon, 1952-75
- 10, Utah, 1962-83
- 9, New Jersey, 1986-99

NATIONAL CHAMPIONSHIP GAMES BY STATE
- 12, Missouri, 1940-88
- 7, Kentucky, 1958-85
- 7, New York, 1943-50
- 5, Washington, 1949-95
- 4, California, 1960-75
- 4, Indiana, 1980-2000
- 3, Louisiana, 1982-93
- 3, Minnesota, 1951-2001
- 3, Texas, 1971-98
- 2, Illinois, 1939-56
- 2, Maryland, 1966-70
- 2, North Carolina, 1974-94
- 2, Pennsylvania, 1976-81

Tournament Game Arenas By Site

Number of games is indicated by (G), number of sessions by (S), year by (Yr.); national championship game by (CH), national third-place game by (3d), regional by (Rgnl), second round by (2d), first round by (1st), opening round by (OR), East region by (East), Southeast region by (SE), Mideast region by (ME), Midwest region (MW), West region by (W), Far West region by (FW), Eastern region by (En), Western region by (Wn), East-1 region by (E-1), East-2 region by (E-2), West-1 region by (W-1), West-2 region by (W-2), triple-header by (TH) and noncampus arena by (#).

G	S	Yr.	Round	City	Facility	Built	Capacity
ALABAMA							
3	2	1982	ME Rgnl	Birmingham	#Birmingham-Jefferson Civic Center	1976	17,500
4	2	1984	E 1st-2d	"	"		"
3	2	1985	SE Rgnl	"	"		"
6	3	1987	SE 1st-2d	"	"		"
3	2	1988	SE Rgnl	"	"		"
3	2	1997	SE Rgnl	"	"		"
3	2	1995	SE Rgnl	"	"		16,835
6	3	2000	S 1st-2d	"	"		"
4	2	1974	ME Rgnl	Tuscaloosa	Memorial Coliseum	1968	15,043
2	1	1975	ME 1st	"	"		"
4	2	1981	ME 1st-2d	"	"		"
					(now named Coleman Coliseum)		
2	1	75	W 1st	Tempe	University Activity Center	1974	14,287
2	1	1975	W 1st	Tempe	University Activity Center	1974	14,287
2	1	1976	W 1st	"	"		"
2	1	1978	W 1st	"	"		"
4	2	1980	W 1st-2d	"	"		"
6	3	1992	W 1st-2d	"	"		"
6	3	1996	W 1st-2d	"	"		13,849
4	2	1974	W Rgnl	Tucson	McKale Center	1973	14,214
2	1	1977	W 1st	"	"		"
2	1	1979	W 2d	"	"		"
3	2	1980	W Rgnl	"	"		"
6	3	1987	W 1st-2d	"	"		13,124
6	3	1989	W 1st-2d	"	"		13,477
6	3	1991	W 1st-2d	"	"		"
6	3	1993	W 1st-2d	"	"		"
6	3	1997	W 1st-2d	"	"		14,428
6	3	2000	W 1st-2d	"	"		13,859
3	2	1999	W Rgnl	Phoenix	#America West Arena	1992	19,022
CALIFORNIA							
3	2	1998	W Rgnl	Anaheim	#Arrowhead Pond	1993	17,533
3	2	2001	W Rgnl	"	"		17,268
2	1	1958	W 1st	Berkeley	Harmon Arena	1933	6,450
6	3	1986	W 1st-2d	Long Beach	#Long Beach Arena	1965	12,000
6	3	1990	W 1st-2d	"	"		"
4	2	1968	Final Four	Los Angeles	#L.A. Sports Arena	1959	15,509
4	2	1972	Final Four	"	"		"
3	2	1994	W Rgnl	"	"		14,616
4	2	1966	W Rgnl	"	Pauley Pavilion	1965	12,543
4	2	1969	W Rgnl	"	"		"
4	2	1973	W Rgnl	"	"		"
3	2	1976	W Rgnl	"	"		"
4	2	1979	W 1st-2d	"	"		"
4	2	1981	W 1st-2d	"	"		"
3	2	1984	W Rgnl	"	"		"
6	3	1988	W 1st-2d	"	"		"
3	2	1990	W Rgnl	Oakland	#Oakland-Alameda County Coliseum	1966	15,000
3	2	1995	W Rgnl	"	"		15,039
1	1	1953	W-2 1st	Palo Alto	Old Pavilion	1922	3,000
6	3	1994	W 1st-2d	Sacramento	#Arco Arena	1981	16,418
6	3	1998	W 1st-2d	"	"		16,621
4	2	1975	Final Four	San Diego	#San Diego Sports Arena	1967	13,741
6	3	2001	W 1st-2d	"	Cox Arena at Aztec Bowl	1997	12,200
4	2	1939	Wn Rgnl	San Francisco	#California Coliseum	1938	9,476
2	1	1955	W-2 1st	"	#Cow Palace	1941	14,500
4	2	1958	W Rgnl	"	"		"
4	2	1959	W Rgnl	"	"		"
1	1	1960	W 1st	"	"		"
4	2	1960	Final Four	"	"		"
3	2	1997	W Rgnl	San Jose	#San Jose Arena	1993	18,543
COLORADO							
3	2	1985	W Rgnl	Denver	#McNichols Sports Arena	1974	17,022
3	2	1989	W Rgnl	"	"		"
3	2	1990	Final Four	"	"		"
3	2	1996	W Rgnl	"	"		"
3	2	1999	W Rgnl	"	"		18,707
6	3	1999	W 1st-2d	"	"		"
2	1	1967	MW,W 1st	Fort Collins	Moby Arena	1966	9,001
CONNECTICUT							
4	2	1983	E 1st-2d	Hartford	#Hartford Civic Center	1975	16,016
6	3	1985	E 1st-2d	"	"		"
6	3	1988	E 1st-2d	"	"		"
6	3	1990	E 1st-2d	"	"		"
6	3	1998	E 1st-2d	"	"		"
DISTRICT OF COLUMBIA							
6	3	1998	E 1st-2d	Washington	#MCI Center	1997	19,288
FLORIDA							
3	2	1994	E Rgnl	Miami	#Miami Arena	1988	15,308
6	3	1993	SE 1st-2d	Orlando	#Orlando Arena	1989	14,910

In 1990, seniors Karl Brown (5) and Johnny McNeil celebrate Georgia Tech's only victory in an NCAA regional final by indicating the team's next stop, McNichols Sports Arena in Denver, a city that has hosted one Final Four.

Question... What are the only two father-and-son combinations to win NCAA championships as players?

Answer... Marques (UCLA 1975) and Kris (UCLA 1995) Johnson; and Henry (UCLA, 1970, '71, '72) and Mike (Arizona 1997) Bibby

Tournament trivia

TOURNAMENT GAME ARENAS BY SITE

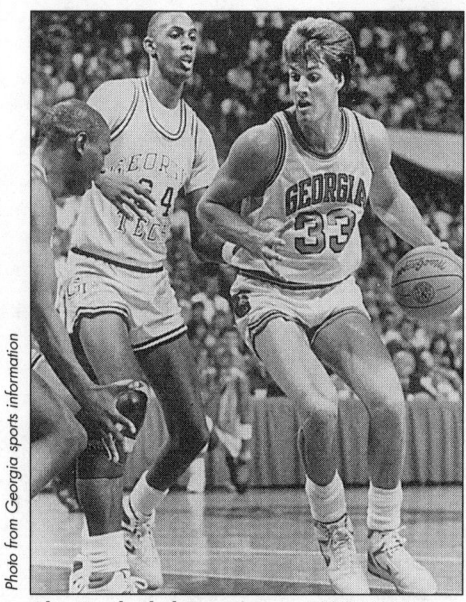

Alec Kessler led Georgia to a 1990 NCAA tournament berth and first-round game in the RCA Dome in Indianapolis.

G	S	Yr.	Round	City	Facility	Built	Capacity
FLORIDA							
6	3	1996	SE 1st-2d	"	"		16,894
6	3	1999	South 1st-2d	"	"		17,164
6	3	1994	SE 1st-2d	St. Petersburg	#ThunderDome	1990	22,665
3	2	1998	South Rgnl	"	#Tropicana Field (name change)		40,589
3	2	1999	Final Four	"	"		41,340
6	3	1995	SE 1st-2d	Tallahassee	#Tallahassee-Leon County Civic Center	1981	13,000
4	2	1983	ME 1st-2d	Tampa	USF Sun Dome	1980	10,347
GEORGIA							
4	2	1971	ME Rgnl	Athens	Georgia Coliseum	1964	11,200
3	2	1996	E Rgnl	Atlanta	#Georgia Dome	1992	40,628
6	3	1998	South 1st-2d	"	"		26,700
3	2	2001	South Rgnl	"	"		12,375
4	2	1977	Final Four	"	#Omni	1972	16,271
3	2	1981	E Rgnl	"	"		"
3	2	1984	E Rgnl	"	"		"
6	3	1985	E 1st-2d	"	"		"
3	2	1986	SE Rgnl	"	"		"
6	3	1987	SE 1st-2d	"	"		"
6	3	1988	SE 1st-2d	"	"		"
6	3	1989	SE 1st-2d	"	"		"
6	3	1990	E 1st-2d	"	"		"
6	3	1991	SE 1st-2d	"	"		"
6	3	1992	SE 1st-2d	"	"		"
IDAHO							
4	2	1983	W 1st-2d	Boise	BSU Pavilion	1982	12,200
6	3	1989	W 1st-2d	"	"		"
6	3	1992	W 1st-2d	"	"		"
6	3	1995	W 1st-2d	"	"		12,375
6	3	1998	W 1st-2d	"	"		11,900
6	3	2001	W 1st-2d	"	"		12,375
1	1	1957	W 1st	Pocatello	ISU Gymnasium (now named Reed Gym)	1948	3,500
2	1	1972	W 1st	"	ISU Minidome	1969	12,000
2	1	1974	W 1st	"	"		"
2	1	1977	W 1st	"	(now named Holt Arena)		
ILLINOIS							
2	1	1969	ME 1st	Carbondale	SIU Arena	1964	10,014
1	1	1960	MW 1st	Chicago	Alumni Arena	1956	5,308
4	2	1952	E-2 Rgnl	"	#Chicago Stadium	1929	17,458
4	2	1953	E-2 Rgnl	"	"		"
6	3	1998	MW 1st-2d	"	#United Center	1994	22,579
4	2	1955	E-2 Rgnl	Evanston	McGaw Hall	1952	10,500
4	2	1956	Final Four	"	"		"
2	1	1958	ME 1st	"	"		"
4	2	1959	ME Rgnl	"	"		"
2	1	1963	ME 1st	"	"		"
2	1	1964	ME 1st	"	"		"
4	2	1967	ME Rgnl	"	"		"
					(now named Welsh-Ryan Arena/McGaw Hall)		
1	1	1939	CH	"	Patten Gym	1910	6,000
1	1	1954	W-1 1st	Peoria	Robertson Memorial Field House	1949	7,300
6	3	1987	MW 1st-2d	Rosemont	#Rosemont Horizon	1980	17,500
6	3	1993	MW 1st-2d	"	"		"
INDIANA							
2	1	1977	ME 1st	Bloomington	Assembly Hall	1971	17,357
2	1	1979	ME 2d	"	"		"
3	2	1981	ME Rgnl	"	"		"
4	2	1983	ME 1st-2d	Evansville	#Roberts Municipal Stadium	1956	11,096
2	1	1953	E-2 1st	Fort Wayne	#Allen County Coliseum	1952	9,500
2	1	1954	E-2 1st	"	"		"
2	1	1956	ME 1st	"	"		"
3	2	1940	En Rgnl	Indianapolis	Butler Field House (now named Hinkle Field House)	1928	15,000
6	3	1987	MW 1st-2d	"	#Hoosier Dome	1984	47,100
6	3	1989	MW 1st-2d	"	"		"
6	3	1990	MW 1st-2d	"	"		"
3	2	1991	Final Four	"	"		"
6	3	1993	MW 1st-2d	"	"		"
6	3	1996	SE 1st-2d	"	#RCA Dome (name change)		40,868
3	2	1997	Final Four	"	"		47,028
6	3	1999	South 1st-2d	"	"		37,900
3	2	2000	Final Four	"	"		43,116
2	1	1978	ME 1st	"	#Market Square Arena	1974	17,000
3	2	1979	ME Rgnl	"	"		"
4	2	1980	Final Four	"	"		"
4	2	1982	ME 1st-2d	"	"		"
2	1	1971	ME 1st	South Bend	Athletic & Convocation Center	1968	11,350
2	1	1976	ME 1st	"	"		"
6	3	1985	SE 1st-2d	"	"		"
6	3	1988	MW 1st-2d	"	The Joyce Center (name change)		
2	1	1974	ME 1st	Terre Haute	Hulman Center	1973	10,200
4	2	1980	ME 1st-2d	West Lafayette	Mackey Arena	1967	14,123
IOWA							
4	2	1972	MW Rgnl	Ames	James Hilton Coliseum	1971	14,020
4	2	1954	E-2 Rgnl	Iowa City	Iowa Field House	1927	13,500
4	2	1956	MW Rgnl	"	"		"
4	2	1962	ME Rgnl	"	"		"
4	2	1966	ME Rgnl	"	"		"

Tournament trivia

Question... Which are the only two schools to win the championship one season and have a losing record the next season?

Answer... Stanford (1942) and Michigan State (1979).

TOURNAMENT GAME ARENAS BY SITE

G	S	Yr.	Round	City	Facility	Built	Capacity
KANSAS							
4	2	1956	MW Rgnl	Lawrence	Allen Field House	1955	15,200
4	2	1958	MW Rgnl	"	"		"
4	2	1959	MW Rgnl	"	"		"
4	2	1961	MW Rgnl	"	"		"
4	2	1963	MW Rgnl	"	"		"
4	2	1967	MW Rgnl	"	"		"
4	2	1970	MW Rgnl	"	"		"
2	1	1976	MW 1st	"	"		"
3	2	1978	MW Rgnl	"	"		"
4	2	1979	MW 1st-2d	"	"		"
4	2	1953	W-1 Rgnl	Manhattan	Ahearn Field House	1951	12,500
4	2	1955	W-1 Rgnl	"	"		"
4	2	1960	MW Rgnl	"	"		"
4	2	1962	MW Rgnl	"	"		"
4	2	1965	MW Rgnl	"	"		"
4	2	1969	MW Rgnl	"	"		"
2	1	1956	MW 1st	Wichita	Levitt Arena	1955	10,716
4	2	1964	MW Rgnl	"	"		10,666
2	1	1966	MW,W 1st	"	"		"
4	2	1968	MW Rgnl	"	"		"
4	2	1971	MW Rgnl	"	"		"
2	1	1973	MW 1st	"	"		"
2	1	1978	MW 1st	"	"		"
4	2	1981	MW 1st-2d	"	"		"
6	3	1994	MW 1st-2d	"	#Kansas Coliseum	1978	10,086
KENTUCKY							
2	1	1965	ME 1st	Bowling Green	E.A. Diddle Arena	1963	8,500
4	2	1980	ME 1st-2d	"	"		12,370
2	1	1955	E-2 1st	Lexington	Memorial Coliseum	1950	11,500
4	2	1957	ME Rgnl	"	"		"
4	2	1958	ME Rgnl	"	"		"
2	1	1959	ME 1st	"	"		"
2	1	1960	ME 1st	"	"		"
2	1	1962	ME 1st	"	"		"
4	2	1965	ME Rgnl	"	"		"
2	1	1967	ME 1st	"	"		"
4	2	1968	ME Rgnl	"	"		"
2	1	1975	ME 1st	"	"		"
3	2	1977	ME Rgnl	"	#Rupp Arena	1976	23,000
3	2	1980	ME Rgnl	"	"		"
3	2	1984	ME Rgnl	"	"		"
3	2	1985	Final Four	"	"		"
3	2	1989	SE Rgnl	"	"		"
3	2	1992	SE Rgnl	"	"		"
6	3	1994	SE 1st-2d	"	"		22,564
3	2	1996	SE Rgnl	"	"		23,890
6	3	1998	South 1st-2d	"	"		22,700
4	2	1958	Final Four	Louisville	#Freedom Hall	1956	17,865
4	2	1959	Final Four	"	"		18,750
4	2	1960	ME Rgnl	"	"		"
6	3	1961	ME 1st-Rgnl	"	"		18,000
4	2	1962	Final Four	"	"		"
4	2	1963	Final Four	"	"		"
4	2	1967	Final Four	"	"		18,800
4	2	1969	Final Four	"	"		"
3	2	1976	MW Rgnl	"	"		16,433
4	2	1983	MW 1st-2d	"	"		16,613
3	2	1987	SE Rgnl	"	"		19,865
6	3	1991	SE 1st-2d	"	"		18,946
LOUISIANA							
3	2	1976	ME Rgnl	Baton Rouge	Assembly Center	1971	14,327
2	1	1977	ME 1st	"	"		14,327
6	3	1986	ME 1st-2d	"	"		14,236
4	2	1942	En Rgnl	New Orleans	Tulane Gym (now named Fogelman Arena)	1933	3,000
3	2	1981	MW Rgnl	"	#Louisiana Superdome	1975	64,959
3	2	1982	Final Four	"	"		"
3	2	1987	Final Four	"	"		"
3	2	1990	SE Rgnl	"	"		"
3	2	1993	Final Four	"	"		64,151
6	3	1999	MW 1st-2d	"	"		24,912
6	3	2001	South 1st-2d	"	"		"
MARYLAND							
6	3	1995	E 1st-2d	Baltimore	#Baltimore Arena	1962	12,959
4	2	1962	E Rgnl	College Park	Cole Field House	1955	14,500
4	2	1963	E Rgnl	"	"		"
4	2	1965	E Rgnl	"	"		"
4	2	1966	Final Four	"	"		"
4	2	1967	E Rgnl	"	"		"
2	1	1968	E 1st	"	"		"
4	2	1969	E Rgnl	"	"		"
4	2	1970	Final Four	"	"		"
3	2	1977	E Rgnl	"	"		"
6	3	1991	E 1st-2d	"	"		"
6	3	1994	E 1st-2d	Landover	#USAir Arena	1973	19,611
MASSACHUSETTS							
6	3	1992	E 1st-2d	Worcester	#Centrum	1983	13,452
6	3	1999	E 1st-2d	Boston	#FleetCenter	1995	18,800

Kentucky forward Larry Conley attempts to shoot between Willie Worsley (24) and Willie Cager of Texas Western (later UTEP) during the 1966 NCAA championship game in Cole Field House in College Park, Maryland. Texas Western won the title.

Photo by Rich Clarkson

Tournament facts

Only five schools have appeared in the Final Four and the College World Series in the same school year. They are: Bradley in 1950, Houston in 1967, UCLA in 1967, LSU in 1986 and Kansas in 1993.

TOURNAMENT GAME ARENAS BY SITE

The state of Missouri has hosted the Final Four a record 12 times. In 1978, the Checkerdome in St. Louis was the site of the championship game, in which Jack Givens (21) helped Kentucky to the title over Duke.

Photo by Rich Clarkson

Tournament trivia

Question...

Can you match the following arenas that have hosted the Final Four with the city in which they are located?

Arena
1. Checkerdome
2. Cole Fieldhouse
3. Cow Palace
4. Freedom Hall
5. Humphrey Metrodome
6. Kemper Arena
7. Kingdome
8. McGaw Hall
9. McNichols Arena
10. Omni
11. The Pit
12. Reunion Arena
13. Rupp Arena
14. Spectrum
15. Superdome

City
A. Albuquerque, NM
B. Atlanta
C. College Park, MD
D. Dallas
E. Denver
F. Evanston, IL
G. Kansas City, MO
H. Lexington, KY
J. Louisville KY
K. Minneapolis
L. New Orleans
M. Philadelphia
N. St. Louis
P. San Francisco
Q. Seattle

Answer...

1-N, 2-C, 3-P, 4-J, 5-K, 6-G, 7-Q, 8-F, 9-E, 10-B, 11-A, 12-D, 13-H, 14-M, 15-L

G	S	Yr.	Round	City	Facility	Built	Capacity
MICHIGAN							
6	3	1997	MW 1st-2d	Auburn Hills	#Palace of Auburn Hills	1988	21,020
3	2	2000	MW Rgnl	"	"		21,214
4	2	1963	ME Rgnl	East Lansing	Jenison Field House	1940	12,500
3	2	1988	MW Rgnl	Pontiac	#Pontiac Silverdome	1975	36,000
3	2	1991	MW Rgnl	"	"		"
MINNESOTA							
6	3	1986	MW 1st-2d	Minneapolis	#Hubert H. Humphrey Metrodome	1982	35,000
3	2	1989	MW Rgnl	"	"		"
6	3	1991	MW 1st-2d	"	"		"
3	2	1992	Final Four	"	"		"
3	2	1996	MW Rgnl	"	"		"
6	3	2000	MW 1st-2d	"	"		"
3	2	2001	Final Four	"	"		45,994
2	1	1951	CH-3d	"	Williams Arena	1928	18,052
4	2	1964	ME Rgnl	"	"		"
MISSOURI							
3	2	1983	MW Rgnl	Kansas City	#Kemper Arena	1975	17,153
3	2	1986	MW Rgnl	"	"		"
3	2	1988	Final Four	"	"		"
3	2	1992	MW Rgnl	"	"		"
3	2	1995	MW Rgnl	"	"		16,668
6	3	1997	MW 1st-2d	"	"		"
6	3	2001	MW 1st-2d	"	"		17,484
5	3	1940	Wn Rgnl-CH	"	#Municipal Auditorium	1935	10,500
5	3	1941	Wn Rgnl-CH	"	"		"
5	3	1942	Wn Rgnl-CH	"	"		"
4	2	1943	Wn Rgnl	"	"		"
4	2	1944	Wn Rgnl	"	"		"
4	2	1945	Wn Rgnl	"	"		"
4	2	1946	Wn Rgnl	"	"		"
4	2	1947	Wn Rgnl	"	"		"
4	2	1948	Wn Rgnl	"	"		"
4	2	1949	Wn Rgnl	"	"		"
4	2	1950	Wn Rgnl	"	"		"
8	4	1951	W 1st-Rgnl	"	"		"
4	2	1952	W-1 Rgnl	"	"		"
4	2	1953	Final Four	"	"		"
4	2	1954	Final Four	"	"		"
4	2	1955	Final Four	"	"		"
4	2	1957	Final Four	"	"		"
4	2	1961	Final Four	"	"		"
4	2	1964	Final Four	"	"		"
4	2	1973	Final Four	St. Louis	#Arena	1929	18,500
4	2	1978	Final Four	"	#Checkerdome (name change)		"
3	2	1982	MW Rgnl	"	"		"
3	2	1984	MW Rgnl	"	#Arena (name changed back)		"
3	2	1993	MW Rgnl	"	"		"
3	2	1998	MW Rgnl	"	#Kiel Center	1994	22,172
3	2	1999	MW Rgnl	"	#Trans World Dome	1995	37,542
NEBRASKA							
4	2	1980	MW 1st-2d	Lincoln	Bob Devaney Sports Center	1976	14,478
4	2	1984	MW 1st-2d	"	"		"
6	3	1988	MW 1st-2d	"	"		"
2	1	1977	MW 1st	Omaha	#Omaha Civic Auditorium	1954	9,373
NEW JERSEY							
4	2	1984	E 1st-2d	East Rutherford	#Meadowlands Arena	1981	20,149
3	2	1986	E Rgnl	"	"		"
3	2	1987	E Rgnl	"	"		"
3	2	1988	E Rgnl	"	"		"
3	2	1989	E Rgnl	"	"		"
3	2	1990	E Rgnl	"	"		"
3	2	1991	E Rgnl	"	"		"
3	2	1993	E Rgnl	"	"		"
3	2	1995	E Rgnl	"	"		19,761
3	2	1996	Final Four	"	#Continental Airlines Arena (name change)		19,229
3	2	1999	E Rgnl	"	"		19,557
1	1	1970	E 1st	Princeton	Jadwin Gymnasium	1969	7,550
1	1	1972	E 1st	"	"		"
NEW MEXICO							
4	2	1968	W Rgnl	Albuquerque	University Arena	1966	14,831
3	2	1978	W Rgnl	"	"		17,126
3	2	1983	Final Four	"	"		"
6	3	1985	W 1st-2d	"	"		"
3	2	1992	W Rgnl	"	"		"
6	3	1996	W 1st-2d	"	"		"
3	2	2000	W Rgnl	"	"		16,004
1	1	1959	W 1st	Las Cruces	Las Cruces HS Gym	1958	5,000
2	1	1969	W 1st	"	Pan American Center	1968	13,222
2	1	1972	MW 1st	"	"		"
4	2	1975	MW Rgnl	"	"		"
NEW YORK							
6	3	1995	E 1st-2d	Albany	#Knickerbocker Arena	1990	14,820
2	1	1954	E-1 1st	Buffalo	#Buffalo Memorial Auditorium	1936	13,900
6	3	2000	E 1st-2d	"	#Marine Midland Arena	1996	19,357
1	1	1970	E 1st	Jamaica	Alumni Hall	1962	6,000
1	1	1971	E 1st	"	"		"
1	1	1972	E 1st	"	"		"
1	1	1973	E 1st	"	"		"

TOURNAMENT GAME ARENAS BY SITE

G	S	Yr.	Round	City	Facility	Built	Capacity
NEW YORK							
1	1	1974	E 1st	"	"		
5	3	1943	En Rgnl-CH	New York City	#Madison Square Garden	1925	18,479
5	3	1944	En Rgnl-CH	"	"		
5	3	1945	En Rgnl-CH	"	"		
6	3	1946	En Rgnl-CH-3d	"	"		
6	3	1947	En Rgnl-CH-3d	"	"		
6	3	1948	En Rgnl-CH-3d	"	"		
4	2	1949	En Rgnl	"	"		
6	3	1950	En Rgnl-CH-3d	"	"		
6	3	1951	E 1st-Rgnl	"	"		
3	1	1955	E-1 1st TH	"	"		
4	2	1956	E 1st	"	"		
3	1	1957	E 1st TH	"	"		
3	1	1958	E 1st TH	"	"		
3	1	1959	E 1st TH	"	"		
3	1	1960	E 1st TH	"	"		
3	1	1961	E 1st TH	"	"		
3	2	1983	E Rgnl	Syracuse	Carrier Dome	1980	33,000
6	3	1986	E 1st-2d	"	"		
6	3	1987	E 1st-2d	"	"		
6	3	1991	E 1st-2d	"	"		
6	3	1993	E 1st-2d	"	"		
3	2	1997	E Rgnl	"	"		32,048
3	2	2000	E Rgnl	"	"		31,805
4	2	1982	E 1st-2d	Uniondale	#Nassau Coliseum	1972	16,547
6	3	1994	E 1st-2d	"	"		15,510
6	3	2001	E 1st-2d	"	"		16,115
NORTH CAROLINA							
6	3	1988	E 1st-2d	Chapel Hill	Dean E. Smith Center	1986	21,444
4	2	1958	E Rgnl	Charlotte	#Charlotte Coliseum I	1951	11,666
4	2	1959	E Rgnl	"	"		
4	2	1960	E Rgnl	"	"		
4	2	1961	E Rgnl	"	"		
4	2	1973	E Rgnl	"	"		
2	1	1975	E 1st	"	"		
2	1	1976	E 1st	"	"		
2	1	1978	E 1st	"	"		
4	2	1981	E 1st-2d	"	"		
4	2	1982	E 1st-2d	"	"		
4	2	1984	E 1st-2d	"	"		
6	3	1986	SE 1st-2d	"	"		
6	3	1987	E 1st-2d	"	"		
3	2	1993	SE Rgnl	"	"		
3	2	1991	SE Rgnl	"	#Charlotte Coliseum II	1988	23,339
3	2	1994	Final Four	"	"		22,876
6	3	1997	SE 1st-2d	"	"		22,806
6	3	1999	E 1st-2d	"	"		
1	1	1954	E-1 1st	Durham	Cameron Indoor Stadium	1939	8,564
4	2	1974	Final Four	Greensboro	#Greensboro Coliseum	1959	16,000
3	2	1976	E Rgnl	"	"		
3	2	1979	E Rgnl	"	"		
4	2	1980	E 1st-2d	"	"		
4	2	1983	E 1st-2d	"	"		
6	3	1986	E 1st-2d	"	"		
6	3	1989	E 1st-2d	"	"		
6	3	1992	E 1st-2d	"	"		
3	2	1998	E Rgnl	"	"		23,235
6	3	2001	E 1st-2d	"	"		
2	1	1951	E 1st	Raleigh	William Neal Reynolds Coliseum	1949	12,400
4	2	1952	E-1 Rgnl	"	"		
4	2	1953	E-1 Rgnl	"	"		
4	2	1964	E Rgnl	"	"		
4	2	1966	E Rgnl	"	"		
4	2	1968	E Rgnl	"	"		
2	1	1969	E 1st	"	"		
4	2	1971	E Rgnl	"	"		
4	2	1974	E Rgnl	"	"		
2	1	1977	E 1st	"	"		
4	2	1979	E Rgnl	"	"		
3	2	1982	E Rgnl	"	"		
6	3	1993	E 1st-2d	Winston-Salem	#Lawrence Joel Veterans Memorial Coliseum	1989	14,407
6	3	1997	E 1st-2d	"	"		14,368
6	3	2000	E 1st-2d	"	"		14,252
OHIO							
3	2	1979	MW Rgnl	Cincinnati	#Riverfront Coliseum	1975	16,562
3	2	1987	MW Rgnl	"	"		
6	3	1988	SE 1st-2d	"	"		
6	3	1992	SE 1st-2d	"	"		
6	3	2000	MW 1st-2d	Cleveland	CSU Convocation Center	1991	13,374
2	1	1957	ME 1st	Columbus	St. John Arena	1956	13,489
4	2	1970	ME Rgnl	"	"		
2	1	1970	ME 1st	Dayton	University of Dayton Arena	1969	13,455
4	2	1972	ME Rgnl	"	"		
2	1	1973	ME 1st	"	"		
4	2	1975	ME Rgnl	"	"		

The Final Four semifinal game in the Greensboro Coliseum in North Carolina featured David Thompson (44) of eventual champion North Carolina State and UCLA's Bill Walton (32).

Photo by Rich Clarkson

Tournament trivia

Question... Have two teams from the same state ever played each other in the championship game?

Answer... Yes, Cincinnati defeated Ohio State in both 1961 and 1962.

The Spectrum in Philadelphia has hosted two Final Fours, including 1976, when Hoosiers guard Quinn Buckner celebrated Indiana's title by relaxing in the Oval Office during the team's visit to the White House.

Tournament trivia

Question...

Since 1956, when the Final Four competitors came from four different regionals, what region has produced the most national champions?

Answer...

The West/Far West with 18, next are the Midwest with 13; the South/Southeast/Mideast, 10; and the East, six. Remember that any team, regardless of its geographical location, can play in any region to best balance the bracket in the committee's judgment.

G	S	Yr.	Round	City	Facility	Built	Capacity
OHIO							
2	1	1976	ME 1st	"	"		"
3	2	1978	ME Rgnl	"	"		"
4	2	1981	ME 1st-2d	"	"		"
2	1	1983	OR	"	"		"
2	1	1984	OR	"	"		"
6	3	1985	SE 1st-2d	"	"		"
6	3	1986	MW 1st-2d	"	"		"
6	3	1991	MW 1st-2d	"	"		"
6	3	1992	MW 1st-2d	"	"		"
6	3	1995	MW 1st-2d	"	"		"
7	4	2001	MW OR, 1st-2d	"	"		"
2	1	1966	ME 1st	Kent	Memorial Gymnasium	1950	6,034
2	1	1968	ME 1st	"	"		"
OKLAHOMA							
1	1	1955	W-1 1st	El Reno	Thunderbird Coliseum	1954	4,000
2	1	1977	MW 1st	Norman	Lloyd Noble Center	1975	10,871
1	1	1957	MW 1st	Oklahoma City	Capitol Hill HS Arena	1953	4,000
3	2	1977	MW Rgnl	"	#Myriad Convention Center	1974	15,200
6	3	1994	MW 1st-2d	"	"		13,268
6	3	1998	MW 1st-2d	"	"		
4	2	1954	W-1 Rgnl	Stillwater	Gallagher Hall	1938	7,400
1	1	1958	MW 1st	"	"		"
4	2	1974	MW Rgnl	Tulsa	Mabee Center	1972	10,575
2	1	1975	MW 1st	"	"		"
2	1	1978	MW 1st	"	"		"
4	2	1982	MW 1st-2d	"	"		"
6	3	1985	MW 1st-2d	"	"		"
OREGON							
4	2	1952	W-2 Rgnl	Corvallis	Gill Coliseum	1949	10,000
4	2	1953	W-2 Rgnl	"	"		"
6	3	1954	W-2 1st-Rgnl	"	"		"
4	2	1955	W-2 Rgnl	"	"		"
4	2	1956	FW Rgnl	"	"		"
4	2	1957	W Rgnl	"	"		"
1	1	1960	W 1st	"	"		"
2	1	1962	W 1st	"	"		"
4	2	1964	W Rgnl	"	"		"
4	2	1967	W Rgnl	"	"		"
4	2	1983	W 1st-2d	"	"		"
2	1	1963	W 1st	Eugene	McArthur Court	1926	10,099
2	1	1964	W 1st	"	"		"
2	1	1976	W 1st	"	"		"
2	1	1978	W 1st	"	"		"
6	3	1961	W 1st-Rgnl	Portland	#Memorial Coliseum	1960	12,666
4	2	1965	Final Four	"	"		"
4	2	1975	W Rgnl	"	"		"
1	1	1959	W 1st	"	#Pacific International Livestock Pavilion (now named Pacific Exposition Center)	1919	4,200
PENNSYLVANIA							
3	2	2001	E Rgnl	Philadelphia	First Union Center	1996	20,060
3	2	1939	En Rgnl	"	Palestra	1927	9,200
2	1	1953	E-1 1st	"	"		"
4	2	1954	E-1 Rgnl	"	"		"
4	2	1955	E-1 Rgnl	"	"		"
4	2	1956	E Rgnl	"	"		"
4	2	1957	E Rgnl	"	"		"
3	1	1962	E 1st TH	"	"		"
3	1	1963	E 1st TH	"	"		"
3	1	1964	E 1st TH	"	"		"
3	1	1965	E 1st TH	"	"		"
1	1	1970	E 1st	"	"		"
1	1	1971	E 1st	"	"		"
1	1	1973	E 1st	"	"		"
1	1	1974	E 1st	"	"		"
2	1	1975	E 1st	"	"		"
2	1	1977	E 1st	"	"		"
2	1	1978	E 1st	"	"		"
3	2	1980	E Rgnl	"	"		"
2	1	1983	OR	"	"		"
3	1	1984	OR TH	"	"		"
4	2	1976	Final Four	"	#Spectrum	1967	17,937
4	2	1981	Final Four	"	"		"
3	2	1992	E Rgnl	"	"		"
6	3	1997	E 1st-2d	Pittsburgh	#Civic Arena	1961	17,509
RHODE ISLAND							
1	1	1967	E 1st	Kingston	Keaney Gymnasium	1953	5,000
1	1	1968	E 1st	"	"		"
1	1	1969	E 1st	"	"		"
4	2	1975	E Rgnl	Providence	#Providence Civic Center	1972	12,155
2	1	1976	E 1st	"	"		"
3	2	1978	E Rgnl	"	"		"
2	1	1979	E 2d	"	"		"
4	2	1980	E 1st-2d	"	"		"
4	2	1981	E 1st-2d	"	"		"
3	2	1985	E Rgnl	"	"		"
6	3	1989	E 1st-2d	"	"		13,100
6	3	1996	E 1st-2d	"	"		11,931

TOURNAMENT GAME ARENAS BY SITE

G	S	Yr.	Round	City	Facility	Built	Capacity
SOUTH CAROLINA							
4	2	1970	E Rgnl	Columbia	Carolina Coliseum	1968	12,401
TENNESSEE							
2	1	1972	ME 1st	Knoxville	Stokely Athletics Center	1966	12,700
2	1	1978	ME 1st	"	"		"
3	2	1983	ME Rgnl	"	"		"
6	3	1990	SE 1st-2d	"	Thompson-Boling Arena	1987	24,535
3	2	1994	SE Rgnl	"	"		23,291
3	2	1999	South Rgnl	"	"		24,385
4	2	1984	MW 1st-2d	Memphis	#Mid-South Coliseum	1975	11,200
6	3	1995	SE 1st-2d	"	The Pyramid	1991	20,142
6	3	1997	SE 1st-2d	"	"		"
6	3	2001	South 1st-2d	"	"		"
4	2	1979	ME 1st-2d	Murfreesboro	Murphy Athletic Center	1972	11,520
4	2	1973	ME Rgnl	Nashville	Memorial Gymnasium	1952	15,626
4	2	1982	ME 1st-2d	"	"		"
6	3	1989	SE 1st-2d	"	"		"
6	3	1993	SE 1st-2d	"	"		"
6	3	2000	S 1st-2d	"	#Gaylord Entertainment Center	1996	17,297
TEXAS							
4	2	1981	MW 1st-2d	Austin	Frank Erwin Center	1977	16,231
6	3	1990	MW 1st-2d	"	"		16,042
6	3	1995	MW 1st-2d	"	"		16,731
3	2	2000	S Rgnl	"	"		"
4	2	1957	MW Rgnl	Dallas	Moody Coliseum	1956	9,007
2	1	1962	MW 1st	"	"		"
2	1	1964	MW 1st	"	"		"
2	1	1979	MW 2d	"	"		"
4	2	1982	MW 1st-2d	"	#Reunion Arena	1980	17,000
3	2	1985	MW Rgnl	"	"		"
3	2	1986	Final Four	"	"		"
6	3	1989	MW 1st-2d	"	"		"
3	2	1990	MW Rgnl	"	"		"
3	2	1994	MW Rgnl	"	"		16,240
6	3	1996	MW 1st-2d	"	"		16,379
2	1	1974	MW 1st	Denton	North Texas Coliseum	1973	10,000
2	1	1976	MW 1st	"	"		"
4	2	1980	MW 1st-2d	"	"		"
4	2	1981	W 1st-2d	El Paso	Special Events Center	1977	12,000
2	1	1969	MW 1st	Fort Worth	Daniel-Meyer Coliseum	1961	7,166
2	1	1970	MW 1st	"	"		"
4	2	1971	Final Four	Houston	#Astrodome	1965	31,765
1	1	1961	MW 1st	"	Delmar Field House	1960	5,300
2	1	1971	MW 1st	"	Hofheinz Pavilion	1969	10,066
4	2	1973	MW Rgnl	"	"		"
6	3	1985	MW 1st-2d	"	"		"
3	2	1980	MW Rgnl	"	#Summit	1975	16,016
4	2	1983	MW 1st-2d	"	"		"
3	2	1986	W Rgnl	"	"		"
2	1	1963	MW 1st	Lubbock	Lubbock Memorial Coliseum	1956	8,174
2	1	1965	MW 1st	"	"		"
4	2	1966	MW Rgnl	"	"		"
2	1	1975	MW 1st	"	"		"
3	2	1997	MW Rgnl	San Antonio	#Alamodome	1993	41,250
3	2	1998	Final Four	"	"		40,509
3	2	2001	MW Rgnl	"	"		"
UTAH							
2	1	1971	W 1st	Logan	Dee Glen Smith Spectrum	1970	10,270
2	1	1973	W 1st	"	"		"
4	2	1982	W 1st-2d	"	"		"
4	2	1980	W 1st-2d	Ogden	Dee Event Center	1977	11,592
4	2	1983	W Rgnl	"	"		"
6	3	1986	W 1st-2d	"	"		"
6	3	1994	W 1st-2d	"	"		"
1	1	1960	W 1st	Provo	George Albert Smith Field House	1951	10,500
4	2	1962	W Rgnl	"	"		"
4	2	1963	W Rgnl	"	"		"
4	2	1965	W Rgnl	"	"		"
2	1	1970	W 1st	"	"		"
4	2	1972	W Rgnl	"	Marriott Center	1971	22,700
3	2	1977	W Rgnl	"	"		"
3	2	1979	W Rgnl	"	"		"
3	2	1982	W Rgnl	"	"		"
2	1	1968	MW,W 1st	Salt Lake City	Nielsen Field House	1940	5,000
4	2	1971	W Rgnl	"	Special Events Center	1969	15,000
4	2	1979	Final Four	"	"		"
3	2	1981	W Rgnl	"	"		"
4	2	1984	W 1st-2d	"	"		"
6	3	1985	W 1st-2d	"	"		"
6	3	1987	W 1st-2d	"	"		"
6	3	1988	W 1st-2d	"	Jon M. Huntsman Center (name change)		"
6	3	1990	W 1st-2d	"	"		"
6	3	1991	W 1st-2d	"	"		"
6	3	1993	W 1st-2d	"	"		"
6	3	1995	W 1st-2d	"	"		14,910
6	3	1997	W 1st-2d	"	"		14,925
6	3	2000	W 1st-2d	"	"		"

Four-year starter Jay Bilas was a key part of the 1986 Duke team that won a record 37 games and advanced to the title game at Reunion Arena in Dallas.

Photo from Duke sports information

Tournament trivia

Question...
Including this season, Atlanta has hosted the Final Four twice – at the Omni in 1977 and at the Georgia Dome in 2002. Five other cities have used two different facilities to host the Final Four. What are those cities?

Answer...
Evanston (Illinois), Indianapolis, Kansas City (Missouri), Minneapolis and Seattle

TOURNAMENT GAME ARENAS BY SITE

In the first Final Four in the Kingdome in Seattle in 1984, Patrick Ewing led Georgetown over Akeem Olajuwon and Houston, 84-75, in the championship game.

G	S	Yr.	Round	City	Facility	Built	Capacity
VIRGINIA							
2	1	1966	E 1st	Blacksburg	Cassell Coliseum	1964	10,000
2	1	1967	W 1st	"	"		
6	3	1990	SE 1st-2d	Richmond	#Richmond Coliseum	1971	11,051
6	3	1996	E 1st-2d	"	"		11,859
1	1	1972	E 1st	Williamsburg	William and Mary Hall	1970	10,070
1	1	1973	E 1st				
WASHINGTON							
2	1	1975	W 1st	Pullman	Wallis Beasley Performing Arts Coliseum	1973	12,058
4	2	1982	W 1st-2d	"			"
4	2	1984	W 1st-2d	"			
2	1	1949	CH-3d	Seattle	Edmundson Pavilion	1927	9,000
4	2	1952	Final Four	"	"		"
1	1	1953	W-2 1st	"	"		"
1	1	1956	FW 1st	"	"		"
4	2	1960	W Rgnl	"	"		"
4	2	1970	W Rgnl	"	"		"
6	3	1999	W 1st-2d	"	#Key Arena	1995	14,643
3	2	1984	Final Four	"	#Kingdome	1976	38,471
3	2	1987	W Rgnl	"	"		"
3	2	1988	W Rgnl	"	"		"
3	2	1989	Final Four	"	"		"
3	2	1991	W Rgnl	"	"		"
3	2	1993	W Rgnl	"	"		"
3	2	1995	Final Four	"	"		38,540
WEST VIRGINIA							
1	1	1971	E 1st	Morgantown	WVU Coliseum	1970	14,000
4	2	1972	E Rgnl	"	"		"
1	1	1974	E 1st				
WISCONSIN							
4	2	1941	En Rgnl	Madison	Wisconsin Field House	1927	14,000
4	2	1969	ME Rgnl	"	"		13,000
4	2	1984	ME 1st-2d	Milwaukee	#Milwaukee Exposition & Convention Center	1950	11,052
6	3	1992	MW 1st-2d	"	#Bradley Center	1988	18,600
6	3	1996	MW Rgnl	"	"		"
6	3	1999	MW 1st-2d	"	"		"

G — Number of games.
S — Number of sessions.
CH — National championship game.
3d — National third-place game.
Rgnl — Regional.
2d — Second round.
1st — First round.
OR — Opening round.
East — East region.
En — Eastern region.
E-1 — East-1 region.
E-2 — East-2 region.

FW — Far West region.
ME — Mideast region.
MW — Midwest region.
S — South region.
SE — Southeast region.
W — West region.
Wn — Western region.
W-1 — West-1 region.
W-2 — West-2 region.
TH — Tripleheader.
#Non-campus arena.

Future Dates and Sites

Tournament

Year	First Round	Second Round	Regionals	Final Four
2002	March 14-15	March 16-17	March 21-24	March 30 and April 1
2003	March 20-21	March 22-23	March 27-30	April 5 and 7
2004	March 18-19	March 20-21	March 25-28	April 3 and 5
2005	March 17-18	March 19-20	March 24-27	April 2 and 4
2006	March 16-17	March 18-19	March 23-26	April 1 and 3
2007	March 15-16	March 17-18	March 22-25	March 31 and April 2

Final Four

Year	Dates	Site & Hosts
2002	March 30 and April 1	Georgia Dome, Atlanta Host: Georgia Institute of Technology
2003	April 5 and 7	Louisiana Superdome, New Orleans Cohosts: Sun Belt Conference and University of New Orleans
2004	April 3 and 5	Alamodome, San Antonio Host: University of Texas at San Antonio
2005	April 2 and 4	Trans World Dome, St. Louis Host: Missouri Valley Conference
2006	April 1 and 3	RCA Dome, Indianapolis Cohosts: Midwestern Collegiate Conference and Butler University
2007	March 31 and April 2	Georgia Dome, Atlanta Host: Georgia Institute of Technology

National Semifinal Pairings

2002, 2005, 2008 — East vs. Midwest; South vs. West
2003, 2006, 2009 — East vs. South; West vs. Midwest
2004, 2007, 2010 — East vs. West; Midwest vs. South

2002

OPENING ROUND

MARCH 12
— University of Dayton Arena, Ohio
Host: University of Dayton

FIRST AND SECOND ROUND

MARCH 14 AND 16
— University Arena, Albuquerque, New Mexico
Host: University of New Mexico

— BI-LO Center, Greenville, South Carolina
Co-hosts: Southern Conference and Furman University

— ARCO Arena, Sacramento, California
Host: University of the Pacific

— Trans World Dome, St. Louis
Host: Missouri Valley Conference

MARCH 15 AND 17
— United Center, Chicago
Host: Big Ten Conference

— American Airlines Arena, Dallas
Host: Big 12 Conference

— Mellon Arena, Pittsburgh
  Host: Duquesne University

— MCI Center, Washington, D.C.
  Host: Georgetown University

REGIONALS
MARCH 21 AND 23
SOUTH — Rupp Arena, Lexington, Kentucky
  Host: University of Kentucky

WEST — Compaq Center, San Jose, California
  Host: Santa Clara University

MARCH 22 AND 24
EAST — Carrier Dome, Syracuse, New York
  Host: Syracuse University

MIDWEST — Kohl Center, Madison, Wisconsin
  Host: University of Wisconsin-Madison

2003
FIRST AND SECOND ROUND
MARCH 20 AND 22
— RCA Dome, Indianapolis
  Co-hosts: Butler University and Horizon League

— The Myriad, Oklahoma City
  Host: University of Oklahoma

— Jon M. Huntsman Center, Salt Lake City
  Host: University of Utah

— Spokane Arena, Spokane, Washington
  Host: Washington State University

MARCH 21 AND 23
— Birmingham-Jefferson Civic Center, Birmingham, Alabama
  Host: Southeastern Conference

— FleetCenter, Boston
  Host: Boston College

— Gaylord Entertainment Center, Nashville, Tennessee
  Host: Vanderbilt University

— Ice Palace Arena, Tampa, Florida
  Host: University of South Florida

REGIONALS
MARCH 27 AND 29
MIDWEST — Hubert H. Humphrey Metrodome, Minneapolis
  Host: University of Minnesota–Twin Cities

WEST — Arrowhead Pond of Anaheim, Anaheim, California
  Host: Big West Conference

MARCH 28 AND 30
EAST — Pepsi Arena, Albany, New York
  Co-hosts: Metro Atlantic Athletic Conference and Siena College

MIDWEST — Alamodome, San Antonio
  Host: University of Texas at San Antonio

2004
FIRST AND SECOND ROUND
MARCH 18 AND 20
— HSBC, Buffalo, New York
  Co-hosts: Canisius College and Niagara University

— Pepsi Center, Denver
  Co-hosts: Colorado State University and Mountain West Conference

— Raleigh Entertainment & Sports Arena, Raleigh, North Carolina
  Host: North Carolina State University

— Key Arena, Seattle
  Host: University of Washington

MARCH 19 AND 21
— Nationwide Arena, Columbus, Ohio
  Host: Ohio State University

— Kemper Arena, Kansas City, Missouri
  Host: Big 12 Conference

— Bradley Center, Milwaukee
  Host: Marquette University

— T.D. Waterhouse Center, Orlando, Florida
  Host: Stetson University

REGIONALS
MARCH 25 AND 27
EAST — Continental Airlines Arena, East Rutherford, New Jersey
  Host: Rutgers University

WEST — America West Arena, Phoenix
  Host: Arizona State University

MARCH 26 AND 38
SOUTH — Georgia Dome, Atlanta
  Host: Georgia Tech

MIDWEST — Trans World Dome, St. Louis
  Host: Missouri Valley Conference

Tournament Moments...

March 22, 1947, Western regional final in the Municipal Auditorium in Kansas City, Missouri – Down a point with seven seconds remaining, Oklahoma advanced to the NCAA title game as substitute guard Ken Pryor sank a two-handed jumper to give the Sooners a 55-54 victory over Texas.

The Tournament Field

All-Time Tournament Field 118
Team Champions 145
The Brackets 170

All-Time Tournament Field

Note: The column "How" indicates how teams qualified for the tournament: "Q" means automatic qualifier and "L" indicates at-large selection. In the "Conference" column, for an independent or conference team that earned automatic qualification by winning the conference tournament of an unofficially recognized conference, that conference is listed in parenthesis. Other notations in the conference column are listed at the end of this section.

1939 Tournament

School	Conference	How	Pre-Tourney W	L	Pct.	Tourney W	L	Final W	L	Pct.	Conf. W	L	Fin.
Brown	Independent	L	16	3	.842	0	1	16	4	.800	—	—	—
Ohio St.	Big Ten	L	14	6	.700	2	1	16	7	.696	10	2	1st
Oklahoma	Big Six	L	11	8	.579	1	1	12	9	.571	7	3	T1st
Oregon	Pacific Coast (N)	L	26	5	.839	3	0	29	5	.853	14	2	1st
Texas	Southwest	L	19	4	.826	0	2	19	6	.760	10	2	1st
Utah St.	Mountain States	L	16	6	.727	1	1	17	7	.708	8	4	2d
Villanova	Independent	L	19	4	.826	1	1	20	5	.800	—	—	—
Wake Forest	Southern	L	18	5	.783	0	1	18	6	.750	15	3	1st

1940 Tournament

School	Conference	How	Pre-Tourney W	L	Pct.	Tourney W	L	Final W	L	Pct.	Conf. W	L	Fin.
Colorado	Mountain States	L	17	2	.895	0	2	17	4	.810	11	1	1st
Duquesne	Independent	L	19	2	.905	1	1	20	3	.870	—	—	—
Indiana	Big Ten	L	17	3	.850	3	0	20	3	.870	9	3	2d
Kansas	Big Six	L	17	5	.773	2	1	19	6	.760	8	2	T1st
Rice	Southwest	L	21	2	.913	1	1	22	3	.880	10	2	1st
Southern California	Pacific Coast (S)	L	19	2	.905	1	1	20	3	.870	10	2	1st
Springfield	Independent	L	16	2	.889	0	1	16	3	.842	—	—	—
Western Ky.	Kentucky Intercollegiate	L	24	5	.828	0	1	24	6	.800	6	2	3d

1941 Tournament

School	Conference	How	Pre-Tourney W	L	Pct.	Tourney W	L	Final W	L	Pct.	Conf. W	L	Fin.
Arkansas	Southwest	L	19	2	.905	1	1	20	3	.870	12	0	1st
Creighton	Missouri Valley	L	17	6	.739	1	1	18	7	.720	9	3	1st
Dartmouth	Ivy	L	18	4	.818	1	1	19	5	.792	10	2	1st
North Carolina	Southern	L	19	7	.731	0	2	19	9	.679	14	1	1st
Pittsburgh	Independent	L	12	5	.706	1	1	13	6	.684	—	—	—
Washington St.	Pacific Coast (N)	L	24	5	.828	2	1	26	6	.813	13	3	1st
Wisconsin	Big Ten	L	17	3	.850	3	0	20	3	.870	11	1	1st
Wyoming	Mountain States	L	14	4	.778	0	2	14	6	.700	10	2	1st

1942 Tournament

School	Conference	How	Pre-Tourney W	L	Pct.	Tourney W	L	Final W	L	Pct.	Conf. W	L	Fin.
Colorado	Mountain States	L	15	1	.938	1	1	16	2	.889	11	1	1st
Dartmouth	Ivy	L	20	3	.870	2	1	22	4	.846	11	2	1st
Illinois	Big Ten	L	18	3	.857	0	2	18	5	.783	13	2	1st
Kansas	Big Six	L	16	4	.800	1	1	17	5	.773	8	2	T1st
Kentucky	Southeastern	L	18	5	.783	1	1	19	6	.760	8	1	1st
Penn St.	Independent	L	17	2	.895	1	1	18	3	.857	—	—	—
Rice	Southwest	L	22	3	.880	0	2	22	5	.815	10	2	T1st
Stanford	Pacific Coast (S)	L	25	4	.862	3	0	28	4	.875	11	1	1st

1943 Tournament

School	Conference	How	Pre-Tourney W	L	Pct.	Tourney W	L	Final W	L	Pct.	Conf. W	L	Fin.
Dartmouth	Ivy	L	19	2	.905	1	1	20	3	.870	11	1	1st
DePaul	Independent	L	18	4	.818	1	1	19	5	.792	—	—	—
Georgetown	Independent	L	20	4	.833	2	1	22	5	.815	—	—	—
New York U.	Independent	L	17	4	.810	0	2	17	6	.739	—	—	—
Oklahoma	Big Six	L	17	8	.680	1	1	18	9	.667	7	3	2d
Texas	Southwest	L	18	6	.750	1	1	19	7	.731	9	3	T1st
Washington	Pacific Coast (N)	L	24	5	.828	0	2	24	7	.774	12	4	1st
Wyoming	Mountain States (E)	L	28	2	.933	3	0	31	2	.939	4	0	1st

1944 Tournament

School	Conference	How	Pre-Tourney W	L	Pct.	Tourney W	L	Final W	L	Pct.	Conf. W	L	Fin.
Catholic	Independent	L	17	5	.773	0	2	17	7	.708	—	—	—
Dartmouth	Ivy	L	17	1	.944	2	1	19	2	.905	8	0	1st
Iowa St.	Big Six	L	13	3	.813	1	1	14	4	.778	9	1	T1st
Missouri	Big Six	L	9	8	.529	1	1	10	9	.526	5	5	T3d
Ohio St.	Big Ten	L	13	6	.684	1	1	14	7	.667	10	2	1st
Pepperdine	Independent	L	22	10	.688	0	2	22	12	.647	—	—	—
Temple	Independent	L	13	8	.619	1	1	14	9	.609	—	—	—
Utah	Mountain States	L	18	4	.818	3	0	21	4	.840	—	—	—

1945 Tournament

School	Conference	How	Pre-Tourney W	L	Pct.	Tourney W	L	Final W	L	Pct.	Conf. W	L	Fin.
Arkansas	Southwest	L	16	8	.667	1	1	17	9	.654	9	3	2d
Kentucky	Southeastern	L	21	3	.875	1	1	22	4	.846	4	1	2d
New York U.	Independent	L	14	7	.667	2	1	16	8	.667	—	—	—
Ohio St.	Big Ten	L	14	4	.778	1	1	15	5	.750	10	2	2d
Oklahoma St.	Missouri Valley	L	24	4	.857	3	0	27	4	.871	—	—	—
Oregon	Pacific Coast (N)	L	29	12	.707	1	1	30	13	.698	11	5	T1st
Tufts	Independent	L	10	6	.625	0	2	10	8	.556	—	—	—
Utah	Mountain States	L	17	2	.895	0	2	17	4	.810	—	—	—

1946 Tournament

School	Conference	How	Pre-Tourney W	L	Pct.	Tourney W	L	Final W	L	Pct.	Conf. W	L	Fin.
Baylor	Southwest	L	25	3	.893	0	2	25	5	.833	11	1	1st
California	Pacific Coast (S)	L	29	4	.879	1	2	30	6	.833	11	1	1st
Colorado	Mountain States	L	11	5	.688	1	1	12	6	.667	9	3	2d
Harvard	Independent	L	20	1	.952	0	2	20	3	.870	—	—	—
New York U.	Independent	L	18	2	.900	1	1	19	3	.864	—	—	—
North Carolina	Southern	L	28	4	.875	2	1	30	5	.857	13	1	1st
Ohio St.	Big Ten	L	14	4	.778	2	1	16	5	.762	10	2	1st
Oklahoma St.	Missouri Valley	L	28	2	.933	3	0	31	2	.939	12	0	1st

ALL-TIME TOURNAMENT FIELD

1947 Tournament

School	Conference	How	Pre-Tourney W	L	Pct.	Tourney W	L	Final W	L	Pct.	Conf. W	L	Fin.
CCNY	Independent	L	16	4	.800	1	2	17	6	.739	—	—	—
Holy Cross	Independent	L	24	3	.889	3	0	27	3	.900	—	—	—
Navy	Independent	L	16	1	.941	0	2	16	3	.842	—	—	—
Oklahoma	Big Six	L	22	6	.786	2	1	24	7	.774	8	2	1st
Oregon St.	Pacific Coast (N)	L	27	4	.871	1	1	28	5	.848	10	6	T1st
Texas	Southwest	L	24	1	.960	2	1	26	2	.929	12	0	1st
Wisconsin	Big Nine	L	15	5	.750	1	1	16	6	.727	9	3	1st
Wyoming	Mountain States	L	22	4	.846	0	2	22	6	.786	11	1	1st

1948 Tournament

School	Conference	How	Pre-Tourney W	L	Pct.	Tourney W	L	Final W	L	Pct.	Conf. W	L	Fin.
Baylor	Southwest	L	22	7	.759	2	1	24	8	.750	11	1	1st
Columbia	Ivy	L	20	1	.952	0	2	20	3	.870	11	1	1st
Holy Cross	Independent	L	24	3	.889	2	1	26	4	.867	—	—	—
Kansas St.	Big Seven	L	21	4	.840	1	2	22	6	.786	9	3	—
#Kentucky	Southeastern	L	31	2	.939	3	0	36	3	.923	9	0	1st
Michigan	Big Nine	L	15	5	.750	1	1	16	6	.727	10	2	1st
Washington	Pacific Coast (N)	L	22	10	.688	1	1	23	11	.676	10	6	T1st
Wyoming	Mountain States	L	18	7	.720	0	2	18	9	.667	6	4	T2d

1949 Tournament

School	Conference	How	Pre-Tourney W	L	Pct.	Tourney W	L	Final W	L	Pct.	Conf. W	L	Fin.
Arkansas	Southwest	L	14	10	.583	1	1	15	11	.577	9	3	T1st
Illinois	Big Ten	L	19	3	.864	2	1	21	4	.840	10	2	1st
Kentucky	Southeastern	L	29	2	.935	3	0	32	2	.941	13	0	1st
Oklahoma St.	Missouri Valley	L	21	4	.840	2	1	23	5	.821	9	1	1st
Oregon St.	Pacific Coast (N)	L	23	10	.697	1	2	24	12	.667	12	4	1st
Villanova	Independent	L	22	3	.880	1	1	23	4	.852	—	—	—
Wyoming	Mountain States	L	25	8	.758	0	2	25	10	.714	15	5	1st
Yale	Ivy	L	22	6	.786	0	2	22	8	.733	9	3	1st

1950 Tournament

School	Conference	How	Pre-Tourney W	L	Pct.	Tourney W	L	Final W	L	Pct.	Conf. W	L	Fin.
Baylor	Southwest	L	13	11	.542	1	2	14	13	.519	8	4	T1st
Bradley	Missouri Valley	L	30	4	.882	2	1	32	5	.865	11	1	1st
Brigham Young	Mountain States	L	21	11	.656	1	1	22	12	.647	14	6	1st
CCNY	Independent	L	21	5	.808	3	0	24	5	.828	—	—	—
Holy Cross	Independent	L	27	2	.931	0	2	27	4	.871	—	—	—
North Carolina St.	Southern	L	25	5	.833	2	1	27	6	.818	12	2	1st
Ohio St.	Big Ten	L	21	3	.875	1	1	22	4	.846	11	1	1st
UCLA	Pacific Coast (S)	L	24	5	.828	0	2	24	7	.774	10	2	1st

1951 Tournament

School	Conference	How	Pre-Tourney W	L	Pct.	Tourney W	L	Final W	L	Pct.	Conf. W	L	Fin.
Arizona	Border	Q	24	5	.828	0	1	24	6	.800	15	1	1st
Brigham Young	Mountain States	Q	25	8	.758	1	2	26	10	.722	15	5	1st
Columbia	Ivy	Q	21	0	1.000	0	1	21	1	.955	12	0	1st
Connecticut	Yankee	L	22	3	.880	0	1	22	4	.846	6	1	1st
Illinois	Big Ten	Q	19	4	.826	3	1	22	5	.815	13	1	1st
Kansas St.	Big Seven	Q	22	3	.880	3	1	25	4	.862	11	1	1st
Kentucky	Southeastern	Q	28	2	.933	4	0	32	2	.941	14	0	1st
Louisville	Independent	L	19	6	.760	0	1	19	7	.731	—	—	—
Montana St.	Rocky Mountain	L	24	11	.686	0	1	24	12	.667	9	1	1st
North Carolina St.	Southern	Q	29	5	.853	1	2	30	7	.811	13	1	1st
Oklahoma St.	Missouri Valley	Q	27	4	.871	2	2	29	6	.829	12	2	1st
San Jose St.	Independent	L	18	11	.621	0	1	18	12	.600	—	—	—
St. John's (N.Y.)	Independent	L	24	4	.857	2	1	26	5	.839	—	—	—
Texas A&M	Southwest	Q	17	11	.607	0	1	17	12	.586	8	4	T1st
Villanova	Independent	L	25	6	.806	0	1	25	7	.781	—	—	—
Washington	Pacific Coast (N)	Q	22	5	.815	2	1	24	6	.800	11	5	1st

1952 Tournament

School	Conference	How	Pre-Tourney W	L	Pct.	Tourney W	L	Final W	L	Pct.	Conf. W	L	Fin.
Dayton	Independent	L	27	4	.871	1	1	28	5	.848	—	—	—
Duquesne	Independent	L	22	3	.880	1	1	23	4	.852	—	—	—
Illinois	Big Ten	Q	19	3	.864	3	1	22	4	.846	14	4	2d
#Kansas	Big Seven	Q	22	2	.917	4	0	28	3	.903	11	1	1st
Kentucky	Southeastern	Q	28	2	.933	1	1	29	3	.906	14	0	1st
New Mexico St.	Border	Q	22	9	.710	0	2	22	11	.667	12	2	T1st
North Carolina St.	Southern	Q	23	9	.719	1	1	24	10	.706	12	2	2d
Oklahoma City	Independent	L	18	7	.720	1	1	19	8	.704	—	—	—
Penn St.	Independent	L	20	4	.833	0	2	20	6	.769	—	—	—
Princeton	Ivy	Q	16	9	.640	0	2	16	11	.593	10	2	1st
St. John's (N.Y.)	Independent	L	22	5	.815	3	1	25	6	.806	—	—	—
St. Louis	Missouri Valley	Q	22	7	.759	1	1	23	8	.742	9	1	1st
Santa Clara	Independent	L	15	10	.600	2	2	17	12	.586	—	—	—
TCU	Southwest	Q	23	3	.885	1	1	24	4	.857	11	1	1st
UCLA	Pacific Coast (S)	Q	19	10	.655	0	2	19	12	.613	8	4	1st
Wyoming	Mountain States	Q	27	6	.818	1	1	28	7	.800	13	1	1st

#Final won-lost record includes 2-1 record in postseason play.

1953 Tournament

School	Conference	How	Pre-Tourney W	L	Pct.	Tourney W	L	Final W	L	Pct.	Conf. W	L	Fin.
DePaul	Independent	L	18	7	.720	1	2	19	9	.679	—	—	—
Eastern Ky.	Ohio Valley	L	16	8	.667	0	1	16	9	.640	9	1	1st
Fordham	Independent	L	18	7	.720	0	1	18	8	.692	—	—	—
Hardin-Simmons	Border	Q	19	11	.633	0	1	19	12	.613	11	3	T1st
Holy Cross	Independent (New England)	Q	18	5	.783	2	1	20	6	.769	—	—	—
Idaho St.	Rocky Mountain	Q	18	6	.750	0	1	18	7	.720	10	0	1st
Indiana	Big Ten	Q	19	3	.864	4	0	23	3	.885	17	1	1st
Kansas	Big Seven	Q	16	5	.762	3	1	19	6	.760	10	2	1st
Lebanon Valley	Independent (Middle Atlantic)	Q	18	1	.947	1	2	19	3	.864	—	—	—

All-Time Tournament Field

School	Conference	How	W	L	Pct.	W	L	W	L	Pct.	W	L	Fin.
LSU	Southeastern	Q	20	1	.952	2	2	22	3	.880	13	0	1st
Miami (Ohio)	Mid-American	Q	17	5	.773	0	1	17	6	.739	10	2	1st
Navy	Independent	L	16	4	.800	0	1	16	5	.762	—	—	—
Notre Dame	Independent	L	17	4	.810	2	1	19	5	.792	—	—	—
Oklahoma City	Independent	L	18	4	.818	0	2	18	6	.750	—	—	—
Oklahoma St.	Missouri Valley	Q	22	6	.786	1	1	23	7	.767	8	2	1st
Pennsylvania	Ivy	Q	21	4	.840	1	1	22	5	.815	10	2	1st
Santa Clara	West Coast	L	15	6	.714	2	1	17	7	.708	6	2	T1st
Seattle	Independent	L	26	3	.897	2	1	28	4	.875	—	—	—
TCU	Southwest	Q	14	7	.667	1	1	15	8	.652	9	3	1st
Wake Forest	Southern	Q	21	6	.778	1	1	22	7	.759	12	5	T2d
Washington	Pacific Coast (N)	Q	25	2	.926	3	1	28	3	.903	15	1	1st
Wyoming	Mountain States	Q	20	8	.714	0	2	20	10	.667	12	2	1st

1954 Tournament

School	Conference	How	Pre-Tourney W	L	Pct.	Tourney W	L	Final W	L	Pct.	Conf. W	L	Fin.
Bradley	Independent	L	15	12	.556	4	1	19	13	.594	—	—	—
Colorado	Big Seven	Q	11	9	.550	0	2	11	11	.500	10	2	T1st
Colorado St.	Mountain States	Q	22	5	.815	0	2	22	7	.759	12	1	1st
Connecticut	Yankee (New England)	Q	23	2	.920	0	1	23	3	.885	7	0	1st
Cornell	Ivy	Q	17	5	.773	0	2	17	7	.708	12	3	1st
Fordham	Independent	L	18	5	.783	0	1	18	6	.750	—	—	—
George Washington	Southern	Q	23	2	.920	0	1	23	3	.885	10	0	1st
Idaho St.	Rocky Mountain	Q	20	4	.833	2	1	22	5	.815	9	1	1st
Indiana	Big Ten	Q	19	3	.864	1	1	20	4	.833	12	2	1st
La Salle	Independent (Middle Atlantic)	Q	21	4	.840	5	0	26	4	.867	—	—	—
LSU	Southeastern	Q	20	3	.870	0	2	20	5	.800	14	0	T1st
Loyola (La.)	Independent	L	15	8	.652	0	1	15	9	.625	—	—	—
Navy	Independent	L	16	7	.696	2	1	18	8	.692	—	—	—
North Carolina St.	Atlantic Coast	Q	24	6	.800	2	1	26	7	.788	5	3	4th
Notre Dame	Independent	L	20	2	.909	2	1	22	3	.880	—	—	—
Oklahoma City	Independent	L	18	6	.750	0	1	18	7	.720	—	—	—
Oklahoma St.	Missouri Valley	Q	23	4	.852	1	1	24	5	.828	9	1	1st
Penn St.	Independent	L	14	5	.737	4	1	18	6	.750	—	—	—
Rice	Southwest	Q	22	4	.846	1	1	23	5	.821	9	3	T1st
Santa Clara	West Coast	L	18	6	.750	2	1	20	7	.741	9	3	1st
Seattle	Independent	L	26	1	.963	0	1	26	2	.929	—	—	—
Southern California	Pacific Coast (S)	Q	17	12	.586	2	2	19	14	.576	8	4	1st
Texas Tech	Border	Q	20	4	.833	0	1	20	5	.800	11	1	1st
Toledo	Mid-American	Q	13	9	.591	0	1	13	10	.565	10	2	1st

1955 Tournament

School	Conference	How	Pre-Tourney W	L	Pct.	Tourney W	L	Final W	L	Pct.	Conf. W	L	Fin.
Bradley	Independent	L	7	19	.269	2	1	9	20	.310	—	—	—
Canisius	Western N.Y. Little 3	L	16	6	.727	2	1	18	7	.720	2	2	2d
Colorado	Big Seven	Q	16	5	.762	3	1	19	6	.760	11	1	1st
Duke	Atlantic Coast	Q	20	7	.741	0	1	20	8	.714	11	3	2d
Idaho St.	Rocky Mountain	Q	18	7	.720	0	1	18	8	.692	9	1	1st
Iowa	Big Ten	Q	17	5	.773	2	2	19	7	.731	11	3	1st
Kentucky	Southeastern	Q	22	2	.917	1	1	23	3	.885	12	2	1st
La Salle	Independent (Middle Atlantic)	Q	22	4	.846	4	1	26	5	.839	—	—	—
Marquette	Independent	Q	22	2	.917	2	1	24	3	.889	—	—	—
Memphis	Independent	L	17	4	.810	0	1	17	5	.773	—	—	—
Miami (Ohio)	Mid-American	Q	14	8	.636	0	1	14	9	.609	11	3	1st
Oklahoma City	Independent	L	9	17	.346	0	1	9	18	.333	—	—	—
Oregon St.	Pacific Coast (N)	Q	21	7	.750	1	1	22	8	.733	15	1	1st
Penn St.	Independent	L	17	8	.680	1	2	18	10	.643	—	—	—
Princeton	Ivy	Q	13	10	.565	0	2	13	12	.520	11	4	1st
San Francisco	West Coast	L	23	1	.958	5	0	28	1	.966	12	0	1st
Seattle	Independent	L	21	5	.808	1	2	22	7	.759	—	—	—
Southern Methodist	Southwest	Q	15	8	.652	0	2	15	10	.600	9	3	1st
Tulsa	Missouri Valley	Q	20	6	.769	1	1	21	7	.750	8	2	T1st
Utah	Mountain States	Q	23	3	.885	1	1	24	4	.857	13	1	1st
Villanova	Independent	L	16	9	.640	2	1	18	10	.643	—	—	—
West Tex. A&M	Border	Q	15	6	.714	0	1	15	7	.682	9	3	T1st
West Virginia	Southern	Q	19	10	.655	0	1	19	11	.633	9	1	1st
Williams	Little Three (New England)	Q	17	1	.944	0	1	17	2	.895	3	1	1st

1956 Tournament

School	Conference	How	Pre-Tourney W	L	Pct.	Tourney W	L	Final W	L	Pct.	Conf. W	L	Fin.
Canisius	Western N.Y. Little 3	L	17	6	.739	2	1	19	7	.731	4	0	1st
Connecticut	Yankee	Q	16	9	.640	1	2	17	11	.607	6	1	1st
Dartmouth	Ivy	Q	16	10	.615	2	1	18	11	.621	10	4	1st
DePaul	Independent	L	16	7	.696	0	1	16	8	.667	—	—	—
Holy Cross	Independent	L	22	4	.846	0	1	22	5	.815	—	—	—
Houston	Missouri Valley	Q	19	5	.792	0	2	19	7	.731	9	3	1st
Idaho St.	Rocky Mountain	Q	18	7	.720	0	1	18	8	.692	11	1	1st
Iowa	Big Ten	Q	17	5	.773	3	1	20	6	.769	13	1	1st
Kansas St.	Big Seven	Q	16	5	.696	1	1	17	8	.680	9	3	1st
Kentucky	Southeastern	Q	19	5	.792	1	1	20	6	.769	12	2	2d
Manhattan	Independent	L	16	7	.696	0	1	16	8	.667	—	—	—
Marshall	Mid-American	Q	18	4	.818	0	1	18	5	.783	10	2	1st
Memphis	Independent	L	20	6	.769	0	1	20	7	.741	—	—	—
Morehead St.	Ohio Valley	Q	17	9	.654	2	1	19	10	.655	7	3	T1st
North Carolina St.	Atlantic Coast	Q	24	3	.889	0	1	24	4	.857	11	3	T1st
Oklahoma City	Independent	L	18	6	.750	2	1	20	7	.741	—	—	—
San Francisco	West Coast	Q	25	0	1.000	4	0	29	0	1.000	14	0	1st
Seattle	Independent	L	17	9	.654	1	2	18	11	.621	—	—	—
Southern Methodist	Southwest	Q	22	2	.917	3	2	25	4	.862	12	0	1st
Temple	Independent (Middle Atlantic)	Q	23	3	.885	4	1	27	4	.871	—	—	—
Texas Tech	Border	Q	13	11	.542	0	1	13	12	.520	8	4	1st
UCLA	Pacific Coast	Q	21	5	.808	1	1	22	6	.786	16	0	1st

ALL-TIME TOURNAMENT FIELD

School	Conference	How	W	L	Pct.	W	L	W	L	Pct.	W	L	Fin.
Utah	Mountain States	Q	21	5	.808	1	1	22	6	.786	12	2	1st
Wayne St. (Mich.)	President's Athletic	L	17	1	.944	1	2	18	3	.857	6	0	1st
West Virginia	Southern	Q	21	8	.724	0	1	21	9	.700	10	2	T1st

1957 Tournament

School	Conference	How	Pre-Tourney W L Pct.	Tourney W L	Final W L Pct.	Conf. W L Fin.
Brigham Young	Mountain States	Q	18 8 .692	1 1	19 9 .679	11 3 1st
California	Pacific Coast	Q	20 4 .833	1 1	21 5 .808	14 2 1st
Canisius	Western N.Y. Little 3	L	20 5 .800	2 1	22 6 .786	3 1 T1st
Connecticut	Yankee	Q	17 7 .708	0 1	17 8 .680	8 0 1st
Hardin-Simmons	Border	Q	17 8 .680	0 1	17 9 .654	7 3 2d
Idaho St.	Rocky Mountain	Q	24 2 .923	1 2	25 4 .862	12 0 1st
Kansas	Big Seven	Q	21 2 .913	3 1	24 3 .889	11 1 1st
Kentucky	Southeastern	Q	22 4 .846	1 1	23 5 .821	12 2 1st
Lafayette	Independent (Middle Atlantic)	Q	22 3 .880	0 2	22 5 .815	— — —
Loyola (La.)	Independent	L	14 11 .560	0 1	14 12 .538	— — —
Miami (Ohio)	Mid-American	Q	17 7 .708	0 1	17 8 .680	11 1 1st
Michigan St.	Big Ten	Q	14 8 .636	2 2	16 10 .615	10 4 T1st
Morehead St.	Ohio Valley	Q	19 7 .731	0 1	19 8 .704	9 1 T1st
North Carolina	Atlantic Coast	Q	27 0 1.000	5 0	32 0 1.000	14 0 1st
Notre Dame	Independent	L	18 7 .720	2 1	20 8 .714	— — —
Oklahoma City	Independent	L	17 8 .680	2 1	19 9 .679	— — —
Pittsburgh	Independent	L	15 9 .625	1 2	16 11 .593	— — —
St. Louis	Missouri Valley	Q	19 7 .731	0 2	19 9 .679	12 2 1st
San Francisco	West Coast	Q	18 6 .750	3 1	21 7 .750	12 2 1st
Southern Methodist	Southwest	Q	21 3 .875	1 1	22 4 .846	11 1 1st
Syracuse	Independent	L	16 6 .727	2 1	18 7 .720	— — —
West Virginia	Southern	Q	25 4 .862	0 1	25 5 .833	12 0 1st
Yale	Ivy	L	18 7 .720	0 1	18 8 .692	12 2 1st

1958 Tournament

School	Conference	How	Pre-Tourney W L Pct.	Tourney W L	Final W L Pct.	Conf. W L Fin.
Arizona St.	Border	Q	13 12 .520	0 1	13 13 .500	8 2 1st
Arkansas	Southwest	Q	17 8 .680	0 2	17 10 .630	9 5 T1st
Boston College	Independent	L	15 5 .750	0 1	15 6 .714	— — —
California	Pacific Coast	Q	18 8 .692	1 1	19 9 .679	12 4 T1st
Cincinnati	Missouri Valley	Q	24 2 .923	1 1	25 3 .893	13 1 1st
Connecticut	Yankee	Q	17 9 .654	0 1	17 10 .630	10 0 1st
Dartmouth	Ivy	L	20 4 .833	2 1	22 5 .815	11 3 1st
Idaho St.	Rocky Mountain	Q	21 4 .840	1 2	22 6 .786	10 0 1st
Indiana	Big Ten	Q	12 10 .545	1 1	13 11 .542	10 4 1st
Kansas St.	Big Seven	Q	20 3 .870	2 2	22 5 .815	10 2 1st
Kentucky	Southeastern	Q	19 6 .760	4 0	23 6 .793	12 2 1st
Loyola (La.)	Independent	L	16 8 .667	0 1	16 9 .640	— — —
Manhattan	Independent	L	15 8 .652	1 2	16 10 .615	— — —
Maryland	Atlantic Coast	Q	20 6 .769	2 1	22 7 .759	9 5 4th
Miami (Ohio)	Mid-American	Q	17 7 .708	1 2	18 9 .667	12 0 1st
Notre Dame	Independent	L	22 4 .846	2 1	24 5 .828	— — —
Oklahoma St.	Independent	L	19 7 .731	2 1	21 8 .724	— — —
Pittsburgh	Independent	L	18 6 .750	0 1	18 7 .720	— — —
San Francisco	West Coast	Q	24 1 .960	1 1	25 2 .926	12 0 1st
Seattle	Independent	L	19 5 .792	4 1	23 6 .793	— — —
Temple	Independent (Middle Atlantic)	Q	24 2 .923	3 1	27 3 .900	— — —
Tennessee Tech	Ohio Valley	Q	17 8 .680	0 1	17 9 .654	8 2 1st
West Virginia	Southern	Q	26 1 .963	0 1	26 2 .929	12 0 1st
Wyoming	Mountain States	Q	13 13 .500	0 1	13 14 .481	10 4 1st

1959 Tournament

School	Conference	How	Pre-Tourney W L Pct.	Tourney W L	Final W L Pct.	Conf. W L Fin.
Boston U.	Independent	L	18 6 .750	2 1	20 7 .741	— — —
Bowling Green	Mid-American	Q	18 7 .720	0 1	18 8 .692	9 3 T1st
California	Pacific Coast	Q	21 3 .840	4 0	25 3 .862	14 2 1st
Cincinnati	Missouri Valley	Q	23 3 .885	3 1	26 4 .867	13 1 1st
Connecticut	Yankee	Q	17 6 .739	0 1	17 7 .708	8 2 1st
Dartmouth	Ivy	L	22 5 .815	0 1	22 6 .786	14 1 1st
DePaul	Independent	L	12 9 .571	1 2	13 11 .542	— — —
Eastern Ky.	Ohio Valley	Q	16 5 .762	0 1	16 6 .727	10 2 1st
Idaho St.	Rocky Mountain	Q	19 6 .760	2 1	21 7 .750	9 1 1st
Kansas St.	Big Eight	Q	24 1 .960	1 1	25 2 .926	14 0 1st
Kentucky	Southeastern	Q	23 2 .920	1 1	24 3 .889	12 2 T2d
Louisville	Independent	L	16 10 .615	3 2	19 12 .613	— — —
Marquette	Independent	L	22 6 .846	1 2	23 6 .793	— — —
Michigan St.	Big Ten	Q	18 3 .857	1 1	19 4 .826	12 2 1st
Navy	Independent	L	16 5 .762	2 1	18 6 .750	— — —
New Mexico St.	Border	Q	17 10 .630	0 1	17 11 .607	7 3 T1st
North Carolina	Atlantic Coast	Q	20 4 .833	0 1	20 5 .800	12 2 T1st
Portland	Independent	L	19 7 .731	0 1	19 8 .704	— — —
St. Joseph's	Middle Atlantic	Q	22 3 .880	0 2	22 5 .815	7 0 1st
St. Mary's (Cal.)	West Coast	Q	18 5 .783	1 1	19 6 .760	11 1 1st
TCU	Southwest	Q	19 5 .792	1 1	20 6 .769	12 2 1st
Utah	Mountain States	Q	21 5 .808	0 2	21 7 .750	13 1 1st
West Virginia	Southern	Q	25 4 .862	4 1	29 5 .853	11 0 1st

1960 Tournament

School	Conference	How	Pre-Tourney W L Pct.	Tourney W L	Final W L Pct.	Conf. W L Fin.
Air Force	Independent	L	12 9 .571	0 1	12 10 .545	— — —
California	AAWU	L	24 1 .960	4 1	28 2 .933	11 1 1st
Cincinnati	Missouri Valley	Q	25 1 .962	3 1	28 2 .933	13 1 1st
Connecticut	Yankee	Q	17 8 .680	0 1	17 9 .654	8 2 1st
DePaul	Independent	L	15 6 .714	2 1	17 7 .708	— — —
Duke	Atlantic Coast	Q	15 10 .600	2 1	17 11 .607	7 7 4th
Georgia Tech	Southeastern	Q	21 5 .808	1 1	22 6 .786	11 3 2d
Idaho St.	Rocky Mountain	L	21 4 .840	0 1	21 5 .808	8 0 1st

ALL-TIME TOURNAMENT FIELD

School	Conference	How	Pre-Tourney W	L	Pct.	Tourney W	L	Final W	L	Pct.	Conf. W	L	Fin.
Kansas	Big Eight	Q	18	8	.692	1	1	19	9	.679	10	4	T1st
Miami (Fla.)	Florida Intercollegiate	L	23	3	.885	0	1	23	4	.852	9	1	1st
Navy	Independent	L	16	5	.762	0	1	16	6	.727	—	—	—
New Mexico St.	Border	Q	20	6	.769	0	1	20	7	.741	8	2	1st
New York U.	Independent	L	19	3	.864	3	2	22	5	.815	—	—	—
Notre Dame	Independent	L	17	8	.680	0	1	17	9	.654	—	—	—
Ohio	Mid-American	Q	15	6	.714	1	2	16	8	.667	10	2	1st
Ohio St.	Big Ten	Q	21	3	.875	4	0	25	3	.893	13	1	1st
Oregon	Independent	L	17	9	.654	2	1	19	10	.655	—	—	—
Princeton	Ivy	L	15	8	.652	0	1	15	9	.625	11	3	1st
St. Joseph's	Middle Atlantic	Q	20	5	.800	0	2	20	7	.741	7	1	1st
Santa Clara	West Coast	Q	21	8	.724	0	2	21	10	.677	9	3	T1st
Southern California	AAWU	L	16	10	.615	0	1	16	11	.593	5	7	3d
Texas	Southwest	Q	18	6	.750	0	2	18	8	.692	11	3	1st
Utah	Mountain States	Q	24	2	.923	2	1	26	3	.897	13	1	1st
West Virginia	Southern	Q	24	4	.857	2	1	26	5	.839	9	2	2d
Western Ky.	Ohio Valley	Q	19	6	.760	2	1	21	7	.750	10	1	1st

1961 Tournament

School	Conference	How	Pre-Tourney W	L	Pct.	Tourney W	L	Final W	L	Pct.	Conf. W	L	Fin.
Arizona St.	Border	Q	21	5	.808	2	1	23	6	.793	9	1	T1st
Cincinnati	Missouri Valley	Q	23	3	.885	4	0	27	3	.900	10	2	1st
George Washington	Southern	Q	9	16	.360	0	1	9	17	.346	3	9	7th
Houston	Independent	L	16	9	.640	1	2	17	11	.607	—	—	—
Kansas St.	Big Eight	Q	21	4	.840	1	1	22	5	.815	13	1	1st
Kentucky	Southeastern	Q	18	8	.692	1	1	19	9	.679	10	4	T2d
Louisville	Independent	L	19	7	.731	2	1	21	8	.724	—	—	—
Loyola Marymount	West Coast	Q	19	6	.760	1	1	20	7	.741	10	2	1st
Marquette	Independent	L	16	10	.615	0	1	16	11	.593	—	—	—
Morehead St.	Ohio Valley	Q	18	10	.643	1	2	19	12	.613	9	3	T1st
Ohio	Mid-American	Q	17	6	.739	0	1	17	7	.708	10	2	1st
Ohio St.	Big Ten	Q	24	0	1.000	3	1	27	1	.964	14	0	1st
Oregon	Independent	L	15	11	.577	0	1	15	12	.556	—	—	—
Princeton	Ivy	L	17	6	.739	1	2	18	8	.692	11	3	1st
Rhode Island	Yankee	Q	18	8	.692	0	1	18	9	.667	9	1	1st
St. Bonaventure	Independent	L	22	3	.880	2	1	24	4	.857	—	—	—
St. John's (N.Y.)	Independent	L	20	4	.833	0	1	20	5	.800	—	—	—
St. Joseph's	Middle Atlantic	Q	22	4	.846	3	1	25	5	.833	8	0	1st
Seattle	Independent	L	18	7	.720	0	1	18	8	.692	—	—	—
Southern California	AAWU	Q	20	6	.769	1	2	21	8	.724	9	3	1st
Texas Tech	Southwest	Q	14	9	.609	1	1	15	10	.600	11	3	1st
Utah	Mountain States	Q	21	6	.778	2	2	23	8	.742	12	2	T1st
Wake Forest	Atlantic Coast	Q	17	10	.630	2	1	19	11	.633	11	3	2d
Xavier	Independent	L	17	9	.654	0	1	17	10	.630	—	—	—

1962 Tournament

School	Conference	How	Pre-Tourney W	L	Pct.	Tourney W	L	Final W	L	Pct.	Conf. W	L	Fin.
Air Force	Independent	L	16	6	.727	0	1	16	7	.696	—	—	—
Arizona St.	Border	Q	23	3	.885	0	1	23	4	.852	8	0	1st
Bowling Green	Mid-American	Q	21	3	.875	0	1	21	4	.840	11	1	1st
Butler	Indiana Collegiate	L	20	5	.800	2	1	22	6	.786	10	2	1st
Cincinnati	Missouri Valley	Q	25	2	.926	4	0	29	2	.935	10	2	T1st
Colorado	Big Eight	Q	18	6	.750	1	1	19	7	.731	13	1	1st
Creighton	Independent	L	19	4	.826	2	1	21	5	.808	—	—	—
Detroit	Independent	L	15	11	.577	0	1	15	12	.556	—	—	—
Kentucky	Southeastern	Q	22	2	.917	1	1	23	3	.885	13	1	T1st
Massachusetts	Yankee	Q	15	8	.652	0	1	15	9	.625	8	2	1st
Memphis	Independent	L	15	6	.714	0	1	15	7	.682	—	—	—
New York U.	Independent	L	18	4	.818	2	1	20	5	.800	—	—	—
Ohio St.	Big Ten	Q	23	1	.958	3	1	26	2	.929	13	1	1st
Oregon St.	Independent	L	22	4	.846	2	1	24	5	.828	—	—	—
Pepperdine	West Coast	Q	19	6	.760	1	1	20	7	.741	11	1	1st
St. Joseph's	Middle Atlantic	Q	18	8	.692	0	2	18	10	.643	9	1	1st
Seattle	Independent	L	18	8	.692	0	1	18	9	.667	—	—	—
Texas Tech	Southwest	Q	18	6	.750	1	2	19	8	.704	11	3	T1st
UCLA	AAWU	Q	16	9	.640	2	2	18	11	.621	10	2	1st
Utah St.	Mountain States	Q	21	6	.808	1	2	22	7	.759	12	2	2d
Villanova	Independent	L	19	6	.760	2	1	21	7	.750	—	—	—
Wake Forest	Atlantic Coast	Q	18	8	.692	4	1	22	9	.710	12	2	1st
West Virginia	Southern	Q	24	5	.828	0	1	24	6	.800	12	1	1st
Western Ky.	Ohio Valley	Q	16	8	.667	1	2	17	10	.630	11	1	1st
Yale	Ivy	L	18	5	.783	0	1	18	6	.750	13	1	1st

1963 Tournament

School	Conference	How	Pre-Tourney W	L	Pct.	Tourney W	L	Final W	L	Pct.	Conf. W	L	Fin.
Arizona St.	Western Athletic	Q	24	2	.923	2	1	26	3	.897	9	1	1st
Bowling Green	Mid-American	Q	18	6	.750	1	2	19	8	.704	9	3	1st
Cincinnati	Missouri Valley	Q	23	1	.958	3	1	26	2	.929	11	1	1st
Colorado	Big Eight	Q	18	6	.750	1	1	19	7	.731	11	3	T1st
Colorado St.	Independent	L	18	4	.818	0	1	18	5	.783	—	—	—
Connecticut	Yankee	Q	18	6	.750	0	1	18	7	.720	9	1	1st
Duke	Atlantic Coast	Q	24	2	.923	3	1	27	3	.900	14	0	1st
Illinois	Big Ten	Q	19	5	.792	1	1	20	6	.769	11	3	T1st
Loyola (Ill.)	Independent	L	24	2	.923	5	0	29	2	.935	—	—	—
Mississippi St.	Southeastern	Q	21	5	.808	1	1	22	6	.786	12	2	1st
New York U.	Independent	L	17	3	.850	1	2	18	5	.783	—	—	—
Notre Dame	Independent	L	17	8	.680	0	1	17	9	.654	—	—	—
Oklahoma City	Independent	L	18	8	.692	1	2	19	10	.655	—	—	—
Oregon St.	Independent	L	19	7	.731	3	2	22	9	.710	—	—	—
Pittsburgh	Independent	L	19	5	.792	0	1	19	6	.760	—	—	—
Princeton	Ivy	Q	19	5	.792	0	1	19	6	.760	12	3	1st
St. Joseph's	Middle Atlantic	Q	21	4	.840	2	1	23	5	.821	8	0	1st

ALL-TIME TOURNAMENT FIELD

School	Conference	How	W	L	Pct.	W	L	W	L	Pct.	W	L	Fin.
San Francisco	West Coast	Q	17	8	.680	1	1	18	9	.667	10	2	1st
Seattle	Independent	L	21	5	.808	0	1	21	6	.778	—	—	—
Tennessee Tech	Ohio Valley	Q	16	7	.696	0	1	16	8	.667	8	4	T1st
Texas	Southwest	Q	18	6	.750	2	1	20	7	.741	13	1	1st
UTEP	Independent	L	19	6	.760	0	1	19	7	.731	—	—	—
UCLA	AAWU	Q	20	7	.741	0	2	20	9	.690	7	5	T1st
Utah St.	Independent	L	20	6	.769	0	1	20	7	.741	—	—	—
West Virginia	Southern	Q	21	7	.750	2	1	23	8	.742	11	2	1st

1964 Tournament

School	Conference	How	Pre-Tourney W L Pct.	Tourney W L	Final W L Pct.	Conf. W L Fin.
Arizona St.	Western Athletic	Q	16 10 .615	0 1	16 11 .593	4 6 T4th
Connecticut	Yankee	Q	14 10 .583	2 1	16 11 .593	8 2 T1st
Creighton	Independent	L	21 5 .808	1 2	22 7 .759	— — —
Duke	Atlantic Coast	Q	23 4 .852	3 1	26 5 .839	13 1 1st
Kansas St.	Big Eight	Q	20 5 .800	2 2	22 7 .759	12 2 1st
Kentucky	Southeastern	Q	21 4 .840	0 2	21 6 .778	11 3 1st
Louisville	Independent	L	15 9 .625	0 1	15 10 .600	— — —
Loyola (Ill.)	Independent	L	20 5 .800	2 1	22 6 .786	— — —
Michigan	Big Ten	Q	20 4 .833	3 1	23 5 .821	11 3 T1st
Murray St.	Ohio Valley	Q	16 8 .667	0 1	16 9 .640	11 3 1st
Ohio	Mid-American	Q	19 5 .792	2 1	21 6 .778	10 2 1st
Oklahoma City	Independent	L	15 10 .600	0 1	15 11 .577	— — —
Oregon St.	Independent	L	25 3 .893	0 1	25 4 .862	— — —
Princeton	Ivy	Q	19 7 .731	1 2	20 9 .690	12 2 1st
Providence	Independent	L	20 5 .800	0 1	20 6 .769	— — —
San Francisco	West Coast	Q	22 4 .846	1 1	23 5 .821	12 0 1st
Seattle	Independent	L	20 5 .800	2 1	22 6 .786	— — —
Temple	Middle Atlantic	Q	17 7 .708	0 1	17 8 .680	6 1 1st
UTEP	Independent	L	23 2 .920	2 1	25 3 .893	— — —
Texas A&M	Southwest	Q	18 6 .750	0 1	18 7 .720	13 1 1st
UCLA	AAWU	Q	26 0 1.000	4 0	30 0 1.000	15 0 1st
Utah St.	Independent	L	20 6 .769	1 2	21 8 .724	— — —
VMI	Southern	Q	12 11 .522	0 1	12 12 .500	7 7 4th
Villanova	Independent	L	22 3 .880	2 1	24 4 .857	— — —
Wichita St.	Missouri Valley	Q	22 5 .815	1 1	23 6 .793	10 2 T1st

1965 Tournament

School	Conference	How	Pre-Tourney W L Pct.	Tourney W L	Final W L Pct.	Conf. W L Fin.
Brigham Young	Western Athletic	Q	21 5 .808	0 2	21 7 .750	8 2 1st
Colorado St.	Independent	L	16 7 .696	0 1	16 8 .667	— — —
Connecticut	Yankee	Q	23 2 .920	0 1	23 3 .885	10 0 1st
Dayton	Independent	L	20 6 .769	2 1	22 7 .759	— — —
DePaul	Independent	L	16 8 .667	1 2	17 10 .630	— — —
Eastern Ky.	Ohio Valley	Q	19 5 .792	0 1	19 6 .760	13 1 1st
Houston	Independent	L	18 8 .692	1 2	19 10 .655	— — —
Michigan	Big Ten	Q	21 3 .875	3 1	24 4 .857	13 1 1st
North Carolina St.	Atlantic Coast	Q	20 4 .833	1 1	21 5 .808	10 4 T2d
Notre Dame	Independent	L	15 11 .577	0 1	15 12 .556	— — —
Ohio	Mid-American	Q	19 6 .760	0 1	19 7 .731	11 1 T1st
Oklahoma City	Independent	L	19 9 .679	2 1	21 10 .677	— — —
Oklahoma St.	Big Eight	Q	19 6 .760	1 1	20 7 .741	12 2 1st
Penn St.	Independent	L	20 3 .870	0 1	20 4 .833	— — —
Princeton	Ivy	Q	19 5 .792	4 1	23 6 .793	13 1 1st
Providence	Independent	L	22 1 .957	2 1	24 2 .923	— — —
St. Joseph's	Middle Atlantic	Q	25 1 .962	1 2	26 3 .897	— — 1st
San Francisco	West Coast	Q	23 4 .852	1 1	24 5 .828	13 1 1st
Southern Methodist	Southwest	Q	16 9 .640	1 1	17 10 .630	10 4 T1st
UCLA	AAWU	Q	24 2 .923	4 0	28 2 .933	14 0 1st
Vanderbilt	Southeastern	Q	23 3 .885	1 1	24 4 .857	15 1 1st
West Virginia	Southern	Q	14 14 .500	0 1	14 15 .483	8 6 4th
Wichita St.	Missouri Valley	Q	19 7 .731	2 2	21 9 .700	11 3 1st

1966 Tournament

School	Conference	How	Pre-Tourney W L Pct.	Tourney W L	Final W L Pct.	Conf. W L Fin.
Cincinnati	Missouri Valley	Q	21 5 .808	0 2	21 7 .750	10 4 1st
Colorado St.	Independent	L	14 7 .667	0 1	14 8 .636	— — —
Davidson	Southern	Q	20 5 .800	1 2	21 7 .750	11 1 1st
Dayton	Independent	L	22 4 .846	1 2	23 6 .793	— — —
Duke	Atlantic Coast	Q	23 3 .885	3 1	26 4 .867	12 2 1st
Houston	Independent	L	21 5 .808	2 1	23 6 .793	— — —
Kansas	Big Eight	Q	22 3 .880	1 1	23 4 .852	13 1 1st
Kentucky	Southeastern	Q	24 1 .960	3 1	27 2 .931	15 1 1st
Loyola (Ill.)	Independent	L	22 2 .917	0 1	22 3 .880	— — —
Miami (Ohio)	Mid-American	Q	18 6 .750	0 1	18 7 .720	11 1 1st
Michigan	Big Ten	Q	17 7 .708	1 1	18 8 .692	11 3 1st
Oklahoma City	Independent	L	24 4 .857	0 1	24 5 .828	— — —
Oregon St.	AAWU	Q	20 6 .769	1 1	21 7 .750	12 2 1st
Pacific (Cal.)	West Coast	Q	22 4 .846	0 2	22 6 .786	13 1 1st
Providence	Independent	L	22 4 .846	0 1	22 5 .815	— — —
Rhode Island	Yankee	Q	20 7 .741	0 1	20 8 .714	9 1 T1st
St. Joseph's	Middle Atlantic	Q	22 4 .846	2 1	24 5 .828	— — 1st
Southern Methodist	Southwest	Q	16 8 .667	1 1	17 9 .654	11 3 1st
Syracuse	Independent	L	21 5 .808	1 1	22 6 .786	— — —
UTEP	Independent	L	23 1 .958	5 0	28 1 .966	— — —
Utah	Western Athletic	Q	21 6 .778	2 2	23 8 .742	7 3 1st
Western Ky.	Ohio Valley	Q	23 2 .920	2 1	25 3 .893	14 0 1st

1967 Tournament

School	Conference	How	Pre-Tourney W L Pct.	Tourney W L	Final W L Pct.	Conf. W L Fin.
Boston College	Independent	L	19 2 .905	2 1	21 3 .875	— — —
Connecticut	Yankee	Q	17 6 .739	0 1	17 7 .708	9 1 1st
Dayton	Independent	L	21 5 .808	4 1	25 6 .806	— — —

THE TOURNAMENT FIELD

School	Conference	How	W	L	Pct.	W	L	W	L	Pct.	W	L	Fin.
Houston	Independent	L	23	3	.885	4	1	27	4	.871	—	—	—
Indiana	Big Ten	Q	17	7	.708	1	1	18	8	.692	10	4	T1st
Kansas	Big Eight	Q	22	3	.880	1	1	23	4	.852	13	1	1st
Louisville	Missouri Valley	Q	23	3	.885	0	2	23	5	.821	12	2	1st
New Mexico St.	Independent	L	15	10	.600	0	1	15	11	.577	—	—	—
North Carolina	Atlantic Coast	Q	24	4	.857	2	2	26	6	.813	12	2	1st
Pacific (Cal.)	West Coast	Q	23	3	.885	1	1	24	4	.857	14	0	1st
Princeton	Ivy	Q	23	2	.920	2	1	25	3	.893	13	1	1st
St. John's (N.Y.)	Independent	L	22	3	.880	1	2	23	5	.821	—	—	—
Seattle	Independent	L	18	7	.720	0	1	18	8	.692	—	—	—
Southern Methodist	Southwest	Q	19	5	.792	1	1	20	6	.769	12	2	1st
Temple	Middle Atlantic	Q	20	7	.741	0	1	20	8	.714	—	—	—
Tennessee	Southeastern	Q	21	5	.808	0	2	21	7	.750	15	3	1st
UTEP	Independent	L	20	5	.800	2	1	22	6	.786	—	—	—
Toledo	Mid-American	Q	23	1	.958	0	1	23	2	.920	11	1	1st
UCLA	AAWU	Q	26	0	1.000	4	0	30	0	1.000	14	0	1st
Virginia Tech	Independent	L	18	6	.750	2	1	20	7	.741	—	—	—
West Virginia	Southern	Q	19	8	.704	0	1	19	9	.679	9	1	1st
Western Ky.	Ohio Valley	Q	23	2	.920	0	1	23	3	.885	13	1	1st
Wyoming	Western Athletic	Q	15	12	.556	0	2	15	14	.517	8	2	T1st

1968 Tournament

School	Conference	How	Pre-Tourney W	L	Pct.	Tourney W	L	Final W	L	Pct.	Conf. W	L	Fin.
Boston College	Independent	L	17	7	.708	0	1	17	8	.680	—	—	—
Bowling Green	Mid-American	Q	18	6	.750	0	1	18	7	.720	10	2	1st
Columbia	Ivy	L	21	4	.840	2	1	23	5	.821	13	2	1st
Davidson	Southern	Q	22	4	.846	2	1	24	5	.828	9	1	1st
East Tenn. St.	Ohio Valley	Q	18	6	.750	1	2	19	8	.704	10	4	T1st
Florida St.	Independent	L	19	7	.731	0	1	19	8	.704	—	—	—
Houston	Independent	L	28	0	1.000	3	2	31	2	.939	—	—	—
Kansas St.	Big Eight	Q	19	7	.731	0	2	19	9	.679	11	3	1st
Kentucky	Southeastern	Q	21	4	.840	1	1	22	5	.815	15	3	1st
La Salle	Middle Atlantic	Q	20	7	.741	0	1	20	8	.714	—	—	1st
Louisville	Missouri Valley	Q	20	6	.769	1	1	21	7	.750	14	0	1st
Loyola (Ill.)	Independent	L	15	8	.652	0	1	15	9	.625	—	—	—
Marquette	Independent	L	21	5	.808	2	1	23	6	.793	—	—	—
New Mexico	Western Athletic	Q	23	3	.885	0	2	23	5	.821	8	2	1st
New Mexico St.	Independent	L	21	5	.808	2	1	23	6	.793	—	—	—
North Carolina	Atlantic Coast	Q	25	3	.893	3	1	28	4	.875	12	2	1st
Ohio St.	Big Ten	Q	18	7	.720	3	1	21	8	.724	10	4	T1st
St. Bonaventure	Independent	L	22	0	1.000	1	2	23	2	.920	—	—	—
St. John's (N.Y.)	Independent	L	19	7	.731	0	1	19	8	.704	—	—	—
Santa Clara	West Coast	Q	21	3	.875	1	1	22	4	.846	13	1	1st
TCU	Southwest	Q	14	10	.583	1	1	15	11	.577	9	5	1st
UCLA	AAWU	Q	25	1	.962	4	0	29	1	.967	14	0	1st
Weber St.	Big Sky	Q	21	5	.808	0	1	21	6	.778	12	3	1st

1969 Tournament

School	Conference	How	Pre-Tourney W	L	Pct.	Tourney W	L	Final W	L	Pct.	Conf. W	L	Fin.
Brigham Young	Western Athletic	Q	16	11	.593	0	1	16	12	.571	6	4	T1st
Colorado	Big Eight	Q	20	6	.769	1	1	21	7	.750	10	4	1st
Colorado St.	Independent	L	15	6	.714	2	1	17	7	.708	—	—	—
Davidson	Southern	Q	25	2	.926	2	1	27	3	.900	9	0	1st
Dayton	Independent	L	20	6	.769	0	1	20	7	.741	—	—	—
Drake	Missouri Valley	Q	23	4	.852	3	1	26	5	.839	13	3	T1st
Duquesne	Independent	L	19	4	.826	2	1	21	5	.808	—	—	—
Kentucky	Southeastern	Q	22	4	.846	1	1	23	5	.821	16	2	1st
Marquette	Independent	L	22	4	.846	2	1	24	5	.828	—	—	—
Miami (Ohio)	Mid-American	Q	14	10	.583	1	2	15	12	.556	10	2	1st
Murray St.	Ohio Valley	Q	22	5	.815	0	1	22	6	.786	11	3	T1st
New Mexico St.	Independent	L	23	3	.885	1	2	24	5	.828	—	—	—
North Carolina	Atlantic Coast	Q	25	3	.893	2	2	27	5	.844	12	2	1st
Notre Dame	Independent	L	20	6	.769	0	1	20	7	.741	—	—	—
Princeton	Ivy	Q	19	6	.760	0	1	19	7	.731	14	0	1st
Purdue	Big Ten	Q	20	4	.833	3	1	23	5	.821	13	1	1st
St. John's (N.Y.)	Independent	L	22	4	.846	1	2	23	6	.793	—	—	—
St. Joseph's	Middle Atlantic	Q	17	10	.630	0	1	17	11	.607	—	—	3d
Santa Clara	West Coast	Q	26	1	.963	1	1	27	2	.931	13	1	1st
Seattle	Independent	L	19	7	.731	0	1	19	8	.704	—	—	—
Texas A&M	Southwest	Q	17	7	.708	1	2	18	9	.667	12	2	1st
Trinity (Tex.)	Southland	L	19	4	.826	0	1	19	5	.792	7	1	1st
UCLA	Pacific-8	Q	25	1	.962	4	0	29	1	.967	13	1	1st
Villanova	Independent	L	21	4	.840	0	1	21	5	.808	—	—	—
Weber St.	Big Sky	Q	25	2	.926	2	1	27	3	.900	15	0	1st

1970 Tournament

School	Conference	How	Pre-Tourney W	L	Pct.	Tourney W	L	Final W	L	Pct.	Conf. W	L	Fin.
Davidson	Southern	Q	22	4	.846	0	1	22	5	.815	10	0	1st
Dayton	Independent	L	19	7	.731	0	1	19	8	.704	—	—	—
Drake	Missouri Valley	Q	21	6	.778	1	1	22	7	.759	14	2	1st
Houston	Independent	L	24	3	.889	1	2	25	5	.833	—	—	—
Iowa	Big Ten	Q	19	4	.826	1	1	20	5	.800	14	0	1st
Jacksonville	Independent	L	23	1	.958	4	1	27	2	.931	—	—	—
Kansas St.	Big Eight	Q	19	7	.731	1	1	20	8	.714	10	4	1st
Kentucky	Southeastern	Q	25	1	.962	1	1	26	2	.929	17	1	1st
Long Beach St.	Pacific Coast	Q	23	3	.885	1	2	24	5	.828	10	0	1st
New Mexico St.	Independent	L	23	2	.920	4	1	27	3	.900	—	—	—
Niagara	Independent	L	21	5	.808	1	2	22	7	.759	—	—	—
North Carolina St.	Atlantic Coast	Q	22	6	.786	1	1	23	7	.767	9	5	T2d
Notre Dame	Independent	L	20	6	.769	1	2	21	8	.724	—	—	—
Ohio	Mid-American	Q	20	4	.833	0	1	20	5	.800	9	1	1st
Pennsylvania	Ivy	Q	25	0	.962	0	1	25	2	.926	14	0	1st

ALL-TIME TOURNAMENT FIELD

School	Conference	How	W	L	Pct.	W	L	W	L	Pct.	W	L	Fin.
Rice	Southwest	Q	14	10	.583	0	1	14	11	.560	10	4	1st
St. Bonaventure	Independent	L	22	1	.957	3	2	25	3	.893	—	—	—
Santa Clara	West Coast	Q	22	5	.815	1	1	23	6	.793	11	3	T1st
Temple	Middle Atlantic (E)	Q	15	12	.556	0	1	15	13	.536	2	3	T3d
UTEP	Western Athletic	Q	17	7	.708	0	1	17	8	.680	10	4	1st
UCLA	Pacific-8	Q	24	2	.923	4	0	28	2	.933	12	2	1st
Utah St.	Independent	L	20	6	.769	2	1	22	7	.759	—	—	—
Villanova	Independent	L	20	6	.769	2	1	22	7	.759	—	—	—
Weber St.	Big Sky	Q	20	6	.769	0	1	20	7	.741	12	3	1st
Western Ky.	Ohio Valley	Q	22	2	.917	0	1	22	3	.880	14	0	1st

1971 Tournament

School	Conference	How	Pre-Tourney W	L	Pct.	Tourney W	L	Final W	L	Pct.	Conf. W	L	Fin.
Brigham Young	Western Athletic	Q	17	9	.654	1	2	18	11	.621	10	4	1st
Drake	Missouri Valley	Q	20	7	.741	1	1	21	8	.724	9	5	T1st
Duquesne	Independent	L	21	3	.875	0	1	21	4	.840	—	—	—
Fordham	Independent	L	24	2	.923	2	1	26	3	.897	—	—	—
Furman	Southern	Q	15	11	.577	0	1	15	12	.556	5	5	T5th
Houston	Independent	L	20	6	.769	2	1	22	7	.759	—	—	—
Jacksonville	Independent	L	22	3	.880	0	1	22	4	.846	—	—	—
Kansas	Big Eight	Q	25	1	.962	2	2	27	3	.900	14	0	1st
Kentucky	Southeastern	Q	22	4	.846	0	2	22	6	.786	16	2	1st
Long Beach St.	Pacific Coast	L	22	4	.846	2	1	24	5	.828	10	0	1st
Marquette	Independent	L	26	0	1.000	2	1	28	1	.966	—	—	—
Miami (Ohio)	Mid-American	Q	20	4	.833	0	1	20	5	.800	9	1	1st
New Mexico St.	Independent	L	19	7	.731	0	1	19	8	.704	—	—	—
Notre Dame	Independent	L	19	7	.731	1	2	20	9	.690	—	—	—
Ohio St.	Big Ten	Q	19	5	.792	1	1	20	6	.769	13	1	1st
Pacific (Cal.)	West Coast	Q	21	5	.808	1	1	22	6	.786	12	2	1st
Pennsylvania	Ivy	Q	26	0	1.000	2	1	28	1	.966	14	0	1st
St. Joseph's	Middle Atlantic (E)	Q	19	8	.704	0	1	19	9	.679	6	0	1st
South Carolina	Atlantic Coast	Q	23	4	.852	0	2	23	6	.793	10	4	2d
TCU	Southwest	Q	15	11	.577	0	1	15	12	.556	11	3	1st
UCLA	Pacific-8	Q	25	1	.962	4	0	29	1	.967	14	0	1st
Utah St.	Independent	L	20	6	.769	0	1	20	7	.741	—	—	—
Villanova	Independent	L	23	6	.793	4	1	27	7	.794	—	—	—
Weber St.	Big Sky	Q	21	5	.808	0	1	21	6	.778	12	2	1st
Western Ky.	Ohio Valley	Q	20	5	.800	4	1	24	6	.800	12	2	1st

1972 Tournament

School	Conference	How	Pre-Tourney W	L	Pct.	Tourney W	L	Final W	L	Pct.	Conf. W	L	Fin.
Brigham Young	Western Athletic	Q	21	4	.840	0	1	21	5	.808	12	2	1st
East Caro.	Southern	Q	14	14	.500	0	1	14	15	.483	7	5	4th
Eastern Ky.	Ohio Valley	Q	15	10	.600	0	1	15	11	.577	9	5	T1st
Florida St.	Independent	L	23	5	.821	4	1	27	6	.818	—	—	—
Hawaii	Independent	L	24	2	.923	0	1	24	3	.889	—	—	—
Houston	Independent	L	20	6	.769	0	1	20	7	.741	—	—	—
Kansas St.	Big Eight	Q	18	8	.692	1	1	19	9	.679	12	2	1st
Kentucky	Southeastern	Q	20	6	.769	1	1	21	7	.750	14	4	T1st
Long Beach St.	Pacific Coast	Q	23	3	.885	2	1	25	4	.862	10	0	1st
La.-Lafayette	Southland	L	23	3	.885	2	1	25	4	.862	8	0	1st
Louisville	Missouri Valley	Q	24	2	.889	2	2	26	5	.839	12	2	T1st
Marquette	Independent	L	24	2	.923	1	2	25	4	.862	—	—	—
Marshall	Independent	L	23	3	.885	0	1	23	4	.852	—	—	—
Minnesota	Big Ten	Q	17	6	.739	1	1	18	7	.720	11	3	1st
North Carolina	Atlantic Coast	Q	23	4	.852	3	1	26	5	.839	9	3	1st
Ohio	Mid-American	Q	15	10	.600	0	1	15	11	.577	7	3	T1st
Pennsylvania	Ivy	Q	23	2	.920	2	1	25	3	.893	13	1	1st
Providence	Independent	L	21	5	.808	0	1	21	6	.778	—	—	—
San Francisco	West Coast	Q	19	7	.731	1	1	20	8	.714	13	1	1st
South Carolina	Independent	L	22	4	.846	2	1	24	5	.828	—	—	—
Temple	Middle Atlantic (E)	Q	23	7	.767	0	1	23	8	.742	6	0	1st
Texas	Southwest	Q	18	7	.720	1	2	19	9	.679	10	4	T1st
UCLA	Pacific-8	Q	26	0	1.000	4	0	30	0	1.000	14	0	1st
Villanova	Independent	L	19	6	.760	1	2	20	8	.714	—	—	—
Weber St.	Big Sky	Q	17	9	.654	1	2	18	11	.621	10	4	1st

1973 Tournament

School	Conference	How	Pre-Tourney W	L	Pct.	Tourney W	L	Final W	L	Pct.	Conf. W	L	Fin.
Arizona St.	Western Athletic	Q	18	7	.720	1	2	19	9	.679	10	4	1st
Austin Peay	Ohio Valley	Q	21	5	.808	1	2	22	7	.759	11	3	1st
Furman	Southern	Q	20	8	.714	0	1	20	9	.690	11	2	2d
Houston	Independent	L	23	3	.885	0	1	23	4	.852	—	—	—
Indiana	Big Ten	Q	19	5	.792	3	1	22	6	.786	11	3	1st
Jacksonville	Independent	L	21	5	.808	0	1	21	6	.778	—	—	—
Kansas St.	Big Eight	Q	22	4	.846	1	1	23	5	.821	12	2	1st
Kentucky	Southeastern	Q	19	7	.731	1	1	20	8	.714	14	4	1st
Long Beach St.	Pacific Coast	Q	24	2	.923	2	1	26	3	.897	10	0	1st
La.-Lafayette	Southland	Q	23	3	.885	1	2	24	5	.828	12	0	1st
Marquette	Independent	L	23	3	.885	2	1	25	4	.862	—	—	—
Maryland	Atlantic Coast	Q	22	6	.786	1	1	23	7	.767	7	5	3d
Memphis	Missouri Valley	Q	21	5	.808	3	1	24	6	.800	12	2	1st
Miami (Ohio)	Mid-American	Q	18	8	.692	0	1	18	9	.667	9	2	1st
Oklahoma City	Independent	L	21	5	.808	0	1	21	6	.778	—	—	—
Pennsylvania	Ivy	Q	20	5	.800	1	2	21	7	.750	12	2	1st
Providence	Independent	L	24	2	.923	3	2	27	4	.871	—	—	—
St. John's (N.Y.)	Independent	L	19	6	.760	0	1	19	7	.731	—	—	—
St. Joseph's	Middle Atlantic (E)	Q	22	5	.815	0	1	22	6	.786	6	0	1st
San Francisco	West Coast	Q	22	4	.846	1	1	23	5	.821	12	2	1st
South Carolina	Independent	L	22	6	.769	0	1	22	7	.759	—	—	—
Syracuse	Independent	L	22	4	.846	2	1	24	5	.828	—	—	—
Texas Tech	Southwest	Q	19	7	.731	0	1	19	8	.704	12	2	1st
UCLA	Pacific-8	Q	26	0	1.000	4	0	30	0	1.000	14	0	1st
Weber St.	Big Sky	Q	20	6	.769	0	1	20	7	.741	13	1	1st

1974 Tournament

School	Conference	How	Pre-Tourney W	L	Pct.	Tourney W	L	Final W	L	Pct.	Conf. W	L	Fin.
Austin Peay	Ohio Valley	Q	17	9	.654	0	1	17	10	.630	10	4	T1st
Creighton	Independent	L	21	6	.778	2	1	23	7	.767	—	—	—
Dayton	Independent	L	19	7	.731	1	2	20	9	.690	—	—	—
Furman	Southern	Q	21	7	.750	1	2	22	9	.710	11	1	1st
Idaho St.	Big Sky	Q	20	7	.741	0	1	20	8	.714	11	3	T1st
Kansas	Big Eight	Q	21	5	.808	2	2	23	7	.767	13	1	1st
Cal St. Los Angeles	Pacific Coast	Q	17	9	.654	0	1	17	10	.630	8	4	2d
Louisville	Missouri Valley	Q	21	5	.808	0	2	21	7	.750	11	1	1st
Marquette	Independent	L	22	4	.846	4	1	26	5	.839	—	—	—
Michigan	Big Ten	Q	21	4	.840	1	1	22	5	.815	12	2	T1st
New Mexico	Western Athletic	Q	20	6	.769	2	1	22	7	.759	10	4	1st
North Carolina St.	Atlantic Coast	Q	26	1	.963	4	0	30	1	.968	12	0	1st
Notre Dame	Independent	L	24	2	.923	2	1	26	3	.897	—	—	—
Ohio	Mid-American	Q	16	10	.615	0	1	16	11	.593	9	3	1st
Oral Roberts	Independent	L	21	5	.808	2	1	23	6	.793	—	—	—
Pennsylvania	Ivy	Q	21	5	.808	0	1	21	6	.778	13	1	1st
Pittsburgh	Independent	L	22	3	.880	2	1	24	4	.857	—	—	—
Providence	Independent	L	26	3	.897	2	1	28	4	.875	—	—	—
St. Joseph's	Middle Atlantic (E)	Q	19	10	.655	0	1	19	11	.633	5	1	T1st
San Francisco	West Coast	Q	18	8	.692	1	1	19	9	.679	12	2	1st
South Carolina	Independent	L	22	4	.846	0	1	22	5	.815	—	—	—
Syracuse	Independent	L	19	6	.760	0	1	19	7	.731	—	—	—
Texas	Southwest	Q	12	14	.462	0	1	12	15	.444	11	3	1st
UCLA	Pacific-8	Q	23	3	.885	3	1	26	4	.867	12	2	1st
Vanderbilt	Southeastern	Q	23	3	.885	0	2	23	5	.821	15	3	T1st

1975 Tournament

School	Conference	How	Pre-Tourney W	L	Pct.	Tourney W	L	Final W	L	Pct.	Conf. W	L	Fin.
Alabama	Southeastern	L	22	4	.846	0	1	22	5	.815	15	3	T1st
Arizona St.	Western Athletic	Q	23	3	.885	2	1	25	4	.862	12	2	1st
Boston College	Independent (ECAC New England)	Q	20	7	.741	1	2	21	9	.700	—	—	—
Central Mich.	Mid-American	Q	20	5	.800	2	1	22	6	.786	10	4	1st
Cincinnati	Independent	L	21	5	.808	2	1	23	6	.793	—	—	—
Creighton	Independent	L	20	6	.769	0	1	20	7	.741	—	—	—
Furman	Southern	Q	22	6	.786	0	1	22	7	.759	12	0	1st
Georgetown	Independent (ECAC South)	Q	18	9	.667	0	1	18	10	.643	—	—	—
Indiana	Big Ten	Q	29	0	1.000	2	1	31	1	.969	18	0	1st
Kansas	Big Eight	Q	19	7	.731	0	1	19	8	.704	11	3	1st
Kansas St.	Big Eight	L	18	8	.692	2	1	20	9	.690	10	4	2d
Kentucky	Southeastern	Q	22	4	.846	4	1	26	5	.839	15	3	T1st
La Salle	East Coast (E)	Q	22	6	.786	0	1	22	7	.759	5	1	T1st
Louisville	Missouri Valley	Q	24	2	.923	4	1	28	3	.903	12	2	1st
Marquette	Independent	L	23	3	.885	0	1	23	4	.852	—	—	—
Maryland	Atlantic Coast	Q	22	4	.846	2	1	24	5	.828	10	2	1st
Michigan	Big Ten	L	19	7	.731	0	1	19	8	.704	12	6	2d
Middle Tenn.	Ohio Valley	Q	23	4	.852	0	1	23	5	.821	12	2	1st
Montana	Big Sky	Q	20	6	.769	1	2	21	8	.724	13	1	1st
UNLV	West Coast	Q	22	4	.846	2	1	24	5	.828	13	1	1st
New Mexico St.	Missouri Valley	L	20	6	.769	0	1	20	7	.741	11	3	2d
North Carolina	Atlantic Coast	Q	21	7	.750	2	1	23	8	.742	8	4	T2d
Notre Dame	Independent	L	18	8	.692	1	2	19	10	.655	—	—	—
Oregon St.	Pacific-8	L	18	10	.643	1	2	19	12	.613	10	4	2d
Pennsylvania	Ivy	Q	23	4	.852	0	1	23	5	.821	13	1	1st
Rutgers	Independent (ECAC Metro)	Q	22	6	.786	0	1	22	7	.759	—	—	—
San Diego St.	Pacific Coast	Q	14	12	.538	0	1	14	13	.519	6	4	2d
Syracuse	Independent (ECAC Upstate)	Q	20	7	.741	3	2	23	9	.719	—	—	—
UTEP	Western Athletic	L	20	5	.800	0	1	20	6	.769	10	4	2d
Texas A&M	Southwest	Q	20	6	.769	0	1	20	7	.741	12	2	1st
UCLA	Pacific-8	Q	23	3	.885	5	0	28	3	.903	12	2	1st
Utah St.	Independent	Q	21	5	.808	0	1	21	6	.778	—	—	—

1976 Tournament

School	Conference	How	Pre-Tourney W	L	Pct.	Tourney W	L	Final W	L	Pct.	Conf. W	L	Fin.
Alabama	Southeastern	Q	22	4	.846	1	1	23	5	.821	15	3	1st
Arizona	Western Athletic	Q	22	8	.733	2	1	24	9	.727	11	3	1st
Boise St.	Big Sky	Q	18	10	.643	0	1	18	11	.621	9	5	T1st
Cincinnati	Metro	Q	25	5	.833	0	1	25	6	.806	2	1	T2d
Connecticut	Yankee (ECAC New England)	Q	18	9	.667	1	1	19	10	.655	7	5	T2d
DePaul	Independent	L	19	8	.704	1	1	20	9	.690	—	—	—
Georgetown	Independent (ECAC South)	Q	21	6	.778	0	1	21	7	.750	—	—	—
Hofstra	East Coast (E)	Q	18	11	.621	0	1	18	12	.600	3	2	T2d
Indiana	Big Ten	Q	27	0	1.000	5	0	32	0	1.000	18	0	1st
Marquette	Independent	L	25	1	.962	2	1	27	2	.931	—	—	—
Memphis	Metro	L	21	8	.724	0	1	21	9	.700	1	0	1st
Michigan	Big Ten	L	21	6	.778	4	1	25	7	.781	14	4	2d
Missouri	Big Eight	Q	24	4	.857	2	1	26	5	.839	12	2	1st
UNLV	Independent	L	28	1	.966	1	1	29	2	.935	—	—	—
North Carolina	Atlantic Coast	L	25	3	.893	0	1	25	4	.862	11	1	1st
Notre Dame	Independent	L	22	5	.815	1	1	23	6	.793	—	—	—
Pepperdine	West Coast	Q	21	5	.808	1	1	22	6	.786	10	2	1st
Princeton	Ivy	Q	22	4	.846	0	1	22	5	.815	14	0	1st
Rutgers	Independent (ECAC Metro)	Q	28	0	1.000	3	2	31	2	.939	—	—	—
St. John's (N.Y.)	Independent	L	23	5	.821	0	1	23	6	.793	—	—	—
San Diego St.	Pacific Coast	Q	16	12	.571	0	1	16	13	.552	5	5	T3d
Syracuse	Independent (ECAC Upstate)	Q	20	8	.714	0	1	20	9	.690	—	—	—
Tennessee	Southeastern	L	21	5	.808	0	1	21	6	.778	14	4	2d
Texas Tech	Southwest	Q	24	5	.828	1	1	25	6	.806	13	3	2d
UCLA	Pacific-8	Q	24	3	.889	4	1	28	4	.875	12	2	1st
Virginia	Atlantic Coast	Q	18	11	.621	0	1	18	12	.600	4	8	6th
VMI	Southern	Q	20	9	.690	2	1	22	10	.688	9	3	1st

ALL-TIME TOURNAMENT FIELD

School	Conference	How	Pre-Tourney W L Pct.	Tourney W L	Final W L Pct.	Conf. W L Fin.
Virginia Tech	Independent	L	21 6 .778	0 1	21 7 .750	— — —
Washington	Pacific-8	L	23 4 .852	0 1	23 5 .821	9 5 4th
Western Ky.	Ohio Valley	Q	20 8 .714	0 1	20 9 .690	11 3 1st
Western Mich.	Mid-American	Q	24 2 .923	1 1	25 3 .893	15 1 1st
Wichita St.	Missouri Valley	Q	18 9 .667	0 1	18 10 .643	10 2 1st

1977 Tournament

School	Conference	How	Pre-Tourney W L Pct.	Tourney W L	Final W L Pct.	Conf. W L Fin.
Arizona	Western Athletic	L	21 5 .808	0 1	21 6 .778	10 4 2d
Arkansas	Southwest	Q	26 1 .963	0 1	26 2 .929	16 0 1st
Central Mich.	Mid-American	Q	18 9 .667	0 1	18 10 .643	13 3 T1st
Charlotte	Sun Belt	L	25 3 .893	3 2	28 5 .848	5 1 1st
Cincinnati	Metro	Q	25 4 .862	0 1	25 5 .833	4 2 2d
Detroit	Independent	L	25 2 .926	1 1	26 3 .897	— — —
Duquesne	Eastern Collegiate	Q	15 14 .517	0 1	15 15 .500	3 7 7th
Hofstra	East Coast (E)	Q	23 6 .793	0 1	23 7 .767	4 1 T1st
Holy Cross	Independent (ECAC New England)	Q	23 5 .821	0 1	23 6 .793	— — —
Idaho St.	Big Sky	Q	23 4 .852	2 1	25 5 .833	13 1 1st
Kansas St.	Big Eight	Q	23 6 .793	1 1	24 7 .774	11 3 1st
Kentucky	Southeastern	L	24 3 .889	2 1	26 4 .867	16 2 1st
Long Beach St.	Pacific Coast	Q	21 7 .750	0 1	21 8 .724	9 3 T1st
Louisville	Metro	L	21 6 .778	0 1	21 7 .750	6 1 1st
Marquette	Independent	L	20 7 .741	5 0	25 7 .781	— — —
Michigan	Big Ten	Q	24 3 .889	2 1	26 4 .867	16 2 1st
Middle Tenn.	Ohio Valley	Q	20 8 .714	0 1	20 9 .690	9 5 T2d
UNLV	Independent	L	25 2 .926	4 1	29 3 .906	— — —
North Carolina	Atlantic Coast	Q	24 4 .857	4 1	28 5 .848	9 3 1st
Notre Dame	Independent	L	21 6 .778	1 1	22 7 .759	— — —
Princeton	Ivy	Q	21 4 .840	0 1	21 5 .808	13 1 1st
Providence	Independent	L	24 4 .857	0 1	24 5 .828	— — —
Purdue	Big Ten	L	20 7 .741	0 1	20 8 .714	14 4 2d
St. John's (N.Y.)	Independent (ECAC Metro)	Q	22 8 .733	0 1	22 9 .710	— — —
San Francisco	West Coast	Q	29 1 .967	0 1	29 2 .935	14 0 1st
Southern Ill.	Missouri Valley	Q	21 6 .778	1 1	22 7 .759	8 4 T1st
Syracuse	Independent (ECAC Upstate)	Q	25 3 .893	1 1	26 4 .867	— — —
Tennessee	Southeastern	Q	22 5 .815	0 1	22 6 .786	16 2 T1st
UCLA	Pacific-8	Q	23 4 .852	1 1	24 5 .828	11 3 1st
Utah	Western Athletic	Q	21 6 .778	1 1	22 7 .759	11 3 1st
VMI	Southern	Q	25 3 .893	1 1	26 4 .867	8 2 T1st
Wake Forest	Atlantic Coast	L	20 7 .741	2 1	22 8 .733	8 4 T2d

1978 Tournament

School	Conference	How	Pre-Tourney W L Pct.	Tourney W L	Final W L Pct.	Conf. W L Fin.
Arkansas	Southwest	L	28 3 .903	4 1	32 4 .889	14 2 T1st
Cal St. Fullerton	Pacific Coast	Q	21 8 .724	2 1	23 9 .719	9 5 T3d
Creighton	Missouri Valley	Q	19 8 .704	0 1	19 9 .679	12 4 1st
DePaul	Independent	L	25 2 .926	2 1	27 3 .900	— — —
Duke	Atlantic Coast	Q	23 6 .793	4 1	27 7 .794	8 4 2d
Florida St.	Metro	L	23 5 .821	0 1	23 6 .793	11 1 1st
Furman	Southern	Q	19 10 .655	0 1	19 11 .633	7 5 T4th
Houston	Southwest	Q	25 7 .781	0 1	25 8 .758	11 5 3d
Indiana	Big Ten	L	20 7 .741	1 1	21 8 .724	12 6 T2d
Kansas	Big Eight	L	24 4 .857	0 1	24 5 .828	13 1 1st
Kentucky	Southeastern	L	25 2 .926	5 0	30 2 .938	16 2 1st
La Salle	East Coast (E)	Q	18 11 .621	0 1	18 12 .600	5 0 1st
Louisville	Metro	Q	22 6 .786	1 1	23 7 .767	9 3 2d
Marquette	Independent	L	24 3 .889	0 1	24 4 .857	— — —
Miami (Ohio)	Mid-American	Q	18 8 .692	1 1	19 9 .679	12 4 1st
Michigan St.	Big Ten	Q	23 4 .852	2 1	25 5 .833	15 3 1st
Missouri	Big Eight	Q	14 15 .483	0 1	14 16 .467	4 10 T6th
New Mexico	Western Athletic	Q	24 3 .889	0 1	24 4 .857	13 1 1st
North Carolina	Atlantic Coast	L	23 7 .767	0 1	23 8 .742	9 3 1st
Notre Dame	Independent	L	20 6 .769	3 2	23 8 .742	— — —
Pennsylvania	Ivy	Q	19 7 .731	1 1	20 8 .714	12 2 1st
Providence	Independent	L	24 7 .774	0 1	24 8 .750	— — —
Rhode Island	Independent (ECAC New England)	Q	24 6 .800	0 1	24 7 .774	— — —
St. Bonaventure	Independent (ECAC Upstate)	Q	21 7 .750	0 1	21 8 .724	— — —
St. John's (N.Y.)	Independent (ECAC Metro)	Q	21 6 .778	0 1	21 7 .750	— — —
San Francisco	West Coast	Q	22 5 .815	1 1	23 6 .793	12 2 1st
Syracuse	Independent	Q	22 5 .815	0 1	22 6 .786	— — —
UCLA	Pacific-8	Q	24 2 .923	1 1	25 3 .893	14 0 1st
Utah	Western Athletic	L	22 5 .815	1 1	23 6 .793	12 2 2d
Villanova	Eastern 8	Q	21 8 .724	2 1	23 9 .719	7 3 T1st
Weber St.	Big Sky	Q	19 9 .679	0 1	19 10 .655	9 5 3d
Western Ky.	Ohio Valley	Q	15 13 .536	1 1	16 14 .533	9 5 3d

1979 Tournament

Seed	School	Conference	How	Pre-Tourney W L Pct.	Tourney W L	Final W L Pct.	Conf. W L Fin.
6	Appalachian St.	Southern	Q	23 5 .821	0 1	23 6 .793	11 3 1st
2	Arkansas	Southwest	Q	23 4 .852	2 1	25 5 .833	13 3 T1st
5	Brigham Young	Western Athletic	Q	20 7 .741	0 1	20 8 .714	10 2 1st
5	Connecticut	Independent (ECAC New England)	Q	21 7 .750	0 1	21 8 .724	— — —
2	DePaul	Independent	L	22 5 .815	4 1	26 6 .813	— — —
7	Detroit	Independent	L	22 5 .815	0 1	22 6 .786	— — —
2	Duke	Atlantic Coast	L	22 7 .759	0 1	22 8 .733	9 3 T1st
9	Eastern Ky.	Ohio Valley	Q	21 7 .750	0 1	21 8 .724	9 3 1st
3	Georgetown	Independent (ECAC South)	Q	24 4 .857	0 1	24 5 .828	— — —
	Indiana St.	Missouri Valley	Q	29 0 1.000	4 1	33 1 .971	16 0 1st
8	Iona	Independent (ECAC Metro)	Q	23 5 .821	0 1	23 6 .793	— — —
4	Iowa	Big Ten	L	20 7 .741	0 1	20 8 .714	13 5 T1st

127

THE TOURNAMENT FIELD

1979 Tournament

Seed	School	Conference	How	W	L	Pct.	W	L	W	L	Pct.	W	L	Fin.
9	Jacksonville	Sun Belt	Q	19	10	.655	0	1	19	11	.633	5	5	4th
10	Lamar	Southland	Q	22	8	.733	1	1	23	9	.719	9	1	1st
3	LSU	Southeastern	L	22	5	.815	1	1	23	6	.793	14	4	1st
3	Louisville	Metro	L	23	7	.767	1	1	24	8	.750	9	1	1st
3	Marquette	Independent	L	21	6	.778	1	1	22	7	.759	—	—	—
2	Michigan St.	Big Ten	Q	21	6	.778	5	0	26	6	.813	13	5	T1st
10	New Mexico St.	Missouri Valley	L	22	9	.710	0	1	22	10	.688	11	5	2d
1	North Carolina	Atlantic Coast	Q	23	5	.821	0	1	23	6	.793	9	3	T1st
1	Notre Dame	Independent	L	22	5	.815	2	1	24	6	.800	—	—	—
5	Oklahoma	Big Eight	Q	20	9	.690	1	1	21	10	.677	10	4	1st
6	Pacific (Cal.)	Pacific Coast	Q	18	11	.621	0	1	18	12	.600	11	3	1st
9	Pennsylvania	Ivy	Q	21	5	.808	4	2	25	7	.781	13	1	1st
9	Pepperdine	West Coast	L	21	9	.700	1	1	22	10	.688	10	2	2d
6	Rutgers	Eastern 8	Q	21	8	.724	1	1	22	9	.710	7	3	T2d
10	St. John's (N.Y.)	Independent	L	18	10	.643	3	1	21	11	.656	—	—	—
4	San Francisco	West Coast	Q	21	6	.778	1	1	22	7	.759	12	2	1st
6	South Ala.	Sun Belt	L	20	6	.769	0	1	20	7	.741	10	0	1st
7	Southern California	Pacific-10	L	19	8	.704	1	1	20	9	.690	14	4	2d
4	Syracuse	Independent	L	25	3	.893	1	1	26	4	.867	—	—	—
7	Temple	East Coast (E)	Q	25	3	.893	0	1	25	4	.862	10	0	1st
8	Tennessee	Southeastern	Q	20	11	.645	1	1	21	12	.636	12	6	2d
4	Texas	Southwest	L	21	7	.750	0	1	21	8	.724	8	8	T3d
5	Toledo	Mid-American	L	21	7	.750	1	1	22	8	.733	13	3	T1st
1	UCLA	Pacific-10	Q	23	4	.852	2	1	25	5	.833	15	3	1st
8	Utah	Western Athletic	L	20	9	.690	0	1	20	10	.667	9	3	2d
10	Utah St.	Pacific Coast	L	19	10	.655	0	1	19	11	.633	9	5	T2d
8	Virginia Tech	Metro	Q	21	8	.724	1	1	22	9	.710	4	6	T4th
7	Weber St.	Big Sky	Q	24	8	.750	1	1	25	9	.735	10	4	1st

1980 Tournament

Seed	School	Conference	How	W	L	Pct.	W	L	W	L	Pct.	W	L	Fin.
8	Alcorn St.	Southwestern	L	27	1	.964	1	1	28	2	.933	12	0	1st
5	Arizona St.	Pacific-10	L	21	6	.778	1	1	22	7	.759	15	3	2d
10	Arkansas	Southwest	L	21	7	.750	0	1	21	8	.724	13	3	2d
11	Bradley	Missouri Valley	Q	23	9	.719	0	1	23	10	.697	13	3	1st
3	Brigham Young	Western Athletic	Q	24	4	.857	0	1	24	5	.828	13	1	1st
6	Clemson	Atlantic Coast	Q	20	8	.714	3	1	23	9	.719	8	6	4th
1	DePaul	Independent	L	26	1	.963	0	1	26	2	.929	—	—	—
4	Duke	Atlantic Coast	Q	22	8	.733	2	1	24	9	.727	7	7	T5th
8	Florida St.	Metro	L	21	8	.724	1	1	22	9	.710	7	5	3d
10	Furman	Southern	Q	23	6	.793	0	1	23	7	.767	14	1	1st
3	Georgetown	Big East	L	24	5	.828	2	1	26	6	.813	5	1	T1st
11	Holy Cross	ECAC New England	Q	19	10	.655	0	1	19	11	.633	16	10	3d
2	Indiana	Big Ten	Q	20	7	.741	1	1	21	8	.724	13	5	1st
6	Iona	Independent (ECAC Metro)	Q	28	4	.875	1	1	29	5	.853	—	—	—
5	Iowa	Big Ten	L	19	8	.704	4	2	23	10	.697	10	8	T4th
7	Kansas St.	Big Eight	Q	21	8	.724	1	1	22	9	.710	8	6	T2d
1	Kentucky	Southeastern	L	28	5	.848	1	1	29	6	.829	15	3	1st
11	La Salle	East Coast (E)	Q	22	8	.733	0	1	22	9	.710	7	4	3d
10	Lamar	Southland	Q	20	10	.667	2	1	22	11	.667	8	2	1st
1	LSU	Southeastern	Q	24	5	.828	2	1	26	6	.813	14	4	2d
2	Louisville	Metro	Q	28	3	.903	5	0	33	3	.917	12	0	1st
12	Loyola Marymount	West Coast	Q	14	13	.519	0	1	14	14	.500	10	6	T3d
9	Marquette	Independent	L	18	6	.692	0	1	18	9	.667	—	—	—
2	Maryland	Atlantic Coast	L	23	6	.793	1	1	24	7	.774	11	3	1st
5	Missouri	Big Eight	L	23	5	.821	2	1	25	6	.806	11	3	1st
3	North Carolina	Atlantic Coast	L	21	7	.750	0	1	21	8	.724	9	5	T2d
4	North Carolina St.	Atlantic Coast	L	20	7	.741	0	1	20	8	.714	9	5	T2d
4	Notre Dame	Independent	L	22	5	.815	0	1	22	6	.786	—	—	—
4	Ohio St.	Big Ten	L	20	7	.741	1	1	21	8	.724	12	6	2d
9	Old Dominion	Independent (ECAC South)	Q	25	4	.862	0	1	25	5	.833	—	—	—
2	Oregon St.	Pacific-10	Q	26	3	.897	0	1	26	4	.867	16	2	1st
12	Pennsylvania	Ivy	Q	16	11	.593	1	1	17	12	.586	12	3	1st
6	Purdue	Big Ten	L	18	9	.667	5	1	23	10	.697	11	7	3d
3	St. John's (N.Y.)	Big East	L	24	4	.857	0	1	24	5	.828	5	1	T1st
12	San Jose St.	Pacific Coast	Q	17	11	.607	0	1	17	12	.586	7	6	4th
9	South Ala.	Sun Belt	L	23	5	.821	0	1	23	6	.793	12	2	1st
1	Syracuse	Big East	L	25	3	.893	1	1	26	4	.867	5	1	T1st
7	Tennessee	Southeastern	L	17	10	.630	1	1	18	11	.621	12	6	T3d
6	Texas A&M	Southwest	Q	24	7	.774	2	1	26	8	.765	14	2	1st
9	Toledo	Mid-American	Q	23	5	.821	0	1	23	6	.793	14	2	1st
8	UCLA	Pacific-10	L	17	9	.654	5	1	22	10	.688	12	6	4th
11	Utah St.	Pacific Coast	L	18	8	.692	0	1	18	9	.667	11	2	1st
8	Villanova	Eastern 8	Q	22	7	.759	1	1	23	8	.742	7	3	T1st
12	Va. Commonwealth	Sun Belt	Q	18	11	.621	0	1	18	12	.600	8	6	5th
7	Virginia Tech	Metro	L	20	7	.741	1	1	21	8	.724	8	4	2d
5	Washington St.	Pacific-10	L	22	5	.815	0	1	22	6	.786	14	4	3d
7	Weber St.	Big Sky	Q	26	2	.929	0	1	26	3	.897	13	1	1st
10	Western Ky.	Ohio Valley	Q	21	7	.750	0	1	21	8	.724	10	2	T1st

1981 Tournament

Seed	School	Conference	How	W	L	Pct.	W	L	W	L	Pct.	W	L	Fin.
7	UAB	Sun Belt	L	21	8	.724	2	1	23	9	.719	9	3	T1st
2	Arizona St.	Pacific-10	L	24	3	.889	0	1	24	4	.857	16	2	2d
5	Arkansas	Southwest	L	22	7	.759	2	1	24	8	.750	13	3	T1st
12	Ball St.	Mid-American	Q	20	9	.690	0	1	20	10	.667	10	6	T1st
5	Boston College	Big East	L	21	6	.778	2	1	23	7	.767	10	4	1st
6	Brigham Young	Western Athletic	L	22	6	.786	3	1	25	7	.781	12	4	3d
11	Chattanooga	Southern	Q	21	8	.724	0	1	21	9	.700	11	5	T1st
8	Creighton	Missouri Valley	Q	21	8	.724	0	1	21	9	.700	11	5	T2d
1	DePaul	Independent	L	27	1	.964	0	1	27	2	.931	—	—	—

ALL-TIME TOURNAMENT FIELD   129

Seed	School	Conference	How	Pre-Tourney W L Pct.	Tourney W L	Final W L Pct.	Conf. W L Fin.
6	Fresno St.	Pacific Coast	Q	25 3 .893	0 1	25 4 .862	12 2 1st
7	Georgetown	Big East	L	20 11 .645	0 1	20 12 .625	9 5 2d
8	Houston	Southwest	Q	21 8 .724	0 1	21 9 .700	10 6 T2d
12	Howard	Mid-Eastern	Q	17 11 .607	0 1	17 12 .586	6 4 T2d
7	Idaho	Big Sky	Q	25 3 .893	0 1	25 4 .862	12 2 1st
4	Illinois	Big Ten	L	20 7 .741	1 1	21 8 .724	12 6 3d
3	Indiana	Big Ten	Q	21 9 .700	5 0	26 9 .743	14 4 1st
3	Iowa	Big Ten	L	21 6 .778	0 1	21 7 .750	13 5 2d
10	James Madison	Independent (ECAC South)	Q	20 8 .714	1 1	21 9 .700	— — —
7	Kansas	Big Eight	Q	22 7 .759	2 1	24 8 .750	9 5 T2d
6	Kansas St.	Big Eight	L	21 8 .724	3 1	24 9 .727	9 5 T2d
2	Kentucky	Southeastern	L	22 5 .815	0 1	22 6 .786	15 3 2d
8	Lamar	Southland	Q	24 4 .857	1 1	25 5 .833	8 2 1st
12	Long Island	Independent (ECAC Metro)	Q	18 10 .643	0 1	18 11 .621	— — —
1	LSU	Southeastern	L	28 3 .903	3 2	31 5 .861	17 1 1st
4	Louisville	Metro	Q	21 8 .724	0 1	21 9 .700	11 1 1st
6	Maryland	Atlantic Coast	L	20 9 .690	1 1	21 10 .677	8 6 4th
12	Mercer	Trans America	Q	18 11 .621	0 1	18 12 .600	7 4 3d
10	Mississippi	Southeastern	Q	16 13 .552	0 1	16 14 .533	10 8 4th
9	Missouri	Big Eight	Q	22 9 .710	0 1	22 10 .688	10 4 3d
2	North Carolina	Atlantic Coast	Q	25 7 .781	4 1	29 8 .784	10 4 2d
11	Northeastern	ECAC New England	Q	23 5 .821	1 1	24 6 .800	21 5 1st
2	Notre Dame	Independent	L	22 5 .815	1 1	23 6 .793	— — —
1	Oregon St.	Pacific-10	Q	26 1 .963	0 1	26 2 .929	17 1 1st
10	Pittsburgh	Eastern 8	Q	18 11 .621	1 1	19 12 .613	8 5 4th
11	Princeton	Ivy	Q	18 9 .667	0 1	18 10 .643	14 1 1st
9	St. Joseph's	East Coast (E)	Q	22 7 .759	3 1	25 8 .758	9 2 T2d
9	San Francisco	West Coast	Q	24 6 .800	0 1	24 7 .774	11 3 T1st
11	Southern U.	Southwestern	Q	17 10 .630	0 1	17 11 .607	8 4 T1st
4	Tennessee	Southeastern	L	20 7 .741	1 1	21 8 .724	12 6 3d
3	UCLA	Pacific-10	L	20 6 .769	0 1	20 7 .741	13 5 3d
3	Utah	Western Athletic	L	24 4 .857	1 1	25 5 .833	13 3 T1st
9	Villanova	Big East	L	19 10 .655	1 1	20 11 .645	8 6 T3d
1	Virginia	Atlantic Coast	L	25 3 .893	4 1	29 4 .879	13 1 1st
5	Va. Commonwealth	Sun Belt	Q	23 4 .852	1 1	24 5 .828	9 3 T1st
4	Wake Forest	Atlantic Coast	L	22 6 .786	0 1	22 7 .759	9 5 3d
10	Western Ky.	Ohio Valley	Q	21 7 .750	0 1	21 8 .724	12 2 1st
6	Wichita St.	Missouri Valley	L	23 6 .793	3 1	26 7 .788	12 4 1st
5	Wyoming	Western Athletic	Q	23 5 .821	1 1	24 6 .800	13 3 T1st

1982 Tournament

Seed	School	Conference	How	Pre-Tourney W L Pct.	Tourney W L	Final W L Pct.	Conf. W L Fin.
4	Alabama	Southeastern	Q	23 6 .793	1 1	24 7 .774	12 6 3d
4	UAB	Sun Belt	Q	23 5 .821	2 1	25 6 .806	9 1 1st
11	Alcorn St.	Southwestern	Q	22 7 .759	0 1	22 8 .733	10 2 T1st
4	Arkansas	Southwest	Q	23 5 .821	0 1	23 6 .793	12 4 1st
8	Boston College	Big East	L	19 9 .679	3 1	22 10 .688	8 6 4th
10	Chattanooga	Southern	Q	26 3 .897	1 1	27 4 .871	15 1 1st
1	DePaul	Independent	L	26 1 .963	0 1	26 2 .929	— — —
10	Evansville	Midwestern	Q	23 5 .821	0 1	23 6 .793	10 2 1st
4	Fresno St.	Pacific Coast	Q	26 2 .929	1 1	27 3 .900	13 1 1st
1	Georgetown	Big East	Q	26 6 .813	4 1	30 7 .811	10 4 2d
6	Houston	Southwest	L	21 7 .750	4 1	25 8 .758	11 5 2d
3	Idaho	Big Sky	Q	26 2 .929	1 1	27 3 .900	13 1 1st
5	Indiana	Big Ten	L	18 9 .667	1 1	19 10 .655	12 6 T2d
6	Iowa	Big Ten	L	20 7 .741	1 1	21 8 .724	12 6 T2d
9	James Madison	Independent	L	23 5 .821	1 1	24 6 .800	— — —
5	Kansas St.	Big Eight	L	21 7 .750	2 1	23 8 .742	10 4 2d
6	Kentucky	Southeastern	L	22 7 .759	0 1	22 8 .733	13 5 T1st
8	La.-Lafayette	Southland	Q	24 7 .774	0 1	24 8 .750	8 2 1st
11	La.-Monroe	Trans America	Q	19 10 .655	0 1	19 11 .633	9 7 T3d
3	Louisville	Metro	L	20 9 .690	3 1	23 10 .697	8 4 T2d
7	Marquette	Independent	L	22 8 .733	1 1	23 9 .719	— — —
2	Memphis	Metro	Q	23 4 .852	1 1	24 5 .828	10 2 1st
11	Middle Tenn.	Ohio Valley	Q	21 7 .750	1 1	22 8 .733	12 4 3d
2	Minnesota	Big Ten	Q	22 5 .815	1 1	23 6 .793	14 4 1st
2	Missouri	Big Eight	Q	26 3 .897	1 1	27 4 .871	12 2 1st
1	North Carolina	Atlantic Coast	Q	27 2 .931	5 0	32 2 .941	12 2 1st
12	N.C. A&T	Mid-Eastern	Q	19 8 .704	0 1	19 9 .679	10 2 1st
7	North Carolina St.	Atlantic Coast	L	22 9 .710	0 1	22 10 .688	7 7 4th
11	Northeastern	ECAC New England	Q	22 6 .786	1 1	23 7 .767	8 1 1st
12	Northern Ill.	Mid-American	Q	16 13 .552	0 1	16 14 .533	9 7 3d
8	Ohio St.	Big Ten	L	21 9 .700	0 1	21 10 .677	12 6 T2d
10	Old Dominion	Independent (ECAC South)	Q	18 11 .621	0 1	18 12 .600	— — —
2	Oregon St.	Pacific-10	Q	23 4 .852	2 1	25 5 .833	16 2 1st
12	Pennsylvania	Ivy	Q	17 9 .654	0 1	17 10 .630	12 2 1st
7	Pepperdine	West Coast	Q	21 6 .778	1 1	22 7 .759	14 0 1st
10	Pittsburgh	Eastern 8	Q	20 9 .690	0 1	20 10 .667	8 6 3d
12	Robert Morris	ECAC Metro (S)	Q	17 12 .586	0 1	17 13 .567	9 5 1st
5	St. John's (N.Y.)	Big East	L	20 8 .714	1 1	21 9 .700	9 5 3d
6	St. Joseph's	East Coast (E)	Q	25 4 .862	0 1	25 5 .833	10 1 2d
9	San Francisco	West Coast	L	25 5 .833	0 1	25 6 .806	11 3 2d
9	Southern California	Pacific-10	L	19 8 .704	0 1	19 9 .679	13 5 3d
9	Tennessee	Southeastern	L	19 9 .679	1 1	20 10 .667	13 5 T1st
3	Tulsa	Missouri Valley	Q	24 5 .828	0 1	24 6 .800	12 4 T2d
3	Villanova	Big East	L	22 7 .759	2 1	24 8 .750	11 3 1st
1	Virginia	Atlantic Coast	L	29 3 .906	1 1	30 4 .882	12 2 T1st
7	Wake Forest	Atlantic Coast	L	20 8 .714	1 1	21 9 .700	9 5 3d
3	West Virginia	Eastern 8	Q	26 3 .897	1 1	27 4 .871	11 1 1st
8	Wyoming	Western Athletic	Q	22 6 .786	1 1	23 7 .767	14 2 1st

1983 Tournament

Seed	School	Conference	How	Pre-Tourney W	L	Pct.	Tourney W	L	Final W	L	Pct.	Conf. W	L	Fin.
6	Alabama	Southeastern	L	20	11	.645	0	1	20	12	.625	8	10	T8th
10	UAB	Sun Belt	Q	19	13	.594	0	1	19	14	.576	9	5	3d
12	Alcorn St.	Southwestern	Q	21	9	.700	1	1	22	10	.688	10	4	3d
4	Arkansas	Southwest	L	25	3	.893	1	1	26	4	.867	14	2	2d
4	Boston College	Big East	L	24	6	.800	1	1	25	7	.781	12	4	T1st
—	Boston U.	ECAC North	Q	21	9	.700	0	1	21	10	.677	8	2	T1st
9	Chattanooga	Southern	L	26	3	.897	0	1	26	4	.867	15	1	1st
5	Georgetown	Big East	L	21	9	.700	1	1	22	10	.688	11	5	4th
4	Georgia	Southeastern	Q	21	9	.700	3	1	24	10	.706	9	9	T4th
—	Ga. Southern	Trans America	Q	18	11	.621	0	1	18	12	.600	8	6	T3d
1	Houston	Southwest	Q	27	2	.931	4	1	31	3	.912	16	0	1st
7	Illinois	Big Ten	L	21	10	.677	0	1	21	11	.656	11	7	T2d
6	Illinois St.	Missouri Valley	Q	24	6	.800	0	1	24	7	.774	13	5	2d
2	Indiana	Big Ten	Q	23	5	.821	1	1	24	6	.800	13	5	1st
7	Iowa	Big Ten	L	19	9	.679	2	1	21	10	.677	11	7	T2d
10	James Madison	ECAC South	Q	19	10	.655	1	1	20	11	.645	6	3	2d
3	Kentucky	Southeastern	L	21	7	.750	2	1	23	8	.742	13	5	1st
12	La Salle	East Coast (E)	Q	17	13	.567	1	1	18	14	.563	7	2	T1st
11	Lamar	Southland	Q	22	7	.759	1	1	23	8	.742	9	3	1st
8	La.-Lafayette	Independent	L	22	6	.786	0	1	22	7	.759	—	—	—
1	Louisville	Metro	Q	29	3	.906	3	1	32	4	.889	12	0	1st
9	Marquette	Independent	L	19	9	.679	0	1	19	10	.655	—	—	—
8	Maryland	Atlantic Coast	L	19	9	.679	1	1	20	10	.667	8	6	T3d
4	Memphis	Metro	L	22	7	.759	1	1	23	8	.742	6	6	4th
2	Missouri	Big Eight	L	26	7	.788	0	1	26	8	.765	12	2	1st
11	Morehead St.	Ohio Valley	Q	19	10	.655	0	1	19	11	.633	10	4	2d
3	UNLV	Pacific Coast	Q	28	2	.933	0	1	28	3	.903	15	1	1st
2	North Carolina	Atlantic Coast	L	26	7	.788	2	1	28	8	.778	12	2	T1st
—	N.C. A&T	Mid-Eastern	Q	23	7	.767	0	1	23	8	.742	9	3	2d
6	North Carolina St.	Atlantic Coast	Q	20	10	.667	6	0	26	10	.722	8	6	T3d
11	Ohio	Mid-American	Q	22	8	.733	1	1	23	9	.719	12	6	2d
3	Ohio St.	Big Ten	L	19	9	.679	1	1	20	10	.667	11	7	T2d
7	Oklahoma	Big Eight	L	23	8	.742	1	1	24	9	.727	10	4	2d
5	Oklahoma St.	Big Eight	Q	24	6	.800	0	1	24	7	.774	9	5	T3d
11	Pepperdine	West Coast	Q	20	8	.714	0	1	20	9	.690	10	2	1st
12	Princeton	Ivy	Q	18	8	.692	2	1	20	9	.690	12	2	1st
5	Purdue	Big Ten	L	20	8	.714	1	1	21	9	.700	11	7	T2d
12	Robert Morris	ECAC Metro (S)	Q	22	7	.759	1	1	23	8	.742	12	2	1st
9	Rutgers	Atlantic 10 (E)	Q	22	7	.759	1	1	23	8	.742	11	3	1st
1	St. John's (N.Y.)	Big East	Q	27	4	.871	1	1	28	5	.848	12	4	T1st
6	Syracuse	Big East	L	20	9	.690	1	1	21	10	.677	9	7	5th
8	Tennessee	Southeastern	L	19	11	.633	1	1	20	12	.625	9	9	T4th
2	UCLA	Pacific-10	Q	23	5	.821	0	1	23	6	.793	15	3	1st
10	Utah	Western Athletic	Q	16	13	.552	2	1	18	14	.563	11	5	T1st
10	Utah St.	Pacific Coast	L	20	8	.714	0	1	20	9	.690	10	6	3d
3	Villanova	Big East	L	22	7	.759	2	1	24	8	.750	12	4	T1st
1	Virginia	Atlantic Coast	L	27	4	.871	2	1	29	5	.853	12	2	T1st
5	Va. Commonwealth	Sun Belt	L	23	6	.793	1	1	24	7	.774	12	2	T1st
8	Washington St.	Pacific-10	L	22	6	.786	1	1	23	7	.767	14	4	2d
9	Weber St.	Big Sky	Q	23	7	.767	0	1	23	8	.742	10	4	T1st
7	West Virginia	Atlantic 10 (W)	Q	23	7	.767	0	1	23	8	.742	10	4	T1st
—	Xavier	Midwestern	Q	22	7	.759	0	1	22	8	.733	10	4	T2d

1984 Tournament

Seed	School	Conference	How	Pre-Tourney W	L	Pct.	Tourney W	L	Final W	L	Pct.	Conf. W	L	Fin.
9	Alabama	Southeastern	L	18	11	.621	0	1	18	12	.600	10	8	5th
9	UAB	Sun Belt	Q	23	10	.697	0	1	23	11	.676	8	6	5th
12	Alcorn St.	Southwestern	Q	20	9	.690	1	1	21	10	.677	11	3	T1st
2	Arkansas	Southwest	L	25	6	.806	0	1	25	7	.781	14	2	2d
5	Auburn	Southeastern	L	20	10	.667	0	1	20	11	.645	12	6	2d
8	Brigham Young	Western Athletic	Q	19	10	.655	1	1	20	11	.645	12	4	T1st
10	Dayton	Independent	L	18	10	.643	3	1	21	11	.656	—	—	—
1	DePaul	Independent	L	26	2	.929	1	1	27	3	.900	—	—	—
3	Duke	Atlantic Coast	L	24	9	.727	0	1	24	10	.706	7	7	T3d
7	Fresno St.	Pacific Coast	L	25	7	.781	0	1	25	8	.758	13	5	3d
1	Georgetown	Big East	Q	29	3	.906	5	0	34	3	.919	14	2	1st
2	Houston	Southwest	Q	28	4	.875	4	1	32	5	.865	15	1	1st
—	Houston Baptist	Trans America	Q	24	6	.800	0	1	24	7	.774	11	3	1st
2	Illinois	Big Ten	Q	24	4	.857	2	1	26	5	.839	15	3	T1st
8	Illinois St.	Missouri Valley	L	22	7	.759	1	1	23	8	.742	13	3	T1st
4	Indiana	Big Ten	L	20	8	.714	2	1	22	9	.710	13	5	3d
10	Iona	Metro Atlantic	Q	23	7	.767	0	1	23	8	.742	11	3	T1st
5	Kansas	Big Eight	Q	21	9	.700	1	1	22	10	.688	9	5	2d
1	Kentucky	Southeastern	Q	26	4	.867	3	1	29	5	.853	14	4	1st
—	Long Island	ECAC Metro	Q	20	10	.667	0	1	20	11	.645	11	5	T1st
7	LSU	Southeastern	L	18	10	.643	0	1	18	11	.621	11	7	T3d
10	Louisiana Tech	Southland	Q	25	6	.806	1	1	26	7	.788	8	4	3d
5	Louisville	Metro	L	22	10	.688	2	1	24	11	.686	11	3	T1st
10	Marshall	Southern	Q	25	5	.833	0	1	25	6	.806	13	3	1st
3	Maryland	Atlantic Coast	Q	23	7	.767	1	1	24	8	.750	9	5	2d
6	Memphis	Metro	Q	24	6	.800	2	1	26	7	.788	11	3	T1st
8	Miami (Ohio)	Mid-American	Q	24	5	.828	0	1	24	6	.800	16	2	1st
12	Morehead St.	Ohio Valley	Q	24	5	.828	1	1	25	6	.806	12	2	1st
11	Nevada	Big Sky	Q	17	13	.567	0	1	17	14	.548	7	7	T3d
5	UNLV	Pacific Coast	Q	27	5	.844	1	1	29	6	.829	16	2	1st
1	North Carolina	Atlantic Coast	L	27	2	.931	1	1	28	3	.903	14	0	1st
—	N.C. A&T	Mid-Eastern	Q	22	6	.786	0	1	22	7	.759	9	1	1st
11	Northeastern	ECAC North Atlantic	Q	26	4	.867	1	1	27	5	.844	14	0	1st
2	Oklahoma	Big Eight	L	29	4	.879	0	1	29	5	.853	13	1	1st
11	Oral Roberts	Midwestern	Q	21	9	.700	0	1	21	10	.677	11	3	1st

ALL-TIME TOURNAMENT FIELD   131

1984 Tournament

Seed	School	Conference	How	Pre-Tourney W	L	Pct.	Tourney W	L	Final W	L	Pct.	Conf. W	L	Fin.
6	Oregon St.	Pacific-10	L	22	6	.786	0	1	22	7	.759	15	3	T1st
12	Princeton	Ivy	Q	17	9	.654	1	1	18	10	.643	10	4	1st
3	Purdue	Big Ten	L	22	6	.786	0	1	22	7	.759	15	3	T1st
12	Richmond	ECAC South	Q	20	9	.690	2	1	22	10	.688	7	3	1st
—	Rider	East Coast	Q	20	10	.667	0	1	20	11	.645	11	5	2d
9	St. John's (N.Y.)	Big East	L	18	11	.621	0	1	18	12	.600	8	8	T4th
—	San Diego	West Coast	Q	18	9	.667	0	1	18	10	.643	9	3	1st
9	Southern Methodist	Southwest	L	24	7	.774	1	1	25	8	.758	12	4	3d
3	Syracuse	Big East	L	22	8	.733	1	1	23	9	.719	12	4	T2d
8	Temple	Atlantic 10	L	25	4	.862	1	1	26	5	.839	18	0	1st
4	UTEP	Western Athletic	Q	27	3	.900	0	1	27	4	.871	13	3	1st
4	Tulsa	Missouri Valley	Q	27	3	.900	0	1	27	4	.871	13	3	T1st
7	Villanova	Big East	L	18	11	.621	1	1	19	12	.613	12	4	T2d
7	Virginia	Atlantic Coast	L	17	11	.607	4	1	21	12	.636	6	8	T5th
6	Va. Commonwealth	Sun Belt	L	22	6	.786	1	1	23	7	.767	11	3	1st
4	Wake Forest	Atlantic Coast	L	21	8	.724	2	1	23	9	.719	7	7	T3d
6	Washington	Pacific-10	Q	22	6	.786	2	1	24	7	.774	15	3	T1st
11	West Virginia	Atlantic 10	Q	19	11	.633	1	1	20	12	.625	9	9	T4th

1985 Tournament

Seed	School	Conference	How	Pre-Tourney W	L	Pct.	Tourney W	L	Final W	L	Pct.	Conf. W	L	Fin.
7	Alabama	Southeastern	L	21	9	.700	2	1	23	10	.697	11	7	T3d
7	UAB	Sun Belt	L	24	8	.750	1	1	25	9	.735	11	5	2d
10	Arizona	Pacific-10	L	21	9	.700	0	1	21	10	.677	12	6	T3d
9	Arkansas	Southwest	L	21	12	.636	1	1	22	13	.629	10	6	T2d
11	Auburn	Southeastern	Q	20	11	.645	2	1	22	12	.647	8	10	T7th
11	Boston College	Big East	L	18	10	.643	2	1	20	11	.645	7	9	6th
9	Dayton	Independent	L	19	9	.679	0	1	19	10	.655	—	—	—
10	DePaul	Independent	L	19	9	.679	0	1	19	10	.655	—	—	—
3	Duke	Atlantic Coast	L	22	7	.759	1	1	23	8	.742	8	6	T4th
16	Fairleigh Dickinson	ECAC Metro	Q	21	9	.700	0	1	21	10	.677	10	4	2d
1	Georgetown	Big East	Q	30	2	.938	5	1	35	3	.921	14	2	2d
6	Georgia	Southeastern	L	21	8	.724	1	1	22	9	.710	12	6	2d
2	Georgia Tech	Atlantic Coast	Q	24	7	.774	3	1	27	8	.771	9	5	T1st
3	Illinois	Big Ten	L	24	8	.750	2	1	26	9	.743	12	6	2d
9	Illinois St.	Missouri Valley	L	21	7	.750	1	1	22	8	.733	11	5	T2d
13	Iona	Metro Atlantic	Q	26	4	.867	0	1	26	5	.839	11	3	1st
8	Iowa	Big Ten	L	21	10	.677	0	1	21	11	.656	10	8	T5th
13	Iowa St.	Big Eight	L	21	12	.636	0	1	21	13	.618	7	7	T3d
3	Kansas	Big Eight	L	25	7	.781	1	1	26	8	.765	11	3	1st
12	Kentucky	Southeastern	L	16	12	.571	2	1	18	13	.581	11	7	T3d
16	Lehigh	East Coast	Q	12	18	.400	0	1	12	19	.387	6	8	6th
4	LSU	Southeastern	L	19	9	.679	0	1	19	10	.655	13	5	1st
5	Louisiana Tech	Southland	Q	27	2	.931	2	1	29	3	.906	11	1	1st
4	Loyola (Ill.)	Midwestern	Q	25	5	.833	2	1	27	6	.818	13	1	1st
15	Marshall	Southern	Q	21	12	.636	0	1	21	13	.618	14	2	1st
5	Maryland	Atlantic Coast	L	23	11	.676	2	1	25	12	.676	8	6	T3d
2	Memphis	Metro	Q	27	3	.900	4	1	31	4	.886	13	1	1st
15	Mercer	Trans America	Q	22	8	.733	0	1	22	9	.710	10	4	T2d
12	Miami (Ohio)	Mid-American	L	20	10	.667	0	1	20	11	.645	13	5	2d
1	Michigan	Big Ten	Q	25	3	.893	1	1	26	4	.867	16	2	1st
10	Michigan St.	Big Ten	L	19	9	.679	0	1	19	10	.655	10	8	T5th
15	Middle Tenn.	Ohio Valley	Q	17	13	.567	0	1	17	14	.548	7	7	5th
13	Navy	ECAC South	Q	25	5	.833	1	1	26	6	.813	11	3	T1st
14	Nevada	Big Sky	Q	21	9	.700	0	1	21	10	.677	11	3	1st
4	UNLV	Pacific Coast	Q	27	3	.900	1	1	28	4	.875	17	1	1st
2	North Carolina	Atlantic Coast	L	24	8	.750	3	1	27	9	.750	9	5	T1st
16	N.C. A&T	Mid-Eastern	Q	19	9	.679	0	1	19	10	.655	10	2	1st
3	North Carolina St.	Atlantic Coast	L	20	9	.690	3	1	23	10	.697	9	5	T1st
14	Northeastern	ECAC North Atlantic	Q	22	8	.733	0	1	22	9	.710	13	3	T1st
7	Notre Dame	Independent	L	20	8	.714	1	1	21	9	.700	—	—	—
14	Ohio	Mid-American	Q	22	7	.759	0	1	22	8	.733	14	4	1st
4	Ohio St.	Big Ten	L	19	9	.679	1	1	20	10	.667	11	7	T3d
1	Oklahoma	Big Eight	Q	28	5	.848	3	1	31	6	.838	13	1	1st
12	Old Dominion	Sun Belt	L	19	11	.633	0	1	19	12	.613	9	5	3d
10	Oregon St.	Pacific-10	L	22	8	.733	0	1	22	9	.710	12	6	T3d
15	Pennsylvania	Ivy	Q	13	13	.500	0	1	13	14	.481	10	4	1st
14	Pepperdine	West Coast	Q	23	8	.742	0	1	23	9	.719	11	1	1st
12	Pittsburgh	Big East	L	17	11	.607	0	1	17	12	.586	8	8	5th
6	Purdue	Big Ten	L	20	8	.714	0	1	20	9	.690	11	7	T3d
1	St. John's (N.Y.)	Big East	L	27	3	.900	4	1	31	4	.886	15	1	1st
13	San Diego St.	Western Athletic	Q	23	7	.767	0	1	23	8	.742	11	5	2d
16	Southern U.	Southwestern	Q	19	10	.655	0	1	19	11	.633	9	5	2d
8	Southern California	Pacific-10	L	19	9	.679	0	1	19	10	.655	13	5	T1st
5	Southern Methodist	Southwest	L	22	9	.710	1	1	23	10	.697	10	6	T2d
7	Syracuse	Big East	L	21	8	.724	1	1	22	9	.710	9	7	T3d
8	Temple	Atlantic 10	Q	24	5	.828	1	1	25	6	.806	15	3	2d
11	UTEP	Western Athletic	L	21	9	.700	1	1	22	10	.688	12	4	1st
6	Texas Tech	Southwest	Q	23	7	.767	0	1	23	8	.742	12	4	1st
6	Tulsa	Missouri Valley	L	23	7	.767	0	1	23	8	.742	12	4	1st
8	Villanova	Big East	L	19	10	.655	6	0	25	10	.714	9	7	3d
2	Va. Commonwealth	Sun Belt	Q	25	5	.833	1	1	26	6	.813	12	2	1st
9	Virginia Tech	Metro	L	20	8	.714	0	1	20	9	.690	10	4	2d
5	Washington	Pacific-10	Q	22	9	.710	0	1	22	10	.688	13	5	1st
11	Wichita St.	Missouri Valley	Q	18	12	.600	0	1	18	13	.581	11	5	T2d

1986 Tournament

Seed	School	Conference	How	Pre-Tourney W	L	Pct.	Tourney W	L	Final W	L	Pct.	Conf. W	L	Fin.
15	Akron	Ohio Valley	Q	22	7	.759	0	1	22	8	.733	10	4	T1st
5	Alabama	Southeastern	L	22	8	.733	2	1	24	9	.727	13	5	T2d
6	UAB	Sun Belt	L	24	10	.706	1	1	25	11	.694	9	5	T3d

THE TOURNAMENT FIELD

ALL-TIME TOURNAMENT FIELD

				Pre-Tourney			Tourney		Final			Conf.		
Seed	School	Conference	How	W	L	Pct.	W	L	W	L	Pct.	W	L	Fin.
9	Arizona	Pacific-10	Q	23	8	.742	0	1	23	9	.719	14	4	1st
14	Ark.-Little Rock	Trans America	Q	22	10	.688	1	1	23	11	.676	12	2	1st
8	Auburn	Southeastern	L	19	10	.655	3	1	22	11	.667	13	5	T2d
14	Ball St.	Mid-American	Q	21	9	.700	0	1	21	10	.677	11	7	3d
7	Bradley	Missouri Valley	L	31	2	.939	1	1	32	3	.914	16	0	1st
15	Brown	Ivy	Q	16	10	.615	0	1	16	11	.593	10	4	1st
14	Cleveland St.	Mid-Continent	L	27	3	.900	2	1	29	4	.879	13	1	1st
16	Davidson	Southern	Q	20	10	.667	0	1	20	11	.645	10	6	T2d
12	DePaul	Independent	L	16	12	.571	2	1	18	13	.581	—	—	
15	Drexel	East Coast	Q	19	11	.633	0	1	19	12	.613	11	3	1st
1	Duke	Atlantic Coast	Q	32	2	.941	5	1	37	3	.925	12	2	1st
13	Fairfield	Metro Atlantic	Q	24	6	.800	0	1	24	7	.774	13	1	1st
4	Georgetown	Big East	L	23	7	.767	1	1	24	8	.750	11	5	3d
2	Georgia Tech	Atlantic Coast	L	25	6	.806	2	1	27	7	.794	11	3	2d
4	Illinois	Big Ten	L	21	9	.700	1	1	22	10	.688	11	7	T4th
3	Indiana	Big Ten	L	21	7	.750	0	1	21	8	.724	13	5	2d
11	Iowa	Big Ten	L	20	11	.645	0	1	20	12	.625	10	8	6th
7	Iowa St.	Big Eight	L	20	10	.667	2	1	22	11	.667	9	5	2d
8	Jacksonville	Sun Belt	Q	21	9	.700	0	1	21	10	.677	9	5	T3d
1	Kansas	Big Eight	Q	31	3	.912	4	1	35	4	.897	13	1	1st
1	Kentucky	Southeastern	Q	29	3	.906	3	1	32	4	.889	17	1	1st
11	LSU	Southeastern	L	22	11	.667	4	1	26	12	.684	9	9	T5th
13	La.-Monroe	Southland	Q	20	9	.690	0	1	20	10	.667	9	3	1st
2	Louisville	Metro	Q	26	7	.788	6	0	32	7	.821	10	2	1st
15	Marist	ECAC Metro	Q	19	11	.633	0	1	19	12	.613	11	5	2d
5	Maryland	Atlantic Coast	L	18	13	.581	1	1	19	14	.576	6	8	6th
3	Memphis	Metro	L	27	5	.844	1	1	28	6	.824	9	3	2d
10	Miami (Ohio)	Mid-American	L	24	6	.800	0	1	24	7	.774	16	2	1st
2	Michigan	Big Ten	Q	27	4	.871	1	1	28	5	.848	14	4	1st
5	Michigan St.	Big Ten	L	21	7	.750	2	1	23	8	.742	12	6	3d
16	Mississippi Val.	Southwestern	Q	20	10	.667	0	1	20	11	.645	10	4	3d
11	Missouri	Big Eight	L	21	13	.618	0	1	21	14	.600	8	6	T3d
16	Montana St.	Big Sky	Q	14	16	.467	0	1	14	17	.452	6	8	T6th
7	Navy	Colonial	Q	27	4	.871	3	1	30	5	.857	13	1	1st
9	Nebraska	Big Eight	L	19	10	.655	0	1	19	11	.633	8	6	T3d
4	UNLV	Pacific Coast	Q	31	4	.886	2	1	33	5	.868	16	2	1st
3	North Carolina	Atlantic Coast	L	26	5	.839	2	1	28	6	.824	10	4	3d
16	N.C. A&T	Mid-Eastern	Q	22	7	.759	0	1	22	8	.733	12	2	1st
6	North Carolina St.	Atlantic Coast	L	18	12	.600	3	1	21	13	.618	7	7	T4th
13	Northeastern	ECAC North Atlantic	Q	26	4	.867	0	1	26	5	.839	16	2	1st
3	Notre Dame	Independent	L	23	5	.821	0	1	23	6	.793	—	—	
4	Oklahoma	Big Eight	L	25	8	.758	1	1	26	9	.743	8	6	T3d
8	Old Dominion	Sun Belt	L	22	7	.759	1	1	23	8	.742	11	3	1st
12	Pepperdine	West Coast	Q	25	4	.862	0	1	25	5	.833	13	1	1st
6	Purdue	Big Ten	L	22	9	.710	0	1	22	10	.688	11	7	T4th
11	Richmond	Colonial	L	23	6	.793	0	1	23	7	.767	12	2	2d
1	St. John's (N.Y.)	Big East	L	30	4	.882	1	1	31	5	.861	14	2	T1st
6	St. Joseph's	Atlantic 10	Q	25	5	.833	1	1	26	6	.813	16	2	1st
2	Syracuse	Big East	L	25	5	.833	1	1	26	6	.813	14	2	T1st
9	Temple	Atlantic 10	L	24	5	.828	1	1	25	6	.806	15	3	T2d
10	UTEP	Western Athletic	Q	27	5	.844	0	1	27	6	.818	12	4	T1st
13	Texas Tech	Southwest	Q	17	13	.567	0	1	17	14	.548	9	7	5th
10	Tulsa	Missouri Valley	Q	23	8	.742	0	1	23	9	.719	10	6	T2d
14	Utah	Western Athletic	L	20	9	.690	0	1	20	10	.667	12	4	T1st
10	Villanova	Big East	L	22	13	.629	1	1	23	14	.622	10	6	4th
5	Virginia	Atlantic Coast	L	19	10	.655	0	1	19	11	.633	7	7	T4th
7	Virginia Tech	Metro	L	22	8	.733	0	1	22	9	.710	7	5	3d
12	Washington	Pacific-10	L	19	11	.633	0	1	19	12	.613	13	5	2d
9	West Virginia	Atlantic 10	L	22	10	.688	0	1	22	11	.667	15	3	T2d
8	Western Ky.	Sun Belt	L	22	7	.759	1	1	23	8	.742	10	4	2d
12	Xavier	Midwestern	Q	25	4	.862	0	1	25	5	.833	10	2	1st

1987 Tournament

				Pre-Tourney			Tourney		Final			Conf.		
Seed	School	Conference	How	W	L	Pct.	W	L	W	L	Pct.	W	L	Fin.
2	Alabama	Southeastern	Q	26	4	.867	2	1	28	5	.848	16	1	1st
11	UAB	Sun Belt	L	21	10	.677	0	1	21	11	.656	10	4	3d
10	Arizona	Pacific-10	L	18	11	.621	0	1	18	12	.600	13	5	2d
8	Auburn	Southeastern	L	17	12	.586	1	1	18	13	.581	9	9	5th
14	Austin Peay	Ohio Valley	Q	19	11	.633	1	1	20	12	.625	8	6	T4th
10	Brigham Young	Western Athletic	L	21	10	.677	0	1	21	11	.656	12	4	2d
16	Bucknell	East Coast	Q	22	8	.733	0	1	22	9	.710	11	3	1st
13	Central Mich.	Mid-American	Q	22	7	.759	0	1	22	8	.733	14	2	1st
4	Clemson	Atlantic Coast	L	25	5	.833	0	1	25	6	.806	10	4	2d
3	DePaul	Independent	L	26	2	.929	2	1	28	3	.903	—	—	
5	Duke	Atlantic Coast	L	22	8	.733	2	1	24	9	.727	9	5	3d
16	Fairfield	Metro Atlantic	Q	15	15	.500	0	1	15	16	.484	5	9	7th
6	Florida	Southeastern	Q	21	10	.677	2	1	23	11	.676	12	6	2d
1	Georgetown	Big East	Q	26	4	.867	3	1	29	5	.853	12	4	T1st
8	Georgia	Southeastern	L	18	11	.621	0	1	18	12	.600	10	8	T3d
15	Ga. Southern	Trans America	Q	20	10	.667	0	1	20	11	.645	12	6	4th
7	Georgia Tech	Atlantic Coast	L	16	12	.571	0	1	16	13	.552	7	7	5th
12	Houston	Southwest	L	18	11	.621	0	1	18	12	.600	9	7	2d
16	Idaho St.	Big Sky	Q	15	15	.500	0	1	15	16	.484	5	9	T5th
3	Illinois	Big Ten	L	23	7	.767	0	1	23	8	.742	13	5	4th
1	Indiana	Big Ten	Q	24	4	.857	6	0	30	4	.882	15	3	T1st
2	Iowa	Big Ten	L	27	4	.871	3	1	30	5	.857	14	4	3d
5	Kansas	Big Eight	L	23	10	.697	2	1	25	11	.694	9	5	T2d
9	Kansas St.	Big Eight	L	19	10	.655	1	1	20	11	.645	8	6	4th
8	Kentucky	Southeastern	L	18	10	.643	0	1	18	11	.621	10	8	T3d
10	LSU	Southeastern	L	21	14	.600	3	1	24	15	.615	8	10	T6th

ALL-TIME TOURNAMENT FIELD

				Pre-Tourney			Tourney		Final			Conf.		
Seed	School	Conference	How	W	L	Pct.	W	L	W	L	Pct.	W	L	Fin.
14	Louisiana Tech	Southland	Q	22	7	.759	0	1	22	8	.733	9	1	1st
14	Marist	ECAC Metro	Q	20	9	.690	0	1	20	10	.667	15	1	1st
13	Marshall	Southern	Q	25	5	.833	0	1	25	6	.806	15	1	1st
9	Michigan	Big Ten	L	19	11	.633	1	1	20	12	.625	10	8	5th
12	Middle Tenn.	Ohio Valley	Q	22	6	.786	0	1	22	7	.759	11	3	1st
4	Missouri	Big Eight	Q	24	9	.727	0	1	24	10	.706	11	3	1st
8	Navy	Colonial	Q	26	5	.839	0	1	26	6	.813	13	1	1st
1	UNLV	Pacific Coast	Q	33	1	.971	4	1	37	2	.949	18	0	1st
7	New Orleans	Independent	L	25	3	.893	1	1	26	4	.867	—	—	—
1	North Carolina	Atlantic Coast	L	29	3	.906	3	1	32	4	.889	14	0	1st
15	N.C. A&T	Mid-Eastern	Q	24	5	.828	0	1	24	6	.800	12	2	2d
11	North Carolina St.	Atlantic Coast	Q	20	14	.588	0	1	20	15	.571	6	8	6th
14	Northeastern	ECAC North Atlantic	Q	27	6	.818	0	1	27	7	.794	17	1	1st
5	Notre Dame	Independent	L	22	7	.759	2	1	24	8	.750	—	—	—
9	Ohio St.	Big Ten	L	19	12	.613	1	1	20	13	.606	9	9	6th
6	Oklahoma	Big Eight	L	22	9	.710	2	1	24	10	.706	9	5	T2d
16	Pennsylvania	Ivy	Q	13	13	.500	0	1	13	14	.481	10	4	1st
3	Pittsburgh	Big East	L	24	7	.774	1	1	25	8	.758	12	4	T1st
6	Providence	Big East	L	21	8	.724	4	1	25	9	.735	10	6	T4th
3	Purdue	Big Ten	L	24	4	.857	1	1	25	5	.833	15	3	T1st
6	St. John's (N.Y.)	Big East	L	20	8	.714	1	1	21	9	.700	10	6	T4th
9	San Diego	West Coast	L	24	5	.828	0	1	24	6	.800	13	1	1st
15	Santa Clara	West Coast	Q	18	13	.581	0	1	18	14	.563	6	8	T4th
15	Southern U.	Southwestern	Q	19	11	.633	0	1	19	12	.613	9	5	T2d
15	Southwest Mo. St.	Mid-Continent	L	27	5	.844	1	1	28	6	.824	13	1	1st
2	Syracuse	Big East	L	26	6	.813	5	1	31	7	.816	12	4	T1st
2	Temple	Atlantic 10	Q	31	3	.912	1	1	32	4	.889	17	1	1st
7	UTEP	Western Athletic	L	24	6	.800	1	1	25	7	.781	13	3	1st
12	Texas A&M	Southwest	Q	17	13	.567	0	1	17	14	.548	6	10	8th
4	TCU	Southwest	L	23	6	.793	1	1	24	7	.774	14	2	1st
11	Tulsa	Missouri Valley	L	22	7	.759	0	1	22	8	.733	11	3	1st
4	UCLA	Pacific-10	Q	24	6	.800	1	1	25	7	.781	12	6	T2d
5	Virginia	Atlantic Coast	L	21	9	.700	0	1	21	10	.677	8	6	4th
7	West Virginia	Atlantic 10	L	23	7	.767	0	1	23	8	.742	15	3	2d
10	Western Ky.	Sun Belt	L	28	8	.778	1	1	29	9	.763	12	2	1st
11	Wichita St.	Missouri Valley	Q	22	10	.688	0	1	22	11	.667	9	5	3d
12	Wyoming	Western Athletic	Q	22	9	.710	2	1	24	10	.706	11	5	T3d
13	Xavier	Midwestern	Q	18	12	.600	1	1	19	13	.594	7	5	T3d

1988 Tournament

				Pre-Tourney			Tourney		Final			Conf.		
Seed	School	Conference	How	W	L	Pct.	W	L	W	L	Pct.	W	L	Fin.
1	Arizona	Pacific-10	Q	31	2	.939	4	1	35	3	.921	17	1	1st
11	Arkansas	Southwest	L	21	8	.724	0	1	21	9	.700	11	5	T2d
8	Auburn	Southeastern	L	18	10	.643	1	1	19	11	.633	11	7	T2d
8	Baylor	Southwest	L	23	10	.697	0	1	23	11	.676	11	5	T2d
14	Boise St.	Big Sky	Q	24	5	.828	0	1	24	6	.800	13	3	1st
15	Boston U.	ECAC North Atlantic	Q	23	7	.767	0	1	23	8	.742	14	4	2d
9	Bradley	Missouri Valley	Q	26	4	.867	0	1	26	5	.839	12	2	1st
4	Brigham Young	Western Athletic	L	25	5	.833	1	1	26	6	.813	13	3	1st
10	UC Santa Barb.	Pacific Coast	Q	22	7	.759	0	1	22	8	.733	13	5	T2d
13	Charlotte	Sun Belt	Q	22	8	.733	0	1	22	9	.710	11	3	1st
16	Chattanooga	Southern	Q	20	12	.625	0	1	20	13	.606	8	8	T5th
16	Cornell	Ivy	Q	17	9	.654	0	1	17	10	.630	11	3	1st
5	DePaul	Independent	L	21	7	.750	1	1	22	8	.733	—	—	—
2	Duke	Atlantic Coast	Q	24	6	.800	4	1	28	7	.800	9	5	3d
15	Eastern Mich.	Mid-American	Q	22	7	.759	0	1	22	8	.733	14	2	1st
16	Fairleigh Dickinson	ECAC Metro	Q	23	6	.793	0	1	23	7	.767	13	3	T1st
6	Florida	Southeastern	L	22	11	.667	1	1	23	12	.657	11	7	2d
12	Florida St.	Metro	L	19	10	.655	0	1	19	11	.633	7	5	2d
8	Georgetown	Big East	L	19	9	.679	1	1	20	10	.667	9	7	T3d
5	Georgia Tech	Atlantic Coast	L	21	9	.700	1	1	22	10	.688	8	6	4th
3	Illinois	Big Ten	L	22	9	.710	1	1	23	10	.697	12	6	T3d
4	Indiana	Big Ten	L	19	9	.679	0	1	19	10	.655	11	7	5th
5	Iowa	Big Ten	L	22	9	.710	2	1	24	10	.706	12	6	T3d
12	Iowa St.	Big Eight	L	20	11	.645	0	1	20	12	.625	6	8	5th
6	Kansas	Big Eight	L	21	11	.656	6	0	27	11	.711	9	5	3d
4	Kansas St.	Big Eight	L	22	8	.733	3	1	25	9	.735	11	3	2d
2	Kentucky	Southeastern	Q	25	5	.833	2	1	27	6	.818	13	5	1st
13	La Salle	Metro Atlantic	Q	24	9	.727	0	1	24	10	.706	14	0	1st
16	Lehigh	East Coast	Q	21	9	.700	0	1	21	10	.677	8	6	4th
9	LSU	Southeastern	L	16	13	.552	0	1	16	14	.533	10	8	T4th
5	Louisville	Metro	Q	22	10	.688	2	1	24	11	.686	9	3	1st
10	Loyola Marymount	West Coast	Q	27	3	.900	1	1	28	4	.875	14	0	1st
7	Maryland	Atlantic Coast	L	17	12	.586	1	1	18	13	.581	6	8	5th
9	Memphis	Metro	L	19	11	.633	1	1	20	12	.625	6	6	T3d
3	Michigan	Big Ten	L	24	7	.774	2	1	26	8	.765	13	5	2d
6	Missouri	Big Eight	L	19	10	.655	0	1	19	11	.633	10	4	2d
14	Murray St.	Ohio Valley	Q	21	8	.724	1	1	22	9	.710	13	1	1st
4	UNLV	Pacific Coast	L	27	5	.844	1	1	28	6	.824	15	3	1st
2	North Carolina	Atlantic Coast	L	24	6	.800	3	1	27	7	.794	11	3	1st
14	N.C. A&T	Mid-Eastern	Q	26	2	.929	0	1	26	3	.897	16	0	1st
3	North Carolina St.	Atlantic Coast	L	24	7	.774	0	1	24	8	.750	10	4	2d
15	North Texas	Southland	Q	17	12	.586	0	1	17	13	.567	12	2	1st
10	Notre Dame	Independent	L	20	8	.714	0	1	20	9	.690	—	—	—
1	Oklahoma	Big Eight	Q	30	3	.909	5	1	35	4	.897	12	2	1st
12	Oregon St.	Pacific-10	L	20	10	.667	0	1	20	11	.645	12	6	T2d
2	Pittsburgh	Big East	L	23	6	.793	1	1	24	7	.774	12	4	1st
3	Purdue	Big Ten	L	27	3	.900	2	1	29	4	.879	16	2	1st
11	Rhode Island	Atlantic 10	L	26	6	.813	2	1	28	7	.800	14	4	2d
13	Richmond	Colonial	Q	24	6	.800	2	1	26	7	.788	11	3	1st
11	St. John's (N.Y.)	Big East	L	17	11	.607	0	1	17	12	.586	8	8	T5th

ALL-TIME TOURNAMENT FIELD

Seed	School	Conference	How	Pre-Tourney W	L	Pct.	Tourney W	L	Final W	L	Pct.	Conf. W	L	Fin.
8	Seton Hall	Big East	L	21	12	.636	1	1	22	13	.629	8	8	T5th
15	Southern U.	Southwestern	Q	24	6	.800	0	1	24	7	.774	12	2	1st
7	Southern Methodist	Southwest	Q	27	6	.818	1	1	28	7	.800	12	4	1st
13	Southwest Mo. St.	Mid-Continent	Q	22	6	.786	0	1	22	7	.759	12	2	1st
3	Syracuse	Big East	L	25	8	.758	1	1	26	9	.743	11	5	2d
1	Temple	Atlantic 10	Q	29	1	.967	3	1	32	2	.941	18	0	1st
9	UTEP	Western Athletic	L	23	9	.719	0	1	23	10	.697	10	6	4th
14	Texas-San Antonio	Trans America	Q	22	8	.733	0	1	22	9	.710	13	5	3d
10	Utah St.	Pacific Coast	Q	21	9	.700	0	1	21	10	.677	13	5	T2d
7	Vanderbilt	Southeastern	L	18	10	.643	2	1	20	11	.645	10	8	T4th
6	Villanova	Big East	L	21	12	.636	3	1	24	13	.649	9	7	T3d
12	Wichita St.	Missouri Valley	L	20	9	.690	0	1	20	10	.667	11	5	2d
7	Wyoming	Western Athletic	Q	26	5	.839	0	1	26	6	.813	11	5	T2d
11	Xavier	Midwestern	Q	26	3	.897	0	1	26	4	.867	9	1	1st

1989 Tournament

Seed	School	Conference	How	Pre-Tourney W	L	Pct.	Tourney W	L	Final W	L	Pct.	Conf. W	L	Fin.
6	Alabama	Southeastern	Q	23	7	.767	0	1	23	8	.742	12	6	T2d
1	Arizona	Pacific-10	Q	27	3	.900	2	1	29	4	.879	17	1	1st
5	Arkansas	Southwest	Q	24	6	.800	1	1	25	7	.781	13	3	1st
13	Ark.-Little Rock	Trans America	Q	23	7	.767	0	1	23	8	.742	14	4	2d
9	Ball St.	Mid-American	Q	28	2	.933	1	1	29	3	.906	14	2	1st
15	Bucknell	East Coast	Q	23	7	.767	0	1	23	8	.742	11	3	1st
9	Clemson	Atlantic Coast	L	18	10	.643	1	1	19	11	.633	7	7	6th
10	Colorado St.	Western Athletic	L	22	9	.710	1	1	23	10	.697	12	4	1st
14	Creighton	Missouri Valley	Q	20	10	.667	0	1	20	11	.645	11	3	1st
12	DePaul	Independent	L	20	11	.645	1	1	21	12	.636	—	—	—
2	Duke	Atlantic Coast	L	24	7	.774	4	1	28	8	.778	9	5	T2d
16	East Tenn. St.	Southern	Q	20	10	.667	0	1	20	11	.645	7	7	T4th
11	Evansville	Midwestern	L	24	5	.828	1	1	25	6	.806	10	2	1st
7	Florida	Southeastern	L	21	12	.636	0	1	21	13	.618	13	5	1st
4	Florida St.	Metro	L	22	7	.759	0	1	22	8	.733	9	3	1st
15	George Mason	Colonial	Q	20	10	.667	0	1	20	11	.645	10	4	2d
1	Georgetown	Big East	Q	26	4	.867	3	1	29	5	.853	13	3	1st
6	Georgia Tech	Atlantic Coast	L	20	11	.645	0	1	20	12	.625	8	6	5th
13	Idaho	Big Sky	Q	25	5	.833	0	1	25	6	.806	13	3	T1st
1	Illinois	Big Ten	L	27	4	.871	4	1	31	5	.861	14	4	2d
2	Indiana	Big Ten	Q	25	7	.781	2	1	27	8	.771	15	3	1st
4	Iowa	Big Ten	L	22	9	.710	1	1	23	10	.697	10	8	4th
10	Iowa St.	Big Eight	L	17	11	.607	0	1	17	12	.586	7	7	T4th
6	Kansas St.	Big Eight	L	19	10	.655	0	1	19	11	.633	8	6	3d
8	La Salle	Metro Atlantic	Q	26	5	.839	0	1	26	6	.813	13	1	1st
10	LSU	Southeastern	L	20	11	.645	0	1	20	12	.625	11	7	T4th
9	Louisiana Tech	American South	L	22	8	.733	1	1	23	9	.719	6	4	T2d
4	Louisville	Metro	Q	22	8	.733	2	1	24	9	.727	8	4	T2d
12	Loyola Marymount	West Coast	Q	20	10	.667	0	1	20	11	.645	10	4	T2d
16	McNeese St.	Southland	Q	16	13	.552	0	1	16	14	.533	9	5	T2d
5	Memphis	Metro	L	21	10	.677	0	1	21	11	.656	8	4	T2d
3	Michigan	Big Ten	L	24	7	.774	6	0	30	7	.811	12	6	3d
13	Middle Tenn.	Ohio Valley	Q	22	7	.759	1	1	23	8	.742	10	2	T1st
11	Minnesota	Big Ten	L	17	11	.607	2	1	19	12	.613	9	9	5th
3	Missouri	Big Eight	Q	27	7	.794	2	1	29	8	.784	12	2	1st
4	UNLV	Big West	Q	26	7	.788	3	1	29	8	.784	16	2	1st
2	North Carolina	Atlantic Coast	Q	27	7	.794	2	1	29	8	.784	9	5	T2d
5	North Carolina St.	Atlantic Coast	L	20	8	.714	2	1	22	9	.710	10	4	1st
9	Notre Dame	Independent	L	20	8	.714	1	1	21	9	.700	—	—	—
1	Oklahoma	Big Eight	L	28	5	.848	2	1	30	6	.833	12	2	1st
6	Oregon St.	Pacific-10	L	22	7	.759	0	1	22	8	.733	13	5	T3d
8	Pittsburgh	Big East	L	17	12	.586	0	1	17	13	.567	9	7	4th
16	Princeton	Ivy	Q	19	7	.731	0	1	19	8	.704	11	3	1st
12	Providence	Big East	L	18	10	.643	0	1	18	11	.621	7	9	T5th
16	Robert Morris	Northeast	Q	21	8	.724	0	1	21	9	.700	12	4	1st
13	Rutgers	Atlantic 10	Q	18	12	.600	0	1	18	13	.581	13	5	3d
8	St. Mary's (Cal.)	West Coast	L	25	4	.862	0	1	25	5	.833	12	2	1st
3	Seton Hall	Big East	L	26	6	.813	5	1	31	7	.816	11	5	2d
14	Siena	ECAC North Atlantic	Q	24	4	.857	1	1	25	5	.833	16	1	1st
11	South Ala.	Sun Belt	Q	22	8	.733	1	1	23	9	.719	11	3	1st
12	South Carolina	Metro	L	19	10	.655	0	1	19	11	.633	8	4	T2d
15	South Carolina St.	Mid-Eastern	Q	25	7	.781	0	1	25	8	.758	14	2	1st
15	Southern U.	Southwestern	Q	20	10	.667	0	1	20	11	.645	10	4	T1st
14	Southwest Mo. St.	Mid-Continent	Q	21	9	.700	0	1	21	10	.677	10	2	1st
3	Stanford	Pacific-10	L	26	6	.813	0	1	26	7	.788	15	3	2d
2	Syracuse	Big East	L	27	7	.794	3	1	30	8	.789	10	6	3d
10	Tennessee	Southeastern	L	19	10	.655	0	1	19	11	.633	10	7	T4th
11	Texas	Southwest	L	24	8	.750	1	1	25	9	.735	12	4	2d
7	UTEP	Western Athletic	Q	25	6	.806	1	1	26	7	.788	11	5	T2d
7	UCLA	Pacific-10	L	20	9	.690	1	1	21	10	.677	13	5	T3d
8	Vanderbilt	Southeastern	L	19	13	.594	0	1	19	14	.576	12	6	T2d
5	Virginia	Atlantic Coast	L	19	10	.655	3	1	22	11	.667	9	5	T2d
7	West Virginia	Atlantic 10	L	25	4	.862	1	1	26	5	.839	17	1	1st
14	Xavier	Midwestern	Q	21	11	.656	0	1	21	12	.636	7	5	3d

1990 Tournament

Seed	School	Conference	How	Pre-Tourney W	L	Pct.	Tourney W	L	Final W	L	Pct.	Conf. W	L	Fin.
7	Alabama	Southeastern	Q	24	8	.750	2	1	26	9	.743	12	6	T2d
10	UAB	Sun Belt	L	22	8	.733	0	1	22	9	.710	12	2	1st
2	Arizona	Pacific-10	Q	24	6	.800	1	1	25	7	.781	15	3	T1st
4	Arkansas	Southwest	Q	26	4	.867	4	1	30	5	.857	14	2	1st
16	Ark.-Little Rock	Trans America	Q	20	9	.690	0	1	20	10	.667	12	4	3d
12	Ball St.	Mid-American	Q	24	6	.800	2	1	26	7	.788	13	3	1st

ALL-TIME TOURNAMENT FIELD

135

Seed	School	Conference	How	Pre-Tourney W L Pct.	Tourney W L	Final W L Pct.	Conf. W L Fin.
16	Boston U.	North Atlantic	Q	18 11 .621	0 1	18 12 .600	9 3 T1st
12	Brigham Young	Western Athletic	L	21 8 .724	0 1	21 9 .700	11 5 T1st
9	California	Pacific-10	L	21 9 .700	1 1	22 10 .688	12 6 3d
9	UC Santa Barb.	Big West	L	20 8 .714	1 1	21 9 .700	13 5 3d
5	Clemson	Atlantic Coast	L	24 8 .750	2 1	26 9 .743	10 4 1st
10	Colorado St.	Western Athletic	L	21 8 .724	0 1	21 9 .700	11 5 T1st
1	Connecticut	Big East	Q	28 5 .848	3 1	31 6 .838	12 4 T1st
15	Coppin St.	Mid-Eastern	Q	26 6 .813	0 1	26 7 .788	15 1 1st
12	Dayton	Midwestern	Q	21 9 .700	1 1	22 10 .688	10 4 2d
3	Duke	Atlantic Coast	L	24 8 .750	5 1	29 9 .763	9 5 2d
13	East Tenn. St.	Southern	Q	27 6 .818	0 1	27 7 .794	12 2 1st
3	Georgetown	Big East	L	23 6 .793	1 1	24 7 .774	11 5 3d
7	Georgia	Southeastern	L	20 8 .714	0 1	20 9 .690	13 5 1st
4	Georgia Tech	Atlantic Coast	Q	24 6 .800	4 1	28 7 .800	8 6 T3d
8	Houston	Southwest	L	25 7 .781	0 1	25 8 .758	13 3 2d
13	Idaho	Big Sky	Q	25 5 .833	0 1	25 6 .806	13 3 1st
5	Illinois	Big Ten	L	21 7 .750	0 1	21 8 .724	11 7 T4th
14	Illinois St.	Missouri Valley	Q	18 12 .600	0 1	18 13 .581	9 5 T2d
8	Indiana	Big Ten	L	18 10 .643	0 1	18 11 .621	8 10 7th
2	Kansas	Big Eight	L	29 4 .879	1 1	30 5 .857	11 3 T2d
11	Kansas St.	Big Eight	L	17 14 .548	0 1	17 15 .531	7 7 4th
4	La Salle	Metro Atlantic (S)	Q	29 1 .967	1 1	30 2 .938	16 0 1st
5	LSU	Southeastern	L	22 8 .733	1 1	23 9 .719	12 6 T2d
15	La.-Monroe	Southland	Q	22 7 .759	0 1	22 8 .733	13 1 1st
4	Louisville	Metro	Q	26 7 .788	1 1	27 8 .771	12 2 1st
11	Loyola Marymount	West Coast	Q	23 5 .821	3 1	26 6 .813	13 1 1st
3	Michigan	Big Ten	L	22 7 .759	1 1	23 8 .742	12 6 3d
1	Michigan St.	Big Ten	Q	26 5 .839	2 1	28 6 .824	15 3 1st
6	Minnesota	Big Ten	L	20 8 .714	3 1	23 9 .719	11 7 T4th
3	Missouri	Big Eight	L	26 5 .839	0 1	26 6 .813	12 2 1st
16	Murray St.	Ohio Valley	Q	21 8 .724	0 1	21 9 .700	10 2 1st
1	UNLV	Big West	Q	29 5 .853	6 0	35 5 .875	16 2 T1st
6	New Mexico St.	Big West	L	26 4 .867	0 1	26 5 .839	16 2 T1st
8	North Carolina	Atlantic Coast	L	19 12 .613	2 1	21 13 .618	8 6 T3d
14	Northern Iowa	Mid-Continent	Q	22 8 .733	1 1	23 9 .719	6 6 T3d
10	Notre Dame	Independent	L	16 12 .571	0 1	16 13 .552	— — 6th
8	Ohio St.	Big Ten	L	16 12 .571	1 1	17 13 .567	10 8 6th
1	Oklahoma	Big Eight	Q	26 4 .867	1 1	27 5 .844	11 3 T2d
5	Oregon St.	Pacific-10	L	22 6 .786	0 1	22 7 .759	15 3 T1st
13	Princeton	Ivy	Q	20 6 .769	0 1	20 7 .741	11 3 1st
9	Providence	Big East	L	17 11 .607	0 1	17 12 .586	8 8 T5th
2	Purdue	Big Ten	L	21 7 .750	1 1	22 8 .733	13 5 2d
14	Richmond	Colonial	L	22 9 .710	0 1	22 10 .688	10 4 T2d
15	Robert Morris	Northeast	Q	22 7 .759	0 1	22 8 .733	12 4 1st
6	St. John's (N.Y.)	Big East	L	23 9 .719	1 1	24 10 .706	10 6 4th
15	South Fla.	Sun Belt	Q	20 10 .667	0 1	20 11 .645	9 5 2d
13	Southern Miss.	Metro	L	20 11 .645	0 1	20 12 .625	9 5 T2d
9	Southwest Mo. St.	Mid-Continent	L	22 6 .786	0 1	22 7 .759	11 1 1st
2	Syracuse	Big East	L	24 6 .800	2 1	26 7 .788	12 4 T1st
11	Temple	Atlantic 10	Q	20 10 .667	0 1	20 11 .645	15 3 1st
10	Texas	Southwest	L	21 8 .724	3 1	24 9 .727	12 4 3d
11	UTEP	Western Athletic	Q	21 10 .677	0 1	21 11 .656	10 6 T3d
14	Texas Southern	Southwestern	Q	19 11 .633	0 1	19 12 .613	10 4 2d
16	Towson	East Coast	Q	18 12 .600	0 1	18 13 .581	8 6 T1st
7	UCLA	Pacific-10	Q	20 10 .667	2 1	22 11 .667	11 7 4th
12	Villanova	Big East	L	18 14 .563	0 1	18 15 .545	8 8 T5th
7	Virginia	Atlantic Coast	L	19 11 .633	1 1	20 12 .625	6 8 T5th
6	Xavier	Midwestern	L	26 4 .867	2 1	28 5 .848	12 2 1st

1991 Tournament

Seed	School	Conference	How	Pre-Tourney W L Pct.	Tourney W L	Final W L Pct.	Conf. W L Fin.
4	Alabama	Southeastern	Q	21 9 .700	2 1	23 10 .697	12 6 3d
2	Arizona	Pacific-10	Q	26 6 .813	2 1	28 7 .800	14 4 1st
8	Arizona St.	Pacific-10	L	19 9 .679	1 1	20 10 .667	10 8 T3d
1	Arkansas	Southwest	Q	31 3 .912	3 1	34 4 .895	15 1 1st
10	Brigham Young	Western Athletic	Q	20 12 .625	1 1	21 13 .618	11 5 2d
15	Coastal Caro.	Big South	Q	24 7 .774	0 1	24 8 .750	13 1 1st
11	Connecticut	Big East	L	18 10 .643	2 1	20 11 .645	9 7 T3d
11	Creighton	Missouri Valley	Q	23 7 .767	1 1	24 8 .750	12 4 1st
9	DePaul	Independent	L	20 8 .714	0 1	20 9 .690	— — —
2	Duke	Atlantic Coast	L	26 7 .788	6 0	32 7 .821	11 3 1st
10	East Tenn. St.	Southern	Q	28 4 .875	0 1	28 5 .848	11 3 T1st
12	Eastern Mich.	Mid-American	Q	24 6 .800	2 1	26 7 .788	13 3 1st
7	Florida St.	Metro	L	20 10 .667	1 1	21 11 .656	9 5 2d
8	Georgetown	Big East	L	18 12 .600	1 1	19 13 .594	8 8 6th
11	Georgia	Southeastern	L	17 12 .586	0 1	17 13 .567	9 9 5th
16	Georgia St.	Trans America	Q	16 14 .533	0 1	16 15 .516	7 7 5th
8	Georgia Tech	Atlantic Coast	L	16 12 .571	1 1	17 13 .567	6 8 T5th
2	Indiana	Big Ten	L	27 4 .871	2 1	29 5 .853	15 3 T1st
7	Iowa	Big Ten	L	20 10 .667	1 1	21 11 .656	9 9 T5th
3	Kansas	Big Eight	L	22 7 .759	5 1	27 8 .771	10 4 T1st
6	LSU	Southeastern	L	20 9 .690	0 1	20 10 .667	13 5 T1st
15	La.-Monroe	Southland	Q	25 7 .781	0 1	25 8 .758	13 1 1st
12	Louisiana Tech	American South	Q	21 9 .700	0 1	21 10 .677	8 4 3d
5	Michigan St.	Big Ten	L	18 10 .643	1 1	19 11 .633	11 7 3d
5	Mississippi St.	Southeastern	L	20 8 .714	0 1	20 9 .690	13 5 T1st
16	Montana	Big Sky	Q	23 7 .767	0 1	23 8 .742	13 3 1st
13	Murray St.	Ohio Valley	Q	24 5 .750	0 1	24 9 .727	10 2 1st
9	Nebraska	Big Eight	L	26 7 .788	0 1	26 8 .765	9 5 3d
1	UNLV	Big West	Q	30 0 1.000	4 1	34 1 .971	18 0 1st
14	New Mexico	Western Athletic	L	20 9 .690	0 1	20 10 .667	10 6 3d

THE TOURNAMENT FIELD

ALL-TIME TOURNAMENT FIELD

Seed	School	Conference	How	Pre-Tourney W	L	Pct.	Tourney W	L	Final W	L	Pct.	Conf. W	L	Fin.
6	New Mexico St.	Big West	L	23	5	.821	0	1	23	6	.793	15	3	2d
14	New Orleans	American South	L	23	7	.767	0	1	23	8	.742	9	3	T1st
1	North Carolina	Atlantic Coast	Q	25	5	.833	4	1	29	6	.829	10	4	2d
6	North Carolina St.	Atlantic Coast	L	19	10	.655	1	1	20	11	.645	8	6	T3d
16	Northeastern	North Atlantic	Q	22	10	.688	0	1	22	11	.667	8	2	1st
13	Northern Ill.	Mid-Continent	L	25	5	.833	0	1	25	6	.806	14	2	1st
1	Ohio St.	Big Ten	Q	25	3	.893	2	1	27	4	.871	15	3	T1st
3	Oklahoma St.	Big Eight	L	22	7	.759	2	1	24	8	.750	10	4	T1st
13	Penn St.	Atlantic 10	Q	20	10	.667	1	1	21	11	.656	10	8	T3d
14	Pepperdine	West Coast	Q	22	8	.733	0	1	22	9	.710	13	1	1st
6	Pittsburgh	Big East	L	20	11	.645	1	1	21	12	.636	9	7	T3d
8	Princeton	Ivy	Q	24	2	.923	0	1	24	3	.889	14	0	1st
7	Purdue	Big Ten	L	17	11	.607	0	1	17	12	.586	9	9	T5th
15	Richmond	Colonial	Q	21	9	.700	1	1	22	10	.688	10	4	2d
9	Rutgers	Atlantic 10	L	19	9	.679	0	1	19	10	.655	14	4	1st
15	St. Francis (Pa.)	Northeast	Q	24	7	.774	0	1	24	8	.750	13	3	T1st
4	St. John's (N.Y.)	Big East	L	20	8	.714	3	1	23	9	.719	10	6	2d
12	St. Peter's	Metro Atlantic	Q	24	6	.800	0	1	24	7	.774	11	5	T2d
3	Seton Hall	Big East	Q	22	8	.733	3	1	25	9	.735	9	7	T3d
13	South Ala.	Sun Belt	Q	22	8	.733	0	1	22	9	.710	11	3	1st
10	Southern California	Pacific-10	L	19	9	.679	0	1	19	10	.655	10	8	T3d
11	Southern Miss.	Metro	L	21	7	.750	0	1	21	8	.724	10	4	1st
2	Syracuse	Big East	L	26	5	.839	0	1	26	6	.813	12	4	1st
10	Temple	Atlantic 10	L	21	9	.700	3	1	24	10	.706	13	5	2d
5	Texas	Southwest	L	22	8	.733	1	1	23	9	.719	13	3	2d
16	Towson	East Coast	Q	19	10	.655	0	1	19	11	.633	10	2	1st
4	UCLA	Pacific-10	L	23	8	.742	0	1	23	9	.719	11	7	2d
4	Utah	Western Athletic	L	28	3	.903	2	1	30	4	.882	15	1	1st
9	Vanderbilt	Southeastern	L	17	12	.586	0	1	17	13	.567	11	7	4th
9	Villanova	Big East	L	16	14	.533	1	1	17	15	.531	7	9	T7th
7	Virginia	Atlantic Coast	L	21	11	.656	0	1	21	12	.636	6	8	T5th
5	Wake Forest	Atlantic Coast	L	18	10	.643	1	1	19	11	.633	8	6	T3d
12	Wis.-Green Bay	Mid-Continent	Q	24	6	.800	0	1	24	7	.774	13	3	2d
14	Xavier	Midwestern	Q	21	9	.700	1	1	22	10	.688	11	3	1st

1992 Tournament

Seed	School	Conference	How	Pre-Tourney W	L	Pct.	Tourney W	L	Final W	L	Pct.	Conf. W	L	Fin.
5	Alabama	Southeastern (W)	L	25	8	.758	1	1	26	9	.743	10	6	3d
3	Arizona	Pacific-10	L	24	6	.800	0	1	24	7	.774	13	5	3d
3	Arkansas	Southeastern (W)	L	25	7	.781	1	1	26	8	.765	13	3	1st
10	Brigham Young	Western Athletic	Q	25	6	.806	0	1	25	7	.781	12	4	T1st
16	Campbell	Big South	Q	19	11	.633	0	1	19	12	.613	7	7	T3d
7	Charlotte	Metro	L	23	8	.742	0	1	23	9	.719	7	5	T2d
4	Cincinnati	Great Midwest	L	25	4	.862	4	1	29	5	.853	8	2	T1st
9	Connecticut	Big East	L	19	9	.679	1	1	20	10	.667	10	8	T5th
13	Delaware	North Atlantic	Q	27	3	.900	0	1	27	4	.871	14	0	1st
5	DePaul	Great Midwest	L	20	8	.714	0	1	20	9	.690	8	2	T1st
1	Duke	Atlantic Coast	Q	28	2	.933	6	0	34	2	.944	14	2	1st
14	East Tenn. St.	Southern	Q	23	6	.793	1	1	24	7	.774	12	2	T1st
15	Eastern Ill.	Mid-Continent	Q	17	13	.567	0	1	17	14	.548	9	7	T4th
8	Evansville	Midwestern	Q	24	5	.828	0	1	24	6	.800	8	2	1st
3	Florida St.	Atlantic Coast	L	20	9	.690	2	1	22	10	.688	11	5	2d
14	Fordham	Patriot	Q	18	12	.600	0	1	18	13	.581	11	3	T1st
6	Georgetown	Big East	L	21	9	.700	1	1	22	10	.688	12	6	T1st
15	Ga. Southern	Trans America	Q	25	5	.833	0	1	25	6	.806	13	1	1st
7	Georgia Tech	Atlantic Coast	L	21	11	.656	2	1	23	12	.657	8	8	T3d
10	Houston	Southwest	Q	25	5	.833	0	1	25	6	.806	11	3	T1st
16	Howard	Mid-Eastern	Q	17	13	.567	0	1	17	14	.548	12	4	T1st
2	Indiana	Big Ten	L	23	6	.793	4	1	27	7	.794	14	4	2d
9	Iowa	Big Ten	L	18	10	.643	1	1	19	11	.633	10	8	5th
10	Iowa St.	Big Eight	L	20	12	.625	1	1	21	13	.618	5	9	T6th
1	Kansas	Big Eight	Q	26	4	.867	1	1	27	5	.844	11	3	1st
2	Kentucky	Southeastern (E)	Q	26	6	.813	3	1	29	7	.806	12	4	1st
13	La Salle	Metro Atlantic	Q	20	10	.667	0	1	20	11	.645	12	4	1st
7	LSU	Southeastern (W)	L	20	9	.690	1	1	21	10	.677	12	4	2d
13	La.-Lafayette	Sun Belt	Q	20	10	.667	1	1	21	11	.656	12	4	2d
15	La.-Monroe	Southland	Q	19	9	.679	0	1	19	10	.655	12	6	T2d
8	Louisville	Metro	L	18	10	.643	1	1	19	11	.633	7	5	T2d
3	Massachusetts	Atlantic 10	Q	28	4	.875	2	1	30	5	.857	13	3	1st
6	Memphis	Great Midwest	L	20	10	.667	3	1	23	11	.676	5	5	T3d
13	Miami (Ohio)	Mid-American	Q	23	7	.767	0	1	23	8	.742	13	3	1st
6	Michigan	Big Ten	L	20	8	.714	5	1	25	9	.735	11	7	T3d
5	Michigan St.	Big Ten	L	21	7	.750	1	1	22	8	.733	11	7	T3d
16	Mississippi Val.	Southwestern	Q	16	13	.552	0	1	16	14	.533	11	3	T1st
5	Missouri	Big Eight	L	20	8	.714	1	1	21	9	.700	8	6	T2d
14	Montana	Big Sky	Q	27	3	.900	0	1	27	4	.871	14	2	1st
14	Murray St.	Ohio Valley	Q	17	12	.586	0	1	17	13	.567	11	3	1st
8	Nebraska	Big Eight	L	19	9	.679	0	1	19	10	.655	9	5	5th
12	New Mexico St.	Big West	Q	23	7	.767	2	1	25	8	.758	12	6	3d
4	North Carolina	Atlantic Coast	L	21	9	.700	2	1	23	10	.697	9	7	3d
1	Ohio St.	Big Ten	Q	23	5	.821	3	1	26	6	.813	15	3	1st
4	Oklahoma	Big Eight	L	21	8	.724	0	1	21	9	.700	9	5	T2d
2	Oklahoma St.	Big Eight	L	26	7	.788	2	1	28	8	.778	8	6	T2d
15	Old Dominion	Colonial	Q	15	14	.517	0	1	15	15	.500	8	6	T3d
11	Pepperdine	West Coast	Q	24	6	.800	0	1	24	7	.774	14	0	1st
11	Princeton	Ivy	Q	22	5	.815	0	1	22	6	.786	12	2	1st
16	Robert Morris	Northeast	Q	19	11	.633	0	1	19	12	.613	12	4	1st
7	St. John's (N.Y.)	Big East	L	19	10	.655	0	1	19	11	.633	12	6	T1st
4	Seton Hall	Big East	L	21	8	.724	2	1	23	9	.719	12	6	T1st
11	South Fla.	Metro	L	19	9	.679	0	1	19	10	.655	7	5	T2d

ALL-TIME TOURNAMENT FIELD

				Pre-Tourney			Tourney		Final			Conf.		
Seed	School	Conference	How	W	L	Pct.	W	L	W	L	Pct.	W	L	Fin.
2	Southern California	Pacific-10	L	23	5	.821	1	1	24	6	.800	15	3	2d
12	Southwest Mo. St.	Missouri Valley	Q	23	7	.767	0	1	23	8	.742	13	5	3d
12	Stanford	Pacific-10	L	18	10	.643	0	1	18	11	.621	10	8	4th
6	Syracuse	Big East	Q	21	9	.700	1	1	22	10	.688	10	8	T5th
11	Temple	Atlantic 10	L	17	12	.586	0	1	17	13	.567	11	5	2d
8	Texas	Southwest	L	23	11	.676	0	1	23	12	.657	11	3	T1st
9	UTEP	Western Athletic	L	25	6	.806	2	1	27	7	.794	12	4	T1st
10	Tulane	Metro	L	21	8	.724	1	1	22	9	.710	8	4	1st
1	UCLA	Pacific-10	Q	25	4	.862	3	1	28	5	.848	16	2	1st
9	Wake Forest	Atlantic Coast	L	17	11	.607	0	1	17	12	.586	7	9	5th
12	West Virginia	Atlantic 10	L	20	11	.645	0	1	20	12	.625	10	6	3d

1993 Tournament

				Pre-Tourney			Tourney		Final			Conf.		
Seed	School	Conference	How	W	L	Pct.	W	L	W	L	Pct.	W	L	Fin.
2	Arizona	Pacific-10	Q	24	3	.889	0	1	24	4	.857	17	1	1st
4	Arkansas	Southeastern (W)	L	20	8	.714	2	1	22	9	.710	10	6	1st
15	Ball St.	Mid-American	Q	26	7	.788	0	1	26	8	.765	14	4	T1st
14	Boise St.	Big Sky	Q	21	7	.750	0	1	21	8	.724	10	4	T2d
7	Brigham Young	Western Athletic	L	24	8	.750	1	1	25	9	.735	15	3	T1st
6	California	Pacific-10	L	19	8	.704	2	1	21	9	.700	12	6	2d
12	Chattanooga	Southern	Q	26	6	.813	0	1	26	7	.788	16	2	1st
2	Cincinnati	Great Midwest	L	24	4	.857	3	1	27	5	.844	8	2	1st
16	Coastal Caro.	Big South	Q	22	9	.710	0	1	22	10	.688	12	4	2d
15	Coppin St.	Mid-Eastern	Q	22	7	.759	0	1	22	8	.733	16	0	1st
13	Delaware	North Atlantic	Q	22	7	.759	0	1	22	8	.733	10	4	3d
3	Duke	Atlantic Coast	L	23	7	.767	1	1	24	8	.750	10	6	T3d
16	East Caro.	Colonial	Q	13	16	.448	0	1	13	17	.433	4	10	7th
14	Evansville	Midwestern	Q	23	6	.793	0	1	23	7	.767	12	2	T1st
3	Florida St.	Atlantic Coast	L	22	9	.710	3	1	25	10	.714	12	4	2d
12	George Washington	Atlantic 10	L	19	8	.704	2	1	21	9	.700	8	6	T2d
4	Georgia Tech	Atlantic Coast	Q	19	10	.655	0	1	19	11	.633	8	8	6th
13	Holy Cross	Patriot	Q	23	6	.793	0	1	23	7	.767	12	2	1st
6	Illinois	Big Ten	L	18	12	.600	1	1	19	13	.594	11	7	T3d
1	Indiana	Big Ten	Q	28	3	.903	3	1	31	4	.886	17	1	1st
4	Iowa	Big Ten	L	22	8	.733	1	1	23	9	.719	11	7	T3d
8	Iowa St.	Big Eight	L	20	10	.667	0	1	20	11	.645	8	6	T3d
2	Kansas	Big Eight	L	25	6	.806	4	1	29	7	.806	11	3	1st
6	Kansas St.	Big Eight	L	19	10	.655	0	1	19	11	.633	7	7	T5th
1	Kentucky	Southeastern (E)	Q	26	3	.897	4	1	30	4	.882	13	3	2d
11	Long Beach St.	Big West	Q	22	9	.710	0	1	22	10	.688	11	7	4th
11	LSU	Southeastern (W)	L	22	10	.688	0	1	22	11	.667	9	7	2d
13	La.-Monroe	Southland	Q	26	4	.867	0	1	26	5	.839	17	1	1st
4	Louisville	Metro	L	20	8	.714	2	1	22	9	.710	11	1	1st
11	Manhattan	Metro Atlantic	Q	23	6	.793	0	1	23	7	.767	12	2	1st
12	Marquette	Great Midwest	L	20	7	.741	0	1	20	8	.714	6	4	3d
3	Massachusetts	Atlantic 10	Q	23	6	.793	1	1	24	7	.774	11	3	1st
10	Memphis	Great Midwest	L	20	11	.645	0	1	20	12	.625	7	3	2d
1	Michigan	Big Ten	L	26	4	.867	5	1	31	5	.861	15	3	2d
10	Missouri	Big Eight	Q	19	13	.594	0	1	19	14	.576	5	9	7th
10	Nebraska	Big Eight	L	20	10	.667	0	1	20	11	.645	8	6	T2d
5	New Mexico	Western Athletic	Q	24	6	.800	0	1	24	7	.774	13	5	3d
7	New Mexico St.	Big West	L	25	7	.781	1	1	26	8	.765	15	3	1st
8	New Orleans	Sun Belt	L	26	3	.897	0	1	26	4	.867	18	0	1st
1	North Carolina	Atlantic Coast	L	28	4	.875	6	0	34	4	.895	14	2	1st
5	Oklahoma St.	Big Eight	L	19	8	.704	1	1	20	9	.690	8	6	T2d
14	Pennsylvania	Ivy	Q	22	4	.846	0	1	22	5	.815	14	0	1st
9	Pittsburgh	Big East	L	17	10	.630	0	1	17	11	.607	9	9	T4th
9	Purdue	Big Ten	L	18	9	.667	0	1	18	10	.643	9	9	T5th
8	Rhode Island	Atlantic 10	L	18	10	.643	1	1	19	11	.633	8	6	T2d
16	Rider	Northeast	Q	19	10	.655	0	1	19	11	.633	14	4	1st
5	St. John's (N.Y.)	Big East	L	18	10	.643	1	1	19	11	.633	12	6	2d
15	Santa Clara	West Coast	Q	18	11	.621	1	1	19	12	.613	9	5	3d
2	Seton Hall	Big East	Q	27	6	.818	1	1	28	7	.800	14	4	1st
13	Southern U.	Southwestern	Q	20	9	.690	1	1	21	10	.677	9	5	T2d
14	Southern Ill.	Missouri Valley	Q	23	9	.719	0	1	23	10	.697	12	6	2d
10	Southern Methodist	Southwest	L	20	7	.741	0	1	20	8	.714	12	2	1st
7	Temple	Atlantic 10	L	17	12	.586	3	1	20	13	.606	8	6	T2d
15	Tennessee St.	Ohio Valley	Q	19	9	.679	0	1	19	10	.655	13	3	1st
12	Texas Tech	Southwest	Q	18	11	.621	0	1	18	12	.600	6	8	5th
11	Tulane	Metro	L	21	8	.724	1	1	22	9	.710	9	3	2d
9	UCLA	Pacific-10	L	21	10	.677	1	1	22	11	.667	11	7	T3d
8	Utah	Western Athletic	L	23	6	.793	1	1	24	7	.774	15	3	T1st
3	Vanderbilt	Southeastern (E)	L	26	5	.839	2	1	28	6	.824	14	2	1st
6	Virginia	Atlantic Coast	L	19	9	.679	2	1	21	10	.677	9	7	5th
5	Wake Forest	Atlantic Coast	L	19	8	.704	2	1	21	9	.700	10	6	T3d
7	Western Ky.	Sun Belt	Q	24	5	.828	2	1	26	6	.813	14	4	2d
16	Wright St.	Mid-Continent	Q	20	9	.690	0	1	20	10	.667	10	6	T2d
9	Xavier	Midwestern	L	23	6	.821	1	1	24	7	.800	12	2	T1st

1994 Tournament

				Pre-Tourney			Tourney		Final			Conf.		
Seed	School	Conference	How	W	L	Pct.	W	L	W	L	Pct.	W	L	Fin.
9	Alabama	Southeastern (W)	L	19	9	.679	1	1	20	10	.667	12	4	2d
7	UAB	Great Midwest	L	22	7	.759	0	1	22	8	.733	8	4	T2d
2	Arizona	Pacific-10	Q	25	5	.833	4	1	29	6	.829	14	4	1st
1	Arkansas	Southeastern (W)	L	25	3	.893	6	0	31	3	.912	14	2	1st
14	Boise St.	Big Sky	Q	17	12	.586	0	1	17	13	.567	7	7	5th
9	Boston College	Big East	L	20	10	.667	3	1	23	11	.676	11	7	3d
5	California	Pacific-10	L	22	7	.759	0	1	22	8	.733	13	5	T2d
16	UCF	Trans America	Q	21	8	.724	0	1	21	9	.700	11	5	2d
12	Col. of Charleston	Trans America	L	24	3	.889	0	1	24	4	.857	14	2	1st
13	Chattanooga	Southern	Q	23	6	.793	0	1	23	7	.767	14	4	1st

THE TOURNAMENT FIELD

ALL-TIME TOURNAMENT FIELD

Seed	School	Conference	How	Pre-Tourney W	L	Pct.	Tourney W	L	Final W	L	Pct.	Conf. W	L	Fin.
8	Cincinnati	Great Midwest	L	22	9	.710	0	1	22	10	.688	7	5	4th
2	Connecticut	Big East	L	27	4	.871	2	1	29	5	.853	16	2	1st
13	Drexel	North Atlantic	Q	25	4	.862	0	1	25	5	.833	12	2	1st
2	Duke	Atlantic Coast	L	23	5	.821	5	1	28	6	.824	12	4	1st
3	Florida	Southeastern (E)	L	25	7	.781	4	1	29	8	.784	12	4	T1st
10	George Washington	Atlantic 10	L	17	11	.607	1	1	18	12	.600	8	8	T3d
9	Georgetown	Big East	L	18	11	.621	1	1	19	12	.613	10	8	T4th
13	Hawaii	Western Athletic	Q	18	14	.563	0	1	18	15	.545	11	7	4th
8	Illinois	Big Ten	L	17	10	.630	0	1	17	11	.607	10	8	T4th
5	Indiana	Big Ten	L	19	8	.704	2	1	21	9	.700	12	6	3d
14	James Madison	Colonial	Q	20	9	.690	0	1	20	10	.667	10	4	T1st
4	Kansas	Big Eight	L	25	7	.781	2	1	27	8	.771	9	5	3d
3	Kentucky	Southeastern (E)	Q	26	6	.813	1	1	27	7	.794	12	4	T1st
16	Liberty	Big South	Q	18	11	.621	0	1	18	12	.600	13	5	T3d
11	La.-Lafayette	Sun Belt	Q	22	7	.759	0	1	22	8	.733	13	5	2d
3	Louisville	Metro	Q	26	5	.839	2	1	28	6	.824	10	2	1st
15	Loyola (Md.)	Metro Atlantic	Q	17	12	.586	0	1	17	13	.567	6	8	5th
6	Marquette	Great Midwest	L	22	8	.733	2	1	24	9	.727	10	2	1st
10	Maryland	Atlantic Coast	L	16	11	.593	2	1	18	12	.600	8	8	4th
2	Massachusetts	Atlantic 10	Q	27	6	.818	1	1	28	7	.800	14	2	1st
3	Michigan	Big Ten	L	21	7	.750	3	1	24	8	.750	13	5	2d
7	Michigan St.	Big Ten	L	19	11	.633	1	1	20	12	.625	10	8	T4th
6	Minnesota	Big Ten	L	20	11	.645	1	1	21	12	.636	10	8	T4th
1	Missouri	Big Eight	L	25	3	.893	3	1	28	4	.875	14	0	1st
16	Navy	Patriot	Q	17	12	.586	0	1	17	13	.567	9	5	T1st
6	Nebraska	Big Eight	Q	20	9	.690	0	1	20	10	.667	7	7	4th
10	New Mexico	Western Athletic	L	23	7	.767	0	1	23	8	.742	14	4	1st
13	New Mexico St.	Big West	Q	23	7	.767	0	1	23	8	.742	12	6	1st
1	North Carolina	Atlantic Coast	Q	27	6	.818	1	1	28	7	.800	11	5	2d
16	N.C. A&T	Mid-Eastern	Q	16	13	.552	0	1	16	14	.533	10	6	T2d
12	Ohio	Mid-American	Q	25	7	.781	0	1	25	8	.758	14	4	1st
4	Oklahoma St.	Big Eight	L	23	9	.719	1	1	24	10	.706	10	4	2d
11	Pennsylvania	Ivy	Q	24	2	.923	1	1	25	3	.893	14	0	1st
14	Pepperdine	West Coast	Q	19	10	.655	0	1	19	11	.633	8	6	T2d
8	Providence	Big East	Q	20	9	.690	0	1	20	10	.667	10	8	T4th
1	Purdue	Big Ten	Q	26	4	.867	3	1	29	5	.853	14	4	1st
15	Rider	Northeast	Q	21	8	.724	0	1	21	9	.700	14	4	1st
7	St. Louis	Great Midwest	L	23	5	.821	0	1	23	6	.793	8	4	T2d
10	Seton Hall	Big East	L	17	12	.586	0	1	17	13	.567	8	10	7th
11	Southern Ill.	Missouri Valley	Q	23	6	.793	0	1	23	7	.767	16	4	T1st
15	Southwest Tex. St.	Southland	Q	25	6	.806	0	1	25	7	.781	14	4	2d
4	Syracuse	Big East	L	21	6	.778	2	1	23	7	.767	13	5	2d
4	Temple	Atlantic 10	L	22	7	.759	1	1	23	8	.742	12	4	2d
14	Tennessee St.	Ohio Valley	Q	19	11	.633	0	1	19	12	.613	12	4	2d
6	Texas	Southwest	Q	25	7	.781	1	1	26	8	.765	12	2	1st
15	Texas Southern	Southwestern	Q	19	10	.655	0	1	19	11	.633	12	2	1st
12	Tulsa	Missouri Valley	L	21	7	.750	2	1	23	8	.742	16	4	T1st
5	UCLA	Pacific-10	L	21	6	.778	0	1	21	7	.750	13	5	T2d
7	Virginia	Atlantic Coast	L	17	12	.586	1	1	18	13	.581	8	8	T4th
5	Wake Forest	Atlantic Coast	L	20	11	.645	1	1	21	12	.636	9	7	3d
8	Washington St.	Pacific-10	L	20	10	.667	0	1	20	11	.645	10	8	T4th
11	Western Ky.	Sun Belt	L	20	10	.667	0	1	20	11	.645	14	4	1st
9	Wisconsin	Big Ten	L	17	10	.630	1	1	18	11	.621	8	10	7th
12	Wis.-Green Bay	Mid-Continent	Q	26	5	.813	1	1	27	7	.794	15	3	1st

1995 Tournament

Seed	School	Conference	How	Pre-Tourney W	L	Pct.	Tourney W	L	Final W	L	Pct.	Conf. W	L	Fin.
5	Alabama	Southeastern (W)	L	22	9	.710	1	1	23	10	.697	10	6	3d
5	Arizona	Pacific-10	L	23	7	.767	0	1	23	8	.742	13	5	2d
5	Arizona St.	Pacific-10	L	22	8	.733	2	1	24	9	.727	12	6	3d
2	Arkansas	Southeastern (W)	L	27	6	.818	5	1	32	7	.821	12	4	T1st
12	Ball St.	Mid-American	Q	19	10	.655	0	1	19	11	.633	11	7	4th
8	Brigham Young	Western Athletic	L	22	9	.710	0	1	22	10	.688	13	5	T2d
7	Charlotte	Metro	L	19	8	.704	0	1	19	9	.679	8	4	1st
15	Chattanooga	Southern (S)	Q	19	10	.655	0	1	19	11	.633	11	3	1st
7	Cincinnati	Great Midwest	L	21	11	.656	1	1	22	12	.647	7	5	T3d
16	Colgate	Patriot	Q	17	12	.586	0	1	17	13	.567	11	3	T1st
2	Connecticut	Big East	L	25	4	.862	3	1	28	5	.848	16	2	1st
13	Drexel	North Atlantic	Q	22	7	.759	0	1	22	8	.733	12	4	1st
10	Florida	Southeastern (E)	L	17	12	.586	0	1	17	13	.567	8	8	3d
16	Florida Int'l	Trans America	Q	11	18	.379	0	1	11	19	.367	4	12	T9th
6	Georgetown	Big East	L	19	9	.679	2	1	21	10	.677	11	7	4th
14	Gonzaga	West Coast	Q	21	8	.724	0	1	21	9	.700	7	7	4th
11	Illinois	Big Ten	L	19	11	.633	0	1	19	12	.613	11	7	T5th
9	Indiana	Big Ten	L	19	11	.633	0	1	19	12	.613	11	7	T3d
7	Iowa St.	Big Eight	L	22	10	.688	1	1	23	11	.676	6	8	5th
1	Kansas	Big Eight	L	23	5	.821	2	1	25	6	.806	11	3	1st
1	Kentucky	Southeastern (E)	L	25	4	.862	3	1	28	5	.848	14	2	1st
13	Long Beach St.	Big West	Q	20	9	.690	0	1	20	10	.667	13	5	T2d
11	Louisville	Metro	Q	19	13	.594	0	1	19	14	.576	7	5	T2d
13	Manhattan	Metro Atlantic	L	25	4	.862	1	1	26	5	.839	12	2	1st
3	Maryland	Atlantic Coast	L	24	7	.774	2	1	26	8	.765	12	4	T1st
2	Massachusetts	Atlantic 10	Q	26	4	.867	3	1	29	5	.853	13	3	1st
6	Memphis	Great Midwest	L	22	9	.710	2	1	24	10	.706	9	3	2d
12	Miami (Ohio)	Mid-American	L	22	6	.786	1	1	23	7	.767	16	2	1st
9	Michigan	Big Ten	L	17	13	.567	0	1	17	14	.548	11	7	T3d
3	Michigan St.	Big Ten	L	22	5	.815	0	1	22	6	.786	14	4	2d
9	Minnesota	Big Ten	L	19	11	.633	0	1	19	12	.613	10	8	T5th
5	Mississippi St.	Southeastern (W)	L	20	7	.741	2	1	22	8	.733	12	4	T1st
8	Missouri	Big Eight	L	19	8	.704	1	1	20	9	.690	8	6	4th
16	Mt. St. Mary's	Northeast	Q	17	12	.586	0	1	17	13	.567	12	6	T2d

ALL-TIME TOURNAMENT FIELD

Seed	School	Conference	How	Pre-Tourney W	L	Pct.	Tourney W	L	Final W	L	Pct.	Conf. W	L	Fin.
15	Murray St.	Ohio Valley	Q	21	8	.724	0	1	21	9	.700	11	5	T1st
13	Nicholls St.	Southland	Q	24	5	.828	0	1	24	6	.800	17	1	1st
2	North Carolina	Atlantic Coast	L	24	5	.828	4	1	28	6	.824	12	4	T1st
16	N.C. A&T	Mid-Eastern	Q	15	14	.517	0	1	15	15	.500	10	6	1st
14	Old Dominion	Colonial	Q	20	11	.645	1	1	21	12	.636	12	2	1st
4	Oklahoma	Big Eight	L	23	8	.742	0	1	23	9	.719	9	5	3d
4	Oklahoma St.	Big Eight	Q	23	9	.719	4	1	27	10	.730	10	4	2d
6	Oregon	Pacific-10	L	19	8	.704	0	1	19	9	.679	11	7	4th
12	Pennsylvania	Ivy	Q	22	5	.815	0	1	22	6	.786	14	0	1st
3	Purdue	Big Ten	Q	24	6	.800	1	1	25	7	.781	15	3	1st
9	St. Louis	Great Midwest	L	22	7	.759	1	1	23	8	.742	8	4	2d
15	St. Peter's	Metro Atlantic	Q	19	10	.655	0	1	19	11	.633	10	4	T2d
12	Santa Clara	West Coast	L	21	6	.778	0	1	21	7	.750	12	2	1st
10	Southern Ill.	Missouri Valley	Q	23	8	.742	0	1	23	9	.719	13	5	T2d
10	Stanford	Pacific-10	L	19	8	.704	1	1	20	9	.690	10	8	T5th
7	Syracuse	Big East	L	19	9	.679	1	1	20	10	.667	12	6	3d
10	Temple	Atlantic 10	L	19	10	.655	0	1	19	11	.633	10	6	T2d
11	Texas	Southwest	L	22	6	.786	1	1	23	7	.767	11	3	T1st
15	Texas Southern	Southwestern	Q	22	6	.786	0	1	22	7	.759	12	2	1st
9	Tulane	Metro	L	22	9	.710	1	1	23	10	.697	7	5	T2d
6	Tulsa	Missouri Valley	L	22	7	.759	2	1	24	8	.750	15	3	1st
1	UCLA	Pacific-10	Q	25	2	.926	6	0	31	2	.939	16	2	1st
4	Utah	Western Athletic	Q	27	5	.844	1	1	28	6	.824	15	3	1st
3	Villanova	Big East	Q	25	7	.781	0	1	25	8	.758	14	4	2d
4	Virginia	Atlantic Coast	Q	22	8	.733	3	1	25	9	.735	12	4	T1st
1	Wake Forest	Atlantic Coast	Q	24	5	.828	2	1	26	6	.813	12	4	T1st
14	Weber St.	Big Sky	Q	20	8	.714	1	1	21	9	.700	11	3	T1st
8	Western Ky.	Sun Belt	Q	26	3	.897	1	1	27	4	.871	17	1	1st
14	Wis.-Green Bay	Midwestern	Q	22	7	.759	0	1	22	8	.733	11	4	T2d
11	Xavier	Midwestern	L	23	4	.852	0	1	23	5	.821	14	0	1st

1996 Tournament

Seed	School	Conference	How	Pre-Tourney W	L	Pct.	Tourney W	L	Final W	L	Pct.	Conf. W	L	Fin.
3	Arizona	Pacific-10	L	24	6	.800	2	1	26	7	.788	13	5	2d
12	Arkansas	Southeastern (W)	L	18	12	.600	2	1	20	13	.606	9	7	T2d
14	Austin Peay	Ohio Valley	Q	19	10	.655	0	1	19	11	.633	10	6	T2d
11	Boston College	Big East (6)	L	18	10	.643	1	1	19	11	.633	10	8	3d
8	Bradley	Missouri Valley	L	22	7	.759	0	1	22	8	.733	15	3	1st
12	California	Pacific-10	L	17	10	.630	0	1	17	11	.607	11	7	4th
13	Canisius	Metro Atlantic	Q	19	10	.655	0	1	19	11	.633	10	4	T1st
16	UCF	Trans America (E)	Q	11	18	.379	0	1	11	19	.367	6	10	T3d
2	Cincinnati	Conference USA (B)	L	25	4	.862	3	1	28	5	.848	11	3	1st
9	Clemson	Atlantic Coast	L	18	10	.643	0	1	18	11	.621	7	9	6th
16	Colgate	Patriot	Q	15	14	.517	0	1	15	15	.500	9	3	T1st
1	Connecticut	Big East (6)	Q	30	2	.938	2	1	32	3	.914	17	1	1st
12	Drexel	North Atlantic	Q	26	3	.897	1	1	27	4	.871	17	1	1st
8	Duke	Atlantic Coast	L	18	12	.600	0	1	18	13	.581	8	8	T4th
9	Eastern Mich.	Mid-American	Q	24	5	.828	1	1	25	6	.806	14	4	1st
11	George Washington	Atlantic 10 (W)	L	21	7	.750	0	1	21	8	.724	13	3	T1st
2	Georgetown	Big East (7)	L	26	7	.788	3	1	29	8	.784	13	5	1st
8	Georgia	Southeastern (E)	L	19	9	.679	2	1	21	10	.677	9	7	2d
3	Georgia Tech	Atlantic Coast	L	22	11	.667	2	1	24	12	.667	13	3	1st
6	Indiana	Big Ten	L	19	11	.633	0	1	19	12	.613	12	6	T2d
6	Iowa	Big Ten	L	22	8	.733	1	1	23	9	.719	11	7	4th
5	Iowa St.	Big Eight	Q	23	8	.742	1	1	24	9	.727	9	5	2d
2	Kansas	Big Eight	L	26	4	.867	3	1	29	5	.853	12	2	1st
10	Kansas St.	Big Eight	L	17	11	.607	0	1	17	12	.586	7	7	T4th
1	Kentucky	Southeastern (E)	L	28	2	.933	6	0	34	2	.944	16	0	1st
15	La.-Monroe	Southland	Q	16	13	.552	0	1	16	14	.533	13	5	1st
6	Louisville	Conference USA (W)	L	20	11	.645	2	1	22	12	.647	10	4	2d
4	Marquette	Conference USA (B)	L	22	7	.759	1	1	23	8	.742	10	4	2d
7	Maryland	Atlantic Coast	L	17	12	.586	0	1	17	13	.567	8	8	T4th
1	Massachusetts	Atlantic 10 (E)	Q	31	1	.969	4	1	35	2	.946	15	1	1st
5	Memphis	Conference USA (W)	L	22	7	.759	0	1	22	8	.733	11	3	1st
7	Michigan	Big Ten	L	20	11	.645	0	1	20	12	.625	10	8	T5th
5	Mississippi St.	Southeastern (W)	Q	22	7	.759	4	1	26	8	.765	10	6	1st
15	Mississippi Val.	Southwestern	Q	22	6	.786	0	1	22	7	.759	11	3	T1st
13	Monmouth	Northeast	Q	20	9	.690	0	1	20	10	.667	14	4	T2d
13	Montana St.	Big Sky	Q	21	8	.724	0	1	21	9	.700	11	3	1st
7	New Mexico	Western Athletic	Q	27	4	.871	1	1	28	5	.848	14	4	2d
11	New Orleans	Sun Belt	Q	21	8	.724	0	1	21	9	.700	14	4	T1st
6	North Carolina	Atlantic Coast	L	20	10	.667	1	1	21	11	.656	10	6	3d
15	UNC Greensboro	Big South	Q	20	9	.690	0	1	20	10	.667	11	3	1st
14	Northern Ill.	Midwestern	Q	20	9	.690	0	1	20	10	.667	10	6	3d
10	Oklahoma	Big Eight	L	17	12	.586	0	1	17	13	.567	8	6	3d
5	Penn St.	Big Ten	L	21	6	.778	0	1	21	7	.750	12	6	T2d
14	Portland	West Coast	Q	19	10	.655	0	1	19	11	.633	7	7	5th
13	Princeton	Ivy	Q	21	6	.778	1	1	22	7	.759	13	2	1st
1	Purdue	Big Ten	Q	25	5	.833	1	1	26	6	.813	15	3	1st
16	San Jose St.	Big West	Q	13	16	.448	0	1	13	17	.433	9	9	T5th
10	Santa Clara	West Coast	L	19	8	.704	1	1	20	9	.690	10	4	T1st
15	South Carolina St.	Mid-Eastern	Q	22	7	.759	0	1	22	8	.733	14	2	T1st
9	Stanford	Pacific-10	L	19	8	.704	1	1	20	9	.690	12	6	3d
4	Syracuse	Big East (7)	L	24	8	.750	5	1	29	9	.763	12	6	2d
7	Temple	Atlantic 10 (E)	L	19	12	.613	1	1	20	13	.606	12	4	2d
10	Texas	Southwest	L	20	9	.690	1	1	21	10	.677	10	4	3d
3	Texas Tech	Southwest	Q	28	1	.966	2	1	30	2	.938	14	0	1st
11	Tulsa	Missouri Valley	Q	22	7	.759	0	1	22	8	.733	12	6	3d
2	UCLA	Pacific-10	Q	23	7	.767	0	1	23	8	.742	16	2	1st
4	Utah	Western Athletic	Q	25	6	.806	2	1	27	7	.794	15	3	1st
14	Valparaiso	Mid-Continent	Q	21	10	.677	0	1	21	11	.656	13	5	1st
3	Villanova	Big East (6)	L	25	6	.806	1	1	26	7	.788	14	4	2d

ALL-TIME TOURNAMENT FIELD

Seed	School	Conference	How	Pre-Tourney W	L	Pct.	Tourney W	L	Final W	L	Pct.	Conf. W	L	Fin.
12	Va. Commonwealth	Colonial	Q	24	8	.750	0	1	24	9	.727	14	2	1st
9	Virginia Tech	Atlantic 10 (W)	L	22	5	.815	1	1	23	6	.793	13	3	T1st
2	Wake Forest	Atlantic Coast	Q	23	5	.821	3	1	26	6	.813	12	4	2d
16	Western Caro.	Southern (S)	Q	17	12	.586	0	1	17	13	.567	10	4	1st
8	Wis.-Green Bay	Midwestern	L	25	3	.893	0	1	25	4	.862	16	0	1st

1997 Tournament

Seed	School	Conference	How	Pre-Tourney W	L	Pct.	Tourney W	L	Final W	L	Pct.	Conf. W	L	Fin.
4	Arizona	Pacific-10	L	19	9	.679	6	0	25	9	.735	11	7	5th
5	Boston College	Big East (6)	Q	21	8	.724	1	1	22	9	.710	12	6	T1st
12	Boston U.	America East	Q	25	4	.862	0	1	25	5	.833	17	1	1st
14	Butler	Midwestern	Q	23	9	.719	0	1	23	10	.697	12	4	1st
5	California	Pacific-10	L	21	8	.724	2	1	23	9	.719	12	6	T2d
15	Charleston So.	Big South	Q	17	12	.586	0	1	17	13	.567	7	7	4th
12	Col. of Charleston	Trans America (E)	Q	28	2	.933	1	1	29	3	.906	16	0	1st
7	Charlotte	Conference USA (W)	L	21	8	.724	1	1	22	9	.710	10	4	T1st
14	Chattanooga	Southern (S)	Q	22	10	.688	2	1	24	11	.686	11	3	1st
3	Cincinnati	Conference USA (B)	L	25	7	.781	1	1	26	8	.765	12	2	1st
4	Clemson	Atlantic Coast	L	21	9	.700	2	1	23	10	.697	9	7	T4th
9	Colorado	Big 12	L	21	9	.700	1	1	22	10	.688	11	5	2d
15	Coppin St.	Mid-Eastern	Q	21	8	.724	1	1	22	9	.710	15	3	1st
2	Duke	Atlantic Coast	L	23	8	.742	1	1	24	9	.727	12	4	1st
16	Fairfield	Metro Atlantic	Q	11	18	.379	0	1	11	19	.367	2	12	8th
10	Georgetown	Big East (7)	L	20	9	.690	0	1	20	10	.667	11	7	1st
3	Georgia	Southeastern (E)	L	24	8	.750	0	1	24	9	.727	10	6	3d
6	Illinois	Big Ten	L	21	9	.700	1	1	22	10	.688	11	7	T4th
11	Illinois St.	Missouri Valley	Q	24	5	.828	0	1	24	6	.800	14	4	1st
8	Indiana	Big Ten	L	22	10	.688	0	1	22	11	.667	9	9	T6th
8	Iowa	Big Ten	L	21	9	.700	1	1	22	10	.688	12	6	T2d
6	Iowa St.	Big 12	L	20	8	.714	2	1	22	9	.710	10	6	T3d
16	Jackson St.	Southwestern	Q	14	15	.483	0	1	14	16	.467	9	5	2d
1	Kansas	Big 12	Q	32	1	.970	2	1	34	2	.944	15	1	1st
1	Kentucky	Southeastern (E)	Q	30	4	.882	5	1	35	5	.875	13	3	2d
13	Long Island	Northeast	Q	21	8	.724	0	1	21	9	.700	15	3	1st
6	Louisville	Conference USA (W)	L	23	8	.742	3	1	26	9	.743	9	5	3d
7	Marquette	Conference USA (B)	Q	22	8	.733	0	1	22	9	.710	9	5	2d
5	Maryland	Atlantic Coast	L	21	10	.677	0	1	21	11	.656	9	7	T4th
11	Massachusetts	Atlantic 10 (E)	L	19	13	.594	0	1	19	14	.576	11	5	3d
13	Miami (Ohio)	Mid-American	Q	21	8	.724	0	1	21	9	.700	13	5	T1st
1	Minnesota	Big Ten	Q	27	3	.900	4	1	31	4	.886	16	2	1st
8	Mississippi	Southeastern (W)	L	20	8	.714	0	1	20	9	.690	11	5	1st
16	Montana	Big Sky	Q	21	10	.677	0	1	21	11	.656	11	5	2d
15	Murray St.	Ohio Valley	Q	20	9	.690	0	1	20	10	.667	12	6	T1st
15	Navy	Patriot	Q	20	8	.714	0	1	20	9	.690	10	2	1st
3	New Mexico	Western Athletic (M)	L	24	7	.774	1	1	25	8	.758	11	5	3d
1	North Carolina	Atlantic Coast	Q	24	6	.800	4	1	28	7	.800	11	5	T2d
11	Oklahoma	Big 12	L	19	10	.655	0	1	19	11	.633	9	7	6th
14	Old Dominion	Colonial	Q	22	10	.688	0	1	22	11	.667	10	6	T1st
13	Pacific (Cal.)	Big West (W)	Q	24	5	.828	0	1	24	6	.800	12	4	1st
12	Princeton	Ivy	Q	24	3	.889	0	1	24	4	.857	14	0	1st
10	Providence	Big East (7)	L	21	11	.656	3	1	24	12	.667	10	8	T2d
8	Purdue	Big Ten	L	17	11	.607	1	1	18	12	.600	12	6	T2d
9	Rhode Island	Atlantic 10 (E)	L	20	9	.690	0	1	20	10	.667	12	6	T2d
13	South Ala.	Sun Belt	Q	23	6	.793	0	1	23	7	.767	14	4	T1st
2	South Carolina	Southeastern (E)	L	24	7	.774	0	1	24	8	.750	15	1	1st
11	Southern California	Pacific-10	L	17	10	.630	0	1	17	11	.607	10	8	T2d
16	Southwest Tex. St.	Southland	Q	16	12	.571	0	1	16	13	.552	10	6	T1st
6	Stanford	Pacific-10	L	20	7	.741	2	1	22	8	.733	12	6	T2d
4	St. Joseph's	Atlantic 10 (E)	Q	24	6	.800	2	1	26	7	.788	13	3	1st
14	St. Mary's (Cal.)	West Coast	Q	23	7	.767	0	1	23	8	.742	10	4	T1st
9	Temple	Atlantic 10 (E)	L	19	10	.655	1	1	20	11	.645	10	6	4th
10	Texas	Big 12	L	16	11	.593	2	1	18	12	.600	10	6	T3d
5	Tulsa	Western Athletic (M)	L	23	9	.719	1	1	24	10	.706	12	4	2d
2	UCLA	Pacific-10	Q	21	7	.750	3	1	24	8	.750	15	3	1st
2	Utah	Western Athletic (M)	Q	26	3	.897	3	1	29	4	.879	15	1	1st
12	Valparaiso	Mid-Continent	Q	24	6	.800	0	1	24	7	.774	13	3	1st
10	Vanderbilt	Southeastern (E)	L	19	11	.633	0	1	19	12	.613	9	7	4th
4	Villanova	Big East (6)	L	23	9	.719	1	1	24	10	.706	12	6	T1st
9	Virginia	Atlantic Coast	L	18	12	.600	0	1	18	13	.581	7	9	6th
3	Wake Forest	Atlantic Coast	L	23	6	.793	1	1	24	7	.774	11	5	T2d
7	Wisconsin	Big Ten	L	18	9	.667	0	1	18	10	.643	11	7	T4th
7	Xavier	Atlantic 10 (W)	L	22	5	.815	1	1	23	6	.793	13	3	1st

1998 Tournament

Seed	School	Conference	How	Pre-Tourney W	L	Pct.	Tourney W	L	Final W	L	Pct.	Conf. W	L	Fin.
1	Arizona	Pacific-10	Q	27	4	.871	3	1	30	5	.857	17	1	1st
6	Arkansas	Southeastern (W)	L	23	8	.742	1	1	24	9	.727	11	5	2d
13	Butler	Midwestern	Q	22	10	.688	0	1	22	11	.667	8	6	3d
14	Col. of Charleston	Trans America (E)	Q	24	5	.828	0	1	24	6	.800	14	2	1st
8	Charlotte	Conference USA (A)	L	19	10	.655	1	1	20	11	.645	13	3	2d
2	Cincinnati	Conference USA (A)	Q	26	5	.839	1	1	27	6	.818	14	2	1st
6	Clemson	Atlantic Coast	L	18	13	.581	0	1	18	14	.563	7	9	T4th
2	Connecticut	Big East (6)	Q	29	4	.879	3	1	32	5	.865	15	3	1st
14	Davidson	Southern (N)	Q	20	9	.690	0	1	20	10	.667	13	2	T1st
15	Delaware	America East	Q	20	9	.690	0	1	20	10	.667	12	6	T1st
10	Detroit	Midwestern	L	24	5	.828	1	1	25	6	.806	12	2	T1st
1	Duke	Atlantic Coast	Q	29	3	.906	3	1	32	4	.889	15	1	1st
13	Eastern Mich.	Mid-American (W)	Q	20	9	.690	0	1	20	10	.667	13	5	T3d
15	Fairleigh Dickinson	Northeast	Q	23	6	.793	0	1	23	7	.767	13	3	2d
12	Florida St.	Atlantic Coast	L	17	13	.567	1	1	18	14	.563	6	10	T6th
9	George Washington	Atlantic 10 (W)	L	24	8	.750	0	1	24	9	.727	11	5	T1st
5	Illinois	Big Ten	L	22	9	.710	1	1	23	10	.697	13	3	T1st
9	Illinois St.	Missouri Valley	Q	24	5	.828	1	1	25	6	.806	16	2	1st
9	Ill.-Chicago	Midwestern	Q	22	5	.815	0	1	22	6	.786	12	2	1st
7	Indiana	Big Ten	L	19	11	.633	1	1	20	12	.625	9	7	T5th
12	Iona	Metro Atlantic	Q	27	5	.844	0	1	27	6	.818	15	3	1st
1	Kansas	Big 12	Q	34	3	.919	1	1	35	4	.897	15	1	1st

ALL-TIME TOURNAMENT FIELD

				Pre-Tourney			Tourney		Final			Conf.		
Seed	School	Conference	How	W	L	Pct.	W	L	W	L	Pct.	W	L	Fin.
2	Kentucky	Southeastern (E)	Q	29	4	.879	6	0	35	4	.897	14	2	1st
4	Maryland	Atlantic Coast	L	19	10	.655	2	1	21	11	.656	10	6	3d
7	Massachusetts	Atlantic 10 (E)	L	21	10	.677	0	1	21	11	.656	12	4	T2d
11	Miami (Fla.)	Big East (7)	L	18	9	.667	0	1	18	10	.643	11	7	2d
3	Michigan	Big Ten	Q	24	8	.750	1	1	25	9	.735	11	5	4th
4	Michigan St.	Big Ten	L	20	7	.741	2	1	22	8	.733	13	3	T1st
4	Mississippi	Southeastern (W)	L	19	10	.655	0	1	19	11	.633	12	4	1st
9	Murray St.	Ohio Valley	Q	29	3	.906	0	1	29	4	.879	16	2	1st
16	Navy	Patriot	Q	19	10	.655	0	1	19	11	.633	10	2	T1st
11	Nebraska	Big 12	L	20	11	.645	0	1	20	12	.625	10	6	4th
12	UNLV	Western Athletic (M)	Q	20	12	.625	0	1	20	13	.606	7	7	5th
4	New Mexico	Western Athletic (M)	L	23	7	.767	1	1	24	8	.750	11	3	2d
16	Nicholls St.	Southland	Q	19	9	.679	0	1	19	10	.655	15	1	1st
1	North Carolina	Atlantic Coast	L	30	3	.909	4	1	34	4	.895	13	3	2d
15	Northern Ariz.	Big Sky	Q	21	7	.750	0	1	21	8	.724	13	3	1st
10	Oklahoma	Big 12	L	22	10	.688	0	1	22	11	.667	11	5	T2d
8	Oklahoma St.	Big 12	L	21	6	.778	1	1	22	7	.759	11	5	T2d
16	Prairie View	Southwestern	Q	13	16	.448	0	1	13	17	.433	6	10	T6th
5	Princeton	Ivy	Q	26	1	.963	1	1	27	2	.931	14	0	1st
2	Purdue	Big Ten	L	26	7	.788	2	1	28	8	.778	12	4	3d
16	Radford	Big South	Q	20	9	.690	0	1	20	10	.667	10	2	2d
8	Rhode Island	Atlantic 10 (E)	L	22	8	.733	3	1	25	9	.735	12	4	T2d
14	Richmond	Colonial	Q	22	7	.759	1	1	23	8	.742	12	4	3d
7	St. John's (N.Y.)	Big East (6)	L	22	9	.710	0	1	22	10	.688	13	5	2d
10	St. Louis	Conference USA (A)	L	21	10	.677	1	1	22	11	.667	11	5	3d
14	San Francisco	West Coast	Q	19	10	.655	0	1	19	11	.633	7	7	T4th
12	South Ala.	Sun Belt	Q	21	6	.778	0	1	21	7	.750	14	4	T1st
3	South Carolina	Southeastern (E)	L	23	7	.767	0	1	23	8	.742	11	5	2d
15	South Carolina St.	Mid-Eastern	Q	22	7	.759	0	1	22	8	.733	16	2	2d
3	Stanford	Pacific-10	L	26	4	.867	4	1	30	5	.857	15	3	2d
5	Syracuse	Big East (7)	L	24	8	.750	2	1	26	9	.743	12	6	1st
7	Temple	Atlantic 10 (E)	L	21	8	.724	0	1	21	9	.700	13	3	1st
8	Tennessee	Southeastern (E)	L	20	8	.714	0	1	20	9	.690	9	7	3d
5	TCU	Western Athletic (P)	L	27	5	.844	0	1	27	6	.818	14	0	1st
6	UCLA	Pacific-10	L	22	8	.733	2	1	24	9	.727	12	6	3d
3	Utah	Western Athletic (M)	L	25	3	.893	5	1	30	4	.882	12	2	1st
13	Utah St.	Big West (E)	Q	25	7	.781	0	1	25	8	.758	13	3	1st
13	Valparaiso	Mid-Continent	Q	21	9	.700	2	1	23	10	.697	13	3	1st
11	Washington	Pacific-10	L	18	9	.667	2	1	20	10	.667	11	7	4th
10	West Virginia	Big East (6)	L	22	8	.733	2	1	24	9	.727	11	7	3d
11	Western Mich.	Mid-American (W)	L	20	7	.741	0	1	21	8	.724	14	4	T1st
6	Xavier	Atlantic 10 (W)	Q	22	7	.759	0	1	22	8	.733	11	5	T1st

1999 Tournament

				Pre-Tourney			Tourney		Final			Conf.		
Seed	School	Conference	How	W	L	Pct.	W	L	W	L	Pct.	W	L	Fin.
12	UAB	Conference USA (N)	L	20	11	.645	0	1	20	12	.625	10	6	1st
15	Alcorn St.	Southwestern	Q	23	6	.793	0	1	23	7	.767	14	2	1st
4	Arizona	Pacific-10	L	22	6	.786	0	1	22	7	.759	13	5	2d
4	Arkansas	Southeastern (W)	L	22	10	.688	1	1	23	11	.676	9	7	2d
15	Arkansas St.	Sun Belt	Q	18	11	.621	0	1	18	12	.600	9	5	2d
1	Auburn	Southeastern (W)	L	27	3	.900	2	1	29	4	.879	14	2	1st
3	Cincinnati	Conference USA (A)	L	26	5	.839	1	1	27	6	.818	12	4	1st
8	Col. of Charleston	Southern (S)	Q	28	2	.933	0	1	28	3	.903	16	0	1st
5	Charlotte	Conference USA (A)	Q	22	10	.688	1	1	23	11	.676	10	6	T3d
1	Connecticut	Big East	Q	28	2	.933	6	0	34	2	.944	16	2	1st
10	Creighton	Missouri Valley	Q	21	9	.724	1	1	22	9	.710	11	7	T2d
13	Delaware	America East	Q	25	5	.833	0	1	25	6	.806	15	3	T1st
12	Detroit	Midwestern	Q	24	5	.828	1	1	25	6	.806	12	2	1st
1	Duke	Atlantic Coast	Q	32	1	.970	5	1	37	2	.949	16	0	1st
11	Evansville	Missouri Valley	L	23	9	.719	0	1	23	10	.697	13	5	1st
6	Florida	Southeastern (E)	L	20	8	.714	2	1	22	9	.710	10	6	3d
16	Florida A&M	Mid-Eastern	Q	12	18	.400	0	1	12	19	.387	8	11	8th
14	George Mason	Colonial	Q	19	10	.655	0	1	19	11	.633	13	3	1st
11	George Washington	Atlantic 10 (W)	L	20	8	.714	0	1	20	9	.690	13	3	1st
10	Gonzaga	West Coast	Q	25	6	.806	3	1	28	7	.800	12	2	1st
6	Indiana	Big Ten	L	22	10	.688	1	1	23	11	.676	9	7	T3d
5	Iowa	Big Ten	L	18	9	.667	2	1	20	10	.667	9	7	T3d
6	Kansas	Big 12	Q	22	9	.710	1	1	23	10	.697	11	5	T2d
11	Kent St.	Mid-American (E)	Q	23	6	.793	0	1	23	7	.767	13	5	2d
3	Kentucky	Southeastern (E)	Q	25	8	.758	3	1	28	9	.757	11	5	2d
15	Lafayette	Patriot	Q	22	7	.759	0	1	22	8	.733	10	2	1st
7	Louisville	Conference USA (A)	L	19	10	.655	0	1	19	11	.633	11	5	2d
2	Maryland	Atlantic Coast	L	26	5	.839	2	1	28	6	.824	13	3	2d
2	Miami (Fla.)	Big East	L	22	6	.786	1	1	23	7	.767	22	6	2d
10	Miami (Ohio)	Mid-American (E)	L	22	7	.759	2	1	24	8	.750	15	3	1st
1	Michigan St.	Big Ten	Q	29	4	.879	4	1	33	5	.868	15	1	1st
7	Minnesota	Big Ten	L	17	10	.630	0	1	17	11	.607	8	8	6th
9	Mississippi	Southeastern (W)	L	19	12	.613	1	1	20	13	.606	8	8	T3d
8	Missouri	Big 12	L	20	8	.714	0	1	20	9	.690	11	5	T2d
16	Mt. St. Mary's	Northeast	Q	15	14	.517	0	1	15	15	.500	10	10	T5th
13	Murray St.	Ohio Valley	Q	27	5	.844	0	1	27	6	.818	16	2	1st
9	New Mexico	Western Athletic (P)	Q	24	8	.750	1	1	25	9	.735	9	5	T2d
14	New Mexico St.	Big West (E)	Q	23	9	.719	0	1	23	10	.697	12	4	T1st
3	North Carolina	Atlantic Coast	L	24	9	.727	0	1	24	10	.706	10	6	3d
4	Ohio St.	Big Ten	L	23	8	.742	4	1	27	9	.750	12	4	2d
13	Oklahoma	Big 12	L	20	10	.667	2	1	22	11	.667	11	5	T2d
9	Oklahoma St.	Big 12	L	22	10	.688	1	1	23	11	.676	10	6	T5th
11	Pennsylvania	Ivy	Q	21	5	.808	0	1	21	6	.778	12	1	1st

				Pre-Tourney			Tourney		Final			Conf.		
Seed	School	Conference	How	W	L	Pct.	W	L	W	L	Pct.	W	L	Fin.
10	Purdue	Big Ten	L	19	12	.613	2	1	21	13	.618	7	9	7th
12	Rhode Island	Atlantic 10 (E)	Q	20	12	.625	0	1	20	13	.606	10	6	2d
3	St. John's (N.Y.)	Big East	L	25	8	.758	3	1	28	9	.757	14	4	3d
14	Samford	Trans America	Q	24	5	.828	0	1	24	6	.800	15	1	1st
13	Siena	Metro Atlantic	Q	25	5	.833	0	1	25	6	.806	13	5	T1st
12	Southwest Mo. St.	Missouri Valley	L	20	10	.667	2	1	22	11	.667	11	7	T2d
2	Stanford	Pacific-10	Q	25	6	.806	1	1	26	7	.788	15	3	1st
8	Syracuse	Big East	L	21	11	.656	0	1	21	12	.636	10	8	T4th
6	Temple	Atlantic 10 (E)	L	21	10	.677	3	1	24	11	.686	13	3	1st
4	Tennessee	Southeastern (E)	L	20	8	.714	1	1	21	9	.700	12	4	1st
7	Texas	Big 12	L	19	12	.613	0	1	19	13	.594	13	3	1st
16	Texas-San Antonio	Southland	Q	18	10	.643	0	1	18	11	.621	13	5	1st
9	Tulsa	Western Athletic (M)	L	22	9	.710	1	1	23	10	.697	9	5	T1st
5	UCLA	Pacific-10	L	22	8	.733	0	1	22	9	.710	12	6	3d
2	Utah	Western Athletic (P)	Q	27	4	.871	1	1	28	5	.848	14	0	1st
15	Valparaiso	Mid-Continent	Q	23	8	.742	0	1	23	9	.719	10	4	T1st
8	Villanova	Big East	L	21	10	.677	0	1	21	11	.656	10	8	T4th
7	Washington	Pacific-10	L	17	11	.607	0	1	17	12	.586	10	8	4th
14	Weber St.	Big Sky	Q	24	7	.774	1	1	25	8	.758	13	3	1st
16	Winthrop	Big South	Q	21	7	.750	0	1	21	8	.724	9	1	1st
5	Wisconsin	Big Ten	L	22	9	.710	0	1	22	10	.688	9	7	T3d

2000 Tournament

				Pre-Tourney			Tourney		Final			Conf.		
Seed	School	Conference	How	W	L	Pct.	W	L	W	L	Pct.	W	L	Fin.
14	Appalachian St.	Southern (N)	Q	23	8	.742	0	1	23	9	.719	13	3	1st
1	Arizona	Pacific-10	Q	26	6	.813	1	1	27	7	.794	15	3	T1st
11	Arkansas	Southeastern (W)	Q	19	14	.576	0	1	19	15	.559	7	9	3rd
7	Auburn	Southeastern (W)	L	23	9	.719	1	1	24	10	.706	9	7	2nd
11	Ball St.	Mid-American (W)	Q	22	8	.733	0	1	22	9	.710	11	7	T1st
12	Butler	Midwestern	Q	23	7	.767	0	1	23	8	.742	12	2	1st
15	Central Conn. St.	Northeast	Q	25	5	.833	0	1	25	6	.806	15	3	1st
2	Cincinnati	Conference USA (A)	L	28	3	.903	1	1	29	4	.879	16	0	1st
5	Connecticut	Big East	L	24	9	.727	1	1	25	10	.714	10	6	T4th
10	Creighton	Missouri Valley	Q	23	9	.719	0	1	23	10	.697	11	7	4th
11	Dayton	Atlantic 10 (W)	L	22	8	.733	0	1	22	9	.710	11	5	1st
9	DePaul	Conference USA (A)	L	21	11	.656	0	1	21	12	.636	9	7	3rd
1	Duke	Atlantic Coast	Q	27	4	.871	2	1	29	5	.853	15	1	1st
5	Florida	Southeastern (E)	L	24	7	.774	5	1	29	8	.784	12	4	T1st
9	Fresno St.	Western Athletic	L	24	9	.727	0	1	24	10	.706	11	3	2nd
10	Gonzaga	West Coast	Q	24	8	.750	2	1	26	9	.743	10	3	2nd
14	Hofstra	America East	Q	24	6	.800	0	1	24	7	.774	16	2	1st
4	Illinois	Big Ten	L	21	9	.700	1	1	22	10	.688	11	5	4th
6	Indiana	Big Ten	L	20	8	.714	0	1	20	9	.690	10	6	5th
12	Indiana St.	Missouri Valley	L	22	9	.710	0	1	22	10	.688	14	4	1st
14	Iona	Metro Atlantic	Q	20	10	.667	0	1	20	11	.645	13	5	2nd
2	Iowa St.	Big 12	Q	29	4	.879	3	1	32	5	.865	14	2	1st
16	Jackson St.	Southwestern	Q	17	15	.531	0	1	17	16	.515	10	8	T4th
8	Kansas	Big 12	L	23	9	.719	1	1	24	10	.706	11	5	5th
5	Kentucky	Southeastern (E)	L	22	9	.710	1	1	23	10	.697	12	4	T1st
15	Lafayette	Patriot	Q	24	6	.800	0	1	24	7	.774	11	1	T1st
16	Lamar	Southland	Q	15	15	.500	0	1	15	16	.484	8	10	T6th
4	LSU	Southeastern (W)	L	26	5	.839	2	1	28	6	.824	12	4	1st
13	La.-Lafayette	Sun Belt	Q	25	8	.758	0	1	25	9	.735	13	3	T1st
7	Louisville	Conference USA (A)	L	19	11	.633	0	1	19	12	.613	10	6	2nd
3	Maryland	Atlantic Coast	L	24	9	.727	1	1	25	10	.714	11	5	2nd
6	Miami (Fla.)	Big East	L	21	10	.677	2	1	23	11	.676	13	3	T1st
1	Michigan St.	Big Ten	Q	26	7	.788	6	0	32	7	.821	13	3	T1st
9	Missouri	Big 12	L	18	12	.600	0	1	18	13	.581	10	6	6th
10	UNLV	Mountain West	L	23	7	.767	0	1	23	8	.742	10	4	T1st
8	North Carolina	Atlantic Coast	L	18	13	.581	4	1	22	14	.611	9	7	T3rd
15	UNC Wilmington	Colonial	Q	18	12	.600	0	1	18	13	.581	8	8	4th
15	Northern Ariz.	Big Sky	Q	20	10	.667	0	1	20	11	.645	11	5	3rd
3	Ohio St.	Big Ten	L	22	6	.786	1	1	23	7	.767	13	3	T1st
3	Oklahoma	Big 12	L	26	6	.813	1	1	27	7	.794	12	4	T3rd
3	Oklahoma St.	Big 12	L	24	6	.800	3	1	27	7	.794	12	4	T3rd
7	Oregon	Pacific-10	L	22	7	.759	0	1	22	8	.733	13	5	3rd
13	Pennsylvania	Ivy	Q	21	7	.750	0	1	21	8	.724	14	0	1st
11	Pepperdine	West Coast	L	24	8	.750	1	1	25	9	.735	12	2	1st
6	Purdue	Big Ten	L	21	9	.700	3	1	24	10	.706	12	4	3rd
12	St. Bonaventure	Atlantic 10 (E)	L	21	9	.700	0	1	21	10	.677	11	5	2nd
2	St. John's (N.Y.)	Big East	L	24	7	.774	1	1	25	8	.758	12	4	3rd
9	St. Louis	Conference USA (A)	Q	19	13	.594	0	1	19	14	.576	7	9	T5th
13	Samford	Trans America	Q	21	10	.677	0	1	21	11	.656	12	6	T3rd
10	Seton Hall	Big East	L	20	9	.690	2	1	22	10	.688	10	6	T4th
16	South Carolina St.	Mid-Eastern	Q	20	13	.606	0	1	20	14	.588	14	5	1st
13	Southeast Mo. St.	Ohio Valley	Q	24	6	.800	0	1	24	7	.774	14	4	T1st
1	Stanford	Pacific-10	L	26	3	.897	1	1	27	4	.871	15	3	T1st
4	Syracuse	Big East	L	24	5	.828	2	1	26	6	.813	13	3	T1st
2	Temple	Atlantic 10 (E)	Q	26	5	.839	1	1	27	6	.818	14	2	1st
4	Tennessee	Southeastern (E)	L	24	6	.800	2	1	26	7	.788	12	4	T1st
5	Texas	Big 12	L	23	8	.742	1	1	24	9	.727	13	3	2nd
7	Tulsa	Western Athletic	L	29	4	.879	3	1	32	5	.865	12	3	1st
6	UCLA	Pacific-10	L	19	11	.633	2	1	21	12	.636	10	8	T4th
8	Utah	Mountain West	L	22	8	.733	1	1	23	9	.719	10	4	T1st
12	Utah St.	Big West (E)	L	28	5	.848	0	1	28	6	.824	16	0	1st
16	Valparaiso	Mid-Continent	Q	19	12	.613	0	1	19	13	.594	10	6	T2nd
14	Winthrop	Big South	Q	21	8	.724	0	1	21	9	.700	11	3	2nd
8	Wisconsin	Big Ten	L	18	13	.581	4	1	22	14	.611	8	8	6th

ALL-TIME TOURNAMENT FIELD

2001 Tournament

Seed	School	Conference	How	Pre-Tourney W	L	Pct.	Tourney W	L	Final W	L	Pct.	Conf. W	L	Fin.
16	Alabama St.	Southwestern	Q	22	8	.733	0	1	22	9	.710	15	3	1st
2	Arizona	Pacific 10	L	23	7	.767	5	1	28	8	.778	15	3	2d
7	Arkansas	Southeastern (W)	L	20	10	.667	0	1	20	11	.645	10	6	2d
3	Boston College	Big East (E)	Q	26	4	.867	1	1	27	5	.844	13	3	1st
12	Brigham Young	Mountain West	Q	24	8	.750	0	1	24	9	.727	10	4	T1st
10	Butler	Midwestern	Q	23	7	.767	1	1	24	8	.750	11	3	1st
8	California	Pacific 10	L	20	10	.667	0	1	20	11	.645	11	7	T4th
13	Cal St. Northridge	Big Sky	Q	22	9	.710	0	1	22	10	.688	13	3	1st
9	Charlotte	Conference USA (A)	Q	21	10	.677	1	1	22	11	.667	10	6	2d
5	Cincinnati	Conference USA (A)	L	23	9	.719	2	1	25	10	.714	11	5	1st
10	Creighton	Missouri Valley	L	24	7	.774	0	1	24	8	.750	14	4	1st
1	Duke	Atlantic Coast	Q	29	4	.879	6	0	35	4	.897	13	3	T1st
15	Eastern Ill.	Ohio Valley	Q	21	9	.700	0	1	21	10	.677	11	5	T2d
3	Florida	Southeastern (E)	L	23	6	.793	1	1	24	7	.774	12	4	T1st
9	Fresno St.	Western Athletic	L	25	6	.806	1	1	26	7	.788	13	3	1st
14	George Mason	Colonial	Q	18	11	.621	0	1	18	12	.600	11	5	T2d
10	Georgetown	Big East (W)	L	23	7	.767	2	1	25	8	.758	9	6	T2d
8	Georgia	Southeastern (E)	L	16	14	.533	0	1	16	15	.516	9	7	3d
11	Georgia St.	Trans America	Q	28	4	.875	1	1	29	5	.853	16	2	1st
8	Georgia Tech	Atlantic Coast	L	17	12	.586	0	1	17	13	.567	8	8	T5th
12	Gonzaga	West Coast	Q	24	6	.800	2	1	26	7	.788	13	1	1st
15	Hampton	Mid-Eastern	Q	24	6	.800	1	1	25	7	.781	14	4	T1st
12	Hawaii	Western Athletic	Q	17	13	.567	0	1	17	14	.548	8	8	T5th
13	Hofstra	America East	Q	26	4	.867	0	1	26	5	.839	16	2	1st
15	Holy Cross	Patriot	Q	22	7	.759	0	1	22	8	.733	10	2	1st
1	Illinois	Big Ten	L	24	7	.774	3	1	27	8	.771	13	3	T1st
4	Indiana	Big Ten	L	21	12	.636	0	1	21	13	.618	10	6	4th
13	Indiana St.	Missouri Valley	Q	21	11	.656	1	1	22	12	.647	10	8	T4th
14	Iona	Metro Atlantic	Q	22	10	.688	0	1	22	11	.667	12	6	T1st
7	Iowa	Big Ten	Q	22	11	.667	1	1	23	12	.657	7	9	T6th
2	Iowa St.	Big 12	L	25	5	.833	0	1	25	6	.806	13	3	1st
4	Kansas	Big 12	L	24	6	.800	2	1	26	7	.788	12	4	T2d
13	Kent St.	Mid-American (E)	Q	23	9	.719	1	1	24	10	.706	13	5	1st
2	Kentucky	Southeastern (E)	L	22	9	.710	2	1	24	10	.706	12	4	T1st
3	Maryland	Atlantic Coast	L	21	10	.677	4	1	25	11	.694	10	6	3d
1	Michigan St.	Big Ten	L	24	4	.857	4	1	28	5	.848	13	3	T1st
3	Mississippi	Southeastern (W)	L	25	7	.781	2	1	27	8	.771	11	5	1st
9	Missouri	Big 12	L	19	12	.613	1	1	20	13	.606	9	7	6th
16	Monmouth	Northeast	Q	21	9	.700	0	1	21	10	.677	15	5	2d
2	North Carolina	Atlantic Coast	L	25	6	.806	1	1	26	7	.788	13	3	T1st
16	UNC Greensboro	Southern (N)	Q	19	11	.633	0	1	19	12	.613	10	6	2d
16	Northwestern St.	Southland	Q	18	12	.600	1	1	19	13	.594	11	9	T4th
6	Notre Dame	Big East (W)	L	19	9	.679	1	1	20	10	.667	11	5	3d
5	Ohio St.	Big Ten	L	20	10	.667	0	1	20	11	.645	11	5	3d
4	Oklahoma	Big 12	Q	26	6	.813	0	1	26	7	.788	12	4	T2d
11	Oklahoma St.	Big 12	L	20	9	.690	0	1	20	10	.667	10	6	5th
7	Penn St.	Big Ten	L	19	11	.633	2	1	21	12	.636	7	9	T6th
15	Princeton	Ivy	Q	16	10	.615	0	1	16	11	.593	11	3	1st
10	Providence	Big East (E)	L	21	9	.700	0	1	21	10	.677	11	5	2d
9	St. Joseph's	Atlantic 10	L	25	6	.806	1	1	26	7	.788	14	2	1st
6	Southern California	Pacific 10	L	21	9	.700	3	1	24	10	.706	11	7	T4th
14	Southern Utah	Mid-Continent	Q	25	5	.833	0	1	25	6	.806	13	3	T1st
1	Stanford	Pacific 10	Q	28	2	.933	3	1	31	3	.912	16	2	1st
5	Syracuse	Big East (W)	L	24	8	.750	1	1	25	9	.735	9	6	T2d
11	Temple	Atlantic 10	Q	21	12	.636	3	1	24	13	.618	12	4	T2d
8	Tennessee	Southeastern (E)	L	22	10	.688	0	1	22	11	.667	8	8	4th
6	Texas	Big 12	L	25	8	.758	0	1	25	9	.735	12	4	T2d
4	UCLA	Pacific 10	L	21	8	.724	2	1	23	9	.719	14	4	3d
12	Utah St.	Big West	Q	27	5	.844	1	1	28	6	.824	13	3	2d
5	Virginia	Atlantic Coast	L	20	8	.714	0	1	20	9	.690	9	7	4th
7	Wake Forest	Atlantic Coast	L	19	10	.655	0	1	19	11	.633	8	8	T5th
14	Western Ky.	Sun Belt (E)	Q	24	6	.800	0	1	24	7	.774	14	2	1st
16	Winthrop	Big South	Q	18	12	.600	0	1	18	13	.581	11	3	2d
6	Wisconsin	Big Ten	L	18	10	.643	0	1	18	11	.621	9	7	5th
11	Xavier	Atlantic 10	L	21	7	.750	0	1	21	8	.724	12	4	T2d

THE TOURNAMENT FIELD

Key to the Conferences and Their Histories:
(A)—American Division
AAWU—Athletic Association of Western Universities (1960-68) Past name for Pacific-10
America East (1980-present) Formerly ECAC North (1980-83), ECAC North Atlantic (1984-89) and North Atlantic (1990-96)
American South (1988-91)
Athletic Association of Western Universities—AAWU (1960-68) Past name for Pacific-10
Atlantic Sun (1979-present) Formerly Trans America (1979-2001)
Atlantic Coast (1954-present)
Atlantic 10 (1977-present) Formerly Eastern Collegiate Basketball League (1977) and Eastern 8 (1978-82); also known as Eastern AA
(B)—Blue Division
Big East (1980-present)
Big Eight (1908-96) Formerly Missouri Valley (1908-28), Big Six (1929-47) and Big Seven (1948-58)
Big Five (1960-62) Past name for Pacific-10
Big Nine (1947-48) Past name for Big Ten
Big Seven (1938-43, 46-47) Past name for Mountain States
Big Seven (1948-58) Past name for Big Eight
Big Six (1929-47) Past name for Big Eight
Big Six (1963) Past name for Pacific-10
Big Sky (1964-present)
Big South (1986-present)
Big Ten (1895-present) Formerly Big Nine (1947-48); Also known as Intercollegiate Conference of Faculty Representatives and Western Intercollegiate
Big 12 (1997-present)
Big West (1970-present) Formerly Pacific Coast (1970-88)
Border (1932-40, 42-62)
Colonial (1983-present) Formerly ECAC South (1983-85)
(E)—East or Eastern Division
East Coast (1959-92, 94) Formerly Middle Atlantic (1959-74)
Eastern AA (1979-82) Past name for Atlantic 10
Eastern Collegiate Basketball League (1977-78) Past name for Atlantic 10
Eastern 8 (1978-82) Past name for Atlantic 10
Eastern Intercollegiate League—Also known as Ivy Group
ECAC Metro (1975-81)
ECAC Metro (1982-88) Past name for Northeast
ECAC North (1980-83) Past name for America East
ECAC North Atlantic (1984-89) Past name for America East
ECAC South (1975-82)
ECAC South (1983-85) Past name for Colonial
ECAC Upstate (1975-78)
Florida Intercollegiate (1960) Non-Division I
Great Midwest (1992-95)
Gulf Star (1985-87)
Horizon (1980-present) Formerly Midwestern (1980-2001)
Indiana Collegiate (1962) Non-Division I
Intercollegiate Conference of Faculty Representatives—Also known as Big Ten

Ivy Group (1902-08, 11-18, 20-present) Also known as Eastern Intercollegiate League
Kentucky Intercollegiate (1940) Non-Division I
Little Three (1955) Non-Division I
(M)—Mountain Division
Metro (1976-95) Short for Metropolitan Collegiate
Metro Atlantic (1982-present)
Metropolitan Collegiate—See Metro
Metropolitan New York (1943, 46-63)
Mid-American (1947-present)
Mid-Continent (1983-present)
Mid-Eastern (1972-present)
Middle Atlantic (1959-74) Past name for East Coast
Midwestern (1980-2001) Past name for Horizon
Missouri Valley (1908-present) Big Eight also claims Missouri Valley history from 1908-28
Mountain States (1911-43, 46-62) Formerly Rocky Mountain (1911-37); also known as Big Seven (1938-43, 46-47), Skyline Six (1948-51) and Skyline Eight (1952-62)
(N)—North or Northern Division; or National Division (Conference USA only)
New Jersey-New York 7 (1977-79)
North Atlantic (1990-96) Past name for America East
Northeast (1982-present) Formerly ECAC Metro (1982-88)
Ohio Valley (1949-present)
(P)—Pacific Division
Pacific Coast (1916-1959) Past name for Pacific-10
Pacific Coast (1970-88) Past name for Big West
Pacific 8 (1969-78) Past name for Pacific-10
Pacific-10 (1916-17, 19-present) Formerly Pacific Coast (1916-1959), Big Five (1960-62), Big Six (1963), Athletic Association of Western Universities (AAWU) (1960-68) and Pacific 8 (1969-78)
Patriot League (1991-present)
President's Athletic (1956) Non-Division I
(R)—Red Division
Rocky Mountain (1911-37) Past name for Mountain States
Skyline Eight (1952-62) Past name for Mountain States
Skyline Six (1948-51) Past name for Mountain States
(S)—South or Southern Division
Southeastern (1933-present)
Southern (1922-present)
Southland (1964-present)
Southwest (1915-96)
Southwestern (1978-present)
Sun Belt (1977-present)
Trans America (1979-2001) Past name for Atlantic Sun
(W)—West or Western Division; or White Division (Conference USA only)
West Coast (1953-present)
Western Intercollegiate - Past name for Big Ten
Western Athletic (1963-present)
Western New York Little Three (1947-51, 53-58)
Yankee (1938-43, 46-76)

ALL-TIME TOURNAMENT FIELD—TEAM CHAMPIONS

Team Champions

1939 CHAMPIONSHIP GAME, March 27 at Evanston, IL .... OREGON 46, OHIO ST. 33

Oregon	FG	FT-A	PF	TP
Laddie Gale*	3	4-5	1	10
John Dick*	4	5-5	3	13
Slim Wintermute*	2	0-1	1	4
Bobby Anet*	4	2-3	3	10
Wally Johansen*	4	1-2	1	9
Matt Pavalunas	0	0-0	0	0
Ford Mullen	0	0-0	0	0
TOTALS	17	12-16	9	46

Ohio St.	FG	FT-A	PF	TP
Jimmy Hull*	5	2-4	2	12
Richard Baker*	0	0-0	0	0
John Schick*	1	0-0	1	2
Robert Lynch*	3	1-3	3	7
Jack Dawson*	1	0-0	4	2
Gilbert Mickelson	0	0-0	2	0
William Sattler	3	1-2	0	7
Richard Boughner	1	0-0	0	2
Charles Maag	0	0-0	0	0
Don Scott	0	1-1	1	1
Robert Stafford	0	0-0	0	0
TOTALS	14	5-10	13	33

Halftime: Oregon 21, Ohio St. 16. Officials: Lyle Clarno, John Getchell. Attendance: 5,500.

1939 Oregon—Front Row (left to right): Wally Johansen, Slim Wintermute, Bobby Anet, head coach Howard Hobson, Laddie Gale and John Dick. Back Row: Bob Hardy, Red McNeely, Jay Langston, Ford Mullen, Matt Pavalunas, athletic trainer Bob Officer, Ted Sarpola and Earl Sandness.

1940 CHAMPIONSHIP GAME, March 30 at Kansas City, MO .... INDIANA 60, KANSAS 42

Indiana	FG	FT-A	PF	TP
Herman Schaefer	4	1-1	1	9
Jay McCreary	6	0-0	2	12
Paul Armstrong	4	2-3	3	10
Jim Gridley	0	0-0	0	0
Bob Menke	0	0-0	1	0
Bill Menke	2	1-2	3	5
Marv Huffman	5	2-3	4	12
Andy Zimmer	2	1-1	1	5
Bob Dro	3	1-1	4	7
Ralph Dorsey	0	0-0	0	0
Chet Francis	0	0-0	1	0
TOTALS	26	8-11	19	60

Kansas	FG	FT-A	PF	TP
Donald Ebling	1	2-5	0	4
Thomas Hunter	0	1-1	0	1
Howard Engleman	5	2-3	3	12
William Hogben	2	0-0	0	4
Bob Allen	5	3-4	3	13
John Kline	0	0-0	0	0
Ralph Miller	0	2-2	4	2
Bruce Voran	0	1-2	0	1
Dick Harp	2	1-3	1	5
Jack Sands	0	0-0	0	0
Wallace Johnson	0	0-0	0	0
TOTALS	15	12-20	11	42

Halftime: Indiana 32, Kansas 19. Technical foul: McCreary. Officials: Gil MacDonald, Ted O'Sullivan. Attendance: 10,000.

1940 Indiana—Front Row (left to right): Jim Gridley, Herman Schaefer, Bob Dro, Marv Huffman, Jay McCreary, Paul Armstrong and Ralph Dorsey. Back Row: Head coach Branch McCracken, Chet Francis, Bill Menke, Andy Zimmer, Bob Menke and Ralph Graham.

1941 CHAMPIONSHIP GAME, March 29 at Kansas City, MO .... WISCONSIN 39, WASHINGTON ST. 34

Wisconsin	FG-A	FT-A	PF	TP
John Kotz	5	2-3	2	12
Charles Epperson	2	0-0	3	4
Gene Englund	5	3-4	2	13
Don Timmerman	1	0-0	1	2
Ted Strain	0	2-2	1	2
Bob Alwin	1	0-0	0	2
Fred Rehm	2	0-1	2	4
Warren Schrage	0	0-0	1	0
TOTALS	16-63	7-10	12	39

Washington St.	FG-A	FT-A	PF	TP
Dale Gentry	0	1-2	1	1
Vern Butts	1	1-1	1	3
John Hooper	0	0-0	0	0
Paul Lindemann	0	3-4	1	3
Jim Zimmerman	0	0-0	0	0
Kirk Gebert	10-24	1-2	1	21
Owen Hunt	0	0-0	0	0
Ray Sundquist	2	0-1	3	4
Marv Gilberg	1	0-2	1	2
TOTALS	14-65	6-12	8	34

Halftime: Wisconsin 21, Washington St. 17. Officials: Wally Cameron, Bill Haarlow. Attendance: 7,219.

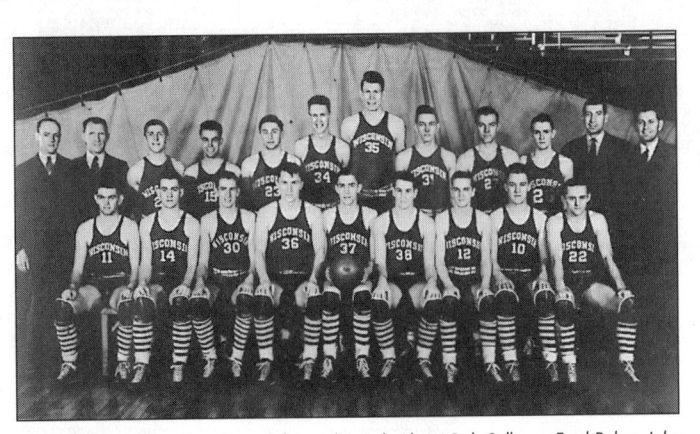

1941 Wisconsin—Front Row (left to right): Bob Alwin, Bob Sullivan, Fred Rehm, John Kotz, Gene Englund, Charles Epperson, Ted Strain, Harlo Scott and Ed Scheiwe. Back Row: Manager Morris Bradley, athletic trainer Walter Bakke, Ted Downs, Bob Roth, George Affeldt, Warren Schrage, Don Timmerman, Ted Deppe, John Lynch, Ed Jones, head coach Bud Foster and assistant coach Fred Wegner.

1942 CHAMPIONSHIP GAME, March 28 at Kansas City, MO .... STANFORD 53, DARTMOUTH 38

Stanford	FG	FT-A	PF	TP
Jack Dana	7	0-0	0	14
Fred Linari	3	0-0	0	6
Ed Voss	6	1-2	2	13
Bill Cowden	2	1-1	3	5
Howie Dallmar	6	3-5	0	15
Don Burness	0	0-0	0	0
TOTALS	24	5-8	5	53
Dartmouth	**FG**	**FT-A**	**PF**	**TP**
Robert Myers	4	0-1	1	8
George Munroe	5	2-2	1	12
James Olsen	4	0-1	0	8
Stanley Skaug	1	0-0	2	2
Charles Pearson	2	2-2	3	6
William Parmer	1	0-0	0	2
TOTALS	17	4-6	7	38

Halftime: Stanford 24, Dartmouth 22. Officials: Glenn Adams, Abb Curtis. Attendance: 6,500.

1942 Stanford—(Left to right): Bill Cowden, Howie Dallmar, Ed Voss, Jim Pollard, Don Burness and head coach Everett Dean.

1943 CHAMPIONSHIP GAME, March 30 at New York .... WYOMING 46, GEORGETOWN 34

Wyoming	FG	FT-A	PF	TP
Kenny Sailors	6	4-6	2	16
Jim Weir	2	1-3	2	5
Milo Komenich	4	1-4	2	9
Floyd Volker	2	1-2	3	5
Don Waite	0	0-0	0	0
Ted Roney	0	1-2	1	1
Jimmy Collins	4	0-1	1	8
Jim Reese	1	0-0	0	2
TOTALS	19	8-18	11	46
Georgetown	**FG**	**FT-A**	**PF**	**TP**
Dan Gabbianelli	1	2-3	3	4
James Reilly	1	0-0	0	2
John Mahnken	2	2-3	2	6
Daniel Kraus	2	0-1	3	4
Bill Hassett	3	0-3	4	6
William Feeney	4	0-0	1	8
Robert Duffey	0	0-1	0	0
Lloyd Potolicchio	1	2-3	1	4
Henry Hyde	0	0-0	0	0
TOTALS	14	6-14	14	34

Halftime: Wyoming 18, Georgetown 16. Officials: Matty Begovich, Pat Kennedy. Attendance: 13,300.

1943 Wyoming—Front Row (left to right): Don Waite, Earl Ray and Jim Reese. Back Row: Jimmy Collins, Floyd Volker, Milo Komenich, head coach Everett Shelton, Ted Roney, Kenny Sailors, Jim Weir and NCAA president Philip O. Badger.

1944 CHAMPIONSHIP GAME, March 28 at New York .... UTAH 42, DARTMOUTH 40 (OT)

Utah	FG	FT-A	PF	TP
Dick Smuin	0	0-0	2	0
Arnie Ferrin	8	6-7	0	22
Fred Sheffield	1	0-0	1	2
Wat Misaka	2	0-0	1	4
Herb Wilkinson	3	1-4	0	7
Bob Lewis	2	3-3	2	7
TOTALS	16	10-14	6	42
Dartmouth	**FG**	**FT-A**	**PF**	**TP**
Harry Leggat	4	0-0	1	8
Robert Gale	5	0-2	1	10
Everett Nordstrom	0	0-0	0	0
Audley Brindley	5	1-1	3	11
Franklin Murphy	0	0-0	0	0
Joseph Vancisin	2	0-0	3	4
Vincent Goering	0	0-0	0	0
Walter Mercer	0	1-1	3	1
Richard McGuire	3	0-1	3	6
TOTALS	19	2-5	14	40

Halftime: Dartmouth 18, Utah 17. End of regulation: Tied at 36. Officials: Paul Menton, James Osborne. Attendance: 15,000.

1944 Utah—Front Row (left to right): Mas Tatsuno and Ray Kingston. Middle Row: Jim Nance, Fred Lewis, Wat Misaka, Bill Kastellic and graduate assistant coach Keith Brown. Back Row: Head coach Vadal Peterson, Fred Sheffield, Herb Wilkinson, Arnie Ferrin, Dick Smuin, Bob Lewis and Pete Couch.

ALL-TIME TOURNAMENT FIELD—TEAM CHAMPIONS

1945 CHAMPIONSHIP GAME, March 27 at New York .... OKLAHOMA ST. 49, NEW YORK U. 45

Oklahoma St.	FG	FT-A	PF	TP
Cecil Hankins	6	3-6	3	15
Weldon Kern	3	0-4	3	6
Bob Kurland	10	2-3	3	22
Doyle Parrack	2	0-1	3	4
J.L. Parks	0	0-0	3	0
Blake Williams	1	0-1	1	2
John Wylie	0	0-0	0	0
TOTALS	22	5-15	16	49

New York U.	FG	FT-A	PF	TP
Al Grenert	5	2-3	3	12
Marty Goldstein	0	2-2	0	2
Don Forman	5	1-1	1	11
Dolph Schayes	2	2-6	2	6
Sid Tanenbaum	2	0-0	2	4
Herb Walsh	0	0-0	2	0
Frank Mangiapane	2	2-2	3	6
Alvin Most	1	2-3	2	4
TOTALS	17	11-17	15	45

Halftime: Oklahoma St. 26, New York U. 21. Officials: Glenn Adams, Abb Curtis. Attendance: 18,035.

1945 Oklahoma State—Front Row (left to right): D.W. Jones, Weldon Kern, J.L. Parks, Doyle Parrack and John Wylie. Back Row: Bill Johnson, Joe Halbert, NCAA president Tug Wilson, Bob Kurland, head coach Henry Iba, Blake Williams, Cecil Hankins and assistant coach Bobby Milikan.

1946 CHAMPIONSHIP GAME, March 26 at New York .... OKLAHOMA ST. 43, NORTH CAROLINA 40

Oklahoma St.	FG	FT-A	PF	TP
Sam Aubrey	0	1-2	1	1
A.L. Bennett	3	0-0	4	6
Weldon Kern	3	1-3	2	7
Joe Bradley	1	1-2	1	3
Bob Kurland	9	5-9	5	23
Joe Halbert	0	0-0	0	0
Blake Williams	0	2-4	2	2
Eugene Bell	0	1-1	1	1
J.L. Parks	0	0-1	2	0
TOTALS	16	11-22	18	43

North Carolina	FG	FT-A	PF	TP
John Dillon	5	6-6	5	16
Don Anderson	3	2-3	3	8
Bob Paxton	2	0-0	4	4
Horace McKinney	2	1-3	5	5
Jim White	0	1-1	0	1
Taylor Thorne	1	0-0	2	2
Jim Jordan	0	4-8	3	4
TOTALS	13	14-21	22	40

Halftime: Oklahoma St. 23, North Carolina 17. Officials: Jocko Collins, Pat Kennedy. Attendance: 18,479.

1946 Oklahoma State—Front (left to right): A.L. Bennett, Paul Geymann, Weldon Kern, J.L. Parks, Joe Pitts, Blake Williams, Joe Bradley and Eugene Bell. Back Row: Assistant coach Leroy Floyd, C.L. Parker, Sam Aubrey, Monroe, Bob Kurland, Joe Halbert, Mark Steinmeyer, Herschel Crowe and head coach Hank Iba.

1947 CHAMPIONSHIP GAME, March 25 at New York .... HOLY CROSS 58, OKLAHOMA 47

Holy Cross	FG	FT-A	PF	TP
George Kaftan	7	4-5	4	18
Dermie O'Connell	7	2-4	3	16
Bob Curran	0	0-1	2	0
Frank Oftring	6	2-3	5	14
Joe Mullaney	0	0-0	2	0
Ken Haggerty	0	0-0	0	0
Bob Cousy	0	2-2	1	2
Bob McMullan	2	4-4	0	8
Andy Laska	0	0-0	0	0
Charlie Bollinger	0	0-0	0	0
Charlie Graver	0	0-0	0	0
Jim Riley	0	0-0	1	0
TOTALS	22	14-19	18	58

Oklahoma	FG	FT-A	PF	TP
Dick Reich	3	2-2	3	8
Paul Courty	3	2-3	4	8
Gerald Tucker	6	10-12	3	22
Allie Paine	2	2-2	0	6
Bill Waters	0	0-0	0	0
Paul Merchant	0	0-0	1	0
Kenneth Pryor	0	1-1	1	1
Jack Landon	1	0-1	4	2
Harley Day	0	0-0	0	0
TOTALS	15	17-21	16	47

Halftime: Oklahoma 31, Holy Cross 28. Officials: Hagan Anderson, Pat Kennedy. Attendance: 18,445.

1947 Holy Cross—Front Row (left to right): Dermie O'Connell, Bob Cousy, Frank Oftring and Andy Laska. Middle Row: Bob Curran, Ken Haggerty, head coach Doggie Julian, Joe Mullaney and George Kaftan. Back Row: Assistant coach Albert Riopel, Jim Riley, Charlie Bollinger, Bob McMullan, Charlie Graver and manager Frank Dooley.

1948 CHAMPIONSHIP GAME, March 23 at New York .... KENTUCKY 58, BAYLOR 42

Kentucky	FG-A	FT-A	PF	TP
Wallace Jones	4	1-1	3	9
Cliff Barker	2	1-3	4	5
Jim Line	3	1-1	3	7
Alex Groza	6	2-4	4	14
Joe Holland	1	0-0	1	2
Ralph Beard	4	4-4	1	12
Kenneth Rollins	3	3-5	3	9
Dale Barnstable	0	0-1	0	0
TOTALS	23-83	12-19	19	58

Baylor	FG-A	FT-A	PF	TP
James Owens	2	1-2	0	5
Bill DeWitt	3	2-4	3	8
William Hickman	1	0-0	0	2
Ralph Pulley	0	1-1	0	1
Don Heathington	3	2-4	5	8
Odell Preston	0	0-2	2	0
Bill Johnson	3	4-7	5	10
Jackie Robinson	3	2-4	4	8
William Srack	0	0-0	0	0
TOTALS	15-64	12-24	19	42

Halftime: Kentucky 29, Baylor 16. Officials: Bill Haarlow, Gil MacDonald. Attendance: 16,174.

1948 Kentucky—Front Row (left to right): Head coach Adolph Rupp, Johnny Stough, Ralph Beard, Kenneth Rollins, Cliff Barker, Dale Barnstable and assistant coach Harry Lancaster. Back Row: Manager Humzey Yessin, Garland Townes, Jim Jordan, Joe Holland, Alex Groza, Wallace Jones, Jim Line, Roger Day and athletic trainer Wilbert Bud Berger.

1949 CHAMPIONSHIP GAME, March 26 at Seattle .... KENTUCKY 46, OKLAHOMA ST. 36

Kentucky	FG	FT-A	PF	TP
Wallace Jones	1	1-3	3	3
Jim Line	2	1-2	3	5
Alex Groza	9	7-8	5	25
Ralph Beard	1	1-2	4	3
Cliff Barker	1	3-3	4	5
Dale Barnstable	1	1-1	1	3
Walt Hirsch	1	0-0	1	2
TOTALS	16	14-19	21	46

Oklahoma St.	FG	FT-A	PF	TP
Vernon Yates	1	0-0	1	2
Jack Shelton	3	6-7	4	12
Bob Harris	3	1-1	5	7
Joe Bradley	0	3-6	3	3
J.L. Parks	2	3-4	5	7
Tom Jacquet	0	1-2	0	1
Gale McArthur	0	2-2	1	2
Morman Pilgrim	0	2-2	1	2
Keith Smith	0	0-0	1	0
TOTALS	9	18-24	21	36

Halftime: Kentucky 25, Oklahoma St. 20. Officials: Hal Lee, Tim McCullough. Attendance: 10,600.

1949 Kentucky—Front Row (left to right): Head coach Adolph Rupp, Jim Line, Cliff Barker, John Stough, Ralph Beard, Joe Hall, Garland Townes and assistant coach Harry Lancaster. Back Row: Dale Barnstable, Walt Hirsch, Wallace Jones, Alex Groza, Bob Henne, Roger Day and manager Humzey Yessin.

1950 CHAMPIONSHIP GAME, March 28 at New York .... CCNY 71, BRADLEY 68

CCNY	FG-A	FT-A	PF	TP
Floyd Layne	3-7	5-6	3	11
Ed Warner	4-9	6-14	2	14
Ed Roman	6-17	0-2	5	12
Joe Galiber	0-0	0-0	1	0
Alvin Roth	2-7	1-5	2	5
Norman Mager	4-10	6-6	3	14
Irwin Dambrot	7-14	1-2	0	15
Ronald Nadell	0-0	0-0	1	0
TOTALS	26-64	19-35	17	71

Bradley	FG-A	FT-A	PF	TP
Bud Grover	0-10	2-3	3	2
Fred Schlictman	0-3	0-0	2	0
Paul Unruh	4-9	0-0	5	8
Elmer Behnke	3-10	3-3	4	9
Jim Kelly	0-1	0-2	0	0
Billy Mann	2-7	5-5	5	9
Aaron Preece	6-11	0-0	5	12
Dino Melchiorre	0-0	0-0	0	0
Gene Melchiorre	7-16	2-4	4	16
Mike Chianakas	5-7	1-3	4	11
Joe Stowell	0-0	1-1	0	1
TOTALS	27-74	14-21	32	68

Halftime: CCNY 39, Bradley 32. Officials: Lou Eisenstein, Ronald Gibbs. Attendance: 18,142.

1950 CCNY—Front Row (left to right): Mike Wittlin, Ed Roman, Joe Galiber, head coach Nat Holman, Irwin Dambrot, Norman Mager and Seymour Levey. Second Row: Floyd Layne, Arnold Smith, Ed Warner, Alvin Roth and Herb Cohen. Third Row: Ronald Nadell, Arthur Glass, LeRoy Watkins, Ed Chenetz and Larry Meyer. Back Row: Manager Al Ragusa and assistant coach Bobby Sand.

ALL-TIME TOURNAMENT FIELD—TEAM CHAMPIONS

1951 CHAMPIONSHIP GAME, March 27 at Minneapolis .... KENTUCKY 68, KANSAS ST. 58

Kentucky	FG-A	FT-A	RB	PF	TP
Cliff Hagan	5-6	0-2	4	5	10
Shelby Linville	2-7	4-8	8	5	8
Bill Spivey	9-29	4-6	21	2	22
Lou Tsiropoulos	1-4	0-0	3	1	2
Bobby Watson	3-8	2-4	3	3	8
Frank Ramsey	4-10	1-3	4	5	9
Lucian Whitaker	4-5	1-1	2	2	9
C.M. Newton	0-0	0-0	0	0	0
TOTALS	28-69	12-24	45	23	68

Kansas St.	FG-A	FT-A	RB	PF	TP
Ed Head	3-11	2-2	3	2	8
Dan Schuyler	1-2	0-0	1	2	2
Jack Stone	3-8	6-8	6	2	12
John Gibson	0-2	1-1	1	5	1
Dick Knostman	1-4	1-2	3	1	3
James Iverson	3-12	1-2	0	3	7
Don Upson	0-1	0-0	2	1	0
Ernie Barrett	2-12	0-2	3	1	4
Robert Rousey	2-10	0-0	2	3	4
Lew Hitch	6-15	1-1	9	3	13
Richard Peck	2-3	0-0	0	0	4
TOTALS	23-80	12-18	30	23	58

Halftime: Kansas St. 29, Kentucky 27. Officials: None listed. Attendance: 15,348.

1951 Kentucky—Front Row (left to right): Lindle Castle, Lucian Whitaker, Bobby Watson, Guy Strong and T. Riddle. Middle Row: Head coach Adolph Rupp, Cliff Hagan, C.M. Newton, Walt Hirsch, Paul Lansaw, Dwight Price and assistant coach Harry Lancaster. Back Row: Frank Ramsey, Shelby Linville, Bill Spivey, Roger Layne, Lou Tsiropoulos and Read Morgan.

1952 CHAMPIONSHIP GAME, March 26 at Seattle .... KANSAS 80, ST. JOHN'S (N.Y.) 63

Kansas	FG-A	FT-A	RB	PF	TP
Bob Kenney	4-11	4-6	4	2	12
Bill Lienhard	5-8	2-2	4	4	12
Larry Davenport	0-0	0-0	0	1	0
John Keller	1-1	0-0	4	2	2
Clyde Lovellette	12-25	9-11	17	4	33
B.H. Born	0-0	0-0	0	0	0
Allen Kelley	0-2	0-0	1	0	0
Dean Kelley	2-5	3-6	3	5	7
Charlie Hoag	2-6	5-7	4	5	9
Dean Smith	0-0	0-0	0	0	0
Bill Hougland	2-5	1-3	6	2	5
TOTALS	28-63	24-35	43	25	80

St. John's (N.Y.)	FG-A	FT-A	RB	PF	TP
Jack McMahon	6-12	1-4	2	4	13
Jim Walsh	3-6	0-0	4	3	6
Carl Peterson	0-1	0-0	0	0	0
Bob Zawoluk	7-12	6-11	9	4	20
Ron MacGilvray	3-8	2-5	10	3	8
Dick Duckett	2-5	2-2	2	4	6
Solly Walker	0-2	0-0	2	4	0
Jim McMorrow	1-3	0-0	0	3	2
Frank Giancontieri	0-0	0-2	1	0	0
Phil Sagona	2-2	0-0	0	5	4
Jim Davis	1-4	2-3	2	4	4
TOTALS	25-55	13-27	32	35	63

Halftime: Kansas 41, St. John's (N.Y.) 27. Officials: Lou Eisenstein, Cliff Ogden. Attendance: 10,700.

1952 Kansas—Front Row (left to right): Dean Kelley, Ken Buller, John Thompson, Don Anderson, Dean Smith, Jack Rodgers and Allen Kelley. Middle Row: Manager Wayne Louderback, LaVennes Squires, Everett Dye, Bob Goodwin, Larry Davenport, head coach Phog Allen, Bob Kenney, Wes Whitney, Wes Johnson and Dean Wells. Back Row: Assistant coach Dick Harp, John Keller, Arthur Heitholt, Bill Hougland, B.H. Born, Clyde Lovellette, Bill Lienhard, Wally Beck, Charlie Hoag and athletic trainer Dean Nesmith.

1953 CHAMPIONSHIP GAME, March 18 at Kansas City, MO .... INDIANA 69, KANSAS 68

Indiana	FG-A	FT-A	PF	TP
Dick Farley	1-8	0-0	5	2
Charley Kraak	5-8	7-10	5	17
Dick White	1-5	0-0	2	2
Jim DeaKyne	0-0	0-0	1	0
Don Schlundt	11-26	8-11	3	30
Burke Scott	2-4	2-3	3	6
Paul Poff	0-1	0-0	0	0
Bob Leonard	5-15	2-4	2	12
Phil Byers	0-2	0-0	0	0
TOTALS	25-69	19-28	21	69

Kansas	FG-A	FT-A	PF	TP
Harold Patterson	1-3	7-8	3	9
Dean Smith	0-0	1-1	1	1
Allen Kelley	7-20	6-8	3	20
Larry Davenport	0-1	0-0	0	0
B.H. Born	8-27	10-12	5	26
Dean Kelley	3-4	2-4	2	8
Gil Reich	2-9	0-0	2	4
Jerry Alberts	0-1	0-0	1	0
TOTALS	21-65	26-33	17	68

Halftime: Tied at 41. Technical fouls: Kraak, Leonard, Schlundt. Officials: Al Lightner, Shaw. Attendance: 10,500.

1953 Indiana—Front Row (left to right): Bob Leonard, Charley Kraak, Don Schlundt, Dick Farley and Burke Scott. Middle Row: Manager Ron Fifer, Dick White, Jim DeaKyne, head coach Branch McCracken, Paul Poff, Phil Byers and assistant coach Ernie Andres. Back Row: Ron Taylor, Jim Schooley, Goethe Chambers and Jack Wright.

1954 CHAMPIONSHIP GAME, March 20 at Kansas City, MO .... LA SALLE 92, BRADLEY 76

La Salle	FG	FT-A	PF	TP
Charlie Singley	8	7-10	4	23
Chas Greenberg	2	1-2	1	5
Bob Maples	2	0-0	4	4
Frank Blatcher	11	1-2	4	23
Tom Gola	7	5-5	5	19
Fran O'Malley	5	1-1	4	11
John Yodsnukis	0	0-0	5	0
Frank O'Hara	2	3-4	1	7
TOTALS	37	18-24	28	92

Bradley	FG	FT-A	PF	TP
Richard Petersen	4	2-2	2	10
Harvey Babetch	0	0-0	0	0
Ed King	3	6-7	4	12
Jack Gower	0	1-2	1	1
Dick Estergard	3	11-12	1	17
Bob Carney	3	11-17	4	17
Lee Utt	0	0-0	1	0
John Kent	8	0-2	2	16
John Riley	1	1-2	1	3
TOTALS	22	32-44	16	76

Halftime: Bradley 43, La Salle 42. Officials: Hagan Anderson, Dean. Attendance: 10,500.

1954 La Salle—Front Row (left to right): Frank Blatcher, Bob Maples, Frank O'Hara, Tom Gola and Bob Ames. Back Row: Chas Greenberg, Fran O'Malley, Manny Gomez, John Yodsnukis, Charlie Singley and manager John Moosbrugger.

1955 CHAMPIONSHIP GAME, March 19 at Kansas City, MO .... SAN FRANCISCO 77, LA SALLE 63

San Francisco	FG-A	FT-A	PF	TP
Jerry Mullen	4	2-5	5	10
Stan Buchanan	3	2-2	1	8
Bill Russell	9-22	5-7	1	23
K.C. Jones	10-23	4-4	2	24
Hal Perry	1	2-2	4	4
Bob Wiebusch	2	0-0	0	4
Rudy Zannini	1	0-0	0	2
Dick Lawless	1	0-0	0	2
Gordon Kirby	0	0-0	1	0
TOTALS	31-83	15-20	14	77

La Salle	FG-A	FT-A	PF	TP
Fran O'Malley	4	2-3	1	10
Charlie Singley	8	4-4	1	20
Tom Gola	6	4-5	4	16
Al Lewis	1	4-9	1	6
Chas Greenberg	1	1-2	4	3
Frank Blatcher	4	0-0	1	8
Bob Maples	0	0-0	0	0
Walt Fredericks	0	0-0	0	0
TOTALS	24-68	15-23	12	63

Halftime: San Francisco 35, La Salle 24. Officials: None listed. Attendance: 10,500.

1955 San Francisco—Front Row (left to right): Hal Perry, Steve Balchios, Rudy Zannini and Warren Baxter. Middle Row: Tom Nelson, Stan Buchanan, Bill Russell, Jerry Mullen, Jack King and Bob Wiebusch. Back Row: Head coach Phil Woolpert, K.C. Jones, Dick Lawless, Gordon Kirby, Bill Bush and manager Healy.

1956 CHAMPIONSHIP GAME, March 24 at Evanston, IL .... SAN FRANCISCO 83, IOWA 71

San Francisco	FG-A	FT-A	RB	PF	TP
Carl Boldt	7	2-2		4	16
Mike Farmer	0	0-0	12	2	0
Mike Preaseau	3	1-2		3	7
Bill Russell	11-24	4-5	27	2	26
Tom Nelson	0	0-0		0	0
Hal Perry	6	2-2		2	14
Gene Brown	6	4-4		0	16
Warren Baxter	2	0-0		0	4
TOTALS	35-87	13-15	60	13	83

Iowa	FG-A	FT-A	RB	PF	TP
Carl Cain	7	3-4	12	1	17
Bill Schoof	5	4-4		3	14
Bill Logan	5	2-2	15	3	12
Bob George	0	0-0		0	0
Milton Scheuerman	4	3-4		2	11
Bill Seaberg	5	7-10		1	17
Augie Martel	0	0-0		0	0
Jim McConnell	0	0-0		0	0
TOTALS	26-80	19-24	48	10	71

Halftime: San Francisco 38, Iowa 33. Officials: None listed. Attendance: 10,600.

1956 San Francisco—Front Row (left to right): Warren Baxter, Hal Payne, Jack King, Hal Perry and Steve Balchios. Middle Row: Head coach Phil Woolpert, Vince Boyle, John Kolijian, Bill Russell, Bill Bush, K.C. Jones and manager Bill Mulholland. Back Row: Tom Nelson, Gene Brown, Mike Farmer, Carl Boldt and Mike Preaseau.

ALL-TIME TOURNAMENT FIELD—TEAM CHAMPIONS

1957 CHAMPIONSHIP GAME, March 23 at Kansas City, MO .... **NORTH CAROLINA 54, KANSAS 53 (3 OT)**

North Carolina	FG-A	FT-A	RB	PF	TP
Lennie Rosenbluth	8-15	4-4	5	5	20
Bob Young	1-1	0-0	3	1	2
Pete Brennan	4-8	3-7	11	3	11
Joe Quigg	4-10	2-3	9	4	10
Tommy Kearns	4-8	3-7	1	4	11
Bob Cunningham	0-3	0-1	5	4	0
Danny Lotz	0-0	0-0	2	0	0
TOTALS	21-45	12-22	36	21	54

Kansas	FG-A	FT-A	RB	PF	TP
Gene Elstun	4-12	3-6	4	2	11
Ron Loneski	0-5	2-3	3	2	2
Wilt Chamberlain	6-13	11-16	14	3	23
Maurice King	3-12	5-6	4	4	11
John Parker	2-4	0-0	0	0	4
Lewis Johnson	0-1	2-2	0	1	2
Robert Billings	0-0	0-0	0	2	0
TOTALS	15-47	23-33	25	14	53

Halftime: North Carolina 29, Kansas 22. End of regulation: Tied at 46. End of first overtime: Tied at 48. End of second overtime: Tied at 48. Officials: Hagan Anderson, Joe Conway. Attendance: 10,500.

1957 North Carolina—Front Row (left to right): Roy Searcy, Gehrmann Holland, Danny Lotz, Ken Rosemond, Bob Cunningham and Tommy Kearns. Back Row: Head coach Frank McGuire, manager Joel Fleishman, Bob Young, Lennie Rosenbluth, Joe Quigg, Pete Brennan, assistant coach Buck Freeman and athletic trainer John Lacey.

1958 CHAMPIONSHIP GAME, March 22 at Louisville, KY .... **KENTUCKY 84, SEATTLE 72**

Kentucky	FG-A	FT-A	RB	PF	TP
Johnny Cox	10-23	4-4	16	3	24
John Crigler	5-12	4-7	14	4	14
Ed Beck	0-1	0-1	3	4	0
Don Mills	4-9	1-4	5	3	9
Vern Hatton	9-20	12-15	3	3	30
Adrian Smith	2-8	3-5	6	4	7
Team			8		
TOTALS	30-73	24-36	55	21	84

Seattle	FG-A	FT-A	RB	PF	TP
Jerry Frizzell	4-6	8-11	5	3	16
Don Ogorek	4-7	2-2	11	5	10
Elgin Baylor	9-32	7-9	19	4	25
Jim Harney	2-5	0-1	1	1	4
Charles Brown	6-17	5-7	5	5	17
Francis Saunders	0-2	0-0	2	3	0
Don Piasecki	0-0	0-0	0	0	0
Team			3		
TOTALS	25-69	22-30	46	21	72

Halftime: Seattle 39, Kentucky 36. Officials: None listed. Attendance: 18,803.

1958 Kentucky—Front Row (left to right): Head coach Adolph Rupp, Adrian Smith, John Crigler, Ed Beck, Don Mills, Johnny Cox, Vern Hatton and assistant coach Harry Lancaster. Back Row: Manager Jay Atkerson, Earl Adkins, Dick Howe, Phil Johnson, Bill Cassady, Lincoln Collinsworth and Harold Ross.

1959 CHAMPIONSHIP GAME, March 21 at Louisville, KY .... **CALIFORNIA 71, WEST VIRGINIA 70**

California	FG-A	FT-A	RB	PF	TP
Bill McClintock	4-13	0-1	10	1	8
Bob Dalton	6-11	3-4	2	4	15
Darrall Imhoff	4-13	2-2	9	3	10
Al Buch	0-4	2-2	2	3	2
Denny Fitzpatrick	8-13	4-7	2	1	20
Bernie Simpson	0-1	0-0	2	2	0
Jack Grout	4-5	2-2	3	1	10
Dick Doughty	3-6	0-0	1	3	6
Team			7		
TOTALS	29-66	13-18	38	18	71

West Virginia	FG-A	FT-A	RB	PF	TP
Jerry West	10-21	8-12	11	4	28
Willie Akers	5-8	0-1	6	0	10
Robert Clousson	4-7	2-3	4	4	10
Bob Smith	2-5	1-1	2	3	5
Marvin Bolyard	1-4	4-4	3	1	6
James Ritchie	1-4	2-2	4	0	4
Ronnie Retton	0-0	2-2	0	0	2
Lee Patrone	2-6	1-2	4	1	5
Team			7		
TOTALS	25-55	20-27	41	16	70

Halftime: California 39, West Virginia 33. Officials: Tommy Bell, Red Mihalik. Attendance: 18,498.

1959 California—Front Row (left to right): Bob Dalton, Jack Grout, Bernie Simpson, Al Buch, Denny Fitzpatrick and Jim Langley. Middle Row: Jerry Mann, Earl Shultz, Dave Stafford, Wally Torkells, Ned Averbuck and Bob Wendell. Back Row: Head coach Pete Newell, Tandy Gillis, Stan Morrison, Dick Doughty, Darrall Imhoff and Bill McClintock.

THE TOURNAMENT FIELD

1960 CHAMPIONSHIP GAME, March 19 at San Francisco .... OHIO ST. 75, CALIFORNIA 55

Ohio St.	FG-A	FT-A	RB	PF	TP
John Havlicek	4-8	4-5	6	2	12
Joe Roberts	5-6	0-1	5	1	10
Jerry Lucas	7-9	2-2	10	2	16
Mel Nowell	6-7	3-3	4	2	15
Larry Siegfried	5-6	3-6	1	2	13
Gary Gearhart	0-1	0-0	1	0	0
Dick Furry	2-4	0-0	3	1	4
Bob Knight	0-1	0-0	0	1	0
Howard Nourse	2-3	0-0	3	1	4
Richie Hoyt	0-1	0-0	0	0	0
Dave Barker	0-0	0-0	0	0	0
John Cedargren	0-0	1-2	1	1	1
Team			1		
TOTALS	31-46	13-19	35	13	75

California	FG-A	FT-A	RB	PF	TP
Bill McClintock	4-15	2-3	3	3	10
Tandy Gillis	4-9	0-0	1	1	8
Darrall Imhoff	3-9	2-2	5	2	8
Bob Wendell	0-6	4-4	0	2	4
Earl Shultz	2-8	2-2	4	4	6
Jerry Mann	3-5	1-1	0	0	7
Dick Doughty	4-5	3-3	6	1	11
Dave Stafford	0-1	1-2	0	1	1
Stan Morrison	0-1	0-0	1	1	0
Ned Averbuck	0-0	0-1	1	0	0
Bill Alexander	0-0		0	0	0
Team			7		
TOTALS	20-59	15-18	28	15	55

Halftime: Ohio St. 37, California 19. Officials: Alex George, other not available. Attendance: 14,500.

1960 Ohio State—Front Row (left to right): Bob Knight, Larry Siegfried, Richie Hoyt, Mel Nowell, John Havlicek, Jerry Lucas, Joe Roberts, Dick Furry and Howard Nourse. Back Row: Athletic trainer Ernie Biggs, head coach Fred Taylor, Jim Allen, Jack Landes, Dave Barker, John Cedargren, Nelson Miller, Gary Gearhart, Gary Milliken, manager Mike Sorocak and assistant coach Jack Graf.

1961 CHAMPIONSHIP GAME, March 25 at Kansas City, MO .... CINCINNATI 70, OHIO ST. 65 (OT)

Cincinnati	FG-A	FT-A	RB	PF	TP
Bob Wiesenhahn	8-15	1-1	9	3	17
Tom Thacker	7-21	1-4	7	0	15
Paul Hogue	3-8	3-6	7	3	9
Carl Bouldin	7-12	2-3	4	4	16
Tony Yates	4-8	5-5	2	3	13
Dale Heidotting	0-0	0-0	0	0	0
Tom Sizer	0-0	0-0	1	0	0
Team			6		
TOTALS	29-64	12-19	36	13	70

Ohio St.	FG-A	FT-A	RB	PF	TP
John Havlicek	1-5	2-2	4	2	4
Richie Hoyt	3-5	1-1	1	3	7
Jerry Lucas	10-17	7-7	12	4	27
Larry Siegfried	6-10	2-3	3	2	14
Mel Nowell	3-9	3-3	3	1	9
Bob Knight	1-3	0-0	1	1	2
Gary Gearhart	1-1	0-0	0	1	2
Team			8		
TOTALS	25-50	15-16	32	14	65

Turnovers: Cincinnati 3, Ohio St. 8. Halftime: Ohio St. 39, Cincinnati 38. End of regulation: Tied at 61. Officials: Curtis Filiberti, Phil Fox. Attendance: 10,700.

1961 Cincinnati—Front Row (left to right): Jim Calhoun, Tony Yates, Carl Bouldin, Paul Hogue, Bob Wiesenhahn, Tom Thacker and Tom Sizer. Back Row: Head coach Ed Jucker, Larry Shingleton, Fred Dierking, Ron Reis, Dale Heidotting, Mark Altenau and assistant coach Tay Baker.

1962 CHAMPIONSHIP GAME, March 24 at Louisville, KY .... CINCINNATI 71, OHIO ST. 59

Cincinnati	FG-A	FT-A	RB	PF	TP
Ron Bonham	3-12	4-4	6	3	10
George Wilson	1-6	4-4	11	2	6
Paul Hogue	11-18	0-2	19	2	22
Tom Thacker	6-14	9-11	6	2	21
Tony Yates	4-8	4-7	1	1	12
Tom Sizer	0-0	0-0	0	0	0
Team			0		
TOTALS	25-58	21-28	43	10	71

Ohio St.	FG-A	FT-A	RB	PF	TP
John Havlicek	5-14	1-2	9	1	11
Doug McDonald	0-1	3-3	1	2	3
Jerry Lucas	5-17	1-2	16	3	11
Mel Nowell	4-16	1-1	6	4	9
Richard Reasbeck	4-6	0-0	0	4	8
James Doughty	0-1	0-0	2	2	0
Gary Bradds	5-7	5-6	4	2	15
Gary Gearhart	1-4	0-0	4	3	2
Team			0		
TOTALS	24-66	11-14	42	19	59

Turnovers: Cincinnati 8, Ohio St. 9. Halftime: Cincinnati 37, Ohio St. 29. Officials: None listed. Attendance: 18,469.

1962 Cincinnati—Front Row (left to right): Larry Shingleton, Tony Yates, Larry Elsasser, Tom Thacker, Tom Sizer and Jim Calhoun. Back Row: Assistant coach Tay Baker, Bill Abernathy, Fred Dierking, George Wilson, Ron Reis, Paul Hogue, Dale Heidotting, Ron Bonham and head coach Ed Jucker.

ALL-TIME TOURNAMENT FIELD—TEAM CHAMPIONS

1963 CHAMPIONSHIP GAME, March 23 at Louisville, KY .... LOYOLA (ILL.) 60, CINCINNATI 58 (OT)

Loyola (Ill.)	FG-A	FT-A	RB	PF	TP
Vic Rouse*	6-22	3-4	12	4	15
Les Hunter*	6-22	4-4	11	3	16
John Egan*	3-8	3-5	3	3	9
Ron Miller*	3-14	0-0	2	3	6
Jerry Harkness*	5-18	4-8	6	4	14
Team			11		
TOTALS	23-84	14-21	45	17	60

Cincinnati	FG-A	FT-A	RB	PF	TP
Ron Bonham	8-16	6-6	4	3	22
Tom Thacker	5-12	3-4	15	4	13
George Wilson	4-8	2-3	13	4	10
Tony Yates	4-6	1-4	8	4	9
Larry Shingleton	1-3	2-3	4	0	4
Dale Heidotting	0-0	0-0	1	2	0
Team			7		
TOTALS	22-45	14-20	52	17	58

Turnovers: Loyola (Ill.) 3, Cincinnati 16. Halftime: Cincinnati 29, Loyola (Ill.) 21. End of regulation: Tied at 54. Officials: Bill Bussenius, Alex George. Attendance: 19,153.

1963 Loyola (Illinois)—Front Row (left to right): Head coach George Ireland and assistant coach Jerry Lyne. Back Row: Jerry Harkness, John Egan, Chuck Wood, Vic Rouse, Les Hunter, Rich Rochelle, Jim Reardon, Dan Cannaughton, Ron Miller, manager John Gabcik, manager Fred Kuehl and athletic trainer Dennis McKenna.

1964 CHAMPIONSHIP GAME, March 21 at Kansas City, MO .... UCLA 98, DUKE 83

UCLA	FG-A	FT-A	RB	PF	TP
Keith Erickson	2-7	4-4	5	5	8
Jack Hirsch	5-9	3-5	6	3	13
Fred Slaughter	0-1	0-0	1	0	0
Gail Goodrich	9-18	9-9	3	1	27
Walt Hazzard	4-10	3-5	3	5	11
Doug McIntosh	4-9	0-0	11	2	8
Kim Stewart	0-1	0-0	0	1	0
Kenny Washington	11-16	4-4	12	4	26
Mike Huggins	0-1	0-1	1	2	0
Vaughn Hoffman	1-2	0-0	0	0	2
Chuck Darrow	0-1	3-4	1	2	3
Rich Levin	0-1	0-0	0	0	0
Team			8		
TOTALS	36-76	26-32	51	25	98

Duke	FG-A	FT-A	RB	PF	TP
Dennis Ferguson	2-6	0-1	1	3	4
Jay Buckley	5-8	8-12	9	4	18
Hack Tison	3-8	1-1	1	2	7
Buzzy Harrison	1-1	0-0	1	2	2
Jeff Mullins	9-21	4-4	4	5	22
Steve Vacendak	2-7	3-3	6	4	7
Ron Herbster	1-4	0-2	0	0	2
Jack Marin	8-16	0-1	10	3	16
Brent Kitching	1-1	0-0	1	0	2
Ted Mann	0-0	3-4	2	1	3
Frank Harscher	0-0	0-0	0	0	0
Ray Cox	0-0	0-0	0	0	0
Team			9		
TOTALS	32-72	19-28	44	24	83

Turnovers: UCLA 19, Duke 24. Halftime: UCLA 50, Duke 38. Officials: Tom Glennon, Red Mihalik. Attendance: 10,864.

1964 UCLA—Front Row (left to right): Manager Dennis Minishian, Gail Goodrich, Jack Hirsch, Rich Levin, Walt Hazzard, Kent Graham, Mike Huggins and Chuck Darrow. Back Row: Athletic trainer Ducky Drake, assistant coach Jerry Norman, Steve Brucker, Fred Slaughter, Doug McIntosh, Vaughn Hoffman, Keith Erickson, Kim Stewart, Kenny Washington and head coach John Wooden.

1965 CHAMPIONSHIP GAME, March 20 at Portland, OR .... UCLA 91, MICHIGAN 80

UCLA	FG-A	FT-A	RB	PF	TP
Edgar Lacey	5-7	1-2	7	3	11
Keith Erickson	1-1	1-2	1	1	3
Doug McIntosh	1-2	1-2	0	2	3
Gail Goodrich	12-22	18-20	4	4	42
Fred Goss	4-12	0-0	3	1	8
Kenny Washington	7-9	3-4	5	2	17
Mike Lynn	2-3	1-2	6	1	5
Vaughn Hoffman	1-1	0-0	1	0	2
Brice Chambers	0-0	0-1	0	0	0
John Lyons	0-0	0-0	0	1	0
Rich Levin	0-1	0-0	1	0	0
John Galbraith	0-0	0-0	0	0	0
Team			4		
TOTALS	33-58	25-33	32	15	91

Michigan	FG-A	FT-A	RB	PF	TP
Larry Tregoning	2-7	1-1	5	5	5
Oliver Darden	8-10	1-1	4	5	17
Bill Buntin	6-14	2-4	6	5	14
Cazzie Russell	10-16	8-9	5	2	28
George Pomey	2-5	0-0	2	2	4
Jim Myers	0-4	0-0	3	2	0
Craig Dill	1-2	2-2	1	1	4
Dan Brown	0-0	0-0	0	0	0
Tom Ludwig	1-2	0-0	0	0	2
John Thompson	0-0	0-0	0	0	0
John Clawson	3-4	0-0	0	2	6
Team			7		
TOTALS	33-64	14-17	33	24	80

Halftime: UCLA 47, Michigan 34. Officials: Steve Honzo, Red Mihalik. Attendance: 13,204.

1965 UCLA—Front Row (left to right): Assistant coach Jerry Norman, Gail Goodrich, John Lyons, John Galbraith, Mike Serafin, Brice Chambers, Larry McCollister and Fred Goss. Back Row: Head coach John Wooden, athletic trainer Ducky Drake, Rich Levin, Edgar Lacey, Doug McIntosh, Vaughn Hoffman, Bill Winkelholz, Mike Lynn, Keith Erickson, Kenny Washington and Bill Ureda.

1966 CHAMPIONSHIP GAME, March 19 at College Park, MD .... UTEP 72, KENTUCKY 65

UTEP	FG-A	FT-A	RB	PF	TP
Harry Flournoy	1-1	0-0	2	0	2
David Lattin	5-10	6-6	9	4	16
Bobby Joe Hill	7-17	6-9	3	3	20
Orsten Artis	5-13	5-5	8	1	15
Willie Cager	1-3	6-7	6	3	8
Willie Worsley	2-4	4-6	4	0	8
Nevil Shed	1-1	1-1	3	1	3
Team			0		
TOTALS	22-49	28-34	35	12	72

Kentucky	FG-A	FT-A	RB	PF	TP
Louie Dampier	7-18	5-5	9	4	19
Tommy Kron	3-6	0-0	7	2	6
Larry Conley	4-9	2-2	8	5	10
Pat Riley	8-22	3-4	4	4	19
Thad Jaracz	3-8	1-2	5	5	7
Jim LeMaster	0-1	0-0	0	1	0
Cliff Berger	2-3	0-0	0	0	4
Gary Gamble	0-0	0-0	0	1	0
Bob Tallent	0-3	0-0	0	1	0
Team			0		
TOTALS	27-70	11-13	33	23	65

Halftime: UTEP 34, Kentucky 31. Officials: Steve Honzo, Thornton Jenkins. Attendance: 14,253.

1966 UTEP—Front Row (left to right): Bobby Joe Hill, Orsten Artis, Togo Railey and Willie Worsley. Middle Row: David Palacio, Dick Myers, Harry Flournoy and Louis Boudoin. Back Row: Nevil Shed, Jerry Armstrong, Willie Cager, David Lattin and head coach Don Haskins.

1967 CHAMPIONSHIP GAME, March 25 at Louisville, KY .... UCLA 79, DAYTON 64

UCLA	FG-A	FT-A	RB	PF	TP
Ken Heitz	2-7	0-0	6	2	4
Lynn Shackelford	5-10	0-2	3	1	10
Lew Alcindor	8-12	4-11	18	0	20
Lucius Allen	7-15	5-8	9	2	19
Mike Warren	8-16	1-1	7	1	17
Joe Chrisman	0-0	1-2	1	2	1
Jim Nielsen	0-1	0-1	1	3	0
Neville Saner	1-1	0-0	2	2	2
Bill Sweek	1-1	0-0	0	1	2
Dick Lynn	0-1	0-0	0	0	0
Gene Sutherland	0-0	0-0	0	0	0
Don Saffer	2-5	0-0	0	1	4
Team			7		
TOTALS	34-69	11-25	54	15	79

Dayton	FG-A	FT-A	RB	PF	TP
Don May	9-23	3-4	17	4	21
Dan Sadlier	2-5	1-2	7	5	5
Dan Obrovac	0-2	0-0	2	1	0
Gene Klaus	4-7	0-0	0	1	8
Bob Hooper	2-7	2-4	5	2	6
Rudy Waterman	4-11	2-3	1	3	10
Glinder Torain	3-14	0-0	4	3	6
Ned Sharpenter	2-5	4-5	5	1	8
John Samanich	0-2	0-0	2	0	0
Tom Heckman	0-0	0-0	0	0	0
Dave Inderrieden	0-0	0-0	0	0	0
Jim Wannemacher	0-0	0-0	0	0	0
Team			8		
TOTALS	26-76	12-18	51	20	64

Turnovers: UCLA 11, Dayton 11. Halftime: UCLA 38, Dayton 20. Officials: None listed. Attendance: 18,892.

1967 UCLA—Front Row (left to right): Don Saffer, Lucius Allen, Dick Lynn, Gene Sutherland and Mike Warren. Back Row: Head coach John Wooden, assistant coach Jerry Norman, Joe Chrisman, Lynn Shackelford, Neville Saner, Lew Alcindor, Jim Nielsen, Ken Heitz, Bill Sweek, manager Ted Henry and athletic trainer Ducky Drake.

1968 CHAMPIONSHIP GAME, March 23 at Los Angeles .... UCLA 78, NORTH CAROLINA 55

UCLA	FG-A	FT-A	RB	PF	TP
Lew Alcindor	15-21	4-4	16	3	34
Mike Lynn	1-7	5-7	6	3	7
Lucius Allen	3-7	5-7	5	0	11
Mike Warren	3-7	1-1	3	2	7
Lynn Shackelford	3-5	0-1	2	0	6
Ken Heitz	3-6	1-1	2	3	7
Jim Nielsen	1-1	0-0	1	1	2
Bill Sweek	0-1	0-0	0	1	0
Gene Sutherland	1-2	0-0	2	1	2
Neville Saner	1-3	0-0	2	2	2
Team			9		
TOTALS	31-60	16-21	48	16	78

North Carolina	FG-A	FT-A	RB	PF	TP
Larry Miller	5-13	4-6	6	3	14
Bill Bunting	1-3	1-2	2	5	3
Rusty Clark	4-12	1-3	8	3	9
Charlie Scott	6-17	0-1	3	3	12
Dick Grubar	2-5	1-2	0	2	5
Eddie Fogler	1-4	2-2	0	0	4
Joe Brown	2-5	2-2	5	1	6
Gerald Tuttle	0-0	0-0	0	0	0
Jim Frye	1-2	0-1	1	0	2
Gra Whitehead	0-0	0-0	0	0	0
Jim Delany	0-1	0-0	0	0	0
Ralph Fletcher	0-1	0-0	0	0	0
Team			10		
TOTALS	22-63	11-19	35	17	55

Turnovers: UCLA 26, North Carolina 23. Halftime: UCLA 32, North Carolina 22. Officials: Charles Fouty, Steve Honzo. Attendance: 14,438.

1968 UCLA—Front Row (left to right): Mike Warren, Gene Sutherland and Lucius Allen. Back Row: Head coach John Wooden, assistant coach Jerry Norman, Ken Heitz, Lynn Shackelford, Jim Nielsen, Lew Alcindor, Mike Lynn, Neville Saner, Bill Sweek, athletic trainer Ducky Drake and manager Frank Adler.

1969 CHAMPIONSHIP GAME, March 22 at Louisville, KY .... UCLA 92, PURDUE 72

UCLA	FG-A	FT-A	RB	PF	TP
Curtis Rowe	4-10	4-4	12	2	12
Lynn Shackelford	3-8	5-8	9	3	11
Lew Alcindor	15-20	7-9	20	2	37
Ken Heitz	0-3	0-1	3	4	0
John Vallely	4-9	7-10	4	3	15
Sidney Wicks	0-1	3-6	4	1	3
Bill Sweek	3-3	0-1	1	3	6
Steve Patterson	1-1	2-2	2	0	4
Bill Seibert	0-0	0-0	1	0	0
George Farmer	0-0	0-0	0	1	0
John Ecker	1-1	0-0	0	0	2
Terry Schofield	1-2	0-0	0	0	2
Team			5		
TOTALS	32-58	28-41	61	19	92

Purdue	FG-A	FT-A	RB	PF	TP
Larry Weatherford	1-5	2-2	1	3	4
George Faerber	1-2	0-0	3	5	2
Rick Mount	12-36	4-5	1	3	28
Bill Keller	4-17	3-4	4	5	11
Tyrone Bedford	3-8	1-3	8	3	7
Jerry Johnson	4-9	3-4	9	2	11
Frank Kaufman	0-0	2-2	5	5	2
Ralph Taylor	0-0	0-0	0	0	0
Ted Reasoner	0-1	0-1	1	2	0
Herman Gilliam	2-14	3-3	11	2	7
Team			5		
TOTALS	27-92	18-24	48	30	72

Turnovers: UCLA 19, Purdue 4. Halftime: UCLA 42, Purdue 31. Officials: Irv Brown, Michael DiTomasso. Attendance: 18,669.

1969 UCLA—Front Row (left to right): Athletic trainer Ducky Drake, assistant coach Denny Crum, head coach John Wooden, assistant coach Gary Cunningham and manager Bob Marcucci. Middle Row: George Farmer, Bill Sweek, Ken Heitz, John Vallely and Terry Schofield. Back Row: Lynn Shackelford, Curtis Rowe, Steve Patterson, Lew Alcindor, Sidney Wicks, John Ecker and Bill Seibert.

1970 CHAMPIONSHIP GAME, March 21 at College Park, MD .... UCLA 80, JACKSONVILLE 69

UCLA	FG-A	FT-A	RB	PF	TP
Rick Betchley	0-0	0-1	0	0	0
Andy Hill	0-0	0-1	0	0	0
Sidney Wicks	5-9	7-10	18	3	17
Curtis Rowe	7-15	5-5	8	4	19
Steve Patterson	8-15	1-4	11	1	17
John Vallely	5-10	5-7	7	2	15
Henry Bibby	2-11	4-4	4	1	8
Kenny Booker	0-0	2-3	0	0	2
John Ecker	1-1	0-0	0	0	2
Terry Schofield	0-0	0-0	0	0	0
Bill Seibert	0-1	0-0	1	1	0
Jon Chapman	0-1	0-0	1	0	0
Team			3		
TOTALS	28-63	24-35	53	12	80

Jacksonville	FG-A	FT-A	RB	PF	TP
Mike Blevins	1-2	1-2	0	1	3
Pembrook Burrows	6-9	0-0	6	1	12
Artis Gilmore	9-29	1-1	16	5	19
Rex Morgan	5-11	0-0	4	5	10
Vaughn Wedeking	6-11	0-0	2	2	12
Chip Dublin	0-5	2-2	1	4	2
Gene Nelson	3-9	2-2	5	1	8
Rod McIntyre	1-3	0-0	3	3	2
Rusty Baldwin	0-0	0-0	0	0	0
Dan Hawkins	0-1	1-1	1	1	1
Ken Selke	0-0	0-0	0	0	0
Team			2		
TOTALS	31-80	7-8	40	23	69

Turnovers: UCLA 23, Jacksonville 18. Halftime: UCLA 41, Jacksonville 36. Officials: Bobby Scott, Lenny Wirtz. Attendance: 14,380.

1970 UCLA—Front Row (left to right): Henry Bibby, Terry Schofield and Andy Hill. Middle Row: Manager George Morgan, assistant coach Gary Cunningham, head coach John Wooden, assistant coach Denny Crum and athletic trainer Ducky Drake. Back Row: Kenny Booker, Rick Betchley, John Ecker, Sidney Wicks, Steve Patterson, Jon Chapman, Curtis Rowe, Bill Seibert and John Vallely.

ALL-TIME TOURNAMENT FIELD—TEAM CHAMPIONS

1971 CHAMPIONSHIP GAME, March 27 at Houston .... UCLA 68, VILLANOVA 62

UCLA	FG-A	FT-A	RB	PF	TP
Curtis Rowe	2-3	4-5	8	0	8
Sidney Wicks	3-7	1-1	9	2	7
Steve Patterson	13-18	3-5	8	1	29
Henry Bibby	6-12	5-5	2	1	17
Kenny Booker	0-0	0-0	0	0	0
Terry Schofield	3-9	0-0	1	4	6
Rick Betchley	0-0	1-2	1	1	1
Team			5		
TOTALS	27-49	14-18	34	9	68

Villanova	FG-A	FT-A	RB	PF	TP
Tom Ingelsby	3-9	1-1	4	2	7
Hank Siemiontkowski	9-16	1-2	6	3	19
Chris Ford	0-4	2-3	5	4	2
Clarence Smith	4-11	1-1	2	4	9
Howard Porter	10-21	5-6	8	1	25
Joe McDowell	0-1	0-0	2	0	0
Team			4		
TOTALS	26-62	10-13	31	14	62

Turnovers: UCLA 13, Villanova 10. Halftime: UCLA 45, Villanova 37. Officials: Jim Bain, Irv Brown. Attendance: 31,765.

1971 UCLA—Front Row (left to right): Andy Hill and Henry Bibby. Middle Row: Manager George Morgan, assistant coach Denny Crum, head coach John Wooden, assistant coach Gary Cunningham and athletic trainer Ducky Drake. Back Row: Larry Hollyfield, Larry Farmer, John Ecker, Curtis Rowe, Steve Patterson, Sidney Wicks, Jon Chapman, Kenny Booker, Rick Betchley and Terry Schofield.

1972 CHAMPIONSHIP GAME, March 25 at Los Angeles .... UCLA 81, FLORIDA ST. 76

UCLA	FG-A	FT-A	RB	PF	TP
Larry Farmer	2-6	0-0	6	2	4
Keith Wilkes	11-16	1-2	10	4	23
Bill Walton	9-17	6-11	20	4	24
Greg Lee	0-0	0-0	2	0	0
Henry Bibby	8-17	2-3	3	2	18
Tommy Curtis	4-14	0-1	4	1	8
Larry Hollyfield	1-6	0-0	2	2	2
Swen Nater	1-2	0-1	1	0	2
Team			2		
TOTALS	36-78	9-18	50	15	81

Florida St.	FG-A	FT-A	RB	PF	TP
Reggie Royals	5-7	5-6	10	5	15
Rowland Garrett	1-9	1-1	5	1	3
Lawrence McCray	3-6	2-5	6	4	8
Ron King	12-20	3-3	6	1	27
Greg Samuel	3-10	0-0	1	1	6
Ron Harris	7-13	2-3	6	1	16
Otto Petty	0-0	1-1	0	1	1
Ottis Cole	0-2	0-0	2	1	0
Team			6		
TOTALS	31-67	14-19	42	15	76

Halftime: UCLA 50, Florida St. 39. Officials: Irv Brown, Bobby Scott. Attendance: 15,063.

1972 UCLA—Front Row: Manager Les Friedman. Middle Row (left to right): Head coach John Wooden, athletic trainer Ducky Drake and assistant coach Gary Cunningham. Back Row: Tommy Curtis, Greg Lee, Larry Hollyfield, Jon Chapman, Keith Wilkes, Bill Walton, Swen Nater, Vince Carson, Larry Farmer, Gary Franklin, Andy Hill and Henry Bibby.

1973 CHAMPIONSHIP GAME, March 26 at St. Louis .... UCLA 87, MEMPHIS 66

UCLA	FG-A	FT-A	RB	PF	TP
Keith Wilkes	8-14	0-0	7	2	16
Larry Farmer	1-4	0-0	2	2	2
Bill Walton	21-22	2-5	13	4	44
Greg Lee	1-1	3-3	3	2	5
Larry Hollyfield	4-7	0-0	3	4	8
Tommy Curtis	1-4	2-2	3	1	4
Dave Meyers	2-7	0-0	3	1	4
Swen Nater	1-1	0-0	3	2	2
Gary Franklin	1-2	0-1	1	0	2
Vince Carson	0-0	0-0	0	0	0
Bob Webb	0-0	0-0	0	0	0
Team			2		
TOTALS	40-62	7-11	40	18	87

Memphis	FG-A	FT-A	RB	PF	TP
Bill Buford	3-7	1-2	3	1	7
Larry Kenon	8-16	4-4	8	3	20
Ron Robinson	3-6	0-1	7	4	6
Bill Laurie	0-1	0-0	0	0	0
Larry Finch	9-21	11-13	1	2	29
Bill Cook	1-4	2-2	0	1	4
Wes Westfall	0-1	0-0	0	5	0
Clarence Jones	0-0	0-0	0	0	0
Jerry Tetzlaff	0-0	0-2	0	1	0
Jim Liss	0-1	0-0	0	0	0
Ken Andrews	0-0	0-0	0	0	0
Doug McKinney	0-0	0-0	0	0	0
Team			2		
TOTALS	24-57	18-24	21	17	66

Turnovers: UCLA 17, Memphis 8. Halftime: Tied at 39. Technical fouls: Hollyfield, Kenon. Officials: Jim Howell, Joe Shosid. Attendance: 19,301.

1973 UCLA—Front Row (left to right): Bob Webb, Tommy Curtis, Gary Franklin and Casey Corliss. Middle Row: Larry Hollyfield, manager Les Friedman, head coach John Wooden, assistant coach Gary Cunningham, athletic trainer Ducky Drake and Greg Lee. Back Row: Larry Farmer, Keith Wilkes, Dave Meyers, Bill Walton, Ralph Drollinger, Swen Nater, Vince Carson and Pete Trgovich.

1974 CHAMPIONSHIP GAME, March 25 at Greensboro, NC .... NORTH CAROLINA ST. 76, MARQUETTE 64

North Carolina St.	FG-A	FT-A	RB	PF	TP
Tim Stoddard	3-4	2-2	7	5	8
David Thompson	7-12	7-8	7	3	21
Tom Burleson	6-9	2-6	11	4	14
Moe Rivers	4-9	6-9	2	2	14
Monte Towe	5-10	6-7	3	1	16
Phil Spence	1-2	1-2	3	2	3
Mark Moeller	0-0	0-0	0	0	0
Team			1		
TOTALS	26-46	24-34	34	17	76

Marquette	FG-A	FT-A	RB	PF	TP
Bo Ellis	6-16	0-0	11	5	12
Earl Tatum	2-7	0-0	3	4	4
Maurice Lucas	7-13	7-9	13	4	21
Lloyd Walton	4-10	0-0	2	2	8
Marcus Washington	3-13	5-8	4	3	11
Ed Daniels	1-3	1-2	0	3	3
Rick Campbell	2-3	0-0	1	3	4
Jerry Homan	0-4	1-2	6	2	1
Dave Delsman	0-0	0-0	0	2	0
Barry Brennan	0-0	0-0	0	1	0
Team			3		
TOTALS	25-69	14-21	43	29	64

Turnovers: North Carolina St. 23, Marquette 18. Halftime: North Carolina St. 39, Marquette 30. Technical fouls: Marquette coach Al McGuire 2. Officials: Irv Brown, Jim Howell. Attendance: 15,742.

1974 North Carolina State—Front Row (left to right): Manager Mike Sloan, Steve Smoral, Craig Kuszmaul, Mark Moeller, Monte Towe, David Thompson, Greg Hawkins, Moe Rivers and Bruce Dayhuff. Middle Row: Assistant coach Eddie Biedenbach, assistant coach Art Musselman, Steve Nuce, Dwight Johnson, Jerry Hunt, Tim Stoddard, Steve Smith, Ken Gehring, assistant coach Sam Esposito and head coach Norm Sloan. Back Row: Bill Lake, Tom Burleson, Phil Spence and Mike Buurma.

1975 CHAMPIONSHIP GAME, March 31 at San Diego .... UCLA 92, KENTUCKY 85

UCLA	FG-A	FT-A	RB	PF	TP
Dave Meyers	9-18	6-7	11	4	24
Marques Johnson	3-9	0-1	7	2	6
Richard Washington	12-23	4-5	12	4	28
Andre McCarter	3-6	2-3	2	1	8
Pete Trgovich	7-16	2-4	5	4	16
Ralph Drollinger	4-6	2-5	13	4	10
Team			5		
TOTALS	38-78	16-25	55	19	92

Kentucky	FG-A	FT-A	RB	PF	TP
Kevin Grevey	13-30	8-10	5	4	34
Bob Guyette	7-11	2-2	7	3	16
Rick Robey	1-3	0-0	9	5	2
Jimmy Dan Conner	4-12	1-2	5	1	9
Mike Flynn	3-9	4-5	3	4	10
Jack Givens	3-10	2-3	6	3	8
Larry Johnson	0-3	0-0	3	3	0
Mike Phillips	1-7	2-3	6	4	4
James Lee	0-0	0-0	0	1	0
Dan Hall	1-1	0-0	1	0	2
Team			4		
TOTALS	33-86	19-25	49	28	85

Turnovers: UCLA 13, Kentucky 13. Halftime: UCLA 43, Kentucky 40. Technical foul: Meyers. Officials: Hank Nichols, Bob Wortman. Attendance: 15,151.

1975 UCLA—Front Row (left to right): Marvin Thomas, Gavin Smith, Jim Spillane, Ray Townsend, Pete Trgovich and Andre McCarter. Back Row: Head coach John Wooden, assistant coach Gary Cunningham, Marques Johnson, Dave Meyers, Richard Washington, Ralph Drollinger, Brett Vroman, Wilbert Olinde, Casey Corliss, Frank Arnold and manager Les Friedman.

1976 CHAMPIONSHIP GAME, March 29 at Philadelphia .... INDIANA 86, MICHIGAN 68

Indiana	FG-A	FT-A	RB	PF	TP
Scott May	10-17	6-6	8	4	26
Tom Abernethy	4-8	3-3	4	2	11
Kent Benson	11-20	3-5	9	3	25
Bobby Wilkerson	0-1	0-0	0	1	0
Quinn Buckner	5-10	6-9	8	4	16
Wayne Radford	0-1	0-0	1	0	0
Jim Wisman	0-1	2-3	1	4	2
Jim Crews	0-1	2-2	1	1	2
Rich Valavicius	1-1	0-0	0	0	2
Bob Bender	0-0	0-0	0	0	0
Mark Haymore	1-1	0-0	1	0	2
Team			3		
TOTALS	32-61	22-28	36	19	86

Michigan	FG-A	FT-A	RB	PF	TP
Wayman Britt	5-6	1-1	3	5	11
John Robinson	4-8	0-1	6	2	8
Phil Hubbard	4-8	2-2	11	5	10
Rickey Green	7-16	4-5	6	3	18
Steve Grote	4-9	4-6	1	4	12
Dave Baxter	0-2	0-0	0	2	0
Alan Hardy	1-2	0-0	2	0	2
Joel Thompson	0-0	0-0	0	0	0
Tom Staton	2-5	3-4	2	3	7
Tom Bergen	0-1	0-0	0	1	0
Team			1		
TOTALS	27-57	14-19	32	25	68

Turnovers: Indiana 13, Michigan 19. Halftime: Michigan 35, Indiana 29. Officials: Irv Brown, Bob Wortman. Attendance: 17,540.

1976 Indiana—Front Row (left to right): Bobby Wilkerson, Jim Crews, Scott May, Quinn Buckner, Tom Abernethy and Kent Benson. Second Row: Manager Tim Walker, Rich Valavicius, Mark Haymore, Scott Eells, Wayne Radford, Bob Bender and manager Chuck Swenson. Third Row: Head coach Bob Knight, assistant coach Harold Andreas, Jim Roberson, Jim Wisman, assistant coach Bob Donewald and assistant coach Bob Weltlich.

ALL-TIME TOURNAMENT FIELD—TEAM CHAMPIONS

1977 CHAMPIONSHIP GAME, March 28 at Atlanta .... MARQUETTE 67, NORTH CAROLINA 59

Marquette	FG-A	FT-A	RB	PF	TP
Bo Ellis	5-9	4-5	9	4	14
Bill Neary	0-2	0-0	0	1	0
Jerome Whitehead	2-8	4-4	11	2	8
Butch Lee	6-14	7-7	3	1	19
Jim Boylan	5-7	4-4	4	3	14
Bernard Toone	3-6	0-1	0	1	6
Gary Rosenberger	1-1	4-4	1	1	6
Team			1		
TOTALS	22-47	23-25	29	13	67

North Carolina	FG-A	FT-A	RB	PF	TP
Walter Davis	6-13	8-10	8	4	20
Mike O'Koren	6-10	2-4	11	5	14
Rich Yonakor	3-5	0-0	4	0	6
Phil Ford	3-10	0-0	2	3	6
John Kuester	2-6	1-2	0	5	5
Steve Krafcisin	1-1	0-0	0	0	2
Tom Zaliagiris	2-3	0-0	0	3	4
Dudley Bradley	1-1	0-0	0	2	2
Bruce Buckley	0-1	0-0	0	1	0
Jeff Wolf	0-1	0-0	1	0	0
Dave Colescott	0-0	0-0	0	0	0
Woody Coley	0-0	0-0	0	0	0
Ged Doughton	0-0	0-0	0	0	0
John Virgil	0-0	0-0	0	1	0
Team			2		
TOTALS	24-51	11-16	28	24	59

Turnovers: Marquette 11, North Carolina 14. Halftime: Marquette 39, North Carolina 27. Technical foul: Toone. Officials: Reggie Copeland, Paul Galvan. Attendance: 16,086.

1977 Marquette—(Left to right): Jim Boylan, Bill Neary, Ulice Payne, Butch Lee, Jim Dudley, Gary Rosenberger, Bernard Toone, Jerome Whitehead, Craig Butrym, Robert Byrd and Bo Ellis.

1978 CHAMPIONSHIP GAME, March 27 at St. Louis .... KENTUCKY 94, DUKE 88

Kentucky	FG-A	FT-A	RB	PF	TP
Jack Givens	18-27	5-8	8	4	41
Rick Robey	8-11	4-6	11	2	20
Mike Phillips	1-4	2-2	2	5	4
Kyle Macy	3-3	3-4	0	1	9
Truman Claytor	3-5	2-4	0	2	8
James Lee	4-8	0-0	4	4	8
Jay Shidler	1-5	0-1	1	3	2
LaVon Williams	1-3	0-0	4	2	2
Chuck Aleksinas	0-0	0-0	0	1	0
Fred Cowan	0-2	0-0	2	1	0
Tim Stephens	0-0	0-0	0	0	0
Scott Courts	0-0	0-0	0	0	0
Chris Gettelfinger	0-0	0-0	0	0	0
Dwane Casey	0-0	0-0	0	0	0
Team			0		
TOTALS	39-68	16-25	32	25	94

Duke	FG-A	FT-A	RB	PF	TP
Eugene Banks	6-12	10-12	8	2	22
Kenny Dennard	5-7	0-0	9	5	10
Mike Gminski	6-16	8-8	12	3	20
John Harrell	2-2	0-0	0	3	4
Jim Spanarkel	8-16	5-6	2	4	21
Bob Bender	1-2	5-5	1	3	7
Jim Suddath	1-3	2-3	2	1	4
Scott Goetsch	0-1	0-0	1	1	0
Team			1		
TOTALS	29-59	30-34	36	22	88

Turnovers: Kentucky 14, Duke 17. Halftime: Kentucky 45, Duke 38. Technical fouls: Duke bench. Officials: Jim Bain, Roy Clymer. Attendance: 18,721.

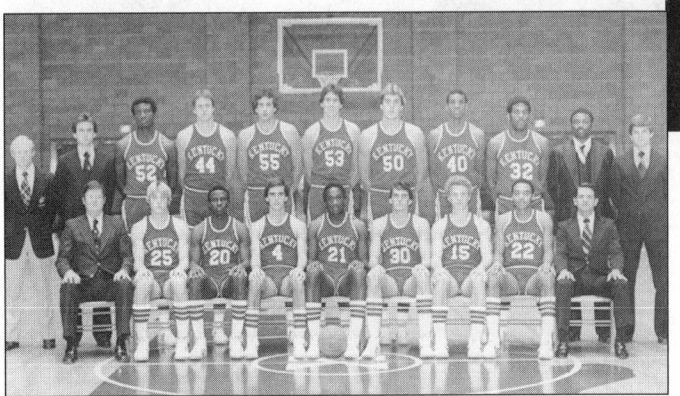

1978 Kentucky—Front Row (left to right): Head coach Joe Hall, Jay Shidler, Dwane Casey, Kyle Macy, Jack Givens, Tim Stephens, Chris Gettelfinger, Truman Claytor and assistant coach Dick Parsons. Back Row: Assistant athletic trainer Walt McCombs, manager Don Sullivan, LaVon Williams, Scott Courts, Mike Phillips, Rick Robey, Chuck Aleksinas, Fred Cowan, James Lee, assistant coach Leonard Hamilton and assistant coach Joe Dean Jr.

1979 CHAMPIONSHIP GAME, March 26 at Salt Lake City .... MICHIGAN ST. 75, INDIANA ST. 64

Michigan St.	FG-A	FT-A	RB	PF	TP
Greg Kelser	7-13	5-6	8	4	19
Magic Johnson	8-15	8-10	7	3	24
Jay Vincent	2-5	1-2	2	4	5
Terry Donnelly	5-5	5-6	4	2	15
Mike Brkovich	1-2	3-7	4	1	5
Ron Charles	3-3	1-2	7	5	7
Mike Longaker	0-0	0-0	0	0	0
Rob Gonzalez	0-0	0-0	0	0	0
Team			2		
TOTALS	26-43	23-33	34	19	75
Indiana St.	**FG-A**	**FT-A**	**RB**	**PF**	**TP**
Brad Miley	0-0	0-1	3	1	0
Alex Gilbert	2-3	0-4	4	4	4
Larry Bird	7-21	5-8	13	3	19
Carl Nicks	7-14	3-6	2	5	17
Steve Reed	4-9	0-0	0	4	8
Bob Heaton	4-14	2-2	6	2	10
Leroy Staley	2-2	0-1	3	2	4
Rich Nemcek	1-1	0-0	0	3	2
Team			3		
TOTALS	27-64	10-22	34	24	64

Turnovers: Michigan St. 16, Indiana St. 10. Halftime: Michigan St. 37, Indiana St. 28. Technical fouls: Bird. Officials: Gary Muncy, Hank Nichols, Lenny Wirtz. Attendance: 15,410.

1979 Michigan State—Front Row (left to right): Manager Randy Bishop, equipment manager Ed Belloli, assistant coach Fred Paulsen, assistant coach Bill Berry, head coach Jud Heathcote, assistant coach Dave Harshman, athletic trainer Clint Thompson and manager Darwin Payton. Back Row: Terry Donnelly, Greg Lloyd, Gerald Gilkie, Don Brkovich, Rick Kaye, Ron Charles, Magic Johnson, Greg Kelser, Jay Vincent, Rob Gonzalez, Mike Brkovich, Jamie Huffman and Mike Longaker.

1980 CHAMPIONSHIP GAME, March 24 at Indianapolis .... LOUISVILLE 59, UCLA 54

Louisville	FG-A	FT-A	RB	PF	TP
Rodney McCray	2-4	3-4	11	4	7
Derek Smith	3-9	3-4	5	2	9
Wiley Brown	4-12	0-2	7	3	8
Jerry Eaves	4-7	0-2	3	3	8
Darrell Griffith	9-16	5-8	2	3	23
Tony Branch	0-0	0-0	0	0	0
Roger Burkman	0-1	0-0	1	4	0
Poncho Wright	2-4	0-0	4	1	4
Team			3		
TOTALS	24-53	11-20	36	20	59
UCLA	**FG-A**	**FT-A**	**RB**	**PF**	**TP**
Kiki Vandeweghe	4-9	6-6	7	3	14
James Wilkes	1-4	0-0	6	3	2
Mike Sanders	4-10	2-4	6	4	10
Rod Foster	6-15	4-4	1	3	16
Michael Holton	1-3	2-2	2	2	4
Darren Daye	1-3	0-0	1	2	2
Cliff Pruitt	2-8	2-2	6	1	6
Tony Anderson	0-0	0-0	0	0	0
Darrell Allums	0-0	0-0	2	0	0
Team			3		
TOTALS	19-52	16-18	34	18	54

Turnovers: Louisville 17, UCLA 16. Halftime: UCLA 28, Louisville 26. Officials: Larry Lembo, Hank Nichols, Rich Weiler. Attendance: 16,637.

1980 Louisville—Front Row (left to right): Manager Randy Bufford, Greg Deuser, Jerry Eaves, Roger Burkman, head coach Denny Crum, Darrell Griffith, Tony Branch, Poncho Wright and manager Lambert Jemley. Back Row: Assistant coach Jerry Jones, graduate assistant coach Mark McDonald, Rodney McCray, Daryl Cleveland, Marty Pulliam, Scooter McCray, Wiley Brown, Derek Smith, assistant coach Wade Houston, assistant head coach Bill Olsen and athletic trainer Steve Donohue.

1981 CHAMPIONSHIP GAME, March 30 at Philadelphia .... INDIANA 63, NORTH CAROLINA 50

Indiana	FG-A	FT-A	RB	PF	TP
Landon Turner	5-8	2-2	6	5	12
Ted Kitchel	0-1	0-0	0	3	0
Ray Tolbert	1-4	3-6	11	3	5
Randy Wittman	7-13	2-2	4	2	16
Isiah Thomas	8-17	7-8	2	4	23
Jim Thomas	1-4	0-0	4	2	2
Steve Risley	1-1	3-4	4	1	5
Team			2		
TOTALS	23-48	17-22	33	17	63
North Carolina	**FG-A**	**FT-A**	**RB**	**PF**	**TP**
Al Wood	6-13	6-9	6	4	18
James Worthy	3-11	1-2	6	5	7
Sam Perkins	5-8	1-2	8	3	11
Mike Pepper	2-5	2-2	1	1	6
Jimmy Black	3-4	0-0	2	5	6
Jimmy Braddock	0-2	0-0	0	1	0
Eric Kenny	0-1	0-0	1	0	0
Pete Budko	0-1	0-0	1	0	0
Matt Doherty	1-2	0-1	4	4	2
Chris Brust	0-0	0-0	0	0	0
Team			0		
TOTALS	20-47	10-16	29	23	50

Turnovers: Indiana 14, North Carolina 19. Halftime: Indiana 27, North Carolina 26. Technical foul: Turner. Officials: Ken Lauderdale, Lou Moser, Booker Turner. Attendance: 18,276.

1981 Indiana—Front Row (left to right): Manager Steve Skoronski, Eric Kirchner, Ray Tolbert, Glen Grunwald, Steve Risley and Phil Isenbarger. Middle Row: Assistant coach Gerry Gimelstob, assistant coach Jene Davis, Chuck Franz, Randy Wittman, Isiah Thomas, Ted Kitchel, assistant coach Jim Crews and athletic trainer Bob Young. Back Row: Team physician Dr. Brad Bomba, head coach Bob Knight, Landon Turner, Mike LaFave, Steve Bouchie, Tony Brown, Jim Thomas and volunteer coach Steve Downing.

ALL-TIME TOURNAMENT FIELD—TEAM CHAMPIONS 161

1982 CHAMPIONSHIP GAME, March 29 at New Orleans .... NORTH CAROLINA 63, GEORGETOWN 62

North Carolina	FG-A	FT-A	RB	PF	TP
Matt Doherty	1-3	2-3	3	0	4
James Worthy	13-17	2-7	4	3	28
Sam Perkins	3-7	4-6	7	2	10
Jimmy Black	1-4	2-2	3	2	4
Michael Jordan	7-13	2-2	9	2	16
Buzz Peterson	0-3	0-0	1	0	0
Chris Brust	0-0	1-2	1	1	1
Jimmy Braddock	0-0	0-0	0	1	0
Team			2		
TOTALS	25-47	13-22	30	11	63

Georgetown	FG-A	FT-A	RB	PF	TP
Eric Smith	6-8	2-2	3	5	14
Mike Hancock	0-2	0-0	0	1	0
Patrick Ewing	10-15	3-3	11	4	23
Fred Brown	1-2	2-2	2	4	4
Eric Floyd	9-17	0-0	3	2	18
Ed Spriggs	0-2	1-2	1	2	1
Gene Smith	0-0	0-0	0	1	0
Anthony Jones	1-3	0-0	0	0	2
Bill Martin	0-2	0-0	0	1	0
Team			2		
TOTALS	27-51	8-9	20	20	62

Turnovers: North Carolina 13, Georgetown 12. Halftime: Georgetown 32, North Carolina 31.
Officials: John Dabrow, Bobby Dibbler, Hank Nichols. Attendance: 61,612.

1982 North Carolina—Front Row (left to right): Athletic trainer Marc Davis, assistant coach Roy Williams, head coach Dean Smith, Jimmy Braddock, Jeb Barlow, Jimmy Black, Chris Brust, Lynwood Robinson, manager Chuck Duckett, assistant coach Eddie Fogler and assistant coach Bill Guthridge. Back Row: Manager David Hart, manager Ralph Meekins, Dean Shaffer, Michael Jordan, James Worthy, John Brownlee, Timo Makkonen, Warren Martin, Sam Perkins, Matt Doherty, Cecil Exum, Buzz Peterson and manager David Daly.

1983 CHAMPIONSHIP GAME, April 4 at Albuquerque, NM .... NORTH CAROLINA ST. 54, HOUSTON 52

North Carolina St.	FG-A	FT-A	RB	PF	TP
Terry Gannon	3-4	1-2	1	3	7
Dereck Whittenburg	6-17	2-2	5	3	14
Ernie Myers	0-0	0-0	1	0	0
Alvin Battle	0-1	2-2	1	1	2
Sidney Lowe	4-9	0-1	0	2	8
Thurl Bailey	7-16	1-2	5	1	15
Lorenzo Charles	2-7	0-0	7	2	4
Cozell McQueen	1-5	2-2	12	4	4
Team			2		
TOTALS	23-59	8-11	34	16	54

Houston	FG-A	FT-A	RB	PF	TP
Clyde Drexler	1-5	2-2	2	4	4
Larry Micheaux	2-6	0-0	6	1	4
Akeem Olajuwon	7-15	6-7	18	1	20
Alvin Franklin	2-6	0-1	0	0	4
Michael Young	3-10	0-4	8	0	6
Reid Gettys	2-2	0-0	2	3	4
Benny Anders	4-9	2-5	2	2	10
Bryan Williams	0-1	0-0	4	3	0
David Rose	0-1	0-0	1	2	0
Team			1		
TOTALS	21-55	10-19	44	16	52

Turnovers: North Carolina St. 6, Houston 13. Halftime: North Carolina St. 33, Houston 25.
Officials: Joe Forte, Paul Housman, Hank Nichols. Attendance: 17,327.

1983 North Carolina State—Front Row (left to right): Alvin Battle, Thurl Bailey, Sidney Lowe, Dereck Whittenburg, Quinton Leonard and Harold Thompson. Middle Row: George McClain, Walt Densmore, Dinky Proctor, Cozell McQueen, Lorenzo Charles, Mike Warren, Terry Gannon and Ernie Myers. Back Row: Manager Gary Bryant, head athletic trainer Craig Sink, assistant coach Ed McLean, assistant coach Ray Martin, head coach Jim Valvano, assistant coach Tom Abatemarco, graduate assistant coach Max Perry, manager Steve Whitt and assistant athletic trainer Jim Rehbock.

THE TOURNAMENT FIELD

1984 CHAMPIONSHIP GAME, April 2 at Seattle .... GEORGETOWN 84, HOUSTON 75

Georgetown	FG-A	FT-A	RB	A	PF	TP
Ralph Dalton	0-0	0-0	2	0	1	0
David Wingate	5-10	6-9	1	3	4	16
Patrick Ewing	4-8	2-2	9	3	4	10
Fred Brown	1-2	2-2	4	4	4	4
Michael Jackson	3-4	5-5	0	6	4	11
Bill Martin	3-6	0-0	2	0	0	6
Horace Broadnax	2-3	0-0	0	0	2	4
Reggie Williams	9-18	1-2	7	3	2	19
Michael Graham	7-9	0-2	5	0	4	14
Victor Morris	0-0	0-0	0	0	0	0
Team			0			
TOTALS	34-60	16-22	30	19	25	84

Houston	FG-A	FT-A	RB	A	PF	TP
Rickie Winslow	0-1	2-2	6	3	4	2
Michael Young	8-21	2-3	5	1	3	18
Akeem Olajuwon	6-9	3-7	9	0	4	15
Alvin Franklin	8-15	5-6	2	9	3	21
Reid Gettys	3-3	0-0	1	7	2	6
Derek Giles	0-0	0-0	0	0	0	0
Benny Anders	2-2	0-2	0	0	0	4
Greg Anderson	1-1	0-0	2	0	0	2
Braxton Clark	0-0	0-0	0	0	0	0
Eric Dickens	2-3	1-2	0	0	5	5
Renaldo Thomas	0-0	0-0	0	0	0	0
James Weaver	0-0	0-0	0	0	0	0
Gary Orsak	1-1	0-0	0	0	0	2
Marvin Alexander	0-0	0-0	1	0	0	0
Stacey Belcher	0-0	0-0	0	0	0	0
Team			0			
TOTALS	31-56	13-22	26	20	21	75

Turnovers: Georgetown 9, Houston 20. Halftime: Georgetown 40, Houston 30. Officials: Ron Spitler, Mike Tanco, Booker Turner. Attendance: 38,471.

1984 Georgetown—Front Row (left to right): Bill Martin, Gene Smith, manager Steve Wolf, Fred Brown and Ralph Dalton. Back Row: Manager George Jackson, Michael Jackson, Clifton Dairsow, Victor Morris, Patrick Ewing, Michael Graham, Reggie Williams, David Wingate, Horace Broadnax and manager David Greene.

1985 CHAMPIONSHIP GAME, April 1 at Lexington, KY .... VILLANOVA 66, GEORGETOWN 64

Villanova	FG-A	FT-A	RB	A	PF	TP
Harold Pressley	4-6	3-4	4	1	1	11
Dwayne McClain	5-7	7-8	1	3	3	17
Ed Pinckney	5-7	6-7	6	5	3	16
Dwight Wilbur	0-0	0-0	0	1	0	0
Gary McLain	3-3	2-2	2	2	2	8
Harold Jensen	5-5	4-5	1	2	2	14
Mark Plansky	0-0	0-1	0	0	1	0
Chuck Everson	0-0	0-0	0	0	0	0
Team			3			
TOTALS	22-28	22-27	17	14	12	66

Georgetown	FG-A	FT-A	RB	A	PF	TP
Bill Martin	4-6	2-2	5	1	2	10
Reggie Williams	5-9	0-2	4	2	3	10
Patrick Ewing	7-13	0-0	5	2	4	14
Michael Jackson	4-7	0-0	0	9	4	8
David Wingate	8-14	0-0	2	2	4	16
Perry McDonald	0-1	0-0	0	0	0	0
Horace Broadnax	1-2	2-2	1	2	4	4
Ralph Dalton	0-1	2-2	0	0	1	2
Team			0			
TOTALS	29-53	6-8	17	18	22	64

Turnovers: Villanova 17, Georgetown 11. Halftime: Villanova 29, Georgetown 28. Officials: John Clougherty, Bobby Dibbler, Don Rutledge. Attendance: 23,124.

1985 Villanova—Front Row (left to right): Dwight Wilbur, Veltra Dawson, R.C. Massimino, Gary McLain, Brian Harrington, Harold Jensen and Steve Pinone. Back Row: Wyatt Maker, Ed Pinckney, Mark Plansky, Harold Pressley, head coach Rollie Massimino, Dwayne McClain, Connally Brown and Chuck Everson.

ALL-TIME TOURNAMENT FIELD—TEAM CHAMPIONS

1986 CHAMPIONSHIP GAME, March 31 at Dallas .... LOUISVILLE 72, DUKE 69

Louisville	FG-A	FT-A	RB	A	BK	ST	PF	TP
Herbert Crook	5-9	0-3	12	5	0	0	2	10
Billy Thompson	6-8	1-3	4	2	2	0	4	13
Pervis Ellison	10-14	5-6	11	1	2	1	4	25
Milt Wagner	2-6	5-5	3	2	1	1	4	9
Jeff Hall	2-4	0-0	2	2	0	2	2	4
Mark McSwain	2-4	1-2	3	2	0	1	1	5
Kevin Walls	0-1	0-0	1	0	0	0	2	0
Tony Kimbro	2-4	2-2	2	2	2	0	1	6
Team			1					
TOTALS	29-50	14-21	39	16	7	5	20	72

Duke	FG-A	FT-A	RB	A	BK	ST	PF	TP
David Henderson	5-15	4-4	4	4	0	3	5	14
Mark Alarie	4-11	4-4	6	0	0	1	5	12
Jay Bilas	2-3	0-0	3	0	0	0	4	4
Tommy Amaker	3-10	5-6	2	7	0	7	3	11
Johnny Dawkins	10-19	4-4	4	0	0	2	1	24
Danny Ferry	1-2	2-2	4	0	0	0	2	4
Billy King	0-1	0-1	0	1	0	0	2	0
Weldon Williams	0-1	0-0	0	0	0	0	0	0
Team			4					
TOTALS	25-62	19-21	27	12	0	13	22	69

Turnovers: Louisville 24, Duke 14. Halftime: Duke 37, Louisville 34. Officials: Hank Nichols, Pete Pavia, Don Rutledge. Attendance: 16,493.

1986 Louisville—Front Row (left to right): Kevin Walls, Chris West, Mike Abram and Keith Williams. Middle Row: Herbert Crook, Jeff Hall, Billy Thompson, head coach Denny Crum, Milt Wagner, Robbie Valentine and Mark McSwain. Back Row: Manager Jeff Witt, athletic trainer Jerry May, assistant coach Jerry Jones, assistant coach Wade Houston, Avery Marshall, David Robinson, Will Olliges, Pervis Ellison, Kenny Payne, Tony Kimbro, assistant coach Bobby Dotson, conditioning coordinator Doug Semenick and graduate assistant coach Jeff Van Pelt.

1987 CHAMPIONSHIP GAME, March 30 at New Orleans .... INDIANA 74, SYRACUSE 73

Indiana	FG-A	3FG-A	FT-A	RB	A	BK	ST	PF	TP
Rick Calloway	0-3	0-0	0-0	2	1	0	0	3	0
Daryl Thomas	8-18	0-0	4-7	7	1	0	0	1	20
Dean Garrett	5-10	0-0	0-0	10	0	3	0	4	10
Steve Alford	8-15	7-10	0-0	3	5	0	2	2	23
Keith Smart	9-15	0-1	3-4	5	6	0	2	2	21
Kreigh Smith	0-0	0-0	0-0	0	0	0	0	1	0
Steve Eyl	0-0	0-0	0-0	1	1	0	0	2	0
Joe Hillman	0-1	0-0	0-0	2	6	0	3	2	0
Todd Meier	0-0	0-0	0-1	1	0	0	0	0	0
Team				4					
TOTALS	30-62	7-11	7-12	35	20	3	7	17	74

Syracuse	FG-A	3FG-A	FT-A	RB	A	BK	ST	PF	TP
Derrick Coleman	3-7	0-0	2-4	19	1	3	1	2	8
Howard Triche	3-9	0-0	2-4	1	1	0	0	4	8
Rony Seikaly	7-13	0-0	4-6	10	1	3	1	3	18
Sherman Douglas	8-15	2-2	2-2	2	7	0	1	3	20
Greg Monroe	5-11	2-8	0-1	2	3	0	2	1	12
Derek Brower	3-3	0-0	1-3	1	0	0	0	3	7
Steve Thompson	0-2	0-0	0-0	3	1	1	0	0	0
Team				0					
TOTALS	29-60	4-10	11-20	38	14	7	5	16	73

Turnovers: Indiana 11, Syracuse 14. Halftime: Indiana 34, Syracuse 33. Officials: Nolan Fine, Joe Forte, Jody Silvester. Attendance: 64,959.

1987 Indiana—Front Row (left to right): Todd Jadlow, Keith Smart, Todd Meier, Steve Alford, Daryl Thomas, Dean Garrett, Kreigh Smith and Joe Hillman. Second Row: Tony Freeman, Dave Minor, Jeff Oliphant, Brian Sloan, Steve Eyl, Magnus Pelkowski and Rick Calloway. Third Row: Athletic trainer Tim Garl, assistant coach Ron Felling, assistant coach Joby Wright, head coach Bob Knight, assistant coach Kohn Smith, assistant coach Royce Waltman and team physician Dr. Brad Bomba. Back Row: Graduate assistant coach Julio Salazar, manager Mike McGlothlin, manager Bill Himbrook, graduate assistant coach Murry Bartow and graduate assistant coach Dan Dakich.

1988 CHAMPIONSHIP GAME, April 4 at Kansas City, MO .... KANSAS 83, OKLAHOMA 79

Kansas	FG-A	3FG-A	FT-A	RB	A	BK	ST	PF	TP
Chris Piper	4-6	0-0	0-0	7	2	0	3	3	8
Jeff Gueldner	1-2	0-1	0-0	2	1	0	1	0	2
Danny Manning	13-24	0-1	5-7	18	2	2	5	3	31
Kevin Pritchard	6-7	1-1	0-0	1	4	0	1	1	13
Milt Newton	6-6	2-2	1-2	4	1	2	0	1	15
Scooter Barry	0-2	0-0	1-2	0	2	0	0	1	1
Mike Maddox	0-0	0-0	0-0	0	0	0	0	1	0
Keith Harris	1-1	0-0	0-0	1	0	0	0	2	2
Clint Normore	3-3	1-1	0-1	1	4	0	0	3	7
Lincoln Minor	1-4	0-0	2-2	1	0	0	1	1	4
Team				1					
TOTALS	35-55	4-6	9-14	36	17	4	11	16	83

Oklahoma	FG-A	3FG-A	FT-A	RB	A	BK	ST	PF	TP
Harvey Grant	6-14	0-0	2-3	5	1	1	1	4	14
Dave Sieger	7-15	7-13	1-2	5	7	0	3	2	22
Stacey King	7-14	0-0	3-3	7	0	2	1	3	17
Mookie Blaylock	6-13	2-4	0-1	5	4	0	7	4	14
Ricky Grace	4-14	1-7	3-4	7	7	0	0	1	12
Terrence Mullins	0-0	0-0	0-0	1	0	0	0	1	0
Team				1					
TOTALS	30-70	10-24	9-13	31	19	3	13	18	79

Turnovers: Kansas 23, Oklahoma 15. Halftime: Tied at 50. Officials: John Clougherty, Tim Higgins, Ed Hightower. Attendance: 16,392.

1988 Kansas—Front Row (left to right): Lincoln Minor, Jeff Gueldner, Milt Newton, Kevin Pritchard, Otis Levingston, Scooter Barry, Keith Harris and Mike Maddox. Back Row: Mark Randall, Sean Alvarado, Mike Masucci, Marvin Branch, Danny Manning, Chris Piper, Archie Marshall and manager Bill Pope. Not pictured: Clint Normore and Marvin Mattox.

1989 CHAMPIONSHIP GAME, April 3 at Seattle .... MICHIGAN 80, SETON HALL 79 (OT)

Michigan	FG-A	3FG-A	FT-A	RB	A	BK	ST	PF	TP
Glen Rice	12-25	5-12	2-2	11	0	0	0	2	31
Mark Hughes	1-1	0-0	0-0	2	0	0	0	2	2
Terry Mills	4-8	0-0	0-0	6	2	3	2	2	8
Mike Griffin	0-0	0-0	0-0	4	3	0	0	4	0
Rumeal Robinson	6-13	0-0	9-10	3	11	0	0	2	21
Loy Vaught	4-8	0-0	0-0	7	0	0	1	2	8
Demetrius Calip	0-2	0-0	0-0	0	1	0	0	3	0
Sean Higgins	3-10	1-4	3-4	9	2	1	0	3	10
Team				3					
TOTALS	30-67	6-16	14-16	45	19	4	3	20	80

Seton Hall	FG-A	3FG-A	FT-A	RB	A	BK	ST	PF	TP
Daryll Walker	5-9	0-1	3-4	11	1	0	0	2	13
Andrew Gaze	1-5	1-5	2-2	3	3	0	1	3	5
Ramon Ramos	4-9	0-0	1-1	5	1	1	1	2	9
John Morton	11-26	4-12	9-10	4	3	0	0	3	35
Gerald Greene	5-13	2-5	1-3	5	5	0	2	3	13
Anthony Avent	1-2	0-0	0-0	3	1	0	0	0	2
Frantz Volcy	0-0	0-0	0-2	1	0	0	0	0	0
Michael Cooper	0-0	0-0	0-0	2	0	1	0	1	0
Pookey Wigington	1-1	0-0	0-0	0	0	0	0	1	2
Team				2					
TOTALS	28-65	7-23	16-22	36	14	2	4	17	79

1989 Michigan—Front Row (left to right): Head coach Steve Fisher, Mike Griffin, Sean Higgins, Glen Rice, Loy Vaught, Mark Hughes, Terry Mills, J.P. Oosterbaan and Mike Boyd. Back Row: Dan Minert, Joe Czupek, Marc Koenig, Demetrius Calip, Rob Pelinka, Chris Seter, James Voskuil, Kirk Tayler, Rumeal Robinson, Brian Dutcher and Bob Bland. Not pictured: Eric Riley.

Turnovers: Michigan 14, Seton Hall 11. Halftime: Michigan 37, Seton Hall 32. End of regulation: Tied at 71. Officials: John Clougherty, Mickey Crowley, Tom Rucker. Attendance: 39,187.

1990 CHAMPIONSHIP GAME, April 2 at Denver .... UNLV 103, DUKE 73

UNLV	FG-A	3FG-A	FT-A	RB	A	BK	ST	PF	TP
Larry Johnson*	8-12	2-2	4-4	11	2	1	4	3	22
Stacey Augmon*	6-7	0-0	0-1	4	7	2	2	5	12
David Butler*	1-4	0-0	2-2	3	3	0	1	3	4
Anderson Hunt*	12-16	4-7	1-2	2	2	0	0	0	29
Greg Anthony*	5-11	0-0	3-4	2	6	0	5	3	13
Stacey Cvijanovich	1-2	1-1	2-2	1	2	0	2	2	5
Travis Bice	0-1	0-1	0-0	0	2	0	1	2	0
Dave Rice	0-2	0-1	0-0	1	0	0	0	0	0
Barry Young	2-2	1-1	0-0	0	0	0	0	1	5
James Jones	4-5	0-0	0-0	2	0	0	0	2	8
Moses Scurry	2-5	0-0	1-2	6	0	0	1	2	5
Chris Jeter	0-0	0-0	0-0	0	0	0	0	0	0
Team				2					
TOTALS	41-67	8-14	13-17	33	24	3	16	23	103

Duke	FG-A	3FG-A	FT-A	RB	A	BK	ST	PF	TP
Robert Brickey*	2-4	0-0	0-2	3	2	0	0	2	4
Christian Laettner*	5-12	0-0	5-6	9	5	0	1	4	15
Alaa Abdelnaby*	5-7	0-0	4-6	7	0	2	0	3	14
Phil Henderson*	9-20	1-8	2-2	2	0	0	1	2	21
Bobby Hurley*	0-3	0-2	2-2	0	3	0	1	3	2
Thomas Hill	0-2	0-0	0-0	3	1	0	1	0	0
Brian Davis	2-5	0-0	2-3	1	0	1	1	1	6
Bill McCaffrey	1-3	0-0	2-2	2	0	0	0	1	4
Greg Koubek	1-4	0-1	0-0	2	0	0	0	0	2
Crawford Palmer	0-0	0-0	3-4	3	0	0	0	0	3
Clay Buckley	0-0	0-0	0-0	1	0	0	0	0	0
Joe Cook	1-1	0-0	0-0	0	0	0	0	0	2
Team				6					
TOTALS	26-61	1-11	20-27	39	11	3	5	16	73

1990 UNLV—Front Row (left to right): Bryan Emerzian, Byron Wesley, Dan Bisek, Sean Watkins and Dave Rice. Middle Row: Greg Anthony, James Jones, David Butler, Anderson Hunt, Travis Bice, Barry Young, Moses Scurry and Stacey Augmon. Back Row: Assistant coach Cleveland Edwards, assistant coach Ron Ganulin, Ed Goorjian, Rob Orellana, Chris Jeter, George Ackles, Larry Johnson, assistant coach Tim Grgurich, assistant coach Denny Hovanec and head coach Jerry Tarkanian.

Turnovers: UNLV 17, Duke 23. Halftime: UNLV 47, Duke 35. Officials: Ed Hightower, Tim Higgins, Richie Ballesteros. Attendance: 17,765.

ALL-TIME TOURNAMENT FIELD—TEAM CHAMPIONS

1991 CHAMPIONSHIP GAME, April 1 at Indianapolis .... DUKE 72, KANSAS 65

Duke	FG-A	3FG-A	FT-A	RB	A	BK	ST	PF	TP
Greg Koubek*	2-4	1-2	0-0	4	0	0	1	1	5
Grant Hill*	4-6	0-0	2-8	8	3	2	2	1	10
Christian Laettner*	3-8	0-0	12-12	10	0	0	1	3	18
Bobby Hurley*	3-5	2-4	4-4	1	9	0	2	1	12
Thomas Hill*	1-5	1-1	0-0	4	1	0	0	2	3
Bill McCaffrey	6-8	2-3	2-2	1	0	0	0	1	16
Antonio Lang	0-0	0-0	0-0	0	0	0	0	0	0
Brian Davis	4-5	0-0	0-2	2	1	0	0	4	8
Crawford Palmer	0-0	0-0	0-0	0	0	0	0	0	0
Team				1					
TOTALS	23-41	6-10	20-28	31	14	2	6	13	72

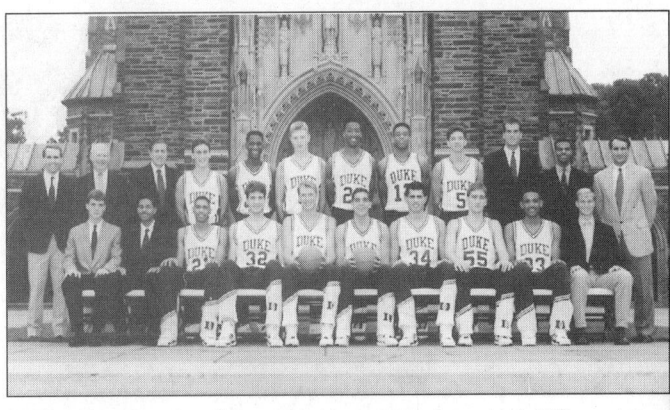

Kansas	FG-A	3FG-A	FT-A	RB	A	BK	ST	PF	TP
Alonzo Jamison*	1-10	0-2	0-0	4	5	0	4	4	2
Mike Maddox*	2-4	0-0	0-0	3	4	1	0	3	4
Mark Randall*	7-9	1-1	3-6	10	2	0	1	4	18
Terry Brown*	6-15	4-11	0-0	4	1	0	3	1	16
Adonis Jordan*	4-6	2-2	1-2	0	3	0	1	0	11
Patrick Richey	0-1	0-1	0-0	1	0	0	0	0	0
Steve Woodberry	1-4	0-0	0-0	4	0	0	1	4	2
Sean Tunstall	1-5	0-1	0-0	1	0	0	0	3	2
Kirk Wagner	1-1	0-0	0-0	1	0	0	0	0	2
Richard Scott	3-9	0-0	0-0	2	0	1	0	1	6
David Johanning	1-1	0-0	0-0	2	1	0	0	1	2
Team				0					
TOTALS	27-65	7-18	4-8	32	16	2	10	21	65

Turnovers: Duke 18, Kansas 14. Halftime: Duke 42, Kansas 34. Officials: Mickey Crowley, Charles Range, Jim Burr. Attendance: 47,100.

1991 Duke—Front Row (left to right): Manager Ivan Jones, Mark Williams, Antonio Lang, Christian Laettner, Clay Buckley, Greg Koubek, Crawford Palmer, Christian Ast, Grant Hill and manager Pete Lowder. Back Row: Assistant coach Mike Brey, athletic trainer Max Crowder, associate coach Pete Gaudet, Bobby Hurley, Kenny Blakeney, Marty Clark, Brian Davis, Thomas Hill, Bill McCaffrey, assistant coach Jay Bilas, assistant coach Tommy Amaker and head coach Mike Krzyzewski.

1992 CHAMPIONSHIP GAME, April 6 at Minneapolis .... DUKE 71, MICHIGAN 51

Duke	FG-A	3FG-A	FT-A	RB	A	BK	ST	PF	TP
Antonio Lang*	2-3	0-0	1-2	4	0	0	1	1	5
Grant Hill*	8-14	0-0	2-2	10	5	2	3	2	18
Christian Laettner*	6-13	2-4	5-6	7	0	1	1	1	19
Bobby Hurley*	3-12	1-3	2-2	3	7	0	1	4	9
Thomas Hill*	5-10	1-2	5-8	7	0	0	2	2	16
Cherokee Parks	1-3	0-0	2-2	3	0	1	0	3	4
Brian Davis	0-2	0-0	0-0	0	0	0	1	0	0
Christian Ast	0-0	0-0	0-0	1	0	0	0	0	0
Marty Clark	0-0	0-0	0-0	0	0	0	0	0	0
Kenny Blakeney	0-0	0-0	0-0	0	0	0	0	0	0
Ron Burt	0-0	0-0	0-0	0	0	0	0	0	0
Team				2					
TOTALS	25-57	4-9	17-22	37	12	4	9	13	71

Michigan	FG-A	3FG-A	FT-A	RB	A	BK	ST	PF	TP
Chris Webber*	6-12	0-2	2-5	11	1	0	2	4	14
Ray Jackson*	0-1	0-0	0-0	1	2	2	1	1	0
Juwan Howard*	4-9	0-1	1-3	3	0	0	0	3	9
Jalen Rose*	5-12	0-3	1-2	5	4	0	2	4	11
Jimmy King*	3-10	1-2	0-0	2	1	1	2	1	7
Eric Riley	2-6	0-0	0-0	4	1	0	0	2	4
James Voskuil	1-2	0-1	2-2	3	3	0	1	2	4
Rob Pelinka	1-2	0-0	0-0	2	1	0	0	0	2
Freddie Hunter	0-0	0-0	0-0	0	0	0	0	0	0
Michael Talley	0-2	0-1	0-0	1	0	0	0	0	0
Jason Bossard	0-1	0-1	0-0	0	0	0	0	0	0
Chris Seter	0-1	0-0	0-0	1	0	0	0	0	0
Chip Armer	0-0	0-0	0-0	0	0	0	0	0	0
Team				2					
TOTALS	22-58	1-11	6-12	35	13	3	8	17	51

Turnovers: Duke 14, Michigan 20. Halftime: Michigan 31, Duke 30. Officials: Gerry Donaghy, Tom Harrington, Dave Libbey. Attendance: 50,379.

1992 Duke—Front Row (left to right): Manager Mark Williams, Marty Clark, Bobby Hurley, Brian Davis, Christian Laettner, Thomas Hill, Kenny Blakeney and manager Suzanne Gilbert. Back Row: Head coach Mike Krzyzewski, assistant coach Mike Brey, athletic trainer Max Crowder, Antonio Lang, Erik Meek, Cherokee Parks, Grant Hill, Christian Ast, volunteer coach Jay Bilas, assistant coach Tommy Amaker and associate coach Pete Gaudet.

1993 CHAMPIONSHIP GAME, April 5 at New Orleans .... NORTH CAROLINA 77, MICHIGAN 71

North Carolina	FG-A	3FG-A	FT-A	RB	A	BK	ST	PF	TP
Brian Reese*	2-7	0-1	4-4	5	3	0	0	1	8
George Lynch*	6-12	0-0	0-0	10	1	2	1	3	12
Eric Montross*	5-11	0-0	6-9	5	0	1	0	2	16
Derrick Phelps*	4-6	0-1	1-2	3	6	0	3	0	9
Donald Williams*	8-12	5-7	4-4	1	1	0	1	1	25
Pat Sullivan	1-2	0-0	1-2	1	1	0	0	2	3
Kevin Salvadori	0-0	0-0	2-2	4	1	1	0	1	2
Henrik Rodl	1-4	0-2	0-0	0	0	0	2	0	2
Dante Calabria	0-0	0-0	0-0	0	0	0	0	0	0
Matt Wenstrom	0-1	0-0	0-0	0	0	0	0	0	0
Scott Cherry	0-0	0-0	0-0	0	0	0	0	0	0
Team				0					
TOTALS	27-55	5-11	18-23	29	13	4	7	10	77
Michigan	FG-A	3FG-A	FT-A	RB	A	BK	ST	PF	TP
Chris Webber*	11-18	0-1	1-2	11	1	3	1	2	23
Ray Jackson*	2-3	0-0	2-2	1	1	0	1	5	6
Juwan Howard*	3-8	0-0	1-1	7	3	0	0	3	7
Jalen Rose*	5-12	2-6	0-0	1	4	0	0	3	12
Jimmy King*	6-13	1-5	2-2	6	4	0	1	2	15
Eric Riley	1-3	0-0	0-0	3	1	1	1	1	2
Rob Pelinka	2-4	2-3	0-0	2	1	0	0	1	6
Michael Talley	0-0	0-0	0-0	0	1	0	0	1	0
James Voskuil	0-1	0-0	0-0	0	1	0	0	0	0
Team				2					
TOTALS	30-62	5-15	6-7	33	17	4	4	18	71

Turnovers: North Carolina 10, Michigan 14. Halftime: North Carolina 42, Michigan 36. Technical fouls: Michigan bench. Officials: Ed Hightower, Tom Harrington, Jim Stupin. Attendance: 64,151.

1993 North Carolina—Front Row (left to right): Strength coach Harley Dartt, athletic athletic trainer Marc Davis, head coach Dean Smith, Travis Stephenson, Henrik Rodl, Matt Wenstrom, George Lynch, Scott Cherry, assistant coach Phil Ford, assistant athletics director Dave Hanners and assistant coach Bill Guthridge. Back Row: Manager Sam Rogers, manager Bobby Dawson, manager Laura Johnson, Larry Davis, Derrick Phelps, Pat Sullivan, Ed Geth, Eric Montross, Serge Zwikker, Kevin Salvadori, Brian Reese, Dante Calabria, Donald Williams, manager Chuck Lisenbee, manager Eddie Wills and manager Eran Bloxam.

1994 CHAMPIONSHIP GAME, April 4 at Charlotte, NC .... ARKANSAS 76, DUKE 72

Arkansas	FG-A	3FG-A	FT-A	RB	A	BK	ST	PF	TP
Ken Biley*	0-0	0-0	0-0	0	0	0	0	1	0
Corliss Williamson*	10-24	0-0	3-5	8	3	2	2	3	23
Dwight Stewart*	3-11	0-5	0-0	9	4	0	4	3	6
Corey Beck*	5-11	0-1	5-8	10	4	0	1	3	15
Scotty Thurman*	6-13	3-5	0-0	5	1	0	1	2	15
Clint McDaniel	2-5	1-3	2-4	2	3	0	3	2	7
Darnell Robinson	1-5	0-0	0-0	2	0	0	0	1	2
Al Dillard	1-5	1-4	1-2	1	0	0	0	1	4
Davor Rimac	0-1	0-0	0-0	0	0	1	0	0	0
Lee Wilson	2-2	0-0	0-0	4	0	0	0	1	4
Team				3					
TOTALS	30-77	5-18	11-19	44	15	3	11	17	76
Duke	FG-A	3FG-A	FT-A	RB	A	BK	ST	PF	TP
Antonio Lang*	6-9	0-0	3-3	5	3	1	0	5	15
Grant Hill*	4-11	1-4	3-5	14	6	3	3	3	12
Cherokee Parks*	7-10	0-0	0-1	7	0	2	0	3	14
Jeff Capel*	6-16	2-6	0-0	5	4	0	1	3	14
Chris Collins*	4-11	4-8	0-0	0	1	1	1	1	12
Marty Clark	1-6	0-2	1-2	1	3	0	0	2	3
Erik Meek	1-2	0-0	0-0	7	0	0	0	1	2
Team				5					
TOTALS	29-65	7-20	7-11	44	17	7	5	18	72

Turnovers: Arkansas 12, Duke 23. Halftime: Arkansas 34, Duke 33. Officials: Jim Burr, Jody Silvester, Ted Valentine. Attendance: 23,674.

1994 Arkansas—Front Row (left to right): Ken Biley, Darnell Robinson, head coach Nolan Richardson, Corliss Williamson, Lee Wilson and Scotty Thurman. Second Row: Ray Biggers, Reggie Garrett, Elmer Martin, John Engskov, Craig Tyson and Davor Rimac. Third Row: Clint McDaniel, Al Dillard, Roger Crawford, Corey Beck, Reggie Merritt and Dwight Stewart.

ALL-TIME TOURNAMENT FIELD—TEAM CHAMPIONS

1995 CHAMPIONSHIP GAME, April 3 at Seattle .... UCLA 89, ARKANSAS 78

UCLA	FG-A	3FG-A	FT-A	RB	A	BK	ST	PF	TP
Charles O'Bannon*	4-10	0-0	3-4	9	6	2	2	1	11
Ed O'Bannon*	10-21	1-4	9-11	17	3	0	3	2	30
George Zidek*	5-8	0-0	4-7	6	0	0	0	4	14
Tyus Edney*	0-0	0-0	0-0	0	0	0	0	0	0
Toby Bailey*	12-20	1-2	1-2	9	3	0	2	3	26
Cameron Dollar	1-4	0-1	4-5	3	8	1	4	4	6
J. R. Henderson	1-5	0-0	0-0	2	1	1	0	1	2
Team				4					
TOTALS	33-68	2-7	21-29	50	21	4	11	15	89

Arkansas	FG-A	3FG-A	FT-A	RB	A	BK	ST	PF	TP
Scotty Thurman*	2-9	1-7	0-0	3	1	0	1	2	5
Corliss Williamson*	3-16	0-0	6-10	4	6	0	4	1	12
Elmer Martin*	1-2	1-2	0-0	3	1	0	1	2	3
Clint McDaniel*	5-10	3-7	3-4	3	1	0	4	5	16
Corey Beck*	4-6	2-3	1-2	3	2	1	3	3	11
Dwight Stewart	5-10	1-5	1-2	5	0	0	0	4	12
Al Dillard	2-4	2-3	0-0	2	1	0	0	1	6
Darnell Robinson	2-3	0-1	0-0	2	0	2	0	3	4
Davor Rimac	1-1	0-0	0-0	2	3	0	2	0	2
Lee Wilson	3-4	0-0	1-2	0	0	1	0	1	7
Landis Williams	0-0	0-0	0-0	0	0	0	0	0	0
Reggie Garrett	0-0	0-0	0-0	0	0	0	0	0	0
Team				4					
TOTALS	28-65	10-28	12-20	31	15	4	15	22	78

Turnovers: UCLA 20, Arkansas 18. Halftime: UCLA 40, Arkansas 39. Officials: Jim Burr, Ted Valentine, John Cahill. Attendance: 38,540.

1995 UCLA—Front Row (left to right): Manager Tony Luftman, manager Richard Klinger, manager Greg Buonaccorsi, manager Brendan Jacobson and manager Andrew Pruter. Middle Row: Assistant coach David Boyle, assistant coach Steve Lavin, assistant coach Mark Gottfried, head coach Jim Harrick, assistant coach Lorenzo Romar, assistant coach Phil Frye and assistant coach Tony Spino. Back Row: Tyus Edney, Marquis Burns, Charles O'Bannon, Kevin Dempsey, Ed O'Bannon, Ike Nwankwo, George Zidek, omm'A Givens, J. R. Henderson, Bob Myers, Toby Bailey, Kris Johnson and Cameron Dollar.

1996 CHAMPIONSHIP GAME, April 1 at East Rutherford, NJ .... KENTUCKY 76, SYRACUSE 67

Kentucky	FG-A	3FG-A	FT-A	RB	A	BK	ST	PF	TP
Derek Anderson*	4-8	2-3	1-1	4	1	0	3	2	11
Antoine Walker*	4-12	0-1	3-6	9	4	0	4	2	11
Walter McCarty*	2-6	0-0	0-0	7	3	0	0	3	4
Tony Delk*	8-20	7-12	1-2	7	2	1	2	2	24
Anthony Epps*	0-6	0-3	0-0	4	7	0	0	1	0
Mark Pope	1-6	0-2	2-2	3	2	0	1	3	4
Ron Mercer	8-12	3-4	1-1	2	2	0	1	3	20
Jeff Sheppard	1-2	0-1	0-1	2	0	0	0	3	2
Allen Edwards	0-1	0-1	0-0	0	1	0	0	0	0
Team				2					
TOTALS	28-73	12-27	8-13	40	22	1	11	19	76

Syracuse	FG-A	3FG-A	FT-A	RB	A	BK	ST	PF	TP
Todd Burgan*	7-10	3-5	2-5	8	1	0	1	5	19
John Wallace*	11-19	2-3	5-5	10	1	1	0	5	29
Otis Hill*	3-9	0-0	1-1	10	1	1	0	2	7
Lazarus Sims*	2-5	1-4	1-2	2	7	0	1	2	6
Jason Cipolla*	3-8	0-3	0-0	1	2	0	4	1	6
J.B. Reafsnyder	0-1	0-0	0-0	4	0	0	0	0	0
Marius Janulis	0-0	0-0	0-0	2	0	0	0	2	0
Elimu Nelson	0-0	0-0	0-0	0	0	0	0	0	0
Team				1					
TOTALS	26-52	6-15	9-13	38	12	2	6	17	67

Turnovers: Kentucky 15, Syracuse 24. Halftime: Kentucky 42, Syracuse 33. Officials: John Clougherty, Scott Thornley, Dave Libbey. Attendance: 19,229.

1996 Kentucky—Front Row (left to right): Assistant coach Delray Brooks, head coach Rick Pitino, Allen Edwards, Derek Anderson, Jeff Sheppard, Tony Delk, Anthony Epps, Cameron Mills, Wayne Turner, associate coach Jim O'Brien and assistant coach Winston Bennett. Back Row: Equipment manager Bill Keightley, administrative assistant George Barber, Jason Lathrem, Oliver Simmons, Nazr Mohammed, Mark Pope, Walter McCarty, Antoine Walker, Jared Prickett, Ron Mercer, athletic trainer Eddie Jamiel, assistant strength coach Layne Kaufman and strength coach Shaun Brown.

1997 CHAMPIONSHIP GAME, March 31 at Indianapolis .... ARIZONA 84, KENTUCKY 79 (OT)

Arizona	FG-A	3FG-A	FT-A	RB	A	BK	ST	PF	TP
Bennett Davison*	3-9	0-0	3-3	7	0	0	0	2	9
Michael Dickerson*	1-8	1-3	2-2	4	0	0	0	5	5
A.J. Bramlett*	1-3	0-0	1-1	6	1	2	1	5	3
Mike Bibby*	5-12	3-5	6-6	9	4	0	3	1	19
Miles Simon*	8-18	0-2	14-17	3	1	0	0	1	30
Jason Terry	2-6	2-3	2-2	2	5	0	3	1	8
Eugene Edgerson	0-0	0-0	2-2	5	0	0	0	2	2
Donnell Harris	2-2	0-0	4-8	7	1	0	0	4	8
Team				2					
TOTALS	22-58	6-13	34-41	45	12	2	7	16	84

Kentucky	FG-A	3FG-A	FT-A	RB	A	BK	ST	PF	TP
Ron Mercer*	5-9	2-4	1-1	9	6	0	1	5	13
Scott Padgett*	5-16	3-12	4-4	1	0	0	2	5	17
Jamal Magloire*	0-1	0-0	0-0	4	1	2	0	4	0
Wayne Turner*	4-9	0-0	0-1	4	5	1	1	5	8
Anthony Epps*	4-13	3-8	0-0	5	4	0	2	0	11
Allen Edwards	0-0	0-0	0-0	0	0	0	0	0	0
Jared Prickett	1-4	0-0	4-5	5	1	1	2	5	6
Nazr Mohammed	6-11	0-0	0-6	11	0	3	0	3	12
Cameron Mills	5-9	2-6	0-0	1	1	0	1	2	12
Steve Masiello	0-0	0-0	0-0	0	0	0	0	0	0
Team				0					
TOTALS	30-72	10-30	9-17	40	18	7	9	29	79

Turnovers: Arizona 18, Kentucky 16. Halftime: Arizona 33, Kentucky 32. End of regulation: Tied at 74. Officials: Tim Higgins, Ted Valentine, Tom O'Neill. Attendance: 47,028.

1997 Arizona—Front Row (left to right): Athletic trainer Ed Orr, senior manager Deron Davenport, assistant coach Phil Johnson, assistant coach Jessie Evans, head coach Lute Olson, assistant coach Jim Rosborough, coordinator of basketball operations Brad Jepson, equipment manager Walter Teike and video coordinator Ryan Hansen. Back Row: Josh Pastner, Mike Bibby, Quynn Tebbs, Jason Lee, Miles Simon, Justin Wessel, A.J. Bramlett, Donnell Harris, Bennett Davison, Eugene Edgerson, Michael Dickerson, Ortege Jenkins, Jason Terry, John Ash and Jason Stewart.

1998 CHAMPIONSHIP GAME, March 30 at San Antonio .... KENTUCKY 78, UTAH 69

Kentucky	FG-A	3FG-A	FT-A	RB	A	BK	ST	PF	TP
Allen Edwards*	2-7	0-3	0-0	1	5	0	1	0	4
Scott Padgett*	6-11	1-5	4-4	5	1	0	0	4	17
Nazr Mohammed*	5-9	0-0	0-0	2	0	2	0	4	10
Wayne Turner*	2-5	0-1	2-4	2	4	0	3	0	6
Jeff Sheppard*	7-14	0-2	2-2	4	3	0	2	1	16
Jamaal Magloire	2-3	0-0	3-3	2	1	3	0	4	7
Heshimu Evans	3-4	2-2	2-2	6	0	1	1	1	10
Cameron Mills	2-4	2-4	2-2	0	1	0	0	0	8
Saul Smith	0-0	0-0	0-0	0	0	0	0	0	0
Michael Bradley	0-0	0-0	0-0	1	0	0	0	1	0
Team				1					
TOTALS	29-57	5-17	15-17	24	15	6	7	15	78

Utah	FG-A	3FG-A	FT-A	RB	A	BK	ST	PF	TP
Hanno Mottola	4-10	1-3	6-6	8	0	0	0	4	15
Alex Jensen	5-6	1-1	3-3	2	2	0	0	2	14
Michael Doleac	5-12	1-1	4-6	10	1	2	3	2	15
Andre Miller	6-15	0-3	4-7	6	5	0	2	5	16
Drew Hansen	1-6	0-2	0-0	5	1	0	3	2	2
Britton Johnsen	3-4	1-2	0-0	4	0	0	0	0	7
Jordie McTavish	0-0	0-0	0-0	0	2	0	0	1	0
David Jackson	0-1	0-1	0-0	0	1	0	0	2	0
Trace Caton	0-1	0-1	0-0	0	0	0	0	0	0
Team				4					
TOTALS	24-55	4-14	17-22	39	12	2	8	18	69

Turnovers: Kentucky 11, Utah 18. Halftime: Utah 41, Kentucky 31. Officials: Jim Burr, Donnee Gray, Mike Sanzere. Attendance: 40,509.

1998 Kentucky—Front Row (left to right): Assistant coach Mike Sutton, head coach Tubby Smith, Saul Smith, Cameron Mills, Jeff Sheppard, Wayne Turner, Steve Masiello, assistant coach George Felton and assistant coach Shawn Finney. Back Row: Special assistant Leon Smith, administrative assistant Simeon Mars, equipment manager Bill Keightley, Ryan Hogan, Heshimu Evans, Scott Padgett, Nazr Mohammed, Jamaal Magloire, Michael Bradley, Myron Anthony, Allen Edwards, athletic trainer Eddie Jamiel and strength coach Tom Boyd.

1999 CHAMPIONSHIP GAME, March 29 at St. Petersburg, Fla. .... CONNECTICUT 77, DUKE 74

Connecticut	FG-A	3FG-A	FT-A	RB	A	BK	ST	PF	TP
Kevin Freeman*	3-6	0-0	0-0	8	0	3	0	1	6
Richard Hamilton*	10-22	2-4	5-6	7	3	0	2	1	27
Jake Voskuhl*	1-1	0-0	0-0	3	2	2	0	3	2
Ricky Moore*	6-10	1-1	0-1	8	2	0	1	4	13
Khalid El-Amin*	5-12	0-2	2-4	4	4	0	0	3	12
Souleymane Wane	2-2	0-0	0-0	0	0	0	1	4	4
Albert Mouring	3-4	0-1	0-1	3	0	1	0	1	6
Edmond Saunders	1-3	0-0	2-4	3	0	0	0	3	4
Rashamel Jones	1-1	0-0	1-2	2	0	0	0	0	3
Antric Klaiber	0-0	0-0	0-0	0	0	0	0	0	0
Team				3					
TOTALS	32-61	3-8	10-18	41	11	6	4	20	77

Duke	FG-A	3FG-A	FT-A	RB	A	BK	ST	PF	TP
Chris Carrawell*	3-7	0-2	3-4	4	2	2	1	4	9
Shane Battier*	2-7	1-3	1-2	4	2	0	0	3	6
Elton Brand*	5-8	0-0	5-8	13	0	2	2	3	15
William Avery*	3-12	1-3	4-4	4	5	0	0	4	11
Trajan Langdon*	7-15	5-10	6-7	1	1	0	3	2	25
Nate James	0-0	0-0	0-0	1	0	0	0	0	0
Corey Maggette	3-7	0-1	2-2	0	0	0	0	2	8
Chris Burgess	0-0	0-0	0-0	0	0	0	0	1	0
Team				4					
TOTALS	23-56	7-19	21-27	31	10	4	6	19	74

Turnovers: Connecticut 16, Duke 12. Halftime: Duke 39, Connecticut 37. Officials: Tim Higgins, Gerald Boudreaux, Scott Thornley. Attendance: 41,340.

1999 Connecticut— Front Row (left to right): Albert Mouring, Khalid El-Amin, Kevin Freeman, Ricky Moore, head coach Jim Calhoun, Rashamel Jones, Richard Hamilton, E. J. Harrison and Beau Archibald. Back Row: Justin Brown, Ajou Ajou Deng, Jake Voskuhl, assistant coach Tom Moore, associate head coach Dave Leitao, assistant coach Karl Hobbs, trainer Joe Sharpe, Souleymane Wane and Edmund Saunders.

ALL-TIME TOURNAMENT FIELD—TEAM CHAMPIONS   169

2000 CHAMPIONSHIP GAME, April 3 at Indianapolis .... MICHIGAN ST. 89, FLORIDA 76

Michigan St.	FG-A	3FG-A	FT-A	RB	A	BK	ST	PF	TP
Kevin Freeman*	3-6	0-0	0-0	8	0	3	0	1	6
Andre Hutson*	2-4	0-0	2-2	1	3	0	0	4	6
Morris Peterson*	7-14	3-8	4-6	2	5	0	1	3	21
A.J. Granger*	7-11	3-5	2-2	9	1	0	0	2	19
Mateen Cleaves*	7-11	3-4	1-1	2	4	0	0	1	18
Charlie Bell*	3-6	1-2	2-3	8	5	0	2	2	9
Jason Richardson	4-7	0-0	1-2	2	0	0	1	1	9
Aloysius Anagonye	0-0	0-0	0-0	3	0	1	0	4	0
Mike Chappell	2-4	1-3	0-0	1	0	0	1	0	5
Adam Ballinger	1-1	0-0	0-0	0	0	0	0	2	2
David Thomas	0-0	0-0	0-0	1	1	0	0	1	0
Brandon Smith	0-0	0-0	0-0	0	0	0	0	0	0
Steve Cherry	0-0	0-0	0-0	0	0	0	0	0	0
Matt Ishbia	0-1	0-0	0-0	0	0	0	0	0	0
Team				3					
TOTALS	33-59	11-22	12-16	32	19	1	5	20	89

Florida	FG-A	3FG-A	FT-A	RB	A	BK	ST	PF	TP
Brandon Smith	0-0	0-0	0-0	0	0	0	0	0	0
Brent Wright	5-8	0-1	3-5	10	4	0	1	4	13
Mike Miller	2-5	1-2	5-6	3	2	0	0	0	10
Udonis Haslem	10-12	0-0	7-7	2	0	1	0	4	27
Teddy Dupay	0-4	0-2	0-0	0	1	0	0	2	0
Justin Hamilton	0-1	0-1	0-0	0	0	0	0	1	0
Brett Nelson	4-10	3-6	0-0	4	3	0	2	1	11
Matt Bonner	0-3	0-2	0-0	3	0	0	0	1	0
Kenyan Weaks	1-3	1-1	0-0	1	1	0	2	2	3
Donnell Harvey	3-11	0-0	3-4	6	0	1	0	2	9
Major Parker	1-3	1-3	0-0	0	2	0	0	2	3
Team				1					
TOTALS	26-60	6-18	18-22	30	13	2	5	19	76

Turnovers: Michigan St. 14, Florida 13. Halftime: Michigan St. 43, Florida 32. Officials: James Burr, Gerald Boudreaux, David Hall. Attendance: 43,116.

2000 Michigan State— Front Row (left to right): A.J. Granger, Brandon Smith, Mateen Cleaves, head coach Tom Izzo, Charlie Bell, Mat Ishbia and Morris Peterson. Middle Row: Assistant coach Brian Gregory, assistant coach Mike Garland, Mike Chappell, Adam Wolfe, Andre Hutson, Davis Thomas, Jason Richardson, assistant coach Stan Heath and assistant to head coach, Dave Owens. Back Row: Athletic trainer Tom Mackowiak, strength and conditioning coach Mike Vorkapich, Aloysius Anagonye, Adam Ballinger, Jason Andreas, Steve Cherry, equipment manager Dave Pruder and manager Mark Armstrong.

2001 CHAMPIONSHIP GAME, April 2 at Minneapolis .... DUKE 82, ARIZONA 72

Duke	FG-A	3FG-A	FT-A	RB	A	BK	ST	PF	TP
Shane Battier*	7-14	1-5	3-6	11	6	2	0	1	18
Mike Dunleavy*	8-17	5-9	0-1	3	0	0	0	3	21
Casey Sanders*	0-1	0-0	0-0	2	1	0	1	1	0
Chris Duhon*	3-5	1-1	2-3	4	6	0	0	2	9
Jason Williams*	5-15	2-11	4-6	3	4	0	3	4	16
Carlos Boozer	5-9	0-0	2-3	12	1	2	0	3	12
Nate James	2-3	0-1	2-3	3	0	1	1	3	6
Team				4					
TOTALS	30-64	9-27	13-22	42	18	5	5	17	82

Arizona	FG-A	3FG-A	FT-A	RB	A	BK	ST	PF	TP
Michael Wright	5-9	0-0	0-1	11	0	2	1	4	10
Richard Jefferson*	7-13	4-8	1-3	8	3	1	1	4	19
Loren Wood*	8-15	0-1	6-8	11	1	4	1	4	22
Gilbert Arenas*	4-17	0-4	2-3	4	4	0	1	1	10
Jason Gardner*	2-11	0-8	3-4	3	2	0	1	2	7
Justin Wessel	0-0	0-0	0-0	0	0	0	0	0	0
Eugene Edgerson	0-0	0-0	0-0	1	0	0	0	4	0
Luke Walton	2-6	0-1	0-0	3	4	0	0	3	4
Team				4					
TOTALS	28-7	4-22	12-19	45	14	7	5	20	72

Turnovers: Duke 11, Arizona 9. Half time: Duke 35, Arizona 33. Officials: Scott Thornley, Gerald Boudreaux, Ed Corbett. Attendance: 45,994.

2001 Duke — Front Row (left to right): Manager Ryan Maschke, manager Lisa Kalich, Andy Borman, Jason Williams, J.D. Simpson, Nate James, Shane Battier, Ryan Caldbeck, Chris Duhon, Andre Buckner, Manager Wynter Galindez, administrative intern Anne Wilson. Back Row: Assistant coach Steve Wojciechowski, director of basketball operations Jeff LaMere, administrative assistant Mike Schrage, assistant coach Chris Collins, Mike Dunleavy, Carlos Boozer, Casey Sanders, Nick Horvath, Matt Christensen, Andre Sweet, Dahntay Jones, head trainer Dave Engelhardt, associate head Coach Johnny Dawkins, head coach Mike Krzyzewski. Not pictured is Reggie Love.

1939 Championship Bracket

Regional Semifinals | **Regional Finals** | **National Championship**

Western Regionals

- Oregon
  - March 20
- Texas
  - Oregon 56-41
  - **San Francisco** March 21
- Oklahoma
  - March 20
- Utah St.
  - Oklahoma 50-39
  - Oregon 55-37
  - **Evanston, IL** March 27

Eastern Regionals

- Villanova
  - March 17
- Brown
  - Villanova 42-30
  - **Philadelphia** March 18
- Wake Forest
  - March 17
- Ohio St.
  - Ohio St. 64-52
  - Ohio St. 53-36

Oregon 46-33
NATIONAL CHAMPION

Regional Third Place
March 21
at San Francisco
Utah St. 51, Texas 49

1940 Championship Bracket

Regional Semifinals | **Regional Finals** | **National Championship**

Eastern Regionals

- Indiana
  - March 20
- Springfield
  - Indiana 48-24
  - **Indianapolis** March 21
- Duquesne
  - March 20
- Western Ky.
  - Duquesne 30-29
  - Indiana 39-30
  - **Kansas City, MO** March 30

Western Regionals

- Southern California
  - March 20
- Colorado
  - Southern California 38-32
  - **Kansas City, MO** March 21
- Rice
  - March 20
- Kansas
  - Kansas 50-44
  - Kansas 43-42

Indiana 60-42
NATIONAL CHAMPION

Regional Third Place
March 21
at Kansas City, MO
Rice 60, Colorado 56 (ot)

1941 Championship Bracket

Regional Semifinals | **Regional Finals** | **National Championship**

Eastern Regionals

- Wisconsin
  - March 21
- Dartmouth
  - Wisconsin 51-50
  - **Madison, WI** March 22
- Pittsburgh
  - March 21
- North Carolina
  - Pittsburgh 26-20
  - Wisconsin 36-30
  - **Kansas City, MO** March 29

Western Regionals

- Arkansas
  - March 21
- Wyoming
  - Arkansas 52-40
  - **Kansas City, MO** March 22
- Creighton
  - March 21
- Washington St.
  - Washington St. 48-39
  - Washington St. 64-53

Wisconsin 39-34
NATIONAL CHAMPION

Regional Third Place
March 22
at Madison, WI
Dartmouth 60, North Carolina 59
at Kansas City, MO
Creighton 45, Wyoming 44

ALL-TIME TOURNAMENT FIELD—BRACKETS

1942 Championship Bracket

Regional Semifinals | **Regional Finals** | **National Championship**

Eastern Regionals
- Dartmouth
- March 20
- Penn St.
  - Dartmouth 44-39
- Kentucky
- March 20
- Illinois
  - Kentucky 46-44

New Orleans March 21
- Dartmouth 47-28

Western Regionals
- Stanford
- March 20
- Rice
  - Stanford 53-47
- Colorado
- March 20
- Kansas
  - Colorado 46-44

Kansas City, MO March 21
- Stanford 46-35

Kansas City, MO March 28
- Stanford 53-38
- **NATIONAL CHAMPION**

Regional Third Place
March 21
at New Orleans
  Penn St. 41, Illinois 34
at Kansas City, MO
  Kansas 55, Rice 53

1943 Championship Bracket

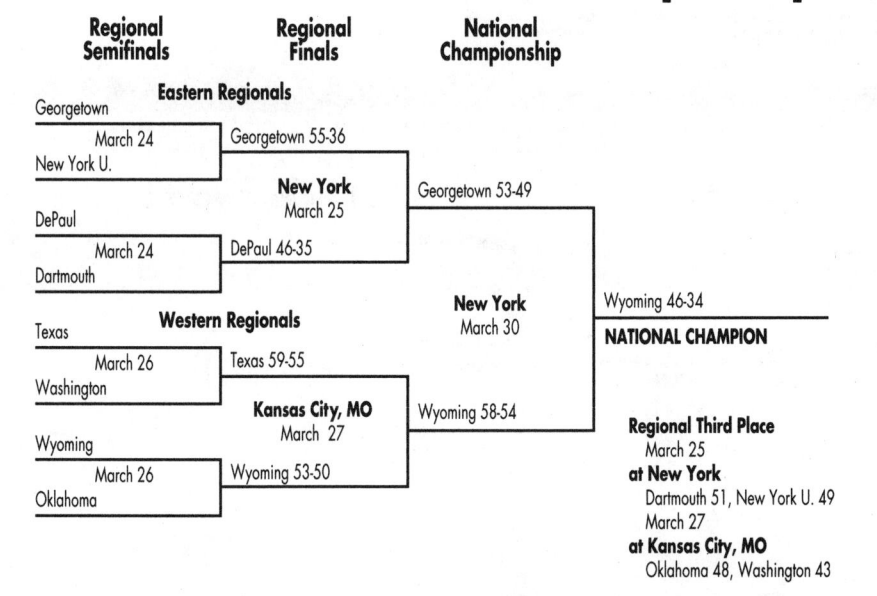

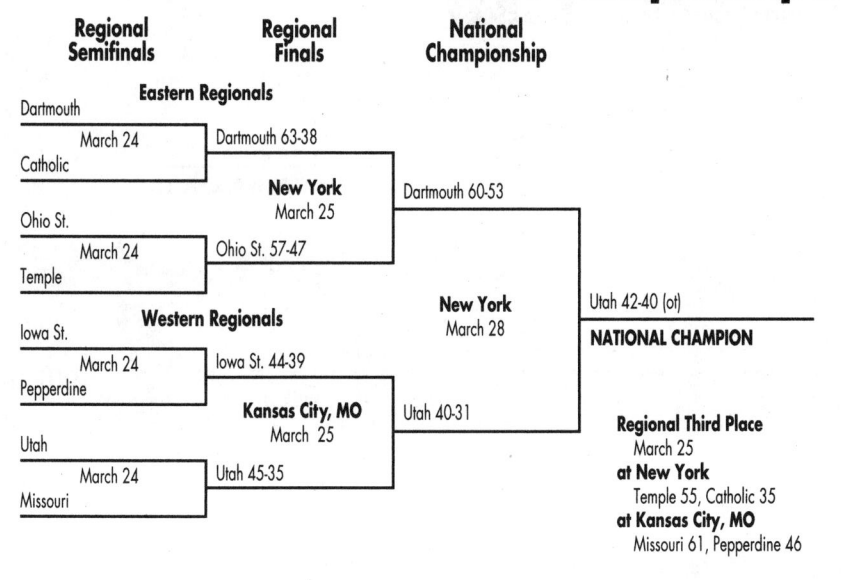

Regional Semifinals | **Regional Finals** | **National Championship**

Eastern Regionals
- Georgetown
- March 24
- New York U.
  - Georgetown 55-36
- DePaul
- March 24
- Dartmouth
  - DePaul 46-35

New York March 25
- Georgetown 53-49

Western Regionals
- Texas
- March 26
- Washington
  - Texas 59-55
- Wyoming
- March 26
- Oklahoma
  - Wyoming 53-50

Kansas City, MO March 27
- Wyoming 58-54

New York March 30
- Wyoming 46-34
- **NATIONAL CHAMPION**

Regional Third Place
March 25
at New York
  Dartmouth 51, New York U. 49
March 27
at Kansas City, MO
  Oklahoma 48, Washington 43

1944 Championship Bracket

Regional Semifinals | **Regional Finals** | **National Championship**

Eastern Regionals
- Dartmouth
- March 24
- Catholic
  - Dartmouth 63-38
- Ohio St.
- March 24
- Temple
  - Ohio St. 57-47

New York March 25
- Dartmouth 60-53

Western Regionals
- Iowa St.
- March 24
- Pepperdine
  - Iowa St. 44-39
- Utah
- March 24
- Missouri
  - Utah 45-35

Kansas City, MO March 25
- Utah 40-31

New York March 28
- Utah 42-40 (ot)
- **NATIONAL CHAMPION**

Regional Third Place
March 25
at New York
  Temple 55, Catholic 35
at Kansas City, MO
  Missouri 61, Pepperdine 46

THE TOURNAMENT FIELD

1945 Championship Bracket

Regional Semifinals | **Regional Finals** | **National Championship**

Eastern Regionals
- New York U.
- Tufts — March 22 → New York U. 59-44
- Ohio St.
- Kentucky — March 22 → Ohio St. 45-37

New York — March 24 → New York U. 70-65 (ot)

Western Regionals
- Arkansas
- Oregon — March 23 → Arkansas 79-76
- Oklahoma St.
- Utah — March 23 → Oklahoma St. 62-37

Kansas City, MO — March 24 → Oklahoma St. 68-41

New York — March 27

Oklahoma St. 49-45
NATIONAL CHAMPION

Regional Third Place
March 24
at New York
Kentucky 66, Tufts 56
at Kansas City, MO
Oregon 69, Utah 66

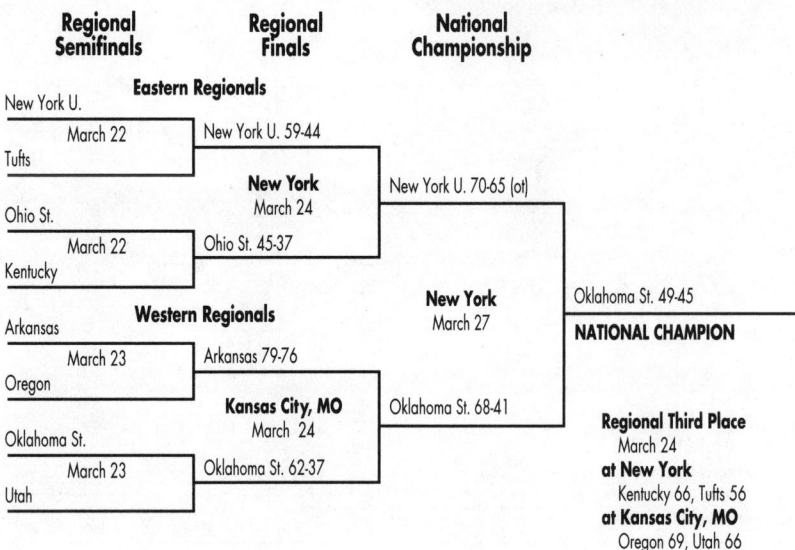

1946 Championship Bracket

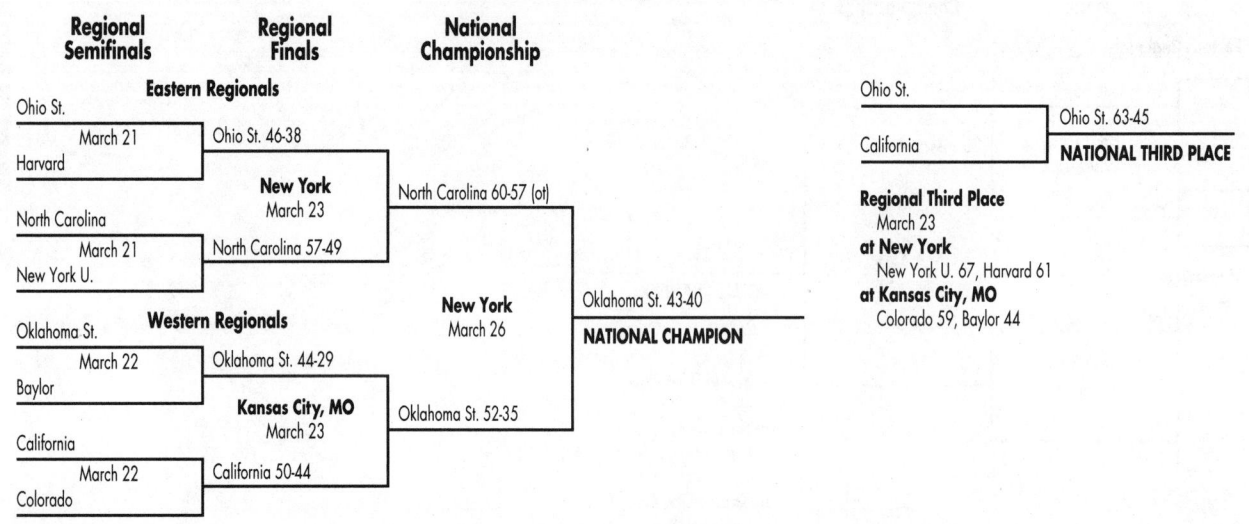

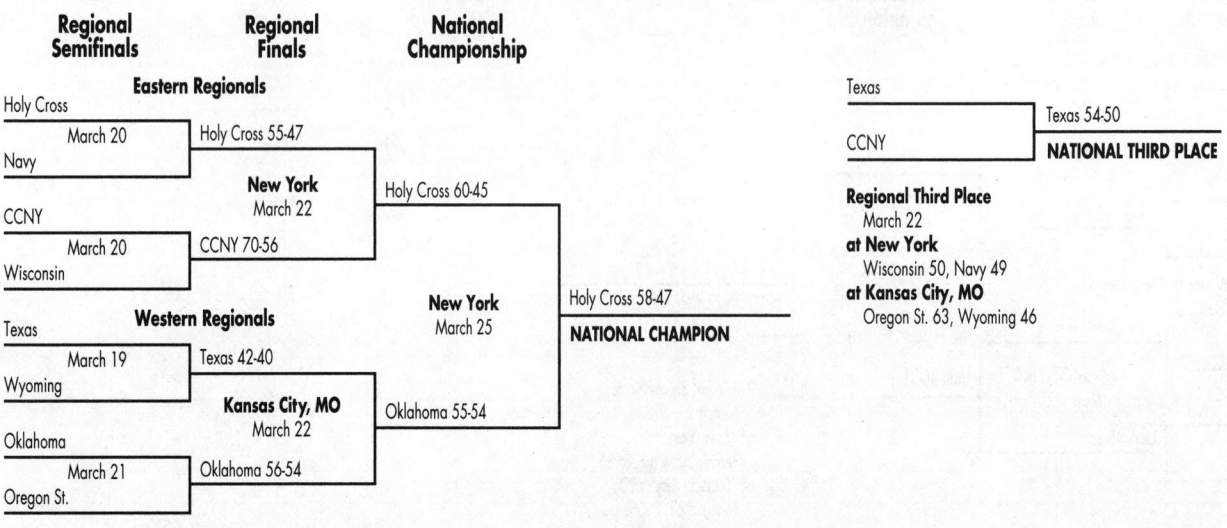

Regional Semifinals | **Regional Finals** | **National Championship**

Eastern Regionals
- Ohio St.
- Harvard — March 21 → Ohio St. 46-38
- North Carolina
- New York U. — March 21 → North Carolina 57-49

New York — March 23 → North Carolina 60-57 (ot)

Western Regionals
- Oklahoma St.
- Baylor — March 22 → Oklahoma St. 44-29
- California
- Colorado — March 22 → California 50-44

Kansas City, MO — March 23 → Oklahoma St. 52-35

New York — March 26

Oklahoma St. 43-40
NATIONAL CHAMPION

Ohio St.
California → Ohio St. 63-45
NATIONAL THIRD PLACE

Regional Third Place
March 23
at New York
New York U. 67, Harvard 61
at Kansas City, MO
Colorado 59, Baylor 44

1947 Championship Bracket

Regional Semifinals | **Regional Finals** | **National Championship**

Eastern Regionals
- Holy Cross
- Navy — March 20 → Holy Cross 55-47
- CCNY
- Wisconsin — March 20 → CCNY 70-56

New York — March 22 → Holy Cross 60-45

Western Regionals
- Texas
- Wyoming — March 19 → Texas 42-40
- Oklahoma
- Oregon St. — March 21 → Oklahoma 56-54

Kansas City, MO — March 22 → Oklahoma 55-54

New York — March 25

Holy Cross 58-47
NATIONAL CHAMPION

Texas
CCNY → Texas 54-50
NATIONAL THIRD PLACE

Regional Third Place
March 22
at New York
Wisconsin 50, Navy 49
at Kansas City, MO
Oregon St. 63, Wyoming 46

ALL-TIME TOURNAMENT FIELD—BRACKETS

1948 Championship Bracket

Regional Semifinals | **Regional Finals** | **National Championship**

Eastern Regionals
- Kentucky / March 19 / Columbia → Kentucky 76-53
- Holy Cross / March 19 / Michigan → Holy Cross 63-45
- New York, March 20: Kentucky 60-52

Western Regionals
- Kansas St. / March 19 / Wyoming → Kansas St. 58-48
- Baylor / March 19 / Washington → Baylor 64-62
- Kansas City, MO, March 20: Baylor 60-52

New York, March 23: Kentucky 58-42 — **NATIONAL CHAMPION**

Holy Cross vs. Kansas St. → Holy Cross 60-54 — **NATIONAL THIRD PLACE**

Regional Third Place — March 20
- at New York: Michigan 66, Columbia 49
- at Kansas City, MO: Washington 57, Wyoming 47

1949 Championship Bracket

Eastern Regionals
- Illinois / March 21 / Yale → Illinois 71-67
- Kentucky / March 21 / Villanova → Kentucky 85-72
- New York, March 22: Kentucky 76-47

Western Regionals
- Oklahoma St. / March 18 / Wyoming → Oklahoma St. 40-39
- Oregon St. / March 18 / Arkansas → Oregon St. 56-38
- Kansas City, MO, March 19: Oklahoma St. 55-30

Seattle, March 26: Kentucky 46-36 — **NATIONAL CHAMPION**

Illinois vs. Oregon St. → Illinois 57-53 — **NATIONAL THIRD PLACE**

Regional Third Place — March 22
- at New York: Villanova 78, Yale 67 (March 19)
- at Kansas City, MO: Arkansas 61, Wyoming 48

1950 Championship Bracket

Eastern Regionals
- CCNY / March 23 / Ohio St. → CCNY 56-55
- North Carolina St. / March 24 / Holy Cross → North Carolina St. 87-74
- New York, March 25: CCNY 78-73

Western Regionals
- Baylor / March 23 / Brigham Young → Baylor 56-55
- Bradley / March 24 / UCLA → Bradley 73-59
- Kansas City, MO, March 25: Bradley 68-66

New York, March 28: CCNY 71-68 — **NATIONAL CHAMPION**

North Carolina St. vs. Baylor → North Carolina St. 53-41 — **NATIONAL THIRD PLACE**

Regional Third Place — March 25
- at New York: Ohio St. 72, Holy Cross 52
- at Kansas City, MO: Brigham Young 83, UCLA 62

1951 Championship Bracket

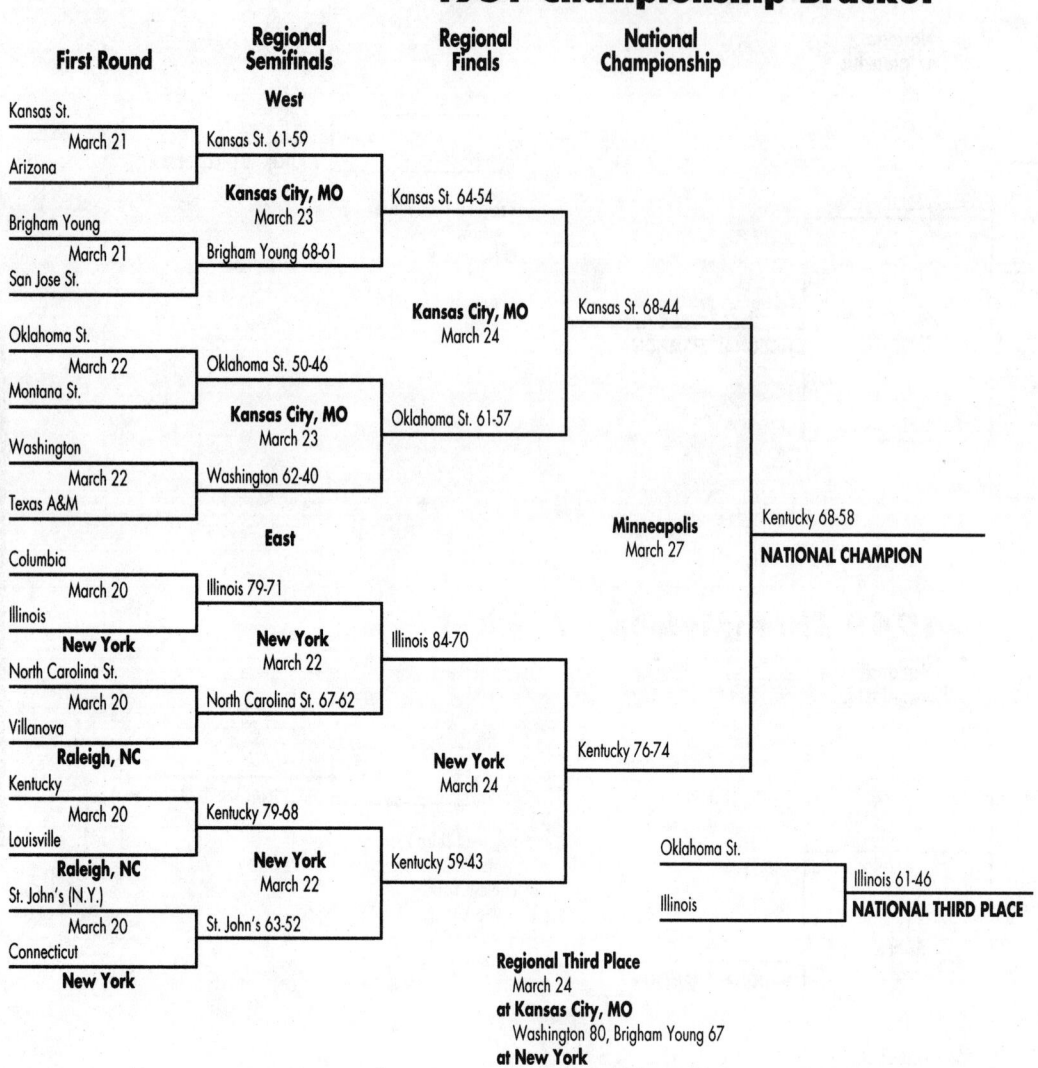

First Round — **Regional Semifinals** — **Regional Finals** — **National Championship**

West

- Kansas St.
  - March 21
- Arizona
  - Kansas St. 61-59
  - **Kansas City, MO** — March 23
- Brigham Young
  - March 21
- San Jose St.
  - Brigham Young 68-61
  - Kansas St. 64-54
  - **Kansas City, MO** — March 24
- Oklahoma St.
  - March 22
- Montana St.
  - Oklahoma St. 50-46
  - **Kansas City, MO** — March 23
- Washington
  - March 22
- Texas A&M
  - Washington 62-40
  - Oklahoma St. 61-57
  - Kansas St. 68-44

East

- Columbia
  - March 20
- Illinois
  - Illinois 79-71
  - **New York** — March 22
- **New York** — North Carolina St.
  - March 20
- Villanova
  - North Carolina St. 67-62
  - Illinois 84-70
  - **New York** — March 24
- **Raleigh, NC** — Kentucky
  - March 20
- Louisville
  - Kentucky 79-68
  - **New York** — March 22
- **Raleigh, NC** — St. John's (N.Y.)
  - March 20
- Connecticut
  - St. John's 63-52
  - Kentucky 59-43
  - Kentucky 76-74

Minneapolis — March 27

Kentucky 68-58
NATIONAL CHAMPION

- Oklahoma St.
- Illinois
  - Illinois 61-46
  - **NATIONAL THIRD PLACE**

New York

Regional Third Place
March 24
at Kansas City, MO
 Washington 80, Brigham Young 67
at New York
 St. John's (N.Y.) 71, North Carolina St. 59

1952 Championship Bracket

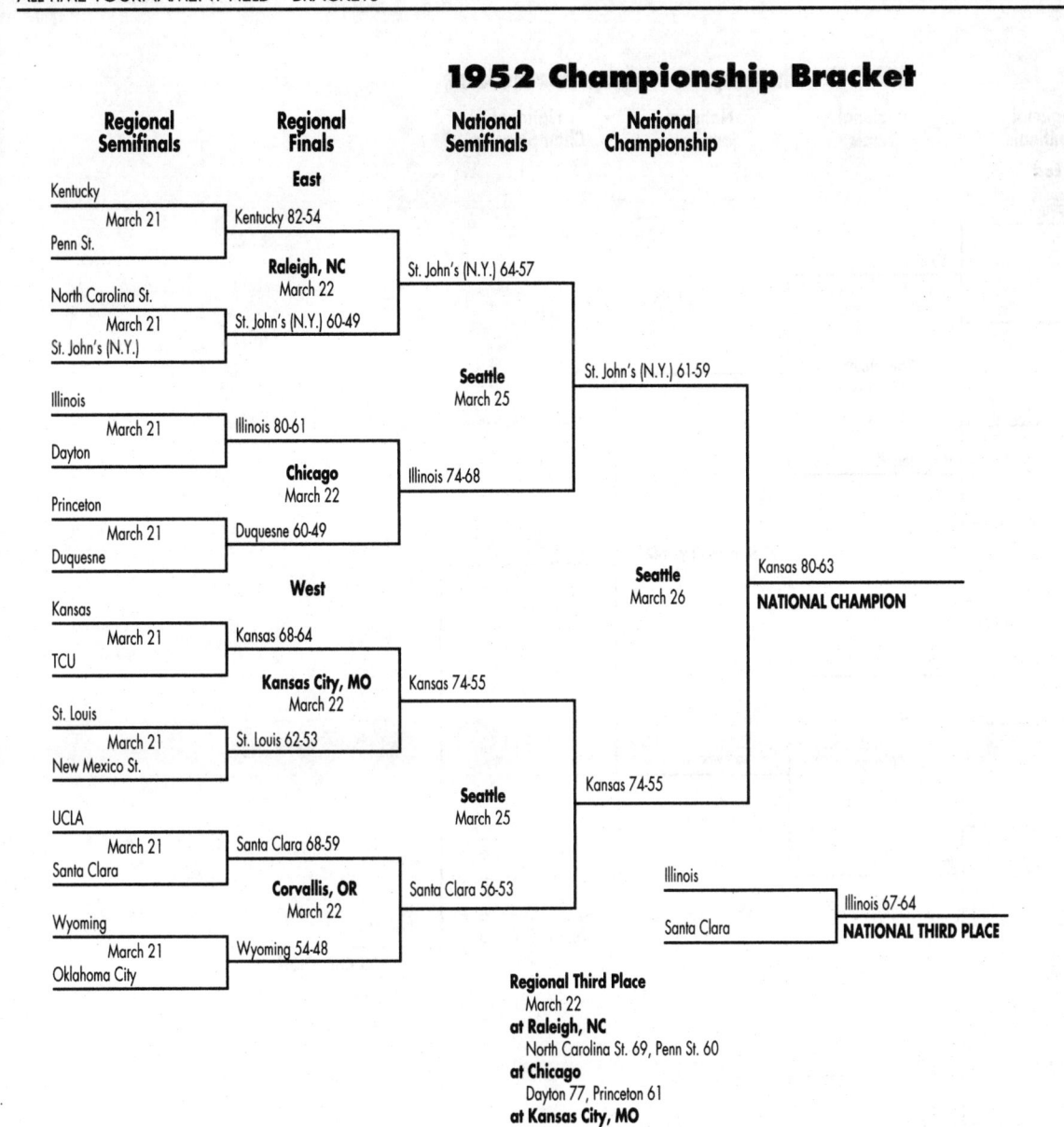

Regional Semifinals | **Regional Finals** | **National Semifinals** | **National Championship**

East

- Kentucky
- March 21
- Penn St.
  - Kentucky 82-54
  - **Raleigh, NC** — March 22
- North Carolina St.
- March 21
- St. John's (N.Y.)
  - St. John's (N.Y.) 60-49

St. John's (N.Y.) 64-57

Seattle — March 25

St. John's (N.Y.) 61-59

- Illinois
- March 21
- Dayton
  - Illinois 80-61
  - **Chicago** — March 22
- Princeton
- March 21
- Duquesne
  - Duquesne 60-49

Illinois 74-68

West

- Kansas
- March 21
- TCU
  - Kansas 68-64
  - **Kansas City, MO** — March 22
- St. Louis
- March 21
- New Mexico St.
  - St. Louis 62-53

Kansas 74-55

Seattle — March 25

Kansas 74-55

Seattle — March 26

Kansas 80-63

NATIONAL CHAMPION

- UCLA
- March 21
- Santa Clara
  - Santa Clara 68-59
  - **Corvallis, OR** — March 22
- Wyoming
- March 21
- Oklahoma City
  - Wyoming 54-48

Santa Clara 56-53

Illinois
Santa Clara
Illinois 67-64
NATIONAL THIRD PLACE

Regional Third Place
March 22
at Raleigh, NC
North Carolina St. 69, Penn St. 60
at Chicago
Dayton 77, Princeton 61
at Kansas City, MO
TCU 61, New Mexico St. 44
at Corvallis, OR
Oklahoma City 55, UCLA 53

1953 Championship Bracket

First Round

- Lebanon Valley
  - March 10
- Fordham
  - **Philadelphia**

- Holy Cross
  - March 10
- Navy
  - **Philadelphia**

- Notre Dame
  - March 10
- Eastern Ky.
  - **Fort Wayne, IN**

- DePaul
  - March 10
- Miami (Ohio)
  - **Fort Wayne, IN**

- Seattle
  - March 10
- Idaho St.
  - **Seattle**

- Santa Clara
  - March 10
- Hardin-Simmons
  - **Palo Alto, CA**

Regional Semifinals

East
- Lebanon Valley 80-67
  - March 13
- LSU

- Holy Cross 87-74
  - March 13
- Wake Forest

- Notre Dame 72-57
  - March 13
- Pennsylvania

- DePaul 74-72
  - March 13
- Indiana

West
- Seattle 88-77
  - March 13
- Washington

- Santa Clara 81-56
  - March 13
- Wyoming

- TCU
  - March 13
- Oklahoma St.

- Kansas
  - March 13
- Oklahoma City

Regional Finals

- LSU 89-76
- **Raleigh, NC** March 14
- Holy Cross 79-71

- Notre Dame 69-57
- **Chicago** March 14
- Indiana 82-80

- Washington 92-70
- **Corvallis, OR** March 14
- Santa Clara 67-52

- Oklahoma St. 71-54
- **Manhattan, KS** March 14
- Kansas 73-65

National Semifinals

- LSU 81-73
- **Kansas City, MO** March 17
- Indiana 79-66

- Washington 74-62
- **Kansas City, MO** March 17
- Kansas 61-55

National Championship

- Indiana 80-67
- **Kansas City, MO** March 18
- Kansas 79-53

Indiana 69-68
NATIONAL CHAMPION

LSU
Washington
Washington 88-69
NATIONAL THIRD PLACE

Regional Third Place
March 14
at Raleigh, NC
  Wake Forest 91, Lebanon Valley 71
at Chicago
  Pennsylvania 90, DePaul 70
at Corvallis, OR
  Seattle 80, Wyoming 64
at Manhattan, KS
  TCU 58, Oklahoma City 56

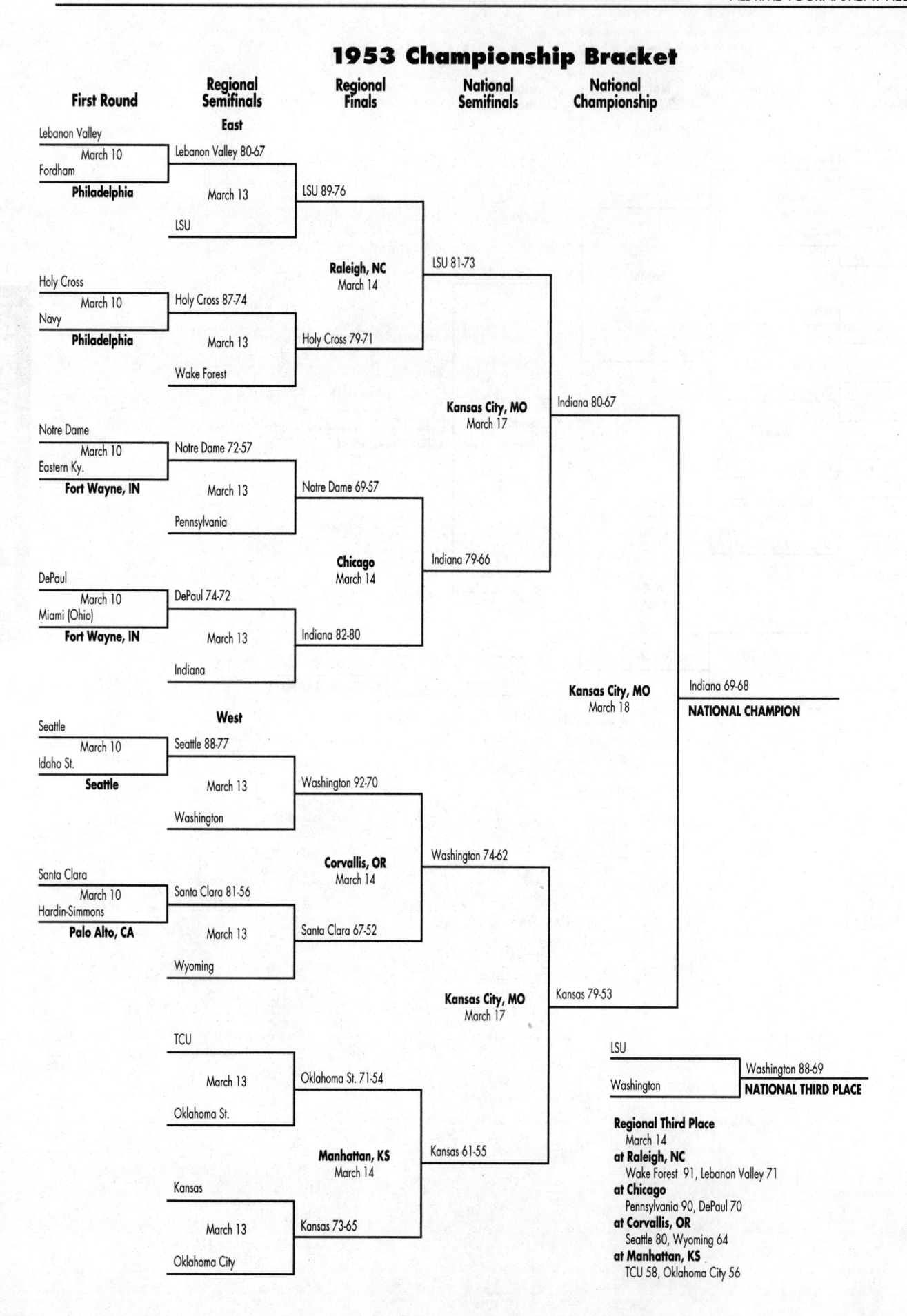

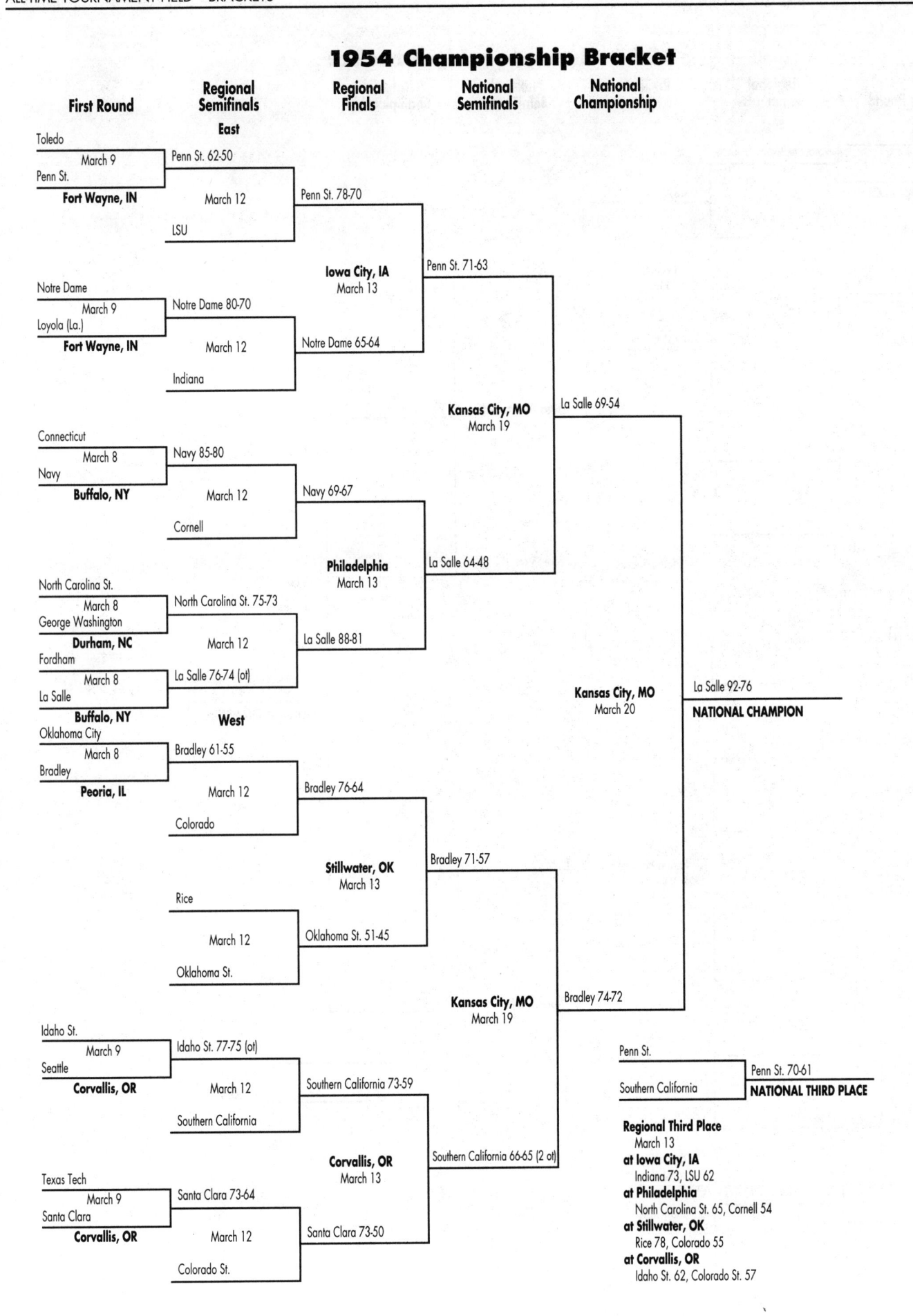

1954 Championship Bracket

First Round | **Regional Semifinals** | **Regional Finals** | **National Semifinals** | **National Championship**

East

- Toledo
- Penn St. — March 9, Fort Wayne, IN
  - Penn St. 62-50 (March 12)
  - LSU
    - Penn St. 78-70
- Notre Dame
- Loyola (La.) — March 9, Fort Wayne, IN
  - Notre Dame 80-70 (March 12)
  - Indiana
    - Notre Dame 65-64

Iowa City, IA — March 13
Penn St. 71-63

- Connecticut
- Navy — March 8, Buffalo, NY
  - Navy 85-80 (March 12)
  - Cornell
    - Navy 69-67
- North Carolina St.
- George Washington — March 8, Durham, NC
  - North Carolina St. 75-73 (March 12)
- Fordham
- La Salle — March 8, Buffalo, NY
  - La Salle 76-74 (ot)
    - La Salle 88-81

Philadelphia — March 13
La Salle 64-48

Kansas City, MO — March 19
La Salle 69-54

West

- Oklahoma City
- Bradley — March 8, Peoria, IL
  - Bradley 61-55 (March 12)
  - Colorado
    - Bradley 76-64
- Rice
  - (March 12)
- Oklahoma St.
  - Oklahoma St. 51-45

Stillwater, OK — March 13
Bradley 71-57

- Idaho St.
- Seattle — March 9, Corvallis, OR
  - Idaho St. 77-75 (ot) (March 12)
  - Southern California
    - Southern California 73-59
- Texas Tech
- Santa Clara — March 9, Corvallis, OR
  - Santa Clara 73-64 (March 12)
  - Colorado St.
    - Santa Clara 73-50

Corvallis, OR — March 13
Southern California 66-65 (2 ot)

Kansas City, MO — March 19
Bradley 74-72

Kansas City, MO — March 20
La Salle 92-76
NATIONAL CHAMPION

Penn St.
Southern California
Penn St. 70-61
NATIONAL THIRD PLACE

Regional Third Place
March 13
at Iowa City, IA
 Indiana 73, LSU 62
at Philadelphia
 North Carolina St. 65, Cornell 54
at Stillwater, OK
 Rice 78, Colorado 55
at Corvallis, OR
 Idaho St. 62, Colorado St. 57

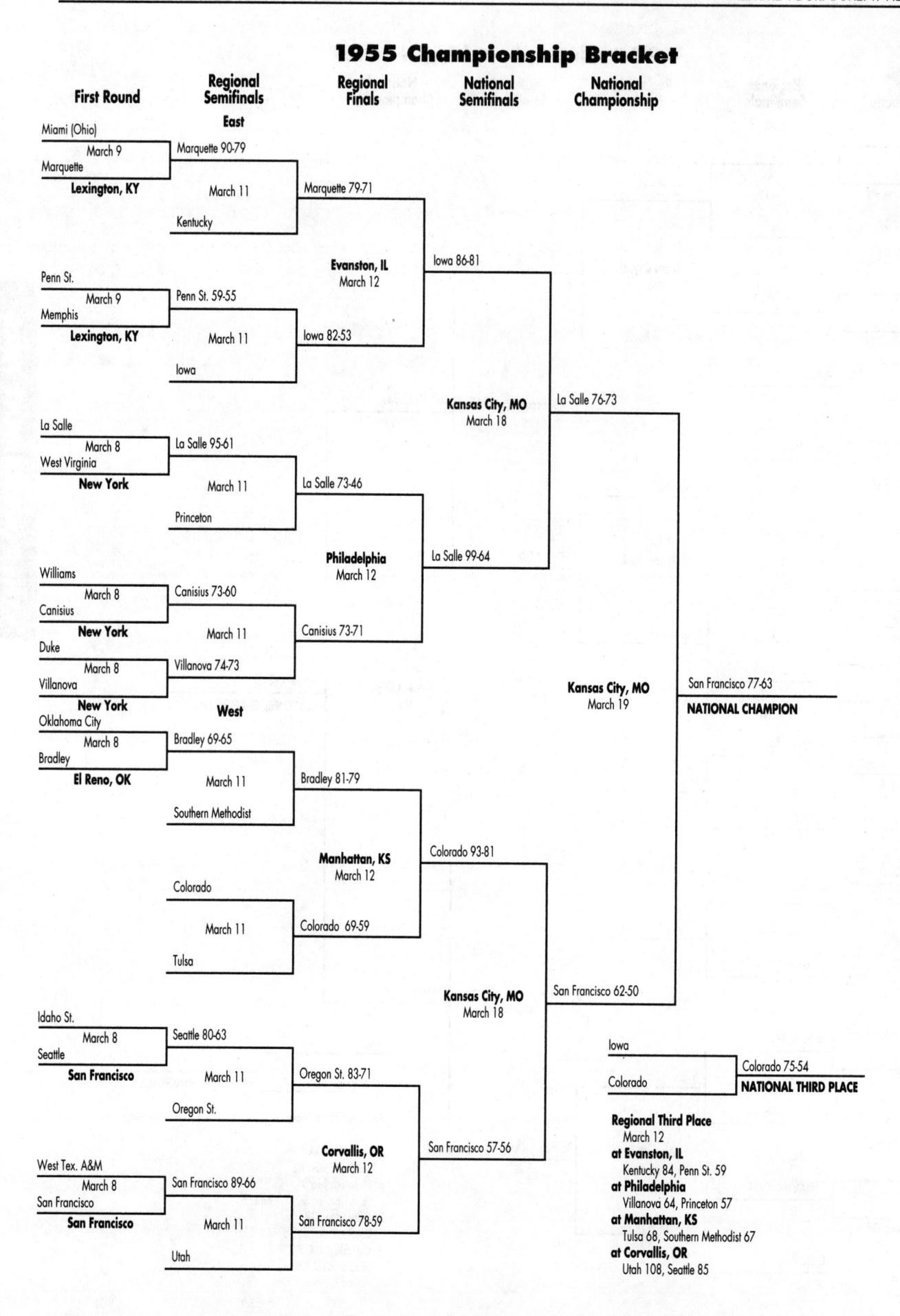

1955 Championship Bracket

First Round | **Regional Semifinals** | **Regional Finals** | **National Semifinals** | **National Championship**

East

- Miami (Ohio)
  - March 9
  - Marquette
  - **Lexington, KY**
- Marquette 90-79
  - March 11
  - Kentucky
- Marquette 79-71

- Penn St.
  - March 9
  - Memphis
  - **Lexington, KY**
- Penn St. 59-55
  - March 11
  - Iowa
- Iowa 82-53

Evanston, IL — March 12
Iowa 86-81

- La Salle
  - March 8
  - West Virginia
  - **New York**
- La Salle 95-61
  - March 11
  - Princeton
- La Salle 73-46

- Williams
  - March 8
  - Canisius
  - **New York**
- Canisius 73-60
  - March 11
- Canisius 73-71
- Duke
  - March 8
  - Villanova
  - **New York**
- Villanova 74-73

Philadelphia — March 12
La Salle 99-64

Kansas City, MO — March 18
La Salle 76-73

West

- Oklahoma City
  - March 8
  - Bradley
  - **El Reno, OK**
- Bradley 69-65
  - March 11
  - Southern Methodist
- Bradley 81-79

- Colorado
  - March 11
  - Tulsa
- Colorado 69-59

Manhattan, KS — March 12
Colorado 93-81

- Idaho St.
  - March 8
  - Seattle
  - **San Francisco**
- Seattle 80-63
  - March 11
  - Oregon St.
- Oregon St. 83-71

- West Tex. A&M
  - March 8
  - San Francisco
  - **San Francisco**
- San Francisco 89-66
  - March 11
  - Utah
- San Francisco 78-59

Corvallis, OR — March 12
San Francisco 57-56

Kansas City, MO — March 18
San Francisco 62-50

Kansas City, MO — March 19
San Francisco 77-63
NATIONAL CHAMPION

Iowa
Colorado
Colorado 75-54
NATIONAL THIRD PLACE

Regional Third Place
March 12
at **Evanston, IL**
Kentucky 84, Penn St. 59
at **Philadelphia**
Villanova 64, Princeton 57
at **Manhattan, KS**
Tulsa 68, Southern Methodist 67
at **Corvallis, OR**
Utah 108, Seattle 85

1956 Championship Bracket

East

First Round
- Connecticut
- Manhattan — March 13, New York
- Temple
- Holy Cross — March 12, New York
- West Virginia
- Dartmouth — March 13, New York
- North Carolina St.
- Canisius — March 12, New York

Regional Semifinals (March 16)
- Connecticut 84-75
- Temple 74-72
- Dartmouth 61-59 (ot)
- Canisius 79-78 (4 ot)

Regional Finals — Philadelphia, March 17
- Temple 65-59
- Canisius 66-58

Regional Winner: Temple 60-58

Midwest

First Round
- Iowa
- Marshall
- Morehead St. — March 12, Fort Wayne, IN
- Kentucky
- Wayne St. (Mich.)
- DePaul — March 12, Fort Wayne, IN

Regional Semifinals (March 16)
- Morehead St. 107-92
- Wayne St. 72-63

Regional Finals — Iowa City, IA, March 17
- Iowa 97-83
- Kentucky 84-64

Regional Winner: Iowa 89-77

West

First Round
- Houston
- Southern Methodist
- Texas Tech — March 13, Wichita, KS
- Kansas St.
- Oklahoma City
- Memphis — March 13, Wichita, KS

Regional Semifinals (March 16)
- Southern Methodist 68-67
- Oklahoma City 97-81

Regional Finals — Lawrence, KS, March 17
- Southern Methodist 89-74
- Oklahoma City 97-93

Regional Winner: Southern Methodist 84-63

Far West

First Round
- Utah
- Idaho St.
- Seattle — March 12, Seattle
- San Francisco
- UCLA

Regional Semifinals (March 16)
- Seattle 68-66
- San Francisco

Regional Finals — Corvallis, OR, March 17
- Utah 81-72
- San Francisco 72-61

Regional Winner: San Francisco 92-77

National Semifinals — Evanston, IL, March 22
- Iowa 83-76
- San Francisco 86-68

National Championship — Evanston, IL, March 23
- **San Francisco 83-71 — NATIONAL CHAMPION**

National Third Place
- Temple 90-81 (vs. Southern Methodist) — NATIONAL THIRD PLACE

Regional Third Place — March 17
- at Philadelphia: Dartmouth 85, Connecticut 64
- at Iowa City, IA: Morehead St. 95, Wayne St. 84
- at Lawrence, KS: Kansas St. 89, Houston 70
- at Corvallis, OR: UCLA 94, Seattle 70

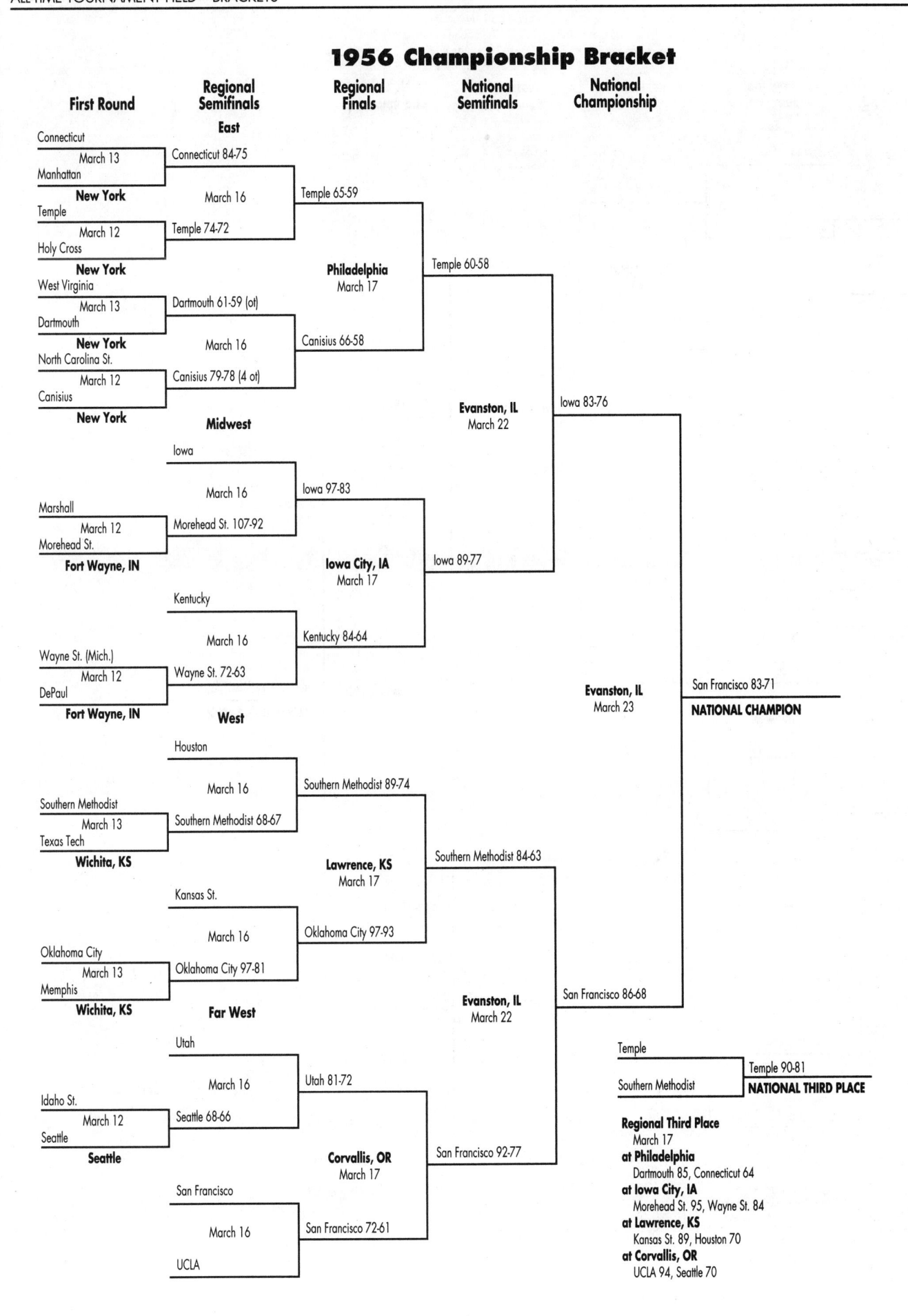

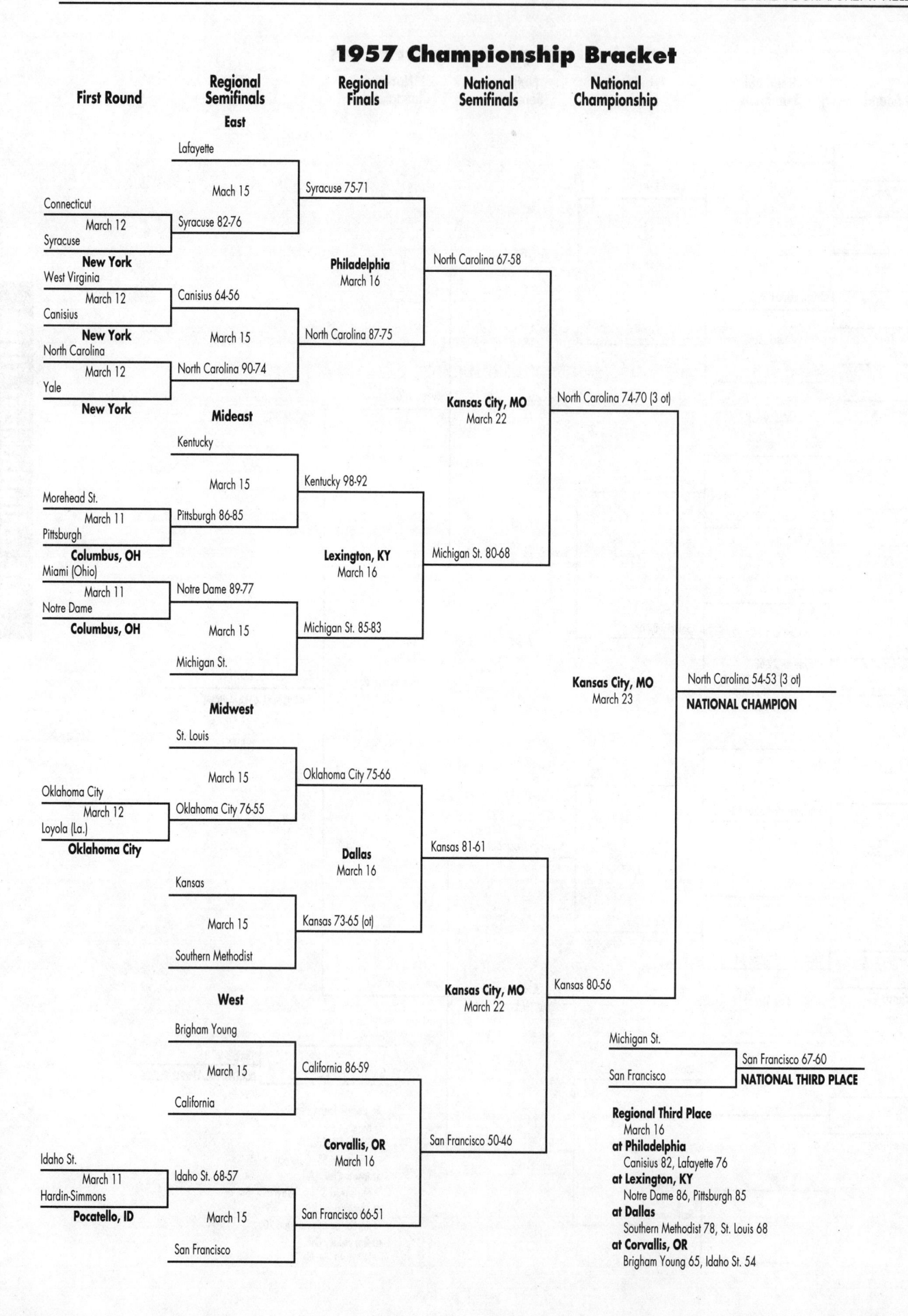

1957 Championship Bracket

First Round	Regional Semifinals	Regional Finals	National Semifinals	National Championship

East

- Lafayette
  - March 15
- Connecticut
  - March 12
- Syracuse
  - **New York**
  - Syracuse 82-76
  - Syracuse 75-71
- West Virginia
  - March 12
- Canisius
  - **New York**
  - Canisius 64-56
  - March 15
- North Carolina
  - March 12
- Yale
  - **New York**
  - North Carolina 90-74

Philadelphia March 16
- North Carolina 87-75
- North Carolina 67-58

Mideast

- Kentucky
  - March 15
- Morehead St.
  - March 11
- Pittsburgh
  - **Columbus, OH**
  - Pittsburgh 86-85
  - Kentucky 98-92
- Miami (Ohio)
  - March 11
- Notre Dame
  - **Columbus, OH**
  - Notre Dame 89-77
  - March 15
- Michigan St.
  - Michigan St. 85-83

Lexington, KY March 16
- Michigan St. 80-68

Kansas City, MO March 22
- North Carolina 74-70 (3 ot)

Midwest

- St. Louis
  - March 15
- Oklahoma City
  - March 12
- Loyola (La.)
  - **Oklahoma City**
  - Oklahoma City 76-55
  - Oklahoma City 75-66
- Kansas
  - March 15
- Southern Methodist
  - Kansas 73-65 (ot)

Dallas March 16
- Kansas 81-61

West

- Brigham Young
  - March 15
- California
  - California 86-59
- Idaho St.
  - March 11
- Hardin-Simmons
  - **Pocatello, ID**
  - Idaho St. 68-57
  - March 15
- San Francisco
  - San Francisco 66-51

Corvallis, OR March 16
- San Francisco 50-46

Kansas City, MO March 22
- Kansas 80-56

Kansas City, MO March 23
- North Carolina 54-53 (3 ot)
- **NATIONAL CHAMPION**

- Michigan St.
- San Francisco
  - San Francisco 67-60
  - **NATIONAL THIRD PLACE**

Regional Third Place
March 16
at Philadelphia
  Canisius 82, Lafayette 76
at Lexington, KY
  Notre Dame 86, Pittsburgh 85
at Dallas
  Southern Methodist 78, St. Louis 68
at Corvallis, OR
  Brigham Young 65, Idaho St. 54

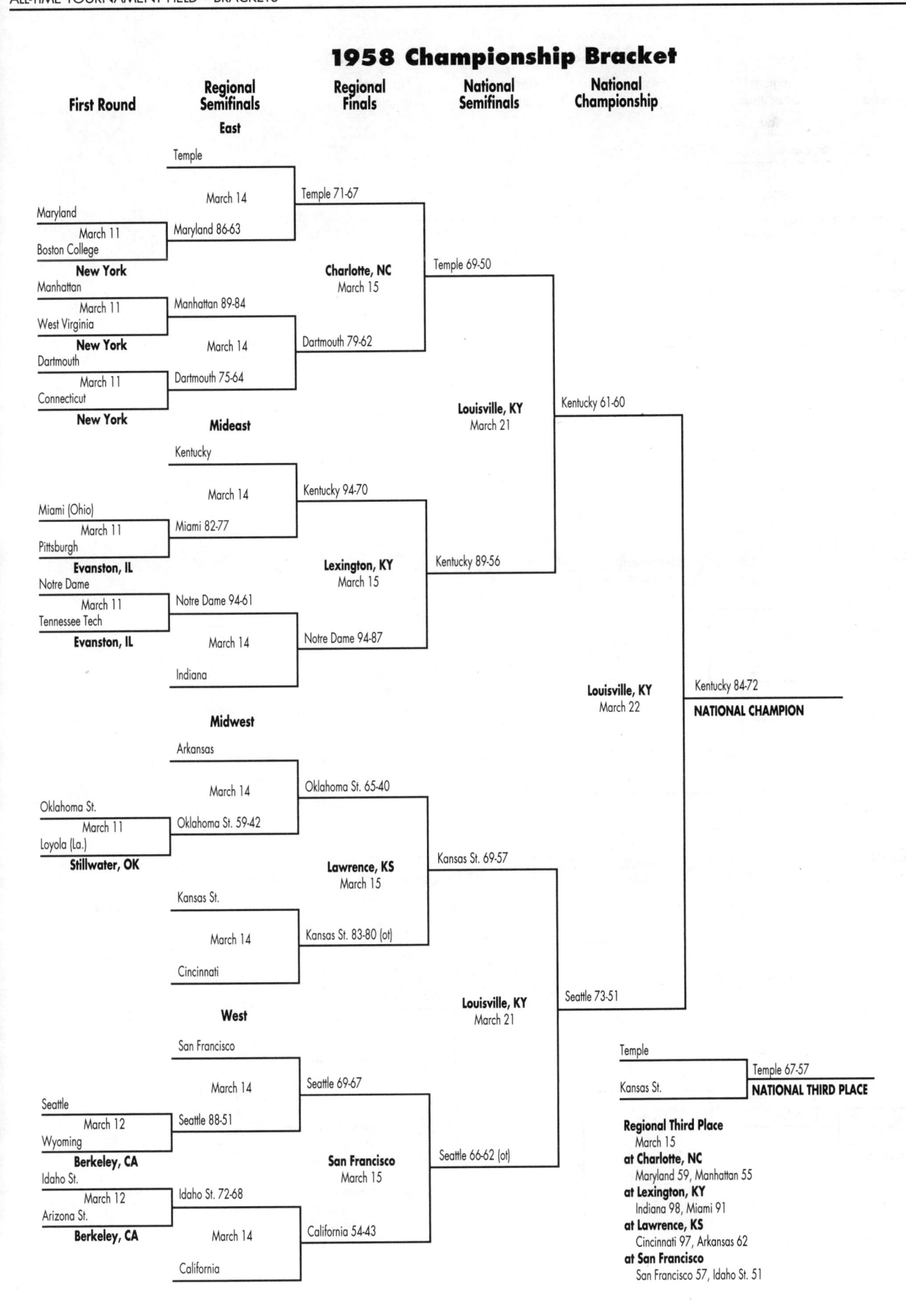

1958 Championship Bracket

East Regional

First Round:
- Maryland vs Boston College, March 11 at New York
- Manhattan vs West Virginia, March 11 at New York
- Dartmouth vs Connecticut, March 11 at New York

Regional Semifinals (March 14):
- Maryland 86-63
- Manhattan 89-84
- Dartmouth 75-64

Regional Finals — Charlotte, NC, March 15:
- Temple 71-67
- Dartmouth 79-62

Temple 69-50

Mideast Regional

First Round:
- Miami (Ohio) vs Pittsburgh, March 11 at Evanston, IL
- Notre Dame vs Tennessee Tech, March 11 at Evanston, IL

Regional Semifinals (March 14):
- Kentucky
- Miami 82-77
- Notre Dame 94-61
- Indiana

Regional Finals — Lexington, KY, March 15:
- Kentucky 94-70
- Notre Dame 94-87

Kentucky 89-56

Midwest Regional

First Round:
- Oklahoma St. vs Loyola (La.), March 11 at Stillwater, OK

Regional Semifinals (March 14):
- Arkansas
- Oklahoma St. 59-42
- Kansas St.
- Cincinnati

Regional Finals — Lawrence, KS, March 15:
- Oklahoma St. 65-40
- Kansas St. 83-80 (ot)

Kansas St. 69-57

West Regional

First Round:
- Seattle vs Wyoming, March 12 at Berkeley, CA
- Idaho St. vs Arizona St., March 12 at Berkeley, CA

Regional Semifinals (March 14):
- San Francisco
- Seattle 88-51
- Idaho St. 72-68
- California

Regional Finals — San Francisco, March 15:
- Seattle 69-67
- California 54-43

Seattle 66-62 (ot)

National Semifinals — Louisville, KY, March 21
- Kentucky 61-60
- Seattle 73-51

National Championship — Louisville, KY, March 22
Kentucky 84-72 — NATIONAL CHAMPION

National Third Place
- Temple
- Kansas St.

Temple 67-57 — NATIONAL THIRD PLACE

Regional Third Place
March 15
- **at Charlotte, NC:** Maryland 59, Manhattan 55
- **at Lexington, KY:** Indiana 98, Miami 91
- **at Lawrence, KS:** Cincinnati 97, Arkansas 62
- **at San Francisco:** San Francisco 57, Idaho St. 51

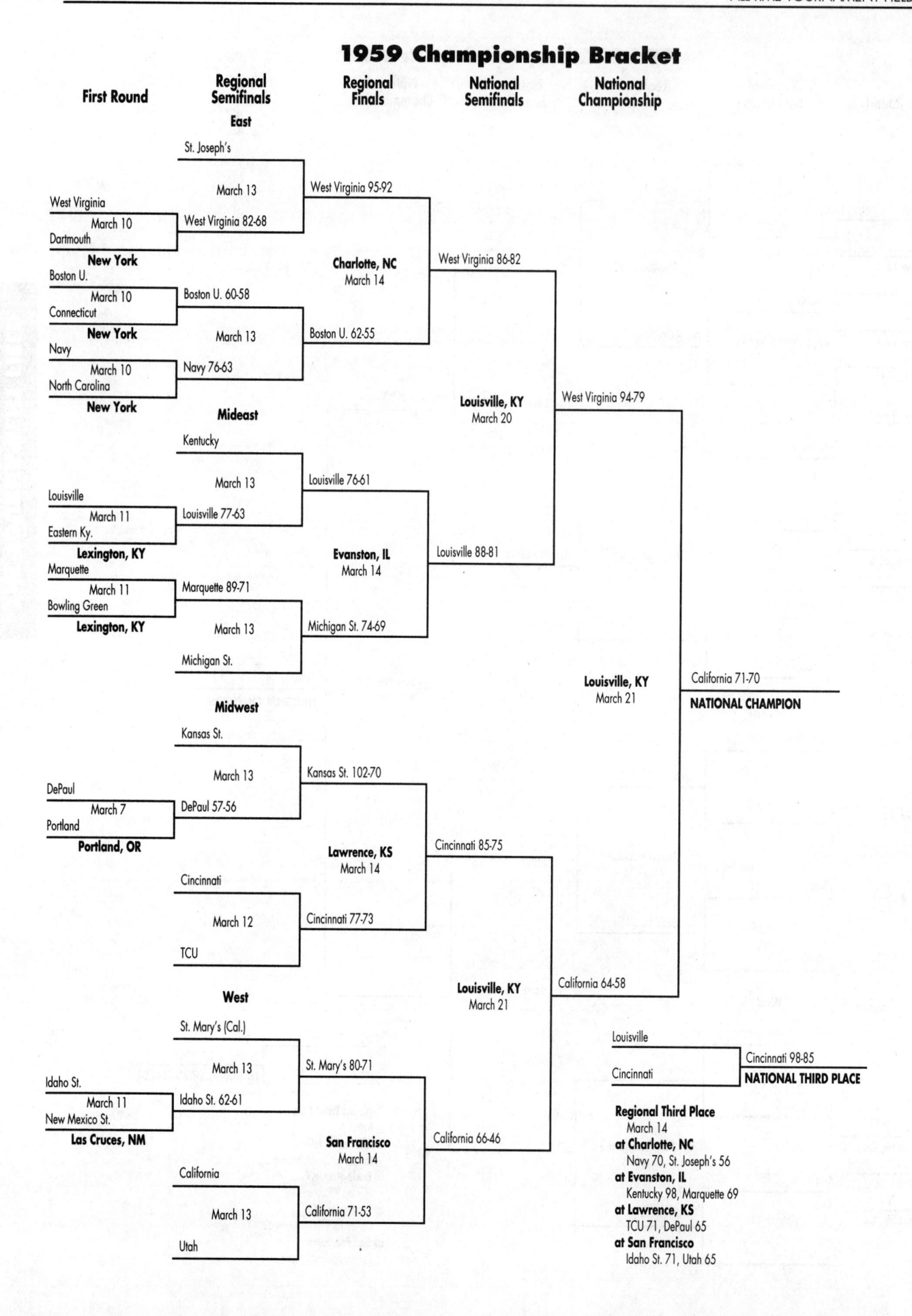

1959 Championship Bracket

First Round	Regional Semifinals	Regional Finals	National Semifinals	National Championship

East

- St. Joseph's
- West Virginia 82-68 (March 13)
  - West Virginia / Dartmouth — March 10, New York
- Boston U. 60-58 (March 10, New York)
  - Boston U. / Connecticut
- Navy 76-63 (March 13, New York)
  - Navy / North Carolina — March 10

Regional Semifinal results:
- West Virginia 82-68
- Boston U. 60-58
- Navy 76-63

Regional Finals at **Charlotte, NC — March 14**:
- West Virginia 95-92 (over St. Joseph's)
- Boston U. 62-55 (over Navy)

Regional Final: **West Virginia 86-82**

Mideast

- Kentucky
- Louisville 77-63 (March 13)
  - Louisville / Eastern Ky. — March 11, Lexington, KY
- Marquette 89-71 (March 11, Lexington, KY)
  - Marquette / Bowling Green
- Michigan St. 74-69 (March 13)
  - Michigan St.

Regional Finals at **Evanston, IL — March 14**:
- Louisville 76-61
- Michigan St. 74-69

Regional Final: **Louisville 88-81**

National Semifinal at **Louisville, KY — March 20**: West Virginia 94-79

Midwest

- Kansas St.
- DePaul 57-56 (March 13)
  - DePaul / Portland — March 7, Portland, OR
- Cincinnati
- Cincinnati 77-73 (March 12)
  - TCU

Regional Finals at **Lawrence, KS — March 14**:
- Kansas St. 102-70
- Cincinnati 77-73

Regional Final: **Cincinnati 85-75**

National Semifinal at **Louisville, KY — March 21**: California 64-58

West

- St. Mary's (Cal.)
- Idaho St. 62-61 (March 13)
  - Idaho St. / New Mexico St. — March 11, Las Cruces, NM
- California
- California 71-53 (March 13)
  - Utah

Regional Finals at **San Francisco — March 14**:
- St. Mary's 80-71
- California 71-53

Regional Final: **California 66-46**

National Championship

California 71-70 — NATIONAL CHAMPION

National Third Place

- Louisville
- Cincinnati

Cincinnati 98-85 — NATIONAL THIRD PLACE

Regional Third Place
March 14
- at Charlotte, NC: Navy 70, St. Joseph's 56
- at Evanston, IL: Kentucky 98, Marquette 69
- at Lawrence, KS: TCU 71, DePaul 65
- at San Francisco: Idaho St. 71, Utah 65

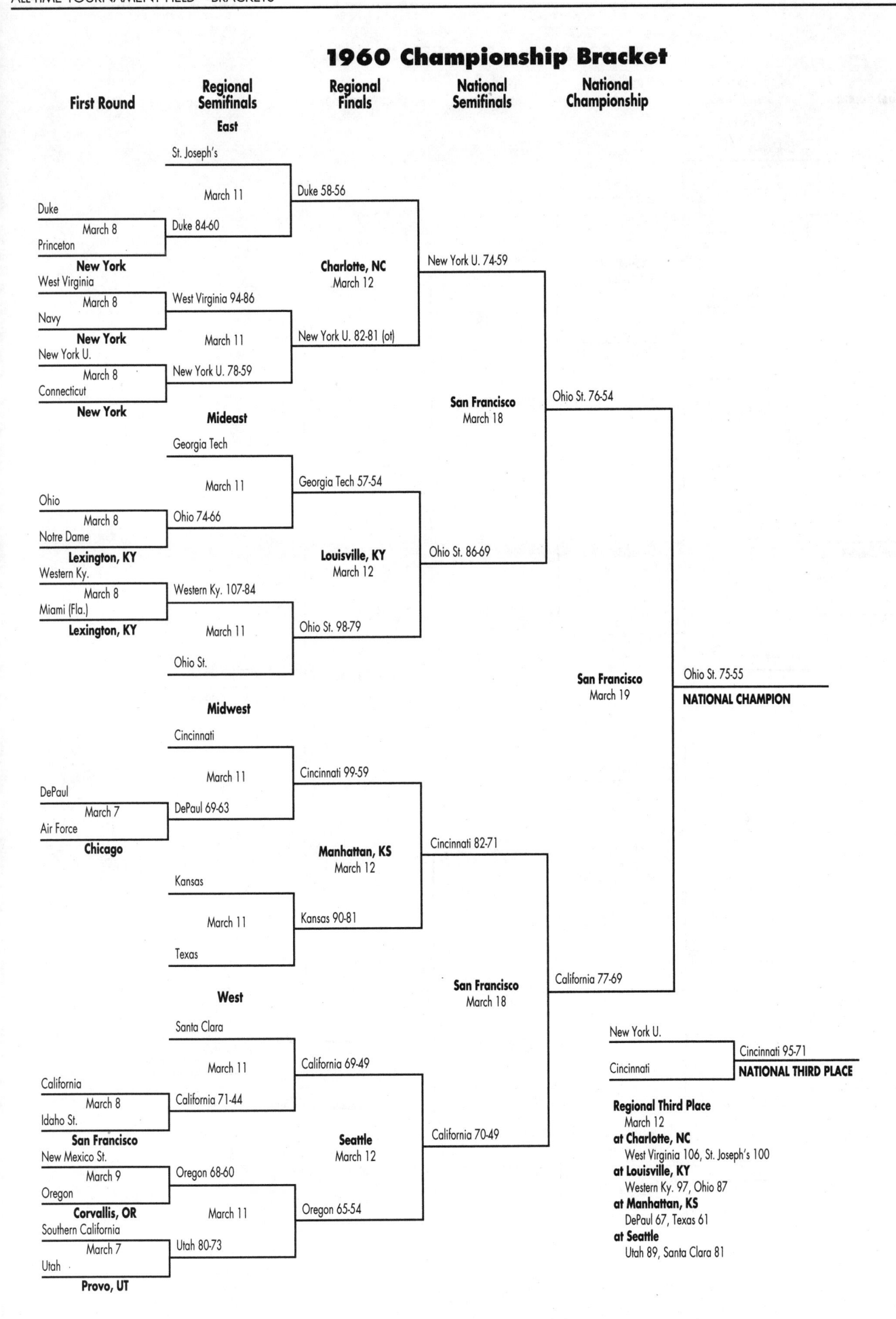

1960 Championship Bracket

East

Regional Semifinals — March 11, Charlotte, NC
- St. Joseph's
- Duke 84-60 (Duke vs Princeton, March 8, New York)
- West Virginia 94-86 (West Virginia vs Navy, March 8, New York)
- New York U. 78-59 (New York U. vs Connecticut, March 8, New York)

Regional Finals — Charlotte, NC, March 12
- Duke 58-56
- New York U. 82-81 (ot)

East Regional Champion: New York U. 74-59

Mideast

Regional Semifinals — March 11, Lexington, KY
- Georgia Tech
- Ohio 74-66 (Ohio vs Notre Dame, March 8, Lexington, KY)
- Western Ky. 107-84 (Western Ky. vs Miami (Fla.), March 8, Lexington, KY)
- Ohio St.

Regional Finals — Louisville, KY, March 12
- Georgia Tech 57-54
- Ohio St. 98-79

Mideast Regional Champion: Ohio St. 86-69

Midwest

Regional Semifinals — March 11, Chicago
- Cincinnati
- DePaul 69-63 (DePaul vs Air Force, March 7, Chicago)
- Kansas
- Texas

Regional Finals — Manhattan, KS, March 12
- Cincinnati 99-59
- Kansas 90-81

Midwest Regional Champion: Cincinnati 82-71

West

Regional Semifinals — March 11, Seattle
- Santa Clara
- California 71-44 (California vs Idaho St., March 8, San Francisco)
- New Mexico St.
- Oregon 68-60 (Oregon, March 9, Corvallis, OR)
- Utah 80-73 (Southern California vs Utah, March 7, Provo, UT)

Regional Finals — Seattle, March 12
- California 69-49
- Oregon 65-54

West Regional Champion: California 70-49

National Semifinals — San Francisco, March 18
- Ohio St. 76-54 (vs New York U.)
- California 77-69 (vs Cincinnati)

National Championship — San Francisco, March 19
Ohio St. 75-55 — NATIONAL CHAMPION

National Third Place
Cincinnati 95-71 (New York U. vs Cincinnati)

Regional Third Place — March 12
- **at Charlotte, NC:** West Virginia 106, St. Joseph's 100
- **at Louisville, KY:** Western Ky. 97, Ohio 87
- **at Manhattan, KS:** DePaul 67, Texas 61
- **at Seattle:** Utah 89, Santa Clara 81

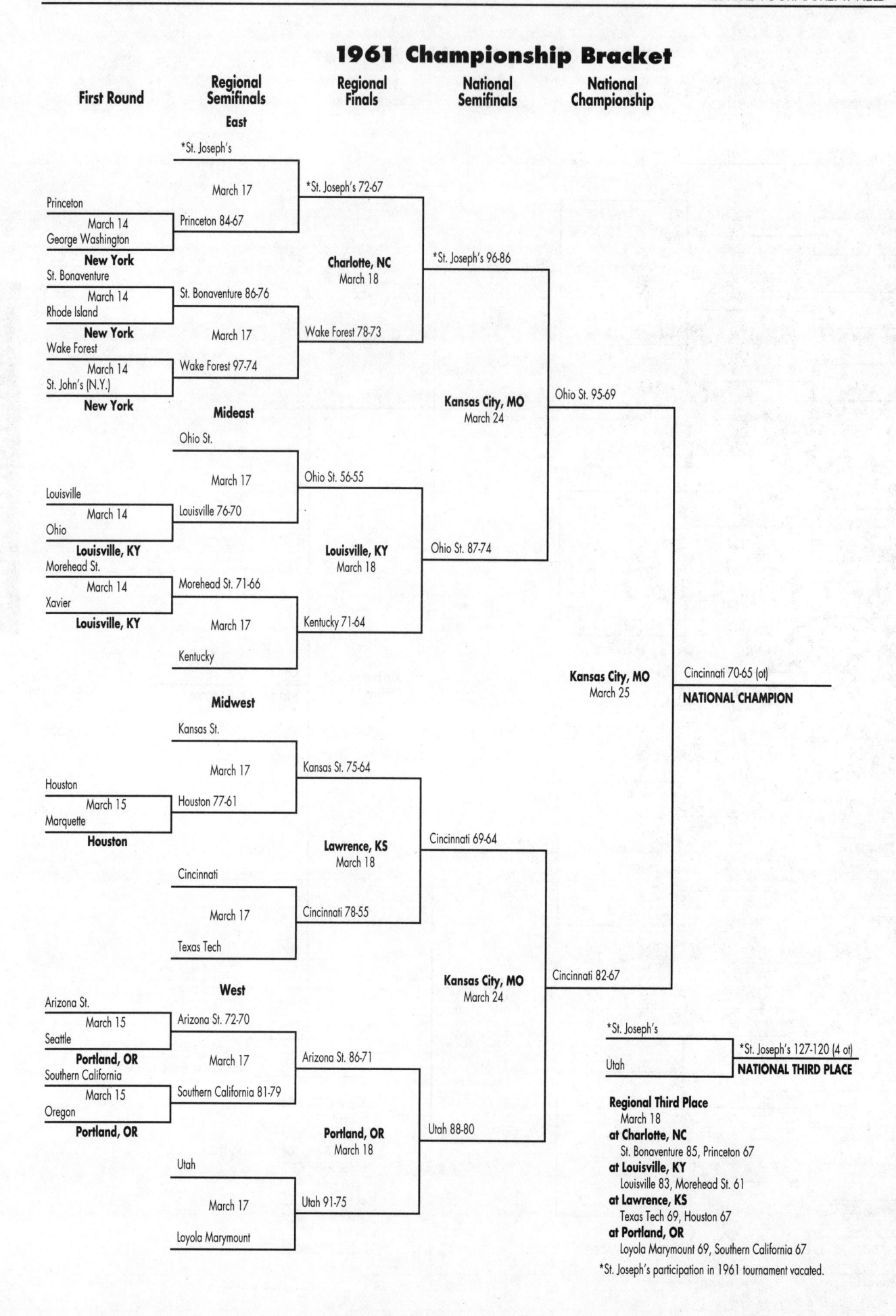

1961 Championship Bracket

First Round | **Regional Semifinals** | **Regional Finals** | **National Semifinals** | **National Championship**

East

- *St. Joseph's
  - March 17
  - Princeton 84-67
    - Princeton
    - March 14
    - George Washington
    - New York
- *St. Joseph's 72-67
- Charlotte, NC — March 18
- St. Bonaventure 86-76
  - St. Bonaventure
  - March 14
  - Rhode Island
  - New York
- Wake Forest 78-73
- Wake Forest 97-74
  - Wake Forest
  - March 14
  - St. John's (N.Y.)
  - New York

*St. Joseph's 96-86

Mideast

- Ohio St.
  - March 17
  - Louisville 76-70
    - Louisville
    - March 14
    - Ohio
    - Louisville, KY
- Ohio St. 56-55
- Louisville, KY — March 18
- Morehead St. 71-66
  - Morehead St.
  - March 14
  - Xavier
  - Louisville, KY
- Kentucky 71-64
  - March 17
  - Kentucky

Ohio St. 87-74

Kansas City, MO — March 24
Ohio St. 95-69

Midwest

- Kansas St.
  - March 17
  - Houston 77-61
    - Houston
    - March 15
    - Marquette
    - Houston
- Kansas St. 75-64
- Lawrence, KS — March 18
- Cincinnati
  - March 17
  - Cincinnati 78-55
    - Texas Tech

Cincinnati 69-64

West

- Arizona St.
  - March 17
  - Arizona St. 72-70
    - Arizona St.
    - March 15
    - Seattle
    - Portland, OR
- Arizona St. 86-71
- Portland, OR — March 18
- Southern California 81-79
  - Southern California
  - March 15
  - Oregon
  - Portland, OR
- Utah 91-75
  - Utah
  - March 17
  - Loyola Marymount

Utah 88-80

Kansas City, MO — March 24
Cincinnati 82-67

Kansas City, MO — March 25
Cincinnati 70-65 (ot)
NATIONAL CHAMPION

*St. Joseph's
Utah
*St. Joseph's 127-120 (4 ot)
NATIONAL THIRD PLACE

Regional Third Place
March 18
at Charlotte, NC
St. Bonaventure 85, Princeton 67
at Louisville, KY
Louisville 83, Morehead St. 61
at Lawrence, KS
Texas Tech 69, Houston 67
at Portland, OR
Loyola Marymount 69, Southern California 67

*St. Joseph's participation in 1961 tournament vacated.

ALL-TIME TOURNAMENT FIELD—BRACKETS   185

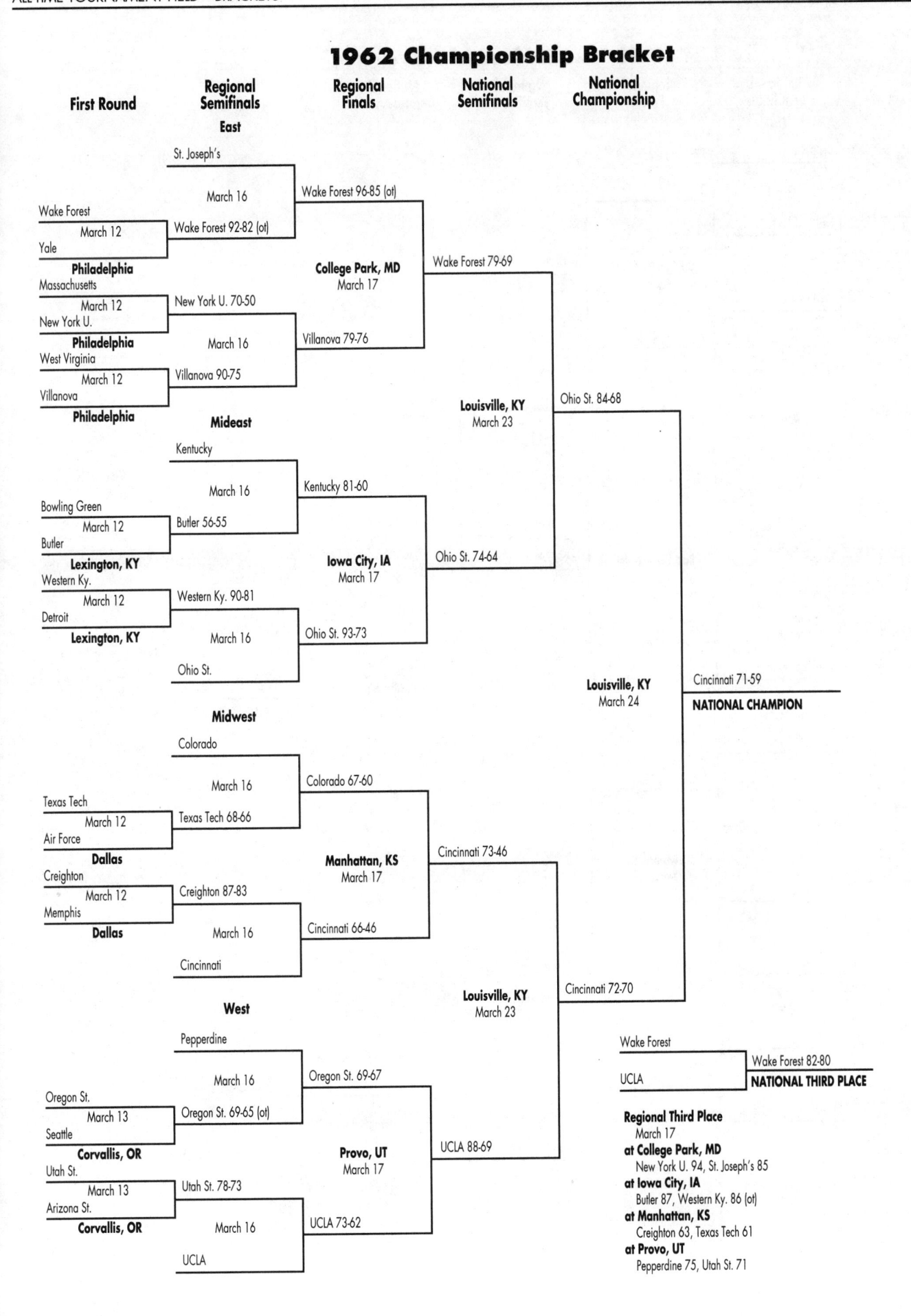

1962 Championship Bracket

First Round | **Regional Semifinals** | **Regional Finals** | **National Semifinals** | **National Championship**

East

- St. Joseph's
- March 16
- Wake Forest 92-82 (ot)
- Wake Forest 96-85 (ot)
- Wake Forest
  - March 12
  - Yale
- **Philadelphia**
- Massachusetts
  - March 12
  - New York U.
- **Philadelphia**
- New York U. 70-50
- March 16
- Villanova 90-75
- Villanova 79-76
- West Virginia
  - March 12
  - Villanova
- **Philadelphia**

College Park, MD — March 17
Wake Forest 79-69

Mideast

- Kentucky
- March 16
- Butler 56-55
- Kentucky 81-60
- Bowling Green
  - March 12
  - Butler
- **Lexington, KY**
- Western Ky.
  - March 12
  - Detroit
- **Lexington, KY**
- Western Ky. 90-81
- March 16
- Ohio St. 93-73
- Ohio St. 74-64
- Ohio St.

Iowa City, IA — March 17

Louisville, KY March 23
Ohio St. 84-68

Midwest

- Colorado
- March 16
- Texas Tech 68-66
- Colorado 67-60
- Texas Tech
  - March 12
  - Air Force
- **Dallas**
- Creighton
  - March 12
  - Memphis
- **Dallas**
- Creighton 87-83
- March 16
- Cincinnati 66-46
- Cincinnati
- Cincinnati 73-46

Manhattan, KS — March 17

Louisville, KY March 23
Cincinnati 72-70

West

- Pepperdine
- March 16
- Oregon St. 69-65 (ot)
- Oregon St. 69-67
- Oregon St.
  - March 13
  - Seattle
- **Corvallis, OR**
- Utah St.
  - March 13
  - Arizona St.
- **Corvallis, OR**
- Utah St. 78-73
- March 16
- UCLA 73-62
- UCLA
- UCLA 88-69

Provo, UT — March 17

Louisville, KY March 24
Cincinnati 71-59
NATIONAL CHAMPION

Wake Forest
Wake Forest 82-80
UCLA
NATIONAL THIRD PLACE

Regional Third Place
March 17
at College Park, MD
 New York U. 94, St. Joseph's 85
at Iowa City, IA
 Butler 87, Western Ky. 86 (ot)
at Manhattan, KS
 Creighton 63, Texas Tech 61
at Provo, UT
 Pepperdine 75, Utah St. 71

THE TOURNAMENT FIELD

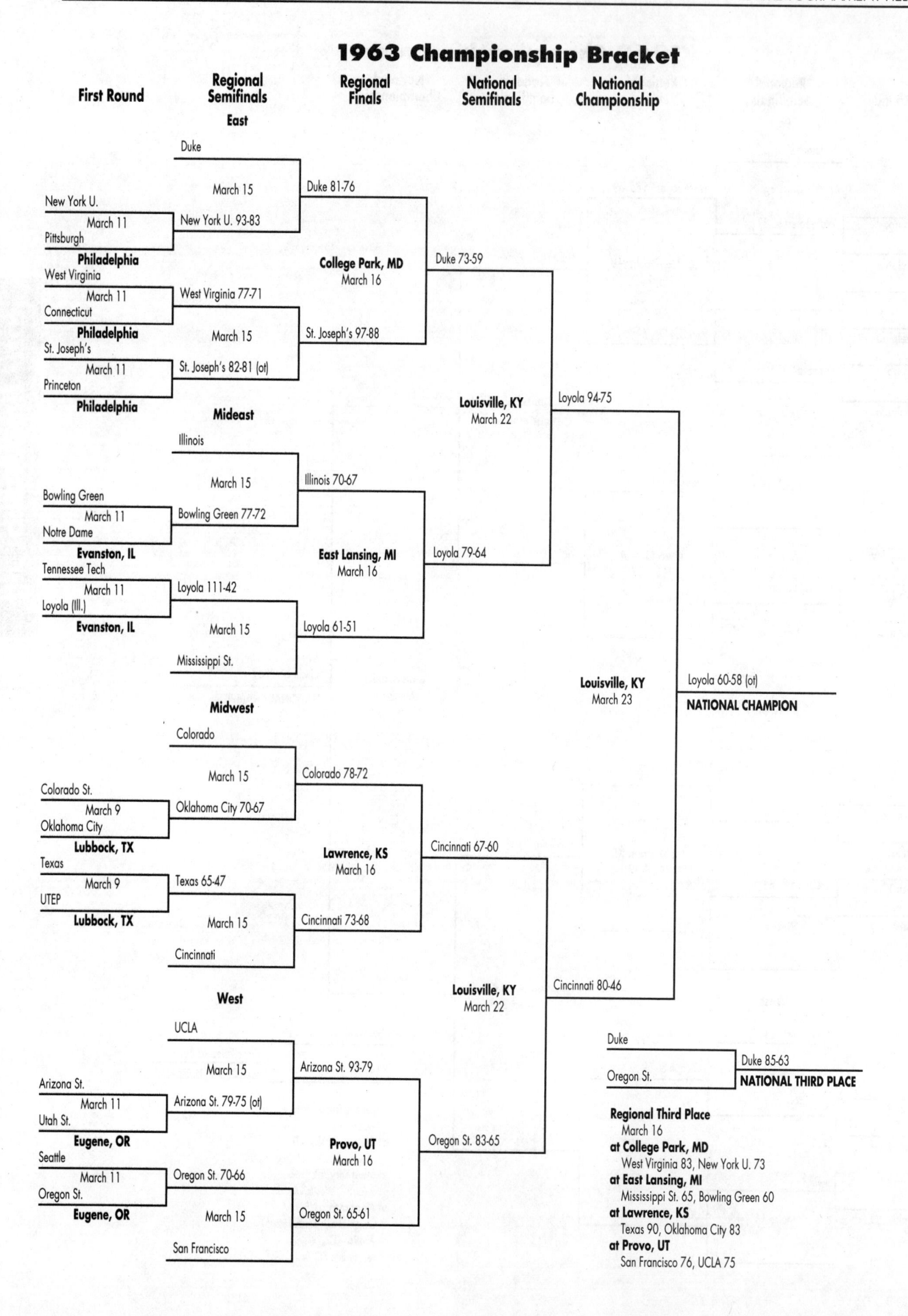

1963 Championship Bracket

First Round | Regional Semifinals | Regional Finals | National Semifinals | National Championship

East
- Duke
  - March 15
  - Duke 81-76
- New York U.
  - March 11 — Pittsburgh — **Philadelphia**
  - New York U. 93-83
- West Virginia
  - March 11 — Connecticut — **Philadelphia**
  - West Virginia 77-71
  - March 15
  - St. Joseph's 82-81 (ot)
- St. Joseph's
  - March 11 — Princeton — **Philadelphia**

College Park, MD — March 16
- Duke 73-59
- St. Joseph's 97-88

Mideast
- Illinois
  - March 15
  - Illinois 70-67
- Bowling Green
  - March 11 — Notre Dame — **Evanston, IL**
  - Bowling Green 77-72
- Tennessee Tech
  - March 11 — Loyola (Ill.) — **Evanston, IL**
  - Loyola 111-42
  - March 15
  - Loyola 61-51
- Mississippi St.

East Lansing, MI — March 16
- Illinois 70-67
- Loyola 79-64

Louisville, KY — March 22
- Loyola 94-75

Midwest
- Colorado
  - March 15
  - Colorado 78-72
- Colorado St.
  - March 9 — Oklahoma City — **Lubbock, TX**
  - Oklahoma City 70-67
- Texas
  - March 9 — UTEP — **Lubbock, TX**
  - Texas 65-47
  - March 15
- Cincinnati

Lawrence, KS — March 16
- Colorado 78-72
- Cincinnati 73-68

Cincinnati 67-60

Louisville, KY — March 22
- Cincinnati 80-46

West
- UCLA
  - March 15
  - Arizona St. 93-79
- Arizona St.
  - March 11 — Utah St. — **Eugene, OR**
  - Arizona St. 79-75 (ot)
- Seattle
  - March 11 — Oregon St. — **Eugene, OR**
  - Oregon St. 70-66
  - March 15
  - Oregon St. 65-61
- San Francisco

Provo, UT — March 16
- Arizona St. 93-79
- Oregon St. 83-65

Louisville, KY — March 23
- Loyola 60-58 (ot)
- **NATIONAL CHAMPION**

National Third Place
- Duke
- Oregon St.
- Duke 85-63
- **NATIONAL THIRD PLACE**

Regional Third Place
March 16
- **at College Park, MD**
  West Virginia 83, New York U. 73
- **at East Lansing, MI**
  Mississippi St. 65, Bowling Green 60
- **at Lawrence, KS**
  Texas 90, Oklahoma City 83
- **at Provo, UT**
  San Francisco 76, UCLA 75

ALL-TIME TOURNAMENT FIELD—BRACKETS 187

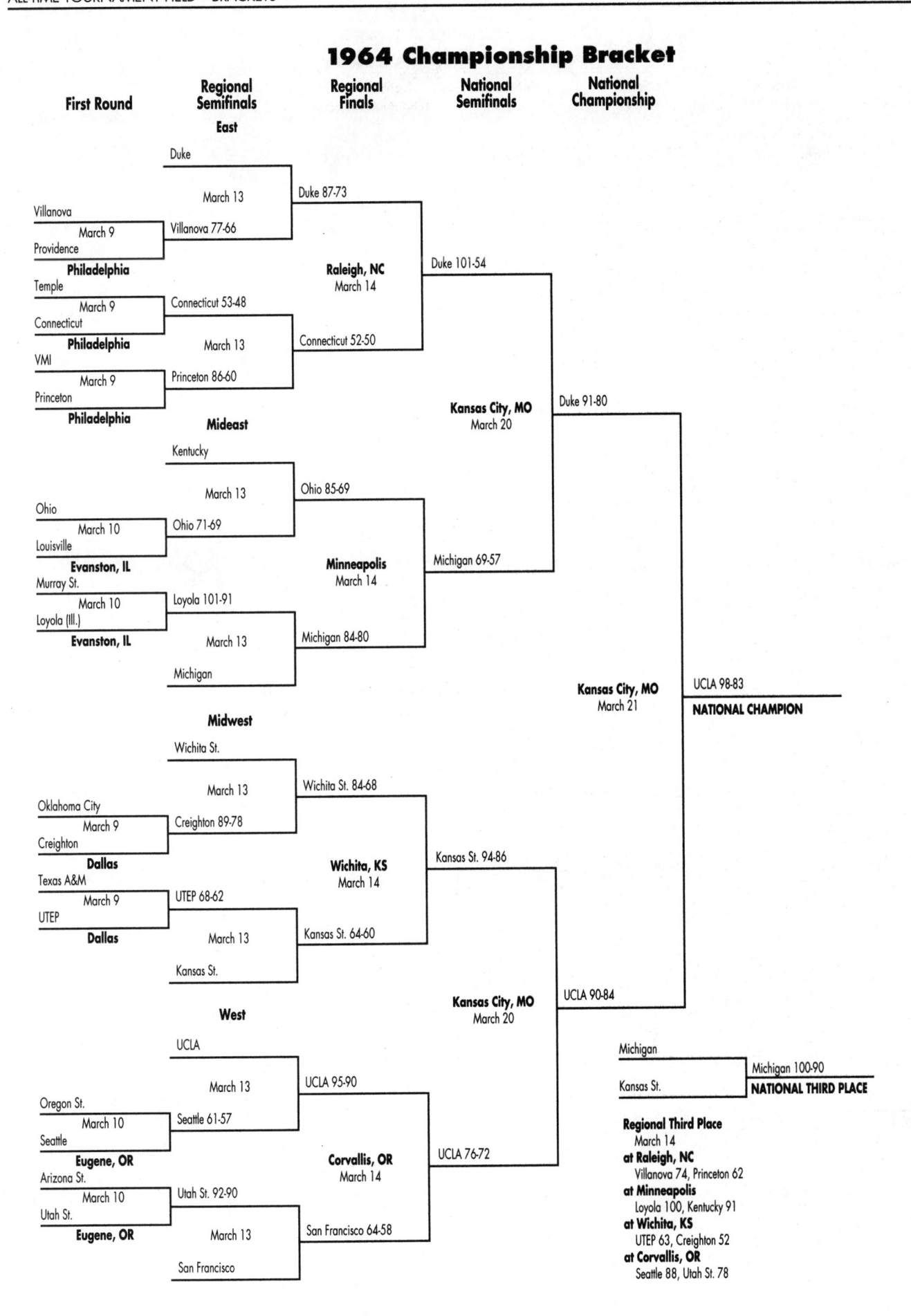

1964 Championship Bracket

First Round | **Regional Semifinals** | **Regional Finals** | **National Semifinals** | **National Championship**

East
- Duke
- Villanova (March 9, Philadelphia) def. Providence — Villanova 77-66
- Duke 87-73
- Temple vs Connecticut (March 9, Philadelphia) — Connecticut 53-48
- VMI vs Princeton (March 9, Philadelphia) — Princeton 86-60
- Connecticut 52-50 (March 13)
- **Raleigh, NC** March 14: Duke 101-54

Mideast
- Kentucky
- Ohio vs Louisville (March 10, Evanston, IL) — Ohio 71-69
- Ohio 85-69 (March 13)
- Murray St. vs Loyola (Ill.) (March 10, Evanston, IL) — Loyola 101-91
- Michigan 84-80 (March 13)
- Michigan
- **Minneapolis** March 14: Michigan 69-57

Kansas City, MO March 20: Duke 91-80

Midwest
- Wichita St.
- Oklahoma City vs Creighton (March 9, Dallas) — Creighton 89-78
- Wichita St. 84-68 (March 13)
- Texas A&M vs UTEP (March 9, Dallas) — UTEP 68-62
- Kansas St. 64-60 (March 13)
- Kansas St.
- **Wichita, KS** March 14: Kansas St. 94-86

West
- UCLA
- Oregon St. vs Seattle (March 10, Eugene, OR) — Seattle 61-57
- UCLA 95-90 (March 13)
- Arizona St. vs Utah St. (March 10, Eugene, OR) — Utah St. 92-90
- San Francisco 64-58 (March 13)
- San Francisco
- **Corvallis, OR** March 14: UCLA 76-72

Kansas City, MO March 20: UCLA 90-84

Kansas City, MO March 21: UCLA 98-83 — **NATIONAL CHAMPION**

National Third Place
- Michigan
- Kansas St.
- Michigan 100-90 — **NATIONAL THIRD PLACE**

Regional Third Place
March 14
- **at Raleigh, NC** — Villanova 74, Princeton 62
- **at Minneapolis** — Loyola 100, Kentucky 91
- **at Wichita, KS** — UTEP 63, Creighton 52
- **at Corvallis, OR** — Seattle 88, Utah St. 78

THE TOURNAMENT FIELD

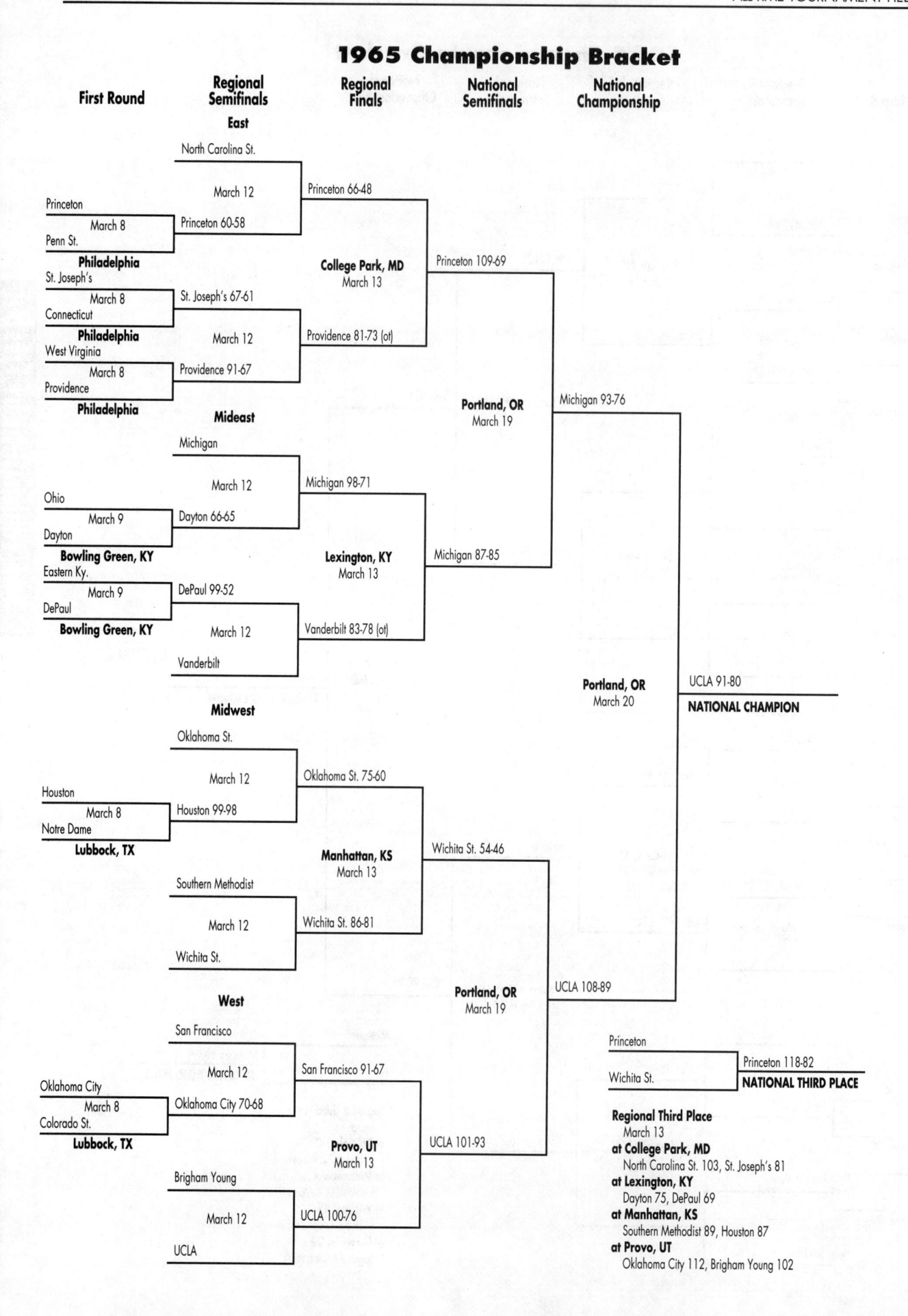

1965 Championship Bracket

East

First Round:
- Princeton vs Penn St. — March 8, Philadelphia
- St. Joseph's vs Connecticut — March 8, Philadelphia
- West Virginia vs Providence — March 8, Philadelphia

Regional Semifinals (March 12):
- North Carolina St. vs Princeton → Princeton 60-58
- St. Joseph's 67-61
- Providence 91-67

Regional Finals — College Park, MD, March 13:
- Princeton 66-48
- Providence 81-73 (ot)

National Semifinal — Portland, OR, March 19:
- Princeton 109-69

Mideast

First Round:
- Ohio vs Dayton — March 9, Bowling Green, KY
- Eastern Ky. vs DePaul — March 9, Bowling Green, KY

Regional Semifinals (March 12):
- Michigan vs Dayton → Dayton 66-65
- DePaul 99-52 vs Vanderbilt

Regional Finals — Lexington, KY, March 13:
- Michigan 98-71
- Vanderbilt 83-78 (ot)

National Semifinal:
- Michigan 87-85

National Championship — Portland, OR, March 20:
- Michigan 93-76

Midwest

First Round:
- Houston vs Notre Dame — March 8, Lubbock, TX

Regional Semifinals (March 12):
- Oklahoma St. vs Houston → Houston 99-98
- Southern Methodist vs Wichita St.

Regional Finals — Manhattan, KS, March 13:
- Oklahoma St. 75-60
- Wichita St. 86-81

National Semifinal — Portland, OR, March 19:
- Wichita St. 54-46

West

First Round:
- Oklahoma City vs Colorado St. — March 8, Lubbock, TX

Regional Semifinals (March 12):
- San Francisco vs Oklahoma City → Oklahoma City 70-68
- Brigham Young vs UCLA

Regional Finals — Provo, UT, March 13:
- San Francisco 91-67
- UCLA 100-76

National Semifinal:
- UCLA 108-89

UCLA 101-93

National Championship

UCLA 91-80 — NATIONAL CHAMPION

National Third Place:
- Princeton vs Wichita St. → Princeton 118-82

Regional Third Place — March 13

- **at College Park, MD:** North Carolina St. 103, St. Joseph's 81
- **at Lexington, KY:** Dayton 75, DePaul 69
- **at Manhattan, KS:** Southern Methodist 89, Houston 87
- **at Provo, UT:** Oklahoma City 112, Brigham Young 102

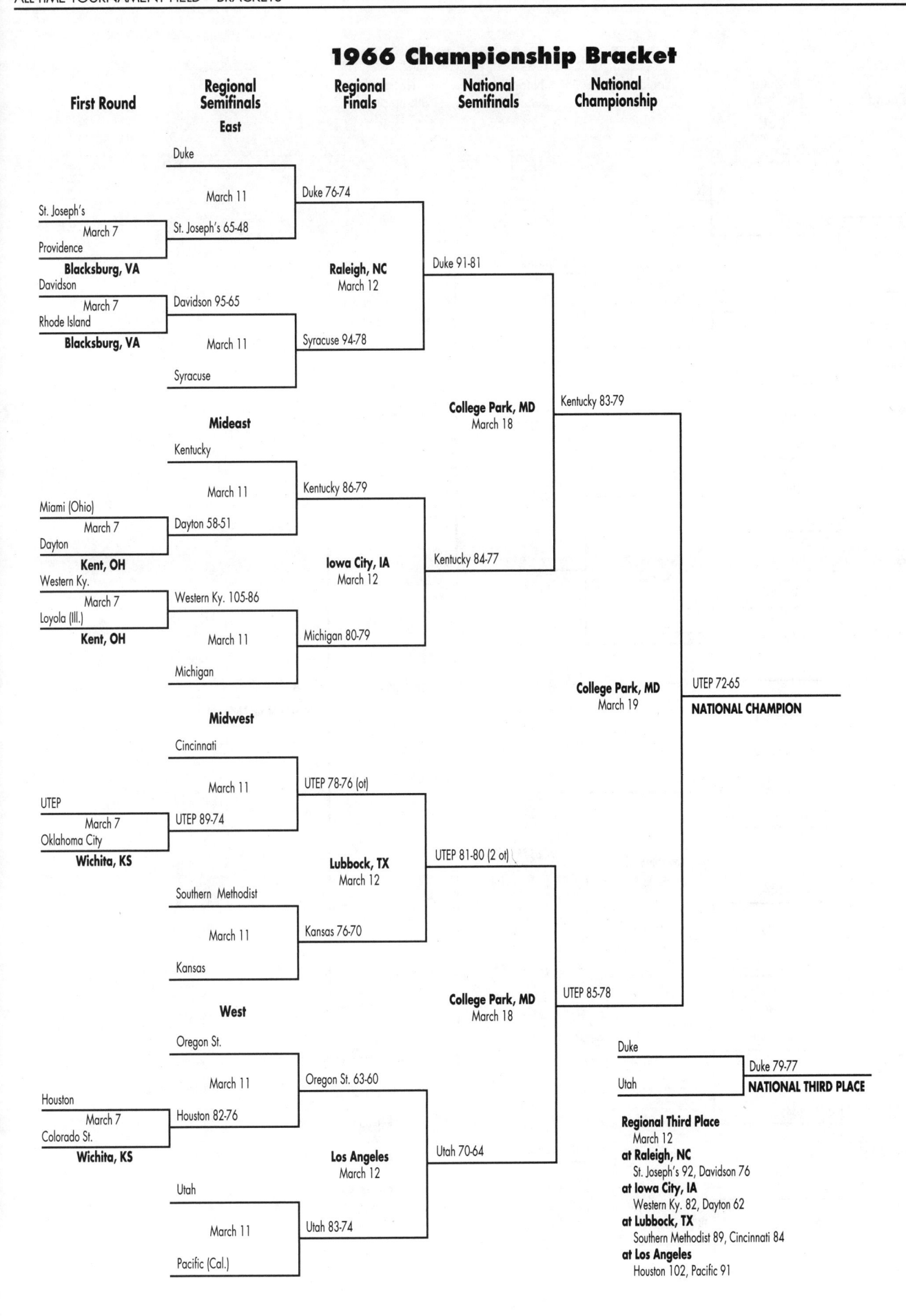

1966 Championship Bracket

First Round — **Regional Semifinals** — **Regional Finals** — **National Semifinals** — **National Championship**

East

- Duke
  - March 11
- St. Joseph's 65-48
  - St. Joseph's / March 7 / Providence — **Blacksburg, VA**
- Duke 76-74
- **Raleigh, NC** — March 12 — Duke 91-81
- Davidson 95-65
  - Davidson / March 7 / Rhode Island — **Blacksburg, VA**
  - March 11
- Syracuse 94-78
  - Syracuse

Mideast

- Kentucky
  - March 11
- Kentucky 86-79
- Dayton 58-51
  - Miami (Ohio) / March 7 / Dayton — **Kent, OH**
- **Iowa City, IA** — March 12 — Kentucky 84-77
- Western Ky. 105-86
  - Western Ky. / March 7 / Loyola (Ill.) — **Kent, OH**
  - March 11
- Michigan 80-79
  - Michigan

College Park, MD — March 18 — Kentucky 83-79

Midwest

- Cincinnati
  - March 11
- UTEP 89-74
  - UTEP / March 7 / Oklahoma City — **Wichita, KS**
- UTEP 78-76 (ot)
- **Lubbock, TX** — March 12 — UTEP 81-80 (2 ot)
- Kansas 76-70
  - Southern Methodist
  - March 11
  - Kansas

College Park, MD — March 18 — UTEP 85-78

College Park, MD — March 19 — UTEP 72-65 **NATIONAL CHAMPION**

West

- Oregon St.
  - March 11
- Houston 82-76
  - Houston / March 7 / Colorado St. — **Wichita, KS**
- Oregon St. 63-60
- **Los Angeles** — March 12 — Utah 70-64
- Utah 83-74
  - Utah
  - March 11
  - Pacific (Cal.)

- Duke
- Utah
- Duke 79-77 **NATIONAL THIRD PLACE**

Regional Third Place
March 12
at Raleigh, NC
St. Joseph's 92, Davidson 76
at Iowa City, IA
Western Ky. 82, Dayton 62
at Lubbock, TX
Southern Methodist 89, Cincinnati 84
at Los Angeles
Houston 102, Pacific 91

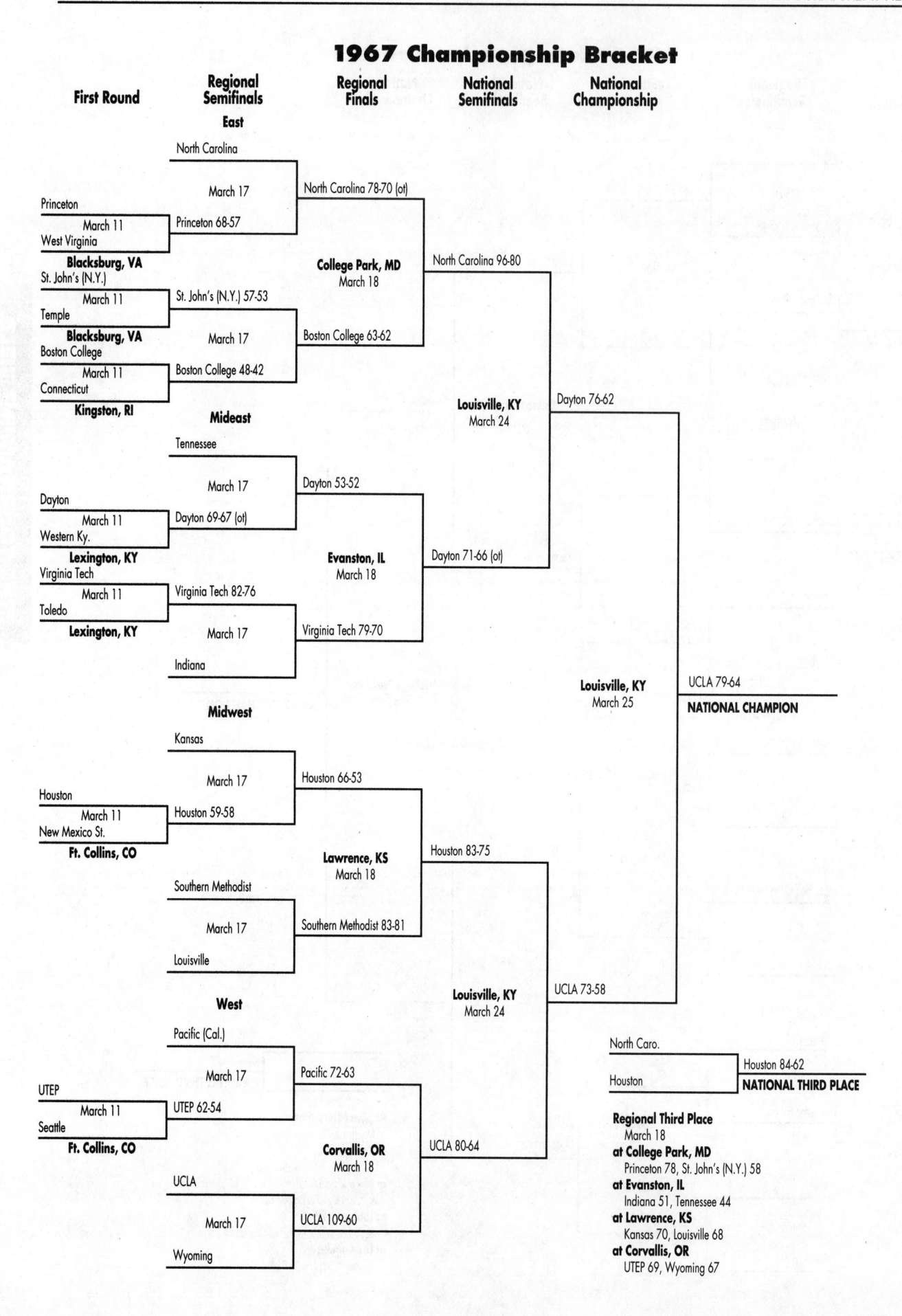

1967 Championship Bracket

First Round — **Regional Semifinals** — **Regional Finals** — **National Semifinals** — **National Championship**

East

- North Carolina
- March 17: North Carolina 78-70 (ot)
- Princeton
- March 11 — Princeton 68-57
- West Virginia
- **Blacksburg, VA**
- **College Park, MD** — March 18 — North Carolina 96-80
- St. John's (N.Y.)
- March 11 — St. John's (N.Y.) 57-53
- Temple
- **Blacksburg, VA**
- Boston College
- March 17 — Boston College 63-62
- March 11 — Boston College 48-42
- Connecticut
- **Kingston, RI**

Mideast

- Tennessee
- March 17 — Dayton 53-52
- Dayton
- March 11 — Dayton 69-67 (ot)
- Western Ky.
- **Lexington, KY**
- **Evanston, IL** — March 18 — Dayton 71-66 (ot)
- Virginia Tech
- March 11 — Virginia Tech 82-76
- Toledo
- **Lexington, KY**
- March 17 — Virginia Tech 79-70
- Indiana

Louisville, KY — March 24 — Dayton 76-62

Midwest

- Kansas
- March 17 — Houston 66-53
- Houston
- March 11 — Houston 59-58
- New Mexico St.
- **Ft. Collins, CO**
- **Lawrence, KS** — March 18 — Houston 83-75
- Southern Methodist
- March 17 — Southern Methodist 83-81
- Louisville

Louisville, KY — March 24 — UCLA 73-58

West

- Pacific (Cal.)
- March 17 — Pacific 72-63
- UTEP
- March 11 — UTEP 62-54
- Seattle
- **Ft. Collins, CO**
- **Corvallis, OR** — March 18 — UCLA 80-64
- UCLA
- March 17 — UCLA 109-60
- Wyoming

Louisville, KY — March 25 — UCLA 79-64 — **NATIONAL CHAMPION**

National Third Place
- North Caro.
- Houston
- Houston 84-62 — **NATIONAL THIRD PLACE**

Regional Third Place
March 18
- **at College Park, MD** — Princeton 78, St. John's (N.Y.) 58
- **at Evanston, IL** — Indiana 51, Tennessee 44
- **at Lawrence, KS** — Kansas 70, Louisville 68
- **at Corvallis, OR** — UTEP 69, Wyoming 67

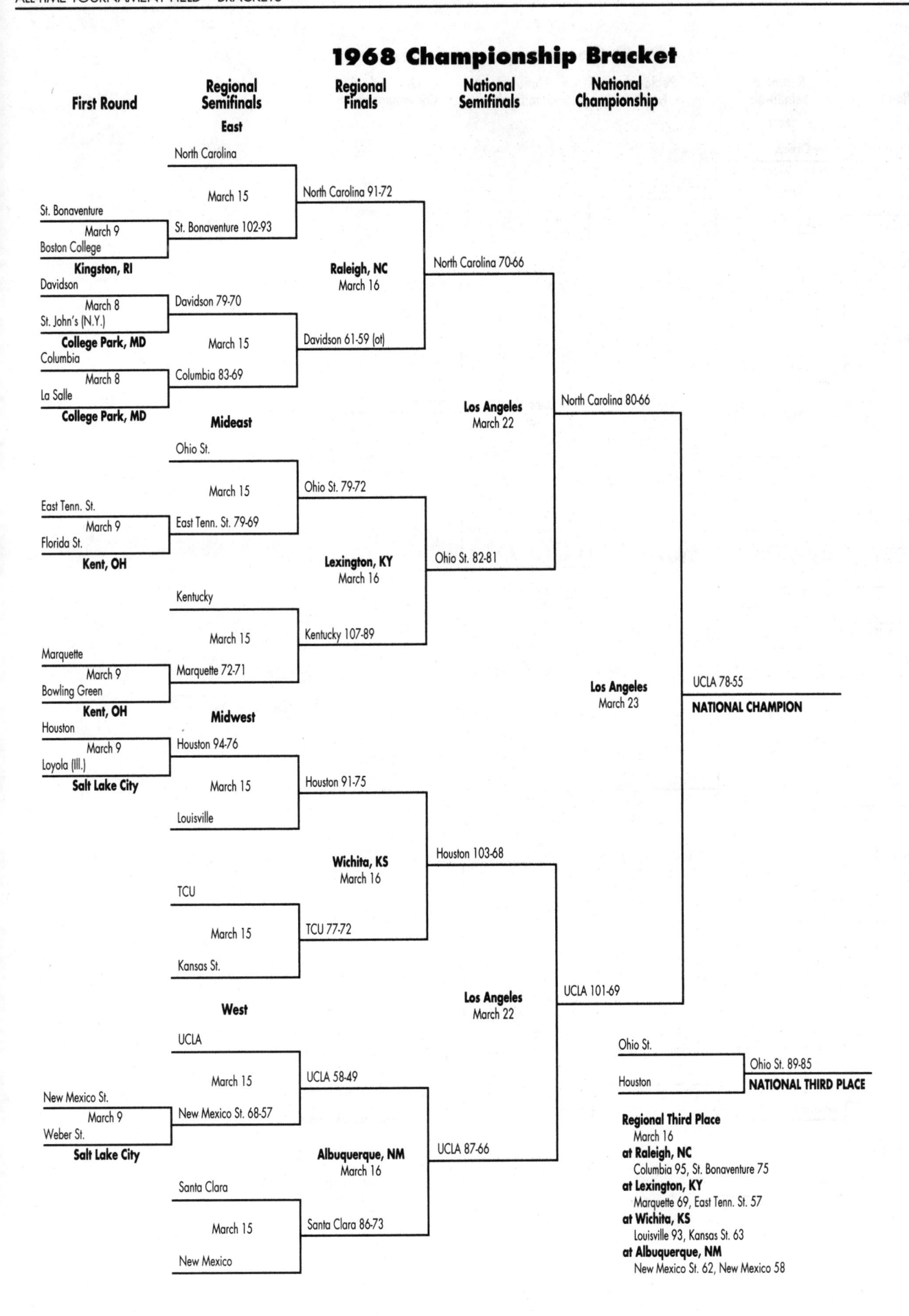

1968 Championship Bracket

First Round | **Regional Semifinals** | **Regional Finals** | **National Semifinals** | **National Championship**

East

- North Carolina
- March 15 — St. Bonaventure 102-93
  - St. Bonaventure (March 9, Kingston, RI)
  - Boston College
- North Carolina 91-72 (Raleigh, NC — March 16)
- Davidson
  - Davidson (March 8, College Park, MD)
  - St. John's (N.Y.)
- March 15 — Davidson 79-70
- Columbia
  - Columbia (March 8, College Park, MD)
  - La Salle
- March 15 — Columbia 83-69
- Davidson 61-59 (ot)

North Carolina 70-66

Mideast

- Ohio St.
- March 15 — Ohio St.
  - East Tenn. St. (March 9, Kent, OH)
  - Florida St.
- East Tenn. St. 79-69
- Ohio St. 79-72 (Lexington, KY — March 16)
- Kentucky
  - Marquette (March 9, Kent, OH)
  - Bowling Green
- March 15 — Marquette 72-71
- Kentucky 107-89

Ohio St. 82-81

Los Angeles — March 22
North Carolina 80-66

Midwest

- Houston
  - Houston (March 9, Salt Lake City)
  - Loyola (Ill.)
- Houston 94-76
- March 15 — Houston 91-75
- Louisville
- (Wichita, KS — March 16)
- TCU
- March 15 — TCU 77-72
- Kansas St.

Houston 103-68

Los Angeles — March 23
UCLA 78-55
NATIONAL CHAMPION

West

- UCLA
- March 15 — UCLA 58-49
  - New Mexico St. (March 9, Salt Lake City)
  - Weber St.
- New Mexico St. 68-57
- (Albuquerque, NM — March 16)
- Santa Clara
- March 15 — Santa Clara 86-73
- New Mexico

UCLA 87-66

Los Angeles — March 22
UCLA 101-69

- Ohio St.
- Houston

Ohio St. 89-85
NATIONAL THIRD PLACE

Regional Third Place
March 16
at Raleigh, NC
 Columbia 95, St. Bonaventure 75
at Lexington, KY
 Marquette 69, East Tenn. St. 57
at Wichita, KS
 Louisville 93, Kansas St. 63
at Albuquerque, NM
 New Mexico St. 62, New Mexico 58

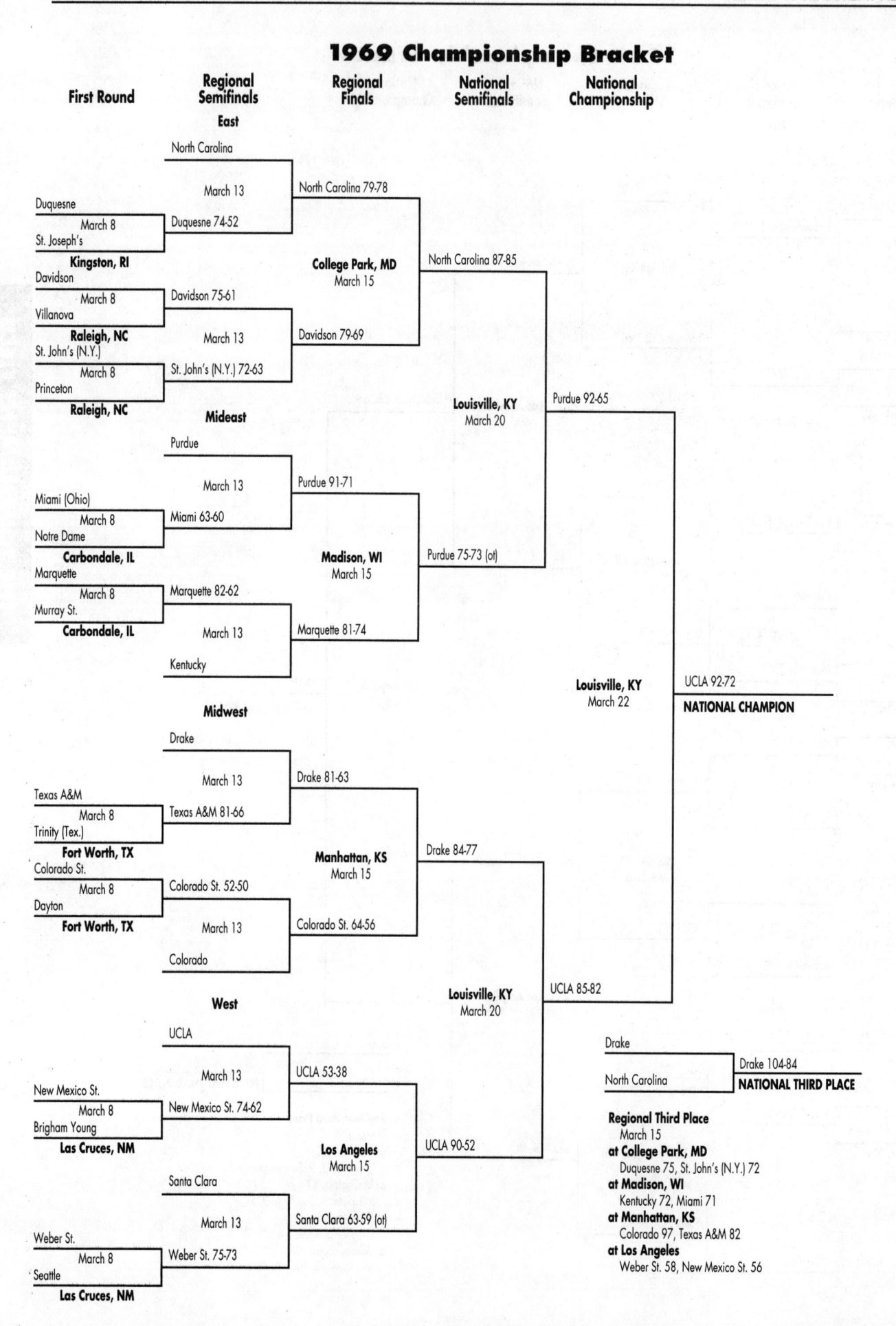

1969 Championship Bracket

First Round — **Regional Semifinals** — **Regional Finals** — **National Semifinals** — **National Championship**

East

- North Carolina
- March 13: Duquesne 74-52
  - Duquesne (March 8, Kingston, RI)
  - St. Joseph's
- North Carolina 79-78
- Davidson (March 8, Raleigh, NC)
- Villanova
- March 13: Davidson 75-61
- Davidson 79-69
- St. John's (N.Y.) (March 8, Raleigh, NC)
- Princeton
- March 13: St. John's (N.Y.) 72-63

College Park, MD — March 15

North Carolina 87-85

Mideast

- Purdue
- March 13: Miami 63-60
  - Miami (Ohio) (March 8, Carbondale, IL)
  - Notre Dame
- Purdue 91-71
- Marquette (March 8, Carbondale, IL)
- Murray St.
- March 13: Marquette 82-62
- Marquette 81-74
- Kentucky

Madison, WI — March 15

Purdue 75-73 (ot)

Louisville, KY — March 20

Purdue 92-65

Midwest

- Drake
- March 13: Texas A&M 81-66
  - Texas A&M (March 8, Fort Worth, TX)
  - Trinity (Tex.)
- Drake 81-63
- Colorado St. (March 8, Fort Worth, TX)
- Dayton
- March 13: Colorado St. 52-50
- Colorado St. 64-56
- Colorado

Manhattan, KS — March 15

Drake 84-77

West

- UCLA
- March 13: New Mexico St. 74-62
  - New Mexico St. (March 8, Las Cruces, NM)
  - Brigham Young
- UCLA 53-38
- Santa Clara
- Weber St. (March 8, Las Cruces, NM)
- Seattle
- March 13: Weber St. 75-73
- Santa Clara 63-59 (ot)

Los Angeles — March 15

UCLA 90-52

Louisville, KY — March 20

UCLA 85-82

Louisville, KY — March 22

UCLA 92-72
NATIONAL CHAMPION

Drake
North Carolina
Drake 104-84
NATIONAL THIRD PLACE

Regional Third Place
March 15
at College Park, MD
Duquesne 75, St. John's (N.Y.) 72
at Madison, WI
Kentucky 72, Miami 71
at Manhattan, KS
Colorado 97, Texas A&M 82
at Los Angeles
Weber St. 58, New Mexico St. 56

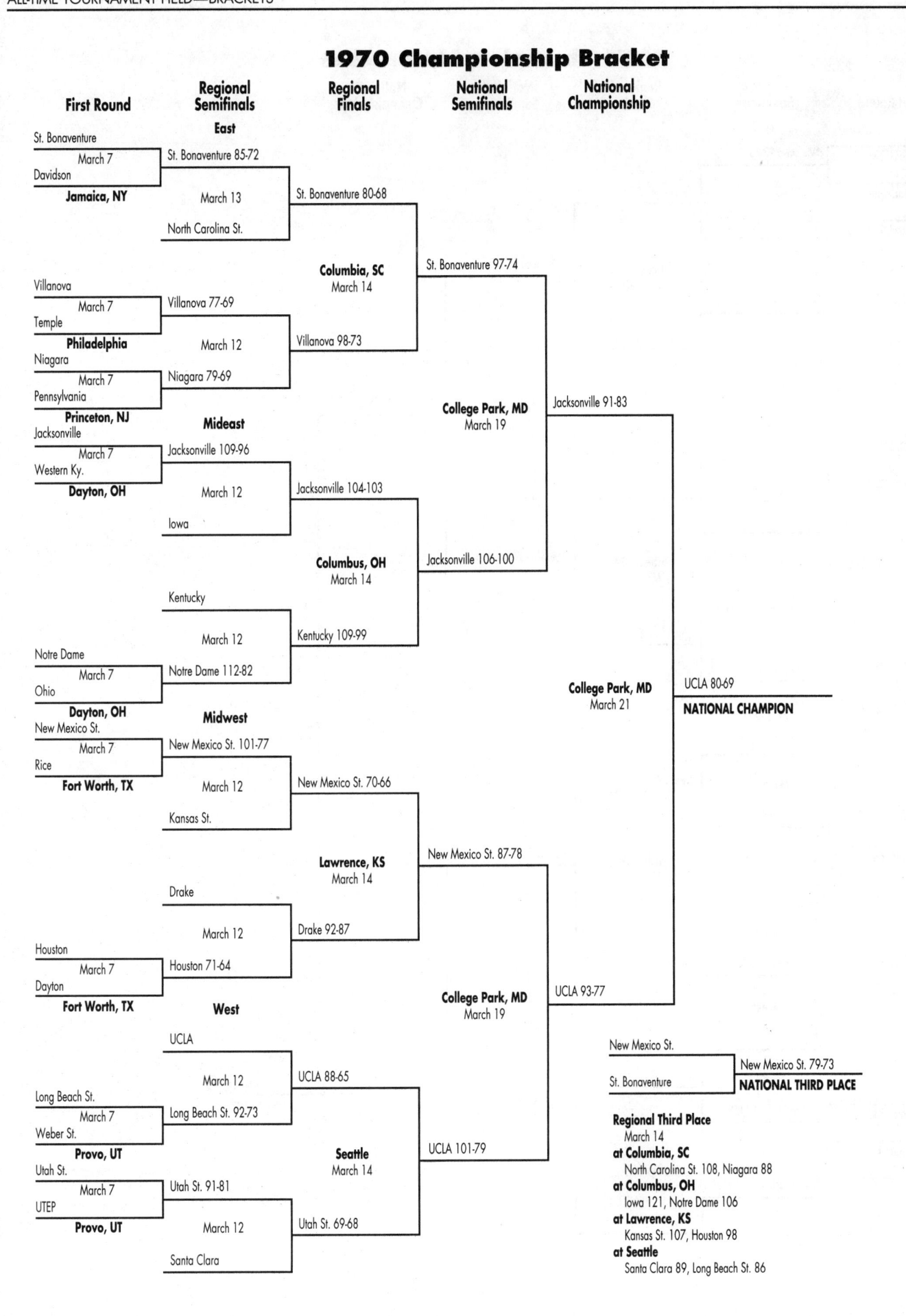

1970 Championship Bracket

First Round | **Regional Semifinals** | **Regional Finals** | **National Semifinals** | **National Championship**

East

- St. Bonaventure
- Davidson — March 7, Jamaica, NY
- St. Bonaventure 85-72
- North Carolina St.
- St. Bonaventure 80-68 (March 13)

- Villanova
- Temple — March 7, Philadelphia
- Villanova 77-69
- Niagara
- Pennsylvania — March 7, Princeton, NJ
- Niagara 79-69
- Villanova 98-73 (March 12)

St. Bonaventure 97-74 — Columbia, SC, March 14

Mideast

- Jacksonville
- Western Ky. — March 7, Dayton, OH
- Jacksonville 109-96
- Iowa
- Jacksonville 104-103 (March 12)

- Kentucky
- Notre Dame
- Ohio — March 7, Dayton, OH
- Notre Dame 112-82
- Kentucky 109-99 (March 12)

Jacksonville 106-100 — Columbus, OH, March 14

Jacksonville 91-83 — College Park, MD, March 19

Midwest

- New Mexico St.
- Rice — March 7, Fort Worth, TX
- New Mexico St. 101-77
- Kansas St.
- New Mexico St. 70-66 (March 12)

- Drake
- Houston
- Dayton — March 7, Fort Worth, TX
- Houston 71-64
- Drake 92-87 (March 12)

New Mexico St. 87-78 — Lawrence, KS, March 14

West

- UCLA
- Long Beach St.
- Weber St. — March 7, Provo, UT
- Long Beach St. 92-73
- UCLA 88-65 (March 12)

- Utah St.
- UTEP — March 7, Provo, UT
- Utah St. 91-81
- Santa Clara
- Utah St. 69-68 (March 12)

UCLA 101-79 — Seattle, March 14

UCLA 93-77 — College Park, MD, March 19

UCLA 80-69 — College Park, MD, March 21
NATIONAL CHAMPION

New Mexico St. vs. St. Bonaventure
New Mexico St. 79-73
NATIONAL THIRD PLACE

Regional Third Place
March 14
at Columbia, SC
  North Carolina St. 108, Niagara 88
at Columbus, OH
  Iowa 121, Notre Dame 106
at Lawrence, KS
  Kansas St. 107, Houston 98
at Seattle
  Santa Clara 89, Long Beach St. 86

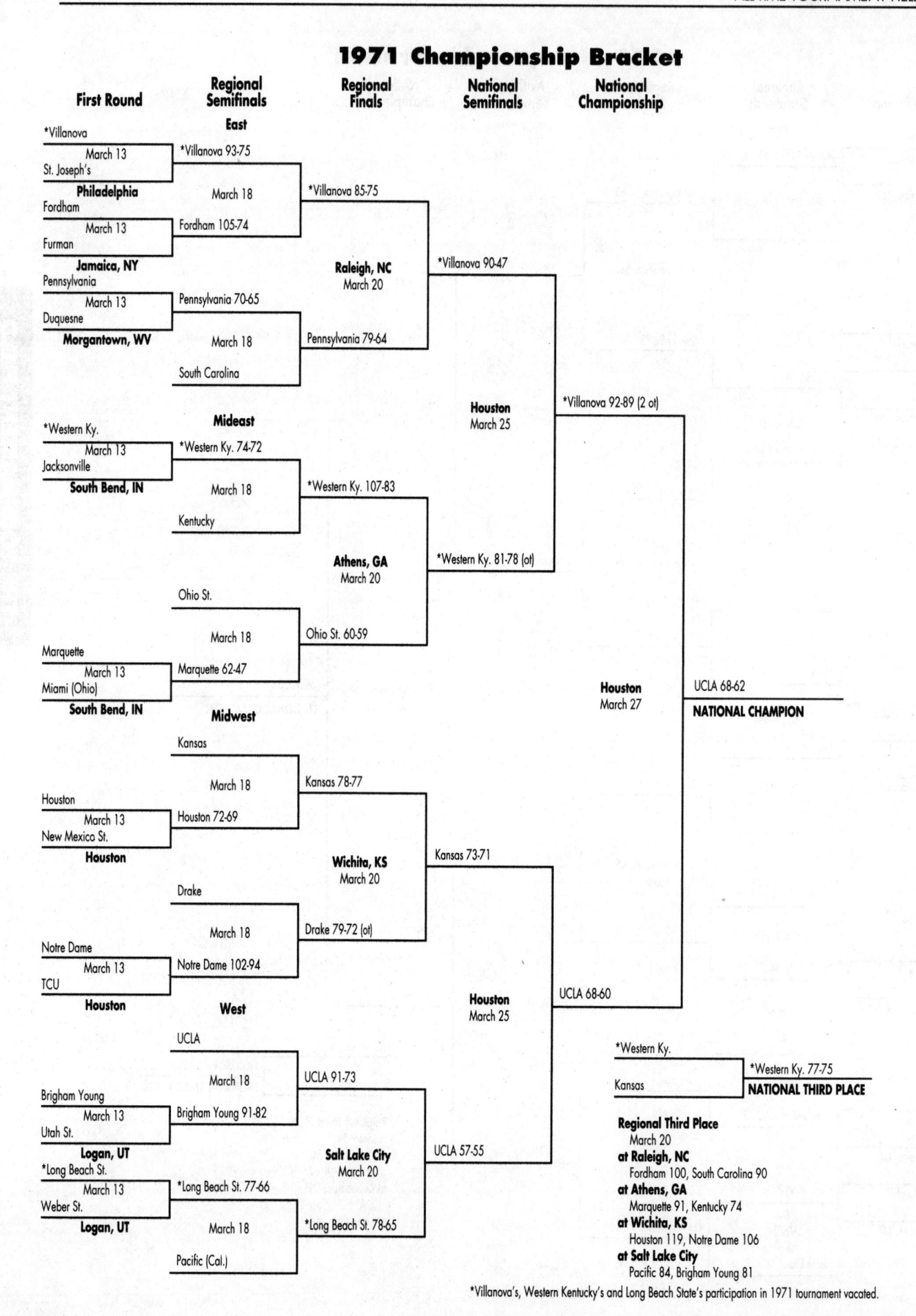

1971 Championship Bracket

East Region

First Round
- *Villanova vs St. Joseph's — March 13, Philadelphia
- Fordham vs Furman — March 13, Jamaica, NY
- Pennsylvania vs Duquesne — March 13, Morgantown, WV

Regional Semifinals (March 18)
- *Villanova 93-75
- Fordham 105-74
- Pennsylvania 70-65
- South Carolina

Regional Finals — Raleigh, NC, March 20
- *Villanova 85-75
- Pennsylvania 79-64

Regional Final: *Villanova 90-47

Mideast Region

First Round
- *Western Ky. vs Jacksonville — March 13, South Bend, IN
- Marquette vs Miami (Ohio) — March 13, South Bend, IN

Regional Semifinals (March 18)
- *Western Ky. 74-72
- Kentucky
- Ohio St.
- Marquette 62-47

Regional Finals — Athens, GA, March 20
- *Western Ky. 107-83
- Ohio St. 60-59

Regional Final: *Western Ky. 81-78 (ot)

Midwest Region

First Round
- Kansas
- Houston vs New Mexico St. — March 13, Houston
- Notre Dame vs TCU — March 13, Houston

Regional Semifinals (March 18)
- Kansas
- Houston 72-69
- Drake
- Notre Dame 102-94

Regional Finals — Wichita, KS, March 20
- Kansas 78-77
- Drake 79-72 (ot)

Regional Final: Kansas 73-71

West Region

First Round
- UCLA
- Brigham Young vs Utah St. — March 13, Logan, UT
- *Long Beach St. vs Weber St. — March 13, Logan, UT

Regional Semifinals (March 18)
- UCLA
- Brigham Young 91-82
- *Long Beach St. 77-66
- Pacific (Cal.)

Regional Finals — Salt Lake City, March 20
- UCLA 91-73
- *Long Beach St. 78-65

Regional Final: UCLA 57-55

National Semifinals — Houston, March 25
- *Villanova 92-89 (2 ot) (over Western Ky.)
- UCLA 68-60 (over Kansas)

National Championship — Houston, March 27
UCLA 68-62 — NATIONAL CHAMPION

National Third Place
*Western Ky. 77-75 over Kansas

Regional Third Place — March 20
- **at Raleigh, NC:** Fordham 100, South Carolina 90
- **at Athens, GA:** Marquette 91, Kentucky 74
- **at Wichita, KS:** Houston 119, Notre Dame 106
- **at Salt Lake City:** Pacific 84, Brigham Young 81

*Villanova's, Western Kentucky's and Long Beach State's participation in 1971 tournament vacated.

1972 Championship Bracket

Mideast

First Round — Knoxville, TN, March 11
- Florida St. / Eastern Ky. → Florida St. 83-81
- Marquette / Ohio → Marquette 73-49

Regional Semifinals — March 16
- Florida St. / *Minnesota
- Kentucky / Marquette 73-49 → Kentucky 85-69

Regional Finals — Dayton, OH, March 18
- Florida St. 70-56 vs Kentucky 85-69 → Florida St. 73-54

East

First Round — March 11
- South Carolina / Temple → South Carolina 53-51 (Williamsburg, VA)
- Pennsylvania / Providence → Pennsylvania 76-60 (Jamaica, NY)
- Villanova / East Caro. → Villanova 85-70 (Princeton, NJ)

Regional Semifinals — March 16
- North Carolina / South Carolina 53-51 → North Carolina 92-69
- Pennsylvania 76-60 / Villanova 85-70 → Pennsylvania 78-67

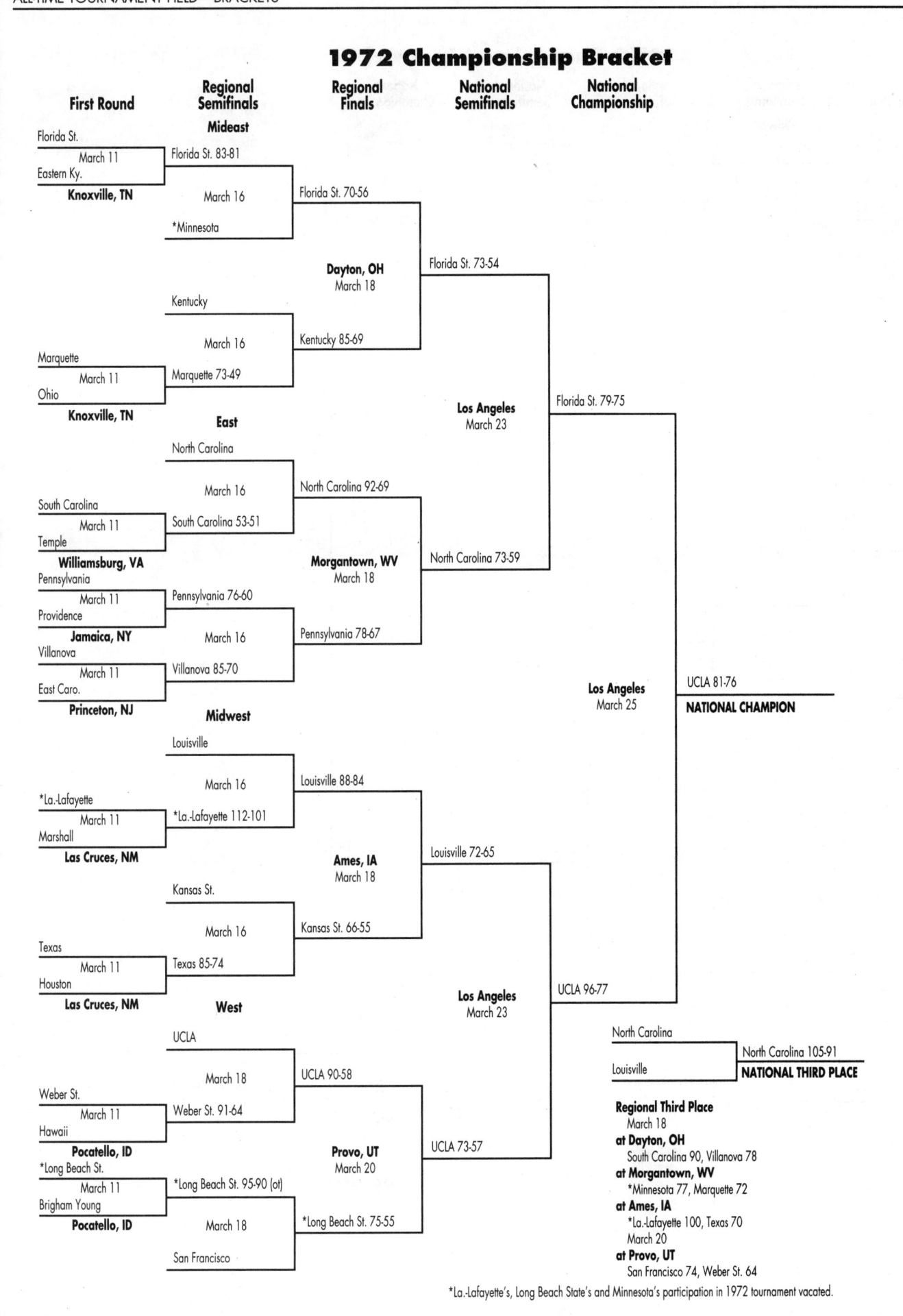

Regional Finals — Morgantown, WV, March 18
- North Carolina 92-69 vs Pennsylvania 78-67 → North Carolina 73-59

Midwest

First Round — March 11
- *La.-Lafayette / Marshall → *La.-Lafayette 112-101 (Las Cruces, NM)
- Texas / Houston → Texas 85-74 (Las Cruces, NM)

Regional Semifinals — March 16
- Louisville / *La.-Lafayette 112-101 → Louisville 88-84
- Kansas St. / Texas 85-74 → Kansas St. 66-55

Regional Finals — Ames, IA, March 18
- Louisville 88-84 vs Kansas St. 66-55 → Louisville 72-65

West

First Round — March 11
- Weber St. / Hawaii → Weber St. 91-64 (Pocatello, ID)
- *Long Beach St. / Brigham Young → *Long Beach St. 95-90 (ot) (Pocatello, ID)

Regional Semifinals — March 18
- UCLA / Weber St. 91-64 → UCLA 90-58
- *Long Beach St. 95-90 / San Francisco → *Long Beach St. 75-55

Regional Finals — Provo, UT, March 20
- UCLA 90-58 vs *Long Beach St. 75-55 → UCLA 73-57

National Semifinals — Los Angeles, March 23
- Florida St. 73-54 vs North Carolina 73-59 → Florida St. 79-75
- Louisville 72-65 vs UCLA 73-57 → UCLA 96-77

National Championship — Los Angeles, March 25
- Florida St. 79-75 vs UCLA 96-77 → **UCLA 81-76**
- **NATIONAL CHAMPION**

National Third Place
- North Carolina vs Louisville → North Carolina 105-91

Regional Third Place
- March 18
  - at Dayton, OH: South Carolina 90, Villanova 78
  - at Morgantown, WV: *Minnesota 77, Marquette 72
  - at Ames, IA: *La.-Lafayette 100, Texas 70
- March 20
  - at Provo, UT: San Francisco 74, Weber St. 64

*La.-Lafayette's, Long Beach State's and Minnesota's participation in 1972 tournament vacated.

1973 Championship Bracket

First Round | **Regional Semifinals** | **Regional Finals** | **National Semifinals** | **National Championship**

Midwest

- Memphis
- March 15: Memphis 90-76
  - South Carolina
  - March 10: South Carolina 78-70
  - Texas Tech
  - **Wichita, KS**
- **Houston — March 17**
- Memphis 92-72
- Kansas St.
- March 15: Kansas St. 66-63
  - *La.-Lafayette
  - March 10: *La.-Lafayette 102-89
  - Houston
  - **Wichita, KS**

St. Louis — March 24
Memphis 98-85

East

- Providence
- March 15: Providence 89-76
  - Providence
  - March 10
  - St. Joseph's
  - **Williamsburg, VA**
- Providence 87-65
- Pennsylvania
- March 15: Pennsylvania 62-61
  - Pennsylvania
  - March 10
  - St. John's (N.Y.)
  - **Jamaica, NY**
- **Charlotte, NC — March 17**
- Providence 103-89
- Maryland
- March 15: Maryland 91-75
  - Syracuse
  - March 10: Syracuse 83-82
  - Furman
  - **Philadelphia**

St. Louis — March 26
UCLA 87-66
NATIONAL CHAMPION

Mideast

- Indiana
- March 15: Indiana 75-69
  - Marquette
  - March 10: Marquette 77-62
  - Miami (Ohio)
  - **Dayton, OH**
- **Nashville, TN — March 17**
- Indiana 72-65
- Kentucky
- March 15: Kentucky 106-100 (ot)
  - *Austin Peay
  - March 10: *Austin Peay 77-75
  - Jacksonville
  - **Dayton, OH**

St. Louis — March 24
UCLA 70-59

West

- UCLA
- March 15: UCLA 98-81
  - Arizona St.
  - March 10: Arizona St. 103-78
  - Oklahoma City
  - **Logan, UT**
- **Los Angeles — March 17**
- UCLA 54-39
- San Francisco
- March 15: San Francisco 77-67
  - *Long Beach St.
  - March 10: *Long Beach St. 88-75
  - Weber St.
  - **Logan UT**

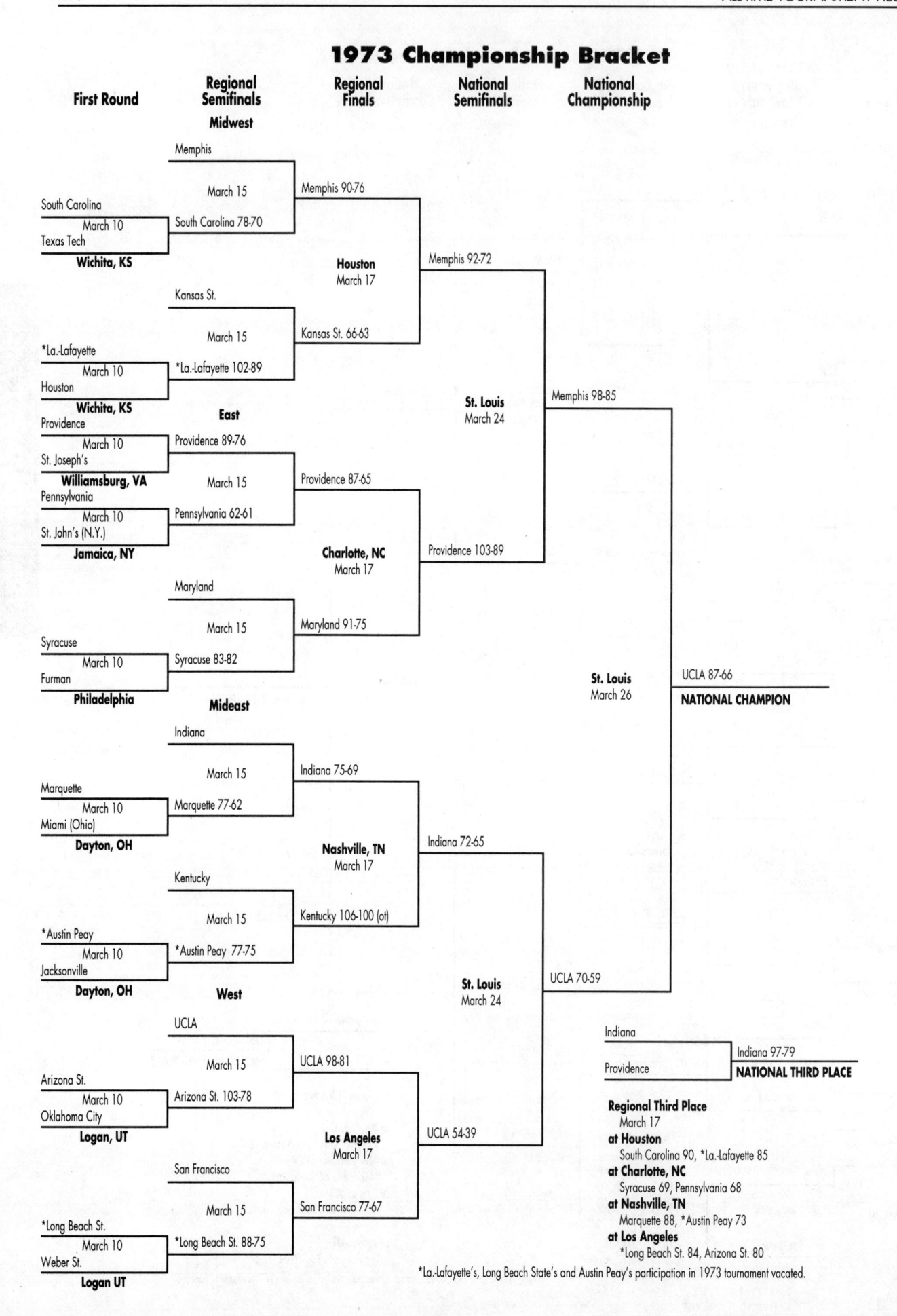

Indiana 97-79
NATIONAL THIRD PLACE
- Indiana
- Providence

Regional Third Place
March 17
- at Houston
  South Carolina 90, *La.-Lafayette 85
- at Charlotte, NC
  Syracuse 69, Pennsylvania 68
- at Nashville, TN
  Marquette 88, *Austin Peay 73
- at Los Angeles
  *Long Beach St. 84, Arizona St. 80

*La.-Lafayette's, Long Beach State's and Austin Peay's participation in 1973 tournament vacated.

ALL-TIME TOURNAMENT FIELD—BRACKETS

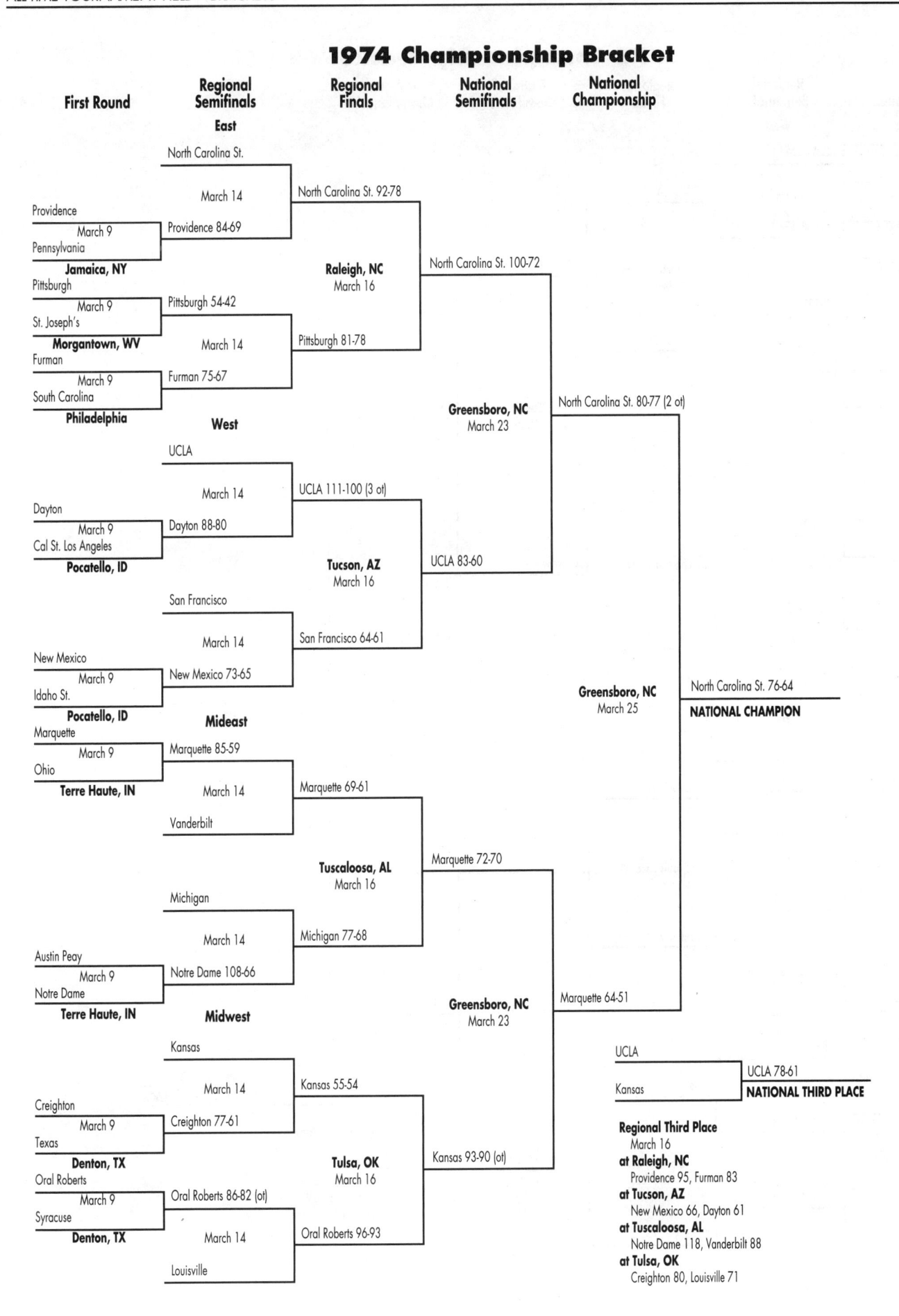

1974 Championship Bracket

First Round | **Regional Semifinals** | **Regional Finals** | **National Semifinals** | **National Championship**

East

- North Carolina St.
- Providence — March 9 — Providence 84-69
- Pennsylvania
  - Jamaica, NY
- Pittsburgh — March 9 — Pittsburgh 54-42
- St. Joseph's
  - Morgantown, WV
- Furman — March 9 — Furman 75-67
- South Carolina
  - Philadelphia

North Carolina St. 92-78 (March 14)
Pittsburgh 81-78 (March 14)

Raleigh, NC — March 16
North Carolina St. 100-72

West

- UCLA
- Dayton — March 9 — Dayton 88-80
- Cal St. Los Angeles
  - Pocatello, ID
- San Francisco
- New Mexico — March 9 — New Mexico 73-65
- Idaho St.
  - Pocatello, ID

UCLA 111-100 (3 ot) (March 14)
San Francisco 64-61 (March 14)

Tucson, AZ — March 16
UCLA 83-60

Greensboro, NC — March 23
North Carolina St. 80-77 (2 ot)

Mideast

- Marquette — March 9 — Marquette 85-59
- Ohio
  - Terre Haute, IN
- Vanderbilt
- Michigan
- Austin Peay — March 9 — Notre Dame 108-66
- Notre Dame
  - Terre Haute, IN

Marquette 69-61 (March 14)
Michigan 77-68 (March 14)

Tuscaloosa, AL — March 16
Marquette 72-70

Midwest

- Kansas
- Creighton — March 9 — Creighton 77-61
- Texas
  - Denton, TX
- Oral Roberts — March 9 — Oral Roberts 86-82 (ot)
- Syracuse
  - Denton, TX
- Louisville

Kansas 55-54 (March 14)
Oral Roberts 96-93 (March 14)

Tulsa, OK — March 16
Kansas 93-90 (ot)

Greensboro, NC — March 23
Marquette 64-51

Greensboro, NC — March 25
North Carolina St. 76-64
NATIONAL CHAMPION

UCLA
Kansas
UCLA 78-61
NATIONAL THIRD PLACE

Regional Third Place
March 16
at Raleigh, NC
Providence 95, Furman 83
at Tucson, AZ
New Mexico 66, Dayton 61
at Tuscaloosa, AL
Notre Dame 118, Vanderbilt 88
at Tulsa, OK
Creighton 80, Louisville 71

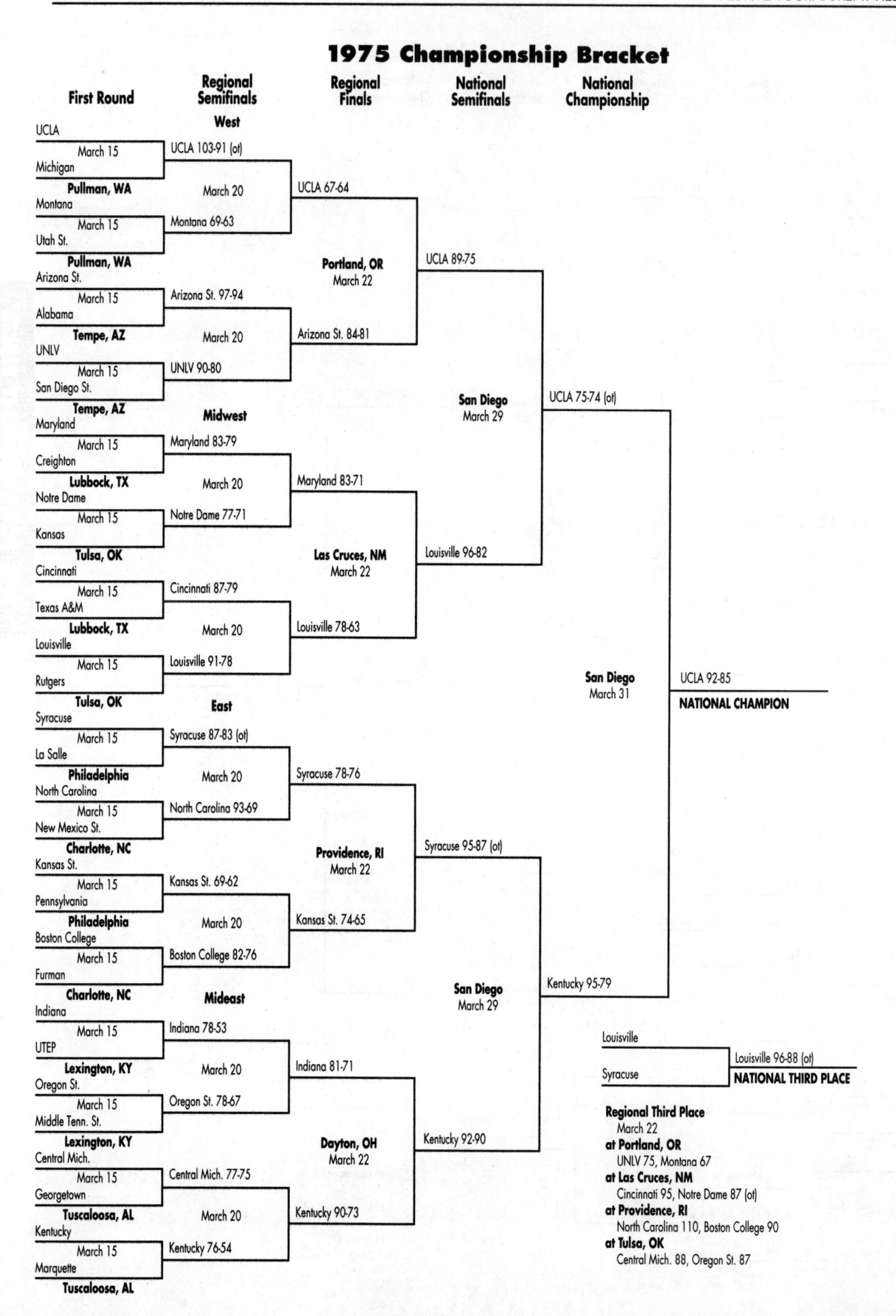

1975 Championship Bracket

First Round | **Regional Semifinals** | **Regional Finals** | **National Semifinals** | **National Championship**

West

- UCLA
- Michigan — March 15 — UCLA 103-91 (ot)
- Montana (Pullman, WA) — March 20 — Montana 69-63
- Utah St. — March 15
- Arizona St. (Pullman, WA) — UCLA 67-64 (Portland, OR, March 22)
- Alabama — March 15 — Arizona St. 97-94
- UNLV (Tempe, AZ) — March 20 — UNLV 90-80
- San Diego St. — March 15
- (Tempe, AZ) — Arizona St. 84-81

UCLA 89-75

Midwest

- Maryland
- Creighton — March 15 — Maryland 83-79
- Notre Dame (Lubbock, TX) — March 20 — Notre Dame 77-71
- Kansas — March 15
- Cincinnati (Tulsa, OK) — Maryland 83-71 (Las Cruces, NM, March 22)
- Texas A&M — March 15 — Cincinnati 87-79
- Louisville (Lubbock, TX) — March 20 — Louisville 91-78
- Rutgers — March 15
- (Tulsa, OK) — Louisville 78-63

Louisville 96-82

San Diego, March 29 — UCLA 75-74 (ot)

East

- Syracuse
- La Salle — March 15 — Syracuse 87-83 (ot)
- North Carolina (Philadelphia) — March 20 — North Carolina 93-69
- New Mexico St. — March 15
- Kansas St. (Charlotte, NC) — Syracuse 78-76 (Providence, RI, March 22)
- Pennsylvania — March 15 — Kansas St. 69-62
- Boston College (Philadelphia) — March 20 — Boston College 82-76
- Furman — March 15
- (Charlotte, NC) — Kansas St. 74-65

Syracuse 95-87 (ot)

Mideast

- Indiana
- UTEP — March 15 — Indiana 78-53
- Oregon St. (Lexington, KY) — March 20 — Oregon St. 78-67
- Middle Tenn. St. — March 15
- Central Mich. (Lexington, KY) — Indiana 81-71 (Dayton, OH, March 22)
- Georgetown — March 15 — Central Mich. 77-75
- Kentucky (Tuscaloosa, AL) — March 20 — Kentucky 76-54
- Marquette — March 15
- (Tuscaloosa, AL) — Kentucky 90-73

Kentucky 92-90

San Diego, March 29 — Kentucky 95-79

San Diego, March 31 — UCLA 92-85 **NATIONAL CHAMPION**

- Louisville
- Syracuse — Louisville 96-88 (ot) **NATIONAL THIRD PLACE**

Regional Third Place
March 22
- at Portland, OR
  UNLV 75, Montana 67
- at Las Cruces, NM
  Cincinnati 95, Notre Dame 87 (ot)
- at Providence, RI
  North Carolina 110, Boston College 90
- at Tulsa, OK
  Central Mich. 88, Oregon St. 87

ALL-TIME TOURNAMENT FIELD—BRACKETS

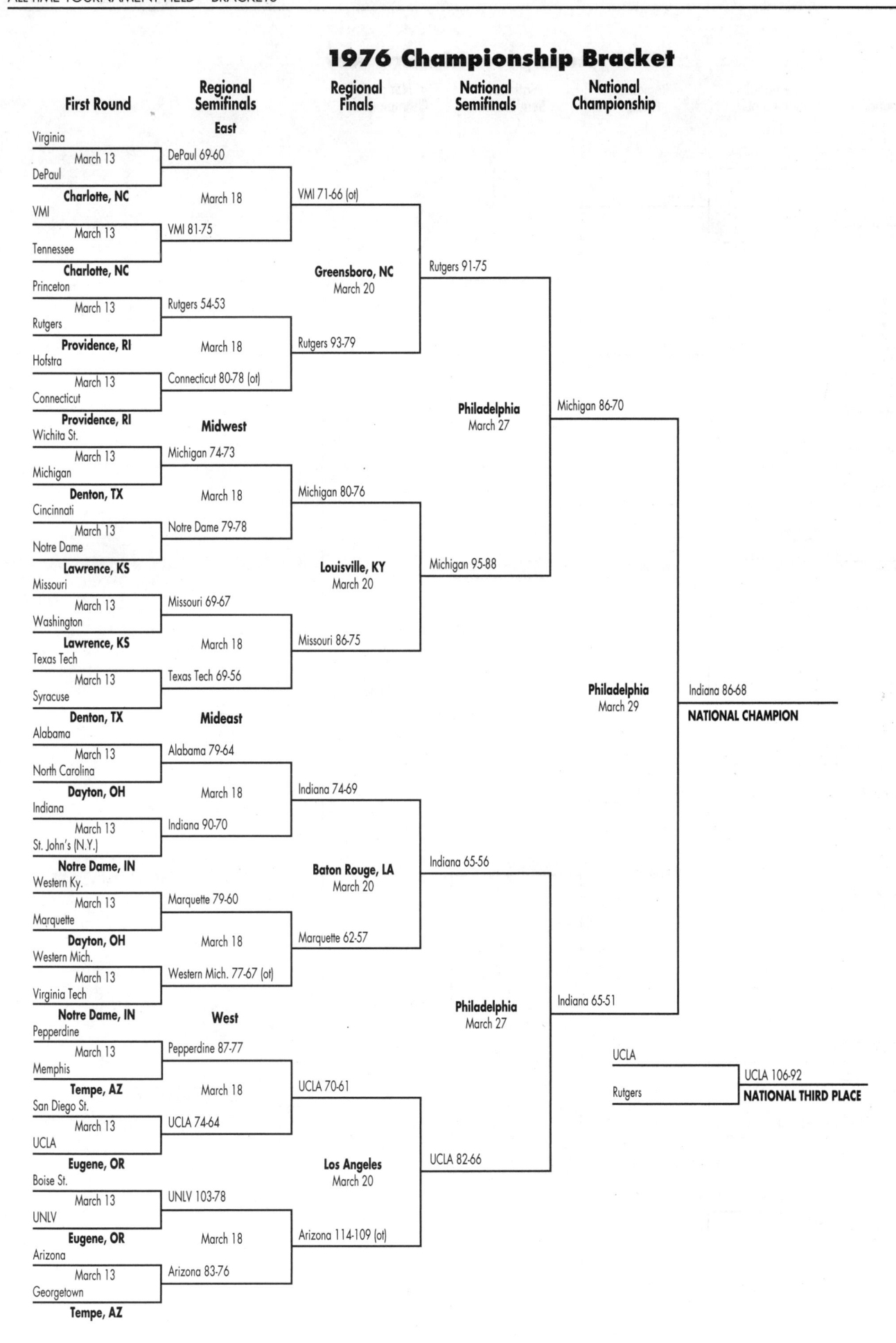

1976 Championship Bracket

First Round	Regional Semifinals	Regional Finals	National Semifinals	National Championship

East

- Virginia
- DePaul — March 13 — DePaul 69-60
  - Charlotte, NC — March 18 — VMI 71-66 (ot)
- VMI
- Tennessee — March 13 — VMI 81-75
  - Charlotte, NC
- Princeton
- Rutgers — March 13 — Rutgers 54-53
  - Providence, RI — March 18 — Rutgers 93-79
- Hofstra
- Connecticut — March 13 — Connecticut 80-78 (ot)
  - Providence, RI

Greensboro, NC — March 20 — Rutgers 91-75

Midwest

- Wichita St.
- Michigan — March 13 — Michigan 74-73
  - Denton, TX — March 18 — Michigan 80-76
- Cincinnati
- Notre Dame — March 13 — Notre Dame 79-78
  - Lawrence, KS
- Missouri
- Washington — March 13 — Missouri 69-67
  - Lawrence, KS — March 18 — Missouri 86-75
- Texas Tech
- Syracuse — March 13 — Texas Tech 69-56
  - Denton, TX

Louisville, KY — March 20 — Michigan 95-88

Philadelphia — March 27 — Michigan 86-70

Mideast

- Alabama
- North Carolina — March 13 — Alabama 79-64
  - Dayton, OH — March 18 — Indiana 74-69
- Indiana
- St. John's (N.Y.) — March 13 — Indiana 90-70
  - Notre Dame, IN
- Western Ky.
- Marquette — March 13 — Marquette 79-60
  - Dayton, OH — March 18 — Marquette 62-57
- Western Mich.
- Virginia Tech — March 13 — Western Mich. 77-67 (ot)
  - Notre Dame, IN

Baton Rouge, LA — March 20 — Indiana 65-56

Philadelphia — March 27 — Indiana 65-51

Philadelphia — March 29 — Indiana 86-68
NATIONAL CHAMPION

West

- Pepperdine
- Memphis — March 13 — Pepperdine 87-77
  - Tempe, AZ — March 18 — UCLA 70-61
- San Diego St.
- UCLA — March 13 — UCLA 74-64
  - Eugene, OR
- Boise St.
- UNLV — March 13 — UNLV 103-78
  - Eugene, OR — March 18 — Arizona 114-109 (ot)
- Arizona
- Georgetown — March 13 — Arizona 83-76
  - Tempe, AZ

Los Angeles — March 20 — UCLA 82-66

- UCLA
- Rutgers — UCLA 106-92
NATIONAL THIRD PLACE

THE TOURNAMENT FIELD

1977 Championship Bracket

East Region

First Round:
- VMI vs Duquesne (March 12, Raleigh, NC) — VMI 73-66
- Princeton vs Kentucky (March 12, Philadelphia) — Kentucky 72-58
- Hofstra vs Notre Dame (March 12, Philadelphia) — Notre Dame 90-83
- North Carolina vs Purdue (March 12, Raleigh, NC) — North Carolina 69-66

Regional Semifinals (March 17):
- Kentucky 93-78 (over VMI)
- North Carolina 79-77 (over Notre Dame)

Regional Final (College Park, MD, March 19):
- North Carolina 79-72 (over Kentucky)

West Region

First Round:
- UCLA vs Louisville (March 12, Pocatello, ID) — UCLA 87-79
- Long Beach St. vs Idaho St. (March 12, Pocatello, ID) — Idaho St. 83-72
- Utah vs St. John's (N.Y.) (March 12, Tucson, AZ) — Utah 72-68
- San Francisco vs UNLV (March 12, Tucson, AZ) — UNLV 121-95

Regional Semifinals (March 17):
- Idaho St. 76-75 (over UCLA)
- UNLV 88-83 (over Utah)

Regional Final (Provo, UT, March 19):
- UNLV 107-90 (over Idaho St.)

Mideast Region

First Round:
- Michigan vs Holy Cross (March 13, Tucson, AZ) — Michigan 92-81
- Middle Tenn. St. vs Detroit (March 13, Bloomington, IN) — Detroit 93-76
- Central Mich. vs Charlotte (March 13, Baton Rouge, LA) — Charlotte 91-86 (ot)
- Tennessee vs Syracuse (March 13, Bloomington, IN) — Syracuse 93-88 (ot)

Regional Semifinals (March 17):
- Michigan 86-81 (over Detroit)
- Charlotte 81-59 (over Syracuse)

Regional Final (Lexington, KY, March 19):
- Charlotte 75-68 (over Michigan)

Midwest Region

First Round:
- Cincinnati vs Marquette (March 12, Baton Rouge, LA) — Marquette 66-51
- Kansas St. vs Providence (March 12, Omaha, NE) — Kansas St. 87-80
- Arkansas vs Wake Forest (March 12, Norman, OK) — Wake Forest 86-80
- Southern Ill. vs Arizona (March 12, Norman, OK) — Southern Ill. 81-77

Regional Semifinals (March 17):
- Marquette 67-66 (over Kansas St.)
- Wake Forest 86-81 (over Southern Ill.)

Regional Final (Oklahoma City, March 19):
- Marquette 82-68 (over Wake Forest)

National Semifinals (Atlanta, March 26)
- North Carolina 84-83 (over UNLV)
- Marquette 51-49 (over Charlotte)

National Championship (Atlanta, March 28)
- **Marquette 67-59** — NATIONAL CHAMPION

National Third Place
- UNLV 106-94 (over Charlotte)

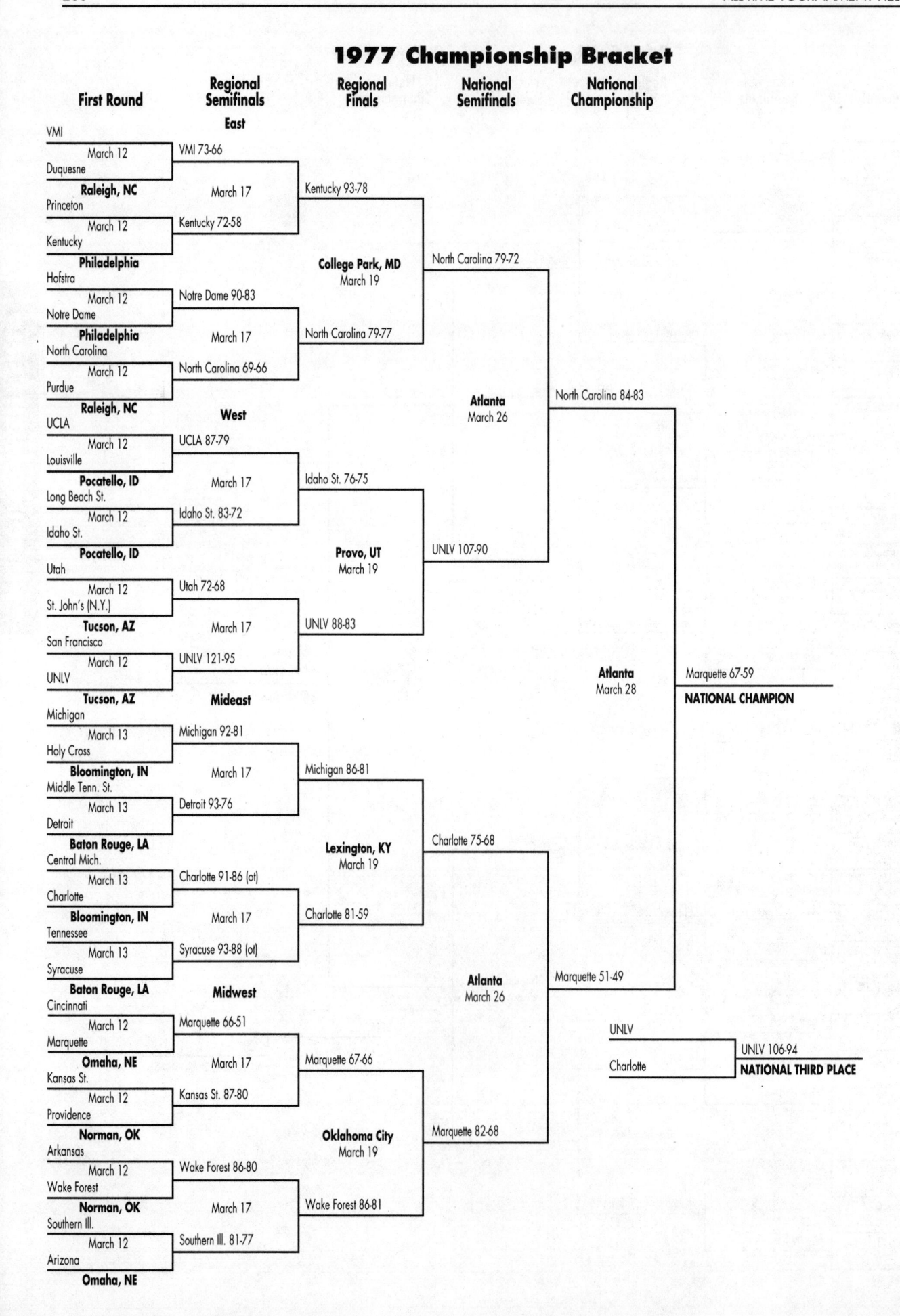

1978 Championship Bracket

Mideast

First Round
- Michigan St.
- Providence — March 11, Indianapolis
- Western Ky.
- Syracuse — March 11, Knoxville, TN
- Miami (Ohio)
- Marquette — March 11, Indianapolis
- Kentucky
- Florida St. — March 11, Knoxville, TN

Regional Semifinals (March 16)
- Michigan St. 77-63
- Western Ky. 87-86 (ot)
- Miami 84-81 (ot)
- Kentucky 85-76

Regional Finals — Dayton, OH, March 18
- Michigan St. 90-69
- Kentucky 91-69

Kentucky 52-49

West

First Round
- UCLA
- Kansas — March 11, Eugene, OR
- Weber St.
- Arkansas — March 11, Eugene, OR
- San Francisco
- North Carolina — March 11, Tempe, AZ
- New Mexico
- Cal St. Fullerton — March 11, Tempe, AZ

Regional Semifinals (March 16)
- UCLA 83-76
- Arkansas 73-52
- San Francisco 68-64
- Cal St. Fullerton 90-85

Regional Finals — Albuquerque, NM, March 18
- Arkansas 74-70
- Cal St. Fullerton 75-72

Arkansas 61-58

National Semifinals — St. Louis, March 25
- Kentucky 64-59

East

First Round
- Duke
- Rhode Island — March 12, Charlotte, NC
- Pennsylvania
- St. Bonaventure — March 12, Philadelphia
- Furman
- Indiana — March 12, Charlotte, NC
- Villanova
- La Salle — March 12, Philadelphia

Regional Semifinals (March 17)
- Duke 63-62
- Pennsylvania 92-83
- Indiana 63-62
- Villanova 103-97

Regional Finals — Providence, RI, March 19
- Duke 84-80
- Villanova 61-60

Duke 90-72

Midwest

First Round
- Missouri
- Utah — March 12, Wichita, KS
- Houston
- Notre Dame — March 12, Tulsa, OK
- Creighton
- DePaul — March 12, Wichita, KS
- Louisville
- St. John's (N.Y.) — March 12, Tulsa, OK

Regional Semifinals (March 17)
- Utah 86-79 (2 ot)
- Notre Dame 100-77
- DePaul 80-78
- Louisville 76-68

Regional Finals — Lawrence, KS, March 19
- Notre Dame 69-56
- DePaul 90-89 (2 ot)

Notre Dame 84-64

National Semifinals — St. Louis, March 25
- Duke 90-86

National Championship — St. Louis, March 27
Kentucky 94-88 — NATIONAL CHAMPION

National Third Place
- Arkansas
- Notre Dame
- **Arkansas 71-69 — NATIONAL THIRD PLACE**

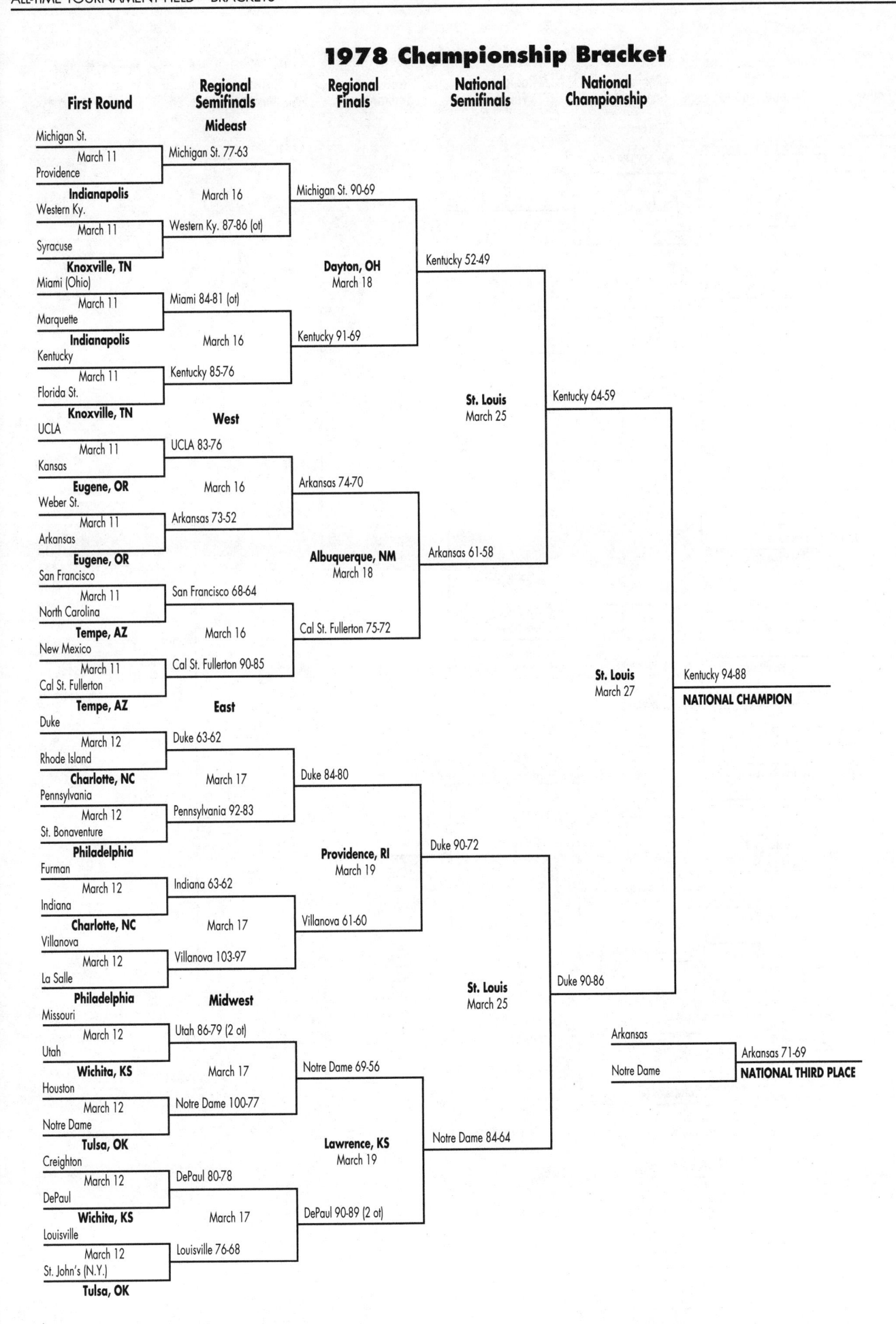

1979 Championship Bracket

East

First Round
- 7 Temple / 10 St. John's (N.Y.) — March 9, Raleigh, NC
- 8 Iona / 9 Pennsylvania — March 9, Raleigh, NC

Second Round (March 11, Raleigh, NC)
- St. John's (N.Y.) 75-70
- 2 Duke
- 3 Georgetown / 6 Rutgers — March 10, Providence, RI
- Pennsylvania 73-69
- 1 North Carolina
- 4 Syracuse / 5 Connecticut — March 10, Raleigh, NC

Regional Semifinals (March 16)
- St. John's (N.Y.) 80-78
- Rutgers 64-58
- Pennsylvania 72-71
- Syracuse 89-81

Regional Finals — Greensboro, NC, March 18
- St. John's (N.Y.) 67-65
- Pennsylvania 84-76

National Semifinals — Salt Lake City, March 24
- Pennsylvania 64-62

Mideast

First Round
- 7 Detroit / 10 Lamar — March 9, Murfreesboro, TN
- 8 Tennessee / 9 Eastern Ky. — March 9, Murfreesboro, TN

Second Round (March 11)
- Lamar 95-87
- 2 Michigan St. — Murfreesboro, TN
- 3 LSU / 6 Appalachian St. — March 10, Bloomington, IN
- Tennessee 97-81
- 1 Notre Dame — Murfreesboro, TN
- 4 Iowa / 5 Toledo — March 10

Regional Semifinals (March 16)
- Michigan St. 95-64
- LSU 71-57
- Notre Dame 73-67
- Toledo 74-72

Regional Finals — Indianapolis, March 18
- Michigan St. 87-71
- Notre Dame 79-71

National Semifinals
- Michigan St. 80-68

National Championship — Salt Lake City, March 26
- Michigan St. 101-67
- Michigan St. 75-64 **NATIONAL CHAMPION**

West

First Round
- 7 Southern California / 10 Utah St. — March 9, Los Angeles
- 8 Utah / 9 Pepperdine — March 9, Los Angeles

Second Round (March 11)
- Southern California 86-67
- 2 DePaul — Los Angeles
- 3 Marquette / 6 Pacific (Cal.) — March 10, Tucson, AZ
- Pepperdine 92-88 (ot)
- 1 UCLA — Los Angeles
- 4 San Francisco / 5 Brigham Young — March 10

Regional Semifinals (March 15)
- DePaul 89-78
- Marquette 73-48
- UCLA 76-71
- San Francisco 86-63

Regional Finals — Provo, UT, March 17
- DePaul 62-56
- UCLA 99-81

National Semifinals — Salt Lake City, March 24
- DePaul 95-91
- Indiana St. 76-74

Midwest

First Round
- 7 Weber St. / 10 New Mexico St. — March 9, Lawrence, KS
- 8 Virginia Tech / 9 Jacksonville — March 9, Lawrence, KS

Second Round (March 11)
- Weber St. 81-78 (ot)
- 2 Arkansas — Tucson, AZ
- 3 Louisville / 6 South Ala. — March 10, Lawrence, KS
- Virginia Tech 70-53
- 1 Indiana St. — Dallas
- 4 Texas / 5 Oklahoma — March 10, Lawrence, KS

Regional Semifinals (March 15)
- Arkansas 74-63
- Louisville 69-66
- Indiana St. 86-69
- Oklahoma 90-76

Regional Finals — Cincinnati, March 17
- Arkansas 73-62
- Indiana St. 93-72

National Semifinals
- Indiana St. 73-71

National Third Place
- DePaul 96-93
- Pennsylvania

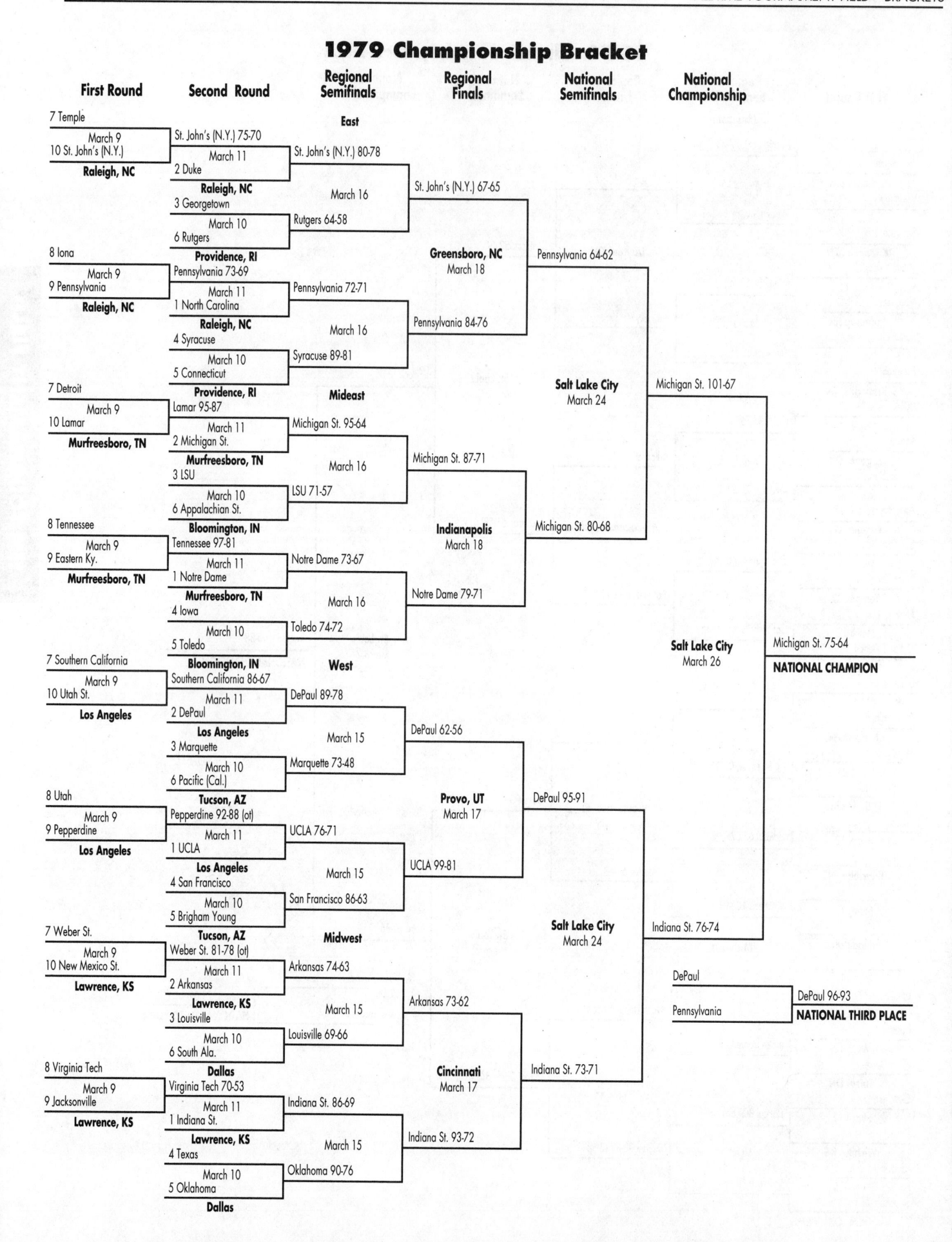

ALL-TIME TOURNAMENT FIELD—BRACKETS 203

1980 Championship Bracket

First Round | Second Round | Regional Semifinals | Regional Finals | National Semifinals | National Championship

East

- 8 Villanova
  - March 7 — Villanova 77-59
- 9 Marquette
  - Providence, RI
  - March 9 — 1 Syracuse → Syracuse 97-83
- 5 Iowa
  - March 6 — Iowa 86-72
- 12 Va. Commonwealth
  - Greensboro, NC
  - March 8 — 4 North Carolina St. → Iowa 77-64
  - March 14 — Iowa 88-77
- 6 *Iona
  - March 7 — *Iona 84-78
- 11 Holy Cross
  - Providence, RI
  - March 9 — 3 Georgetown → Georgetown 74-71
- 7 Tennessee
  - March 6 — Tennessee 80-69
- 10 Furman
  - Greensboro, NC
  - March 8 — 2 Maryland → Maryland 86-75
  - March 14 — Georgetown 74-68

Philadelphia — March 16
Iowa 81-80

Midwest

- 8 Alcorn St.
  - March 7 — Alcorn St. 70-62
- 9 South Ala.
  - Denton, TX
  - March 9 — 1 LSU → LSU 98-88
- 5 Missouri
  - March 6 — Missouri 61-51
- 12 San Jose St.
  - Lincoln, NE
  - March 8 — 4 Notre Dame → Missouri 87-84 (ot)
  - March 14 — LSU 68-63
- 6 Texas A&M
  - March 7 — Texas A&M 55-53
- 11 Bradley
  - Denton, TX
  - March 9 — 3 North Carolina → Texas A&M 78-61 (2 ot)
- 7 Kansas St.
  - March 6 — Kansas St. 71-53
- 10 Arkansas
  - Lincoln, NE
  - March 8 — 2 Louisville → Louisville 71-69 (ot)
  - March 14 — Louisville 66-55 (ot)

Houston — March 16
Louisville 86-66

Indianapolis — March 22
Louisville 80-72

Mideast

- 8 Florida St.
  - March 7 — Florida St. 94-91
- 9 Toledo
  - Bowling Green, KY
  - March 9 — 1 Kentucky → Kentucky 97-78
- 5 Washington St.
  - March 6 — Pennsylvania 62-55
- 12 Pennsylvania
  - West Lafayette, IN
  - March 8 — 4 Duke → Duke 52-42
  - March 13 — Duke 55-54
- 6 Purdue
  - March 6 — Purdue 90-82
- 11 La Salle
  - West Lafayette, IN
  - March 8 — 3 St. John's (N.Y.) → Purdue 87-72
- 7 Virginia Tech
  - March 7 — Virginia Tech 89-85 (ot)
- 10 Western Ky.
  - Bowling Green, KY
  - March 9 — 2 Indiana → Indiana 68-59
  - March 13 — Purdue 76-69

Lexington, KY — March 15
Purdue 68-60

Indianapolis — March 22
*UCLA 67-62

West

- 8 *UCLA
  - March 7 — *UCLA 87-74
- 9 Old Dominion
  - Tempe, AZ
  - March 9 — 1 DePaul → *UCLA 77-71
- 5 Arizona St.
  - March 7 — Arizona St. 99-71
- 12 *Loyola Marymount
  - Tempe, AZ
  - March 9 — 4 Ohio St. → Ohio St. 89-75
  - March 13 — *UCLA 72-68
- 6 Clemson
  - March 6 — Clemson 76-73
- 11 Utah St.
  - Ogden, UT
  - March 8 — 3 Brigham Young → Clemson 71-66
- 7 Weber St.
  - March 6 — Lamar 87-86
- 10 Lamar
  - Ogden, UT
  - March 8 — 2 *Oregon St. → Lamar 81-77
  - March 13 — Clemson 74-66

Tucson, AZ — March 15
*UCLA 85-74

Louisville 59-54
NATIONAL CHAMPION

Purdue
Iowa
Purdue 75-58
NATIONAL THIRD PLACE

*Iona's, Loyola Marymount's, Oregon State's and UCLA's participation in 1980 tournament vacated.

THE TOURNAMENT FIELD

1981 Championship Bracket

First Round | **Second Round** | **Regional Semifinals** | **Regional Finals** | **National Semifinals** | **National Championship**

Midwest

- 8 Lamar
  - March 12 — Lamar 71-67
- 9 Missouri
  - Austin, TX
    - March 14 — LSU 100-78
- 1 LSU
- 5 Arkansas
  - March 12 — Arkansas 73-67
- 12 Mercer
  - Austin, TX
    - March 14 — Arkansas 74-73
- 4 Louisville

  - March 20 — LSU 72-56

- 6 Wichita St.
  - March 13 — Wichita St. 95-70
- 11 Southern U.
  - Wichita, KS
    - March 15 — Wichita St. 60-56
- 3 Iowa
- 7 Kansas
  - March 13 — Kansas 69-66
- 10 Mississippi
  - Wichita, KS
    - March 15 — Kansas 88-71
- 2 Arizona St.

  - March 20 — Wichita St. 66-65

New Orleans — March 22
LSU 96-85

Mideast

- 8 Creighton
  - March 12 — St. Joseph's 59-57
- 9 St. Joseph's
  - Dayton, OH
    - March 14 — St. Joseph's 49-48
- 1 DePaul
- 5 Boston College
  - March 13 — Boston College 93-90
- 12 Ball St.
  - Tuscaloosa, AL
    - March 15 — Boston College 67-64
- 4 Wake Forest

  - March 20 — St. Joseph's 42-41

- 6 Maryland
  - March 12 — Maryland 81-69
- 11 Chattanooga
  - Dayton, OH
    - March 14 — Indiana 99-64
- 3 Indiana
- 7 UAB
  - March 13 — UAB 93-68
- 10 Western Ky.
  - Tuscaloosa, AL
    - March 15 — UAB 69-62
- 2 Kentucky

  - March 20 — Indiana 87-72

Bloomington, IN — March 22
Indiana 78-46

West

- 8 Kansas St.
  - March 12 — Kansas St. 64-60
- 9 San Francisco
  - Los Angeles
    - March 14 — Kansas St. 50-48
- 1 *Oregon St.
- 5 Wyoming
  - March 12 — Wyoming 78-43
- 12 Howard
  - Los Angeles
    - March 14 — Illinois 67-65
- 4 Illinois

  - March 19 — Kansas St. 57-52

- 6 Fresno St.
  - March 13 — Northeastern 55-53
- 11 Northeastern
  - El Paso, TX
    - March 15 — Utah 94-69
- 3 Utah
- 7 Idaho
  - March 13 — Pittsburgh 70-69 (ot)
- 10 Pittsburgh
  - El Paso, TX
    - March 15 — North Carolina 74-57
- 2 North Carolina

  - March 19 — North Carolina 61-56

Salt Lake City — March 21
North Carolina 82-68

East

- 8 Houston
  - March 13 — Villanova 90-72
- 9 Villanova
  - Charlotte, NC
    - March 15 — Virginia 54-50
- 1 Virginia
- 5 Va. Commonwealth
  - March 13 — Va. Commonwealth 85-69
- 12 Long Island
  - Charlotte, NC
    - March 15 — Tennessee 58-56 (ot)
- 4 Tennessee

  - March 19 — Virginia 62-48

- 6 Brigham Young
  - March 12 — Brigham Young 60-51
- 11 Princeton
  - Providence, RI
    - March 14 — Brigham Young 78-55
- 3 UCLA
- 7 Georgetown
  - March 13 — James Madison 61-55
- 10 James Madison
  - Providence, RI
    - March 14 — Notre Dame 54-45
- 2 Notre Dame

  - March 19 — Brigham Young 51-50

Atlanta — March 21
Virginia 74-60

Philadelphia — March 28
Indiana 67-49

Philadelphia — March 28
North Carolina 78-65

Philadelphia — March 30
Indiana 63-50
NATIONAL CHAMPION

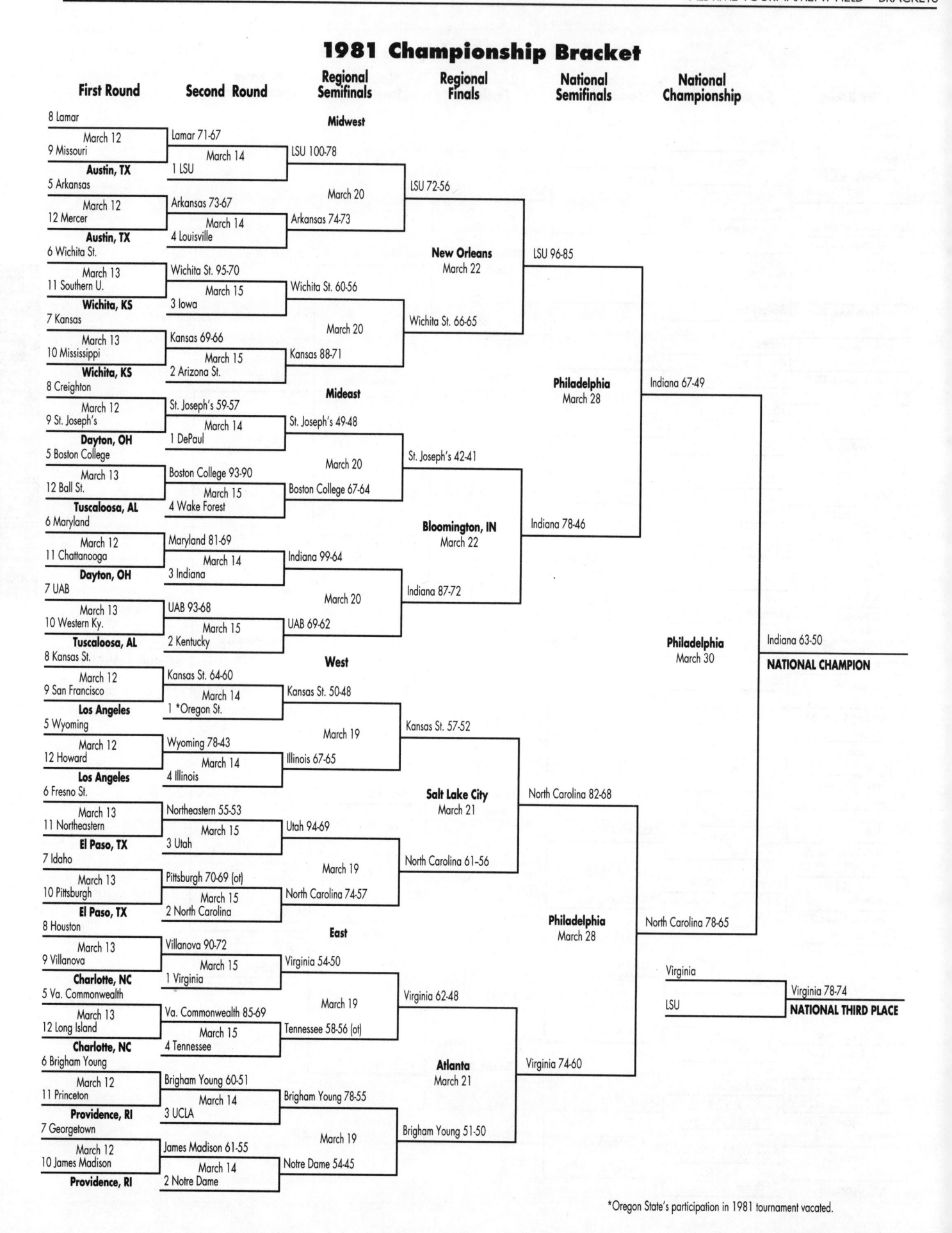

Virginia
LSU
Virginia 78-74
NATIONAL THIRD PLACE

*Oregon State's participation in 1981 tournament vacated.

1982 Championship Bracket

First Round	Second Round	Regional Semifinals	Regional Finals	National Semifinals	National Championship

East

- 8 Ohio St.
  - March 11
- 9 James Madison
  - Charlotte, NC
  - James Madison 55-48
    - March 13
    - 1 North Carolina
      - North Carolina 52-50
- 5 St. John's (N.Y.)
  - March 12
- 12 Pennsylvania
  - Uniondale, NY
  - St. John's (N.Y.) 66-56
    - March 14
    - 4 Alabama
      - Alabama 69-68
        - March 19
        - North Carolina 74-69
          - Raleigh, NC
          - March 21
          - North Carolina 70-60
- 6 St. Joseph's
  - March 12
- 11 Northeastern
  - Uniondale, NY
  - Northeastern 63-62
    - March 14
    - 3 Villanova
      - Villanova 76-72 (3 ot)
- 7 Wake Forest
  - March 11
- 10 Old Dominion
  - Charlotte, NC
  - Wake Forest 74-57
    - March 13
    - 2 *Memphis
      - *Memphis 56-55
        - March 19
        - Villanova 70-66

Midwest

- 8 Boston College
  - March 12
- 9 San Francisco
  - Dallas
  - Boston College 70-66
    - March 14
    - 1 DePaul
      - Boston College 82-75
- 5 Kansas St.
  - March 12
- 12 Northern Ill.
  - Dallas
  - Kansas St. 77-68
    - March 14
    - 4 Arkansas
      - Kansas St. 65-64
        - March 19
        - Boston College 69-65
          - St. Louis
          - March 21
          - Houston 99-92
- 6 Houston
  - March 11
- 11 Alcorn St.
  - Tulsa, OK
  - Houston 94-84
    - March 13
    - 3 Tulsa
      - Houston 78-74
- 7 Marquette
  - March 11
- 10 Evansville
  - Tulsa, OK
  - Marquette 67-62
    - March 13
    - 2 Missouri
      - Missouri 73-69
        - March 19
        - Houston 79-78

North Carolina 70-60

Villanova 70-66

North Carolina 68-63

New Orleans
March 27

Houston 99-92

Boston College 69-65

Mideast

- 8 La.-Lafayette
  - March 12
- 9 Tennessee
  - Indianapolis
  - Tennessee 61-57
    - March 14
    - 1 Virginia
      - Virginia 54-51
- 5 Indiana
  - March 11
- 12 Robert Morris
  - Nashville, TN
  - Indiana 94-62
    - March 13
    - 4 UAB
      - UAB 80-70
        - March 18
        - UAB 68-66
          - Birmingham, AL
          - March 20
          - Louisville 75-68
- 6 Kentucky
  - March 11
- 11 Middle Tenn.
  - Nashville, TN
  - Middle Tenn. 50-44
    - March 13
    - 3 Louisville
      - Louisville 81-56
- 7 North Carolina St.
  - March 12
- 10 Chattanooga
  - Indianapolis
  - Chattanooga 58-51
    - March 14
    - 2 Minnesota
      - Minnesota 62-61
        - March 18
        - Louisville 67-61

West

- 8 Wyoming
  - March 11
- 9 Southern California
  - Logan, UT
  - Wyoming 61-58
    - March 13
    - 1 Georgetown
      - Georgetown 51-43
- 5 West Virginia
  - March 11
- 12 N.C. A&T
  - Logan, UT
  - West Virginia 102-72
    - March 13
    - 4 Fresno St.
      - Fresno St. 50-46
        - March 18
        - Georgetown 58-40
          - Provo, UT
          - March 20
          - Georgetown 69-45
- 6 Iowa
  - March 12
- 11 La.-Monroe
  - Pullman, WA
  - Iowa 70-63
    - March 14
    - 3 Idaho
      - Idaho 69-67 (ot)
- 7 Pepperdine
  - March 12
- 10 Pittsburgh
  - Pullman, WA
  - Pepperdine 99-88
    - March 14
    - 2 *Oregon St.
      - *Oregon St. 70-51
        - March 18
        - *Oregon St. 60-42

New Orleans
March 27

Georgetown 50-46

New Orleans
March 29

North Carolina 63-62
NATIONAL CHAMPION

*Oregon State's and Memphis' participation in 1982 tournament vacated.

1983 Championship Bracket

First Round | **Second Round** | **Regional Semifinals** | **Regional Finals** | **National Semifinals** | **National Championship**

Midwest

- 8 Maryland
- March 17
- 9 Chattanooga — Maryland 52-51
- Houston — March 19
- 5 Georgetown — 1 Houston — Houston 60-50
- March 18
- 12 #Alcorn St. — Georgetown 68-63
- Louisville, KY — March 20
- 6 Alabama — 4 *Memphis — *Memphis 66-57 — Houston 70-63
- March 17
- 11 Lamar — Lamar 73-50
- Houston — March 19
- 7 Iowa — 3 Villanova — Villanova 60-58
- March 18
- 10 Utah St. — Iowa 64-59
- Louisville, KY — March 20
- 8 Tennessee — 2 Missouri — Iowa 77-63 — Villanova 55-54

Kansas City, MO — March 27 — Houston 89-71

Mideast

- March 18
- 9 Marquette — Tennessee 57-56
- Evansville, IN — March 20
- 5 Purdue — 1 Louisville — Louisville 70-57
- March 17
- 12 #Robert Morris — Purdue 55-53
- Tampa, FL — March 19
- 6 Illinois St. — 4 Arkansas — Arkansas 78-68 — Louisville 65-63
- March 17
- 11 Ohio — Ohio 51-49
- Tampa, FL — March 19
- 7 Oklahoma — 3 Kentucky — Kentucky 57-40
- March 18
- 10 UAB — Oklahoma 71-63
- Evansville, IN — March 20
- 8 Washington St. — 2 Indiana — Indiana 63-49 — Kentucky 64-59

Knoxville, TN — March 26 — Louisville 80-68 (ot)

Albuquerque, NM — April 2 — Houston 94-81

West

- March 17
- 9 Weber St. — Washington St. 62-52
- Boise, ID — March 19
- 5 Oklahoma St. — 1 Virginia — Virginia 54-49
- March 18
- 12 #Princeton — Princeton 56-53
- Corvallis, OR — March 20
- 6 North Carolina St. — 4 Boston College — Boston College 51-42 — Virginia 95-92
- March 18
- 11 Pepperdine — North Carolina St. 69-67 (2 ot)
- Corvallis, OR — March 20
- 7 Illinois — 3 UNLV — North Carolina St. 71-70
- March 17
- 10 Utah — Utah 52-49
- Boise, ID — March 19
- 8 La.-Lafayette — 2 UCLA — Utah 67-61 — North Carolina St. 75-56

Ogden, UT — March 26 — North Carolina St. 63-62

East

- March 18
- 9 Rutgers — Rutgers 60-53
- Hartford, CT — March 20
- 5 Va. Commonwealth — 1 St. John's (N.Y.) — St. John's (N.Y.) 66-55
- March 17
- 12 #La Salle — Va. Commonwealth 76-67
- Greensboro, NC — March 19
- 6 Syracuse — 4 Georgia — Georgia 56-54 — Georgia 70-67
- March 18
- 11 Morehead St. — Syracuse 74-59
- Hartford, CT — March 20
- 7 West Virginia — 3 Ohio St. — Ohio St. 79-74
- March 17
- 10 James Madison — James Madison 57-50
- Greensboro, NC — March 19
- 2 North Carolina — North Carolina 68-49 — North Carolina 64-51

Syracuse, NY — March 27 — Georgia 82-77

Albuquerque, NM — April 2 — North Carolina St. 67-60

North Carolina St. 54-52
NATIONAL CHAMPION

Albuquerque, NM — April 4

#OPENING ROUND
March 15
at Dayton, OH
Alcorn St. 81, Xavier 75
Robert Morris 64, Ga. Southern 54
at Philadelphia
La Salle 70, Boston U. 58
Princeton 53, N.C. A&T 41

*Memphis' participation in 1983 tournament vacated.

1984 Championship Bracket

First Round | Second Round | Regional Semifinals | Regional Finals | National Semifinals | National Championship

Mideast
- 8 Brigham Young
- March 15 — Brigham Young 84-68
- 9 UAB
- Birmingham, AL
- March 17 — Kentucky 93-68
- 1 Kentucky
- 5 Louisville
- March 16 — Louisville 72-59
- 12 #Morehead St.
- Milwaukee
- March 18 — Louisville 69-67
- 4 Tulsa
- March 22 — Kentucky 72-67
- 6 Oregon St.
- March 15 — West Virginia 64-62
- 11 West Virginia
- Birmingham, AL
- March 17 — Maryland 102-77
- 3 Maryland
- 7 Villanova
- March 16 — Villanova 84-72
- 10 Marshall
- Milwaukee
- March 18 — Illinois 64-56
- 2 Illinois
- March 22 — Illinois 72-70

Lexington, KY — March 24 — Kentucky 54-51

West
- 8 Miami (Ohio)
- March 16 — Southern Methodist 83-69
- 9 Southern Methodist
- Pullman, WA
- March 18 — Georgetown 37-36
- 1 Georgetown
- 5 UNLV
- March 15 — UNLV 68-56
- 12 #Princeton
- Salt Lake City
- March 17 — UNLV 73-60
- 4 UTEP
- March 23 — Georgetown 62-48
- 6 Washington
- March 16 — Washington 64-54
- 11 Nevada
- Pullman, WA
- March 18 — Washington 80-78
- 3 Duke
- 7 LSU
- March 15 — Dayton 74-66
- 10 Dayton
- Salt Lake City
- March 17 — Dayton 89-85
- 2 Oklahoma
- March 23 — Dayton 64-58

Los Angeles — March 25 — Georgetown 61-49

East
- 8 Temple
- March 15 — Temple 65-63
- 9 St. John's (N.Y.)
- Charlotte, NC
- March 17 — North Carolina 77-66
- 1 North Carolina
- 5 Auburn
- March 15 — Richmond 72-71
- 12 #Richmond
- Charlotte, NC
- March 17 — Indiana 75-67
- 4 Indiana
- March 22 — Indiana 72-68
- 6 Va. Commonwealth
- March 16 — Va. Commonwealth 70-69
- 11 #Northeastern
- East Rutherford, NJ
- March 18 — Syracuse 78-63
- 3 Syracuse
- 7 Virginia
- March 16 — Virginia 58-57
- 10 Iona
- East Rutherford, NJ
- March 18 — Virginia 53-51 (ot)
- 2 Arkansas
- March 22 — Virginia 63-55

Atlanta — March 24 — Virginia 50-48

Midwest
- 8 Illinois St.
- March 16 — Illinois St. 49-48
- 9 Alabama
- Lincoln, NE
- March 18 — DePaul 75-61
- 1 DePaul
- 5 Kansas
- March 16 — Kansas 57-56
- 12 #Alcorn St.
- Lincoln, NE
- March 18 — Wake Forest 69-59
- 4 Wake Forest
- March 23 — Wake Forest 73-71 (ot)
- 6 *Memphis
- March 15 — *Memphis 92-83
- 11 Oral Roberts
- Memphis, TN
- March 17 — *Memphis 66-48
- 3 Purdue
- 7 Fresno St.
- March 15 — Louisiana Tech 66-56
- 10 Louisiana Tech
- Memphis, TN
- March 17 — Houston 77-69
- 2 Houston
- March 23 — Houston 78-71

St. Louis — March 25 — Houston 68-63

National Semifinals
- **Seattle — March 31**
  - Kentucky 53-40 → Georgetown 53-40
  - Georgetown 61-49
  - Houston 49-47 (ot)

National Championship
- **Seattle — April 2**
- Georgetown 84-75
- **NATIONAL CHAMPION**

#OPENING ROUND
March 13

at Philadelphia
Princeton 65, San Diego 56
Richmond 89, Rider 65
Northeastern 90, Long Island 87

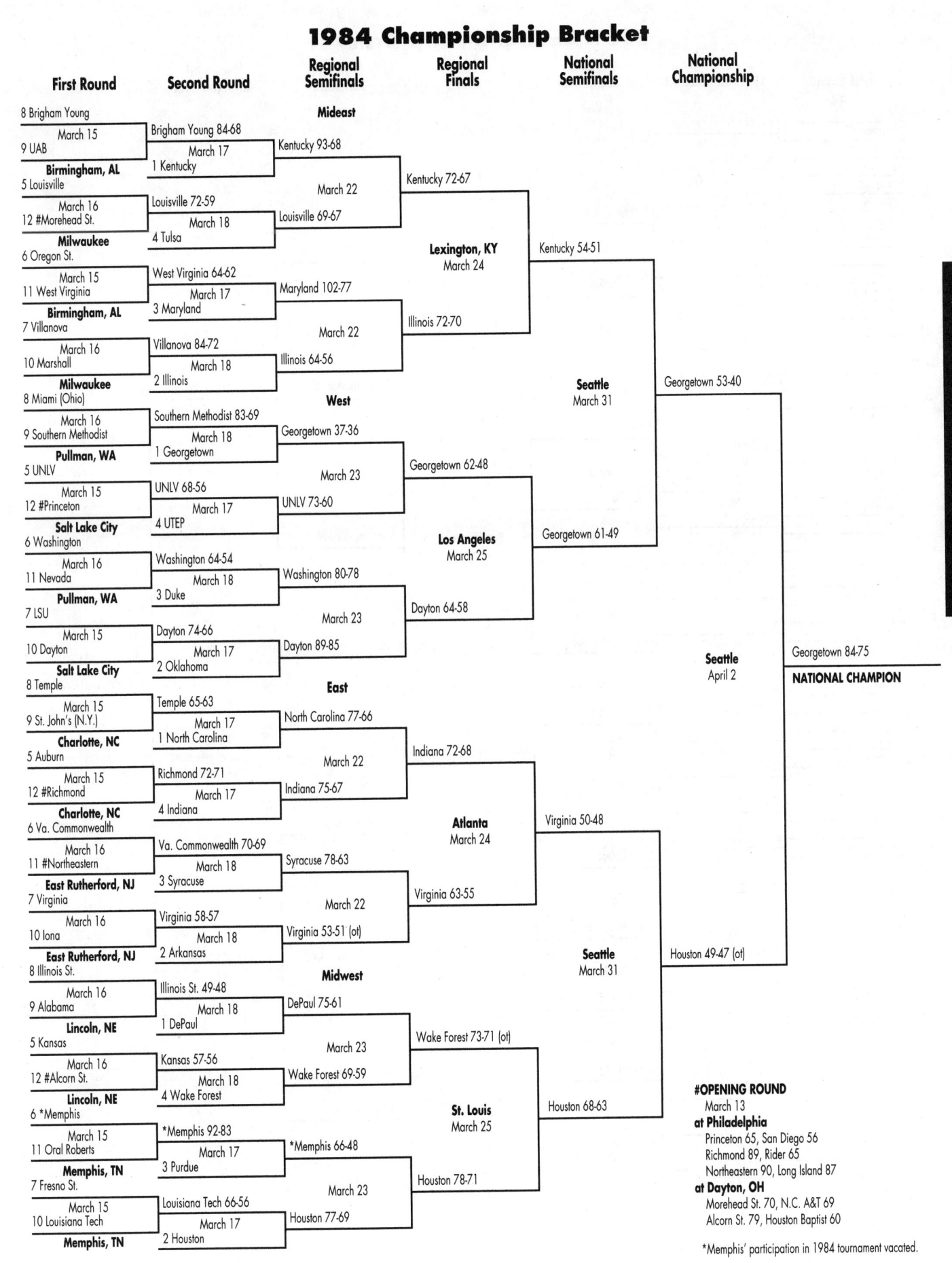

at Dayton, OH
Morehead St. 70, N.C. A&T 69
Alcorn St. 79, Houston Baptist 60

*Memphis' participation in 1984 tournament vacated.

1985 Championship Bracket

First Round	Second Round	Regional Semifinals	Regional Finals	National Semifinals	National Championship

West

- 3/14 — 1 St. John's (N.Y.) / 16 Southern U. → St. John's (N.Y.) 83-59
- 3/14 — 8 Iowa / 9 Arkansas → Arkansas 63-54
  - **Salt Lake City** March 16 — St. John's (N.Y.) 68-65
- 3/14 — 5 Washington / 12 Kentucky → Kentucky 66-58
- 3/14 — 4 UNLV / 13 San Diego St. → UNLV 85-80
  - March 16 — Kentucky 64-61
  - March 22 — St. John's (N.Y.) 86-70
- 3/15 — 6 Tulsa / 11 UTEP → UTEP 79-75
- 3/15 — 3 North Carolina St. / 14 Nevada → North Carolina St. 65-56
  - **Albuquerque, NM** March 17 — North Carolina St. 86-73
- 3/15 — 7 Alabama / 10 Arizona → Alabama 50-41
- 3/15 — 2 Va. Commonwealth / 15 Marshall → Va. Commonwealth 81-65
  - March 17 — Alabama 63-59
  - March 22 — North Carolina St. 61-55

Denver March 24 — St. John's (N.Y.) 69-60

East

- 3/14 — 1 Georgetown / 16 Lehigh → Georgetown 68-43
- 3/14 — 8 Temple / 9 Virginia Tech → Temple 60-57
  - **Hartford, CT** March 16 — Georgetown 63-46
- 3/14 — 5 Southern Methodist / 12 Old Dominion → Southern Methodist 85-68
- 3/14 — 4 Loyola (Ill.) / 13 Iona → Loyola 59-58
  - March 16 — Loyola 70-57
  - March 21 — Georgetown 65-53
- 3/15 — 6 *Georgia / 11 Wichita St. → *Georgia 67-59
- 3/15 — 3 Illinois / 14 Northeastern → Illinois 76-57
  - **Atlanta** March 17 — Illinois 74-58
- 3/15 — 7 Syracuse / 10 DePaul → Syracuse 70-65
- 3/15 — 2 Georgia Tech / 15 Mercer → Georgia Tech 65-58
  - March 17 — Georgia Tech 70-53
  - March 21 — Georgia Tech 61-53

Providence, RI March 23 — Georgetown 60-54

Lexington, KY March 30 — Georgetown 77-59

Midwest

- 3/14 — 1 Oklahoma / 16 N.C. A&T → Oklahoma 96-83
- 3/14 — 8 Southern California / 9 Illinois St. → Illinois St. 58-55
  - **Tulsa, OK** March 16 — Oklahoma 75-69
- 3/14 — 5 Louisiana Tech / 12 Pittsburgh → Louisiana Tech 78-54
- 3/14 — 4 Ohio St. / 13 Iowa St. → Ohio St. 75-64
  - March 16 — Louisiana Tech 79-67
  - March 21 — Oklahoma 86-84 (ot)
- 3/15 — 6 Texas Tech / 11 Boston College → Boston College 55-53
- 3/15 — 3 Duke / 14 Pepperdine → Duke 75-62
  - **Houston** March 17 — Boston College 74-73
- 3/15 — 7 UAB / 10 Michigan St. → UAB 70-68
- 3/15 — 2 *Memphis / 15 Pennsylvania → *Memphis 67-55
  - March 17 — *Memphis 67-66 (ot)
  - March 21 — *Memphis 59-57

Dallas March 23 — *Memphis 63-61

Southeast

- 3/15 — 1 Michigan / 16 Fairleigh Dickinson → Michigan 59-55
- 3/15 — 8 Villanova / 9 Dayton → Villanova 51-49
  - **Dayton, OH** March 17 — Villanova 59-55
- 3/15 — 5 Maryland / 12 Miami (Ohio) → Maryland 69-68 (ot)
- 3/15 — 4 LSU / 13 Navy → Navy 78-55
  - March 17 — Maryland 64-59
  - March 22 — Villanova 46-43
- 3/14 — 6 Purdue / 11 Auburn → Auburn 59-58
- 3/14 — 3 Kansas / 14 Ohio → Kansas 49-38
  - **Notre Dame, IN** March 16 — Auburn 66-64
- 3/14 — 7 Notre Dame / 10 Oregon St. → Notre Dame 79-70
- 3/14 — 2 North Carolina / 15 Middle Tenn. → North Carolina 76-57
  - March 16 — North Carolina 60-58
  - March 22 — North Carolina 62-56

Birmingham, AL March 24 — Villanova 56-44

Lexington, KY March 30 — Villanova 52-45

Lexington, KY April 1 — Villanova 66-64

NATIONAL CHAMPION

*Georgia's and Memphis' participation in 1985 tournament vacated.

ALL-TIME TOURNAMENT FIELD—BRACKETS

1986 Championship Bracket

First Round	Second Round	Regional Semifinals	Regional Finals	National Semifinals	National Championship

Southeast

- 3/14 1 Kentucky — Kentucky 75-55
- 3/14 16 Davidson
- 3/14 8 Western Ky. — Western Ky. 67-59 (March 16, Charlotte, NC) → Kentucky 71-64
- 3/14 9 Nebraska
- 3/14 5 Alabama — Alabama 97-80
- 3/14 12 Xavier
- 3/14 4 Illinois — Illinois 75-51 (March 16) → Alabama 58-56
- 3/14 13 Fairfield

→ Kentucky 68-63 (March 20, Atlanta, March 22)

- 3/13 6 Purdue — LSU 94-87 (2 ot)
- 3/13 11 LSU
- 3/13 3 *Memphis — *Memphis 95-63 (March 15, Baton Rouge, LA) → LSU 83-81
- 3/13 14 Ball St.
- 3/13 7 Virginia Tech — Villanova 71-62
- 3/13 10 Villanova
- 3/13 2 Georgia Tech — Georgia Tech 68-53 (March 15) → Georgia Tech 66-61
- 3/13 15 Marist

→ LSU 70-64 (March 20)

→ LSU 59-57

West

- 3/14 1 St. John's (N.Y.) — St. John's 83-74
- 3/14 16 Montana St.
- 3/14 8 Auburn — Auburn 73-63 (March 16, Long Beach, CA) → Auburn 81-65
- 3/14 9 Arizona
- 3/14 5 Maryland — Maryland 69-64
- 3/14 12 Pepperdine
- 3/14 4 UNLV — UNLV 74-51 (March 16) → UNLV 70-64
- 3/14 13 La.-Monroe

→ Auburn 70-63 (March 20, Houston, March 22)

- 3/13 6 UAB — UAB 66-64
- 3/13 11 Missouri
- 3/13 3 North Carolina — North Carolina 84-72 (March 15, Ogden, UT) → North Carolina 77-59
- 3/13 14 Utah
- 3/13 7 Bradley — Bradley 83-65
- 3/13 10 UTEP
- 3/13 2 Louisville — Louisville 93-73 (March 15) → Louisville 82-68
- 3/13 15 Drexel

→ Louisville 94-79 (March 20)

→ Louisville 84-76

Dallas, March 29

Louisville 88-77

East

- 3/13 1 Duke — Duke 85-78
- 3/13 16 Mississippi Val.
- 3/13 8 Old Dominion — Old Dominion 72-64 (March 15, Greensboro, NC) → Duke 89-61
- 3/13 9 West Virginia
- 3/13 5 Virginia — *DePaul 72-68
- 3/13 12 *DePaul
- 3/13 4 Oklahoma — Oklahoma 80-74 (March 15) → *DePaul 74-69
- 3/13 13 Northeastern

→ Duke 74-67 (March 21, East Rutherford, NJ, March 23)

- 3/14 6 St. Joseph's — St. Joseph's 60-59
- 3/14 11 Richmond
- 3/14 3 Indiana — Cleveland St. 83-79 (March 16, Syracuse, NY) → Cleveland St. 75-69
- 3/14 14 Cleveland St.
- 3/14 7 Navy — Navy 87-68
- 3/14 10 Tulsa
- 3/14 2 Syracuse — Syracuse 101-52 (March 16) → Navy 97-85
- 3/14 15 Brown

→ Navy 71-70 (March 21)

→ Duke 71-50

Dallas, March 29

Duke 71-67

Midwest

- 3/13 1 Kansas — Kansas 71-46
- 3/13 16 N.C. A&T
- 3/13 8 Jacksonville — Temple 61-50 (ot) (March 15, Dayton, OH) → Kansas 65-43
- 3/13 9 Temple
- 3/13 5 Michigan St. — Michigan St. 72-70
- 3/13 12 Washington
- 3/13 4 Georgetown — Georgetown 70-64 (March 15) → Michigan St. 80-68
- 3/13 13 Texas Tech

→ Kansas 96-86 (ot) (March 21, Kansas City, MO, March 23)

- 3/14 6 North Carolina St. — North Carolina St. 66-64
- 3/14 11 Iowa
- 3/14 3 Notre Dame — Ark.-Little Rock 90-83 (March 16, Minneapolis) → North Carolina St. 80-66 (2 ot)
- 3/14 14 Ark.-Little Rock
- 3/14 7 Iowa St. — Iowa St. 81-79 (ot)
- 3/14 10 Miami (Ohio)
- 3/14 2 Michigan — Michigan 70-64 (March 16) → Iowa St. 72-69
- 3/14 15 Akron

→ North Carolina St. 70-66 (March 21)

→ Kansas 75-67

Dallas, March 31

Louisville 72-69 — **NATIONAL CHAMPION**

*DePaul's and Memphis' participation in 1986 tournament vacated.

THE TOURNAMENT FIELD

1987 Championship Bracket

First Round	Second Round	Regional Semifinals	Regional Finals	National Semifinals	National Championship

West

- 3/12 1 UNLV
- 16 Idaho St.
- UNLV 95-70
- 3/12 8 Georgia
- 9 Kansas St.
- March 14 Kansas St. 82-79 (ot)
- **Salt Lake City**
- UNLV 80-61
- 3/12 5 Virginia
- 12 Wyoming
- Wyoming 64-60
- 3/12 4 UCLA
- 13 Central Mich.
- March 14 UCLA 92-73
- March 20 Wyoming 78-68
- **Seattle** March 22
- UNLV 92-78
- 3/13 6 Oklahoma
- 11 Tulsa
- Oklahoma 74-69
- 3/13 3 Pittsburgh
- 14 Marist
- March 15 Pittsburgh 93-68
- **Tucson, AZ**
- Oklahoma 96-93
- 3/13 7 UTEP
- 10 Arizona
- UTEP 98-91 (ot)
- 3/13 2 Iowa
- 15 Santa Clara
- March 15 Iowa 99-76
- March 20 Iowa 84-82
- UNLV 84-81
- Iowa 93-91 (ot)
- **New Orleans** March 28

Midwest

- 3/12 1 Indiana
- 16 Fairfield
- Indiana 92-58
- 3/12 8 Auburn
- 9 San Diego
- March 14 Auburn 62-61
- **Indianapolis**
- Indiana 107-90
- 3/12 5 Duke
- 12 Texas A&M
- Duke 58-51
- 3/12 4 Missouri
- 13 Xavier
- March 14 Xavier 70-69
- March 20 Duke 65-60
- **Cincinnati** March 22
- Indiana 88-82
- 3/13 6 St. John's (N.Y.)
- 11 Wichita St.
- St. John's (N.Y.) 57-55
- 3/13 3 *DePaul
- 14 Louisiana Tech
- March 15 *DePaul 76-62
- **Chicago**
- *DePaul 83-75 (ot)
- 3/13 7 Georgia Tech
- 10 LSU
- LSU 85-79
- 3/13 2 Temple
- 15 Southern U.
- March 15 Temple 75-56
- March 20 LSU 72-62
- LSU 63-58
- Indiana 97-93
- Indiana 77-76

Southeast

- 3/13 1 Georgetown
- 16 Bucknell
- Georgetown 75-53
- 3/13 8 Kentucky
- 9 Ohio St.
- March 15 Ohio St. 91-77
- **Atlanta**
- Georgetown 82-79
- 3/13 5 Kansas
- 12 Houston
- Kansas 66-55
- 3/13 4 Clemson
- 13 Southwest Mo. St.
- March 15 Southwest Mo. St. 65-60
- March 19 Kansas 67-63
- **Louisville, KY** March 21
- Georgetown 70-57
- 3/12 6 Providence
- 11 UAB
- Providence 90-68
- 3/12 3 Illinois
- 14 Austin Peay
- March 14 Austin Peay 68-67
- **Birmingham, AL**
- Providence 90-87 (ot)
- 3/12 7 New Orleans
- 10 Brigham Young
- New Orleans 83-79
- 3/12 2 *Alabama
- 15 N.C. A&T
- March 14 *Alabama 88-71
- March 19 *Alabama 101-76
- Providence 103-82
- Providence 88-73
- **New Orleans** March 28
- Indiana 74-73
- **NATIONAL CHAMPION**

East

- 3/12 1 North Carolina
- 16 Pennsylvania
- North Carolina 113-82
- 3/12 8 Navy
- 9 Michigan
- March 14 Michigan 97-82
- **Charlotte, NC**
- North Carolina 109-97
- 3/12 5 Notre Dame
- 12 Middle Tenn.
- Notre Dame 84-71
- 3/12 4 TCU
- 13 *Marshall
- March 14 TCU 76-60
- March 19 Notre Dame 58-57
- **East Rutherford, NJ** March 21
- North Carolina 74-68
- 3/13 6 *Florida
- 11 *North Carolina St.
- *Florida 82-70
- 3/13 3 Purdue
- 14 Northeastern
- March 15 Purdue 104-95
- **Syracuse, NY**
- *Florida 85-66
- 3/13 7 West Virginia
- 10 Western Ky.
- Western Ky. 64-62
- 3/13 2 Syracuse
- 15 Ga. Southern
- March 15 Syracuse 79-73
- March 19 Syracuse 104-86
- Syracuse 87-81
- Syracuse 79-75
- Syracuse 77-63

*Alabama's, DePaul's, Florida's, Marshall's and North Carolina State's participation in 1987 tournament vacated.

ALL-TIME TOURNAMENT FIELD—BRACKETS

1988 Championship Bracket

Rounds: First Round | Second Round | Regional Semifinals | Regional Finals | National Semifinals | National Championship

Midwest

- 3/17 1 Purdue / 16 Fairleigh Dickinson — Purdue 94-79
- 3/17 8 Baylor / 9 Memphis — Memphis 75-60
  - March 19, South Bend, IN: Purdue 100-73
- 3/17 5 *DePaul / 12 Wichita St. — *DePaul 83-62
- 3/17 4 Kansas St. / 13 La Salle — Kansas St. 66-53
  - March 19: Kansas St. 66-58
  - March 25: Kansas St. 73-70 (Pontiac, MI, March 27)
- 3/18 6 Kansas / 11 Xavier — Kansas 85-72
- 3/18 3 *North Carolina St. / 14 Murray St. — Murray St. 78-75
  - March 20, Lincoln, NE: Kansas 61-58
- 3/18 7 Vanderbilt / 10 Utah St. — Vanderbilt 80-77
- 3/18 2 Pittsburgh / 15 Eastern Mich. — Pittsburgh 108-90
  - March 20: Vanderbilt 80-74 (ot)
  - March 25: Kansas 77-64
  - Kansas 71-58

East

- 3/18 1 Temple / 16 Lehigh — Temple 87-73
- 3/18 8 Georgetown / 9 LSU — Georgetown 66-63
  - March 20, Hartford, CT: Temple 74-53
- 3/18 5 Georgia Tech / 12 Iowa St. — Georgia Tech 90-78
- 3/18 4 Indiana / 13 Richmond — Richmond 72-69
  - March 20: Richmond 59-55
  - March 24: Temple 69-47 (East Rutherford, NJ, March 26)
- 3/17 6 Missouri / 11 Rhode Island — Rhode Island 87-80
- 3/17 3 Syracuse / 14 N.C. A&T — Syracuse 69-55
  - March 19, Chapel Hill, NC: Rhode Island 97-94
- 3/17 7 Southern Methodist / 10 Notre Dame — Southern Methodist 83-75
- 3/17 2 Duke / 15 Boston U. — Duke 85-69
  - March 19: Duke 94-79
  - March 24: Duke 73-72
  - Duke 63-53

Kansas City, MO — April 2: Kansas 66-59

West

- 3/18 1 Arizona / 16 Cornell — Arizona 90-50
- 3/18 8 Seton Hall / 9 UTEP — Seton Hall 80-64
  - March 20, Los Angeles: Arizona 84-55
- 3/18 5 Iowa / 12 Florida St. — Iowa 102-98
- 3/18 4 UNLV / 13 Southwest Mo. St. — UNLV 54-50
  - March 20: Iowa 104-86
  - March 25: Arizona 99-79 (Seattle, March 27)
- 3/17 6 *Florida / 11 St. John's (N.Y.) — *Florida 62-59
- 3/17 3 Michigan / 14 Boise St. — Michigan 63-58
  - March 19, Salt Lake City: Michigan 108-85
- 3/17 7 Wyoming / 10 Loyola Marymount — Loyola Marymount 119-115
- 3/17 2 North Carolina / 15 North Texas — North Carolina 83-65
  - March 19: North Carolina 123-97
  - March 25: North Carolina 78-69
  - Arizona 70-52

Southeast

- 3/17 1 Oklahoma / 16 Chattanooga — Oklahoma 94-66
- 3/17 8 Auburn / 9 Bradley — Auburn 90-86
  - March 19, Atlanta: Oklahoma 107-87
- 3/17 5 Louisville / 12 Oregon St. — Louisville 70-61
- 3/17 4 Brigham Young / 13 Charlotte — Brigham Young 98-92 (ot)
  - March 19: Louisville 97-76
  - March 24: Oklahoma 108-98 (Birmingham, AL, March 26)
- 3/18 6 Villanova / 11 Arkansas — Villanova 82-74
- 3/18 3 Illinois / 14 Texas-San Antonio — Illinois 81-72
  - March 20, Cincinnati: Villanova 66-63
- 3/18 7 *Maryland / 10 UC Santa Barb. — *Maryland 92-82
- 3/18 2 *Kentucky / 15 Southern U. — *Kentucky 99-84
  - March 20: *Kentucky 90-81
  - March 24: Villanova 80-74
  - Oklahoma 78-59

Kansas City, MO — April 2: Oklahoma 86-78

Kansas 83-79 — NATIONAL CHAMPION (Kansas City, MO, April 4)

*DePaul's, Florida's, Kentucky's, Maryland's and North Carolina State's participation in 1988 tournament vacated.

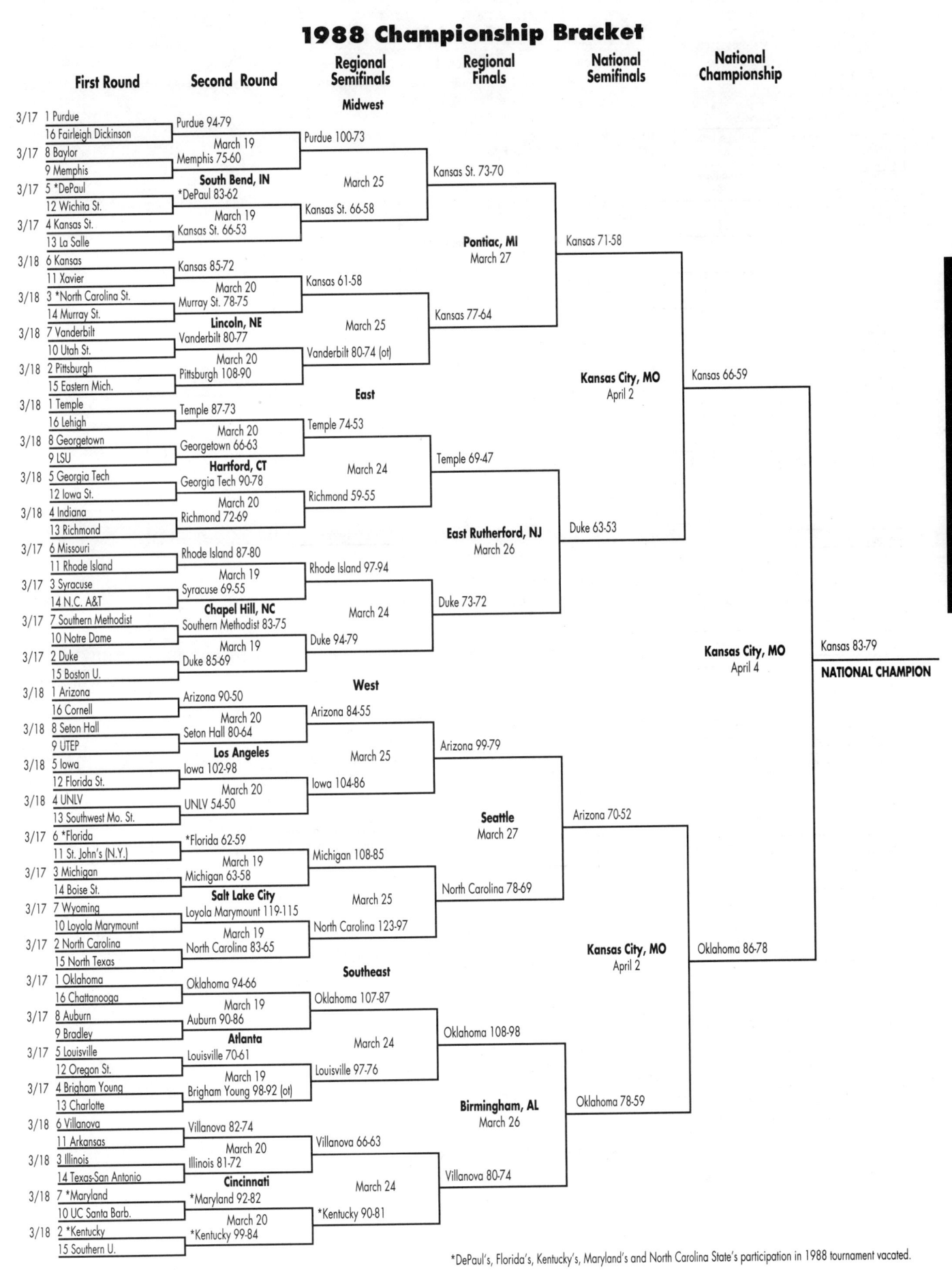

THE TOURNAMENT FIELD

1989 Championship Bracket

Midwest

First Round (3/16):
- 1 Illinois vs 16 McNeese St. → Illinois 77-71
- 8 Pittsburgh vs 9 Ball St. → Ball St. 68-64
- 5 Arkansas vs 12 Loyola Marymount → Arkansas 120-101
- 4 Louisville vs 13 Ark.-Little Rock → Louisville 76-71

First Round (3/17):
- 6 Georgia Tech vs 11 Texas → Texas 76-70
- 3 Missouri vs 14 Creighton → Missouri 85-69
- 7 Florida vs 10 Colorado St. → Colorado St. 68-46
- 2 Syracuse vs 15 Bucknell → Syracuse 104-81

Second Round — Indianapolis (March 18): Illinois 72-60; Louisville 93-84
Second Round — Dallas (March 19): Missouri 108-89; Syracuse 65-50
Regional Semifinals — Minneapolis (March 24): Illinois 83-69; Syracuse 83-80
Regional Final (March 26): Illinois 89-86

Southeast

First Round (3/16):
- 1 Oklahoma vs 16 East Tenn. St. → Oklahoma 72-71
- 8 La Salle vs 9 Louisiana Tech → Louisiana Tech 83-74
- 5 Virginia vs 12 Providence → Virginia 100-97
- 4 Florida St. vs 13 Middle Tenn. → Middle Tenn. 97-83

First Round (3/17):
- 6 Alabama vs 11 South Ala. → South Ala. 86-84
- 3 Michigan vs 14 Xavier → Michigan 92-87
- 7 UCLA vs 10 Iowa St. → UCLA 84-74
- 2 North Carolina vs 15 Southern U. → North Carolina 93-79

Second Round — Nashville, TN (March 18): Oklahoma 124-81; Virginia 104-88
Second Round — Atlanta (March 19): Michigan 91-82; North Carolina 88-81
Regional Semifinals — Lexington, KY (March 23): Virginia 86-80; Michigan 92-87
Regional Final (March 25): Michigan 102-65

National Semifinal — Seattle (April 1): Michigan 83-81

East

First Round (3/17):
- 1 Georgetown vs 16 Princeton → Georgetown 50-49
- 8 Vanderbilt vs 9 Notre Dame → Notre Dame 81-65
- 5 North Carolina St. vs 12 South Carolina → North Carolina St. 81-66
- 4 Iowa vs 13 Rutgers → Iowa 87-73

First Round (3/16):
- 6 Kansas St. vs 11 Minnesota → Minnesota 86-75
- 3 Stanford vs 14 Siena → Siena 80-78
- 7 West Virginia vs 10 Tennessee → West Virginia 84-68
- 2 Duke vs 15 South Carolina St. → Duke 90-69

Second Round — Providence, RI (March 19): Georgetown 81-74; North Carolina St. 102-96 (2 ot)
Second Round — Greensboro, NC (March 18): Minnesota 80-67; Duke 70-63
Regional Semifinals — East Rutherford, NJ (March 24): Georgetown 69-61; Duke 87-70
Regional Final (March 26): Duke 85-77

West

First Round (3/16):
- 1 Arizona vs 16 Robert Morris → Arizona 94-60
- 8 St. Mary's (Cal.) vs 9 Clemson → Clemson 83-70
- 5 Memphis vs 12 *DePaul → *DePaul 66-63
- 4 UNLV vs 13 Idaho → UNLV 68-56

First Round (3/17):
- 6 Oregon St. vs 11 Evansville → Evansville 94-90 (ot)
- 3 Seton Hall vs 14 Southwest Mo. St. → Seton Hall 60-51
- 7 UTEP vs 10 LSU → UTEP 85-74
- 2 Indiana vs 15 George Mason → Indiana 99-85

Second Round — Boise, ID (March 18): Arizona 94-68; UNLV 85-70
Second Round — Tucson, AZ (March 19): Seton Hall 87-73; Indiana 92-69
Regional Semifinals — Denver (March 23): UNLV 68-67; Seton Hall 78-65
Regional Final (March 25): Seton Hall 84-61

National Semifinal — Seattle (April 1): Seton Hall 95-78

National Championship — Seattle (April 3)

Michigan 80-79 (ot) — NATIONAL CHAMPION

*DePaul's participation in 1989 tournament vacated.

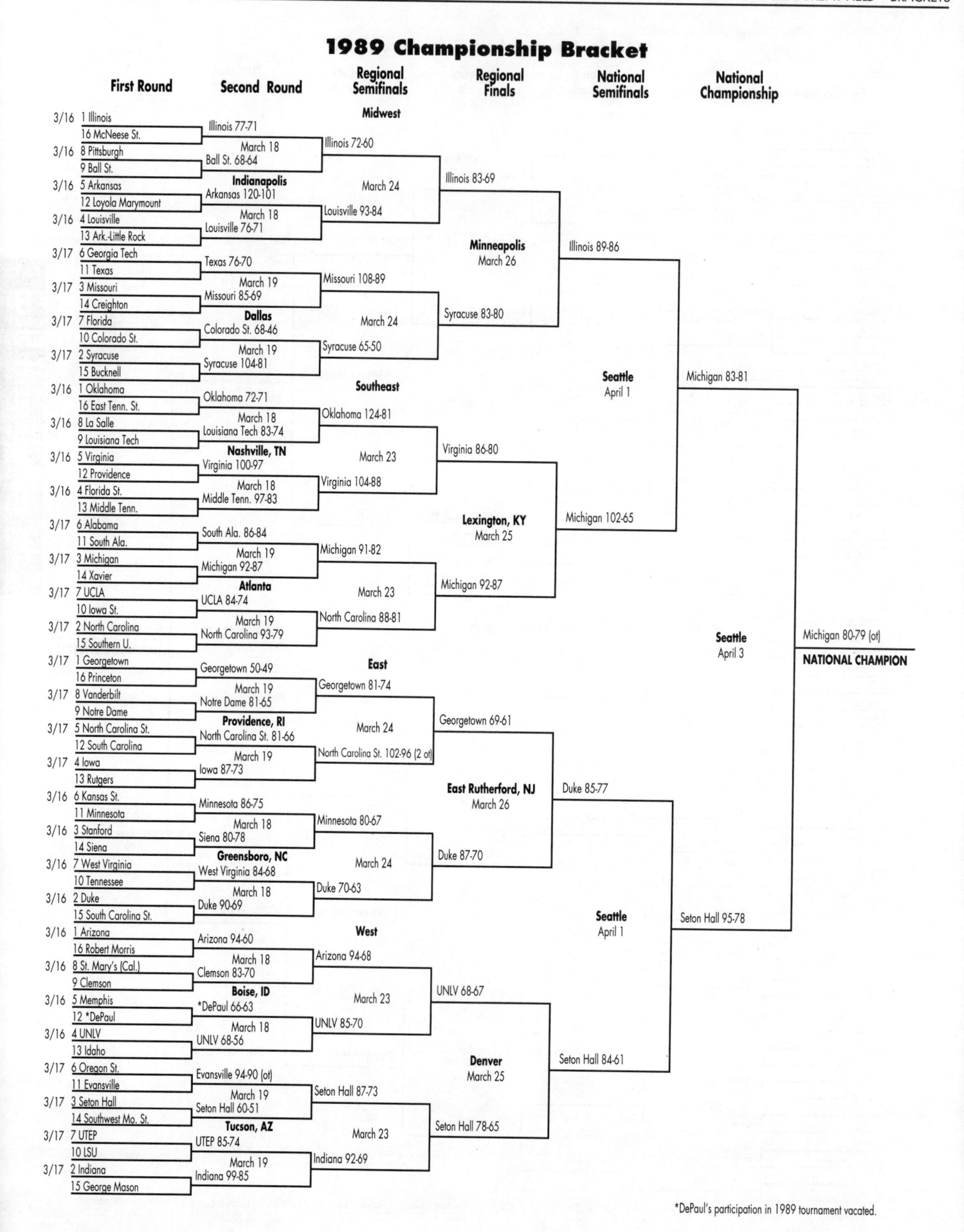

ALL-TIME TOURNAMENT FIELD—BRACKETS

1990 Championship Bracket

Southeast

First Round (3/15):
- 1 Michigan St. vs 16 Murray St. → Michigan St. 75-71 (ot)
- 8 Houston vs 9 UC Santa Barb. → UC Santa Barb. 70-66
- 5 LSU vs 12 Villanova → LSU 70-63
- 4 Georgia Tech vs 13 East Tenn. St. → Georgia Tech 99-83

First Round (3/16):
- 6 Minnesota vs 11 UTEP → Minnesota 64-61 (ot)
- 3 Missouri vs 14 Northern Iowa → Northern Iowa 74-71
- 7 Virginia vs 10 Notre Dame → Virginia 75-67
- 2 Syracuse vs 15 Coppin St. → Syracuse 70-48

Second Round — Knoxville, TN (March 17):
- Michigan St. 62-58
- Georgia Tech 94-91

Second Round — Richmond, VA (March 18):
- Minnesota 81-78
- Syracuse 63-61

Regional Semifinals / Finals — New Orleans (March 23 / March 25):
- Georgia Tech 81-80 (ot)
- Minnesota 82-75
- Georgia Tech 93-91

West

First Round (3/15):
- 1 UNLV vs 16 Ark.-Little Rock → UNLV 102-72
- 8 Ohio St. vs 9 Providence → Ohio St. 84-83 (ot)
- 5 Oregon St. vs 12 Ball St. → Ball St. 54-53
- 4 Louisville vs 13 Idaho → Louisville 78-59

First Round (3/16):
- 6 New Mexico St. vs 11 Loyola Marymount → Loyola Marymount 111-92
- 3 Michigan vs 14 Illinois St. → Michigan 76-70
- 7 Alabama vs 10 Colorado St. → Alabama 71-54
- 2 Arizona vs 15 South Fla. → Arizona 79-67

Second Round — Salt Lake City (March 17):
- UNLV 76-65
- Ball St. 62-60

Second Round — Long Beach, CA (March 18):
- Loyola Marymount 149-115
- Alabama 77-55

Regional Semifinals / Finals — Oakland, CA (March 23 / March 25):
- UNLV 69-67
- Loyola Marymount 62-60
- UNLV 131-101

East

First Round (3/15):
- 1 Connecticut vs 16 Boston U. → Connecticut 76-52
- 8 Indiana vs 9 California → California 65-63
- 5 *Clemson vs 12 Brigham Young → *Clemson 49-47
- 4 La Salle vs 13 Southern Miss. → La Salle 79-63

First Round (3/16):
- 6 St. John's (N.Y.) vs 11 Temple → St. John's (N.Y.) 81-65
- 3 Duke vs 14 Richmond → Duke 81-46
- 7 UCLA vs 10 UAB → UCLA 68-56
- 2 Kansas vs 15 Robert Morris → Kansas 79-71

Second Round — Hartford, CT (March 17):
- Connecticut 74-54
- *Clemson 79-75

Second Round — Atlanta (March 18):
- Duke 76-72
- UCLA 71-70

Regional Semifinals / Finals — East Rutherford, NJ (March 22 / March 24):
- Connecticut 71-70
- Duke 90-81
- Duke 79-78 (ot)

Midwest

First Round (3/15):
- 1 Oklahoma vs 16 Towson → Oklahoma 77-68
- 8 North Carolina vs 9 Southwest Mo. St. → North Carolina 83-70
- 5 Illinois vs 12 Dayton → Dayton 88-86
- 4 Arkansas vs 13 Princeton → Arkansas 68-64

First Round (3/16):
- 6 Xavier vs 11 Kansas St. → Xavier 87-79
- 3 Georgetown vs 14 Texas Southern → Georgetown 70-52
- 7 Georgia vs 10 Texas → Texas 100-88
- 2 Purdue vs 15 La.-Monroe → Purdue 75-63

Second Round — Austin, TX (March 17):
- North Carolina 79-77
- Arkansas 86-84

Second Round — Indianapolis (March 18):
- Xavier 74-71
- Texas 73-72

Regional Semifinals / Finals — Dallas (March 22 / March 24):
- Arkansas 96-73
- Texas 102-89
- Arkansas 88-85

National Semifinals — Denver (March 31)
- UNLV 90-81
- Duke 97-83

National Championship — Denver (April 2)
- **UNLV 103-73 — NATIONAL CHAMPION**

*Clemson's participation in 1990 tournament vacated.

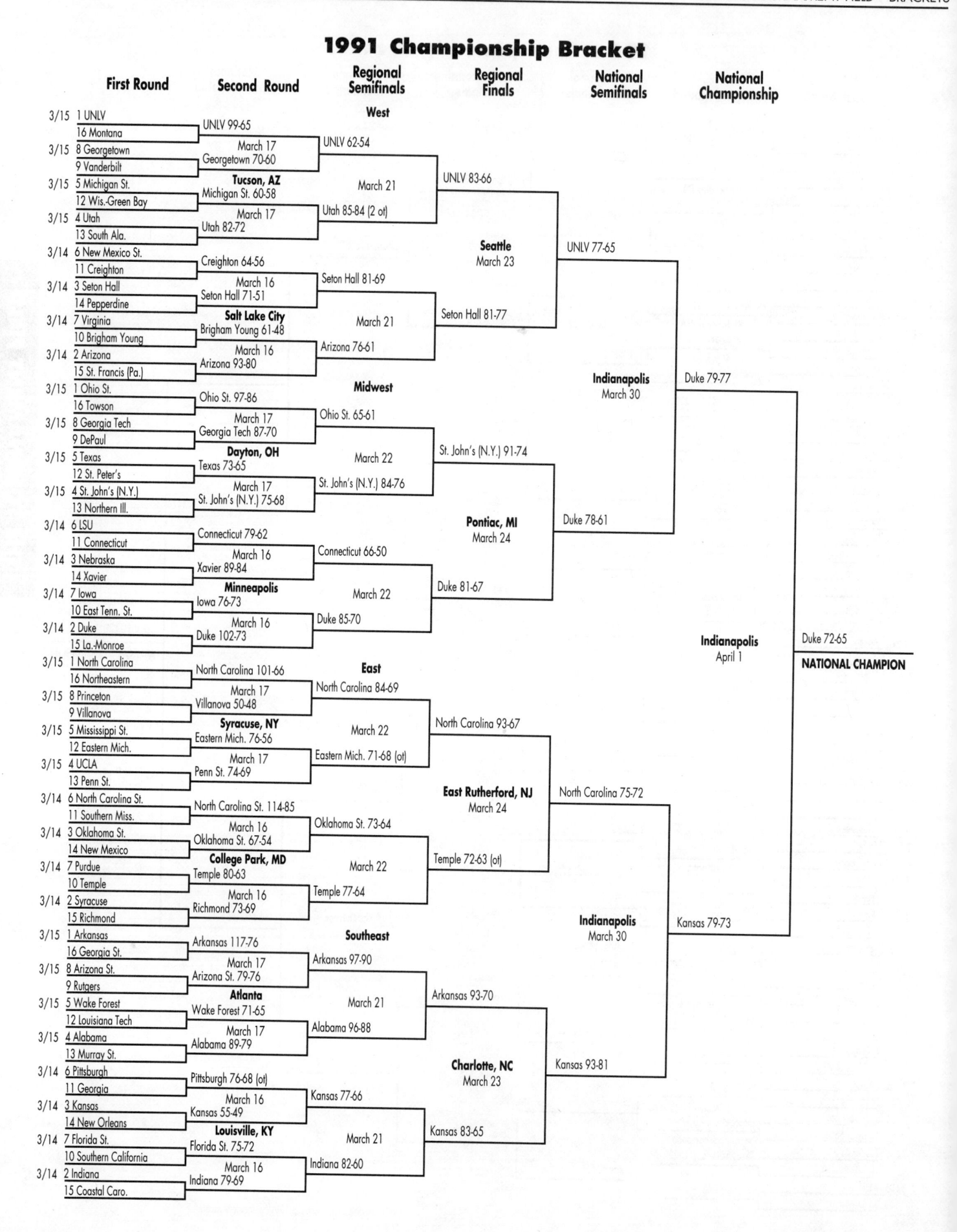

1991 Championship Bracket

First Round | Second Round | Regional Semifinals | Regional Finals | National Semifinals | National Championship

West

- 3/15 1 UNLV / 16 Montana — UNLV 99-65
- 3/15 8 Georgetown / 9 Vanderbilt — Georgetown 70-60
  - *Tucson, AZ* March 17: UNLV 62-54
- 3/15 5 Michigan St. / 12 Wis.-Green Bay — Michigan St. 60-58
- 3/15 4 Utah / 13 South Ala. — Utah 82-72
  - March 17: Utah 85-84 (2 ot)
  - March 21: UNLV 83-66
- 3/14 6 New Mexico St. / 11 Creighton — Creighton 64-56
- 3/14 3 Seton Hall / 14 Pepperdine — Seton Hall 71-51
  - March 16: Seton Hall 81-69
  - *Salt Lake City*
- 3/14 7 Virginia / 10 Brigham Young — Brigham Young 61-48
- 3/14 2 Arizona / 15 St. Francis (Pa.) — Arizona 93-80
  - March 16: Arizona 76-61
  - March 21
- *Seattle* March 23: Seton Hall 81-77

UNLV 77-65

Midwest

- 3/15 1 Ohio St. / 16 Towson — Ohio St. 97-86
- 3/15 8 Georgia Tech / 9 DePaul — Georgia Tech 87-70
  - *Dayton, OH* March 17: Ohio St. 65-61
- 3/15 5 Texas / 12 St. Peter's — Texas 73-65
- 3/15 4 St. John's (N.Y.) / 13 Northern Ill. — St. John's (N.Y.) 75-68
  - March 17
  - March 22: St. John's (N.Y.) 84-76
  - St. John's (N.Y.) 91-74
- 3/14 6 LSU / 11 Connecticut — Connecticut 79-62
- 3/14 3 Nebraska / 14 Xavier — Xavier 89-84
  - *Minneapolis* March 16: Connecticut 66-50
- 3/14 7 Iowa / 10 East Tenn. St. — Iowa 76-73
- 3/14 2 Duke / 15 La.-Monroe — Duke 102-73
  - March 16: Duke 85-70
  - March 22: Duke 81-67
- *Pontiac, MI* March 24: Duke 78-61

Indianapolis March 30: Duke 79-77

East

- 3/15 1 North Carolina / 16 Northeastern — North Carolina 101-66
- 3/15 8 Princeton / 9 Villanova — Villanova 50-48
  - *Syracuse, NY* March 17: North Carolina 84-69
- 3/15 5 Mississippi St. / 12 Eastern Mich. — Eastern Mich. 76-56
- 3/15 4 UCLA / 13 Penn St. — Penn St. 74-69
  - March 17: Eastern Mich. 71-68 (ot)
  - March 22: North Carolina 93-67
- 3/14 6 North Carolina St. / 11 Southern Miss. — North Carolina St. 114-85
- 3/14 3 Oklahoma St. / 14 New Mexico — Oklahoma St. 67-54
  - *College Park, MD* March 16: Oklahoma St. 73-64
- 3/14 7 Purdue / 10 Temple — Temple 80-63
- 3/14 2 Syracuse / 15 Richmond — Richmond 73-69
  - March 16: Temple 77-64
  - March 22: Temple 72-63 (ot)
- *East Rutherford, NJ* March 24: North Carolina 75-72

Southeast

- 3/15 1 Arkansas / 16 Georgia St. — Arkansas 117-76
- 3/15 8 Arizona St. / 9 Rutgers — Arizona St. 79-76
  - *Atlanta* March 17: Arkansas 97-90
- 3/15 5 Wake Forest / 12 Louisiana Tech — Wake Forest 71-65
- 3/15 4 Alabama / 13 Murray St. — Alabama 89-79
  - March 17: Alabama 96-88
  - March 21: Arkansas 93-70
- 3/14 6 Pittsburgh / 11 Georgia — Pittsburgh 76-68 (ot)
- 3/14 3 Kansas / 14 New Orleans — Kansas 55-49
  - *Louisville, KY* March 16: Kansas 77-66
- 3/14 7 Florida St. / 10 Southern California — Florida St. 75-72
- 3/14 2 Indiana / 15 Coastal Caro. — Indiana 79-69
  - March 16: Indiana 82-60
  - March 21: Kansas 83-65
- *Charlotte, NC* March 23: Kansas 93-81

Indianapolis March 30: Kansas 79-73

Indianapolis April 1: Duke 72-65 — NATIONAL CHAMPION

ALL-TIME TOURNAMENT FIELD—BRACKETS   215

1992 Championship Bracket

| First Round | Second Round | Regional Semifinals | Regional Finals | National Semifinals | National Championship |

Midwest

- 3/20 1 Kansas — Kansas 100-67
- 3/20 16 Howard
- 3/20 8 Evansville — UTEP 55-50 (March 22)
- 3/20 9 UTEP
  - UTEP 66-60 — **Dayton, OH** — March 27
- 3/20 5 Michigan St. — Michigan St. 61-54
- 3/20 12 Southwest Mo. St.
- 3/20 4 Cincinnati — Cincinnati 85-47 (March 22)
- 3/20 13 Delaware
  - Cincinnati 77-65
    - Cincinnati 69-67
      - **Kansas City, MO** March 29
- 3/19 6 Memphis — Memphis 80-70
- 3/19 11 Pepperdine
- 3/19 3 Arkansas — Arkansas 80-69 (March 21)
- 3/19 14 Murray St.
  - Memphis 82-80 — **Milwaukee** — March 27
- 3/19 7 Georgia Tech — Georgia Tech 65-60
- 3/19 10 Houston
- 3/19 2 Southern California — Southern California 84-54 (March 21)
- 3/19 15 La.-Monroe
  - Georgia Tech 79-78
    - Memphis 83-79 (ot)

Cincinnati 88-57

Southeast

- 3/19 1 Ohio St. — Ohio St. 83-56
- 3/19 16 Mississippi Val.
- 3/19 8 Nebraska — Connecticut 86-65 (March 21)
- 3/19 9 Connecticut
  - Ohio St. 78-55 — **Cincinnati** — March 27
- 3/19 5 Alabama — Alabama 80-75
- 3/19 12 Stanford
- 3/19 4 North Carolina — North Carolina 68-63 (March 21)
- 3/19 13 Miami (Ohio)
  - North Carolina 64-55
    - Ohio St. 80-73
      - **Lexington, KY** March 29
- 3/20 6 Michigan — Michigan 73-66
- 3/20 11 Temple
- 3/20 3 Arizona — East Tenn. St. 87-80 (March 22)
- 3/20 14 East Tenn. St.
  - Michigan 102-90 — **Atlanta** — March 27
- 3/20 7 St. John's (N.Y.) — Tulane 61-57
- 3/20 10 Tulane
- 3/20 2 Oklahoma St. — Oklahoma St. 100-73 (March 22)
- 3/20 15 Ga. Southern
  - Oklahoma St. 87-71
    - Michigan 75-72

Michigan 75-71 (ot)

Michigan 76-72

Minneapolis April 4

East

- 3/19 1 Duke — Duke 82-56
- 3/19 16 Campbell
- 3/19 8 Texas — Iowa 98-92 (March 21)
- 3/19 9 Iowa
  - Duke 75-62 — **Greensboro, NC** — March 26
- 3/19 5 Missouri — Missouri 89-78
- 3/19 12 West Virginia
- 3/19 4 Seton Hall — Seton Hall 78-76 (March 21)
- 3/19 13 La Salle
  - Seton Hall 88-71
    - Duke 81-69
      - **Philadelphia** March 28
- 3/20 6 Syracuse — Syracuse 51-43
- 3/20 11 Princeton
- 3/20 3 Massachusetts — Massachusetts 85-58 (March 22)
- 3/20 14 Fordham
  - Massachusetts 77-71 (ot) — **Worcester, MA** — March 26
- 3/20 7 Charlotte — Iowa St. 76-74
- 3/20 10 Iowa St.
- 3/20 2 Kentucky — Kentucky 88-69 (March 22)
- 3/20 15 Old Dominion
  - Kentucky 106-98
    - Kentucky 87-77

Duke 104-103 (ot)

Duke 81-78

Minneapolis April 4

West

- 3/20 1 UCLA — UCLA 73-53
- 3/20 16 Robert Morris
- 3/20 8 Louisville — Louisville 81-58 (March 22)
- 3/20 9 Wake Forest
  - UCLA 85-69 — **Tempe, AZ** — March 26
- 3/20 5 DePaul — *New Mexico St. 81-73
- 3/20 12 *New Mexico St.
- 3/20 4 Oklahoma — La.-Lafayette 87-83 (March 22)
- 3/20 13 La.-Lafayette
  - *New Mexico St. 81-73
    - UCLA 85-78
      - **Albuquerque, NM** March 28
- 3/19 6 Georgetown — Georgetown 75-60
- 3/19 11 South Fla.
- 3/19 3 Florida St. — Florida St. 78-68 (March 21)
- 3/19 14 Montana
  - Florida St. 78-68 — **Boise, ID** — March 26
- 3/19 7 LSU — LSU 94-83
- 3/19 10 Brigham Young
- 3/19 2 Indiana — Indiana 94-55 (March 21)
- 3/19 15 Eastern Ill.
  - Indiana 89-79
    - Indiana 85-74

Indiana 106-79

Duke 71-51

NATIONAL CHAMPION

*New Mexico State's participation in 1992 tournament vacated.

THE TOURNAMENT FIELD

1993 Championship Bracket

Southeast

First Round (3/19)
- 1 Kentucky / 16 Rider → Kentucky 96-52
- 8 Utah / 9 Pittsburgh → Utah 86-85
- 5 Wake Forest / 12 Chattanooga → Wake Forest 81-58
- 4 Iowa / 13 La.-Monroe → Iowa 82-69

First Round (3/18)
- 6 Kansas St. / 11 Tulane → Tulane 55-53
- 3 Florida St. / 14 Evansville → Florida St. 82-70
- 7 Western Ky. / 10 Memphis → Western Ky. 55-52
- 2 Seton Hall / 15 Tennessee St. → Seton Hall 81-59

Second Round (Nashville, TN — March 21): Kentucky 83-62, Wake Forest 84-78
Second Round (Orlando, FL — March 20): Florida St. 94-63, Western Ky. 72-68

Regional Semifinals (Charlotte, NC — March 25): Kentucky 103-69, Florida St. 81-78 (ot)
Regional Final (March 27): Kentucky 106-81

West

First Round (3/19)
- 1 Michigan / 16 Coastal Caro. → Michigan 84-53
- 8 Iowa St. / 9 UCLA → UCLA 81-70
- 5 New Mexico / 12 George Washington → George Washington 82-68
- 4 Georgia Tech / 13 Southern U. → Southern U. 93-78

First Round (3/18)
- 6 Illinois / 11 Long Beach St. → Illinois 75-72
- 3 Vanderbilt / 14 Boise St. → Vanderbilt 92-72
- 7 Temple / 10 Missouri → Temple 75-61
- 2 Arizona / 15 Santa Clara → Santa Clara 64-61

Second Round (Tucson, AZ — March 21): Michigan 86-84 (ot), George Washington 90-80
Second Round (Salt Lake City — March 20): Vanderbilt 85-68, Temple 68-57

Regional Semifinals (Seattle — March 26): Michigan 72-64, Temple 67-59
Regional Final (March 28): Michigan 77-72

East

First Round (3/18)
- 1 North Carolina / 16 East Caro. → North Carolina 85-65
- 8 Rhode Island / 9 Purdue → Rhode Island 74-68
- 5 St. John's (N.Y.) / 12 Texas Tech → St. John's (N.Y.) 85-67
- 4 Arkansas / 13 Holy Cross → Arkansas 94-64

First Round (3/19)
- 6 Virginia / 11 Manhattan → Virginia 78-66
- 3 Massachusetts / 14 Pennsylvania → Massachusetts 54-50
- 7 *New Mexico St. / 10 Nebraska → *New Mexico St. 93-79
- 2 Cincinnati / 15 Coppin St. → Cincinnati 93-66

Second Round (Winston-Salem, NC — March 20): North Carolina 112-67, Arkansas 80-74
Second Round (Syracuse, NY — March 21): Virginia 71-56, Cincinnati 92-55

Regional Semifinals (East Rutherford, NJ — March 26): North Carolina 80-74, Cincinnati 71-54
Regional Final (March 28): North Carolina 75-68 (ot)

Midwest

First Round (3/19)
- 1 Indiana / 16 Wright St. → Indiana 97-54
- 8 New Orleans / 9 Xavier → Xavier 73-55
- 5 Oklahoma St. / 12 Marquette → Oklahoma St. 74-62
- 4 Louisville / 13 Delaware → Louisville 76-70

First Round (3/18)
- 6 California / 11 LSU → California 66-64
- 3 Duke / 14 Southern Ill. → Duke 105-70
- 7 Brigham Young / 10 Southern Methodist → Brigham Young 80-71
- 2 Kansas / 15 Ball St. → Kansas 94-72

Second Round (Indianapolis — March 21): Indiana 73-70, Louisville 78-63
Second Round (Rosemont, IL — March 20): California 82-77, Kansas 90-76

Regional Semifinals (St. Louis — March 25): Indiana 82-69, Kansas 93-76
Regional Final (March 27): Kansas 83-77

National Semifinals (New Orleans — April 3)
- Michigan 81-78 (ot)
- North Carolina 78-68

National Championship (New Orleans — April 5)
North Carolina 77-71 — NATIONAL CHAMPION

*New Mexico State's participation in 1993 tournament vacated.

1994 Championship Bracket

First Round — **Second Round** — **Regional Semifinals** — **Regional Finals** — **National Semifinals** — **National Championship**

West

- 3/17 1 *Missouri / 16 Navy → *Missouri 76-53
- 3/17 8 Cincinnati / 9 Wisconsin → Wisconsin 80-72 (March 19, Ogden, UT)
  - *Missouri 109-96 (March 19)
- 3/17 5 California / 12 Wis.-Green Bay → Wis.-Green Bay 61-57
- 3/17 4 Syracuse / 13 Hawaii → Syracuse 92-78 (March 19)
  - Syracuse 64-59 (March 24)
    - *Missouri 98-88 (ot) — Los Angeles, March 26
- 3/18 6 *Minnesota / 11 Southern Ill. → *Minnesota 74-60
- 3/18 3 Louisville / 14 Boise St. → Louisville 67-58 (March 20, Sacramento, CA)
  - Louisville 60-55
- 3/18 7 Virginia / 10 New Mexico → Virginia 57-54
- 3/18 2 Arizona / 15 Loyola (Md.) → Arizona 81-55 (March 20)
  - Arizona 71-58 (March 24)
    - Arizona 82-70
      - Arizona 92-72

Midwest

- 3/18 1 Arkansas / 16 N.C. A&T → Arkansas 94-79
- 3/18 8 Illinois / 9 Georgetown → Georgetown 84-77 (March 20, Oklahoma City)
  - Arkansas 85-73
- 3/17 5 UCLA / 12 Tulsa → Tulsa 112-102
- 3/17 4 Oklahoma St. / 13 *New Mexico St. → Oklahoma St. 65-55 (March 20)
  - Tulsa 82-80 (March 25)
    - Arkansas 103-84 — Dallas, March 27
- 3/17 6 Texas / 11 Western Ky. → Texas 91-77
- 3/17 3 Michigan / 14 Pepperdine → Michigan 78-74 (ot) (March 19, Wichita, KS)
  - Michigan 84-79
- 3/17 7 St. Louis / 10 Maryland → Maryland 74-66
- 3/17 2 Massachusetts / 15 Southwest Tex. St. → Massachusetts 78-60 (March 19)
  - Maryland 95-87 (March 25)
    - Michigan 78-71
      - Arkansas 76-68

Arkansas 91-82 — Charlotte, NC, April 2

East

- 3/18 1 North Carolina / 16 Liberty → North Carolina 71-51
- 3/18 8 Washington St. / 9 Boston College → Boston College 67-64 (March 20, Landover, MD)
  - Boston College 75-72
- 3/18 5 Indiana / 12 Ohio → Indiana 84-72
- 3/18 4 Temple / 13 Drexel → Temple 61-39 (March 20)
  - Indiana 67-58 (March 25)
    - Boston College 77-68 — Miami, March 27
- 3/17 6 Nebraska / 11 Pennsylvania → Pennsylvania 90-80
- 3/17 3 Florida / 14 James Madison → Florida 64-62 (March 19, Long Island, NY)
  - Florida 70-58
- 3/17 7 UAB / 10 George Washington → George Washington 51-46
- 3/17 2 Connecticut / 15 Rider → Connecticut 64-46 (March 19)
  - Connecticut 75-63 (March 25)
    - Florida 69-60 (ot)
      - Florida 74-66

Duke 70-65 — Charlotte, NC, April 2

Southeast

- 3/17 1 Purdue / 16 UCF → Purdue 98-67
- 3/17 8 Providence / 9 Alabama → Alabama 76-70 (March 19, Lexington, KY)
  - Purdue 83-73
- 3/17 5 Wake Forest / 12 Col. of Charleston → Wake Forest 68-58
- 3/17 4 Kansas / 13 Chattanooga → Kansas 102-73 (March 19)
  - Kansas 69-58 (March 24)
    - Purdue 83-78 — Knoxville, TN, March 26
- 3/18 6 Marquette / 11 La.-Lafayette → Marquette 81-59
- 3/18 3 Kentucky / 14 Tennessee St. → Kentucky 83-70 (March 20, St. Petersburg, FL)
  - Marquette 75-63
- 3/18 7 Michigan St. / 10 Seton Hall → Michigan St. 84-73
- 3/18 2 Duke / 15 Texas Southern → Duke 82-70 (March 20)
  - Duke 85-74 (March 24)
    - Duke 59-49
      - Duke 69-60

National Championship

Arkansas 76-72 — NATIONAL CHAMPION (Charlotte, NC, April 4)

*Minnesota's, Missouri's and New Mexico State's participation in 1994 tournament vacated.

All-Time Tournament Field—Brackets — The Tournament Field

1995 Championship Bracket

| First Round | Second Round | Regional Semifinals | Regional Finals | National Semifinals | National Championship |

Midwest

- 3/16 1 Kansas / 16 Colgate — Kansas 82-68
- 3/16 8 Western Ky. / 9 Michigan — Western Ky. 82-76 (ot) — *Dayton, OH, March 18* — Kansas 75-70
- 3/16 5 Arizona / 12 Miami (Ohio) — Miami (Ohio) 71-62
- 3/16 4 Virginia / 13 Nicholls St. — Virginia 96-72 — *March 18* — Virginia 60-54 (ot)
- *March 24* — Virginia 67-58
- 3/17 6 Memphis / 11 Louisville — Memphis 77-56
- 3/17 3 Purdue / 14 Wis.-Green Bay — Purdue 49-48 — *March 19* — Memphis 75-73
- 3/17 7 Syracuse / 10 Southern Ill. — Syracuse 96-92 — *Austin, TX*
- 3/17 2 Arkansas / 15 Texas Southern — Arkansas 79-78 — *March 19* — Arkansas 96-94 (ot)
- *March 24* — Arkansas 96-91 (ot)

Kansas City, MO — March 26 — Arkansas 68-61

Southeast

- 3/16 1 Kentucky / 16 Mt. St. Mary's — Kentucky 113-67
- 3/16 8 Brigham Young / 9 Tulane — Tulane 76-70 — *March 18* — Kentucky 82-60
- 3/16 5* Arizona St. / 12 Ball St. — *Arizona St. 81-66 — *Memphis, TN*
- 3/16 4 Oklahoma / 13 Manhattan — Manhattan 77-67 — *March 18* — *Arizona St. 64-54
- *March 23* — Kentucky 97-73
- 3/17 6 Georgetown / 11 Xavier — Georgetown 68-63
- 3/17 3 Michigan St. / 14 Weber St. — Weber St. 79-72 — *March 19* — Georgetown 53-51
- 3/17 7 Iowa St. / 10 Florida — Iowa St. 64-61 — *Tallahassee, FL*
- 3/17 2 North Carolina / 15 Murray St. — North Carolina 80-70 — *March 19* — North Carolina 73-51
- *March 23* — North Carolina 74-64

Birmingham, AL — March 25 — North Carolina 74-61

Seattle — April 1 — Arkansas 75-68

East

- 3/16 1 Wake Forest / 16 N.C. A&T — Wake Forest 79-47
- 3/16 8 *Minnesota / 9 St. Louis — St. Louis 64-61 (ot) — *March 18* — Wake Forest 64-59
- 3/16 5 Alabama / 12 Pennsylvania — Alabama 91-85 (ot) — *Baltimore*
- 3/16 4 Oklahoma St. / 13 Drexel — Oklahoma St. 73-49 — *March 18* — Oklahoma St. 66-52
- *March 24* — Oklahoma St. 71-66
- 3/17 6 Tulsa / 11 Illinois — Tulsa 68-62
- 3/17 3 Villanova / 14 Old Dominion — Old Dominion 89-81 (3ot) — *March 19* — Tulsa 64-52
- 3/17 7 Charlotte / 10 Stanford — Stanford 70-68 — *Albany, NY*
- 3/17 2 Massachusetts / 15 St. Peter's — Massachusetts 68-51 — *March 19* — Massachusetts 75-53
- *March 24* — Massachusetts 76-51

East Rutherford, NJ — March 26 — Oklahoma St. 68-54

West

- 3/17 1 UCLA / 16 Florida Int'l — UCLA 92-56
- 3/17 8 Missouri / 9 Indiana — Missouri 65-60 — *March 19* — UCLA 75-74
- 3/17 5 Mississippi St. / 12 Santa Clara — Mississippi St. 75-67 — *Boise, ID*
- 3/17 4 Utah / 13 Long Beach St. — Utah 76-64 — *March 19* — Mississippi St. 78-64
- *March 23* — UCLA 86-67
- 3/16 6 Oregon / 11 Texas — Texas 90-73
- 3/16 3 Maryland / 14 Gonzaga — Maryland 87-63 — *March 18* — Maryland 82-68
- 3/16 7 Cincinnati / 10 Temple — Cincinnati 77-71 — *Salt Lake City*
- 3/16 2 Connecticut / 15 Chattanooga — Connecticut 100-71 — *March 18* — Connecticut 96-91
- *March 23* — Connecticut 99-89

Oakland, CA — March 25 — UCLA 102-96

Seattle — April 1 — UCLA 74-61

UCLA 89-78 — NATIONAL CHAMPION (Seattle, April 3)

*Arizona State's and Minnesota's participation in 1995 tournament vacated.

ALL-TIME TOURNAMENT FIELD—BRACKETS

1996 Championship Bracket

First Round	Second Round	Regional Semifinals	Regional Finals	National Semifinals	National Championship

Southeast

- 3/14 1 *Connecticut / 16 Colgate → *Connecticut 68-59 (March 16)
- 3/14 8 Duke / 9 Eastern Mich. → Eastern Mich. 75-60
  - **Indianapolis**: *Connecticut 95-81 (March 22)
- 3/14 5 Mississippi St. / 12 Va. Commonwealth → Mississippi St. 58-51 (March 16)
- 3/14 4 UCLA / 13 Princeton → Princeton 43-41
  - Mississippi St. 63-41 (March 22)
  - **Lexington, KY** March 24: Mississippi St. 60-55
- 3/15 6 Indiana / 11 Boston College → Boston College 64-51 (March 17)
- 3/15 3 Georgia Tech / 14 Austin Peay → Georgia Tech 90-79
  - **Orlando, FL**: Georgia Tech 103-89 (March 22)
- 3/15 7 Temple / 10 Oklahoma → Temple 61-43 (March 17)
- 3/15 2 Cincinnati / 15 UNC Greensboro → Cincinnati 66-61
  - Cincinnati 78-65 (March 22)
  - Cincinnati 87-70

Mississippi St. 73-63

East Rutherford, NJ March 30 — Syracuse 77-69

West

- 3/14 1 *Purdue / 16 Western Caro. → *Purdue 73-71 (March 16)
- 3/14 8 Georgia / 9 Clemson → Georgia 81-74
  - **Albuquerque, NM**: Georgia 76-69 (March 22)
- 3/14 5 Memphis / 12 Drexel → Drexel 75-63 (March 16)
- 3/14 4 Syracuse / 13 Montana St. → Syracuse 88-55
  - Syracuse 69-58 (March 22)
  - **Denver** March 24: Syracuse 83-81 (ot)
- 3/15 6 Iowa / 11 George Washington → Iowa 81-79 (March 17)
- 3/15 3 Arizona / 14 Valparaiso → Arizona 90-51
  - **Tempe, AZ**: Arizona 87-73 (March 22)
- 3/15 7 Maryland / 10 Santa Clara → Santa Clara 91-79 (March 17)
- 3/15 2 Kansas / 15 South Carolina St. → Kansas 92-54
  - Kansas 76-51 (March 22)
  - Kansas 83-80

Syracuse 60-57

East Rutherford, NJ April 1 — Kentucky 76-67 **NATIONAL CHAMPION**

East

- 3/14 1 *Massachusetts / 16 UCF → *Massachusetts 92-70 (March 16)
- 3/14 8 Bradley / 9 Stanford → Stanford 66-58
  - **Providence, RI**: *Massachusetts 79-74 (March 21)
- 3/14 5 Penn St. / 12 Arkansas → Arkansas 86-80 (March 16)
- 3/14 4 Marquette / 13 Monmouth → Marquette 68-44
  - Arkansas 65-56 (March 21)
  - **Atlanta** March 23: *Massachusetts 79-63
- 3/15 6 North Carolina / 11 New Orleans → North Carolina 83-62 (March 17)
- 3/15 3 *Texas Tech / 14 Northern Ill. → *Texas Tech 74-73
  - **Richmond, VA**: *Texas Tech 92-73 (March 21)
- 3/15 7 New Mexico / 10 Kansas St. → New Mexico 69-48 (March 17)
- 3/15 2 Georgetown / 15 Mississippi Val. → Georgetown 93-56
  - Georgetown 73-62 (March 21)
  - Georgetown 98-90

*Massachusetts 86-62

East Rutherford, NJ March 30 — Kentucky 81-74

Midwest

- 3/14 1 Kentucky / 16 San Jose St. → Kentucky 110-72
- 3/14 8 Wis.-Green Bay / 9 Virginia Tech → Virginia Tech 61-48
  - **Dallas**: Kentucky 84-60 (March 16)
- 3/14 5 Iowa St. / 12 *California → Iowa St. 74-64 (March 16)
- 3/14 4 Utah / 13 Canisius → Utah 72-43
  - Utah 73-67 (March 21)
  - **Minneapolis** March 23: Kentucky 101-70
- 3/15 6 Louisville / 11 Tulsa → Louisville 82-80 (ot) (March 17)
- 3/15 3 Villanova / 14 Portland → Villanova 92-58
  - **Milwaukee**: Louisville 68-64 (March 21)
- 3/15 7 Michigan / 10 Texas → Texas 80-76 (March 17)
- 3/15 2 Wake Forest / 15 La.-Monroe → Wake Forest 62-50
  - Wake Forest 65-62 (March 21)
  - Wake Forest 60-59

Kentucky 83-63

*California's, Connecticut's, Massachusetts', Purdue's and Texas Tech's participation in 1996 tournament vacated.

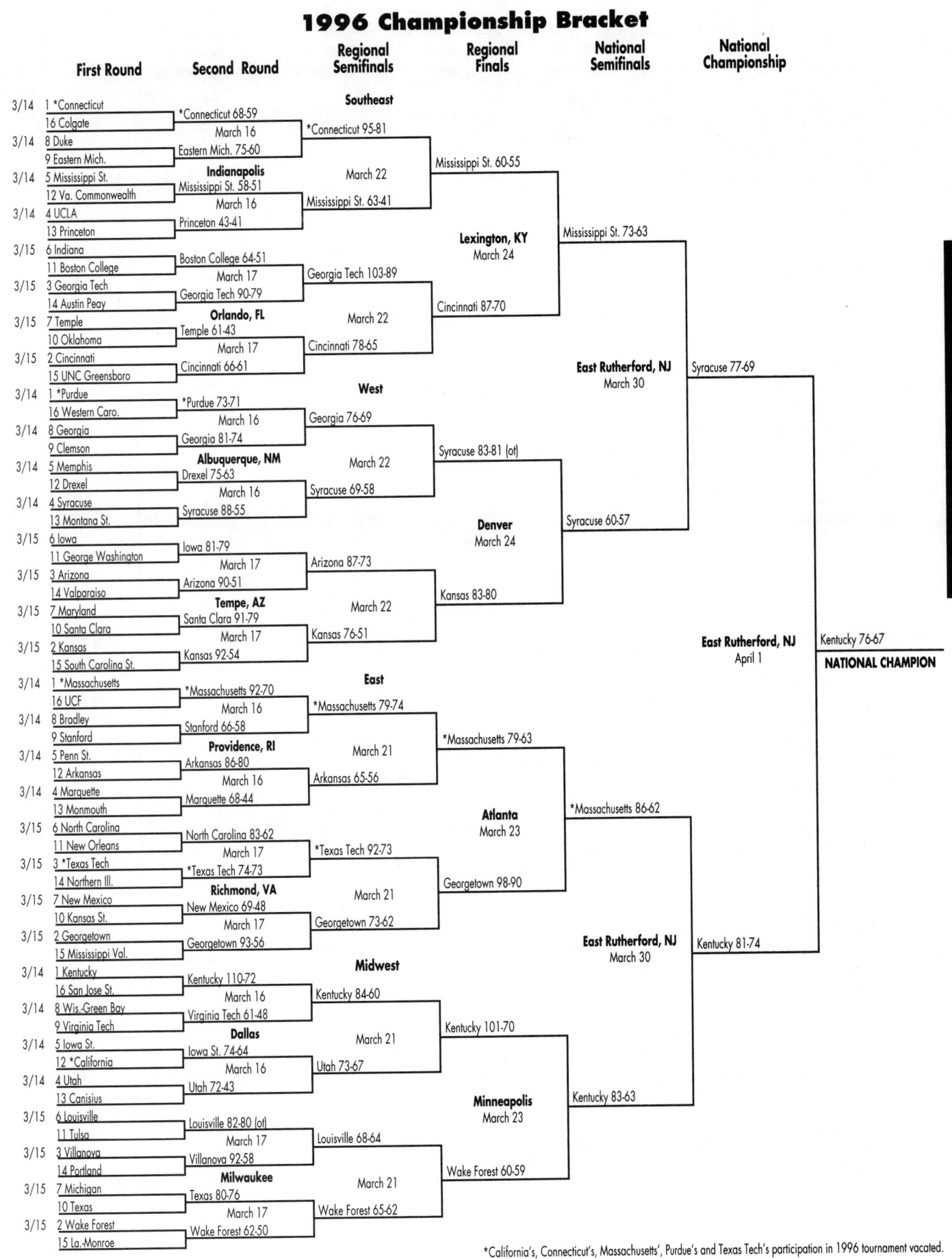

THE TOURNAMENT FIELD

1997 Championship Bracket

First Round | Second Round | Regional Semifinals | Regional Finals | National Semifinals | National Championship

West

- 3/13 — 1 Kentucky / 16 Montana → Kentucky 92-54
- 3/13 — 8 Iowa / 9 Virginia → Iowa 73-60
  - **Salt Lake City, March 15**: Kentucky 75-69
- 3/13 — 5 Boston College / 12 Valparaiso → Boston College 73-66
- 3/13 — 4 St. Joseph's / 13 Pacific (Cal.) → St. Joseph's 75-65
  - **March 15**: St. Joseph's 81-77 (ot)
  - **March 20**: Kentucky 83-68
- 3/14 — 6 Stanford / 11 Oklahoma → Stanford 80-67
- 3/14 — 3 Wake Forest / 14 St. Mary's (Cal.) → Wake Forest 68-46
  - **Tucson, AZ, March 16**: Stanford 72-66
- 3/14 — 7 Charlotte / 10 Georgetown → Charlotte 79-67
- 3/14 — 2 Utah / 15 Navy → Utah 75-61
  - **March 16**: Utah 77-58
  - **March 20**: Utah 82-77 (ot)
  - **San Jose, CA, March 22**: Kentucky 72-59

Midwest

- 3/14 — 1 *Minnesota / 16 Southwest Tex. St. → *Minnesota 78-46
- 3/14 — 8 Mississippi / 9 Temple → Temple 62-40
  - **Kansas City, MO, March 16**: *Minnesota 76-57
- 3/14 — 5 Tulsa / 12 Boston U. → Tulsa 81-52
- 3/14 — 4 Clemson / 13 Miami (Ohio) → Clemson 68-56
  - **March 16**: Clemson 65-59
  - **March 20**: *Minnesota 90-84 (2 ot)
- 3/13 — 6 Iowa St. / 11 Illinois St. → Iowa St. 69-57
- 3/13 — 3 Cincinnati / 14 Butler → Cincinnati 86-69
  - **Auburn Hills, MI, March 15**: Iowa St. 67-66
- 3/13 — 7 Xavier / 10 Vanderbilt → Xavier 80-68
- 3/13 — 2 UCLA / 15 Charleston So. → UCLA 109-75
  - **March 15**: UCLA 96-83
  - **March 20**: UCLA 74-73 (ot)
  - **San Antonio, March 22**: *Minnesota 80-72

Indianapolis, March 29: Kentucky 78-69

East

- 3/13 — 1 North Carolina / 16 Fairfield → North Carolina 82-74
- 3/13 — 8 Indiana / 9 Colorado → Colorado 80-62
  - **Winston-Salem, NC, March 15**: North Carolina 73-56
- 3/13 — 5 California / 12 Princeton → California 55-52
- 3/13 — 4 Villanova / 13 Long Island → Villanova 101-91
  - **March 15**: California 75-68
  - **March 21**: North Carolina 63-57
- 3/14 — 6 Louisville / 11 Massachusetts → Louisville 65-57
- 3/14 — 3 New Mexico / 14 Old Dominion → New Mexico 59-55
  - **Pittsburgh, March 16**: Louisville 64-63
- 3/14 — 7 Wisconsin / 10 Texas → Texas 71-58
- 3/14 — 2 South Carolina / 15 Coppin St. → Coppin St. 78-65
  - **March 16**: Texas 82-81
  - **March 21**: Louisville 78-63
  - **Syracuse, NY, March 23**: North Carolina 97-74

Southeast

- 3/13 — 1 Kansas / 16 Jackson St. → Kansas 78-64
- 3/13 — 8 Purdue / 9 Rhode Island → Purdue 83-76 (ot)
  - **Memphis, TN, March 15**: Kansas 75-61
- 3/13 — 5 Maryland / 12 Col. of Charleston → Col. of Charleston 75-66
- 3/13 — 4 Arizona / 13 South Ala. → Arizona 65-57
  - **March 15**: Arizona 73-69
  - **March 21**: Arizona 85-82
- 3/14 — 6 Illinois / 11 Southern California → Illinois 90-77
- 3/14 — 3 Georgia / 14 Chattanooga → Chattanooga 73-70
  - **Charlotte, NC, March 16**: Chattanooga 75-63
- 3/14 — 7 Marquette / 10 Providence → Providence 81-59
- 3/14 — 2 Duke / 15 Murray St. → Duke 71-68
  - **March 16**: Providence 98-87
  - **March 21**: Providence 71-65
  - **Birmingham, AL, March 23**: Arizona 96-92 (ot)

Indianapolis, March 29: Arizona 66-58

National Championship: Arizona 84-79 (ot) — **NATIONAL CHAMPION**

*Minnesota's participation in 1997 tournament vacated.

1998 Championship Bracket

East Region

First Round (3/12):
- 1 North Carolina vs 16 Navy → North Carolina 88-52
- 8 Charlotte vs 9 Ill.-Chicago → Charlotte 77-62
- 5 Princeton vs 12 UNLV → Princeton 69-57
- 4 Michigan St. vs 13 Eastern Mich. → Michigan St. 83-71
- 6 Xavier vs 11 Washington → Washington 69-68
- 3 South Carolina vs 14 Richmond → Richmond 62-61
- 7 Indiana vs 10 Oklahoma → Indiana 94-87 (ot)
- 2 Connecticut vs 15 Fairleigh Dickinson → Connecticut 93-85

Second Round (March 14, Hartford, CT):
- North Carolina 88-52 def. Charlotte 77-62 → North Carolina 93-83 (ot)
- Princeton 69-57 vs Michigan St. 83-71 → Michigan St. 63-51
- Washington 81-66 vs Richmond → Washington 81-66
- Indiana vs Connecticut 93-85 → Connecticut 78-61

Regional Semifinals (March 19):
- North Carolina 93-83 (ot)
- Michigan St. 63-51
- Washington 81-66
- Connecticut 78-61

Regional Finals (Greensboro, NC, March 21):
- North Carolina 73-58
- Connecticut 75-74

East Regional Champion: North Carolina 75-64

West Region

First Round (3/12):
- 1 Arizona vs 16 Nicholls St. → Arizona 99-60
- 8 Tennessee vs 9 Illinois St. → Illinois St. 82-81
- 5 Illinois vs 12 South Ala. → Illinois 64-51
- 4 Maryland vs 13 Utah St. → Maryland 82-68
- 6 Arkansas vs 11 Nebraska → Arkansas 74-65
- 3 Utah vs 14 San Francisco → Utah 85-68
- 7 Temple vs 10 West Virginia → West Virginia 82-52
- 2 Cincinnati vs 15 Northern Ariz. → Cincinnati 65-62

Second Round (March 14, Sacramento, CA):
- Arizona 82-49
- Maryland 67-61
- Utah 75-69
- West Virginia 75-74

Regional Semifinals (March 19):
- Arizona 87-79
- Utah 65-62

Regional Finals (Anaheim, CA, March 21):
- Utah 76-51

West Regional Champion: Utah 65-59

Midwest Region

First Round (3/13):
- 1 Kansas vs 16 Prairie View → Kansas 110-52
- 8 Rhode Island vs 9 Murray St. → Rhode Island 97-74
- 5 TCU vs 12 Florida St. → Florida St. 96-87
- 4 Mississippi vs 13 Valparaiso → Valparaiso 70-69
- 6 Clemson vs 11 Western Mich. → Western Mich. 75-72
- 3 Stanford vs 14 Col. of Charleston → Stanford 67-57
- 7 St. John's (N.Y.) vs 10 Detroit → Detroit 66-64
- 2 Purdue vs 15 Delaware → Purdue 95-56

Second Round (March 15, Oklahoma City / Chicago):
- Rhode Island 80-75
- Valparaiso 83-77 (ot)
- Stanford 83-65
- Purdue 80-65

Regional Semifinals (March 20):
- Rhode Island 74-68
- Stanford 67-59

Regional Finals (St. Louis, March 22):
- Stanford 79-77

Midwest Regional Champion: Stanford

South Region

First Round (3/13):
- 1 Duke vs 16 Radford → Duke 99-63
- 8 Oklahoma St. vs 9 George Washington → Oklahoma St. 74-59
- 5 Syracuse vs 12 Iona → Syracuse 63-61
- 4 New Mexico vs 13 Butler → New Mexico 79-62
- 6 UCLA vs 11 Miami (Fla.) → UCLA 65-62
- 3 Michigan vs 14 Davidson → Michigan 80-61
- 7 Massachusetts vs 10 St. Louis → St. Louis 51-46
- 2 Kentucky vs 15 South Carolina St. → Kentucky 82-67

Second Round (March 15, Lexington, KY / Atlanta):
- Duke 79-73
- Syracuse 56-46
- UCLA 85-82
- Kentucky 88-61

Regional Semifinals (March 20):
- Duke 80-67
- Kentucky 94-68

Regional Finals (St. Petersburg, FL, March 22):
- Kentucky 86-84

South Regional Champion: Kentucky

National Semifinals (San Antonio, March 28)
- Utah 65-59 (def. North Carolina)
- Kentucky 86-85 (ot) (def. Stanford)

National Championship (San Antonio, March 30)
Kentucky 78-69 — NATIONAL CHAMPION

1999 Championship Bracket

East

First Round (3/12)
- 1 Duke
- 16 Florida A & M
- 8 Col. of Charleston
- 9 Tulsa
- 5 Wisconsin
- 12 Southwest Mo. St.
- 4 Tennessee
- 13 Delaware
- 6 Temple
- 11 Kent St.
- 3 Cincinnati
- 14 George Mason
- 7 Texas
- 10 Purdue
- 2 Miami (Fla.)
- 15 Lafayette

Second Round
- Duke 99-58
- Tulsa 62-53
- Charlotte, NC — March 14
- Southwest Mo. St. 43-32
- Tennessee 62-52
- Temple 61-54
- Cincinnati 72-48
- Boston — March 14
- Purdue 58-54
- Miami (Fla.) 75-54

Regional Semifinals
- Duke 97-56 (March 14)
- Southwest Mo. St. 81-51 (March 19)
- Temple 64-54 (March 14)
- Purdue 73-63 (March 19)

Regional Finals — East Rutherford, NJ — March 21
- Duke 78-61
- Temple 77-55

Duke 85-64

Midwest

First Round (3/12)
- 1 Michigan St.
- 16 Mt. St. Mary's
- 8 Villanova
- 9 Mississippi
- 5 Charlotte
- 12 Rhode Island
- 4 *Arizona
- 13 Oklahoma
- 6 Kansas
- 11 Evansville
- 3 Kentucky
- 14 New Mexico St.
- 7 Washington
- 10 Miami (Ohio)
- 2 Utah
- 15 Arkansas St.

Second Round
- Michigan St. 76-53
- Mississippi 72-70 (March 14)
- Milwaukee — Charlotte 81-70 (ot)
- Oklahoma 61-60 (March 14)
- Kansas 95-74
- Kentucky 82-60 (March 14)
- New Orleans — Miami (Ohio) 59-58
- Utah 80-58 (March 14)

Regional Semifinals
- Michigan St. 74-66 (March 19)
- Oklahoma 85-72
- Kentucky 92-88 (ot) (March 19)
- Miami (Ohio) 66-58

Regional Finals — St. Louis — March 21
- Michigan St. 54-46
- Kentucky 58-43

Michigan St. 73-66

National Semifinal — St. Petersburg, FL — March 27
Duke 68-62

South

First Round (3/11)
- 1 Auburn
- 16 Winthrop
- 8 Syracuse
- 9 Oklahoma St.
- 5 *UCLA
- 12 Detroit
- 4 Ohio St.
- 13 Murray St.
- 6 Indiana
- 11 George Washington
- 3 St. John's (N.Y.)
- 14 Samford
- 7 Louisville
- 10 Creighton
- 2 Maryland
- 15 Valparaiso

Second Round
- Auburn 80-41
- Oklahoma St. 69-61 (March 13)
- Indianapolis — Detroit 56-53
- Ohio St. 72-58 (March 13)
- Indiana 108-88
- St. John's (N.Y.) 69-43 (March 13)
- Orlando, FL — Creighton 62-58
- Maryland 82-60 (March 13)

Regional Semifinals
- Auburn 81-74 (March 18)
- Ohio St. 75-44
- St. John's (N.Y.) 86-61 (March 18)
- Maryland 75-63

Regional Finals — Knoxville, TN — March 20
- Ohio St. 72-64
- St. John's (N.Y.) 76-62

Ohio St. 77-74

West

First Round (3/11)
- 1 Connecticut
- 16 Texas-San Antonio
- 8 Missouri
- 9 New Mexico
- 5 Iowa
- 12 UAB
- 4 Arkansas
- 13 Siena
- 6 Florida
- 11 Pennsylvania
- 3 North Carolina
- 14 Weber St.
- 7 Minnesota
- 10 Gonzaga
- 2 Stanford
- 15 Alcorn St.

Second Round
- Connecticut 91-66
- New Mexico 61-59 (March 13)
- Denver — Iowa 77-64
- Arkansas 94-80 (March 13)
- Florida 75-61
- Weber St. 76-74 (March 13)
- Seattle — Gonzaga 75-63
- Stanford 69-57 (March 13)

Regional Semifinals
- Connecticut 78-56 (March 18)
- Iowa 82-72
- Florida 82-74 (ot) (March 18)
- Gonzaga 82-74

Regional Finals — Phoenix — March 20
- Connecticut 78-68
- Gonzaga 73-72

Connecticut 67-62

National Semifinal — St. Petersburg, FL — March 27
Connecticut 64-58

National Championship

St. Petersburg, FL — March 29

Connecticut 77-74
NATIONAL CHAMPION

*Arizona's and UCLA's participation in 1999 tournament vacated.

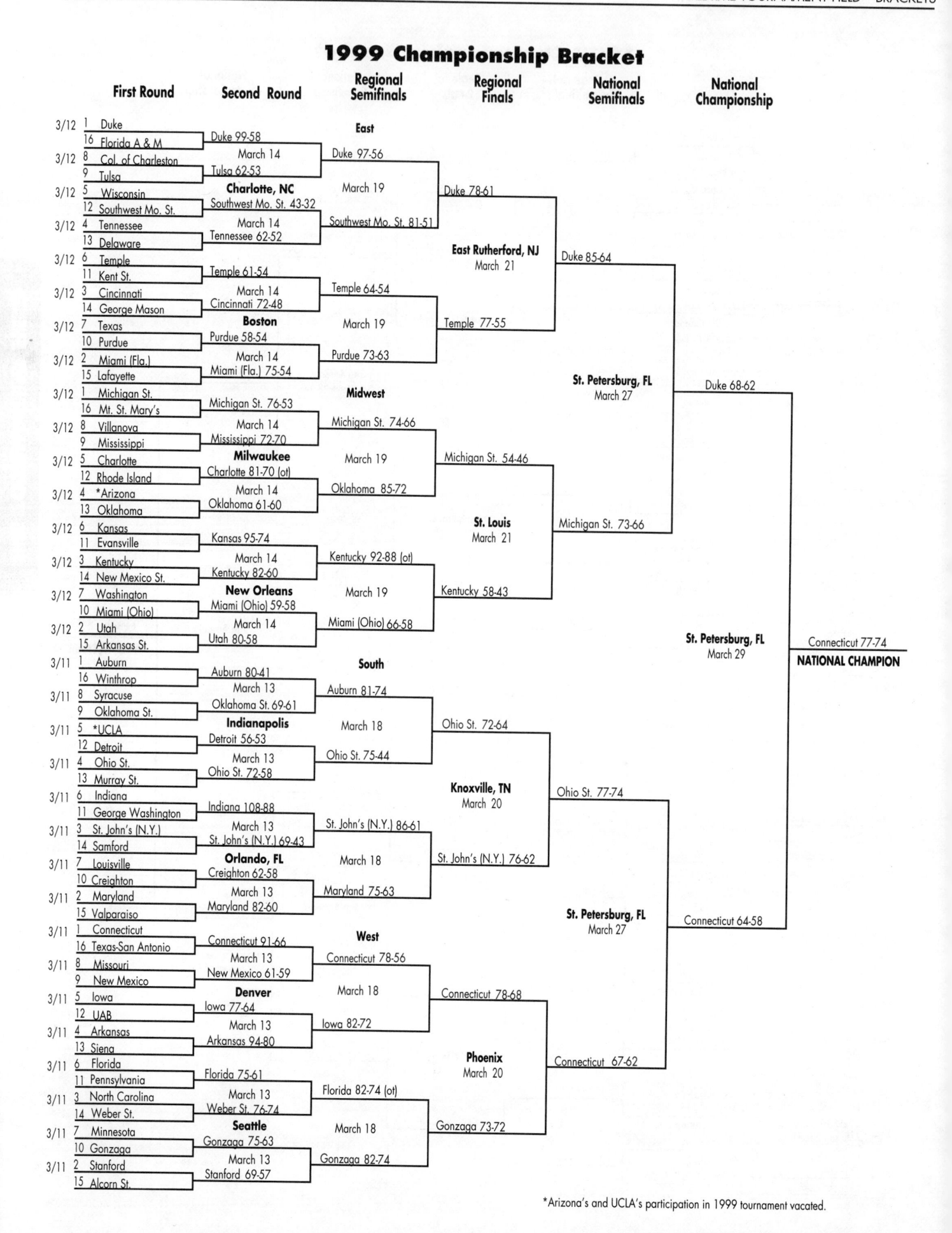

2000 Championship Bracket

West

First Round (3/16)
- 1 Arizona / 16 Jackson St. → Arizona 71-47
- 8 Wisconsin / 9 Fresno St. → Wisconsin 66-56
- 5 Texas / 12 Indiana St. → Texas 77-61
- 4 LSU / 13 Southeast Mo. St. → LSU 64-61
- 6 Purdue / 11 Dayton → Purdue 62-61
- 3 Oklahoma / 14 Winthrop → Oklahoma 74-50
- 7 Louisville / 10 Gonzaga → Gonzaga 77-66
- 2 St. John's (N.Y.) / 15 Northern Ariz. → St. John's (N.Y.) 61-56

Second Round
- Salt Lake City, March 18: Wisconsin 66-59; LSU 72-67
- Tucson, AZ, March 18: Purdue 66-62; Gonzaga 82-76

Regional Semifinals / Finals — Albuquerque, NM, March 23 & 25
- Wisconsin 61-48
- Purdue 75-66
- Wisconsin 64-60

Midwest

First Round (3/16)
- 1 Michigan St. / 16 Valparaiso → Michigan St. 65-38
- 8 Utah / 9 St. Louis → Utah 48-45
- 5 Kentucky / 12 St. Bonaventure → Kentucky 85-80 (2ot)
- 4 Syracuse / 13 Samford → Syracuse 79-65
- 6 UCLA / 11 Ball St. → UCLA 65-57
- 3 Maryland / 14 Iona → Maryland 74-59
- 7 Auburn / 10 Creighton → Auburn 72-69
- 2 Iowa St. / 15 Central Conn. St. → Iowa St. 88-78

Second Round
- Cleveland, March 18: Michigan St. 73-61; Syracuse 52-50
- Minneapolis, March 18: UCLA 105-70; Iowa St. 79-60

Regional Semifinals / Finals — Auburn Hills, MI, March 23 & 25
- Michigan St. 75-58
- Iowa St. 80-56
- Michigan St. 75-64

East

First Round (3/17)
- 1 Duke / 16 Lamar → Duke 85-55
- 8 Kansas / 9 DePaul → Kansas 81-77 (ot)
- 5 Florida / 12 Butler → Florida 69-68 (ot)
- 4 Illinois / 13 Pennsylvania → Illinois 68-58
- 6 Indiana / 11 Pepperdine → Pepperdine 77-57
- 3 Oklahoma St. / 14 Hofstra → Oklahoma St. 86-66
- 7 Oregon / 10 Seton Hall → Seton Hall 72-71 (ot)
- 2 Temple / 15 Lafayette → Temple 73-47

Second Round
- Winston-Salem, NC, March 19: Duke 69-64; Florida 93-76
- Buffalo, NY, March 19: Oklahoma St. 75-67; Seton Hall 67-65 (ot)

Regional Semifinals / Finals — Syracuse, NY, March 24 & 26
- Florida 87-78
- Oklahoma St. 68-66
- Florida 77-65

South

First Round (3/17)
- 1 Stanford / 16 South Carolina St. → Stanford 84-65
- 8 North Carolina / 9 Missouri → North Carolina 84-70
- 5 Connecticut / 12 Utah St. → Connecticut 75-67
- 4 Tennessee / 13 La.-Lafayette → Tennessee 63-58
- 6 Miami (Fla.) / 11 Arkansas → Miami (Fla.) 75-71
- 3 Ohio St. / 14 Appalachian St. → Ohio St. 87-61
- 7 Tulsa / 10 UNLV → Tulsa 89-62
- 2 Cincinnati / 15 UNC Wilmington → Cincinnati 64-47

Second Round
- Birmingham, AL, March 19: North Carolina 60-53; Tennessee 65-61
- Nashville, TN, March 19: Miami (Fla.) 75-62; Tulsa 69-61

Regional Semifinals / Finals — Austin, TX, March 24 & 26
- North Carolina 74-69
- Tulsa 80-71
- North Carolina 59-55

National Semifinals — Indianapolis, April 1
- Michigan St. 53-41
- Florida 71-59

National Championship — Indianapolis, April 3
- **Michigan St. 89-76 — NATIONAL CHAMPION**

2001 Championship Bracket

First Round	Second Round	Regional Semifinals	Regional Finals	National Semifinals	National Championship

Midwest

- 3/16 (1) Illinois / (16) %Northwestern St. — Illinois 96-54
- 3/16 (8) Tennessee / (9) Charlotte — Charlotte 70-63
  - Dayton, OH — March 18: Illinois 79-61
- 3/16 (5) Syracuse / (12) Hawaii — Syracuse 79-69
- 3/16 (4) Kansas / (13) Cal St. Northridge — Kansas 99-75
  - March 18: Kansas 87-58
  - March 23: Illinois 80-64
- 3/16 (6) Notre Dame / (11) Xavier — Notre Dame 83-71
- 3/16 (3) Mississippi / (14) Iona — Mississippi 72-70
  - Kansas City, MO — March 18: Mississippi 59-56
- 3/16 (7) Wake Forest / (10) Butler — Butler 79-63
- 3/16 (2) Arizona / (15) Eastern Ill. — Arizona 101-76
  - March 18: Arizona 73-52
  - March 23: Arizona 66-56

San Antonio — March 25: Arizona 87-81

South

- 3/16 (1) Michigan St. / (16) Alabama St. — Michigan St. 69-35
- 3/16 (8) California / (9) Fresno St. — Fresno St. 82-70
  - Memphis, TN — March 18: Michigan St. 81-65
- 3/16 (5) Virginia / (12) Gonzaga — Gonzaga 86-85
- 3/16 (4) Oklahoma / (13) Indiana St. — Indiana St. 70-68 (ot)
  - March 18: Gonzaga 85-68
  - March 23: Michigan St. 77-62
- 3/16 (6) Texas / (11) Temple — Temple 79-65
- 3/16 (3) Florida / (14) Western Ky. — Florida 69-56
  - New Orleans — March 18: Temple 75-54
- 3/16 (7) Penn St. / (10) Providence — Penn St. 69-59
- 3/16 (2) North Carolina / (15) Princeton — North Carolina 70-48
  - March 18: Penn St. 82-74
  - March 23: Temple 84-72

Atlanta — March 25: Michigan St. 69-62

Minneapolis — March 31: Arizona 80-61

East

- 3/15 (1) Duke / (16) Monmouth — Duke 95-52
- 3/15 (8) Georgia / (9) Missouri — Missouri 70-68
  - Greensboro, NC — March 17: Duke 94-81
- 3/15 (5) Ohio St. / (12) Utah St. — Utah St. 77-68 (ot)
- 3/15 (4) UCLA / (13) Hofstra — UCLA 61-48
  - March 17: UCLA 75-50
  - March 22: Duke 76-63
- 3/15 (6) Southern California / (11) Oklahoma St. — Southern Cal 69-54
- 3/15 (3) Boston College / (14) Southern Utah — Boston Col. 68-65
  - Long Island, NY — March 17: Southern Cal 74-71
- 3/15 (7) Iowa / (10) Creighton — Iowa 69-56
- 3/15 (2) Kentucky / (15) Holy Cross — Kentucky 72-68
  - March 17: Kentucky 92-79
  - March 22: Southern Cal 80-76

Philadelphia — March 24: Duke 79-69

West

- 3/15 (1) Stanford / (16) UNC Greensboro — Stanford 89-60
- 3/15 (8) Georgia Tech / (9) St. Joseph's — St. Joseph's 66-62
  - San Diego — March 17: Stanford 90-83
- 3/15 (5) Cincinnati / (12) Brigham Young — Cincinnati 84-59
- 3/15 (4) Indiana / (13) Kent St. — Kent St. 77-73
  - March 17: Cincinnati 66-43
  - March 22: Stanford 78-65
- 3/15 (6) Wisconsin / (11) Georgia St. — Georgia St. 50-49
- 3/15 (3) Maryland / (14) George Mason — Maryland 83-80
  - Boise, ID — March 17: Maryland 79-60
- 3/15 (7) Arkansas / (10) Georgetown — Georgetown 63-61
- 3/15 (2) Iowa St. / (15) Hampton — Hampton 58-57
  - March 17: Georgetown 76-57
  - March 22: Maryland 76-66

Anaheim, CA — March 24: Maryland 87-73

Minneapolis — March 31: Duke 95-84

Minneapolis — April 2: Duke 82-72 **NATIONAL CHAMPION**

%Opening Round
March 13 - Dayton, OH
Northwestern St. 71
Winthrop 67

2002 Championship Bracket

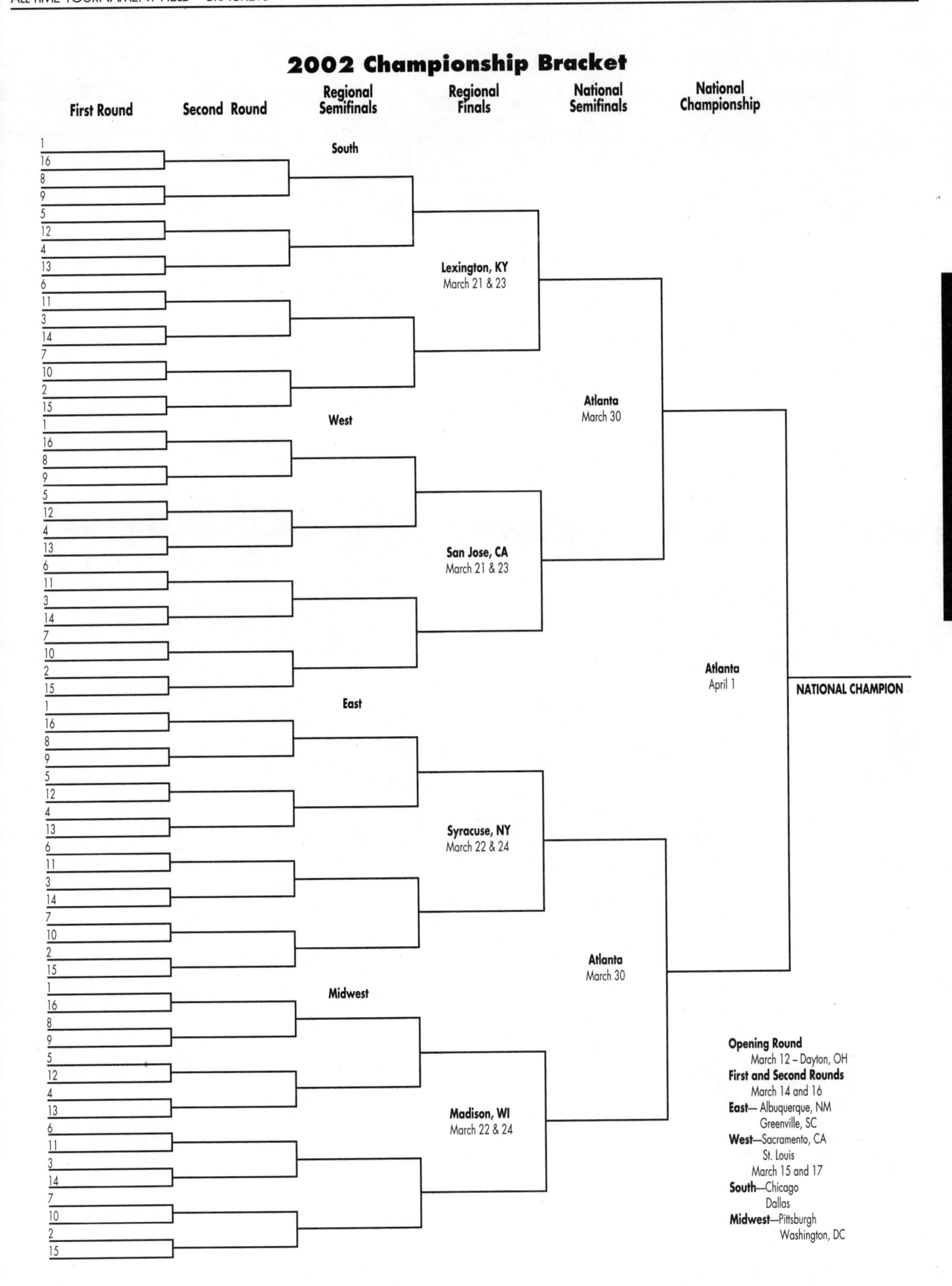

First Round | **Second Round** | **Regional Semifinals** | **Regional Finals** | **National Semifinals** | **National Championship**

South
Seeds: 1, 16, 8, 9, 5, 12, 4, 13, 6, 11, 3, 14, 7, 10, 2, 15

Lexington, KY — March 21 & 23

West
Seeds: 1, 16, 8, 9, 5, 12, 4, 13, 6, 11, 3, 14, 7, 10, 2, 15

San Jose, CA — March 21 & 23

East
Seeds: 1, 16, 8, 9, 5, 12, 4, 13, 6, 11, 3, 14, 7, 10, 2, 15

Syracuse, NY — March 22 & 24

Midwest
Seeds: 1, 16, 8, 9, 5, 12, 4, 13, 6, 11, 3, 14, 7, 10, 2, 15

Madison, WI — March 22 & 24

Atlanta — March 30 (National Semifinals)

Atlanta — April 1 (National Championship)

NATIONAL CHAMPION

Opening Round
March 12 – Dayton, OH

First and Second Rounds
March 14 and 16
East— Albuquerque, NM
Greenville, SC
West—Sacramento, CA
St. Louis
March 15 and 17
South—Chicago
Dallas
Midwest—Pittsburgh
Washington, DC